GROC's CANDID GUIDE TO
THE MAINLAND ISLANDS

Including

EVIA, THE ARGO—SARONIC &
SPORADES ISLANDS

of

SPETSES, HYDRA, POROS, AEGINA,
ANGISTRI, KITHIRA, SALAMINAS, SKYROS,
ALONISSOS, SKOPELOS & SKIATHOS

As well as

Athens City, Piraeus &
The Mainland Ports

of

Rafina, Arkitsa, Skala Oropou, Ag Marina, Glifa,
Ag Konstantinos & Volos

For the package, villa, backpacker &
ferry-boating holiday-maker,
whether travelling by air, car, coach or train

by

Geoffrey O'Connell

Published by
Ashford Press Publis
1 Church Road
Shedfield
Hampshire
SO3 2HW

CONTENTS

Page No.

Introduction 1

PART ONE

Chapter 1 3
PACKING, INSURANCE, MEDICAL MATTERS, CLIMATIC CONDITIONS, CONVERSION TABLES & A STARTER COURSE IN GREEK

Chapter 2 11
GETTING TO & FROM THE MAINLAND ISLANDS & ATHENS

Chapter 3 31
TRAVEL BETWEEN ATHENS & THE MAINLAND ISLANDS

Chapter 4 37
ISLAND ACCOMMODATION

Chapter 5 43
TRAVELLING AROUND AN ISLAND

Chapter 6 49
ISLAND FOOD & DRINK

Chapter 7 61
SHOPPING & PUBLIC SERVICES

Chapter 8 69
GREECE: HISTORY, MYTHOLOGY, RELIGION, PRESENT-DAY GREECE, GREEKS & THEIR HOLIDAYS

PART TWO
Chapter 9 75
ATHENS CITY

Chapter 10 117
PIRAEUS & OTHER MAINLAND PORTS

PART THREE
Chapter 11 137
INTRODUCTION TO THE MAINLAND ISLANDS OF THE ARGO-SARONIC & THE SPORADES.

The Argo-Saronic islands including:-

Chapter 12 143
SPETSES including: Spetses, capital & port.
The island topography including ROUTE ONE: Lampara Beach, Ligoneri Beach, Vrellou Beach, Zogeria Bay, Ag Paraskevi, Ag Anargyri, Bekiris Cave, Ksilokeriza Bay, Spetsopoula islet.

Chapter 13 163
HYDRA including: Hydra, capital & port. EXCURSIONS TO HYDRA PORT including: onta, Kronia, Sipias, Limni, Monastery of St Nicholas. ROUTE THREE: Krieza, Petries, Ag Apostoli, Koskina, Paralia Koskinon, Argiro, Buphalon Harbour, Buphalo islet, Pyrgaki, Ag Dimitrios Panaghia, Almyropotamos, Mesochoria, Ormos

Karalides, Styra, Nea Styra, Marmari Port, Karistos, Metochi, Bouros Beach. Mandraki Beach; Kamini, Vlichos, Episkopi; Eastern Monasteries of Ag Matrona Convent, Ag Trias Convent, Ag Nikolaos Monastery, Zourvas Convent

Chapter 14 179
POROS including: Poros, capital & port. EXCURSIONS TO POROS TOWN SURROUNDS including: Galatas, Lemonodassos; Two Brothers Caique trips.
The island topography including ROUTE ONE: Canal Beach, Nea Chora, Megalo Neorion Bay, Russian Bay. ROUTE TWO: Ormos Vagionia, Temple of Poseidon, Zoodochos Pighi Monastery, Monastery Beach, Askeli Beach.

Chapter 15 197
AEGINA Including: Aegina, capital & port.
The island topography including ROUTE ONE: Leondi, Souvala, Agious, Vagia, Temple of Aphaia, Ag Marina, Portes, Messagros, Paleochora, Kontos. ROUTE TWO: Perdika, Moni islet.

Chapter 16 213
ANGISTRI including; Skala Angistri, capital & port. EXCURSIONS TO SKALA ANGISTRI SURROUNDS including Paradise Beach; Metochi.
The island topography including ROUTE ONE: Megalochorio, Limenari, Aronisos.

Chapter 17 225
KITHIRA including: Ag Pelagia, port. The Chora, the capital.
The island topography including ROUTE ONE: **Kapsali.** ROUTE TWO: Livadi, Fatsadika, Kondolianika, Panaghia Mirtidiotissa, Limnaria, Karvounades, Avlemonas, Dokana, Milopotamos, Aroniadika, Diakofti, Potamos, Karavas, Platia Ammos.

Chapter 18 241
SALAMINAS including: Selinia, port. Salamina, the capital. EXCURSIONS TO SALAMINAS TOWN SURROUNDS including: to the north-west; Ag Georgios, Voudoro peninsula; Eandio & EXCURSIONS TO EANDIO SURROUNDS including: to the west; Paralia; Perani; Peristeria, Ag Nikolaos Monastery, Kanakia; Paloukia.

The Mainland island:-
Chapter 19 249
EVIA including: Chalkis, capital.
The island topography including ROUTE ONE; N Lampsakos, Vasilikon, Lefkandi Beach, Phylla, Louli Beach, **Eretria,** Amarinthos, Aliverion, Velos, Lepoura, Avlonarion, Monastery of Lefkon, Oxilithos, Paralia, Platana, Monodrio, Konistres, Taxiarchi, Mendulis, Kymi Town, **Paralia Kymi.** ROUTE TWO: Nea Artaki, Katheni, Kato Steni, Steni Dirphos, Chiliadon Monastery, Psachna, Politika, Paralia Politika, Nerotrivia, Daphni, Prokopion, Mandoulion, Kirinthos, Kria Vrysi, Strofilia, Ag Anna, Vassilika, Ellinika, Artemision, Asminion, Istiaea, Orei, Neos Pirgos, Agiokampos, Agios, Edipsos, Loutra Edipsos & EXCURSION TO LOUTRA EDIPSOS SURROUNDS including: Ag Nikolaos, Gialtra, Loutra Gialtron, Ag Georgios; (ROUTE TWO cont.) Ilia, Rovies, Monastery of David Geronta, Kronia, Sipias, Limni, Monastery of St Nicholas. ROUTE THREE: Krieza, Petries, Ag Apostoli, Koskina, Paralia Koskinon, Argiro, Buphalon Harbour, Buphalo islet, Pyrgaki, Ag Dimitrios Panaghia, Almyropotamos, Mesochoria, Ormos Karalides, Styra, Nea Styra, Marmari Port, Karistos, Metochi, Bouros Beach.

The Sporades islands including:
Chapter 20 289
SKYROS including: Linaria, Port.
The island topography including ROUTE ONE: Acherounes Bay, Mealos Bay, **The Chora,** the capital, & EXCURSION TO THE CHORA SURROUNDS including: Magazia, Molos Beach, Girismata Bay. ROUTE TWO: the Airport, Atsitsa, Ag Fokas, Pefkos Bay. ROUTE THREE: Kalamitsa, Kolimbadas Bay, Tris Boukes Bay, Renes Bay.

Chapter 21 309
ALONISSOS including: Patitiri Port, capital & port. EXCURSIONS TO PATITIRI PORT SURROUNDS including: Rsoum Gialo Bay, Votsi Bay; Vithisma Beach, Marpounta Hotel & coves; Alonissos Chora.
The island topography including ROUTE ONE: Milia Gialos Beach, Chrisi Milia Beach, Kokkinokastro, Tzortzi Gialo Bay, Lefto Gialo Bay, Steni Vala, Kalamakia, Diasello, Geraka Bay.

Chapter 22 331
SKOPELOS including: Skopelos, capital & port. EXCURSIONS TO SKOPELOS TOWN SURROUNDS including: Monastery Evangelistria, Monastery Metamorphosis, Monastery Varvaras, Monastery Prodromos; Monastery Ag Reginos, Monastery Analipseos, Ag Konstantinos.
The island topography including ROUTE ONE: Stafilos & Velanio Beaches, Agnotas Port, Limnonari Beach, Panormos Beach, Milia Beach, Elios, Klima, Glossa, Ag Ioannis Church, **Loutraki Port.**

Chapter 23 357
SKIATHOS Including: Skiathos, capital & port. EXCURSIONS TO SKIATHOS TOWN SURROUNDS including: Pounta pneinsula, Xanema Bay, the Airport; Monastery Evangelistria; Kastro Beach, Lalaria Beach.
The island topography including ROUTE ONE: Vasilias, Kechrias Beach, Achladias Beach, Tzanerias Bay, Kalamaki Headland, Kanapitsa Beach, Vromolimnos Beach, Kolpos Beach, Platanias Beach; Inland Excursion to Megas Asselinos Beach, Kounistra Monastery, Mikro Asselinos Beach; Troulos Beach, Maratha Beach, Koukounaries, Krassa Beach, Ag Elenis Beach.

Index 384

ILLUSTRATIONS

Illustration Numbers	Illustrations	Page
	The Greek islands	10
1	European Railway Routes	16
2	European Car Routes & Ferry-boat connections	22
3	Mainland islands	30
4	Athens City	74
5	Athens City inset - The Plaka	82
6	Athens City inset - The Railway Stations	112
7	Athens environs, suburbs, bus & metro routes	116
8	Piraeus Port & Town	118
9	Piraeus — Port & Town detail	121
10	Piraeus inset	123
11	Rafina Port	127
12	Volos Port	133
13	Mainland Islands including the Argo-Saronic & Sporades islands	136
14	Spetses island	144
15	Spetses Port	147
16	Hydra island	162
17	Hydra Port	165
18	Poros island	180
19	Poros Port	182
20	Aegina island	196
21	Aegina Port	199
22	Angistri island	212
23	Skala Angistri Port	215
24	Kithira island	224
25	The Chora (Kithira)	229
26	Kapsali Port	235
27	Salaminas island	242
28	Evia island	248
29	Chalkis Town	251
30	Eretria Port	259
31	Paralia Kymi Port	266
32	Skyros island	288
33	Linaria Port	292
34	The Chora (Skyros)	295
35	Alonissos island	308
36	Patitiri Port	311
37	Skopelos island	330
38	Skopelos Port	333
39	Loutraki Port	353
40	Skiathos island	356
41	Skiathos Port	359

Please do not forget that prices are given as a guide only, especially accommodation and restaurant costs which are subject to fluctuation, almost always upwards. In the last year or so, not only lodging and 'troughing' costs, but also transport charges, particularly ferry-boat fees, have escalated dramatically. The increased value of most other currencies to the Greek drachmae has compensated, to some extent, for apparently inexorably rising prices.

In an effort to keep readers as up-to-date as possible regarding these and other matters, I have introduced **GROC's GREEK ISLAND HOTLINE**. *See* elsewhere for details.

The series is entering its sixth year of publication and I would appreciate continuing to hear from readers who have any additions or corrections to bring to my attention. As in the past, all correspondence (except that addressed to 'Dear filth' or similar endearments) will be answered.

I hope readers can excuse errors that creep (well gallop actually) into the welter of detailed information included in the body text. In order to keep the volumes as up-to-date as possible, the period from inception to publication is kept down to some six months which does result in the occasional slip up....

The Candid Guides
unique
'GROC's Greek Island Hotline'

Available to readers of the guides, this service enables a respondent to receive a bang up-to-the-minute, update to the extensive information contained in a particular Candid Guide.

To obtain this paraphrased computer print-out, covering the Introductory Chapters, Athens, Piraeus & the Mainland Ports as well as any named islands, up to twenty five in number, all that is necessary is to:-

Complete the form below, enclosing a payment of £1.50 (to include postage), and send to:-

Willowbridge Enterprises, Bridge House, Southwick Village,
Nr.Fareham, Hants. PO17 6DZ

Note: The information will be of little use to anyone who does not possess the relevant GROC's Candid Greek Island Guide.

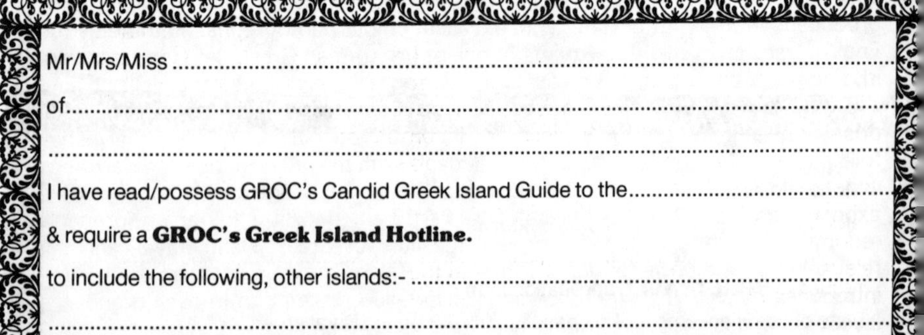

Mr/Mrs/Miss ....

of..

....

I have read/possess GROC's Candid Greek Island Guide to the..

& require a **GROC's Greek Island Hotline.**

to include the following, other islands:- ....

....

and enclose a fee of £1.50. Signature..Date ....

Note. I appreciate that the 'Hotline' may not be dispatched for up to 7-10 days from receipt of this application.

INTRODUCTION

This volume is the sixth in the popular and proven series of GROC's Candid Guides to the Greek Islands. The rationale, the raison d'etre behind their production is to treat each island grouping on an individual and comprehensive basis, rather than attempt overall coverage of the 100 or so islands usually described in one volume. This obviates attempting to do justice to, say, Aegina in amongst an aggregation of many other, often disparate islands.

Due to the vast distances involved very few, if any, vacationers can possibly visit more than a number of islands in a particular group, even if spending as much as four weeks in Greece.

It is important for package and villa holiday-makers to have an unbiased and relevant description of their planned holiday surroundings rather than the usual extravagant hyperbole of the glossy sales brochure. It is vital for backpackers and ferry-boat travellers to have on arrival, detailed and accurate information at their finger tips. With these differing requirements in mind factual, 'straight-from-the-shoulder' location reports have been combined with detailed plans of the major port, town and or city of each island in the group as well as topographical island maps.

Amongst the guides available there are earnest tomes dealing with Ancient and Modern Greece, a number of thumbnail travel booklets and some worthy, if often out-of-date books. Unfortunately they rarely assuage the various travellers' differing requirements. These might include speedy and accurate identification of one's position on arrival; the situation of accommodation as well as the whereabouts of a bank, the postal services and the tourist offices. Additional requisites embrace a swift and easy to read resumé of the settlement's main locations, cafe-bars, tavernas and restaurants; detailed local bus and ferry-boat timetables as well as a full island narrative. Once the traveller has settled in, then and only then, can he or she feel at ease, making their own finds and discoveries.

I have chosen to omit lengthy accounts of the relevant, fabulous Greek mythology and history. These aspects of Greece are, for the serious student, very ably related by authors far more erudite than myself. Moreover, most islands have a semiofficial tourist guide translated into English, and for that matter, French, German and Scandinavian. They are usually well worth the 300 to 400 drachmae (drs) they cost, are extremely informative in 'matters archaeological' and are quite well produced, if rather out of date, with excellent colour photographs. Admittedly the English translation might seem a little quaint (try to read Greek, let alone translate it), and the maps are often unreliable but cartography is not a strong Hellenic suit!

Each **Candid Guide** finally researched as close to the publication date as is possible. Naturally, any new ideas are incorporated but in the main the guides follow a now well-tried formula. Part One deals with the preliminaries and describes in detail the different aspects of travelling and enjoying to the full the unforgettable experience of a Greek islands sojourn. Part Two details a full and thoroughly redrafted account of Athens City, still the hub for Greek island travel, and the relevant mainland ports for connections to the island group in question. Part Three introduces the island chain, followed by a detailed description of each island, the layout being designed to facilitate quick and easy reference.

The exchange rate has fluctuated quite violently in recent years and up-to-date information must be sought prior to departure. For instance at the time of writing the final draft of this guide, the rate to the English pound (£) was hovering about 230drs. Unfortunately prices are subject to fluctuation, usually upward with annual increases varying between 10-20%. Fortunately the drachma tends to devalue by approximately the same amount.

Recommendations and personalities are almost always based on personal observation and experience, occasionally emphasised by the discerning comments of readers or colleagues. They may well change from year to year and be subject to different interpretation by others.

The series incorporates a number of innovative ideas and unique services introduced over the years including:

The Decal: Since 1985 some of the accommodation and eating places recommended in the guides display a specially produced decal to help readers identify the particular establishment.

GROC's Greek Island Hotline: A new and absolutely unique service to readers of the **Candid Guides**. Application to **The GROC's Greek Island Hotline** enables purchasers of the guides to obtain a summary which lists all pertinent and relevant comments that have become available since the publication of the particular guide – in effect, an up-to-date update.

A payment of £1.50 (incl. postage) enables a respondent to receive the paraphrased computer print-out incorporating bang up-to-the-moment information in respect of the Introductory Chapters, Athens, Piraeus & the Mainland Ports as well as any named islands, up to twenty five in number. All it is necessary to do is for a reader to complete the form, or write a letter setting out the request for **GROC's Greek Island Hotline**, enclose the fee and post them to Willowbridge Enterprises, Bridge House, Southwick Village, Nr Fareham, Hants PO17 6DZ. Tel (0705) 375570.

Travel Insurance: A comprehensive holiday insurance plan that 'gives cover that many other policies do not reach....' See elsewhere for details.

The author (and publisher) are very interested in considering ways and means of improving the guides and adding to the backup facilities, so are delighted to hear from readers with their suggestions.

Enjoy yourselves and 'Ya Sou' (welcome).

Geoffrey O'Connell 1988

ACKNOWLEDGMENTS

Every year the list of those to be formally thanked grows and this edition shows no diminution in their number which has forced the original brief entry from the inside front cover to an inside page.

There are those numerous friends and confidants we meet on passage as well as the many correspondents who are kind enough to contact us with useful information, all of who, in the main, remain unnamed.

Rosemary who accompanies me, adding her often unwanted, uninformed comments and asides (and who I occasionally threaten not to take next time), requires especial thanks for unrelieved, unstinting (well almost unstinting) support despite being dragged from this or that sun kissed beach.

Although receiving reward, other than in heaven, some of those who assisted me in the production of this edition require specific acknowledgement for effort far beyond the siren call of vulgar remuneration! These worthies include Graham Bishop, who drew the maps and plans, and Viv Hitié, who controls the word processor.

Lastly, and as always, I must admonish Richard Joseph for ever encouraging and cajoling me to take up the pen – surely the sword is more fun?

The cover picture of a waterfront scene at Ag Georgios, Evia is produced by kind permission of GREEK ISLAND PHOTOS, Willowbridge Enterprises, Bletchley, Milton Keynes, Bucks.

PART ONE

1 Packing, insurance, medical matters, climatic conditions, conversion tables & a starter course in Greek

Leisure nourishes the body and the mind is also fed thereby; on the other hand, immoderate labour exhausts both. Ovid

Vacationing anywhere on an organised tour allows a certain amount of latitude regarding the amount of luggage packed, as this method of holiday does not preclude taking fairly substantial suitcases. On the other hand, ferry-boating and backpacking restricts the amount a traveller is able to carry and the means of conveyance. This latter group usually utilise backpacks and or roll-bags, both of which are more suitable than suitcases for this mode of travel. The choice between the two does not only depend on which is the more commodious, for at the height of season it can be advantageous to be distinguishable from the hordes of other backpackers. To promote the chances of being offered a room, the selection of roll-bags may help disassociation from the more hippy of 'genus rucksacker'. If roll-bags are selected they should include shoulder straps. These help alleviate the discomfort experienced whilst searching out accommodation on hot afternoons with arms just stretching and stretching and stretching.

In the highly populous, oversubscribed months of July and August, it is advisable to pack a thin, foam bedroll and lightweight sleeping bag, just in case accommodation cannot be located on the occasional night.

Unless camping out, I do not think a sweater is necessary between the months of May and September. A desert jacket or lightweight anorak is a better proposition and a stout pair of sandals or training shoes are obligatory, especially if very much walking is contemplated. Leave out the evening suit and cocktail dresses, as the Greeks are very informal. Instead take loose-fitting, casual clothes, and do not forget sunglasses and a floppy hat. Those holiday-makers staying in one place in the hottest months and not too bothered about weight and encumbrances might consider packing a parasol or beach umbrella. It will save a lot of money in daily rental charges.

Should there be any doubt about the electric supply (and you shave) include a pack of disposable razors. Ladies might consider acquiring one of the small, gas cylinder, portable hair-curlers prior to departure. Take along a couple of toilet rolls. They are useful for tasks other than that with which they are usually associated, including mopping up spilt liquid, wiping off plates, and blowing one's nose. It might be an idea to include a container of washing powder, a few clothes pegs, some string for a washing line and a number of wire hangers.

Those visitors contemplating wide ranging travel should consider packing a few plastic, sealed-lid, liquid containers, a plate and a cup, as well as a knife and fork, condiments, an all-purpose cutting/slicing/carving knife as well as a combination bottle and tin opener. These all facilitate economical dining whilst on the move as food and drink, when available on ferry-boats and trains, can be comparatively expensive. Camping out requires these elementary items to be augmented with simple cooking equipment.

Mosquito coils can be bought in Greece but a preferable device is a small two prong, electric heater on which a wafer thin tablet is placed. They can be purchased locally for some 1000drs and come complete with a pack of the capsules. One trade name is *Doker Mat* and almost every room has a suitable electric point. The odourless vapour given off certainly sorts out the mosquitoes and is (hopefully) harmless to humans. Mark you we did hear of a tourist who purchased one and swore by its efficacy, not even aware it was necessary to place a tablet in position.

Whilst discussing items that plug in, why not pack an electric coil. This enables the brew up of a morning 'cuppa'. Tea addicts can use a slice of lemon instead of milk. Those who like their drinks sweet may use those (often unwanted) packets of sugar that accompany most orders for Nes meh ghala or a spoonful of the honey that will be to hand for the morning yoghurt – won't it?

Consider packing a pair of tweezers, some plasters, calamine lotion, after-sun and insect cream, as well as a bottle of aspirin in addition to any pharmaceuticals usually required. It is worth noting that small packets of soap powder are now cheaper in Greece than much of Europe and shampoo and toothpaste cost about the same. Sun-tan oil which was inexpensive has now doubled in price and should be 'imported'. Including a small phial of disinfectant has merit, but it is best not to leave the liquid in the original glass bottle. Should it break, the disinfectant and glass mingled with clothing can prove not only messy but will leave a distinctive and lingering odour. Kaolin and morphine is a very reliable stomach settler. Greek chemists dispense medicines and prescriptions that only a doctor would be able to mete out in many other Western European countries, so prior to summoning a medico, try the local pharmacy.

Insurance & medical matters

While touching upon medical matters, a national of an EEC country should extend their state's National Health cover. United Kingdom residents can contact the local *Department of Health and Social Security* requesting form number *E111 UK*. When completed, and returned, this results in a *Certificate of Entitlement to Benefits in Kind during a stay in a Member State*. Well, that's super! In short, it entitles a person to medical treatment in other EEC countries. Do not only rely on this prop, but seriously consider taking out a holiday insurance policy covering loss of baggage and money; personal accident and medical expenses; cancellation of the holiday and personal liability. Check the exclusion clauses carefully. It is no good an insured imagining he or she is covered for 'this or that' only to discover the insurance company has craftily excluded claims under a particular section. Should a reader intend to hire a scooter ensure this form of 'activity' is insured and not debarred, as is often the case. Rather than rely on the minimal standard insurance cover offered by many tour companies, it is best to approach a specialist insurance broker. For instance, bearing in mind the rather rudimentary treatment offered by the average Greek island hospital, it is almost obligatory to include *Fly-Home Medicare* cover in any policy. A couple of homilies might graphically reinforce the argument. Firstly the Greek hospital system expects the patient's family to minister and feed the inmate 'out-of-hours'. This can result in holiday companions having to camp in the ward for the duration of any internment. Perhaps more thought-provoking is the homespun belief that a patient is best left the first night to survive, if it is God's will, and to pass on if not! After a number of years hearing of the unfortunate experiences of friends and readers, who failed to act on the advice given herein, as well as the inordinate difficulties I experienced in arranging cover for myself, I was prompted to offer readers an all embracing travel insurance scheme. Details are to be found elsewhere in the guide.

DON'T DELAY, ACT NOW.

Most rooms do not have rubbish containers so why not include some plastic bin liners which are also very useful for packing food as well as storing dirty washing. A universal sink plug is almost a necessity. Many Greek sinks do not have one but, as the water usually drains away very slowly, this could be considered an academic point.

Take along a pack of cards, and enough paperback reading to while away sunbathing sojourns and long journeys. Playing cards are subject to a government tax, which makes their price exorbitant, and books are expensive but some shops and lodgings operate a book-swap scheme.

Many flight, bus, ferry-boat and train journeys start off early in the morning, so a small battery-operated alarm clock may well obviate sleepless, fretful nights prior to the dawn of a departure. A small hand or wrist compass can be an enormous help orientating in towns and if room and weight allow, a torch is a useful addition to the inventory.

Readers must not forget their passport which is absolutely essential to (1) enter Greece, (2) book into most accommodation as well as campsites, (3) change money and (4) hire a scooter or car.

In the larger, more popular, tourist orientated resorts *Diners* and *American Express (Amex)* credit cards are accepted. Personal cheques may be changed when accompanied by a Eurocheque bank card. Americans can use an *Amex* credit card at their overseas offices to change personal cheques up to $1000. They may also, by prior arrangement, have cable transfers made to overseas banks, allowing 24hrs from the moment their home bank receives specific instructions.

It is wise to record and keep separate the numbers of credit cards, travellers's cheques and airline tickets in case they should be mislaid. Incidentally, this is a piece of advice I always give but rarely, if ever, carry out myself. Visitors are only allowed to import 3000drs of Greek currency (in notes) and the balance required must be in traveller's cheques and or foreign currency. It used to be 1500drs but the decline in the value of the Greek drachma has resulted in the readjustment. Despite which, with only 3000drs in hand, it is often necessary to change currency soon after arrival. This can be a problem at weekends or if the banks are on strike, a not uncommon occurrence during the summer months. *See* **Banks, Chapter Seven** for further details in respect of banks and money.

Imported spirits are comparatively expensive (except on some of the duty free Dodecanese islands) but the duty free allowance allowed into Greece, is up to one and a half litres of alcohol. So if a person is a whisky or gin drinker, and partial to an evening sundowner, they should acquire a bottle or two before arrival. Cigars are difficult to buy on the islands, so it may well be advantageous to take along the 75 allowed. On the other hand, cigarettes are so inexpensive in Greece that it hardly seems worthwhile 'importing' them. Note the above applies to fellow members of the EEC. Allowances for travellers from other countries are 1 litre of alcohol and 50 cigars. Camera buffs should take as much film as possible as it is more costly in Greece than in most Western European countries.

Officially, the Greek islands enjoy some 3000 hours of sunshine per year, out of an approximate, possible 4250 hours. The prevailing summer wind is the northerly *Meltemi* which can blow very strongly, day in and day out during July and August, added to which these months are usually dry and very hot for 24 hours a day. The sea in April is perhaps a little cool for swimming, but May and June are marvellous months, as are September and October.

For the statistically minded:

The monthly average temperatures in the Mainland Islands include:

	Jan	Feb	Mar	Apr	May	June	July	Aug	Sept	Oct	No v	Dec
Average monthly air temperature Syros	C°9.9 F°49.8	10.3 50.5	11.4 52.5	15.0 59	19.4 66.9	23.5 74.3	25.6 78.1	25.3 77.5	22.0 71.6	18.5 65.3	15.0 59	11.6 52.9
Sea surface temperature (at 1400hrs) Volos	C°12.7 F°54.9	12.8 55	14.0 57.2	17.3 63.1	21.0 69.8	24.6 76.3	26.4 E79.5	27.0 80.6	25.0 77	20.9 69.6	17.6 63.7	14.0 57.2
Average days of rain Skyros	16	11	11	7	6	4	2	1	4	8	11	15

The best time of year to holiday

The above charts indicate that probably the best months to vacation are May, June, September and October, the months of July and August being too hot. Certainly, the most crowded months, when accommodation is at a premium, are July, August and the first two weeks of September. Taking everything into account, it does not need an Einstein to work the matter out.

Conversion tables & equivalent

Units	**Approximate conversion**	**Equivalent**
Miles to kilometres	Divide by 5, multiply by 8	5 miles = 8km
Kilometres to miles	Divide by 8, multiply by 5	
Feet to metres	Divide by 10, multiply by 3	10 ft = 3m
Metres to feet	Divide by 3, multiply by 10	
Inches to centimetres	Divide by 2, multiply by 5	1 inch = 2.5 cm
Centimetres to inches	Divide by 5, multiply by 2	
Fahrenheit to centigrade	Deduct 32, divide by 9 and multiply by 5	77°F = 25°C
Centrigrade to fahrenheit	Divide by 5, multiply by 9 and add 32	
Gallons to litres	Divide by 2, multiply by 9	2 gal = 9 litres
Litres to gallons	Divide by 9, multiply by 2	
	Note: 1 pint = 0.6 of a litre and 1 litre = 1.8 pints	
Pounds (weight) to kilos	Divide by 11, multiply by 5	5 k = 11 lb
Kilos to pounds	Divide by 5, multiply by 11	
	Note: 16 oz = 1 lb; 1000g = 1 kg and 100g = 3.5 oz	

Tyre pressures

Pounds per square inch to kilometres per square centimetre

lb/sq.in	**kg/cm**	**lb/sq.in**	**kg/cm**
10	0.7	26	1.8
15	1.1	28	2.0
20	1.4	30	2.1
24	1.7	40	2.8

The Greeks use the metric system but most 'unreasonably' sell liquid (i.e. wine, spirits and beer) by weight. Take my word for it, a 640g bottle of wine is approximately 0.7 of a litre or 1.1 pints. Proprietary wines such as *Demestica* are sold in bottles holding as much as 950g, which is 1000ml or 1¾ pints and represents good value.

Electric points in the larger towns, smarter hotels and holiday resorts are 220 volts AC and power any American or British appliance. A few older buildings in out-of-the-way places might still have 110 DC supply. Remote pensions may not have any electricity, other than that supplied by a generator and even then the rooms might not be wired into the system. More correctly they may well be wired but not connected!

Greek time is 2 hours ahead of GMT, as it is during British Summer Time, and 7 hours ahead of United States Eastern Time. That is except for a short period when the Greek clocks are corrected for their winter at the end of September, some weeks ahead of the United Kingdom alteration.

Basics & essentials of the language

These notes and subsequent **Useful Greek** at the relevant chapter endings are not, nor could be, intended to substitute for a formal phrase book or three. Accent marks have been omitted.

Whilst in the United Kingdom it is worth noting that the *British Broadcasting Co.* (Marylebone High St, London WIM 4AA) has produced an excellent book, *Greek Language and People*, accompanied by a cassette and record.

For the less committed a very useful, pocket-sized phrase book that I always have to hand is *The Greek Travelmate* (Richard Drew Publishing, Glasgow) costing £1.99. Richard Drew, the publisher, recounts a most amusing, if at the time disastrous, sequence of events in respect of the launch of this booklet. It appears the public relations chaps had come up with the splendid idea of sending each and every travel writer a preview copy of the book complete with an airline tray of the usual food and drink served mid-flight. This was duly delivered at breakfast time but, unlike Bob Newhart's record of the *HMS Codfish's* shelling of Miami Beach, this was not a 'slow newsday'. No, this was the day that Argentina chose to invade the Falklands, which dramatic event drove many stories off the pages for good, including the phrase book launch!

The Alphabet

Capitals	Lower case	Sounds like
Α	α	Alpha
Β	β	Veeta
Γ	γ	Ghama
Δ	δ	Dhelta
Ε	ϵ	Epsilon
Ζ	ζ	Zeeta
Η	η	Eeta
Θ	θ	Theeta
Ι	ι	Yiota
Κ	κ	Kapa
Λ	λ	Lamtha
Μ	μ	Mee
Ν	ν	Nee
Ξ	ξ	Ksee
Ο	ο	Omikron
Π	π	Pee
Ρ	ρ	Roh
Σ	σ	Sighma
Τ	τ	Taf
Υ	υ	Eepsilon
Φ	φ	Fee
Χ	χ	Chi
Ψ	ψ	Psi
Ω	ω	Omegha

Groupings

αι	'e' as in let
αυ	'av/af' as in have/haff
ει/οι	'ee' as in seen
ευ	'ev/ef' as in ever/effort
ου	'oo' as in toot
γγ	'ng' as in ring
γκ	At the beginning of a word 'g' as in go
γχ	'nks' as in rinks
μπ	'b' as in beer
ντ	At the beginning of a word 'd' as in deer In the middle of a word 'nd' as in send
τζ	'ds' as in deeds

Useful Greek

English	Greek	Sounds like
Hello/goodbye	Γειά σου	Yia soo (informal singular said with a smile)
Good morning/day	Καλημέρα	Kalimera
Good afternoon/evening	Καλησπέρα	Kalispera (formal)
Good night	Καληνύχτα	Kalinikta
See you later	Θα σε δω αργοτερα	Tha se tho argotera
See you tomorrow	Θα σε δω αύριο	Tha se tho avrio
Yes	Ναι	Ne (accompanied by a downwards and sideways nod of the head)
No	Οχι	Ochi (accompanied by an upward movement of the head, heavenwards & with a closing of the eyes)
Please	Παρακαλώ	Parakalo
Thank you	(Σαζ) Ευχαριστώ	(sas) Efkaristo
No, thanks	Οχι ζυχαριστώ	Ochi, efkaristo
Thank you very much	Ευχαριστώ πολύ	Efkaristo poli
(After which the reply may well be)		
Thankyou (and please)	Παρακαλώ	Parakalo
Do you speak English?	Μιλάτε Αγγλικά	Milahteh anglikah
How do you say....	Πωσ λενε...	Pos lene...
...in Greek?	...στα Ελληνικά	...sta Ellinika
What is this called?	Πωσ το λένε	Pos to lene
I do not understand	Δεν καταλαβαίνω	Then katahlavehno
Could you speak more slowly (slower?)	Μπορειτε να μιλάτε πιο αργά	Boreete na meelate peeo seegha (arga)
Could you write it down?	Μπορειτε να μου το γράψετε	Boreete na moo to grapsete

Numbers

One	Ενα	enna
Two	Δυο	thio
Three	Τρια	triah
Four	Τεσσερα	tessehra
Five	Πεντε	pendhe
Six	Εξι	exhee
Seven	Επτα	eptah
Eight	Οκτω	ockto
Nine	Εννεα	ennea
Ten	Δεκα	thecca
Eleven	Εντεκα	endekha

Twelve	Δωδεκα	thodhehka
Thirteen	Δεκατρια	thehka triah
Fourteen	Δεκατεσσερα	thehka tessehra
Fifteen	Δεκαπεντε	thehka pendhe
Sixteen	Δεκαεξι	thekaexhee
Seventeen	Δεκαεπτα	thehkaeptah
Eighteen	Δεκαοκτω	thehkaockto
Nineteen	Δεκαεννεα	thehkaennea
Twenty	Εικοσι	eeckossee
Twenty-one	Εικοσι ενα	eeckcossee enna
Twenty-two	Εικοσι δυο	eeckcossee thio
Thirty	Τριαντα	treeandah
Forty	Σαραντα	sarandah
Fifty	Πενηντα	penindah
Sixty	Εξηντα	exhindah
Seventy	Εβδομηντα	evthomeendah
Eighty	Ογδοντα	ogthondah
Ninety	Ενενητα	eneneendah
One hundred	Εκατο	eckato
One hundred and one	Εκατον ενα	eckaton enna
Two hundred	Διακοσια	theeakossia
One thousand	Χιλια	kheelia
Two thousand	Δυο χιλιάδες	thio kheeliathes

Girismata Bay, Skyros.

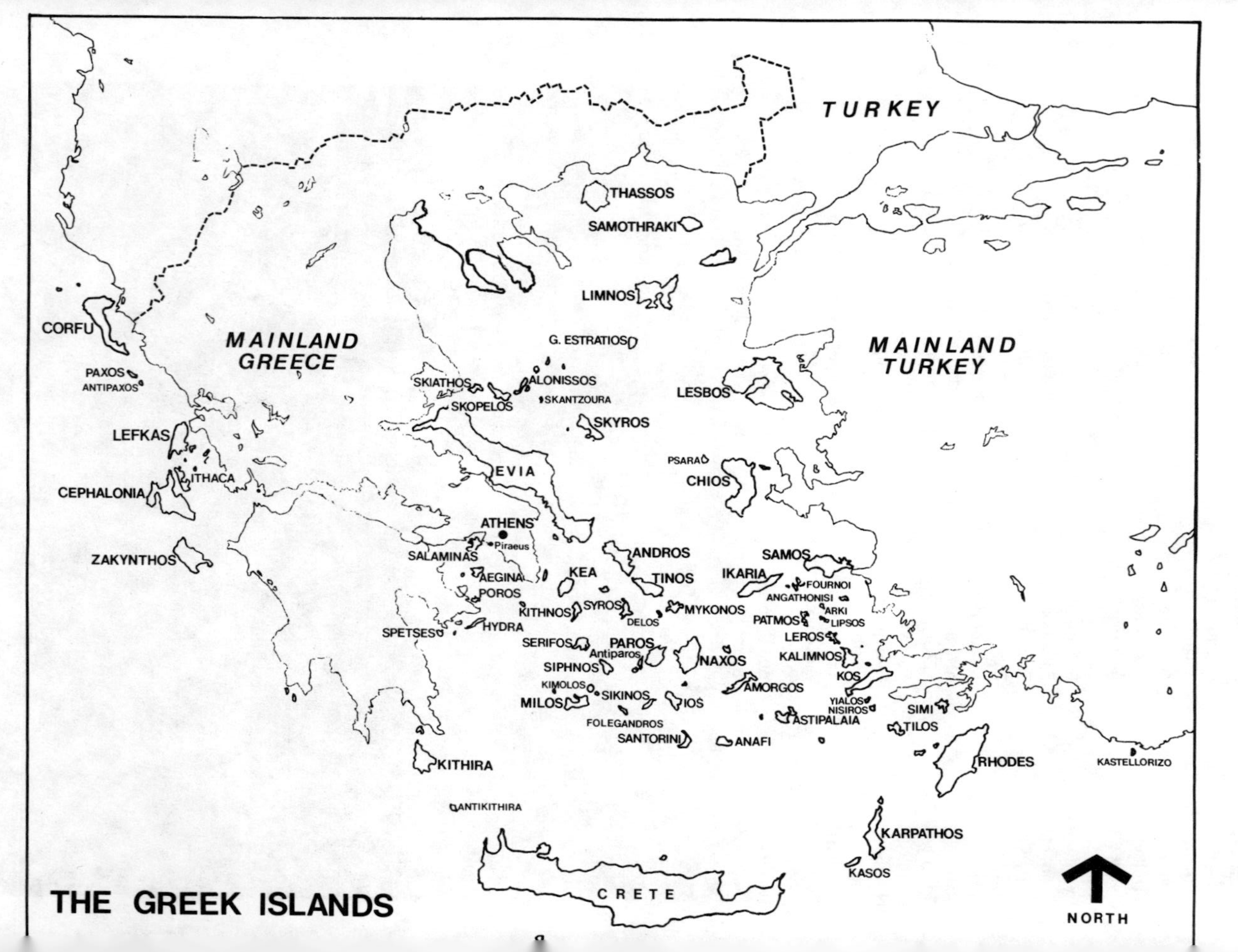

THE GREEK ISLANDS

2 Getting to & from the Mainland Islands & Athens

If all the year were playing holidays, to sport would be as tedious as work. William Shakespeare

To start this chapter off, first a word of warning. Whatever form of travel is utilised, travellers must not pack money or travellers cheques in luggage that is to be stowed away, out of sight. Some years ago, almost unbelievably, we met a young lady who had at the last moment, prior to checking-in at the airport, stuffed some drachmae notes in a zipped side pocket of one of her suitcases. On arrival in Greece, surprise, surprise, she was minus the money.

BY AIR

From the United Kingdom

Scheduled flights To get to the Mainland Islands it is necessary to fly direct to Athens East (international) airport, transfer by bus to Athens West (domestic) airport and then fly Olympic Airways to the islands of Skiathos or Skyros. There is also a Thessaloniki(M) to Skiathos connection. Note both international and domestic Olympic flights use the West airport.

Heathrow to Athens (3¾hrs): daily, non-stop via *British Airways, Olympic* and others.
Scheduled air fare options include: 1st class return, economy, excursion, APEX (Advanced Purchase Excursion Fare), PEX (instant purchase, and the cheapest scheduled fare) and Eurobudget.

Charter flights & package tours Some package tour operators keep a number of seats available on each flight for, what is in effect, a charter flight. A nominal charge is made for accommodation (which need not be taken up but read on...), the cost of which is included in the return air fare. These seats are substantially cheaper than scheduled APEX fares and are known as 'Charter Cheapies'. Apart from the relatively low price, the normal two week holiday period can be extended by a further week or weeks for a small surcharge. There are a variety of United Kingdom departure airports including Birmingham, Gatwick, Luton, Manchester and Newcastle. But, as one correspondent has pointed out, the frequency of charter flights tails off dramatically between October and March, as does the choice of airport departure points. Do not forget this when contemplating an out-of-season holiday.

An increasing tide of near penniless British youngsters taking a charter flight to Athens and causing various sociological problems, prompted the Greek authorities to announce their intention, from 1988, to carefully monitor charter flight arrivals. Those who did not have irrefutable proof of authorised accommodation, as well as enough money to survive, would be repatriated immediately at the carriers expense. In the consequent muddle of internecine squabbling between the charter companies and the Greeks, the authorities agreed to relax the originally stringent threat, but only for 1988. Despite this, it would be best for independent travellers to have proof of some booked accommodation and sufficient money to see them through their planned length of stay.

To ascertain what is on offer, scan the travel section of the Sunday papers as well as the weekly magazine *Time Out* and, possibly, *Private Eye*. There are many, varied packaged holidays available from the large tour operators whilst some of the smaller, more personal companies offer a bewildering array of multi-centre, fly-drive, budget-bed, self-catering and personally tailored holidays, in addition to the usual hotel accommodation.

Exceptionally reasonable charter flights, with the necessary accommodation vouchers, are available from *Owners Abroad Ltd*, Ilford, who also have offices in Manchester, Birmingham and Glasgow. Examples of their fares and destinations for 1988 include:

Two week return fares	Low Season	Mid-season	High Season
Athens leaving Gatwick Thursday, Friday & Sunday	From £98.75	£111.75	£117.75
Athens leaving Manchester Thursday & Friday	From £109.75	£122.75	£128.75
Athens leaving Birmingham Thursday	From 106.75	£119.75	£126.75
Athens leaving Newcastle Friday	From £123.75	£137.75	£143.75

These rates are subject to inexcusable surcharges and airport taxes totalling £14.95 per head. The fares for three weeks are those above plus £25, for four weeks plus £30 and for five or six weeks, an additional 50 per cent is charged. Note that the total number of weeks allowed in Greece for travellers who arrive and depart by charter flights is six, not twelve weeks.

Perhaps the least expensive flights available are *Courier Flights*. These scheduled seats start off at about £65 return to Athens for the low season period. BUT passengers can only take a maximum of 10kg of hand luggage, one holdall measuring no more than 1ft x 2ft – no other baggage. Other restrictions result in only one passenger being able to travel at a time and for a minimum period of ten or fourteen days. The *cognoscenti* assure that these seats are booked well ahead.

It is a pity, if inevitable, that the Olympic Airways subsidiary, *Allsun Holidays* has had to drop their selected island-hopping holidays. There were too many complaints! I can imagine.

Olympic Airways offer their 'Love-A-Fare' service, yes, 'love-a-fare' which is an APEX option in summer dress. The London to Athens return flight costs from £166 but the booking must be made at least two weeks in advance and allows a maximum of four weeks stay. There are Olympic offices in London as well as Manchester, Birmingham and Glasgow.

Amongst companies offering interesting and slightly off-beat holidays are the *Aegina Club Ltd* and *Ramblers Holidays. Aegina* offer a wider range of tours, three different locations in up to three weeks, and additionally, will tailor a programme to fit in with client's requirements. *Ramblers*, as would be imagined, include walking holidays based on a number of locations with half-board accommodation. More conventional inclusions, many in smaller, more personal hotels, pensions and tavernas than those used by the larger tour companies, are available from:

Laskarina Holidays. Their brochure includes islands in both the Argo-Saronic and Sporades chains. Perhaps most importantly, the female representatives of this company are excellent, as I can vouchsafe, having met one in the course of research (not lechery – the 'Management Committee' was close by). *See* **Travel Agents, A To Z, Athens, Chapter Nine.**

Students Young people lucky enough to be under 26 years of age (oh to be 26 again) should consider contacting *STA Travel* who market a number of inexpensive charter flights (for adults as well). Students of any age or scholars under 22 years of age (whatever mode of travel is planned) should take their *International Student Identity Card (ISIC)*. This ensures discounts are available whenever they are applicable, not only in respect of travel but also for entry to museums, archaeological sites and some forms of entertainment.

If under 26 years of age, but not a student, it may be worthwhile applying for membership of *The Federation of International Youth Travel Organization (FIYTO)* which guarantees discounts from some ferry and tour operators.

From the United States of America

Scheduled flights

Olympic flights include departures from:
Atlanta (via John F Kennedy (JFK) airport, New York (NY): daily
Boston (via JFK or La Guardia, NY): daily
Chicago (Via JFK): daily
Dallas (via JFK): daily
Houston (via JFK): daily
Los Angeles (via JFK): daily
Miami (via JFK): daily, 15 hours
Minneapolis (via JFK): daily
New York (JFK:) daily direct, approx. 10½ hours
Norfolk (via JFK): daily, except Saturday
Philadelphia (via JFK:) daily, about 11 hours
Rochester (via JFK): daily
San Francisco (via JFK): daily, approx. 14½ hours
Seattle (via JFK or London): daily
Tampa (via JFK): daily
Washington DC (via JFK or La Guardia): daily

Note that flights via New York's John F Kennedy airport involve a change of plane from, or to, a domestic American airline.

USA domestic airlines, also run a number of flights to Greece and the choice of air fares is bewildering. These include economy, first class return, super APEX, APEX GIT, excursion, ABC, OTC, ITC, and others, wherein part package costs are incorporated.

Charter/standby flights & secondary airlines As in the United Kingdom, scanning the Sunday national papers' travel section, including the *New York Times*, discloses various companies offering package tours and charter flights. Another way to make the journey is to take a standby flight to London and then fly, train or bus on to Greece. Alternatively, there are a number of inexpensive, secondary airline companies offering flights to London, and the major Western European capitals.

Useful agencies, especially for students, include *Let's Go Travel Services*.

From Canada

Scheduled Olympic flights include departures from:
Montreal: twice weekly direct
or (via Amsterdam, JFK and/or La Guardia NY): daily except Mondays
Toronto (via Montreal): twice weekly
or (via Amsterdam, JFK and or La Guardia NY): daily except Monday and Friday
Winnipeg (via Amsterdam): Thursday and Sunday only.

As for the USA, not only do the above flights involve a change of airline but there is a choice of domestic and package flights as well as a wide range of differing fares.

Student agencies include *Canadian Universities Travel Service*.

From Australia

There are Australian airline scheduled flights from Adelaide (via Melbourne), Brisbane (via Sydney), Melbourne and Sydney to Athens. Flights via Melbourne and Sydney involve a change of plane from, or to, a domestic airline. Regular as well as excursion fares and affinity groups.

From New Zealand

There are no scheduled flights.

Various connections are available as well as regular and affinity fares.

From South Africa

Scheduled Olympic flights include departures from:
Cape Town (via Johannesburg): Fridays and Sundays only.
Johannesburg: direct, Thursday, Friday and Sunday.

Flights via Johannesburg involve a change of plane from, or to, a domestic airline. South African airline flights from Johannesburg to Athens are available as regular, excursion or affinity fares.

From Ireland

Scheduled Olympic flights from:
Dublin (via London) daily, which involves a change of airline to *Aer Lingus*.

Note that when flying from Ireland, Australia, New Zealand, South Africa, Canada and the USA there are sometimes advantages in travelling via London or other European capitals on stopover and taking inexpensive connection flights to Greece.

From Scandinavia

including:

Denmark Scheduled Olympic flights from:
Copenhagen (via Frankfurt): daily, involving a change of aircraft as well as non-stop flights on Wednesday, Friday, Saturday and Sunday.

Sweden Scheduled Olympic flights from:
Stockholm (via Copenhagen and Frankfurt): Tuesday, Wednesday, Friday and Saturday.

Norway Scheduled Olympic flights from:
Oslo (via Frankfurt or Copenhagen): daily.

All the Scandinavian countries have a large choice of domestic and package flights with a selection of offerings. Contact *SAS Airlines* for *Olympic Airways details*.

AIRPORTS

United Kingdom

Do not forget if intending to stay in Greece longer than two weeks, the long-stay car parking fees tend to mount up – and will the battery last for a 3 or 4 week layer? Incidentally, charges at Gatwick are about £32.00 for two weeks, £42.00 for three weeks and £52.00 for four weeks. The difficulty is that most charter flights leave and arrive at rather unsociable hours, so friends and family may not be too keen to act as a taxi service.

Athens

Hellinikon airport is split into two parts, West (Olympic domestic and international flights) and East (foreign airlines). There are coaches to make the connection between the two airports, and Olympic buses to Athens centre as well as city buses.

At the Western or domestic airport, city buses pull up alongside the terminal building. Across the road is a pleasant cafe/restaurant but the service becomes fairly chaotic when packed out. To the left of the cafe (facing) is a newspaper kiosk and further on, across a side road, a Post Office is hidden in the depths of the first building.

The Eastern airport is outwardly quite smart but can, in reality, become an expensive, very cramped and uncomfortable location if there are long delays. (Let's not beat about the 'airport', the place becomes a hell-hole). Suspended flights occur when, for instance, air traffic controllers strike elsewhere in Europe. So remember when leaving Greece to have enough money and some food left for an enforced stay. Flight departures are consistently overdue and food and drink in the airport are costly with a plastic cup of coffee costing 115drs. Furthermore, there are simply no facilities to accommodate a lengthy occupation by a plane load of passengers. The bench seats are very soon fully occupied – after which the floor of the concourse fills up with dejected travellers sleeping & slumped for as long as it takes the aircraft to arrive. You have been warned.

BY TRAIN

From the United Kingdom & European countries

(Illustration 1).

Recommended only for train buffs and masochists but one of the alternative routes to be considered when a visitor intends to stay in Greece in excess of 6 weeks. The quickest journey of the three, major scheduled overland routes takes about 60 hours, and a second-class return fare costs in the region of £266. Tickets are valid for two months. One advantage of rail travel is that travellers may break the journey along the route (a little difficult on an airline flight), and another is that it is possible to travel out on one route and back by an alternative track (if you will excuse the pun). It is important to take along basic provisions, toilet paper and to wear old clothes.

A fairly recent return to the 'day of the train' reinforced my general opinion and introductory remarks in respect of this particular method of travel, bringing sharply back into focus the disadvantages and difficulties. The list of drawbacks should be enough to deter any but the most determined.

Try not to have a query which involves making use of the overseas information desk at *Victoria Station* as the facility is undermanned and the wait to get to a counter averages ¾hr. The staff are very willing but it is of interest that they overcome the intricacies of the official British Rail European timetable ('it's all Greek to me guvnor') by overtly referring to the (infinitely) more manageable *Thomas Cook* publication.

The channel crossing is often on craft that would not be pressed into service if we declared war on the Isle of Wight; the sea journey is too short for any cabins to be available; the duty free goods on offer are very limited and there are inordinate delays between train, boat and train.

The French trains that ply between the coast and Paris are of an excellent standard. On the other hand changing trains at the 'black hole' of *Gare du Nord* sharply focuses travellers' attention on a whole subculture of human beings who exist in and around a number of European railway stations. My favourite example

Illustration 1 European Railway Routes

of this little known branch of the human race is the 'bag-shuffler' – usually a middle-aged lady. The genus is initially recognisable by the multitudinous paper and plastic bags festooned about their person. Once at rest the contents are constantly and interminably shuffled from one bag to another, and back again, the ritual being accompanied by low mutterings. French railway stations, which are heated to a temperature relating to gentle simmer on a domestic cooker, have perfected a waiting room seating arrangement that precludes any but a drunk contortionist stretching out for a nap. In common with most other railway stations, food and drink are expensive and credit cards impossible to use, even at the swanky station restaurants. The railway station's toilet facilities are minuscule and men are charged for other than the use of a urinal and washbasin. Ladies have to pay about 2 Francs (F), a private closet costs 6F and a shower 12F. Potential users must not imagine they will be able to sneak in for a crafty stand-up wash using a basin – the toilets are intently watched over by attendants who would only require knitting needles to irresistibly remind one of the women who sat at the foot of the guillotine.

The Metro connection between the railway stations of *Gare du Nord* and *Gare de Lyon* is not straightforward and involves a walk. The *Gare de Lyon* springs a minor trap for the unwary in that the inter-continental trains depart from platforms reached by a long walk up the far left platforms (facing the trains). Don't some of the French trains now resemble children's rocket drawings?

Although it may appear to be an optional extra, it is obligatory to purchase a couchette ticket for the train journey. This is a Catch 22 situation brought about by the rule that only couchette ticket holders have the right to a seat! Yes, well, not so optional. It is also necessary to pack food and drink, at least for the French part of the journey, as usually there are no refreshment services. In Italy most trains are met, at the various station stops by trolley pushing vendors of (rather expensive) sustenance.

Venice station, signed *Stazione St Lucia*, is most conveniently sited bang-on the edge of the Grand Canal waterfront with shops and restaurants to the left. Some of the cake shops sell slabs of pizza pie for about 1000 lira (L) which furnishes good standby nourishment. The scheduled stopover here will have to be adjusted for any (inevitable) delay in arrival. Venice (on the outward journey) is the watershed where Greek, and the occasional Yugoslavian, carriages are coupled up. After this passengers can be guaranteed to encounter a number of nasties. The replacement compartments are seedier and dirtier than their French and Italian counterparts. The lavatories vary between bad to unspeakable and faults include toilets that won't flush (sometimes appearing to mysteriously fill up); Greek style toilet paper (which apart from other deficiencies lacks body and – please excuse the indelicacy – through which fingers break); no toilet paper at all (which is worst?); no soap dispenser; a lack of coat hooks; water taps that don't and all very grimy.

From Venice the term 'Express' should be ignored as the train's progress becomes slower and slower and slower with long, unscheduled stops and quite inordinate delays at the Yugoslavian frontiers. During the Yugoslavian part of the journey it is necessary for passengers to lock themselves into their compartment as some of the locals have an annoying habit of entering and determinedly looting tourists' luggage. There have even been 'totally unsubstantiated rumours', in the last year or two of callow fellows spraying an aerosol knockout gas through the keyholes, breaking in and at leisure relieving passengers of their belongings. I must stress I have not actually met victims and the story may be apocryphal. It is inadvisable to leave the train at *Belgrade* for a stopover as the accommodation available to tourists is extremely expensive, costing in the region of £60 plus for a double room, per night. Additionally, it is almost impossible to renegotiate a couchette for the remainder of the onward journey. There are trolley attendants at the major Yugoslavian railway stations but the innards of the rolls proffered are of an 'interesting' nature resembling 'biltong' or 'hardtack' burgers. Certainly when poked by the enthusiastic vendors I'm sure their fingers buckle. Another item of 'nutriment' on offer are large, but rather old cheese curd pies. A railway employee wanders the length of the train twice a day with a very large aluminium teapot ostensibly containing coffee. Nobody appears to be interested in payment with Yugoslavian dinars, but American dollars or English pounds sterling almost cause a purr of satisfaction. Travellers lucky enough to have the services of a Greek attendant may well find he keeps a cache of alcoholic drinks for sale. An aside is that Yugoslavians are obsessed by wheel-tapping and at all and every stop (almost at 'the drop of a sleeper'), appear and perform. Much of the journey beyond Belgrade is on a single line track and should, for instance, a cow break into a trot the animal might well overtake the train. At the frontier passengers may be reminded of the rigours of Iron Curtain countries, as they will be subjected to rigorous, lengthy baggage and documents checks by a swamp of officials, whose numbers include stern faced, unsmiling, gun-toting police.

In stark contrast the friendly Greek frontier town of *Idomeni* is a tonic. Even late at night the station's bank is open as is the taverna/snackbar with a scattering of tables on the platform and a buzz of brightly lit noise and activity.

To avoid the Yugoslavian experience a very pleasant alternative is to opt for the railway route that travels the length of Italy to *Brindisi Port*. Here international ferry-boats can be caught to the mainland Greek ports of Igoumenitsa or Patras, from either of which buses make the connection with Athens, whilst Patras offers the possibility of another train journey on to Athens. Brindisi (Italy), contains several traps for the unwary. Unfortunately the Maritime Railway Station and the quay for the Italy-Greek ferryboats are some 200m apart, which on a hot day... The railway station has no formal ticket office or barrier. It is only necessary to dismount, turn left along the platform, left again, beside the concrete wall supporting the first floor concourse (which stretches over and above the platforms), across the railway lines and left again down the sterile dockland street romantically named Via del Mare, to the ferry-boat complex. The road, hemmed in by a prefabricated wall on the right, curves parallel to the seawall on the left, from which it is separated by a high chain link fence, a number of railway lines and tarmacadam quay. But, before leaving the station, stop, for all the ticket offices and necessary officials are situated in the referred to upper storey buildings or in the 'Main Street', Corso Garibaldi. My favourite tour office is across the road from the station, alongside a bank on the corner formed by Corso Garibaldi and Via del Mare. The staff are very helpful and most informative. Diagonally across the bottom of this end of the 'Main St' is a small, tree edged square, Plaza Vittorio Emanuele. As it is well endowed with park benches, it has become an unofficial waiting room with travellers and backpackers occupying most of the available seating. Do not forget when booking rail tickets to ask for *Brindisi Maritime*, as the town railway station is some kilometres inland.

The international ferry-boats on this route generally divide neatly into two. The expensive, but rather shambolic Greek ferries and the expensive, but luxurious and well-appointed Italian ferries. The Greek boats are really nothing more than an inter-island ferries of 'middling' quality, with the 'threat' of a cabaret and casino. They can be in appalling condition and the reception staff are often rude. The Italian boats may well include in the trappings, a sea-water swimming pool, a ladies' hairdresser and beauty salon, a number of restaurants, a self-service cafeteria, a coffee bar and a disco. Food and drink is simply expensive. Examples include coffee at 135drs, a beer 120drs, a *petit dejeuner* for two of coffee and cake 520drs and dinner 1300-1900drs a head. On the Greek craft the gourmet standards are average and the service poor whilst the Italian service and offerings are excellent, all at about the same price. Moral, try not to eat on board. Fares range from about 7500drs for a simple, 2 berth cabin to 14000drs for a splendid two berth cabin with a generous en suite bathroom. Don't rely on the purser to carry out normal currency exchange transactions.

Travellers under 26 years of age can take advantage of *British Rail's Inter-Rail pass* by applying to Victoria Travel Centre while Americans and Canadians may obtain an *Eurorail pass* prior to reaching Europe. There is also the *Transalpino ticket* available from the London office of the firm of the same name. All these offers hold out a substantial discount on standard train and ferry fares, but are subject to various terms and conditions. Another student outfit offering cut-price train, coach and airline flights is *London Student Travel (& Eurotrain)*.

Certainly it must be borne in mind that the Greek railway system is not extensive and, unless travelling around other European countries, a concessionary pass might not represent much of a saving. On the other hand discounts in respect of the

Greek railways extends to travel on some of the State Railway buses (OSE).

Examples of the various tickets, costs and conditions are as follows:-

Inter-Rail ticket	Under 26 years of age, valid one month for use in 21 countries (and also allows half fare travel in the UK on *Sealink* and *B & I* ships as well as *P & O* ferries via Southampton and Le Havre).	£139	
Transalpino ticket	Under 26, valid for two months and allows stopover en route to the destination. London to Athens via Brindisi or Yugoslavia from	Single £107.35	Return £188.40

Other ticket options include B.I.G.E., Eurotrain and 'Athens Circle'.

Timetables & routes (Illustration 1)

This section caused me as much work as whole chapters on other subjects. *British Rail*, whose timetable I had the greatest difficulty deciphering and *Thomas Cook*, whose timetable I could understand, were both helpful.

Example routes include:
(1) London (Victoria Station), Dover (Western Docks), (jetfoil), Ostend, Brussels, Liege, Aachen, Cologne (change train, ¾hr delay), Mainz, Mannheim, Ulm, Munich (change train ¾hr delay) Salzburg, Jesenice, Ljubljana, Zagreb, Belgrade (Beograd), Skopje, Gevgelija, Idomeni, Thessaloniki to Athens.
An example of the journey is as follows:
Departure: 1300hrs, afternoon sea crossing, evening on the train, late night change of train at Cologne, night on the train, morning change of train at Munich, all day and night on the train arriving Athens very late, some 2½ days later at 2314hrs.

(2) London (Charing Cross/Waterloo East stations), Dover Hoverport, (hovercraft), Boulogne Hoverpoint, Paris (du Nord), change train (and station) to Paris (de Lyon), Strasbourg, Munich, Salzburg, Ljubljana, Zagreb, Belgrade (change train 1¾hrs delay), Thessaloniki to Athens.
An example:
Departure: 0955hrs and arrive 2½ days later at 2315hrs.
Second class single fare from £147 and return fare from £271.30.

(3) London (Victoria), Folkestone Harbour, (ferry-boat), Calais, Paris (du Nord), change train (and station) to Paris (de Lyon), Venice, Ljubljana, Zagreb, Belgrade, Thessaloniki to Athens.
An example:
Departure: 1415hrs and arrive 2¾ days later at 0840hrs.

Second class single fare from £135.20 and return fare from £266.

(4) London (Liverpool St), Harwich (Parkeston Quay), ferry-boat, Hook of Holland, Rotterdam, Eindhoven, Venio, Cologne (change train), Mainz, Mannheim, Stuttgart, Ulm, Munich, Salzburg, Jesenice, Ljubljana, Zagreb, Belgrade, Nis, Skopje, Gevgelija, Idomeni, Thessaloniki to Athens.
An example:
Departure: 1940hrs, night ferry crossing, change train at Cologne between 1048 and 1330hrs, first and second nights on the train and arrive at Athens middle of the day at 1440hrs.

An alternative is to take the more pleasurable train journey through Italy and make a ferry-boat connection to Greece as follows:
(5) London (Victoria), Folkestone Harbour, Calais, Boulogne, Amiens, Paris (du Nord), change train and station to Paris (de Lyon), Dijon, Vallorbe, Lausanne, Brig, Domodossala, Milan (Central), Bologna, Rimini, Ancona, Pescara, Bari to Brindisi.
(5a) Brindisi to Patras sea crossing.
(5b) Patras to Athens.
An example:
Departure: 0958hrs, day ferry crossing, change of train at Paris to the Parthenon Express, one night on the train and arrive at Brindisi at 1850hrs. Embark on the ferry-boat departing at 2000hrs, night on the ferry-boat and disembark at 1300hrs the next day. Take the coach to Athens arriving at 1600hrs.
The second class single fare costs from £163.30. and the return fare from £324.10.

Note it is possible to disembark at Ancona and take a ferry-boat but the sailing time is about double that of the Brindisi sailing. *See* **By Ferry-boat**.

On all these services children benefit from reduced fares, depending on their age. Couchettes and sleepers are usually available at extra cost and Jetfoil sea crossings are subject to a surcharge.

Details of fares and timetables are available from *British Rail Europe* or *The Hellenic State Railways (OSE)*. One of the most cogent, helpful and informative firms through whom to book rail travel must be *Victoria Travel Centre*. I have always found them to be extremely accommodating and it is well worth contacting *Thomas Cook Ltd*, who have a very useful range of literature and timetables available from their Publications Department.

The above are only a guide and up-to-date details must be checked with the relevant offices prior to actually booking.

From the Continent & Scandinavia to Athens

Pick up one of the above main lines by using the appropriate connections detailed in Illustration 1.

Departure terminals from Scandinavia include Helsinki (Finland); Oslo (Norway); Gothenburg, Malmo and Stockholm (Sweden); Fredrikshavn and Copenhagen (Denmark).

BY COACH

This means of travel is for the more hardy voyager and or young. If the description of the train journey has caused apprehension, the tales of passengers of the less luxurious coach companies should strike terror into the listener/reader. Common 'faults' include lack of 'wash and brush up' stops, smugglers, prolonged border custom investigations (to unearth the smugglers), last minute changes of route and breakdowns. All this is on top of the forced intimacy with a number of widely disparate companions, some wildly drunk, in cramped, uncomfortable surroundings.

For details of the scheduled *Euroway Supabus* apply c/o *Victoria Coach Station* or to the *National Express Company*. A single fare costs from £79 and a return ticket from £137 via Italy or £140 via Germany. This through service takes 4 days plus, with no overnight layovers but short stops at Cologne, Frankfurt and Munich, where there is a change of coach. Fares include ferry costs but exclude refreshments. Arrival and departure in Greece is at the Peloponissos Railway Station, Athens.

The timetable is as follows:

Departure from London, Victoria Coach Station, Bay 20: Friday and Saturday at 2030hrs arriving at 1100hrs, 4½ days later.

Return journey

Departure from Filellinon St, Syntagma Sq, Athens: Wednesday and Friday at 1300hrs arriving London at 0800hrs, 4 days later.

Note this company offers a special one month return fare of £127.

Eurolines Intercars (Uniroute) runs a national coach service that shuttles between Athens and Paris on a three day journey. The buses depart twice a week at 1030hrs, Wednesday and Saturday, at a cost of about 13,000drs, but note that baggage costs an extra 200drs. The French end of the connection is close by the Metro station *Porte Vincennes* and the Athens terminus is alongside the *Stathmos Larissis* railway station. These buses are comfortable with air conditioning but no toilet so the leg-stretching stops are absolutely vital, not only for passengers to relieve themselves but to purchase victuals. To help make the journey acceptable passengers must pack enough food and drink to tide them over the trip. It is a problem that the standard of the 'way-station' toilets and snackbars varies from absolutely awful to luxurious. And do not forget that the use of the lavatories is usually charged for in Greece and Yugoslavia. There are sufficient stops in Greece at, for instance, Livadia, Larissa and Thessaloniki, as well as at the frontier. The frontier crossing can take up to some 2¾hrs. The Yugoslavian part of the route passes through

Belgrade and at about two-thirds distance there is a lunchtime motorway halt. At this sumptuous establishment even Amex credit cards are accepted and the lavatories are free – a welcome contrast to the previous, 'mind boggling' Yugoslavian stop where even the Greeks blanched at the sight of the toilets! The bus and driver change at Trieste which is probably necessary after the rigours of the Yugoslavian roads.

Use of the lavatories in the bus station has to be paid for and they are very smelly with a 'lecher' in the ladies. One of the two Italian stops is at a luxurious motorway complex. It is worth noting that all purchases at Italian motorway cafe-bars and restaurants have to be paid for first. A ticket is issued which is then exchanged for the purchaser's requirements. This house rule even applies to buying a cup of coffee.

The route between Italy and France over the Alps takes a tediously long time on winding, narrow mountain roads with an early morning change of driver in France. It may well be necessary to 'encourage' the driver on this section to make an unscheduled halt in order to save burst bladders. The bus makes three Paris drop-offs, at about midday, three days after leaving Athens. The best disembarkation point depends on a traveller's plans. Devotees of the *Le Havre* channel crossing must make for the *Gare St Lazare* railway station. The Metro, with one change, costs about 5 francs (F) each and the coach's time of arrival allows passengers to catch a Paris to Le Havre train. This departs on the three hour journey at 1630hrs and the tickets cost some 100 F each. No information in respect of cross-Channel ferries is available at the Paris railway station, despite the presence of a number of tourist information desks.

Incidentally, the walk from the Le Havre railway terminus to the cross-Channel embarkation point is a long haul but there are reasonably priced taxis between the two points. The superb restaurant *Le Southampton*, conveniently across the street from the Ferry-boat Quay, may well compensate for the discomfort of the trudge round, especially as they accept payment by *Amex*.

'Express' coach companies include *Consolas Travel*. This well-established company runs daily buses during the summer months, except Sunday, and single fares start at about £59 with a return ticket costing from £99.

Other services are run by various 'pirate' bus companies. The journey time is about the same and, again, prices, which may be slightly cheaper, do not include meals. The cheaper the fare the higher the chance of vehicle break-downs and or the driver going 'walkabout'. On a number of islands, travel agents signs still refer to the *Magic Bus*, or as a fellow traveller so aptly put it – the 'Tragic Bus', but the company that ran this renowned and infamous service perished some years ago. Imitators appear to perpetuate the name.

In the United Kingdom it is advisable to obtain a copy of the weekly magazine *Time Out*, wherein the various coach companies advertise. For return trips from Athens, check shop windows in Omonia Sq, the *American Express* office in Syntagma Sq, or the *Students Union* in Filellinon St, just off Syntagma Sq.

See **Travel Agents, A To Z, Athens, Chapter Nine**

BY CAR (Illustration 2)

Motoring down to Greece is usually only a worthwhile alternative method of travel if there are at least two adults who are planning to stay for longer than three weeks, as the journey from England is about 1900 miles and takes approximately 50hrs non-stop driving.

People taking cars to Greece should ensure that spares are likely to be plentiful. An instance will illuminate. Recently I drove to Greece in a Mazda camping van and the propshaft went on the 'blink'. It transpired there was only one propshaft in the

Illustration 2 European Car Routes & Ferry-boat connection

whole of Greece – well that was the story. Spare parts are incredibly expensive and our replacement finally cost, with carriage and bits and pieces, 36,000drs. The ½hr labour required to fit the wretched thing was charged at 2,000drs plus tax or about £18 an hour. At the time the total worked out at approximately £194 which seemed a bit steep, even when compared to English prices. This cautionary tale prompts me to remind owners to take out one of the vehicle travel insurance schemes. The *AA* offers an excellent *5 Star Service Travel Pack* and other motoring organisations have their own schemes. At the time of making the decision the insurance premium might seem a trifle expensive but when faced with possibly massive inroads into available currency, the knowledge that a pack of credit vouchers is available with which to effect payment, is very reassuring.

The motoring organisations will prepare routes from their extensive resources. Certainly the *AA* offers this service but individual route plans now take 2-3 weeks to prepare.

One of the shortest routes from the United Kingdom is via car-ferry to Ostend

(Belgium) on to Munich, Salzburg (Germany), Klagenfurt (Austria) and Ljubljana (Yugoslavia). There the Autoput E94 is taken on to Zagreb, Belgrade (Beograd) and Nis on the E5, where the E27 and E55 are used via Skopje to the frontier town of Gevgelija/Evzonoi. Major rebuilding works can cause lengthy delays on the road between Zagreb and Nis.

Drivers through France have a number of possible routes but those choosing to skirt Switzerland will have to cross over into Italy, usually angling down through Lyon and heading in the general direction of Turin. One of the loveliest Franco-Italian frontier crossings is effected by driving through Grenoble to Briancon for the Alpine pass of Col de Montgenevre. Across the border lies Turin (Torino), which bypass, and proceed to Piacenza, Brescia, Verona, Padua (Padova), Venice and cut up to Trieste. I say bypass because the ordinary Italian roads are just 'neat aggravation' and the sprawling towns and cities are almost impossible to drive through without a lot of problems and exhausting delays. Although motorways involve constant toll fees they are much quicker and less wearing on the nerves. Note that Italian petrol stations have a 'nasty habit' of closing for a midday siesta between 1200 and 1500hrs. *See* **By Coach** for hints in respect of Italian motorway cafes and restaurants.

Possibly the most consistently picturesque drive down Italy is that using the incredibly engineered, audaciously Alpine tunnelled toll road that hugs the Mediterranean. This route can provide a check list of famous resorts. Proceed to Cannes and then via Nice, Monaco, and San Remo to Geneva and La Spezia. It is possible to detour to Pisa, Florence (Firenze) and Siena or simply continue on along the coast but this magnificent, often breathtaking motorway, terminates at Livorno. Whatever road is used, this route enables the Tuscany region to be driven through, which probably the only area of Southern Italy not defaced by indiscriminate factory building and urban sprawl, and on to Rome (Roma). After which it is possible to continue on past Naples – drivers should ensure that it is past Naples – to cut across the toe of Italy via Salerno, Potenza and Taranto and on to Brindisi Port. An alternative route is via Turin, Milan, Bergamo, Brescia, Verona and on to Trieste which leads around the southern edge of a few of the lakes, in the area of Brescia. Excursions to Padua and Venice are obvious possibilities.

From Trieste the most scenic (and winding) route is to travel the Adriatic coast road via Rijeka, Zadar and Split to Dubrovnik. This latter, lovely medieval inner city is well worth a visit. At Petrovac the pain starts as the road swings up to Titograd around to Kosovska Mitrovika, Pristina, Skopje and down to the border at Gevgelija. The stretch from Skopje to the Greek frontier can be rather unnerving. Signposting in Yugoslavia is usually very bad; always obtain petrol when the opportunity crops up and lastly but not least, city lights are often turned off during the hours of darkness (sounds a bit Irish to me!), making night driving in built-up areas extremely hazardous. To save the journey on from Petrovac, it is possible, at the height of the season, to catch a ferry from Dubrovnik to Igoumenitsa or Patras on the Greek mainland. (*See* **By Ferry-boat**)

Detailed road reports are available from the *Automobile Association*, but I would like to stress that in the Yugoslavian mountains, especially after heavy rain, landslips can (no will!) result in parts of the road disappearing at the odd spot as well as the surface being littered with rocks. There you go! Also note that the very large intercontinental lorries can prove even more of a dangerous hazard in Yugoslavia where they appear to regard the middle of the sometimes narrow roads as their own territory.

The main road through Greece, to Athens via Pirgos, Larissa and Lamia, is wide and good but the speed of lorries and their trailer units can prove disquieting.

Vehicles being overtaken are expected to move right over and tuck well into the wide hard shoulders. From Evzonoi to Athens, via Thessaloniki, is 340 miles (550km) and some of the major autoroute is now a toll road.

Drivers approaching Athens via the Corinth Canal should use the Toll road as the old route is murderously slow, especially in bad weather.

My favourite choice of route used to be crossing the Channel to Le Havre to drive through France, which holds few perils for the traveller, via Evreux, Chartres, Pithiviers, Montargis, Clamecy, Nevers, Lyon and Chambery to the Italian border at Modane. Here the fainthearted take the tunnel whilst the adventurous wind their way over the Col du Mont Cenis. That was until I 'discovered' the Briancon route.

In Italy rather than face the rigours of the Yugoslavian experience, it is worth considering, as for the alternative train journey, cutting down the not-all-that attractive Adriatic seaboard to one of the international Italian ferry-boat ports of Ancona, Bari, or Brindisi where boats connect to Igoumenitsa or Patras on the Greek mainland (*See* **By Ferry-boat & Train**).

General Vehicle & Personal Requirements

Documents required for travel in any European country used to include an *International Driving Licence*, and a *Carnet de Passages* en Douanes (both issued by the AA and valid for one year) but these are not now necessary in many European countries including France, Italy, Switzerland, Germany, Greece and Yugoslavia. Drivers must have their United Kingdom driving licence. One document not to be forgotten is the *Green Insurance Card* and it is recommended to take the vehicle's registration documents as proof of ownership. The vehicle must have a nationality sticker of the approved pattern and design.

Particular countries' requirements include:

Italy Import allowances are as for Greece but the restriction on the importation of Italian currency equals about £100.

All cars entering Italy must possess both right and left hand external driving mirrors. Divers' licences must be accompanied by an Italian translation.

Switzerland If intending to drive through Switzerland remember that the Swiss require the vehicle and all the necessary documents to be absolutely correct. (They would.) The authorities have a nasty habit of stopping vehicles some distance beyond the frontier posts in order to make thorough checks.

Yugoslavia A valid passport is the only personal document required for citizens of, for example, Denmark, West Germany, Finland, Great Britain and Northern Ireland, Republic of Southern Ireland, Holland and Sweden. Americans and Canadians must have a visa and all formalities should be checked with the relevant Yugoslavian Tourist Office.

It is compulsory to carry a warning triangle, a first aid kit and a set of replacement vehicle light bulbs. The use of spotlights is prohibited and drivers planning to travel during the winter should check the special regulations governing the use of studded tyres.

Visiting motorists do not now have to have petrol coupons in order to obtain petrol. But it is still advantageous to purchase them as they are the most cost effective method of buying fuel. The coupons are available at the frontier. Carefully calculate the number required for the journey and pay for them in foreign currency. Not only is the currency rate allowed very advantageous, compared to that if the coupons are paid for in Yugoslavian dinars, but their acquisition allows for 10% more fuel. Petrol stations are often far apart, closed or have run out of fuel, so fill up when possible.

Photographers are only allowed to import five rolls of film; drinkers a bottle of wine and a quarter litre of spirits and smokers 200 cigarettes or 50 cigars. Each person may bring in unlimited foreign currency but only 1500 Yugoslavian dinars.

Fines are issued on the spot and the officer collecting one should issue an official receipt.

To obtain assistance in the case of accident or breakdown dial 987 and the *SPI* will come to your assistance.

Greece It is compulsory to carry a first aid kit as well as a fire extinguisher in a vehicle and failure to comply may result in a fine. It is also mandatory to carry a warning triangle and it is forbidden to carry petrol in cans. In Athens the police are empowered to confiscate and detain the number plates of illegally parked vehicles. The use of undipped headlights in towns is strictly prohibited.

Customs allow the importation of 200 cigarettes or 50 cigars, 1 litre of spirits or 2 lites of wine and only 3000drs but any amount of foreign currency. Visitors from the EEC may import 300 cigarettes or 75 cigars, 1½ litres of spirits or 4 litres of wine.

Speed Limits

See table below – all are standard legal limits which may be varied by signs.

	Built-up areas	**Outside built-up areas**	**Motorways**	**Type of Vehicle affected**
Greece	31 mph (50 kph)	49mph (80 kph)	62 mph (100 mph)	Private vehicles with or without trailers
Yugoslavia	37 mph (60 kph) 62 mph* (100 kph)*	49 mph (80 kph)	74 mph (120 mph)	Private vehicles without trailers

*Speed on dual carriageways

FERRY-BOAT (Illustration 2).

Some of the descriptive matter under the heading **By Train** in this chapter refers to inter-country, ferry-boat travel, especially that relating to Brindisi Port and the international ferry-boats.

Due to the popularity of Brindisi, height of the season travellers must be prepared for crowds, lengthy delays and the usual ferry-boat scrum (scrum not scum). Other irritants include the exasperating requirement to purchase an embarkation pass, with the attendant formalities which include taking the pass to the police station on the second floor of the port office to have it punched! Oh, by the way, the way the distance between the railway station and the port is about 200m and it is absolutely necessary to 'clock in' at least 3hrs before a ferry's departure otherwise passengers may be 'scratched' from the fixture list, have to rebook and pay again.

That is why the knowledgeable head for the other departure ports, more especially Ancona. Motorists should note that the signposting from the autoroute runs out failing to indicate the turn off to Ancona for the Ferry-boat Quay – it is the south exit. But once alongside the quay all the formalities for purchasing a ferry-boat ticket and currency exchange are conveniently to hand in the concourse of the very large, square Victorian, 'neo something' building, alongside the quay-side.

Those making the return boat journey from Greece to Italy must take great care when purchasing the ferry-boat tickets, especially at Igoumenitsa (Greek mainland). The competition is hot and tickets may well be sold below the published price. If so, and a traveller is amongst the 'lucky ones', it is best not to 'count the drachmae' until on board. The port officials carefully check tickets and if they find any that have been sold at a discount then they are confiscated and the purchaser is made to buy replacements at the full price. Ouch!

Passengers must steal themselves for the monumentally crass methods employed by the Italian officials to marshall the passengers prior to disembarking at the Italian ports. The delays and queues that stretch throughout the length of the boat's corridors appear to be quite unnecessary and can turn normally meek and mild people into raging psychopaths.

Sample Ferry-boat Services From Italy & Yugoslavia

From Italy:

Brindisi to Patras: (& vice versa) (April-Oct) daily

Companies include:-
Anco Ferries, 33 Akti Miaouli, 185 35 Piraeus. Tel(010301)4116917/4520135.
CF Flavia & Flavia II

Sample ferry-boat fees To Patras:-			Low season	High season
per person:	deck	from	5500drs	7500drs
	aircraft seats		6000drs	8500drs
	2/4 berth cabin c/w washbasin		7500drs	11000drs
	2 berth cabin c/w bathroom		12/15000drs	16/20000drs
cars (over 4¼m)			5000drs	8/10000drs

Duration: 20hrs.

Brindisi to Igoumenitsa: & Patras: (& vice versa) (April-Oct) daily

Companies include:-
Fragline, 5a Rethymnou St, 10682 Athens Tel(010301) 8214171/8221285.

Nausimar, 9 Filellinon St, 185 36 Piraeus. Tel(010301) 452490
CF Igoumenitsa Express

Adriatic Ferries, 15-17 Hatzikyriakou Ave 185 37 Piraeus. Tel(010301) 4180584.
CF Adriatic Star

Agapitos Lines, 99 Kolokotroni St, 185 35 Piraeus. Tel(010301) 4136246.
CF Corfu Diamond & Sea.

HML, 28 Amalias Ave, Athens. Tel (010301)3236333/4174341.
CF Egnatia, Castalia, Corinthia & Lydia.

Adriatica Naviagazione, 97 Akti Miaoili, Piraeus. Tel(010301)4181901/3223693.
CF Appia & Espr. Grecia

Sample ferry-boat fees To Igoumenitsa:-			Low season	High season
per person:	deck	from	4/5000drs	6500drs
	aircraft seats		5500drs	7500drs
	2/4 cabin c/w washbasin		6/7000drs	10000drs
	2 berth cabin c/w bathroom		10/14000drs	14/19000drs

cars (over 4¼m)		5000drs	8000drs

Duration; 11½ hrs

Ancona to Patras: (& vice versa)

(April-Oct) Monday, Wednesday, Friday & Saturday

Karageorgis Lines, 26-28 Akti-Kondyli, Piraeus. Tel (010301)4110461/4173001. CF Mediterranean Sea & Sky

Sample ferry-boat fees To Patras:-

per person:		Low season	High season
	deck from	5700drs	7000drs
	aircraft seats	-	-
	2/4 berth cabin c/w washbasin	10400drs	12400drs
	2 berth cabin c/w bathroom	21400drs	25600drs
cars (over 4¼m)			

Duration: 35 hrs

Ancona to Igoumenitsa & Patras (& vice versa)

(May-June) Wednesday, & Saturday
(June-Oct) Wednesday, Thursday, Saturday, & Sunday.

Companies include:-
Minoan Lines, 2 Leoforos Vasileos, Konstantinou, Athens. Tel (010301) 7512356. CF El Greco & Fedra

(May-Sept) Wednesday, & Saturday
(July-Aug) Additionally Sunday, Thursday, & Friday

Marlines, 38 Akti Possidonos, 185 31 Piraeus. Tel (010301) 4110777 CF Princess M, Countess M & Queen M

(April-May & October) Monday, Tuesday, & Thursday
(June-September) Monday, Thursday & Saturday
(July-Aug) Monday, Tuesday, Thursday & Saturday

Strintzis Lines, 26 Akti Pissodonos, 185-31 Piraeus. Tel(010301)4129815 CF Ionian Sun, Star & Glory.

Sample ferry-boat fees To Igoumenitsa:-

per person:		Low season	High season
	deck from	4/5700drs	5/7000drs
	aircraft seats	5/6600drs	7/8000drs
	2/4 cabin c/w washbasin	7400drs	9400drs
	2 berth cabin c/w bathroom	12/16000drs	15/19600drs
cars (over 4¼m)			

Duration: 24 hrs

Bari to Igoumenitsa & Patras: (& vice versa)

(mid-April) Wednesday & Friday
(May) Friday & Sunday
(June & Oct) Wednesday, Friday & Sunday
(July-Sept) daily

Ventouris Ferries, 7 Efplias St, 185 37 Piraeus. Tel (010301) 4181001 CF Bari, Patra & Athens Express

Sample ferry-boat fees To Igoumenitsa:-

per person:		Low season	High season
	deck from	3400drs	5100drs
	aircraft seats	4100drs	6100drs
	2/4 cabin c/w washbasin	6800drs	9500drs
	2 berth cabin c/w bathroom	11500drs	15600drs

			Low season	High season
cars (over 4¼m)			4200drs	7500drs
Duration: 13 hrs.				
Sample ferry-boat fees			Low season	High season
To Patras:-				
per person:	deck	from	4700drs	5800drs
	aircraft seats		5400drs	6800drs
	2/4 cabin c/w washbasin		7500drs	10800drs
	2 berth cabin c/w bathroom		12200drs	17700drs
cars (over 4¼m)			4200drs	9500drs
Duration: 20½ hrs.				

From Yugoslavia

Dubrovnik to Igoumenitsa: (& vice versa) (July-Aug) Monday, Tuesday & Thursday. Jadrolinja Line, c/o Hermes en Greece, 3 Iassonos St, 185 37 Piraeus. Tel (010301)4520244.

Duration: 20 hrs.

Rijeka to Igoumenitsa: (July-Aug) Monday, Wednesday & Sunday

Duration; 43 hrs

Split to Igoumenitsa: (July-Aug) Monday. Tuesday & Thursday

Duration: 29 hrs.

Zadar to Igoumenitsa: (July-Aug) Tuesday

Duration: 36 hrs

Ferries that dock at Igoumenitsa can connect with Athens by scheduled bus services and those that dock at Patras connect with Athens by both scheduled bus and train services.

The Greek mainland ports of Igoumenitsa and Patras are detailed in **GROC's Candid Guide to Corfu & The Ionian Islands.**

Note the above services are severely curtailed outside the summer months, many ceasing altogether.

USEFUL NAMES & ADDRESSES

The Automobile Association, Fanum House, Basingstoke, Hants. RG21 2EA. Tel (0256) 20123
AA Routes Tel (0256) 492182
The Greek National Tourist Organisation, 195-197 Regent St, London WIR 8DL. Tel (01) 734 5997
The Italian State Tourist Office, 1 Princess St, London W1R 8AY. Tel (01) 408 1254
The Yugoslavian National Tourist Office, 143 Regent St, London WIR 8AE. Tel (01) 734 5243
British Rail Europe, PO Box 303, London SW1 1JY. Tel (01) 834 2345 *(Author's note – keep ringing)*
The Hellenic State Railways (OSE), 1-3 Karolou St, Athens, Greece. Tel (010301) 01 5222 491
Thomas Cook Ltd, Publications Dept, PO Box 36, Thorpewood, Peterborough PE3 6SB. Tel (0733) 63200

Other useful names & addresses mentioned in the text include:

Time Out, Southampton St, London WC2E 7HD.
Courier Flights/Inflight Courier, 45 Church St, Weybridge, Surrey KT13 8DG. Tel (0932) 857455/56
Owners Abroad Ltd, Valentine House, Ilford Hill, Ilford, Essex IG1 2DG. Tel (01) 514 8844
Olympic Airways, 164 Piccadilly, London W1V 9DE. Tel (01) 846 9080
Ref. 'Love-a-Fare' Tel (01) 493 3965

Aegina Club Ltd, 25A Hills Rd, Cambridge CB2 1NW. Tel (0223) 63256
Ramblers Holidays, 13 Longcroft House, Fretherne Rd, Welwyn Garden City, Herts AL8 6PQ. Tel (07073) 31133
Laskarina Holidays, St Mary's Gate, Wirksworth, Derbyshire, DE4 4DQ. Tel (062 982) 2203/4
STA Travel, 39 Store St, London WC1E 7BZ. Tel (01) 580 7733
Victoria Travel Centre, 52 Grosvenor Gdns, London SW1 Tel (01) 730 8111
Transalpino, 214 Shaftesbury Ave, London WC2H 8EB. Tel(01) 379 6735
London Student Travel, (Tel (01) 730 3402/4473) & **Eurotrain**, Tel (01) 730 6525), both at 52 Grosvenor Gdns, London SW1N 0AG.
Euroways Supabus, c/o Victoria Coach Station, London, SW1. Tel (01) 730 0202
or c/o National Express Co.
The Greek address is: 1 Karolou St, Athens. Tel (010301) 5240 519/6
Eurolines Intercars (Uniroute), 102 Cours de Vincennes, 75012 Paris (Metro Porte Vincennes)
National Express Co, Westwood Garage, Margate Rd, Ramsgate CT12 6S1. Tel (0843) 581333
Consolas Travel, 29-31 Euston Rd, London NW1. Tel (01) 833 2026
The Greek address is: 100 Eolou St, Athens. Tel (010301) 3219 228

Amongst others the agencies and offices listed above have, over the years and in varying degrees, been helpful in the preparation of the guides. I would like to extend my sincere thanks to all those concerned. Some have proved more helpful than others!

Olympic Airways Overseas office addresses are as follows:

America: 647 Fifth Ave, New York, NY 10022. Tel (0101 212)
(Reservations) 838 3600
(Ticket Office) 735 0290
Canada: 1200 McGill College Ave, Suite 1250, Montreal, Quebec H3B 4G7. Tel (0101 418) 878 9691
80 Bloor St West, Suite 406 Toronto ONT M552VI. Tel (0101 416) 920 2452
Australia: 44 Pitt St, 1st Floor, Sydney, NSW 2000. Tel (01061 2) 251 2044
South Africa: Bank of Athens Buildings, 116 Marshall St, Johannesburg. Tel (010127 11) 836 5951
Denmark: 4 Jernbanegade DK 1608, Copenhagen. Tel (010451) 126-100
Sweden: 44 Birger Jalsgatan, 11429 Stockholm. Tel (010468) 113-800

More useful overseas names & addresses include:

Let's Go Travel Services, Harvard Student Agencies, Thayer Hall B, Harvard University, Cambridge, MA02138 USA Tel 617 495 9649
Canadian Universities Travel Service, 187 College St, Toronto ONT M5T IP7 Canada. Tel 417 979 2406
Automobile Association & Touring Club of Greece (ELPA), 2 Messogion Street, Athens. Tel (010301) 7791 615

3 Travel Between Athens & the Mainland Islands

I see land. I see the end of my labour. Diogenes

The Greek islands are very thick on the water, numbering between 1000 and 3000, depending upon which authority you wish to believe. Approximately 100 are inhabited of which some 12 are located in the Mainland islands that I have chosen to agglomerate in the group. (Illustration 3).

In the past, the only way of setting foot on an island was to make for the relevant port and board a ferry-boat. Over the years a specialised and efficient system of water-borne travel developed. Apart from the advent of international air flights direct to the larger island of Skiathos, the opening of a number of smaller airfields to take domestic flights has made it possible to fly to Athens and take a flight to the islands of Kithira and Skiros in addition to the aforementioned, larger islands.

BY AIR

It can prove difficult to obtain a seat for domestic flights on the spot, especially at the height of the tourist season as Greeks now utilise the services extensively. It may be preferable to forward book through a local Olympic office prior to arrival. Ferry-boat travel was always much cheaper than air flight but in recent years this differential all but disappeared. In some cases flying was even cheaper than a 3rd class ferry-boat ticket and certainly less expensive than a 2nd class fare. A savage price hike in air fares in mid-1986 restored the ferries economic advantage.

Travellers arriving in Athens, other than by aircraft, and wanting a domestic flight from the West airport, can catch one of the Olympic coaches or city buses to the airport. These depart from the Olympic terminal and offices, 96-100 (Leoforos) Sygrou and Syntagma Square – day and night at a cost of 80-120drs depending on the hour, compared to the 400-550drs charged by a taxi (*See* **Arrival By Air, Athens, Chapter Nine**). An irate reader has taken me to task for not pointing out that approximately an hour must be allowed between catching the airline bus and the relevant plane check-in time.

Many travellers do not wish to stop over in Athens. If this is the case, and arriving other than on an Olympic flight, it is possible to travel from the East to the domestic, West, airport using the connecting bus service.

The staff of Olympic, the Greek airline, are usually very helpful and their English good, although occasionally it is possible to fall foul of that sporadic Greek characteristic, intransigence. I remember arriving, heavily laden and tired, at the Athens Olympic offices very early one morning. On asking for advice about the location of a hotel, any hotel, I was politely directed, by the girl at the enquiries desk, to the Tourist police, which would have involved an uphill walk of at least 1½km weighed down by an assortment of bags. There was a hotel, in which we stayed, immediately around the corner from the terminal!

It is worth considering utilising internal flights on one leg of a journey, especially if Athens is the point of arrival or departure. The possible extra cost of the flight, over and above the overland and ferry fares, must be balanced against the time element. For instance, Athens to Kithira takes some 50 mins by air whilst the ferry takes about 11 hours. One other advantage of domestic air travel is that the fares can be paid for by the use of *American Express*, *Diners* or *Access Mastercard*, possibly saving precious drachmae, especially towards the end of a holiday. On

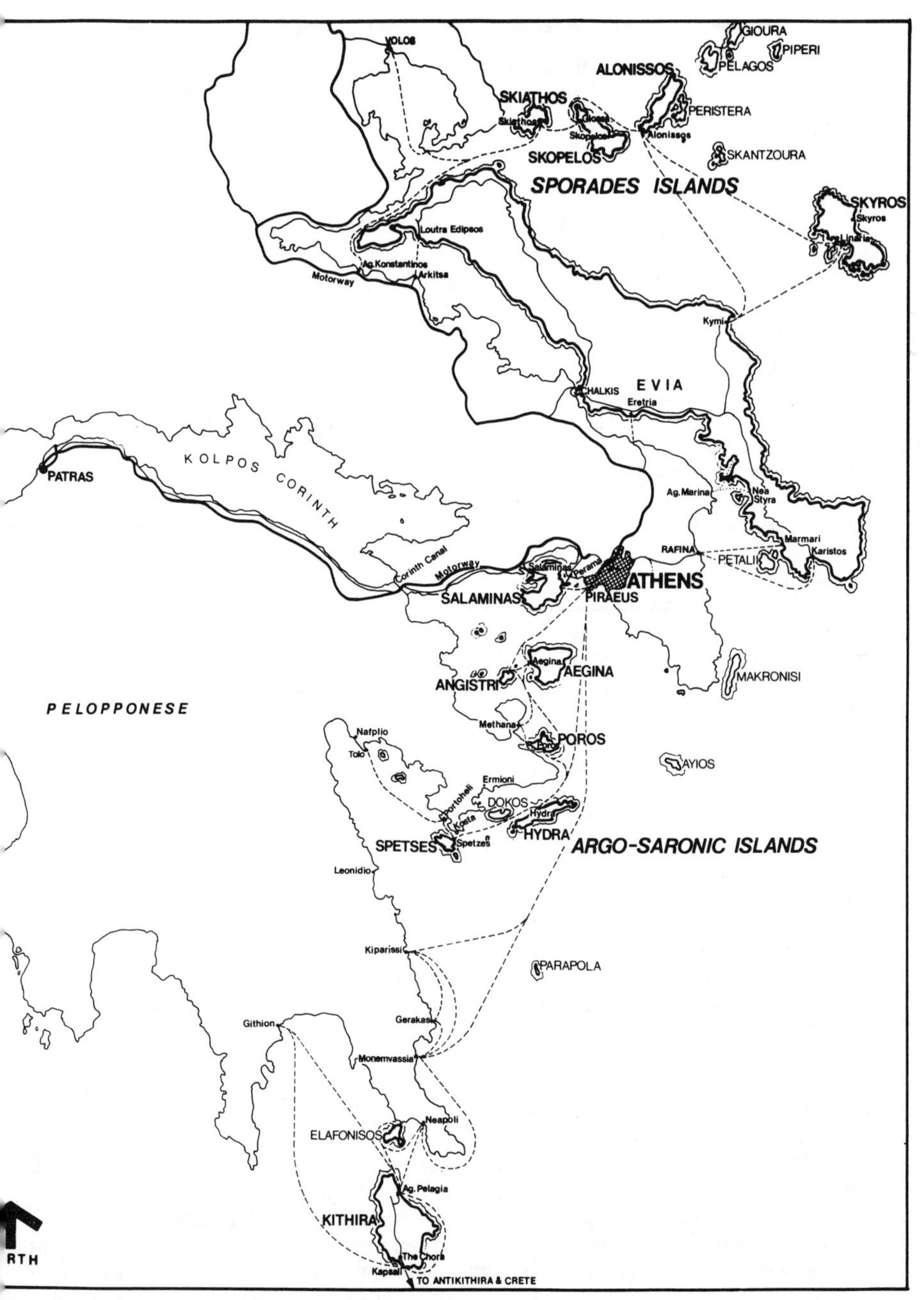

Illustration 3 Mainland islands

the other hand, the cost of domestic flights has been steeply increased over the last couple of years, as have ferry-boat fares. The air fares uplift is such as to restore the old differentials of ferry-boat travel being about 50% cheaper than flying.

BY BUS

See **Athens Chapter Nine, Piraeus and...., Chapter Ten** and the relevant island descriptions for details of daily scheduled bus services to the mainland ports that connect by ferry-boat to the various Sporades islands.

BY FERRY

In the following comments I am calling on my experience of travelling third and tourist class on any number of ferry boats.

In general, where sleeping arrangements are available and necessary they will prove satisfactory if certain basic rules are followed. First claim a bunk by depositing luggage on the chosen berth, it will be quite safe as long as money and passports are removed. The position of a berth is important and despite the labelling of 'Men' and 'Women' sleeping areas, a berth can usually be selected in either. Try to choose one adjacent to stern deck doors to ensure some ventilation. Due to the usual location of the third and tourist class accommodation beneath decks, it can get very hot and stuffy. A last tip is to lay a towel over plastic bunk covering to alleviate what otherwise would prove to be a sticky, uncomfortable night. Some ferries only have aircraft type, fold back seats in the 3rd/tourist class decks. Travellers should attempt, where possible, to find a lounge in which the television is muted.

The third class lavatories are often in an unsightly condition even prior to a craft's departure. To help enjoy reasonable surroundings and have the use of a shower, quietly proceed into the next class and use their facilities (but don't tell everybody). Both the toilets and the showers suffer from the usual deficiencies listed under **Greek Bathrooms, Chapter Four**, so be prepared.

Important points to take into account when inter-island ferry-boating include the following:

1. The ferries are owned by individual steamship companies and an employee of one line will be unable or unwilling to give enquirers information in respect of another company's timetable. Incidentally, this individual ownership results in a wide disparity in quality of service and general comfort between different ferry-boats.
2. The distances and voyage times are quite often lengthy and tiring. Additionally the duration of the overall passage sometimes (no always) results in the timetable going awry, with delays in scheduled departure times at islands well into a ferry's voyage.
3. There are usually four basic fare classes: first, second, tourist and third/deck class. The published fares on scheduled ferries are government controlled and the third/deck class option represents extremely good value. Purchasers must ensure that they state the fare class required as failure to do so may well result in a more expensive, tourist ticket being bought instead of the cheaper, deck class. Apart from the aforementioned four categories, there can be a variety of first and second-class sleeping accommodation, including private and shared cabins.

There are a number of 'Express' ferries and tourist trip boats, usually plying a particular island-to-island journey, on which charges are considerably higher.

4. Food and drink on the ferries used to be comparatively expensive, but price rises on the land have not been mirrored at sea. On the other hand the service on

the older boats is often discourteous and inefficient, so it may be advantageous to pack provisions for a long voyage.

Wholesome and inexpensive ferry-boat picnic food includes: tomatoes, cucumber, bread, salami, ham, *Sunfix* orange juice and a bottle of wine (or two!). Take some bottled water. Greek chocolate (especially with nuts) is very good but does not keep well in the ambient daytime temperatures.

5. The state of the toilets and the lack of basic supplies makes it mandatory that one or two lavatory rolls are packed, easily to hand as it were. The usual lack of washroom facilities commends the stowage of a pack of 'wipes'.

Quite frankly, on some occasions it will be necessary to stand on the rim of the toilet bowl as the only way of using the facility. Sorry!

6. Tickets should be bought from a ticket agency prior to a voyage, as they can cost more when purchased on board. Ticket agency offices vary from 'the plush' to boxed-in back stairs. Clients who have checked the scheduled prices should not go wrong. On the other hand they must be sure their price list is up to date as fare increases over recent years have been very large. For instance the 3rd class Piraeus to Kithira charge increased from 1147drs to 1582drs between April 1985 and June 1987.

7. At the height of the season, the upper deck seats are extremely hot during the day and uncomfortably chilly at night. It is advisable to stake a claim to a seat as early as possible because the ferries are usually very crowded during the summer months. Voyagers who intend to lay out a sleeping bag and sleep the night away on the deck would do well to remember to occupy a seat, not the deck itself which is more often than not sluiced down in the night hours.

8. Travellers should ensure they have a good fat book and a pack of cards to while away the longer sea voyages. Despite the awesome beauty of the islands and the azure blue sea, there are often long, unbroken periods of Mediterranean passage to endure, interrupted only by the occasional passing ship and the dramatic activity and ructions that take place during a port call.

9. Travellers sensitive to discordancy, and who find disagreeable a cacophony, a clamour of sound, may well find unacceptable the usual raucous mix experienced in the average 3rd class lounge. This is auditory assault often embodies two televisions (tuned to different programmes, the picture constantly flickering, suffering a snowstorm or horizontally high jumping in a series of stills) overlaid by the wail of Greco-Turkish music piped over the ship's tannoy system. Best to fly!

One delight is to keep a weather eye open and hope to observe some dolphins diving and leaping in the ship's wake. Their presence is often made discernible by the loud slapping noise they make when re-entering the water.

Ferry-boaters must take care when checking the connections, schedules and timetables as they can, no do, change during the year, especially outside the inclusive months of May to September, as well as from one year to another. So be warned.

Do not forget, when the information is at it's most confusing, the Port police are totally reliable, but often a little short on English. Their offices are almost always on, or adjacent to the quayside.

Please refer to **Piraeus..., Chapter Ten**, and individual island chapters for full details of ferry-boat timetables.

In 1987 the **CF Lemnos**, one of the best ferry-boats ploughing the Aegean, was put into service the Sporades island routes. The Third class lounge would not be out of place in most ships First class sector. There is a splendid cafeteria with a very reasonably priced menu. Below decks is air-conditioned and prior to the ship slipping the quay, it is thoroughly cleaned by the crew, not a lick and a promise, added to which the iced water machines work.

FLYING DOLPHINS (Hydrofoils – Ceres)

These speedy craft cut the ferry-boat timetables in half but the fares are about double.

Examples include Piraeus (Zea) to Spetses by ferry costs 765drs and takes 5¼hrs whilst the hydrofoil costs 1545drs with a 'flying' time of 2hrs.

CRUISE SHIPS

Fly/cruise packages on offer are usually rather up-market and, in the main, are based on seven days or multiples thereof. The cruise ships call in at selected islands for a part or full day, with excursions where applicable.

Other holiday-makers should note that the large influx of this 'genus' of fun loving tourist can have quite an impact on an island, and the *cognoscenti* normally vacate the particular port of call for that day.

GREEK ISLAND PLACE NAMES

This is probably the appropriate place to introduce the forever baffling problem which helps to bedevil the traveller – Greek place names. For instance, the island of Hydra may well be designated Idra or even Ydra. The reason for the apparently haphazard nomenclature lies in the long and complicated territorial ownership of Greece and its islands, more especially the latter. The base root may be Greek, Latin, Turkish or Venetian. Additionally the Greek language has three forms – Demotic (spoken), Katharevousa (literary) and Kathomiloumeni (compromise), of which Demotic and Katharevousa have each been the official linquistic style. Even as recently as 1967-74 the *Colonels* made Katharevousa, once again, the authorised form, but Demotic is now the approved language. Help!

Street names can be equally confusing and I have plumped for my personal choice sometimes stating the alternatives, but where this is not possible, well, there you go! I mean how can Athens' main square, Syntagma be spelt Syntagina, Sintagma or Syntagmatos?

Hotel and pension titles often give rise to some frustration where a Guide has listed the Roman scripted appellation. For instance to the (vast majority of the) uninitiated, *Hotel* Αυλη does not at first, second or third sight look like *Avli*, does it?

Due to scholastic, critical comments I must defend my habit of mixing Roman and Greek script when referring to establishment and street names. For example, I may write the Greek ΑΚΤΗ ΕΘΝΙΚΗΣ ΑΝΤΙΣΤΑΣΗΣ, which translates to the Roman *Akti Ethnikis Antistasis*. My only defence is that 99.9% of readers transmit that which they see to the brain without being able to make the mental gymnastics necessary to substitute the different letters. This is markedly so in respect of those letters that have no easy or direct equivalent. Will my more erudite friends excuse the rest of us dyslexic Grecophiles!

Street names are subject to some obscurity as the common noun Odhos (street) is often omitted, whilst Leoforos (avenue) and Plateia (square) are usually kept in the name. The prefix Saint or St is variously written as Agios, Ayios, Ag or Ai. A *nome* approximates to a small English county, a number of which make up a province such as the Peloponnese or Thessaly.

At this stage, without apologies, I introduce my own definition to help identify an unspoilt Greek town as follows: *where the town's rubbish is collected by donkey, wooden panniers slung across its back, slowly clip-clopping up a stepped hillside street, the driver, not even in sight but probably languishing in a stray taverna!*

Map nomenclature	**Greek**	**Translation**
Agios/Ag/Ayios/Aghios	Αγιος	Saint
Akra/Akrotiri	Ακρωτηρι	Cape/headland
Amoudia		Beach
Ano	Ανω	Upper
Archeologikos (horos)	Αρχαιολογικοζ	Ancient (site)
Cherssonissos		Peninsula
Chora/Horo/Horio/khorio	Χωριο	Village
Kato	Κατω	Lower
Kiladi		Valley
Klimaka		Scale
Kolpos	Κολποζ	Gulf
Leoforos	Λεωφοροζ	Avenue
Limni	Λιμνη	Lake/marsh
Limani	Λιμανι	Harbour
Lofos		Hill
Moni/Monastiri	Μοναστηρι	Monastery
Naos	Ναοζ	Temple
Nea/Neos	Νεο	New
Nissos/Nissi	Νησοζ	Island
Odhos/Odos	Δρσμοζ (Οδος)	Street
Ormos	Ορμοζ	Bay
Oros	Οροζ	Mountain
Palios/Palaios	Παλιοζ	Old
Paralia		Seashore/beach
Pediada		Plain
Pelagos		Sea
Pharos		Lighthouse
Pigi		Spring
Plateia	Πλατεια	Square
Potami	Ποταμι	River
Prokimea		Quay
Spilia	Σπηλια	Cave
Steno		Straight
Thalassa		Sea
Vuno	Βουνο	Mountain

Useful Greek

English	**Greek**	**Sounds like**
Where is...	Που είναι	Poo eene...
...the Olympic Airways office	τα γραφεία τηζ Ολυμπιακήζ	...ta grafia tis Olimbiakis
...the railway station	ο σιδηροδρομικόζ σταθμόζ	...sidheerothromikos stathmos
...the bus station	ο σταθμόζ των λεωφορειων	...stathmos ton leoforion
...the boat	το πλοίο	...to plio
...the nearest underground station	ο πλησιέοτεροζ σταθμόζ του ηλεκτρικοο	...o pleessiestehros stathmos too eelektrikoo
...the ticket office	το εκδοτήριο των εισιτηρίων	...to eckdhoterio ton eessitirion
...the nearest travel agency	το πλησιέστεπο πρακτορεον ταξιδίων	...to pleessiestehro praktorion taxidion
I'd like to reserve...	Θέλω να κρατήσω	Thelo na kratiso
...seat/seats on the	θέση/θέση για	...thessee/thessis ghia
...to	για	...ghia
...plane	αεροπλάνο	...aeroplano

...train	τραίνο	...treno
...bus	λεωφορείο	...leoforio
...ferry-boat	πλοίο	...plio
When does it leave/arrive	Πότε φεύγει/φθάνει	Poteh fehvghi/fthanee
Is there...	Υπάρχει	Eeparhee...
...from here to	απ εδώστο	...Apetho sto
...to	στον	...ston
Where do we get off	Που κατεβαίνομε	Poo katevenomhe
I want to go to	Θέλω να πάω στουζ	Thelo na pao stoos...
I want to get off at	Θέλω να κατέβω στο	Thelo na katevo sto...
Will you tell me when to get off	Θα μου πείτε που να κατέβω	Thah moo peete poo nah kahtevo
I want to go to...	Θέλω να πάω στουζ	Thelo na pao stoos
Stop here	Σταμάτα εδώ	Stamata etho
How much is it	Πόσο είναι	Posso eene
How much does it cost	Πόσο κάνει η μεταφορά	Posso kani i metafora
...to	στο	...sto
Do we call at	Θα σταματήσωμε στην	Tha stamatissome stin

Signs often seen affixed to posts & doors

Greek	**English**
ΑΦΙΞΙΣ	ARRIVAL
ΑΝΑΧΩΡΗΣΙΣ	DEPARTURE
ΣΤΑΣΙΣ	BUS STOP
ΕΙΣΟΔΟΣ	ENTRANCE
ΕΞΟΔΟΣ	EXIT
ΚΕΝΤΡΟ	CENTRE (as in town centre)
ΕΙΣΟΔΟΣ ΕΛΕΥΘΕΡΑ	FREE ADMISSION
ΑΠΑΓΟΡΕΥΕΤΑΙ Η ΕΙΣΟΔΟΣ	NO ENTRANCE
ΕΙΣΙΤΗΡΙΑ	TICKET
ΠΡΟΣ ΤΑΣ ΑΠΟΒΑΘΡΑΣ	TO THE PLATFORMS
ΤΗΛΕΦΩΝΟΝ	TELEPHONE
ΑΝΔΡΩΝ	GENTLEMEN
ΓΥΝΑΙΚΩΝ	LADIES
ΑΠΑΓΟΡΕΥΕΤΑΙ ΤΟ ΚΑΠΝΙΣΜΑ	NO SMOKING
ΤΑΜΕΙΟΝ	CASH DESK
ΤΟΥΑΛΕΤΕΣ	TOILETS
ΑΝΟΙΚΤΟΝ	OPEN
ΚΛΕΙΣΤΟΝ	CLOSED
ΩΘΗΣΑΤΕ	PUSH
ΣΥΡΑΤΕ	PULL

4 Island Accommodation

How doth man by care oppressed, find in an inn a place of rest. Combe

Package villa and tour organised holiday-makers will have accommodation arranged prior to arrival in Greece. In contrast, the most important matter to the independent traveller, is undoubtedly the procurement of lodgings, especially the first overnight stay on a new island or at an untried location.

The choice and standard of accommodation is bewildering, ranging from extremely simple Rooms, in private houses (usually clean but with basic bathroom facilities), even to luxury class, almost indecently plush hotels able to hold their own with the most modern counterpart, almost anywhere else in the world. The deciding factor must be the budget and a person's sensibilities. My comments in respect of standards reflect comparisons with Western European establishments. Those referring to prices are usually in relation to other Greek options.

Travellers stepping off a ferry-boat are usually part of a swarming throng made up of Greeks, tourists and backpackers engulfed by a quayside mass of Greeks, tourists and backpackers struggling to get aboard the same craft. Visitors may well be approached by men, women and youngsters offering accommodation. It is a matter of taking pot-luck there and then, or searching around the town to make an independent selection. The later in the day, the more advisable it is to take an offer, unseen, but it is obligatory to establish the price, if the rooms are with or without a shower, is the water hot and how far away they are located. It can prove unnerving to be 'picked up' and then commence on an ever-lengthening trudge through the back streets of a strange place, especially as Greek ideas of distance are rather optimistic.

Any accommodation usually requires a traveller's passport to be relinquished. As a passport is also required to change money and to hire a car or a scooter, it is a good idea, if married or travelling with friends, to have separate documents. Then, if necessary, one passport can be left with the landlord and another kept for other purposes, as required.

Official sources and many guidebooks lay much emphasis on the role of the Tourist police in finding accommodation, but this cannot be relied upon as the offices may well be closed on arrival. Moreover changes in the structure of the various police forces over the last few years has resulted in the once separate and independent Tourist police being integrated with the Town police. I for one regard this as a very retrograde step. Such a pity that the Greeks, innovators of this excellent service, should now abandon the scheme, more especially in the light of the ever increasing number of tourists. Perhaps having achieved their goal of ensuring Greece is a number one holiday spot, the authorities are allowing the tour guides and couriers (that go 'hand in sand' with the ever increasing number of package tourists) to take over the Tourist police role in an *ex officio* capacity? Preposterous! I hope so.

A fruitful source of accommodation leads are tavernas, which more often than not, result in an introduction to a ***Room*** or pension owner. Failing that, they usually send out for someone.

BEDROOMS

Greek bedrooms tend to be airy, whitewashed and sparsely furnished. The beds are often hard, as are the small pillows, and unyielding mattresses may well be laid directly on to bed-boards, not springs.

It is advisable to inspect bedroom walls for the evidence of blood-red splats. These indicate flattened, but once gorged, mosquitoes and result from a previous occupant's night-time vigil. Well designed rooms usually have a top-opening window screened off with gauze so that they can be left ajar without fear of incursions by winged, creepy-crawlies. Where no gauze is in evidence, it is best to keep the windows tightly closed at night, however alien this may be. Those not in possession of a proprietary insect repellent may well have to reconcile themselves to a sleepless night. Tell-tale buzzing echoing in the ears indicates one has already been bitten. It is comparable to being attacked by Lilliputian Stuka night-fighters.

Hanging points are noticeable by their absence. Often there will be no wardrobe but if present, there is unlikely to be any hangers, not even the steel-wire type, and the cupboard doors may be missing. A rather idiosyncratic feature is that clothes hooks, when present, are often very inadequate, looking as if they have been designed, and are only suitable for, hanging coffee mugs by the handles.

Even more maligned and even more misunderstood than Greek food is:

THE GREEK BATHROOM

I use the descriptive word bathroom, rather than refer simply to the toilets, because the total facility requires some elucidation. The following will not apply to Luxury, Class A or B hotels – well, it should not!

The plumbing is quite often totally inadequate. Instead of the separate wastes of the bath, shower and sink being plumbed into progressively larger soil pipes, thus achieving a 'venturi' effect, they are usually joined into a similar diameter tube to that of the individual pipes. This inevitably causes considerable back pressure with inescapable consequences. If this were not sufficient to cause a building inspector (who?) nightmares, where 'Mama' owns a washing machine it is invariably piped into the same network. That is why the drain grill, cunningly located at the highest point of the bathroom floor, often foams. The toilet waste is almost always insufficient in size and even normal, let alone excessive, use of toilet paper results in dreadful things happening, not only to the bathroom, but probably to a number of bathrooms in the building, street and possibly the village. If this were not enough... the header tank rarely delivers sufficient 'flush'. It has to be pointed out that Greeks have had, for many years, to be economic in the use of water and some islands ration it, turning off the supply for a number of hours per day, in the height of the summer.

Common faults are to find the lavatory without a seat; flooded to a depth of some inches; the bathroom light not working; no toilet roll; door locks not fitted as well as dirty WC pans and or any combination of the above. Furthermore, the wash basin may well be without a drain plug. Amongst other reasons, the lack of a plug is to stop flooding if a sink tap is accidently left turned on when the mains water is switched off, and not turned off when the water supply is resumed!

The most common type of en suite bathroom is an all purpose lavatory and shower room. Beware! Years of research reveals that the shower head is usually positioned in such a way as to not only wash down the occupant but to drench the (amazingly) absorbent toilet roll as well as the bathers clothes, towel and footwear. Incidentally, the drain point is usually located in such a way as to ensure that the bathroom is kept awash to a depth of between 1' and 3' ... and the resultant pool invariably lies where a toilet sitter's feet fall – if you read my meaning.

It is not unusual for there to be no hot water, even if a heating system is in evidence. Government energy conservation methods, the comparatively high cost of electricity and the use of moderately sized solar heating panels, all contribute to this state of affairs. Where solar panels are the means of heating the water, remember to beat the rush and shower as early as possible, for the water soon loses its heat. Why not share with a friend? If hot water is available, but it is not heated by solar energy, then it will be necessary to locate the relevant electric switch. This is usually a 4 way position, ceramic knob hidden away behind a translucent panel door. On the other hand... To be fair to owners of accommodation, it is standard practice to charge for the use of hot water showers so it pays the landlord to have the switch out of sight and reach. Room charges may well be increased by 50 to 100drs per day, per head, for the use of a shower, but this ought to be detailed on the Government controlled price list that should be displayed, and is usually suspended on the back of the bedroom door.

One stipulation on water-short islands that really offends the West European (and North American?) sense of delicacy, is the oft present, hardly legible sign, requesting guests to put their 'paper' in the wastebin supplied, and not down the pan! I must own up to not always obeying this dictum and have had to make a hurried departure from a number of islands, let alone a pension or village, when the consequences of my profligate use of toilet paper have become apparent.

THE BEACH

Some backpacking youngsters utilise the shore for their night's accommodation. In fact all island ferry-boaters must be prepared to consider the beach as a standby at the more crowded locations during the months of July and August. I have only had to spend two or three nights on the beach in the eight or nine years of island excursions but admit to steering clear of the height of season months of late July, August and early September. Certainly the weather could not be more ideal for sleeping under the stars, the officials are generally not too fussed and may well direct travellers to a suitable spot. Beware of mosquitoes and tar.

CAMPING

In direct contrast to *ad hoc* sleeping on the beach beneath the stars, camping, except at approved sites, is strictly forbidden. The law is not always rigorously applied. The restriction comes about from a wish to improve general hygiene, to prohibit and discourage abuse of private property and as a precaution against forest fires. The NTOG operate most of the licensed sites, some of which are spectacularly located, but there are some authorised, privately run camping grounds, which are also price controlled. A *Carnet-Camping International*, although not normally requested, affords campers worldwide, third-party liability cover and is available to United Kingdom residents from the AA and other, similar organisations.

If moved on by any official for sleeping out on the beach or illegally camping, it is advisable not to argue and go quietly. The Greek police have fairly wide, autonomous powers and it is preferable not to upset them unnecessarily.

As a guide, overnight campsite fees are charged as follows:
Adults 290-400drs; children ½ adult rate and tent hire 50-550drs.

YOUTH HOSTELS (ΞΕΝΩΝΑΣ ΝΕΩΝ)

Establishments in Athens include the *YMCA (XAN)* and *YWCA (XEN)* as well as the *YHA*, which also has one or three outposts on the islands. The appellation more often than not is applied to ethnic private pensions catering for young travellers. They are habitually are rather down-at-heel and tend to be operated in a somewhat Spartan, slovenly manner.

It is preferable to have YHA membership, taking the Association's card along.

Approximate prices per night at the YMCA and YWCA are 900drs and in a Youth Hostel 400-450drs.

ROOMS

The story goes that as soon as a tourist steps off the ferry, he (or she) is surrounded by women crying *Rooms* (*Dhomatio*), and whoops, within minutes the traveller is ensconced in some wonderful Greek family's private home.

History may well have been like that, and in truth the ferries are still met at almost every island, the inhabitants offering not only rooms but pensions and the lower category hotels. Rooms are the cheapest accommo- dation and are generally very clean, sometimes including the option of breakfast, which is ordinarily charged extra. Prices reflect an island's popularity and the season, but the average 1987 mid-season cost in the Mainland islands was 1500drs for a double room, depending upon the classification.

Government approved and categorised rooms are subject to an official tariff, and are slightly more expensive than freelance householders. A general point relates to a cautionary tale told us by a delightful French couple. They were in the habit of replying to a room owner's enquiry as to how many nights they wished to stay by saying 'Tonight'. One lady room owner interpreted this to mean two nights! Beware the inaccurate translation.

At the more tourist popular island resorts a new, unwelcome phenomena has reared 'his' ugly head. This is the long stay, enterprising layabout who rents a large double or triple bedroom for the summer season from a hapless, unsuspecting owner of accommodation. The 'entrepreneur', a species to be avoided, then daily sublets out the room, cramming in some 5 or 6 a night.

Apart from a prospect being approached leaving the ferry, the Tourist police would, in the past, advise about available accommodation but their role is being drastically reduced in their amalgamation with the Town police. The Tourist police offices were signed, if at all; 'ΤΟΥΡΙΣΤΙΚΗ ΑΣΤΥΝΟΜΙΑ'. Householders display the sign 'ΕΝΟΙΚΙΑΖΟΝΤΑΙ ΔΩΜΑΤΙΑ' or simply 'ΔΩΜΑΤΙΑ', when they have a room to rent.

PENSIONS ('PANSION, ΠΑΝΣΙΟΝ')

This type of lodging was a natural progression from Rooms and now represents the most often found and reasonably priced accommodation on offer.

The older type of pension is rather reminiscent of those large Victorian English houses, split up into bed-sits. In the main though they have been purpose built, usually during the Colonels' regime (1967-74) when government grants were freely available for the construction of tourist quarters. The owner usually lives in the basement and acts as concierge. The rooms are functional and generally the guests on each level share a bathroom and shower and (a rather nice touch when provided) a communal refrigerator in which visitors can store their various provisions and drinks. Mid-season charges for 1987 varied between 1500 and 2000drs for a double room.

Sometimes a breakfast of coffee, bread and jam, perhaps butter and a boiled egg, is available for about 150drs and represents fair value compared with the cost of a cafe breakfast.

TAVERNAS (ΤΑΒΕΡΝΑ)

Tavernas are, first and foremost, eating places. Some tavernas, especially those situated by, or near, beaches, also have accommodation available. The only drawback is that the more popular the taverna, the less likely guests are to get a full night's sleep, but of course the more involved they will be with the taverna's social life which often continues into the small hours. Charges are similar to those of a Pension.

HOTELS (ΞΕΝΟΔΟΧΕΙΟΝ)

Shades of difference and interpretation can be given to the nomenclature by variations of the bland, descriptive noun hotel. For instance ΞΕΝΟΔΟΧΕΙΟΝ ΥΠΝΟΥ indicates a hotel that does not serve meals and ΠΑΝΔΟΧΕΙΟΝ a low grade hotel.

Many independent travellers would not consider hotels as a first choice. The high classification ones are more expensive than Pensions and the lower grade hotels often cost the same, but may well be rather seedy and less desirable than the equivalent class pension. Greek hotels are classified L (Luxury) A, B, C, D and E and the prices charged within these categories (except L) are controlled by the authorities.

It is unfortunately almost impossible to neatly pigeon-hole and differentiate between hotels and their charges as each individual category is subject to fairly wide standards, and charges are dependent on a multitude of possible percentage supplements and reductions as detailed below:

Shower extra (C, D and E hotels); number of days stayed less than three, plus 10 per cent; air conditioning extra (A and B hotels); out of season deductions (enquire); high season extra (ie months of July, August and the first half of September, plus 20 per cent; single occupancy of a double room, about 80 per cent of the double room rate. The higher classification hotels may well insist on guests taking demi-pension terms, especially in high season.

The following table must be treated as a guide only but is based on 1988 prices.

Class	Comments	Indicated mid-season, double-bedroom price
L	All amenities, a very high standard and price. Probably at least one meal in addition to breakfast will have to be purchased. Very clean. Very hot water.	
A	High standard and price. Most rooms have an en suite shower or bath. Guests may well have to accept demi-pension terms. Clean Hot water.	6000-8000 drs
B	Good standard. Many rooms have an en suite shower or bath. Clean. Hot water.	4000-6000 drs
C	Usually an older hotel. Faded elegance, shared bathroom. Cleanish. Possibly hot water.	2000-4000 drs
D	Older, faded hotel. Shared bathroom, which may well be 'interesting'. A shower, if available, will be an 'experience' and the water cold.	1500-2500 drs
E	Old, faded and unclean. The whole stay will be an 'experience'. Only very cold water.	1200-1600 drs

The prices indicated include government taxes, service and room occupancy until noon.

Where in the text reference is made to 'official rates', these are the prices listed in the *Guide to the Greek Hotels*. Generally prices detailed throughout this guide are those applicable to 1987.

THE XENIAS

Originally government owned and promoted to ensure the availability of high standard accommodation at important tourist centres but now often managed by private enterprise. Only A, B and C rated categories, they are usually of a better standard than hotels in a similar class.

FLATS & HOUSES

During the summer months this type of accommodation, referred to by travel agents and package tour operators as villas, is best booked prior to arriving in Greece. Not only will pre-booking be easier but, surprisingly, works out cheaper than flying out and snooping around.

The winter is a different matter, but probably not within the scope of most of our readers.

Further useful names & addresses

The Youth Hostel Association, 14 Southampton St, London WC2E 7HY. Tel. 01 836 8541

Useful Greek

English	Greek	Sounds like
I want...	Θέλω	Thelo...
...a single room	ένα μονό δωμάτιο	...enna mono dhomatio
...a double room	ένα διπλό δωμάτιο	...enna thiplo dhomatio
...with a shower	με ντουζ	...me doosh
We would like a room for...	Θα θέλαμε ένα δωμάτιο για	Tha thelame ena dhomatio ghia...
two/three days/a week/ until	δύο/τρεiζ μέρεζ/μια εβδομαδα/μεχρι	thio/trees meres/meea evthomatha/mekhri
Can you advise of another...	Ξέρετε κανένα άλλο...	Xerete kanena alo...
house with rooms	σπιτι με δωμάτιο	speeti meh dhomatio
pension	πανσιόν	panseeon
inn	πανδοχείο	panthokheeo
hotel	ξενοδοχείο	ksenodhokheeo
youth hostel	ξενώναζ νέων	xenonas neon
How much is the room for a night?	Πόσο κάνει το δωμάτιο για τη νύχτα	Poso kanee dho dhomatio ghia ti neektah
That is too expensive	Είναι πολύ ακριβά	Eene polee akriva
Have you anything cheaper?	Δεν έχετε άλλο πιό φθηνό	Dhen ekhete ahlo pio ftheeno
Is there...	Υπάρχει	Eeparkhee
a shower	ένα ντουζ	doosh
a refrigerator	ένα ψυγείο	psiyeeo
Where is the shower?	Που είναι το ντουζ	Poo eene dho doosh
I have to leave...	Πρέπει να φύγω	Prepee na feegho...
today	σήμερα	simera
tomorrow	αύριο	avrio
very early	πολύ νωρίς	polee noris
Thank you for a nice time	Ευχαριστώ για την συμπαθητική ώρα*	Efkareesto ghia tin simpathitiki ora

*This is the exact translation, which would never be used, however, in Greek. An expression meaning rather: 'thanks for the fun' is:

	Ευχαριστώ για την διασκέδαση	Efkaristo ghia tin thiaskethasi

5 Travelling around an island

A man is happier for life from having once made an agreeable tour. Anon

A few introductory remarks may well be apposite in respect of holiday-makers' possessions and women in Greece. The matter is discussed elsewhere but it is not out of place to reiterate one or two points (Rosemary calls it 'carrying on').

PERSONAL POSSESSIONS

Do not leave airline tickets, money, travellers' cheques and or passports behind at the accommodation. A man can quite easily acquire a wrist-strap handbag in which to conveniently carry these items. The danger does not, even today, lie with the Greeks, but with fellow tourists, down-and-outs and professional thieves working a territory.

WOMEN

There has been, in recent years, a movement towards the 'Spanish-Costa' percentage ploy. Young Greek men, in the more popular tourist areas, have succumbed to the prospects offered by the sexually liberated overseas women holiday-makers, especially those openly courting sun, sand and sex. Greek girls are still subject to rigorous parental control so it is not surprising that the local lads turn their attentions to other, possibly more fruitful, pastures. Greeks who indulge in this pastime are derogatorily referred to as *Kamaki* – 'spearers of game', after the traditional fishing trident. It's up to you girls, there is no menace, only opportunities!

Now back to the main theme of the chapter but before expanding on the subject a few words will not go amiss in respect of:

BEACHES

A surprisingly large number of beaches are polluted in varying degrees, mainly by seaborne plastic and some tar. Incidentally, olive oil is an excellent medium with which to remove this black menace which sticks to towels, clothes and shoes better than the proverbial .... to a blanket.

Lack of anything but a small rise and fall of tide removes the danger of swimmers being swept out to sea but, on windy days, the tug of the sea's undertow can be very strong.

Jellyfish and sea urchins can occasionally be a problem in a particular bay, jellyfish increasingly so. One of my Mediterranean correspondents advises me that cures for the jellyfish sting include ammonia, urine (ugh) and a paste of meat tenderiser (it takes all sorts I suppose).

The biggest headache (literally) to a tourist is the sun, or more accurately, the heat of the sun at the height of the summer season. To give an example of the extreme temperatures sometimes experienced, in Athens a few years ago birds were actually falling out of the trees, and they were the feathered variety! Every year dozens of tourists are carted off, suffering from acute sunburn. A little often, (sun that is), must be the watchword. The islands benefit from the relief of the prevailing summer wind, the *Meltemi*.

Whereas nudism was once severely punished by puritanical authorities, as long as tourists, who wish to sunbathe topless, bottomless or both, utilise those beaches allocated for the purpose, there will be no trouble. Over the years, as Greek families have increasingly appreciated the delights of the beach, even the young women have taken to going topless. It is very pleasant to observe more and more middle-aged Greek ladies taking to the sea, often in all enveloping black costumes and straw hats. Some, to preserve their modesty, appear to swim in everyday clothes.

Despite the utterly reasonable condemnation of modern day advances in technology by us geriatrics, one amazing leap forward for all travelling and beach bound mankind is the *Walk-Master* personal stereo-casettes. No more the strident, tinny beat of the transistor (or more commonly the 'ghetto-blaster'), now simply the jigging silence of ear-muffed and transfixed faces. Splendid!

It may well be that a reader is a devoted sun worshipper and spends every available minute on the beach, patio or terrace; if so there is no need to read any further. On the other hand when a holiday-maker's daytime interests range beyond conversion of the sun's rays into painful, peeling flesh, and there is a wish to travel around a particular island, then the question of *modus operandi* must be given some thought.

First, purchase an island map and one of the colourful and extremely informative tourist guides available on the larger islands. It is unfortunate that my old friends *Clyde Surveys* do not produce maps of the Argo-Saronic or Sporades islands. It is strange that no one company has made a wholly inclusive map of either chain but there are two well executed maps by the *Efstathiadis Group* of Athens. Number 5 includes the Argo-Saronic islands, apart from all but a smidgin of Salaminas but, as the vast land mass of the Peloponnese is the centrepiece, the scale is too small to do justice to the islands. Number 3, labelled the Sporades, rather pathetically and inadequately includes only Skiathos, Skopelos and the southern end of Alonissos.

Having purchased the maps and guides it is necessary to consider the alternative methods of travel and appraise their value.

ROADS

The main roads of most islands are passable but asphalted country lanes often degenerate alarmingly, becoming nothing more than heavily rutted and cratered tracks. Generally much road building and reconstruction is under way. Beware as not all roads, indicated as being in existence on the maps, are anything more than, at the best, donkey tracks or are simply non-existent. Evidence of broken lines marking a road must be interpreted as meaning there is no paved highway at all.

ON FOOT

Owing to the hilly terrain of the islands and the daytime heat encountered, readers may well have had enough walking without 'looking for trouble'. A quick burst down to the local beach, taverna. shop or restaurant, and the resultant one hundred or so steps back up again, may well go a long way to satiating any desire to go 'walkies'. If needs be, walking is often the only way to negotiate the more rugged donkey tracks and the minimum footwear is a solid pair of sandals or 'trainers'. Plan not to walk during the midday hours, wear a hat, at least take along sufficient clothes to cover up should the sun prove too hot and pack a bottle of drinking water.

HITCHING

The comparative paucity of privately owned cars makes hitch-hiking an unsatisfactory mode of travel. On the other hand, if striking out to get to, or return from a particular village on a dead end road, most Greek drivers stop when thumbed down. It may well be a lift in the back of a Japanese pick-up truck, possibly sharing the space with some chickens, a goat or sheep or all three!

DONKEY

Although once a universal 'transportation module', now usually only available for hire on specific journey basis in particular locations. A personal prejudice is to consider donkey rides part of the unacceptable face of tourism, added to which it tends to be exorbitantly expensive.

BUSES

Buses (and taxis) are the universal method of travel in Greece, so the services are widespread if, naturally enough, a little Greek in operation. Generally they run approximately on time and the fares are, on the whole, extremely reasonable. Passengers must expect to share the available space with fairly bulky loads and occasionally, livestock.

The trick is to first find the square on which the buses terminus. Then locate the bus office where the tickets are pre-purchased and on the walls or windows of which might be stuck the timetable and the fares structure. The real fun starts if the bus is not only 'sardine packed', but fares are collected by a conductor who has to somehow make his way through, round and over the passengers. Be available well prior to the scheduled departure times as buses have a 'nasty habit' of departing early. Ensure any luggage is placed in the correct storage compartment for the particular destination otherwise it may go missing.

Buses are often crowded, especially when a journey coincides with a ferry-boat disgorging its passengers. The timetables are usually scheduled so that a bus or buses await a ferry-boat's arrival, except perhaps very early or late arriving craft. A bus rarely leaves a potential client standing, they just encourage everyone aboard.

Do not fail to observe the decorations festooned around and enveloping the driver. Often these displays resemble a shrine, which taking account of the way some of the drivers propel their bus, is perhaps not so out of place. Finally, do have some change available as coins are always in short supply. It is helpful to know that local buses may be labelled TOPIKO (ΤΟΠΙΚΟ).

A critic recently took me to task for not stressing that the summer bus schedules listed throughout the text are the subject of severe curtailment, if not total termination during the winter months from October through to May. So, smacked hand Geoffrey and readers please note.

TAXIS

As indicated in the previous sub-heading, taxis are the 'other' mode of island travel. They are usually readily available and can be remarkably modern and plush. On the other hand...

Ports and towns nearly always have a main square on which the taxis rank but come the time of a ferry-boat's arrival they queue on the quayside. Fares are governed by the local authorities and, at the main rank, are often displayed giving examples of the cost to various destinations. Charges are reasonable by European standards, but it is essential to establish the cost prior to hiring.

It may come as a shock for a 'fare' to have his halting, pidgin Greek answered in 'pure' Australian or American. But this is not surprising when one considers that many island Greeks have spent their youth on merchant ships or emigrated to the New World for 10 to 15 years. On their return home, with the future relatively financially secure, many take to taxi driving to supplement their income (and possibly to keep out of the little woman's way?).

BICYCLE, SCOOTER & CAR HIRE

Be very careful to establish what (if any) insurance cover is included in the rental fee, and that the quoted hire charge includes any compulsory taxes.

On the whole, bicycles are very hard work and poor value in relation to, say the cost of hiring a *Vespa* scooter – an option endorsed when the mountainous nature of most islands, and the midday heat, is taken into consideration. The once popular Italian machines are progressively being replaced by the ubiquitous, semi-automatic Japanese motorcycles. Although the latter do away with the necessity to fight the gears and clutch, they are not entirely suited to transporting two heavyweights. I have had the frightening experience, when climbing a steep mountainside track, of the bike jumping out of gear, depositing my passenger and I on the ground leaving the scooter whirling found like a crazed mechanical Catherine wheel.

It is amazing how easy it is to get a good tan while scootering. The moderate wind draws the sun's heat, the air is laden with the smell of wild sage and oleanders and with the sun on one's back... marvellous!

Very rarely is a deposit requested when hiring a bike or motorbike but a passport is required. Always shop around to check out various companies' charges: the nearer to a port, town or city centre a hirer is, the more expensive the machines will be. Take a close look over the chosen mode of transport before settling up, as maintenance of any mechanical unit in Greece is poor to non-existent. Bicycles and scooters, a few years old, will be 'pretty clapped out'. A client must check the brakes, they will be needed, and should not allow the hirer to fob him off without making sure there is a spare wheel.

Increasingly, the owners of two wheeled vehicles are hiring out dubious looking crash helmets. Flash young Greek motorbike riders usually wear their 'Space Age' headgear on the handlebars, where no doubt it will protect them (that is the handlebars) from damage. A useful tip when hiring a scooter is to take along a towel! It doubles up as useful additional padding for the pillion passenger's bottom on rocky roads and saves having to sit on painfully hot plastic seating should a rider forget to raise the squab when parked. Sunglasses are necessary to protect the eyes from airborne insets. Out of the height-of-season and early evening it becomes very chilly so a sweater or jumper is a good idea and females may well require a headscarf, whatever the time of day or night.

Fuel is served in litres and five litres of two-stroke costs about 320-340drs. Fill up as soon as possible as fuel stations are in fairly 'short supply' outside the main towns. Increasingly the gap between the scooter and the car is being filled with more sophisticated machinery which include moon-tyred and powerfully engined Japanese motorbikes and beach-buggies.

Typical daily hire rates are: for a bicycle 250drs; a Vespa scooter 1500-2000drs; a car from 5000drs including full insurances and taxes but mileage may cost extra, calculated at so much per kilometre. Out of season and period hire for all forms of conveyance can benefit from 'negotiation'. Car hire companies require a daily deposit, which now starts off at 20,000drs per day, as well as a hirer's passport and driving licence details. Due to this large outlay it is almost mandatory to pay by credit card, which all car hire companies 'gratefully grab'. It is noticeable that I and many readers regard car hire as a legalised rip-off. One contentious area that causes unpleasant disputes is the increasing habit of the hire companies to charge comparatively expensively for any damage incurred, and I mean any damage, however slight. A hirer's detailed reasons for the causes of an accident, the damage and why it should not cost anything falls on deaf ears. Furthermore it is no use threatening to involve the police as they will not be at all interested in the squabble.

Several other words of warning might not go amiss. Taking into account the uncertain state of the roads, do not hire a two-wheeled conveyance if not thoroughly used to handling one. There are a number of very nasty accidents every year, involving tourists and hired scooters. Additionally the combination of poor road surfaces and usually inadequate to non-existent vehicle lights should preclude any night-time scootering. A hirer must ensure he (or she) is fully covered for medical insurance, including an unscheduled, *Medicare* flight home, and do check, before leaving the home shores, that a general holiday policy does not exclude accidents incurred on hired transport, especially scooters.

The glass-fronted metal framed shrines mounted by the roadside are graphic reminders of a fatal accident at this or that spot. Incidentally, on a less macabre note, if the shrine is a memorial to a man, the picture and bottle often present (more often than not of Sophia Loren and whisky) represent that person's favourite earthbound desires.

But back to finger-wagging. The importance of the correct holiday insurance cover cannot be over-stressed. The tribulations I have encountered in obtaining inclusive insurance, combined with some readers' disastrous experiences, have resulted in the inclusion in the guide of an all embracing scheme. This reminder should be coupled with the strictures in **Chapter One** drawing attention to the all-inclusive policy devised for readers of the **Candid Guides**. Enough said!

More useful names & addresses

Clyde Surveys Ltd, Reform Road, Maidenhead, Berks SL6 8BU — Tel (0628) 21371
Efstathiadis Group, 14 Valtetsiou St, Athens — Tel 3615 011

Useful Greek

English	Greek	Sounds like
Where can I hire a...	Που μπορω να νοικιασω ενα	Poo boro na neekeeaso enna...
...bicycle	ποδηλατο	...pothilato
...scooter	σκουτερ	...sckooter
...car	αυτοκινητο	...aftokinito
I'd like a...	Θα ηθελα ενα	Tha eethela enna...
I'd like it for...	Θα το ηθελα για	Tha dho eethela ghia...
...a day	μια μερα (or: μια)	...mia mera
...days	μερες	...meres
...a week	μια εβδομαδα	...mia evthomadha
How much is it by the...	Ποσο κανει την	Poso kanee tin...
...day	μερα	...mera
...week	εβδομαδα	...evthomadha
Does that include...	Συμπεριλαμβανονται σαυτο	Simberilamvanonte safto
...mileage	τα χιλιομετρα	...tah hiliometra
...full insurance	μικτη ασφαλεια	...meektee asfaleah
I want some	Θελω	Thelo
...petrol (gas)	βενζινης	...vehnzini
...oil	λαδι	...lathi
...water	νερο	...nero
Fill it up	Γεμιστε το	Yemiste to
...litres of petrol (gas)	λιτρα βενζινης	...litra vehnzinis
How far is it to...	Ποσο απεχει	Poso apechee
Which is the road for...	Ποιος ειναι ο δρομος για	Pios eene o thromos ghia
Where are we now	Που ειμαστε τωρα	Poo eemaste tora
What is the name of this place	Πως ονομαζεται αυτο το μερος	Pos onomazete afto dho meros
Where is...	Που ειναι	Poo eene...

Road Signs

ΑΛΤ	STOP
ΑΠΑΓΟΡΕΥΕΤΑΙ Η ΕΙΣΟΔΟΣ	NO ENTRY
ΑΔΙΕΞΟΔΟΣ	NO THROUGH ROAD
ΠΑΡΑΚΑΜΠΤΗΡΙΟΣ	DETOUR
ΕΛΑΤΤΩΣΑΤΕ ΤΑΧΥΤΗΤΑΝ	REDUCE SPEED
ΑΠΑΓΟΡΕΥΕΤΑΙ Η ΑΝΑΜΟΝΗ	NO WAITING
ΕΡΓΑ ΕΠΙ ΤΗΣ ΟΔΟΥ	ROAD REPAIRS
ΚΙΝΔΥΝΟΣ	BEWARE (Caution)
ΑΠΑΓΟΡΕΥΕΤΑΙ ΤΟ ΠΡΟΣΠΕΡΑΣΜΑ	NO OVERTAKING
ΑΠΑΓΟΡΕΥΕΤΑΙ Η ΣΤΑΘΜΕΥΣΙΣ	NO PARKING

Shopping in the 'upper reaches' of Poros Port.

6 Island Food & Drink

Let us eat and drink for tomorrow we die. Corinthians

It is a pity that many tourists, prior to visiting Greece, have, in sundry restaurants throughout Europe and North America, 'experienced' the offerings masquerading as Greek food. Greek food and drink does not appear to cross its borders very well. I do not think it is possible to recreate the unique quality of Greek cooking in foreign lands. Perhaps this is because they owe much of their taste to, and are in sympathy with, the very air laden with the scent of the flowers and herbs, the very water, clear and chill, the very soil of the plains and scrub clad mountains, the ethereal and uncapturable quality that is Greece. Incidentally, many critics would postulate that it was impossible to create Greek food, full stop, but be that as it may...

Salad does not normally send me into ecstasy but, after a few days in Greece, the very thought of a peasant salad, consisting of endive leaves, sliced tomatoes and cucumber, black olives, olive oil and vinegar dressing, all topped off with feta cheese and sprinkled with oregano, parsley or fennel, sends me salivating to the nearest taverna.

Admittedly, unless you are lucky enough to chance across an outstanding taverna, the majority are surprisingly unadventurous and the choice of menu limited. Mind you there are one or two restaurants serving exciting and unusual meals, if the spelling mistakes are anything to go by. For instance I have observed over the years the following no doubt appetising dishes: *omeled, spachetti botonnaise, shrings salad, bowels entrails, lump cutlets, limp liver, mushed pot, shrimps, crambs, kid chops, grilled meatbolls, spar rips, wine vives, fiant oven, swardfish, pork shops, staffed vine leaves, wild greens, string queens, wildi cherry, bater honi, gregg goti (!), mate with olive oil, bruised meat, forced meat balls, Creek salad, lamp kebab ....with rise, personal shrimps, mutton bowels served with pice, beef shoup, lame liver, intest liver, cububer, scorpines, chickey, greef beans, fried pataroes, bems giauts, veal roast in kettle, loveubrawn, walout kake, honey boiles, various complex (in the coffee section) and et cetera* – don't they sound interesting.

On a more positive note, whilst the usual dishes will be known to readers, a recommendation, a mention of a dish I haven't seen before and a 'musing' may not go amiss. As to the recommendation, where an eating house serves up a good creamy tzatziki and a Greek salad it makes a very refreshing dish to combine the two. Latterly I came across a meal I have not encountered previously, saganaki. This is a very tasty dish of scrambled egges/omelette in which are mixed sliced bacon and or sausage, all cooked in an olive oil greased 6' pan. The ruminative, brown study relates to the humble potato. Why, oh why, taking into account the copious plates of *patatas* available (thus proving the existence in quantity of the aforesaid tuber), are there no variations on the theme? Where are, oh where are mashed, roast or creamed potatoes to, once in a while usurp the omnipresent, universal chip?

A FEW HINTS & TIPS

Do not insist upon butter, the Greek variant is not very tasty to the European palate, is expensive and in the heat tends to dissolve into greasy pools.

Sample the retsina wine and after a bottle or two a day for a few days there is every chance you will enjoy it. Moreover, retsina is beneficial (well that's what I tell myself), acting as a splendid anti-agent to the comparative oiliness of some of the food.

Bread is automatically served with a meal – and charged for – unless a diner indicates otherwise. It is very useful for mopping up excess olive oil and thus requires no butter to make it more greasy. It has become a noticeable, and regrettable, feature in recent years that the charge for bread has increased to between 10 and 30drs per head, and I have seen it as high as 40drs. Naughty! Many eateries have developed the nasty little habit of lumping an extra tax calculation in with the bread charge, that is extra to the usual tax inclusive prices listed on the menu.

Greek food tends to be served on the 'cool' side. Even if the meal started out hot, and by some mischance is speedily served, it will arrive on a thoroughly chilled plate.

The selection of both food and drink is almost always limited and unenterprising unless diners elect to frequent the more international restaurants (but why go to Greece?). On the other hand the choice of establishments in which to eat and or drink is unlimited, in fact the profusion is such that it can prove very confusing. If in doubt about which particular restaurant or taverna to patronise, use the well tried principle of picking one frequented by the locals. It will invariably serve good quality food at reasonable prices. It is generally a waste of time to ask a Greek for guidance in selecting a good taverna or restaurant as he will be reluctant to give specific advice in case the recommendation proves unsatisfactory.

Especially in the more rural areas, do not be shy, ask to look over the kitchen to see what's cooking. If denied this traditional right, be on your guard as the food may well be pre-cooked, tasteless and plastic, particularly if the various meals available are displayed in a neon-lit showcase. Do not order the whole meal all at once, as would be usual at home. If you do it will be served simultaneously and or in the wrong sequence. Order course by course and take your time, everyone else does. Diners are not being ignored if the waiter does not approach the table for anything up to 20 minutes, he is just taking his time and is probably overworked. At first the blood pressure may inexorably rise as your presence appears to be continually disregarded but it makes a visitor's stay in Greece very much more enjoyable if all preconceived ideas of service can be forgotten. Lay back and settle into the glorious and indolent timelessness of the locals' way of life. If in a hurry, pay when the order arrives for if under the impression that it took a disproportionate time to be served, just wait until it comes to settling up. It will probably take twice as long to get the bill (*logariasmo*) as it did to receive the food.

Chicken, when listed, is usually served with some chips. Fish, contrary to expectations, appears very expensive, even in comparison with European prices, so you can imagine the disparity with the cost of other Greek food. When ordering fish it is normal to select the choice from 'the ice' and, being priced by weight, it will be put on the scales prior to cooking. This is the reason that fish is listed at so many drachmae per kilo, which does reduce the apparently outrageous price just a little. If seeking 'cost conscious' meals, and wishing for a change from the ubiquitous moussaka, beef steak, or for that matter, chicken and chips, why not plump (!) for *kalamari* (squid). Even at present day, inflated prices they usually provide a filling, tasty, low budget cost meal at 250-350drs. It has to be admitted that demand has resulted in the more popular locations and areas serving up imported Mozambique squid. These can often be recognised by their regular shape and sweet taste – probably suiting less demanding palettes very well. From the late summer months locally caught kalamares tend to be large and knobbly.

Government price lists are a legal necessity for drinking and eating places. They should state the establishment's category and the price of every item served. Two prices are shown, the first being net is not really relevant, the second, showing the price actually charged, includes service and taxes.

Food is natural and very rarely are canned or any frozen items used, even if available. When frozen foods are included in the meal the fact must be indicated on the menu by addition of the initials *KAT*. The olive oil used for cooking is excellent, as are the herbs and lemons, but it can take time to become accustomed to the different flavours imparted to food. Before leaving the subject of hints and tips, remember that olive oil can be pressed into service for removing unwanted beach tar from clothes.

A most enjoyable road, quayside or ferry-boat breakfast is to buy a large yoghurt (*yiaorti*) and a small pot of honey (*meli*), mix the honey into the yoghurt and then relish the bitter-sweet delight. If locally produced, natural yoghurt (usually stored in cool tubs and spooned into a container) cannot be purchased, the brand name *Total* is an adequate substitute being made from cow's or sheep's milk. I prefer the sheep derived product and, when words fail, break into a charade of 'baa-ing'. It keeps the other shoppers amused if nothing else. The succulent water melon, a common and inexpensive fruit, provides a juicy, lunchtime refreshment.

Apart from waving the tablecloth in the air, or for that matter the table, it is usual to call *parakalo* (please). It is also permissible to say *gharkon* or simply 'waiter'.

A disturbing habit, becoming more prevalent in recent years, is the increasing use of the word *Special/Spezial*. This is simply to enable establishments to charge extra for a dish or offering that would have, in the past, been the 'norm'. A good example is 'Special souvlaki pita' which is nothing more than a normal giro meat souvlaki. The 'standard', inferior substitute is a slab of meat. Oh dear.

THE DRINKS

Non-alcoholic beverages Being a cafe (and taverna) society, coffee is drunk at all times of the day and night. Greek coffee (*kafe*) is in fact a leftover from the centuries long Turkish influence, being served without milk in small cups and always with a glass of deliciously cool water. Unless specified otherwise it will be served sickly sweet or *varigliko*. There are many variations but the three most usual are *sketto* (no sugar), *metrio* (medium) or *glyko* (sweet). Beware not to completely drain the cup, the bitter grains will choke an imbiber. Except in the most traditional establishments (*kafeneions*), you can ask for *Nes-kafe* or simply *Nes* which, rationally is an instant coffee. This home-grown version often has a comparatively muddy taste. If you require milk with your coffee it is necessary to ask for *meh ghala*. A most refreshing version is to order Nes chilled or *frappé*. French coffee (*ghaliko kafe*), served in a coffee pot with a separate jug of hot milk, espresso and cappuccino are found in the larger, provincial towns, ports and international establishments. However, having made a detailed request, you may well receive any permutation of all the possibilities listed above, however carefully you may think you have ordered.

Tea, (*tsai*), perhaps surprisingly, is quite freely available, made of course with the ubiquitous teabag, which is not so outrageous since they have become universally commonplace. In more out of the way places herbal tea may be served.

Purchasing bottled mineral waters is not always necessary as, generally, island water is superb but should you wish to have some stashed away in the fridge, brand names include *Loutraki, Nigita,* and *Sariza. Sprite* is fizzy and *lemonade/lemonatha* a stillish lemonade. Orangeade (*portokaladha*), cherry soft drink (*visinatha*) and fruit juices are all palatable and sold, as often as not, under brand names, as is the universal *Koka-Kola*. A word of warning comes from a reader who reported that, in the very hot summer months, some youngsters drink nothing but sweet, fizzy beverages. This can result in mouth ulcers caused by fermenting sugar, so drink some water every day. A blot on the general 'aqua pura standard' are most of the islands that make up the Sporades (that is all accept Skyros). The tap water on these is more than likely contaminated. As one Skiathos pharmacist exploded 'Why, when we have the finest water in the world, are we Greeks forced to buy bottled water?'. He went on to elaborate that he regarded the H_2O totally unreliable, not only on Skiathos but Skopelos and Alonissos. This by the way, was as he doled out the drugs necessary to cure a very, very bad bout of *Montezuma's Revenge* that I was suffering – the first time in some 10 years. Generally the cost of bottled water is between 65-75drs.

Alcoholic beverages They are generally sold by weight. Beer comes in 330g tins, very occasionally a small bottle or more usually the large 500g bottles – have the 500g, it is a good value measure. Wine is sold in 340/430g (half bottle), 680/730g (1.1 pints) and 950g (1¾ pints) sized bottles.

Beer Greek brewed or bottled beer represents good value except when served in cans, which are the export version and, I regard, a 'swindle'. This European habit should be resisted for no other reason than it means the cost, quantity for quantity, is almost doubled. Now that *Fix Hellas* is not obtainable, due to the founder's death, the only other widely available, bottled beers are *Amstel* and *Henninger*. Draught lager is insidiously creeping in to various resorts and should be avoided, not only or purist reasons, but because it is comparatively expensive, as are the imported, stronger bottled lagers. No names, no pack drill but *Carlsberg* is one that springs to mind. A small bottle of beer is referred to as a *mikri bira* and a large one *meghali bira*.

Wine Unresinated (*aretsinoto*) wine is European in style, palatable and popular brands include red and white *Demestica, Cambas* and *Rotonda*. More refined palates will approve of the dry white wines (*aspro*) of Evia island. Greek wine is not so much known for its quality but if quantity of brands can make up for this then the country will not let you down. Red wine (*Krasi kokino*), dark wine (*Krasi mavro*) as well as white wine (*Krasi aspro*) are best ordered draught (*huna*) or from the barrel (*apo vareli*) which are much less expensive than the overpriced bottles.

Resinated wine is achieved, if that can be considered the expression, by the barrels, in which the wine is fermented, being internally coated with pine tree resin. The resultant liquid is referred to as retsina, most of which are white, with a *kokkineli* or rosé version sometimes available. Some consider the taste to be similar to chewing wet, lead pencils but this is patently obviously a heresy. Retsina is usually bottled, but some tavernas serve 'open' (*apo vareli*) retsina in metal jugs. When purchasing for personal consumption it can be found dispensed into any container a client might like to press into service, from large vats, buried in side-street cellars. The adjective 'open' (*apo vareli*) is used to describe retsina available on draught or more correctly from the barrel. Asking for *Kortaki* ensures being served the traditional, economically priced small bottle of retsina, rather than the expensive full sized bottle. Rumour has it that the younger retsinas are more easily palatable, but that is very much a matter of taste. A good 'starter' kit is to drink a bottle or two twice a day for three or four days and if the pain goes...

Spirits & others As elsewhere in the world, sticking to the national drinks represents good value.

Ouzo, much maligned and blamed for other excesses, is, in reality, a derivative of the aniseed family of drinks (which include *Ricard* and *Pernod*) and, taken with water, is a splendid 'medicine'. Ouzo is traditionally served with *mezethes* (or *mezes* – the Greek equivalent of Spanish tapas). This is a small plate of, for instance, a slice of cheese, tomato, cucumber, possibly smoked eel, octopus and an olive. When served they are charged for, costing some 20 to 30drs, but the tradition of offering them is disappearing in many tourist locations. If you specifically do not wish to be served mezes then make the request *ouzo sketto*. *Raki* is a stronger alternative to ouzo, often 'created' in Crete.

Metaxa brandy, available in three, five and seven star quality, is very palatable but with a certain amount of 'body', whilst Otys brandy is smoother. Greek aperitifs include *Vermouth, Mastika* and *Citro*.

DRINKING PLACES

Prior to launching into the various branches of this subject, I am at a loss to understand why so many cafe-bar and taverna owners select chairs that are designed to cause the maximum discomfort, even suffering. They are usually too small for any but a very small bottom, too low and made up of wickerwork or raffia that painfully impresses its pattern on the sitter's bare (sun-burnt?) thighs.

Kafeneion (ΚΑΦΕΝΙΟΝ) Greek cafe, serving only Turkish coffee. Very Greek, very masculine and in which women are rarely seen. They are similar to a British working man's club, but with backgammon, worry beads and large open windows allowing a dim view of the smoke-laden interior.

Ouzeries (ΟΥΖΕΡΙ) As above, but the house speciality is (well, well) ouzo.

Cafe-bar (ΚΑΦΕ ΜΠΑΡ) As above, but serving alcoholic beverages as well as coffee, and women are to be seen.

Pavement cafes French in style, with outside tables and chairs sprawling over the road as well as the pavement. Open from mid-morning, throughout the day, to one or two o'clock the next morning. Snacks and sweet cakes are usually available.

Inside any of the above, the locals chat to each other in that peculiar Greek fashion which gives the impression that a full-blooded fight is about to break out at any moment. In reality, they are probably just good friends, chatting to each other over the blaring noise of a televised football match, a sickly American soap opera or a ghastly English 'comic' programme, the latter two with Greek subtitles.

Drinks can always be obtained at a taverna or restaurant, but you may be expected to eat, so read on.

It is of course, possible to sup at hotel cocktail bars, but why leave home!

EATING PLACES

At the cheapest end of the market, and more especially found in Athens, are pavement-mounted stands serving doughnut-shaped bread (*koulouri*) which make for an inexpensive nibble at about 7-10drs.

Pistachio nut & ice-cream vendors They respectively push their wheeled trolleys around the streets, selling a wide variety of nuts in paper bags for 50-100drs or ice-creams in a variety of flavours and prices.

Galaktopoleio (ΓΑΛΑΚΤΟΠΩΛΕΙΟ) Shops selling dairy products including milk, butter, yoghurt, bread, honey and sometimes omelettes and fritters with honey (*loukoumades*). These are for 'take-away' or consumption on the premises and is a traditional but more expensive alternative to a restaurant/bar at which to purchase breakfast.

Zacharoplasteion (ΖΑΧΑΡΟΠΛΑΣΤΕΙΟΝ) Shops specialising in pastries, cakes (*glyko*), chocolates and soft drinks as well as, sometimes, a small selection of alcoholic drinks.

Galaktozacharoplasteion A combination of the two previously described establishments.

Snackbar (ΣΝΑΚΟΜΠΑΡ, **Souvlatzidika & Tyropitadika)** Snackbars are not so numerous in the less touristy areas, often being restricted to one or two in the main town. They represent good value for a stand-up snack. The most popular offering is *souvlaki pita* – pita bread (or a roll) filled with grilled meat or kebab (*doner kebab* – slices off a rotating, vertical spit of an upturned cone of meat also called *giro*) and garnished with a slice of tomato, chopped onion and a dressing, all wrapped in an ice-cream shaped twist of greaseproof paper. Be careful, as *souvlaki* is not to be muddled with *souvlakia* which, when served at a snackbar, consists of wooden skewered pieces of lamb, pork or veal meat grilled over a charcoal fire. These are almost indistinguishable from *shish-kebab*, or *souvlakia*, served at a sit-down meal where the metal skewered meat pieces are interspersed with vegetables.

Note that in touristic locations the adjective *Special*, when applied to souvlaki, usually indicates an average, correctly made offering for which a comparatively extortionate price is charged. The cheaper alternative will be simply a slab of meat in place of the slices of giro meat.

Other 'goodies' include *tiropites* – hot flaky pastry pies filled with cream cheese; *boogatsa* – a custard filled pastry; *spanakopita* – spinach filled pastry squares or pies; a wide variety of rolls and sandwiches (*sanduits*) with cheese, tomato, salami and other spiced meat fillings, as well as toasted sandwiches (*tost*).

This reminds me to point out to readers that if 'toast' is ordered it is odds on that a toasted cheese sandwich will be served.

Creperies These are intruding in the most concentrated package tourist resorts, Aristotle reminding me of the film version of the American milk shake bar. Compared to the more traditional Greek establishments they serve very expensive sandwiches, pies and other 'exotica' including thin pancakes or crepes, thus the name.

They are a rather chic, smooth, smart version of their chromium, brightly neon lit 'cousins', the:-

Fast food joint A surely unwelcome import selling ice-creams, hot-dogs and hamburgers.

Pavement cafes Serve snacks and sweets.

Pizzerias Seem to be on the increase and are restaurants specialising in the imported Italian dish which prompts one to ask why not go to Italy? To be fair they usually represent very good value and a large serving often feeds two.

Tavernas (ΤΑΒΕΡΝΑ), **Restaurants** (ΕΣΤΙΑΤΟΡΙΟΝ), **Rotisserie** (ΨΗΣΤΑΡΙΑ) **& Rural Centres** (ΕΞΟΧΙΚΟΝ ΚΕΝΤΡΟΝ) Four variations on a theme. The traditional Greek taverna is a family concern, frequently only open in the evening. More often than not, the major part of the eating area is outside, under a vine trellis covered patio, along the pavement and or on a roof garden.

Restaurants tend to be more sophisticated, possibly open all day and night but the definition between the two is rather blurred. The price lists may include a chancy English translation, the waiter might be smarter and the tablecloth and napkins could well be linen, in place of the taverna's paper table covering and serviettes.

As tavernas often have a spit-roasting device tacked on the side, there is little, discernible difference between a rotisserie and a taverna. A grilled meat restaurant may also be styled ΨΗΣΤΑΡΙΑ.

The Rural Centre is a mix of cafe-bar and taverna in, you've guessed it, a rural or seaside setting.

Fish tavernas (ΨΑΡΟΤΑΒΕΡΝΑ) Tavernas specialising in fish dishes.

Hotels (ΞΕΝΟΔΟΧΕΙΟΝ), ΞΕΝΟΔΟΧΕΙΟΝ ΥΠΝΟΥ is a hotel that does not serve food, ΠΑΝΔΟΧΕΙΟΝ, a lower category hotel and ΧΕΝΙΑ, a Government-owned hotel. Xenias are usually well run, the food and drink international, the menu written in French and the prices reflect all these 'attributes'.

An extremely unpleasant manifestation (to old fogeys like me) is illustrated by the prolification of menus in the more popular holiday resorts, namely Greek bills of fare set out Chinese restaurant style. You know, 'Set Meal A' for two, 'Meal B' for three and Meal 'C' for four and more...!

THE FOOD

Some of the following represents a selection of the wide variety of menu dishes available.

Sample menu

Ψωμί (Psomi)	Bread
ΠΡΩΙΝΟ	BREAKFAST
Αυγά τηγανιτα με μπέικον και τομάτα	Fried egg. bacon & tomato
Τοστ βούτυρο μαρμελάδα	Buttered toast & marmalade
Το πρόγευμα (to pro-ye-vma)	English (or American on some islands) breakfast
ΑΥΓΑ	EGGS
Μελάτα	soft boiled
Σφικτά	hard boiled
Τηγανιτά	fried
Ποσσέ	poached
ΤΟΣΤ ΣΑΝΤΟΥΙΤΣ	TOASTED SANDWICHES
Τοστ με τυρί	toasted cheese
Τοστ (με) ζαμπόν και τυρί	toasted ham & cheese
Μπούρκερ	burger
Χαμπουρκερ	hamburger
Τσίσμπουρκερ	cheeseburger
Σάντουιτς λουκάνικο	hot dog
ΟΡΕΚΤΙΚΑ	APPETIZERS/HORS D'OEUVRES
Αντσούγιες	anchovies
Ελιές	olives
Σαρδέλλες	sardines
Σκορδαλιά	garlic dip
Τζατζικι	tzatziki (diced cucumber & garlic in yoghurt)
Ταραμοσαλάτα	taramosalata (a fish roe pate)
ΣΟΥΠΕΣ	SOUPS
Σούπα φασόλια	bean
Αυγολέμονο	egg & lemon
Ψαρόσουπα	fish
Κοτόσουπα	chicken
Ντοματόσουπα	tomato
Σούπα λαχανικών	vegetable

ΟΜΕΛΕΤΕΣ	OMELETTES
Ομελέτα μπέικον	bacon
Ομελέτα μπέικον τυρί τομάτα	bacon, cheese & tomato
Ομελέτα τυρί	cheese
Ομελέτα ζαμπόν	ham
Ομελέτα συκωτάκια πουλιών	chicken liver
ΣΑΛΑΤΕΣ	**SALADS**
Ντομάτα Σαλάτα	tomato
Αγγούρι Σαλάτα	cucumber
Αγγουροτομάτα Σαλάτα	tomato & cucumber
Χωριάτικη	Greek peasant/village salad
ΛΑΧΑΝΙΚΑ (ΛΑΔΕΡΑ*)	**VEGETABLES**
Πατάτες	potatoes **
Πατάτες Τηγανιτές	chips (french fries)
φρέσκα φασολάκια	green beans
Υιγαντες	(large) white beans
Σπαράγκια	asparagus
Κολοκυθάκια	courgettes or zucchini
Σπανάκι	spinach

*indicates cooked in oil.
**usually served up as chips

Note various methods of cooking include:
Baked – στο φουρνο; boiled – βραστα; creamed – με αοπρη σαλτοα; fried – τηγανιτα; grilled – στη σχαρα; roasted – ψητα; spit roasted – σουβλας.

ΚΥΜΑΔΕΣ	MINCED MEATS
Μουσακας	moussaka
Ντοματες Γεμιστες	stuffed tomatoes (with rice or minced meat)
Κεφτεδες	meat balls
Ντολμαδακια	stuffed vine leaves (with rice or minced meat)
Παπουτσακια	stuffed vegetable marrow (rice or meat)
Κανελονια	canelloni
Μακαπονια με κυμα	spaghetti bolognese (more correctly with mince)
Παστιτσιο	macaroni, mince and sauce
Σουβλακι	shish-kebab
ΡΥΖΙ	**RICE**
Πιλαφι	pilaff
Πιλαφι (με) λιαουπτι	with yoghurt
Πιλαφι συκωτακια	with liver
Σπανακοριζο	with spinach
Πιλαφι κυμα	with minced meat
ΠΟΥΛΕΡΙΚΑ	**POULTRY**
Κοτοπουλο	chicken, roasted
Ποδι κοτας	leg of chicken
Στηθος κοτας	chicken breast
Κοτοπουλο βραστο	boiled chicken
Ψητο κοτοπουλο στη σουβλα	spit-roasted chicken
ΚΡΕΑΣ	**MEAT**
Νεφρα	kidneys
Αρνΐ	lamb†
Αρνισιες Μπριζολες	lamb chops
Παιδακια	lamb cutlets
Συκωτι	liver
Χοιρινὂ	pork†
Χοιρινες Μπριζολες	pork chops
Λουκανικα	sausages

Μπιφτεκι	steak (beef)
Μοσχαρισιο	veal
Μοσχαρισιες Μπριζολες	veal chops
Μοσχαρι	grilled veal
Ψητο Μοσχαρακι	roast veal

†often with the prefix/suffix to indicated if roasted or grilled

ΨΑΡΙΑ	FISH
Σκουμπρι	mackerel
Συναγριδα	red snapper
Μαριδες	whitebait
Οκταποδι	octopus
Καλαμαρια	squid
Μπαρμπουνι	red mullet
Κεφαλος	mullet
Αυθρινι	grey mullet

ΤΥΡΙΑ	CHEESE
φετα	feta (goat's-milk based)
Γραβιερα	gruyere-type cheese
Κασερι	cheddar-type (sheep's-milk based)

ΦΠΟΥΤΑ	FRUITS
Καρπουζι	water melon
Πεπονι	melon
Μηλα	apple
Πορτοκαλι	oranges
Σταφυλια	grapes
Κομποστα φρουτων	fruit compote

ΠΑΓΩΤΑ	ICE — CREAM
Σπεσιαλ	special
Παγωτο βανιλλια	vanilla
Παγωτο σοκαλατα	chocolate
Παγωτο λεμονι	lemon
Γρανιτα	water ice

ΓΙΥΚΙΣΜΑΤΑ	DESSERTS
Κεικ	cake
φρουτοσαλατα	fruit salad
Κρεμα	milk pudding
Κρεμ καραμελε	cream caramel
Μπακλαβας	crisp pastry with nuts and syrup or honey
Καταιφι	fine shredded pastry with nuts and syrup or honey
Γαλακτομουρεκο	fine crispy pastry with custard and syrup
Γιαουρτι	yoghurt
Μελι	honey

ΑΝΑΨΥΚΤΙΚΑ	COLD DRINKS/SOFT DRINKS
Πορτοκαλι	orange
Πορτοκαλαδα	orangeade
Λεμοναδα	lemonade made with lemon juice
Γκαζοζα (Gazoza)	fizzy lemonade
Μεταλλικο νερο	mineral water
Κοκα κολα	Coca-cola
Πεψι κολα	Pepsi-cola
Σεβεν-απ	Seven Up
Σοδα	soda
Τονικ	tonic
Νερο (Nero)	water

ΚΑΦΕΔΕΣ	COFFEES
Ελληνικος (Καφες)	Greek coffee (sometimes called Turkish coffee ie Toupkikos Καφε)
σκετο (skehto)	no sugar
μεπιο (metrio)	medium sweet
γλυκο (ghliko)	sweet (very)

(Unless stipulated it will turn up 'ghliko'. Do not drink before it has settled.)

Νες καφε	Nescafe
Νες (με γαλα) (Nes me ghala)	Nescafe with milk
Εσπρεσσο	espresso
Καπουτσινο	cappuccino
φραπε	chilled coffee is known as 'frappe'
Τσαι	tea
Σοκαλατα γαλα	chocolate milk
ΜΠΥΡΕΣ	BEERS
ΦΙΞ (ΕΛΛΑΣ) Μπυρα	Fix (Hellas) beer
φιαλη	bottle
κουτι	can
ΑΜΣΤΕΛ (Αμστελ)	Amstel
ΧΕΝΝΙΝΓΕΡ (Χεννινγκερ)	Henninger
	(300g usually a can, 500g usually a bottle)
ΠΟΤΑ	DRINKS
Ουζο	Ouzo
Κονιακ	Cognac
Μπραντυ	Brandy
Μεταζα	Metaxa
3 ΑΣΤ	3 star
5 ΑΣΤ	5 star
Ουισκυ	Whisky
Τζιν	Gin
Βοτκα	Vodka
Καμπαρι	Campari
Βερμουτ	Vermouth
Μαρτινι	Martini
ΚΡΑΣΙΑ	WINES
Κοκκινο	red
Ασπρο	white
Ποζε Κοκκινελι	rose
Ξερο	dry
Γλυκο	sweet
Ρετσινα	resinated wine
e.g. Θεοκριτος	Theokritos
Αρετσινωτο	unresinated wine
e.g. Δεμεστιχα	Demestica

340g is a ½ bottle, 680g is a bottle, 950g is a large bottle

Useful Greek

English	Greek	Sounds like
Have you a table for...	Εχετε ενα τραπεζι για	Echete enna trapezee ghia...
I'd like...	Θελω	Thelo...
We would like...	Θελουμε	Thelome...
a beer	μια μπυρα	meah beerah
a glass	ενα ποτηρι	ena poteeree
a carafe	μια καραφα	meea karafa

a small bottle	ενα μικρο μπουκαλι	ena mikro bookalee
a large bottle	ενα μεγαλο	ena meghalo bookalee
bread	ψωμι	psomee
tea with milk	τσαι με γαλα	tsai me ghala
with lemon	τσαι με λεμονι	me lemoni
Turkish coffee (Greek)	Τουρκικος καφε	Tourkikos kafes
sweet	γλυκος	ghleekos
medium	μετριος	metreeo
bitter (no sugar)	πικρο	pikro
Black coffee	Nescafe χωρισ γαλα	Nescafe horis ghala
Coffee with milk	Nescafe με γαλα	Nescafe me ghala
a glass of water	ενα ποτη ρι νερο	enna poteeree nero
a napkin	μια πετσετα	mia petseta
an ashtray	ενα σταχτοδοχειο	enna stachdothocheeo
toothpick	μια οδοντογλυφιδα	mea odontoglifidha
the olive oil	το ελαιολαδο	dho eleolatho
Where is the toilet?	Που ειναι η τουαλεττα	Poo eene i(ee) tooaleta?
What is this?	Τι ειναι αυτο	Ti ine afto
This is...	Αυτο ειναι	Afto eene
cold	κρυο	kreeo
bad	χαλασμενο	chalasmeno
stale	μπαγιατικο	bayhiatiko
undercooked	αψητο	apseeto
overcooked	παραβρασμενο	paravrasmeno
The bill please	Το λογαπιασμο παρακαλω	To loghariasmo parakalo
How much is that?	Ποσο κανει αυτο	Poso kanee afto?
That was an excellent meal	Περιφη μο γευμα	Pereefimo yevma
We shall come again	Θα ξαναρθουμε	Tha xanarthoume

The Fish Market, Dapia, Spetses Town.

Skopelos Harbour.

7 Shopping & Public Services

Let your purse be your master Proverb

Purchasing items in Greece is still quite an art form or subject for an *Open University* degree course. The difficulties have been compounded by the rest of the western world becoming nations of supermarket shoppers, whilst the Greeks have stubbornly remained traditionally and firmly with their individual shops, selling a fixed number of items and sometimes only one type of a product. Shopping for a corkscrew, for instance, might well involve calling at two or three seemingly look-alike ironmongers, but no, they each specialise in certain lines of goods and do not stock any items outside those prescribed, almost as if by holy writ.

On the other hand Greece is adopting many of the (retrograde?) consumer habits of its Western European neighbours. In cosmopolitan towns and cities and tourist exposed islands credit cards, including *Visa, Access Mastercharge, Diners* and *American Express*, are accepted at the more expensive restaurants and classier gift/souvenir shops. The more popular areas of the in-vogue Argo-Saronic and Sporades islands sport the credit card symbols, but not Kithira and Salaminas or Skyros.

The question of good and bad buys is a rather personal matter but the items listed below are highlighted on the basis of value for money and quality. Clothing and accessories that are attractive and represent good value include embroidered peasant dresses, leather sandals, woven bags, tapestries and furs. Day-to-day items that are inexpensive take in Greek cigarettes, drinks including *ouzo, Metaxa* brandy and selected island wines. Suitable gifts for family and friends embraces ceramic plates, sponges, Turkish delight and worry beads (*komboloe*). Disproportionately expensive items include camera film, toiletries, sun oils, books and playing cards. Do not forget to compare prices and preferably shop in the streets and markets, not in airport and hotel concessionary outlets, which are often much more expensive.

Try not to run short of change. Everybody else does, including bus conductors, taxi drivers and shops.

Opening hours

Strict or old fashioned summer shop hours are:

Monday, Wednesday and Saturday: 0830-1400hrs; Tuesday, Thursday and Friday: 0830-1330hrs & 1730-2030hrs.

Generally, during the summer months, shops in tourist areas are open Monday to Saturday from 0800-1300hrs. They then close for the siesta until 1700hrs, after which they open again until at least 2030hrs, if not 2200hrs. Sundays and Saints' days are more indeterminate, but there is usually a general shop open, somewhere. In very popular tourist resorts and busy ports, many shops often open seven days a week.

Drink

Available either in the markets from delicatessen meat/dairy counters or from 'off licence' type shops.

Smokers

Imported French, English and American cigarettes are inexpensive, compared with

European prices, at between 100 and 150drs for a packet of twenty. Greek cigarettes, which have a distinctive and different taste, are excellent. Try *Karellia* which cost about 68drs for twenty and note that the price is printed around the edge of the packet. Even Greek cigars are almost unheard of on the islands, while in Athens they cost 10-15drs each. Dutch cigars work out at 25-30drs each, so, if a cigar smoker, take along your holiday requirements.

Newspapers & magazines

The Athens News is published daily, except Mondays, in English and costs 50drs. Overseas newspapers are available up to 24 hours after the day of publication, but note that all printed matter is comparatively expensive. Quality English papers cost 200drs.

Photography (Fotografion – ΦΩΤΟΓΡΑΦΕΙΟΝ)

Photographers should carry all the film possible as, being imported, it is comparatively expensive. Despite the allure of the instant print shops that have sprung up on the more popular islands, it is probably best to wait until returning home. The quality of reproduction and focus of the development is 'variable'. That is not to say that the back-at-home 'bucket-print' outfits, whose envelopes fall out of almost every magazine one cares to purchase, are infallible. I had a long drawn out experience with a Shropshire company who managed to 'foul up' the development of five rolls of film. The problem is that a holiday-maker who only has two or three films to develop and receives back the complete batch rather blurred might consider it to be an 'own goal'. On the other hand it might be the print company who have botched the job.

To counter the very bright sunlight, when using colour film, blue filters should be fitted to the lens.

Radio

To receive the English language overseas broadcasts tune to 49m band on the *Short Wave*. In the evening try the *Medium Wave*. English language news is broadcast by the Greek broadcasting system at 0740hrs on the *Medium Wave* (AM), somewhere between 700-800 Khz.

Tourist Guides & Maps

Shop around before purchasing either, as the difference in price of the island guides can be as much as 150drs, that is between 300-450drs. Island maps cost from 80-100drs. Some major ports and towns have one authentic, well stocked bookshop, usually positioned a little off the town centre. The proprietor often speaks adequate English and courteously answers most enquiries.

SHOPS

Bakers & bread shops (ΑΡΤΟΠΟΙΕΙΟΝ, ΑΡΤΟΠΩΛΕΙΟΝ or ΠΡΑΤΗΡΙΟΝ ΑΡΤΟΥ)

For some obscure reason bakers are nearly always difficult to locate, often being hidden away, in or behind other shops. A pointer to their presence may well be a pile of blackened, twisted olive wood, stacked up to one side of the entrance, and used to fuel the oven fires. They are almost always closed on Sundays and Saints days, despite the ovens often being used by the local community to cook their Sunday dinners. Bread shops tend to be few and far between. Both may also sell cheese and meat pies.

The method of purchasing bread can prove disconcerting, especially when sold by weight. Sometimes the purchaser selects the loaf and then pays but the most bewildering system is where it is necessary to pay first then collect the goods. Difficult if the shopper's level of Greek is limited to grunts, 'thank you' and 'please'!

Greek bread has another parameter of measure, that is a graduation in hours – 1 hour bread, 4 hour bread and so on. After the period is up, the loaf is usually completely inedible, having transmogrified into a rock-like substance.

Butcher (ΚΡΕΟΠΩΛΕΙΟΝ)

Similar to those at home but the cuts are quite different (surely the Common Market can legislate against this deviation!).

Galaktopoleio *et al.*

Cake shops (*Zacharoplasteion*) may sell bottled mineral water (ask for a cold bottle). *See* **Chapter Six**.

Markets

The smaller ports and towns may have a market street and the larger municipalities often possess a market building. These are thronged with locals and all the basic necessities can be procured relatively inexpensively. Fruit and vegetable stalls are interspersed by butchers and dairy delicatessen shops. During business hours, the proprietors are brought coffee and a glass of water by waiters carrying the cups and glasses, not on open trays, but in round aluminium salvers with a deep lid, held under a large ring handle, connected to the tray by three flat arms.

Supermarkets (ΥΠΕΡΑΓΟΡΑ/ΣΟΥΠΕΡΜΑΡΚΕΤ)

Very much on the increase and based on small town, self-service stores but not to worry, they inherit all those delightful, native Greek qualities including quiet chaos. It has to be admitted every so often one does come across a 'real supermarket' recognisable by the check-out counters, but this still does not mean it is a Western European equivalent – more an organised shambles.

Mini-Market

The nomenclature usually indicates a well stocked store in a small building.

Speciality shops

Found in some big towns and Athens while pavement browsing. The little basement shops can be espied down flights of steps, specialising, for instance, in dried fruit, beans, nuts and grains.

Street Kiosks (Periptero/ΠΕΡΙΠΤΕΡΟ)

These unique, pagoda-like huts stay open remarkably long hours, often from early morning to after midnight. They sell a wide range of goods including newspapers, magazines (surprisingly sometimes in the larger cities pornographic literature), postcards, tourist maps, postage stamps, sweets, chocolates, cigarettes and matches. Additionally they form the outlet for the pay phone system and, at the cost of 5drs, a local call may be made. It is rather incongruous, to observe a Greek making a possible important business call, in amongst a rack of papers and magazines, with a foreground of jostling pedestrians and a constant stream of noisy traffic in the background. Ownership is often a family affair – vested as a form of Government patronage and handed out to deserving citizens.

Alternate ways of shopping

Then there are the other ways of shopping: from handcarts, their street-vendor owners selling respectively nuts, ice-cream, milk and yoghurt; from the back of a donkey with vegetable-laden panniers or from two wheeled trailers drawn by fearsome sounding, agricultural rotovator power units. Often the donkey or powered trailer has an enormous set of scales mounted on the back end, swinging like a hangman's scaffold.

If the vegetable/fruit is being sold by 'gypsy-types' then it is advisable to only purchase from those who have their prices written up, usually on a piece of cardboard. Even locals admit to being 'ripped off' by, say, a roadside banana seller. These free market entrepreneurs are often prosecuted for breaking the law.

Frequently used shops include:
ΒΙΒΛΙΟΠΩΛΕΙΟΝ – bookshop; ΚΡΕΟΠΩΛΕΙΟΝ – butcher; ΙΧΘΥΟΠΩΛΕΙΟΝ – fishmonger; ΟΠΩΡΟΠΩΛΕΙΟΝ – greengrocer; ΠΑΝΤΟΠΩΛΕΙΟΝ – grocer; ΚΟΥΡΕΙΟΝ – hairdresser; ΚΑΠΝΟΠΩΛΕΙΟΝ – tobacconist. Readers may observe that the above all have a similar ending and it is worth noting that shop titles that terminate in 'ΠΩΛΕΙΟΝ / πωλειον' are selling something, if that's any help.

SERVICES
The Banks & Money (ΤΡΑΠΕΖΑ)

The minimum opening hours are 0800-1300hrs Monday to Thursday and 0800-1300hrs on Friday. Some banks, in the most tourist ravaged spots, open in the evenings and or on Saturdays. Some smaller towns, villages or, for that matter, islands do not have a bank, in which case there may be a local money changer acting as agent for this or that country-wide bank. Do not forget that a passport is almost always required to change travellers' cheques. In the larger cities personal cheques may be changed at a selected bank when backed by a *Eurocheque* (or similar) bank guarantee card. A commission of between ¼–1½% is charged on all transactions, depending upon I know not what! Whereas Eurocheques used to be changed in sums of no more than £50, English sterling, the arrangement now is that a cheque is cashed in drachmae, up to a total of 25,000drs. As the charges for changing cheques are based on a sliding scale weighted against smaller amounts, this new arrangement helps save on fees.

The service is usually discourteous and generally only one employee, if at all, reluctantly speaks English, so make sure the correct bank is selected to carry out a particular transaction (such as changing a personal cheque). Each bank displays a window sticker giving an indication of the tourist services transacted. There is nothing worse, after queuing for half an hour or so, than to be rudely told to go away. I once selected the wrong bank to carry out some banking function, only to receive a loud blast of abuse about a long-departed foreigner's bouncing cheque. Most embarrassing.

Change offices can be used for cashing travellers cheques, as can the larger hotels, but naturally enough at a disadvantageous rate compared with the banks. For instance, the commission charged is 2%, or up to double that charged by the banks. Ouch! *See* **Post Office** for another interesting and less expensive alternative.

The basis of Greek currency is the drachmae. This is nominally divided into 100 lepta and occasionally price lists show a price of, say 62.60drs. As prices are rounded up (or down), in practice the lepta is not now encountered. Notes are in denominations of 50, 100, 500 and 1000drs and coins in denominations of 1 and 2drs (bronze), 5, 10, 20 and 50drs (nickel). Do not run out of change, it is always in demand. Repetitious I know, but well worth remembering.

Museums

The following is a mean average of the entry information but each museum is likely to have its own peculiarities. In the summer season (1st April-31st Oct) they usually open daily 0845-1500/1900hrs, Sundays and holidays 0930-1430/1530hrs and are closed Mondays or Tuesdays. They do not open for business on 1st January, 25th March, Good Friday, Easter holiday and 25th December. Admission costs range from nothing to 100/250drs, whilst Sundays and holidays are sometimes free.

Post Offices (ΤΑΧΥΔΡΟΜΕΙΟΝ/ΕΛΤΑ)

Stamps can be bought from kiosks (plus a small commission) and shops selling postcards as well as from Post Offices. Post boxes are scattered around, are usually painted yellow, are rather small in size and often difficult to find, being fixed, high up, on side-street walls. In 1987 postage rates for cards to the United Kingdom were 40drs for a small card and between 45 & 50drs for a large one. When confronted by two letter-box openings, the inland service is marked ΕΣΩΤΕΡΙΚΟΥ/Εσωτερικου and the overseas ΕΞΩΤΕΡΙΚΟΥ/Εξωτερικου. Letters can be sent for poste restante collection, but a passport will be required for them to be handed over.

Most major town Post Offices are modern and the service received is only slightly less rude than that handed out by bank staff.

Post Offices are usually open Monday to Friday between 0730-2030hrs for stamps, money orders and registered mail; 0730-2000hrs for poste restante and 0730-1430hrs for parcels, which have to be collected.

In recent years the range of Post Office services has been expanded to include cashing *Eurocheques* and *Travellers Cheques* as well as currency exchange. All but the most out-of-the-way island offices now offer these facilities. This can prove very useful knowledge, especially on busy tourist islands where foreign currency desks are usually subject to long queues. More importantly the commission charged can be up to half that of the banks. Another interesting source of taking currency abroad, for United Kingdom residents, is to use *National Giro Post Office* cheques which can be cashed at any Post Office in Greece. Detailed arrangements have to be made with the international branch of Giro.

Telephone Office (OTE)

A separate organisation from the Post Office. To accomplish an overseas or long-distance call it is necessary to go to the OTE office where there are a number of booths from which to make calls. Offices in busy locations are likely to have long queues. The counter clerk indicates which compartment is to be used and alongside him are mounted the instruments to meter the cost. Payment is made after completion of the call at a current rate of 5drs per unit, so ensure that the meter is zeroed prior to making a connection. Opening days and hours vary enormously. Smaller offices may only open weekdays for say 7 hours between 0830-1530hrs whilst some of the larger city offices are open 24 hours a day, seven days a week.

Overseas dialling codes	
Australia	0061
Canada & USA	001
New Zealand	0064
South Africa	0027
United Kingdom & Ireland	0044
Other overseas countries	161

Inland services	
Directory enquiries	131
Provincial enquiries	132
General information	134
Time	141
Medical care	166
City police	100

Gendarmerie	109
Fire	199
Tourist police	171
Roadside assistance	104
Telegrams/cables	165

To dial England, drop the '0' from all four figure codes. Thus making a call to, say, Portsmouth, for which the code is 0705, dial 00 44 705 ...

The internal service is both very good and reasonably priced. Local telephone calls can be made from some bars and the pavement kiosks (periptero) and cost 5drs, which is the 'standard' coin. Some phones take 10 and 20drs coins. The presence of a telephone is often indicated by the sign ΕΔΩΤΗΛΕΦΩΝΕΙΤΕ, a blue background denotes a local phone, and an orange one an inter-city phone. Another sign, Εδω Τηλεφωνειτε (the lower case equivalent), signifies 'telephone from here'. The method of operation is to insert the coin and dial. If a connection cannot be made, place the receiver back on the cradle and the money is returned.

Telegrams may be sent from either the OTE or Post Office.

Useful Greek

English	**Greek**
Stamps	ΓΡΑΜΜΑΤΟΣΗΜΑ
Parcels	ΔΕΜΑΤΑ

English	**Greek**	**Sounds like**
Where is...	Πov ειναι	Poo eenne...
Where is the nearest...	Πov ειναι η πλησιεοτερη	Poo eene i pleesiesteri
baker	ο φουρναρης/ψωμας/	foornaris/psomas/
bakery	Αρτοποιειον	artopieeon
bank	η τραπεζα	i(ee) trapeza
bookshop	το βιβλιοπωλειο	to vivleeopolieo
butchers shop	το χασαπικο	dho hasapiko
chemist shop	το φαρμακειο	to farmakio
dairy shop	το γαλακτοπωλειο	galaktopolieon
doctor	ο γιατρος	o yiahtros
grocer	το μπακαλης	o bakalis
hospital	το νοσοκομειο	to nosokomio
laundry	το πλυντηριο	to plintirio, (plintireeo), since i = ee
liquor store	το ποτοπωλειο	to potopolio (potopoleeo)
photographic shop	το φωτογραφειο	to fotoghrafeeo
post office	το ταχυδρομειο	to tahkithromio
shoe repairer	το τσαγκαραδικο	to tsangkaradiko
tailor	ο ραπτης	o raptis
Have you any...	Εχετε	Ekheteh...
Do you sell...	Πουλατε	Poulate...
How much is this...	Ποσο κανει αυτο	Posso kanee afto...
I want...	Θελω	Thelo...
half kilo/a kilo	μισο κιλο/ενα κιλο	miso kilo/ena kilo
aspirin	η ασπιρινη	aspirini
apple(s)	το μηλο/μηλα	meelo/meela
banana(s)	η μπανανα/μπανανες	banana/bananes
bread	το ψωμι	psomee
butter	το βουτυρο	vutiro
cheese	το τυρι	tiree
cigarettes (filter tip)	το τσιγαρο (με φιλτρο)	to tsigharo (me filtro)

coffee	καφες	cafes
cotton wool	το βαμβακι	to vambaki
crackers	τα κρακερακια	krackerakia
crisps	τσιπς	tsseeps
cucumbers	το αγγουρι	anguree
disinfectant	το απολυμαντικο	to apolimantiko
guide book	ο τουριστικος οδηγος	o touristikos odhigos
ham	το ζαμπον	zambon
ice cream	το παγωτο	paghoto
lemons	το λεμονια	lemonia
lettuce	το μαρουλι	to marooli
map	το χαρτης	o khartis
a box of matches	ενα κουτι σπιρτα	ena kuti spirta
milk	το γαλα	to ghala
pate	πατε	pate
(ball point) pen	το μπικ	to bik
pencil	το μαλυβι	to molivi
pepper	το πιπερι	to piperi
(safety) pins	μια παραμανα	mia (meea) paramana
potatoes	οι πατατες	patates
salad	η σαλατα	i salatah
salami	το σαλαμι	salahmi
sausages	το λουκανικα	lukahniko
soap	το σαπουνι	to sapooni
spaghetti	σπαγγετο	spayehto
string	ο σπαγκος	o spangos
sugar	η ζαχαρη	i zakhahree
tea	το τσαι	to tsai
tomatoes	η ντοματες	domahdes
toothbrush	η οδοντοβουρτσα	odhondovourtsa
toothpaste	η οδοντοχρεμα	odhondokrema
writing paper	το χαρτι γραψιματος	to kharti grapsimatos

A water taxi, KokkinoKastro Beach, Alonissos.

A church in The Chora, Skopelos Port.

8 Greece: History, Mythology, Religion, Present-day Greece, Greeks & their Holidays

All ancient histories, as one of our fine wits said, are but fables that have been accepted. Voltaire

HISTORY

Excavations have shown the presence of Palaeolithic man up to 100,000 years ago. Greece's history and mythology are, like the Greek language, formidable to say the least, with legend, myth, folk tales, fables and religious lore often inextricably mixed up. Archaeologists are now establishing that some mythology is based on ancient facts.

Historically Greeks fought Greeks, Phoenicians and Persians. Under Alexander the Great they conquered Egypt and vast tracts of Asia Minor. Then they were in turn conquered by the Romans. After the splitting of the Roman Kingdom into Western and Eastern Empires, the Greeks, with Constantinople as their capital, were ruled by the Eastern offshoot, only to fall into the hands of the Franks about AD 1200, who were followed by the Turks. The Venetians, Genoese and finally the Turks ruled most of the islands.

In 1821 the War of Independence commenced, which eventually led to the setting up of a Parliamentary Republic in 1928. Incidentally, Thessaly, Crete and the Dodecanese islands remained under Turkish rule. By the time the Dodecanese islanders had thrown out the Turks, the Italians had taken over. If you are now confused, give up, because it gets even more difficult to follow.

The Greek monarchy, which had come into being in 1833, and was related to the German Royal family, opted in 1913 to side with the Axis powers. The chief politician Eleftherios Venizelos, disagreed, was dismissed and set up a rival government, after which the King, under Allied pressure, retired to Switzerland. In the years following the end of the First World War the Turks and Greeks agreed, after some fairly bloody fighting, to exchange a total of one and a half million people.

In 1936 a General Metaxas became dictator and achieved immortal fame by booting out Mussolini's representative. This came about when, in 1940, Mussolini demanded permission for Italy's troops to traverse Greece, and received the famous *Ochi* (No). (This day has become a national festival known as *Ochi Day*, celebrated on 28th October). The Italians demurred and marched on Greece, the soldiers of whom, to the surprise of everybody including themselves, reinforced the refusal by routing the invaders. The Italians were only saved from total humiliation by the intervention of the Germans who then occupied Greece for the duration of the Second World War. At the end of hostilities, all the Italian held Greek islands were reunited with mainland Greece.

As the wartime German ascendancy declined, the Greek freedom fighters split into royalist and communist factions and proceeded to knock even more stuffing out of each other than they had out of the Germans. Until British intervention, followed by large injections of American money and weapons, it looked as if Greece would go behind the Iron Curtain. A second civil war broke out between 1947 and 1949 and this internal strife was reputed to have cost more Greek lives than were lost during the whole of the Second World War.

In 1951, Greece and Turkey became full members of NATO, but the issue of the ex-British colony of Cyprus was about to rear its ugly head, with the resultant, renewed estrangement between Greece and Turkey. The various political manoeuvrings, the involvement of the Greek monarchy in domestic affairs and the worsening situation in Cyprus, led to the *coup d'etat* by the *Colonel's Junta* in 1967, soon after which King Constantine II and his entourage fled to Italy. The extremely repressive dictatorship of the Junta was apparently actively supported by the Americans and condoned by Britain. Popular country-wide feeling and, in particular, student uprisings between 1973-1974, which were initially put down in Athens by brutal tank attacks, led to the eventual collapse of the regime in 1974. In the death-throes of their rule, the Colonels, using the Cyprus dream to distract the ordinary people's feeling of injustice, meddled and attempted to overthrow the vexatious priest, President Makarios. The net result was that the Turks invaded Cyprus and made an enforced division of that unhappy, troubled island.

In 1974, Greece returned to republican democracy and in 1981 joined the EEC.

RELIGION

The Orthodox Church prevails everywhere but there are small pockets of Roman Catholicism as well as very minor enclaves of Muslims on the Dodecanese islands and mainland, western Thrace. The schism within the Holy Roman Empire, in 1054, caused the Catholic Church to be centred on Rome and the Orthodox Church on Constantinople.

The Turkish overlords encouraged the continuation of the indigenous church, probably to keep their bondsmen quiet, but it had the invaluable side effect of keeping alive Greek customs and traditions during the centuries of occupation.

The bewildering profusion of small churches, scattered 'indiscriminately' all over the islands, is not proof of the church's wealth, although the Greek people are not entirely convinced of that fact. It is evidence of the piety of the families or individuals who paid to have them erected, in the name of their selected patron saint, as thanksgiving for God's protection. The style of religious architecture changes between the island groups.

Many churches only have one service a year, on the name day of the particular patron saint, and this ceremony is named *Viorti* or *Panayieri*. It is well worth attending one of these self-indulgent extravaganzas to observe and take part in celebratory village religious life and music. One and all are welcome to the carnival festivities which include eating and dancing in, or adjacent to, the particular churchyard.

The words *Byzantine* and *Byzantium* crop up frequently with especial reference to churches and appertain to the period between the fourth and fourteenth centuries AD. During this epoch Greece was, at least nominally, under the control of Constantinople (Istanbul), built by the Emperor Constantine on the site of the old city of Byzantium. Religious paintings executed on small wooden panels during this period are called icons. Very very few original icons remain available for purchase, so beware if offered an apparent 'bargain'.

When visiting a church, especially noticeable are the pieces of shining, thin metal, placed haphazardly around or pinned to wooden carvings. These *tamata* or *exvotos* represent limbs or portions of the human body and are purchased by worshippers as an offering, in the hope of an illness being cured and or limbs healed.

Male and female visitors to all and every religious building must be properly clothed. Men should wear trousers and a shirt. Ladies clothing should include a skirt, or if unavoidable trousers, a blouse and if possible a headscarf. Many monasteries simply will not allow entrance to scantily or 'undressed' people. With that marvellous duality of standards the Greeks evince, there is quite often a brisk clothes hire business transacted on the very entrance steps. But it is not wise to rely on this arrangement being in force.

GREEKS

In making an assessment of the Greek people and their character, it must be remembered that, perhaps even more so than the Spaniards or the Portuguese, Greece has only recently emerged into the twentieth century. Unlike other countries 'discovered' in the 1960s by the holiday industry, they have not, in the main, degraded or debased their principles or character, despite the onrush of tourist wealth. For a people to have had so little and to face so much demand for European 'necessities', would have strained a less hardy and well-balanced people.

Greece's recent emergence into the western world is evidenced by the still patriarchal nature of their society, a view supported for instance, by the oft-seen spectacle of men lazing in the taverna whilst their womenfolk work in the fields (and why not).

Often the smallest village, on the remotest island, has an English-speaking islander who has lived abroad at some time in his life, earning a living through seafaring, as a hotel waiter, or as a taxi driver. Thus, while making an escape from the comparative poverty at home, for a period of good earnings in the more lucrative world, a working knowledge of English, American or Australian will have been gained. *Greek strine* or, as usually contracted, *grine* simply has to be heard to be believed.

The greatest hurdle to understanding is undoubtedly the language barrier, especially if it is taken into account that the Greeks appear to have some difficulty with their own language in its various forms. Certainly, they seem, on occasions, not to understand each other and the subject matter has to be repeated a number of times. Perhaps that is the reason for all that shouting!

There can be no doubt that the traditional Greek welcome to the *Xenos* or *Singrafeus*, now increasingly becoming known as *touristas*, has naturally, become rather lukewarm in the more 'besieged' areas. It is often difficult to reconcile the shrugged shoulders of a seemingly disinterested airline official or bus driver, with being stopped in the street by a gold-toothed, smiling Greek proffering some fruit. But remember the bus driver may realise the difficulty of overcoming the language barrier, may be very hot, he has been working long hours earning his living and he is not on holiday. Sometimes a drink appears mysteriously at one's taverna table, the donor being indicated by a nod of the waiter's heard, but a word of warning here. Simply smile and accept the gift graciously. Any attempt to return the kindness by 'putting one in the stable' for your new-found friend only results in a 'who buys last' competition which will surely be lost. I know, I am speaking from 'battle-weary' experience. Greeks are very welcoming and may well invite a tourist to their table. But do not expect more, they are reserved and have probably had previous unhappy experiences of ungrateful, rude, overseas visitors.

Women tourists can travel quite freely in Greece without fear, except perhaps from other tourists. On the other hand, females should not wear provocative attire or fail to wear sufficient clothing. This is especially so when in close social contact with Greek men, who might well be inflamed into 'action' or Greek women, whom it will offend, probably because of the effect on their men! Certainly all the above was the case until very recently but the constant stream of 'available' young tourist ladies on the more popular islands has resulted in the local lads taking both a 'view' and a chance. It almost reminds one of the *Costa Brava* in the early 1960s. The disparate moral qualities of the native and tourist females has resulted in a conundrum for young Greek women. To compete for their men's affections they have to loosen their principles with an unheard of and steadily increasing number of speedily arranged marriages, if you know what I mean.

Do not miss the *Volta* (Βολγα), the traditional, family evening walkabout on city, town and village square. Dressed for the event, an important part of the ritual is for the family to show off their marriageable daughters. Good fun and great watching, but the Greeks are rather protective of their family and all things Greek... you may comment favourably, but keep adverse criticism to yourself.

It is interesting to speculate on the influence of the early Greek immigrants on American culture. To justify this hypothesis consider the American habit of serving water with every meal, the ubiquitous hamburger (which is surely a poorly reproduced and inferior souvlaki and which is now being reimported) and some of the official uniforms, more particularly the flat, peaked hats of American postmen and policemen.

THE GREEK NATIONAL HOLIDAYS

Listed below are the national holidays and on these days many areas and islands hold festivals, but with a particular slant and emphasis.

1st January	New Year's Day/The Feast of Saint Basil
6th January	Epiphany/Blessing of the Waters – a cross is immersed in the sea, lake or river during a religious ceremony.
The period 27th Jan to 17th February	The Greek Carnival Season
25th March	The Greek National Anniversary/Independence Day
April – movable days	Good Friday/Procession of the 'Epitaph'; Holy Week Saturday/Ceremony of the Resurrection; Easter Sunday/open air feasts
1st May	May/Labour Day/Feast of the Flowers
1st to 10th July	Greek Navy Week
15th August	Assumption Day/Festival of the Virgin Mary, especially in the Cycladian island of Tinos (beware travelling at this time, anywhere in the area)
28th October	National Holiday/'Ochi' Day
24th December	Christmas Eve/Carols Evening
25th December	Christmas Day
26th December	St Stephen's Day
31st December	New Year's Eve carols, festivals

In addition to these national days, each island has its own particular festivals and holidays which are listed individually under each island.

A word of warning to ferry-boat travellers will not go amiss here – DO NOT travel to an island immediately prior to one of these festivals NOR off the island immediately after the event. It will be almost impossible to do other than stand, that is if one has not already been trampled to death in the various stampedes to and from the ferry-boats.

Artistic, nést-ce-pas? Kapsali Port, Kithira.

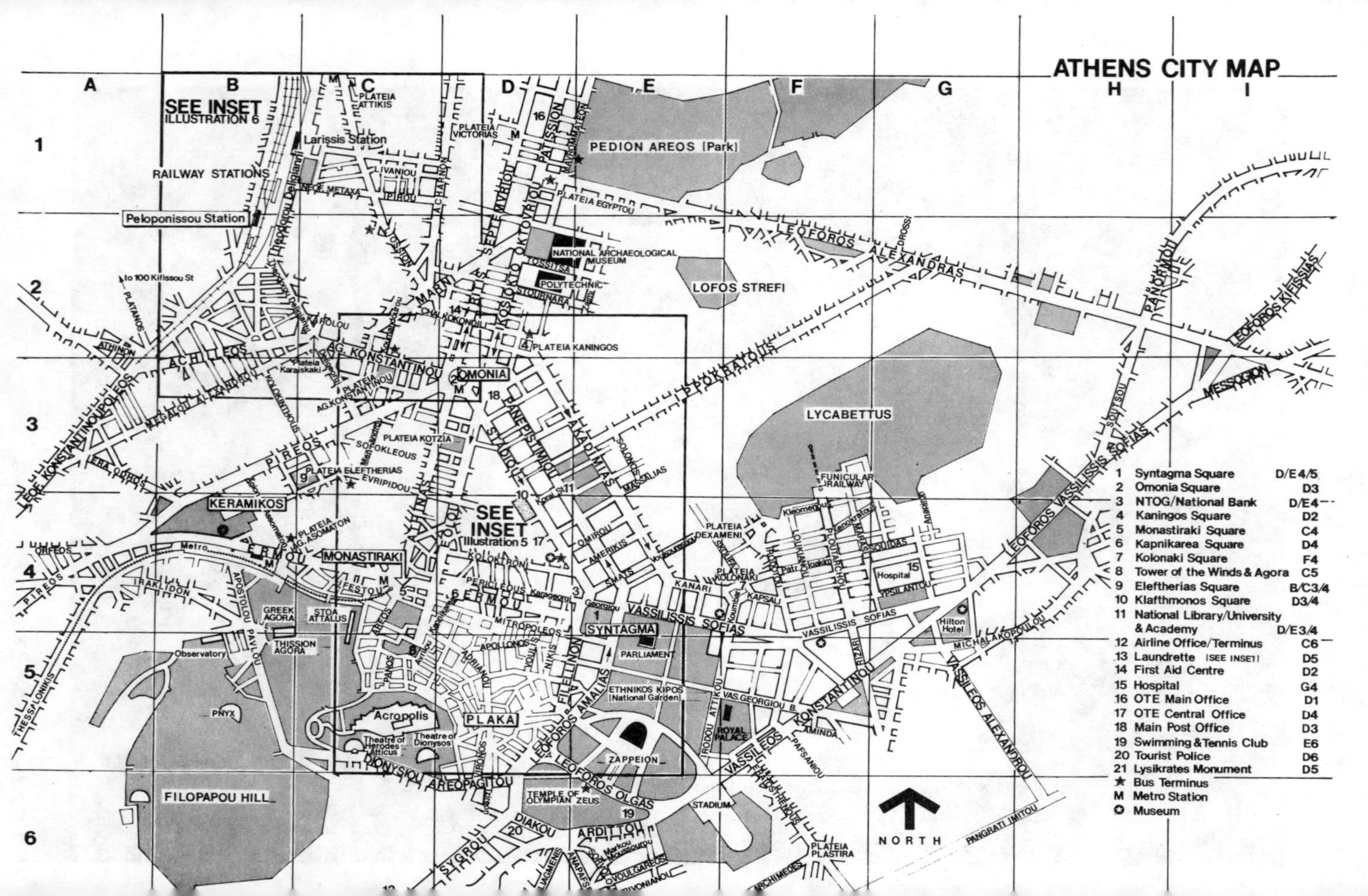

Illustration 4 Athens City

PART TWO
9 ATHENS CITY (ATHINA, ΑΘΗΝΑΙ)

There is no end of it in this city, wherever you set your foot, you encounter some memory of the past. Marcus Cicero

Tel prefix 01

The capital of Greece and major city of Attica (Illustrations 4, 5 & 6). Previously the springboard for travel to most of the Greek islands, but less so since a number of direct flights have become available to the larger islands. Experienced travellers flying into Athens airport, often try to arrange their arrival for early morning and head straight to either the West airport (for a domestic flight), Piraeus port (*See* **Chapter Ten**), the railway station or bus terminal, so as to be able to get under way immediately.

ARRIVAL BY AIR

International flights other than *Olympic Airways* land at the:

East airport

Public transport facilities include:

Bus No. 18: East airport to Leoforos Amalias almost as far as Syntagma Sq. Going to the airport the bus stop is on the right (*Syntagma Sq. behind one*) just beyond the East airport Olympic stop. Say every 30 mins from 0600-2400hrs and after midnight every hour on the half hour i.e. 0030, 0130, 0230hrs.
Fare 120drs. Yellow express bus.*

Bus No. 121: East airport to Leoforos Olgas. 0630-2250hrs.
Fare 120drs.

Bus No. 19: East airport to Plateia Karaiskaki/Akti Tselepi, Piraeus. Every hour from 0800-2000hrs.
Fare 120drs. Yellow express bus.*

Bus No. 101: East airport via Leoforos Possidonos (coast road) to Klisovis/Theotoki St, Piraeus. Every 20 mins from 0500-2245hrs.
Fare 50drs.

**Don't jump for the bus without obtaining tickets first from the office adjacent to the bus terminus.*

One correspondent advised that for those not wanting to trek into Athens centre, it is worth considering staying in a hotel close by the airport. One drawback is the proximity of the flight-path. A recommended hotel that is a short distance away and not in a direct line with the runway is the:-

Hotel Avra (Class C) 3 Nireos, Paleon Faliro Tel 981 4064

Directions: Proceed north (in the direction of Piraeus) along the coastal avenue of Leoforos Vasil Georgiou II which at Paleon Faliro becomes Leoforos Possidonos. A No. 101 bus travels the route. Proceed past the Marina to the area where the road cuts inland from the coastline, an overall distance of some 6km. Nireos St is a branch off the Esplanade Road.

The hotel is close to a beach and not outrageously expensive, in comparison to other Athens and Piraeus hotels. Singles sharing the bathroom start at 1220drs and en suite 1720drs while a double en suite costs 2150drs. These prices rise to 1460, 2060 and 2600drs respectively (1st June-31st Oct). Breakfast costs an extra 220drs.

Domestic and all Olympic flights land at the:

West airport

Public transport facilities include:

Bus No. 133: West airport to Leoforos Square, Leoforos Amalias, Filellinon & Othonos Sts (Syntagma Sq). Every ½ hour from 0530-0030hrs.
Fare 50drs. Blue bus.

Bus No. 122: West Airport to Leoforos Olgas. Every 20mins between 0600-2300hrs. Fare 50drs. Blue bus.

Buses No. 107 & 109: West airport via Leoforos Possidonos (coast road) to Klisovis St, Piraeus.

In addition there are Olympic buses connecting West and East airports as well as Olympic buses from the West airport to the Olympic offices (*Tmr* 12C5), on Leoforos Sygrou, and Syntagma Sq. Every 20 mins between 0600-2000hrs. Fare 100drs.

ARRIVAL BY BUS

Inter-country coaches usually decant passengers at Syntagma Sq (*Tmr* 1D/E4/5), Stathmos Larissis station (*Tmr* B/C1) or close to one of the major city bus terminals.

ARRIVAL BY FERRY

See **Piraeus, Chapter Ten**

ARRIVAL BY TRAIN

See **Trains, A To Z**

GENERAL (Illustrations 4 & 5)

Even if a traveller is a European city dweller, Athens will come as a sociological and cultural shock to the system. In the summer it is a hot, dusty, dry, crowded, traffic bound, exhaust polluted bedlam, but always friendly, cosmopolitan and ever on the move.

On arrival in Athens, and planning to stay over, it is best to select the two main squares of Syntagma (*Tmr* 1D/E4/5) and Omonia (*Tmr* 2/D3). These can be used as centres for the initial sally and from which to radiate out to the other streets and squares.

There is no substitute for a city map which is issued free (yes, free) from the Tourist Board desk in the National Bank of Greece on Syntagma Sq (*Tmr* 3/D/E4). *See* **NTOG, A To Z.**

Syntagama Square (Constitution or Parliament Sq)

(*Tmr* 1D/E4/5). The airport and many other buses stop here. It is the city centre with the most elite hotels, airline offices, international companies, including the American Express headquarters, smart cafes and the Parliament building, all circumscribing the central, sunken square. In the bottom, right-hand (or south-east) corner of the plateia, bounded by Odhos Othonos and Leoforos Amalias, are some very clean, attendant-minded toilets. There is a charge for the use of these 'squatties'.

To orientate, the *Parliament* building and *Monument to the Unknown Warrior* lie to the east of the square. To the north-east, in the middle, distance, is one of the twin hills of Athens, *Mt Lycabettus (Lykavittos, Lykabettos* & etc, etc). The other hill is the *Acropolis*, to the south-west, and not now visible from Syntagma Sq due to the high-rise buildings. On the west side of the square are the offices of *American Express* and a battery of pavement cafes, with Ermou St leading due west to Monastiraki Sq. To the north are the two parallel, main avenues of Stadiou (a one-way street down to Syntagma) and Venizelou or Panepistimiou (a one-way street out of Syntagma) that both run north-west to:

Omonia Square (Concorde or Harmony Sq) (*Tmr* 2D3) The 'Piccadilly Circus' or 'Times Square' of Athens but rather tatty really, with a constant stream of traffic bludgeoning its way round the large central island which is crowned by an impressive fountain. Visitors trying to escape the human bustle on the pavements by stepping off into the kerbside should beware that they are not mown down by a bus, taxi or car.

There is constant activity night and day, with the racial admixture of people cheek by jowl lending the square a cosmopolitan character all of its own. On every side are hotels. These vary from the downright seedy to the better-class tawdry, housed in rather undistinguised, 'neo-city-municipal' style, nineteenth century buildings, almost unique to Athens.

Various Metro train entrance/exits emerge around the square, spewing out and sucking in travellers. The Omonia underground concourse has a Post Office, telephones, a bank and, by the Dorou St entrance, a block of 'squatty' toilets for which the attendant charges 10drs for two sheets of paper.

Shops, cafes and booths fill the gaps between the hotels and the eight streets that converge on the Square.

To the north-east side of Omonia, on the corner of Dorou St, is a taxi rank and beyond, on the right, a now rather squalid, covered arcade brimful of reasonably priced snackbars. Through this covered passageway, and turning to the left up 28 Ikosiokto Oktovriou (28th October St)/Patission St, and then right down Veranzerou St, leads to:

Kaningos Square (*Tmr* 4D2) Serves as a Bus terminal for some routes.

To the south of Omonia Sq is Athinas St, the commercial thoroughfare of Athens. Here every conceivable item imaginable, including ironmongery, tools, crockery and clothing, can be purchased, and parallel to which, for half its length, runs Odhos Sokratous, the city street market during the day and the red-light district by night.

Athinas St drops due south to:

Monastiraki Square (*Tmr* 5C4) This marks the northernmost edge of the area known as the *Plaka* (*Tmr* D5) bounded by Ermou St to the north, Filellinon St to the east, and to the south by the slopes of the Acropolis.

Many of the alleys in this area follow the course of the old Turkish streets, most of the houses are mid-nineteenth century and represent the 'Old Quarter'.

Climbing the twisting maze of streets and steps of the lower north-east slopes of the Acropolis requires the stamina of a mountain goat. The almost primitive, island-village nature of some of the houses is very noticeable, due, it is said, to a Greek law passed after Independence. This was enacted to alleviate a housing shortage and allowed anyone who could raise the roof of a building, between sunrise and sunset, to finish it off and own the dwelling. Some inhabitants of the Cyclades island of Anafi (Anaphe) were reputed to have been the first to benefit from this new law and others followed to specialist in restoration and rebuilding, thus bringing about a colony of expatriate islanders within the Plaka district.

From the south-west corner of Monastiraki Sq, Ifestou St and its associated byways house the *Flea Market*, which climaxes on Sunday into stall upon stall of junk, souvenirs, junk, hardware, junk, boots, junk, records, junk, clothes, junk, footwear, junk, pottery and junk. Where Ifestou becomes Odhos Astigos and curves round to join up with Ermou St, there are a couple of extensive second-hand bookshops with reasonably priced (for Greece that is), if battered, paperbacks for sale. From the south-east corner of Monastiraki, Pandrossou St, one of the only enduring reminders of the Turkish Bazaar, contains a better class of antique dealer, sandal and shoe makers, and pottery stores.

Due south of Monastiraki Sq is Odhos Areos. The raggle-taggle band of European and Japanese drop-outs selling junk trinkets from the pavement kerb appear to have been replaced by a few local traders. Climbing Odhos Areos skirts the *Roman Agora*, from which various streets lead upwards, on ever upwards, and which contain a plethora of stalls and shops, specialising in leather goods, clothes and souvenirs. The further you climb, the cheaper the goods become. This interestingly enough does not apply to the tavernas and restaurants which seemingly become more expensive as one ascends.

The Plaka (*Tmr* D5) The 'chatty' area known as the Plaka is littered with eating places, a few good, some bad, some tourist rip-offs. The liveliest street, Odhos Kidathineon, is, at its lowest end, jam-packed with cafes, tavernas and restaurants and at night attracts a number of music-playing layabouts. The class, tone and price of the establishments improves proceeding in a north-eastwards direction. I have to admit to gently knocking the Plaka over the years but it must be acknowledged that the area offers the cheapest accommodation and eating places in Athens and generally appears to have been cleaned up in recent years. In fact, since the 1986 'Libyan' downturn in American tourists, the area has become positively attractive. Early and late in the year, once the glut of overseas invaders have gone away, the Plaka returns to being a super place to visit. The shopkeepers become human, shopping is inexpensive and the tavernas revert to being 'Greek' and lively. In the last three weeks of February the *Apokria Festival*, a long running 'Halloween' style carnival, is centred on the Plaka. The streets are filled with dozens of revellers dressed in fancy dress, masks and funny hats wandering about, throwing confetti, and creating a marvellous atmosphere. For this event all the tavernas are decorated.

To the east of Monastiraki Sq is Ermou St which is initially lined by clothes and shoe shops. One third of the way towards Syntagma Sq and Odhos Ermou opens out into a small square on which there is the lovely *Church of Kapnikarea* (*Tmr* 6D4). Continuing eastwards, the shops become smarter with a preponderance of fashion stores whilst parallel to Ermou St is Odhos Ploutonos Kteka, which becomes Odhos Mitropoleos. Facing east, on the right is the City's Greek Orthodox Cathedral, *Great Mitropolis*. The church was built about 1850, from the materials of 70 old churches, to the design of four different architects resulting, not unnaturally, in a building of a rather 'strange' appearance. Alongside, and to the south, is the diminutive, medieval *Little Mitropolis* Church or Agios Eleftherios, dating back to at least the twelfth century but which has materials, reliefs and building blocks probably originating from the sixth century AD. A little further on is the intriguing and incongruous site of a small Byzantine church, built over and around by a modern office block, the columns of which tower above and beside the tiny building.

Leaving Syntagama Sq by the north-east corner, along Vassilissis Sofias, and turning left at Odhos Irodou Attikou, runs into:

Kolonaki Square (*Tmr* 7F4) The most fashionable square in the most fashionable area of Athens, around which most of the foreign embassies are located on the square, as are some expensive cafes, restaurants and boutiques.

To the north of Kolonaki, across the pretty, orange tree planted Dexameni Sq, is the southernmost edge of *Mt Lycabettus* (*Tmr* F/G3). Access to the summit can be made on foot by a number of steep paths, the main one of which, a stepped footpath, advances from the north end of Loukianou St, beyond Odhos Kleomenous. A little to the east, at the top of Ploutarchou St, which breaks into a sharply rising flight of steps, is the cable car funicular railway. This runs in a 213m long tunnel emerging near to the nineteenth century chapel, which caps the fir tree covered outcrop, alongside a modern and luxuriously expensive restaurant. There

are some excellent toilets. The railway service runs continuously as follows:
Winter: Wednesday, Saturday, Sunday 0845-0015hrs; Thursday 1030-0015hrs; Monday, Tuesday, Friday 0930-0015hrs.
Summer: As for winter but the opening hours extend daily to 0100hrs every night.
The trip costs 65drs one-way and 100drs for a return ticket.

A more relaxed climb, passing the open air theatre, can be made from the north end of Lycabettus.

The topmost part of the mountain, where the funicular emerges, is surprisingly small if not doll-like. The spectacular panorama that spreads out to the horizon, the stupendous views from far above the roar of the Athens traffic, are best seen in the early morning or late afternoon. Naturally the night hours are the time to see the city's lights.

Leaving Plateia Kolonaki from the south corner and turning right at Vassilissis Sofias, sallies forth to the north corner of:

The National Garden (Ethnikos Kipos) (*Tmr* E5) Here peacocks, waterfowl and songbirds blend with a profusion of shrubbery, subtropical trees, ornamental ponds, various busts and cafe tables through and around which thread neat gravel paths.

To the south of the gardens are the *Zappeion Exhibition Halls*. To the north-west, the Greek Parliament buildings, the old Royal Palace and the Tomb or Monument to the Unknown Warrior, guarded by the traditionally costumed *Evzones*, the Greek equivalent of the British Buckingham Palace Guards (*See* **Places of Interest, A To Z**).

South-east of the National Gardens is the *Olympic Stadium* erected in 1896 on the site of the original stadium, built in 330 BC, and situated in a valley of the Arditos Hills.

South-west across Leoforos Olgas are the Olympic swimming pool and the *Tennis and Athletic Club*. To the west of these sporting facilities is the isolated gateway known as the *Arch of Hadrian* overlooking the busy traffic junction of Leoforos Olgas and Leoforos Amalias. Through the archway, the remains of the Temple of Olympian Zeus are outlined, 15 only of the original 104 Corinthian columns remain standing.

Leaving Hadrian's Arch, westwards along Odhos Dionysiou Areopagitou leads to the south side of:-

The Acropolis (Akropoli) (*Tmr* C5) A 10-acre rock rising 229m above the surrounding city and surmounted by the Parthenon Temple, built in approximately 450 BC, the Propylaia Gateway, the Temple to Athena Nike and the triple Temple of Erechtheion. Additionally, there has been added the modern Acropolis Museum, discreetly tucked away, almost out of sight.

At the bottom of the southern slopes are the *Theatre of Dionysos*, originally said to seat up to 30,000 but more probably 17,000, and the smaller, second century AD, *Odeion of Herodes Atticus*, which has been restored and is used for plays and concerts during the summer festival. It is thought provoking to consider that the Dionysos Odeion is the original theatre where western world drama, as we know it, originated. The west slope leads to the *Hill of Areopagos* (*Areios Pagos*) where, in times of yore, a council of noblemen dispensed supreme judgements. Across Apostolou Pavlou St lie the other tree covered hills of *Filopapou* (*Philopappos/ Mouseion*), or *Hill of Muses*, from whence the views are far-reaching and outstanding; *Pynx* (*Pynka*), where The Assembly once met and a *son et lumiere* is now held, and the *Asteroskopeion* (*Observatory*), or the *Hill of Nymphs*, whereon stands, surprise, surprise, an observatory.

Descending from the Asteroskopeion towards and across Apostolou Pavlou St is:

The Greek Agora (*Tmr* B/C4) The gathering place from whence the Athenians would have approached the Acropolis. This marketplace cum-civic centre is now little more than rubble, but the glory that once was is recreated by a model.

Nearby the *Temple of Hephaistos* or *Thission* (*Theseion*) sits on a small hill overlooking the Agora and to one side is the reconstructed marketplace, *Stoa Attalus*, the cost of which was met from private donations raised by American citizens.

A short distance to the east of the Greek Agora is the site of:-

The Roman Forum (or Agora) (*Tmr* C5) Close by is the *Tower of the Winds* (*Tmr* 8C5) a remarkable, octagonal tower, probably built in the first century BC and which served as a combination water clock, sundial and weather vane. Early descriptions say the building was topped off with a bronze weather vane represented by the mythological Triton complete with a pronged trident. The carved eight gods of wind can be seen, as can traces of the corresponding sundials, but no interior mechanism remains and the building is now used as a store for various stone antiquities.

A short distance to the north-west is an area known as *The Keramikos* (*Tmr* B4), a cemetery or graveyard, containing the *Street of the Tombs*, a funeral avenue laid out about 400 BC.

In a north-easterly direction from Keramikos, along Pireos St, via Eleftherias Sq Bus terminal (*Tmr* 9C3), turning right down Evripidou St, across Athinas and Eolou Sts, leads to:-

Klafthmonos Square (Klathmonos) (*Tmr* 10D3/4) Supposedly the most attractive Byzantine church in Athens, Aghii Theodori, is positioned in the west corner of the Square.

Looking north-east across Stadiou St, up Korai St and across Panepistimiou Ave, reveals an imposing range of neo-classical buildings (*Tmr* 11D/E3/4), fronted by formal gardens. These comprise the *University* flanked by, to the left (facing), the *National Library*, and to the right, the *Academy*. Behind and running parallel to Stadiou and Panepistimiou, is Akadimias St, on which is another Bus terminal. Just off Akadimias St, in Massalias St, is the *Hellenic-American Union*, many of whose facilities are open to the general public. These include an English and music library, as well as a cafeteria.

North-west of Klafthmonos Sq, to the left of Eolou St, is:-

Kotzia Square (*Tmr* D3) A very large plateia around which, on Sunday at least, a profusion of flower sellers' stalls circle the square.

The once paved area has now been dug up by archaeologists who have unearthed a veritable treasure trove of ancient Athens city walls. At the time of writing the fate of the site is in the hands of the opposing and seemingly irreconcilable tugs of the modernists, who have a vision of a vast underground car park, and the traditionalists, who quite rightly, wish to see the 'dig' preserved for posterity.

Fokionos Negri Actually a street, if not an avenue, rather than a square. It is somewhat distant from the city centre, almost in the suburbs to the north, and usually just off the street plans of Athens. To reach Fokionos Negri from Omonia Square, proceed up 28 Ikosiokto Oktovriou, which runs into Patission St, on past the *National Archaeological Museum* and *Green Park* (*Pedion Areos*), both on the right, to where Agiou Meletiou St runs across Patission St. Fokionos Negri starts as a fairly narrow side-street to the right, but widens out into a tree lined. short, squat avenue with a wide, spacious, centre pedestrian way once gravelled but now extensively resurfaced. Supposedly the *Dolce Vita* or *Via Veneto* of Athens but not out of the ordinary, if quiet wealth is normal. Extremely expensive cafes edge the square halfway up on the right and it certainly becomes extremely lively after nightfall.

Trolley-buses 5, 11, 12 or 13, going north, trundle past the turning.

THE ACCOMMODATION & EATING OUT

The Accommodation On the islands the haul of accommodation includes even 'E' Class hotels but in Athens I have erred on the side of caution and stuck with 'B', 'C' and some better 'D' class hotels and pensions. No doubt there are some acceptable Class 'E' hotels but...

On Adrianou St (*Tmr* D5), in the Plaka district, are a few, very cheap dormitories and students' hostels, where a certain amount of rooftop sleeping is allowed, costing upwards of 500drs per night. Unless set well back from the main road, a set of earmuffs or plugs is almost obligatory to ensure a good night's sleep.

On a cautionary note, since the end of 1981 the Greek authorities have been closing a number of the more 'undesirable', unlicensed hotels, so a particular favourite overnight stop from years gone by may no longer be in business.

Most of the hotel charges listed in this book are priced at the 1987 rates but these will average out for 1988 as follows:

Class	Single	Double	
A	5000-6300	6200-8600drs	en suite bathroom
B	3000-4500	4000-6200drs	& breakfast included.
C	1900-3000	2500-4000drs	sharing bathroom &
D	1000-1500	1500-2500drs	room rate only.
E	850-1000	1000-1500drs	

See **Arrival By Air, East airport, Introduction**

SYNTAGMA AREA (*Tmr* D/E4/5)

Festos Guest House (*Tmr* D/E5) 18 Filellinon St Tel 323 2455

Directions: From Syntagma Sq, walk up the rise of Odhos Filellinon past a number of cut-price ticket joints. The entrance is very nearly opposite Ag Nikodimos Church, on the right.

Ethnic guest house with dormitories, triples and quadruple rooms working out at between 500 and 1000drs per person. Hot showers cost an extra 100drs but luggage is stored free. The bar not only serves drinks but simple snacks. For the indiscriminately young at heart.

Hotel Cleo (Cleopatra) (*Tmr* D4) 3 Patroou St Tel 322 9053

Directions: Leaving Syntagma Sq, walk down Mitropoleos St, towards Monastiraki Sq and take the fourth turning left.

Well recommended if threadbare. Ground floor dormitory, free baggage store. Double rooms en suite cost 1650drs rising to 2400drs (1st May-30th Sept).

NB The owners also have a guest house nearby in 18 Apollonos St.

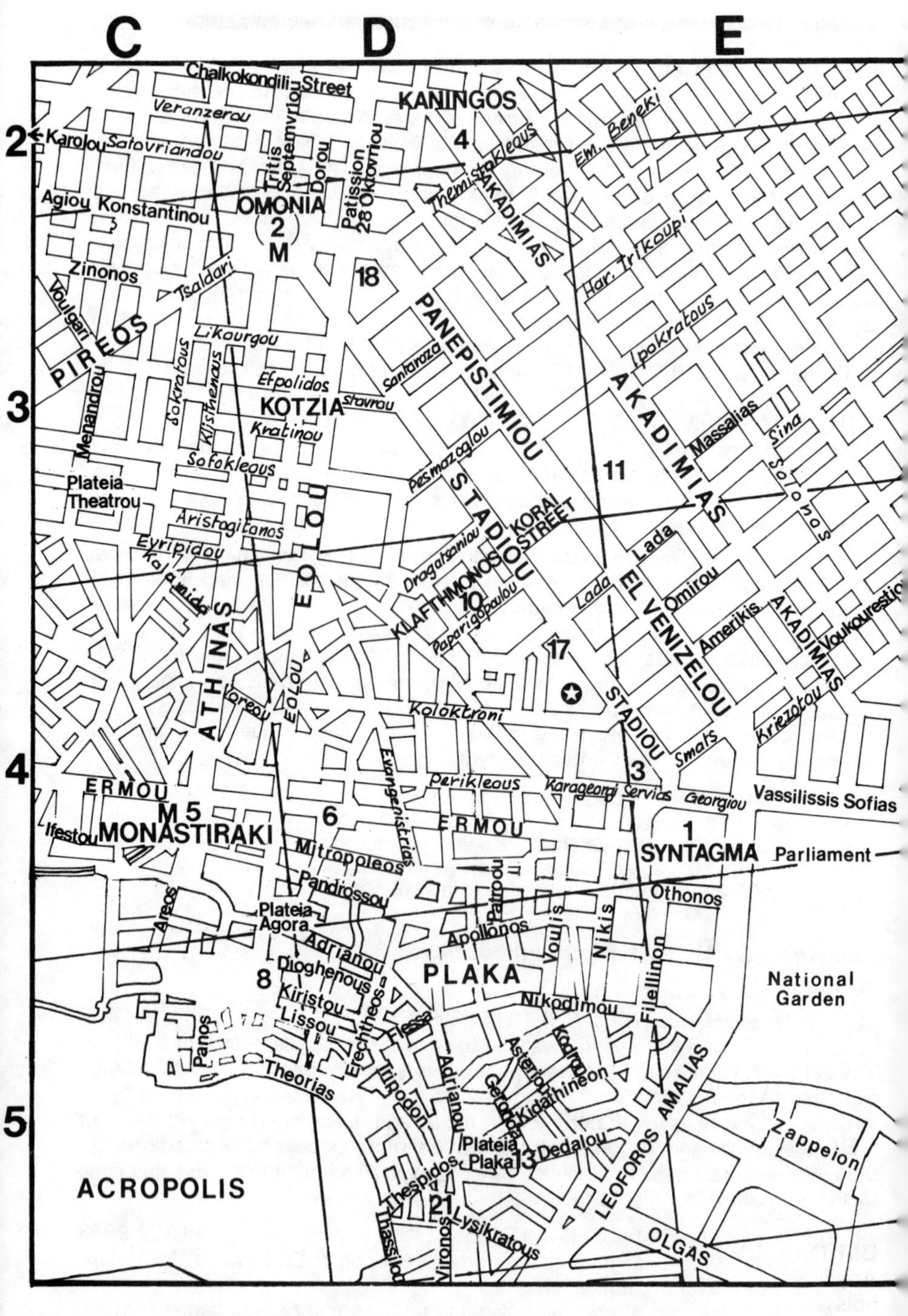

Illustration 5 Athens City inset - The Plaka

Pension John's Place (*Tmr* D4) (Class C) 5 Patroou St Tel 322 9719
Directions: As for *Hotel Cleo* above.

Not surprisingly, the affable old Papa is named John. Well looked after accommodation with singles starting at 900drs and doubles from 1400drs (1st Jan-30th April) increasing to 1200drs and 1800drs (1st May-30th Sept) and 1000drs and 1500drs (1st Oct-31st Dec). Naturally rooms share the bathroom facilities.

George's Guest House (*Tmr* D4) (Class B) 46 Nikis St Tel 322 6474
Directions: From Syntagma Sq, walk west along Mitropoleos St and turn down the first left-hand turning. The guest house is on the right, beyond the first side-street.

Calls itself a *Youth Hostel with student prices*. It was recommended to me by four Texas college girls, met on the train to Patras some years ago and whose first stop in Greece this was. Shared bathroom and hot water in the evening, if you are quick. Doubles from 1230drs rising to 2200drs (1st April-10th Oct).

Hotel Kimon (*Tmr* D5) (Class D) 27 Apollonos Tel 323 5223
Directions: Midway on Apollonos St, one block down from Mitropoleos St.

Old but renovated with all rooms sharing the bathrooms. Single rooms start off at 1000drs increasing to 1630drs (1st May-30th Sept) and en suite 1250drs rising to 1750drs. Double rooms en suite start at 1250drs rising to 1875drs.

Hotel Plaka (*Tmr* D4) (Class C) 7 Kapnikareas/Mitropoleos Sts
Tel 322 2096
Directions: From Syntagma Sq proceed west along Mitropoleos. Kapnikareas St lies between Evangenistrias and Eolou Sts and the hotel is on the left.

Listed because the hotel accepts *American Express* and or *Diners* despite which the charges are not exorbitant.

All rooms have en suite bathrooms with a single costing 1750drs a night and a double 2400drs which charges increase respectively to 2000drs and 2700/3300drs (1st April-30th June & 1st Oct-31st Dec) and 2400drs and 3300/3900drs (1st July-30th Sept). Breakfast might have to be an inclusive, charged extra at between 280 and 350drs per head.

YMCA (XAN) (*Tmr* E4) 28 Omirou St Tel 362 6970
Directions: From the north-east corner of Syntagma Sq proceed up Panepistimiou St, take the third turning right and across Akadimias Avenue, on the right.

Closed for some years for renovations and may open in 1987... then again it may not.

YWCA (XEN) (*Tmr* E4) 11 Amerikis St. Tel 362 4291
Directions: All as above but second turning off Panepistimiou St and on the left.

Don't forget, women only. Apart from accommodation there is a cafe serving breakfasts (200drs), sandwiches, a hair dressing salon, library and laundry facilities. Singles from 900drs and shared rooms 800drs per head.

OMONIA AREA (*Tmr* 2D3)
Any hotel or pension rooms facing Omonia Square must be regarded as very noisy.

Hotel Omonia (*Tmr* D3) (Class C) 4 Omonia Sq. Tel 523 7210

Directions: Just stand on Omonia Sq, swivel on your heels and on the north side of the Square.

The reception is on the first floor, as is a cafe-bar and terrace, overlooking the square and its action. Modern but 'worn international' look to the place. Clients may well have to take demi-pension terms. All rooms have en suite bathrooms. Singles start at 1200drs and a double room 1750drs rising, respectively, to 1400drs and 1750drs (1st April-14th July & 15th Sept-31st Oct) and 1700drs and 2100drs (15th July-14th Sept). Breakfast costs 250drs and a meal from 850drs.

Hotel Banghion (*Tmr* D3) (Class C) 18b Omonia Sq. Tel 324 2259
Directions: As for *Hotel Omonia*, but on the south side of the square.

Elegant and ageing. Rooms sharing a bathroom cost 1250drs for a single and 1900drs for a double and with en suite bathrooms 1800drs and 2450drs. These charges rise respectively to 1500/2300drs and 2100/2950drs (16th July-30th Sept). Breakfasts costs 280drs increasing to 330drs (16th July-30th Sept).

Hotel Carlton (*Tmr* D3) (Class C) 7 Omonia Sq. Tel 522 3201
Directions: As for *Hotel Omonia*.

Very Greek, provincial and old fashioned. All rooms share bathrooms with single rooms from 1000drs and double rooms 1250drs, increasing to 1200drs and 1350drs (1st April-31st May) and 1350drs and 1500drs (1st June-31st Dec).

Hotel Europa (*Tmr* D2) (Class C) 7 Satovriandou St Tel 522 3081
Directions: North of Omonia Sq and the second main street up, lying east/west. This is often listed as Chateaubriandou St but the local authorities either have, or have not been notified of the change. Whatever, the street is now a pedestrian precinct.

Another 'Greek provincial' hotel, the remarkably ancient lift of which creaks its way up and down to the various floors. The rooms are adequate but dingy, there are wardrobes and the floors are covered with brown linoleum. To use the shower the concierge must be asked for the relevant key, in mime if a guest's Greek is as sketchy as the staff's knowledge of English. When produced, the key might well be adjudged large enough to open the doors of the Bastille. Weighted down by this instrument, the moment of truth dawns, for when the door is opened, sheer disbelief may well be the first reaction, especially if it is the first ever stopover in Athens, as it was mine many years ago. A cavernous and be-cobwebbed room reveals plumbing that beggars description. Enough to say the shower is most welcome even if the lack of a point to anchor the shower head, whilst trying to soap oneself down, requires interesting body contortions. The rate for a single room is 1000drs and for a double 1500drs sharing the bathrooms.

Hotel Alma (*Tmr* D2/3) (Class C) 5 Dorou Tel 524 0858
Directions: Dorou St runs north from the north-east corner of Omonia Sq.

Modern and the rooms with a balcony are on the seventh and eighth floors. Single rooms sharing a bathroom start at 1200drs and en suite 1400drs while double rooms cost 1400drs and 1750drs, which rates respectively rise to 1500/1700drs and 1800/2000drs (1st April-15th Oct) and 1300/1500drs and 1500/1800drs (16th Oct-31st Dec).

Hotel Orpheus (*Tmr* C/D2) (Class C) 58 Chalkokondili St Tel 522 4996
Directions: North of Omonia Sq.

Stolid, studentish and provincial in character. Very well recommended and reasonably priced with a mix of accommodation available. For 1988 rooms (& rates) include single (1300drs), double (1800drs), triple (2400drs), quadruple (2800drs), quintuple (3000drs) and dormitory (500drs per person). There is a TV lounge, outdoor patio and bar. Continental breakfast is available at 250drs and an English breakfast at a cost of 400drs. Bar prices are reasonable with a Nes meh ghala costing 90drs, an ouzo 60drs, Metaxa 3 star brandy 60drs and an Amstel beer 100drs. Overseas phone calls can be made.

Hotel Eva (*Tmr* C2) (Class D) 31 Victoros Ougo Tel 522 3079
Directions: West of Omonia as far as Plateia Karaiskaki and to the north, parallel with and two blocks back from Ag Konstantinou.

Well recommended, all rooms have en suite bathrooms. Single rooms start at 1200drs and double rooms 2130drs rising to 1480drs and 2780drs (1st June-30th Sept). Breakfast costs 250drs.

Hotel Marina (*Tmr* C3) (Class C) 13 Voulgari Tel 523 7832/3
Directions: South-west from Omonia Sq along Odhos Pireos and 4th turning to the right.

Single rooms cost from 1150drs, double rooms 1450drs, both sharing the bathroom, while rooms with en suite bathrooms cost from 1400drs and 1950drs respectively. These rates rise (16th March-30th June & 16th Oct-31st Dec) to 1300drs and 1700drs (single and doubles sharing) and 1600drs and 2350drs (singles and doubles en suite) and again (1st July-15th Oct) to 1400/1900drs and 1750/2650drs. Breakfast is charged at 200drs.

Hotel Vienna (*Tmr* C3) (Class C) 20 Pireos Tel 524 9143
Directions: South-west of Omonia Sq.

New, clean and noisy. All rooms have en suite bathrooms with singles starting at 1700drs and doubles 2250drs, increasing to 2000drs and 2650drs (1st July-31st Oct). A breakfast costs 250drs.

Hotel Athinea (*Tmr* C2) (Class C) 9 Vilara Tel 524 3884
Directions: Westwards along Ag Konstantinou and situated on one side of the small square of Agiou Konstantinou.

Old but beautifully positioned although cabaret night life may intrude. A restaurant and cake shop are close by as is a taxi rank. All rooms have en suite bathrooms. A single room starts off at 1460drs and a double 2000drs rising to 1830drs and 2400drs (1-15th June & 1-31st Oct) and again to 2000drs and 2850drs (11-30th April & 16th June-30th Sept). Breakfast is priced at 400drs.

Hotel Florida (*Tmr* C3) (Class C) 25 Menandrou Tel 522 3214
Directions: Third turning left, south-west along Pireos St.

Single rooms from 790/1055drs and doubles 1530drs, both without a bathroom, whilst en suite rooms cost 1220drs and 1865drs. These charges rise respectively to 990/1320drs and 1910drs, and 1525drs and 2330drs (1st June-30th Sept). Breakfast is charged at 230drs.

Hotel Alcestis (Alkistis) (*Tmr* C3) (Class C) 18 Plateia Theatrou
Tel 321 9811
Directions: From Pireos St, south down either Sokratous or Menandrou Sts and across Odhos Sofokleous St.

Despite its chromium-plated appearance, all glass and marble with a prairie-sized lobby, it is a Class C hotel in a commercial square. Popular and all rooms have en suite bathrooms. Singles start off at 1870drs and doubles 2400drs rising to 2100drs and 2800drs (1st July-30th Sept). Breakfast costs 300drs and lunch/dinner 1000drs.

MONASTIRAKI AREA (*Tmr* C4)

Hotel Tembi/Tempi (*Tmr* C/D4) (Class D) 29 Eolou (Aiolu/Aeolou) Tel 321 3175

Directions: A main street north of Ermou St, opposite the Church of Ag Irini.

Pleasant rooms with singles sharing the bathroom starting at 800drs rising to 950drs (16th May-31st Oct). Double rooms sharing cost from 1200drs and en suite 1500drs advancing to 1500drs and 1800drs respectively.

Hotel Ideal (*Tmr* C/D4) (Class D) 39 Eolou/2 Voreou Sts. Tel 321 3195

Directions: On the left of Eolou, walking northwards from Odhos Ermou, and on the corner with Voreou St.

A perfect example of a weather-worn, 19th century, Athens neo-classical building complete with an old fashioned, metal and glass canopy entrance and matchbox sized, wrought iron balconies. The accommodation lives up to all that the exterior promises! The management are helpful, there is a telephone, TV room, a bar and luggage can be stored. Tourist information is freely available as are battered paperbacks for guests. The rooms are clean and the bathroom facilities are shared but there is 24 hour hot water – they promise! Singles start at 800drs and doubles 1200drs rising to 950drs and 1500drs (16th May-31st Oct).

Hotel Hermion (*Tmr* C/D4) (Class D) 66c Ermou St Tel 321 2753

Directions: East of Monastiraki, adjacent to Kapnikarea Church/Square (*Tmr* 6D4).

Old but clean with the reception up the stairs. All rooms share bathrooms with the single room rate starting off at 900drs and the double rooms 1300drs increasing to 1050drs and 1600drs, respectively (1st July-30th Sept).

Hotel Attalos (*Tmr* C3/4) (Class C) 29 Athinas Tel 321 2801

Directions: North from Monastiraki Sq.

Recommended to us by a splendidly eccentric English lady artist who should know – she has been visiting Greece for some 20 years. Singles sharing the bathroom start from 1200drs and en suite 1410drs while doubles cost 1500drs and 1750drs. These charges increase to (singles) 1500/1765 and (doubles) 2000/3150drs (1st June-15th Oct). Breakfast is charged at 275drs.

Hotel Cecil (*Tmr* C3/4) (Class D) 39 Athinas Tel 321 7079

Directions: North from Monastiraki Sq and two buildings up from the Kalamida St turning, on the left-hand side. This is the other side of the road from a very small chapel, incongruously stuck on the pavement. The 'informative' sign outside the hotel is no help.

Clean looking with a single room costing 1200drs and a double 1800drs. The bathrooms are shared.

PLAKA/METZ STADIUM AREAS (*Tmr* D5 & D/E6)

The Plaka is rich in accommodation, as it is in most things!

Hotel Phaedra (*Tmr* D5) (Class D) 4 Adrianou/16 Herephontos Tel 323 8461

Directions: Situated close by a multi-junction of various streets including

Lysikratous, Galanou, Adrianou and Herephontos, opposite the Byzantine Church of Ag Ekaterini and its small, attractive gardens.

Pretty area by day, noisy by night. A family hotel with a ground floor bar. All rooms share the bathrooms with a single room costing 1300drs and doubles 1600drs which rates increase respectively to 2000drs and 2500drs (1st April-15th Oct). Breakfast costs 250drs.

Students' Inn (*Tmr* D5) (Class C) 16 Kidathineon St Tel 324 4808
Directions: On the left of the liveliest stretch of Kidathineon St, walking up from the Adrianou St junction, and almost opposite the front garden of a Japanese eating house.

Hostelish and classified as a pension but recommended as good value with hot showers 'on tap' (sorry) and an English-speaking owner. There is a rooftop, a passable courtyard, a snackbar, the use of a washing machine (which does not always work) and a baggage store costing 50drs per day. The clean but basic rooms, which all share the bathrooms, are complete with a rickety, oilcloth covered table and a mug. Singles cost 1200drs and doubles 1500drs. This latter price increases to 1700drs (2nd May-30th Sept). Breakfast costs 250drs, but I would have to wander out to 'breathe in' the Plaka. The doors are locked at 0200hrs.

Left off Kidathineon Street, climbing towards Syntagma Sq, is Odhos Kodrou on which are two clean, agreeable hotels in a very pleasant area, the:
Hotel Adonis (*Tmr* D5) (Class B) 3 Kodrou/Voulis Sts Tel 324 9737
Directions: As above and on the right.

Actually a pension so the rates are not outrageous. All rooms have en suite bathrooms with singles starting off at 1800drs and doubles 1900drs rising respectively to 2250drs and 2400drs (1st July-30th Sept) and the:

Acropolis House (*Tmr* D5) (Class B) 6-8 Kodrou Tel 322 2344
Directions: As above and on the left.

Highly recommended and once again officially classified as a pension with a choice of rooms sharing or complete with en suite bathrooms. Between April and October the expensive single room rates commence at 2375drs and doubles 2880drs while en suite singles cost 2630drs and doubles 3170drs.

Closer to Kidathineon St, and on the right is the:
Kourous Pension (*Tmr* D5) (Class C) 11 Kodrou Tel 322 7431
Directions: As above.

Rather more provincial than the two establishments detailed above, which lack of sophistication is reflected in the lower prices (and standards). All rooms share the bathrooms and the single room rate starts at 900drs and a double 1400drs climbing to the dizzy heights (!) of 1200drs and 1800drs (1st May-30th Sept).

Hotel Solonion (*Tmr* D5) (Class E) 11 Sp Tsangari/Dedalou Tel 322 0008
Directions: To the right of Kidathineon St (*facing Syntagma Sq*) between Dedalou St and Leoforos Amalias. Odhos Tsangari is a continuation of Asteriou St.

I did start out by pronouncing I would not list any E class hotels but... Run by a rather stern faced lady who is assisted by a varied collection of part-time assistants to run the old, faded but refurbished building. If a guest strikes lucky the night porter will be a delightful old boy who was once a merchant in the

Greek community resident in Turkey, and caught up in the huge population resettlement of 1922/23. The accommodation is 'student provincial' quality, the rooms being high ceilinged with the rather dodgy floorboards overlaid and hidden beneath brown linoleum. The bathrooms are distinctly ethnic and Victorian in style but hot water is promised all day. On a fine day.... it is possible to espy the Acropolis... well a bit of it. No single rooms are available. A double room sharing the bathroom costs from 1200drs, including one bath a day, which rises to 1400drs (1st April-15th Oct).

Close by the *Hotel Solonion* are the:-
Hotel Kekpoy (Cecrops) (*Tmr* D5) (Class D) 13 Sp Tsangari Tel 322 3080
Directions: On the same side as and similar to the *Solonion* but a building or two towards Leoforos Amalias.

All rooms share the bathrooms with singles costing 1300drs and doubles 1390drs (1st April-15th Oct).

Hotel Phoebus (Fivos) *(Tmr* D5) (Class C) Asteriou/12 Peta Sts Tel 322 0142
Directions: Back towards Kidathineon St, on the corner of Odhos Asteriou and Peta.

Rather more up-market than the three previously listed hotels, all rooms have en suite bathrooms. A single room is charged at 1950drs and a double room costs 2500drs. These rates rise respectively to 2300drs and 3000drs (1st June-30th Sept). Breakfast costs 300drs.

A few side streets towards the Acropolis is the:-
Hotel Ava (*Tmr* D5) 9 Lysikratous St Tel 323 6618
Directions: As above.

I have no personal experience but the establishment has been mentioned as a possibility and is in an excellent, central but quiet situation although it is rather expensive. All rooms have en suite bathrooms, are heated and air conditioned. Single rooms cost from 2800drs and doubles from 3600drs. There are family suites complete with kitchen and refrigerator (sic).

New Clare's House (*Tmr* E6) (Class C Pension) 24 Sorvolou St Tel 922 2288
Directions: Rather uniquely, the owners have had a large compliments slip printed with a pen and ink drawing on the face and, on the reverse side, directions in Greek saying *Show this to the taxi driver*. This includes details of the location, south of the Stadium, on Sorvolou St between Charvouri and Voulgareos Sts. The pension is on the right, half-way down the reverse slope with the description *white building with the green shutters*. From Syntagma proceed south down the sweep of Leoforos Amalias, keeping to the main avenue hugging the Temple of Olympian Zeus and along Odhos Diakou. Where Diakou makes a junction with Vouligmenis and Ardittou Avenues, Odhos Anapafseos leads off in a south-east direction and Sorvolou St 'crescents' off to the left. Trolley buses 2, 4, 11 & 12 drop travellers by the Stadium. It is quite a steep climb up Sorvolou St, which breaks into steps, to the pretty and highly recommended area of Metz (highly regarded by Athenians that is). Plus points are that the narrow nature of the lanes, which suddenly become steps, keeps the traffic down to a minimum and the height of the hill raises it above the general level of smog and pollution.

The pleasant, flat-fronted pension is on the right and has a marble floor entrance hall. Inside, off to the left, is a large reception/lounge/bar/breakfast/common room and to the right, the lift. Apart from the usual hotel business, the establishment 'beds' some tour companies clients overnighting in Athens, and en route to other destinations. Thus the hotel can be fully booked so it is best to make a forward booking or telephone prior to journeying out here. The self confident English speaking owner presides over matters from a large desk in the reception area and is warily helpful. The lady staff receptionists do not exactly go wild in an orgy of energy sapping activity, tending to indulge in a saturnalia of TV watching. Guests in the meantime can help themselves to bottles of beer and Coke from the bar, paying when convenient to them, and the receptionist. Despite the inferred aura of excellence the usual collection of faults crop up from time to time including: cracked loo seats; no hot water, despite being assured that there is 24 hours hot water (and for longer no doubt were there more hours in the day!); missing locking mechanism on the lavatory door; toilets having to be flushed using a piece of string and the television on the blink. I do not mean to infer that these irritating defects occur all at once – just one or two, every so often. Double rooms sharing a bathroom cost 2100drs and en suite 3000drs which rates increase, respectively, to 2300drs and 3400drs (1st June-31st Dec). Incidentally, where the well appointed bathrooms are shared, the pleasant rooms only have to go fifty-fifty with one other room. The charges, which include breakfast with warm bread every day, may at first impression (and for that matter second and third impression) appear on the expensive side. The 'pain' might be eased by the realisation that the 4th floor has a balcony and a self-catering kitchen, complete with cooker and a fridge, and the 5th floor a laundry room with an iron and 2 rooftop clothes lines. These facilities must of course be taken into account when weighing up comparative prices. The management creates an atmosphere that will suit the young, very well behaved student and the older traveller but not exuberant rowdies. Hands are 'smacked' if guests lie around eating a snack on the front steps, hang washing out of the windows or make a noise, especially between the hours of 1330 and 1700 and after 2330hrs. You know, lights out boys and no smoking in the 'dorms'. Clare's House was originally recommended by pension owner Alexis on the island of Kos and in recent years has been included in one or two of the smaller tour companies' brochures for the Athens overnight stop. Certainly an old friend of ours, Peter, who 'has to put up with yachting round the Aegean waters during the summer months', almost always spends some of his winter Athens months at Clare's and swears by the place.

Before leaving the area there is an intriguing possibility, accommodation that is, in a very quiet street edging the west side of the Stadium.

Joseph's House Pension (*Tmr* E6) (Class C) 13 Markou Moussourou
Tel 923 1204

Directions: From the region of Hadrian's Arch/the Temple of the Olympian Zeus (*Tmr* D6) proceed up Avenue Arditou in a north-easterly direction towards the Stadium. Odhos Markou Moussourou climbs steeply off to the right, immediately prior to the wooded hillside of Arditos. The pension is on the left, beyond Meletiou Riga St. On the other hand, it is just as easy to follow the directions to *Clare's House* and proceed east along Charvouri St until it bumps into Markou Moussourou.

The bathrooms are shared with single rooms charged at 1000drs and doubles at 1400drs, which rates rise to 1000drs and 1500drs (1st May-30th Sept).

THISSION AREA (THESION) (*Tmr* B/C4/5)
First south-bound Metro stop after Monastiraki and a much quieter area than, say, the Plaka.

Hotel Phedias (*Tmr* B4) (Class C) 39 Apostolou Pavlou Tel 345 9511
Directions: South of the Metro station.

Modern and friendly. All rooms share en suite bathrooms with singles costing 1800drs and double rooms 2300drs, rising to 2100drs and 2700drs (1st July-31st Dec). Breakfast is charged at 250drs per head.

OLYMPIC OFFICE AREA (*Tmr* C6)
Hotel Karayannis (*Tmr* C6) (Class C) 94 Leoforos Sygrou Tel 921 5903
Directions: On the corner of Odhos Byzantiou and Leoforos Sygrou, opposite the side exit of the Olympic terminal office.

'Interesting', tatty and noisy, but very necessary for travellers arriving late at the terminal. Rooms facing the main road should be avoided. The Athenian traffic, which roars up and down the broad avenue non-stop round the clock, gives every appearance of making the journey along Leoforos Sygrou via the hotel balconies, even three or four storeys up. There are picturesque views of the Acropolis from the breakfast and bar rooftop terrace, even if they are through a maze of television aerials. Single rooms with an en suite bathroom cost 1410drs. Double rooms sharing a bathroom cost 1910drs, and en suite 1990drs. These prices increase respectively to 1615drs and 2190/2285drs. Breakfast for one costs 250drs. Best to splash out for the en suite rooms as the hotel's shared lavatories are of a 'thought' provoking nature with a number of the unique features detailed under the general description of bathrooms in **Chapter Four**.

Whilst in this area it would be a pity not to mention the:-
Super-bar Restaurant Odhos Faliron
Directions: As for the *Hotel Karayannis* but behind the Olympic office.

Not inexpensive but very conveniently situated, even if it is closed on Sundays. Snackbar food with 2 Nes meh gala, a toasted cheese and ham sandwich and boiled egg costing 280drs. On that occasion I actually wanted toast...

Youth Hostel 57 Kypselis St and Agiou Meletiou 1 Tel 822 5860
Directions: Located in the Fokionos Negri area of North Athens. Proceed along 28 Ikosiokto Oktovriou/Patission Street from Omonia Sq, beyond Pedion Areos Park to Ag Meletiou St. Turn right and follow until the junction with Kypselis St. Trolley buses 3, 5, 11, 12 & 13 make the journey.

This proclaims itself as *The Official Youth Hostel* and does fulfil the requirements of those who require very basic, cheap accommodation, albeit in dormitories. The overnight charge is 500 drs.

Taverna Youth Hostel (*Tmr* G2) 1 Drossi St/87 Leoforos Alexandra
Tel 646 3669
Directions: East of Pedion Aeros Park along Leoforos Alexandra almost as far as the junction with Ippokratous St. Odhos Drossi is on the left. It is possible to catch trolley-bus No. 7 from Panepistimiou Avenue or No. 8 from Kanigos Sq (*Tmr* 4D2) or Akadimias St.

Actually a taverna that 'sprouts' an 'unofficial Youth Hostel' for the summer months only.

If only to receive confirmation regarding the spurious Youth Hostels, it may be worth visiting the:-

YHA Head Office (*Tmr* D3/4) 4 Dragatsaniou Tel 323 4107

Directions: The north side of Plateia Klafthmonos in a street on the left-hand side of Stadiou St.

Only open Monday-Friday, 0900-1500hrs. They advise of vacancies in the youth hostels and issue international youth hostel cards.

LARISSIS STATION AREA (*Tmr* B/C1)

See **Trains, A To Z.**

CAMPING

Sample daily site charges per person vary between 290-400drs (children half-price) and the hire of a tent between 350-550drs.

Sites include the following:-

Distance from Athens	Site Name	Amenities
8km	**Athens Camping.** 198 Athinon Ave. On the road to Dafni (due west of Athens). Tel 581 4101	Open all year, 25km from the sea. Bar, shop & showers.
10km	**Dafni Camping.** Dafni. On the Athens to Corinth National Road. Tel 581 1562	Open all year, 5km from the sea. Bar, shop, showers & kitchen facilities.
For the above: Bus 853, Athens – Elefsina, departs Koumoundourou Sq/Deligeorgi St (*Tmr* C2/3) every 20 mins between 0510-2215hrs.		
14.5km	**Patritsia.** Kato Kifissia, N. Athens. Tel 801 1900 Closed 'temporarily' for 1987, query 1988?	Open June-October. Bar, shop, showers, laundry & kitchen facilities.
16km	**Nea Kifissia.** Nea Kifissia, N. Athens. Tel 807 5544	Open April-October, 20km from the sea. Bar, shop, showers, swimming pool & laundry.
18km	**Dionyssiotis.** Nea Kifissia N. Athens. Tel 807 1494	Open all year
25km	**Papa-Camping.** Zorgianni, Ag Stefanos. Tel 803 3446	Open June-October, 25km from the sea. Laundry, bar & kitchen facilities.
For the above (sited on or beside the Athens National Road, north to Lamia): Lamia bus from 260 Liossion St (*Tmr* C1/2), every hour from 0615 to 1915hrs & at 2030hrs.		
35km	**Marathon Camping.** Kaminia, Marathon. NE of Athens. Tel 0294 5577	On a sandy beach & open April-October. Showers, bar restaurant & kitchen facilities.
35km	**Nea Makri.** 156 Marathonos Ave, Nea Makri. NE of Athens just south of Marathon. Tel 0294 92719	Open April-October, 220m from the sea. Sandy beach, laundry, bar & shop.
For the above: The bus from Odhos Mavrommateon, Plateia Egyptou (*Tmr* D1), every ½ hour from 0530 to 2200hrs.		
26km	**Cococamp.** Rafina. East of Athens. Tel 0294 23413	Open all year. On the beach, rocky coast. Laundry, bar, showers, kitchen facilities, shop & restaurant.
29km	**Kokkino Limanaki Camping** Kokkino Limanaki, Rafina Tel 0294 31602	On the beach. Open April-October.
29km	**Rafina Camping.** Rafina. East of Athens. Tel 0294 23118	Open May-October, 4km from the sandy beach. Showers, bar, laundry, restaurant & shop

For the above: The Rafina bus from Mavrommateon St, Plateia Egyptou (*Tmr* D1). Twenty-nine departures from 0550 to 2200hrs.

20km	**Voula Camping.** 2 Alkyonidon St, Voula. Just below Glyfada & the Airport. Tel 895 2712	Open all year. On the sandy beach. Showers, laundry, shop & kitchen facilities.
27km	**Varkiza Beach Camping.** Varkiza. Coastal road Athens-Vouliagmeni-Sounion. Tel 897 3613	Open all year, by a sandy beach. Bar, shop, supermarket, taverna, laundry & kitchen facilities.
60km	**Sounion Camping.** Sounion Tel 0292 39358	Open all year, by a sandy beach. Bar, shop, laundry, kitchen facilities & a taverna.
76km	**Vakhos Camping.** Assimaki nr Sounion. On the Sounion to Lavrion road. Tel 0292 39263	Open June-September, on the beach.

For the above: Buses from Mavrommateon St, Plateia Egyptou (*Tmr* D1) every hour from 0630 to 1730hrs. Note, to get to Vakhos Camping catch the Sounion bus via Markopoulo and Lavrion.

The Eating Out Where to dine out is a very personal choice and in a city the size of Athens there are so many restaurants and tavernas from which to choose that only a few recommendations are made. In general, steer clear of Luxury and Class A hotel dining rooms, restaurants offering international cuisine and tavernas with Greek music and or dancing*, all of which may be very good but are usually on the expensive side. Gongoozling from one of the chic establishments, such as a *Floka's*, at one of the smart squares has become an expensive luxury with a milky coffee (Nes meh ghala) or a bottle of beer costing anything up to 150drs, and an ouzo 200drs. In contrast it is possible to 'coffee' in the Plaka at, say *Kafeneion To Mainalon* (on the junction of Odhos Geronda, also named Monisasteriou, and Kidathineon St) where prices are much more reasonable at about 80drs for a Nes meh ghala or an ouzo. It is on an inside wall of *To Mainalon* that two preserved price lists vividly highlight the effect of inflation in Greece. One of them dates back to 1965 and the other to 1968. They are priced in drachmae and lepta – one hundred lepta made up one drachma. A bottle of beer cost 2.50drs in 1965 and 3drs in 1968, a good brandy 3drs and 3.50drs respectively and an ouzo 3drs in both years. Well there you go.

In Athens and the larger, more cosmopolitan, provincial cities, it is usual taverna practice to round off prices, which proves a little disconcerting at first.

In despair it is noted that some restaurants and tavernas climbing the slopes of the Acropolis up Odhos Markou Avriliou, south of Eolou St, are allowing 'Chinese menu' style collective categories (A, B, C etc.) to creep into their menu listings.

Note the reference to Greek dancing and music is not derogatory – only an indication that it is often the case that standards of cuisine may not be any better and prices often reflect the 'overheads' attributable to the musicians. But See* **Palia & **Xnou Tavernas**.

PLAKA AREA (*Tmr* D5)

A glut of eating houses ranging from the very good and expensive, the very expensive and bad, to some inexpensive and very good.

Taverna Thespis 18 Thespidos St Tel 323 8242

Directions: On the right of a lane across the way from Kidathineon St, towards the bottom or south-east end of Adrianou St.

Recommended and noted for its friendly service. The house retsina is served in metal jugs. A two hour, slap-up meal of souvlakia, Greek salad, fried zucchini, bread and two carafes of retsina costs in excess of 1600drs for two.

Plaka Village 28 Kidathineon
Directions: On the left (*Adrianou St behind one*), in the block edged by the streets of Adrianou and Kidathineon.

Once an excellent souvlaki snackbar but.... the offerings are now so-so at a cost of 85drs. Added to which, to sit down costs an extra 16drs per head. Price lists do not make this plain and the annoying habit can cause, at the least, irritation. (This practice is also prevalent in the Omonia Square 'souvlaki arcade'). Even more alarming is the 'take it or leave it' attitude that also extends to customer's money. The staff err towards 'taking' it, having to be badgered to return any change. A large bottle of beer costs 80drs, the home-made tzatziki is good, the service is quick and they even remain open Sunday lunchtimes.

Committed souvlaki pita eaters do not have to despair as any number of snackbars are concentrated on both sides at the Monastiraki Square end of Mitropoleos St. Perhaps the most inexpensive souvlaki in the area are to be found by turning right at the bottom of Kidathineon St and wandering down Adrianou in the direction of Monastiraki Sq. Prices fall as low as 58-65drs.

ΟΥΖΕΡΙ Ο ΚΟΥΚΛΗΣ (or **PEPAVI**) 14 Tripodon St Tel 324 7605
Directions: Up the slope from the Thespidos/Kidathineon junction, one to the left of Adrianou (*facing Monastiraki Sq*), and on the left.

Recognising the establishment used not to be at all difficult as the 1st floor balcony was embellished with a large, stuffed bird and two, big, antique record player horns mounted on the wrought iron balustrade. I write 'used not' because the mounted heron has disappeared, the owners of the taverna maintaining that it has flown away to Mykonos! Mind you the 'HMV' style trumpets are still prominent thus easily distinguishing the old ouzerie/wine shop. The vine continues to grow well.

The taverna, standing on its own, evokes a provincial country atmosphere. It is necessary to arrive early as the ouzerie is well patronised by the locals, which patronage is not surprising considering the inexpensive excellence of one or two of the dishes which include salvers of dolmades and meatballs. Another 'standard' is 'flaming sausages'. These cook away on stainless steel plates set in front of the diner. They are served with a large plateful of hors d'oeuvres, amongst which are a meatball, beans, lettuce, feta, chilli, new potatoes, Russian salad and etc etc, at a cost of 1000drs for two. Great value, very filling indeed but watch the napkins don't go up in flames and bear in mind the house wine is pretty rough. The popularity is vouchsafed by the taverna being full by 2000hrs.

Eden Taverna 3 Flessa St
Directions: Off Adrianou St, almost opposite Odhos Nikodimou, and on the left.

Mentioned because their menu includes many offerings that excellently cater (sorry) for vegetarian requirements. Open 1200hrs to 0100hrs every day except Tuesdays.

Palia Plakiotiki Taverna (Stamatopoulos) (*Tmr* D5) 26 Lissiou St
Tel 322 8722
Directions: Proceed up Lissiou St, which parallels Adrianou St, in the general direction of Monastiraki Sq. The open-air taverna is behind a perimeter wall to the right on a steep slope at the junction with Erechtheos St.

Claims to be one of Athens' oldest tavernas. The large terraced area is laid out with clean gravel chippings. Not particularly cheap but a super place at which to have an 'atmospheric' evening as there is a resident group. Note this recommendation, despite my usual caveats regarding joints at which music 'is on score'. (Those remarks are usually attributed to establishments that advertise live bouzouki). Here it is a major attraction in the shape of a huge, spherical man, with a name to match, Stavros Balagouras. He is the resident singer/accordionist/electric pianist and draws tourists and Greeks alike with his dignified and heartfelt performance. Besides traditional, national songs there is year-round dancing, if customers are so moved, on the one square metre floor space! The taverna is particularly Greek and lively at festival times, added to which the food is good and much cheaper than similar establishments. Cheese and meat dishes, with salad and wine for two, costs just 1500drs. The dolmades are stuffed with meat and served in a lemon sauce so cost 350drs and meat dishes average 450/500drs. The wine is rather expensive with a bottle of Cambas red costing 350drs and a large bottle of retsina 292drs. A bottle of Lowenbrau costs a reasonable 92drs. and the bread and head tax works out at only 14drs.

Michiko Restaurant 27 Kidathineon St Tel 324 6851
Directions: On the right, beyond the junction with Asteriou St proceeding in a north-east direction (*towards Syntagma Sq*), close to a small square and church.

Japanese, if you must, and extremely expensive.

Xynou/Xynos 4 Arghelou Geronda (Angelou Geronta) Tel 322 1065
Directions: Left off the lower, Plaka Square end of Kidathineon St (*facing Syntagma Sq*) and on the left, towards the far point of the short pedestrian way. The unprepossessing entrance door is tucked away in the corner of a recess and can be missed.

One of the oldest, most highly rated Plaka tavernas and well patronised by Athenians. Evenings only and closed on Saturdays and Sundays. A friend advises me that it is now almost obligatory to book in advance although I have managed to squeeze a table for two early on in the evening. Mention of its popularity with Athenians prompts me to stress these are well-heeled locals – you know shipowners, ambassadors and ageing playboys. Xynou is definitely on the 'hotel captains' list of recommended eateries and the tourists who eat here tend to look as if they have stepped off the stage-set of Dallas. But it is not surprising that the cognoscenti gather here because, despite being in the heart of Athens, the premises evoke a rural ambience. The single storey, shed-like, roof tiled buildings edge two sides of a high wall enclosed gravel area, on which are spread the chairs and tables. The food is absolutely excellent and, considering the location, the prices are not that outrageous. A meal of two plates of dolmades in lemon sauce, a plate of moussaka, a lamb fricassee in lemon sauce, a tomato and cucumber salad, a bottle of kortaki retsina and bread for two costs 1530drs. It seems a pity that the bread has to be charged at 50drs but then the ample wine list does include an inexpensive retsina. Three guitarists serenade diners, the napkins are linen, and the service is first class. Readers are recommended to save up and try Xynou's at least once, an experience that will not be easily forgotten.

To Fragathiko Taverna (*Tmr* D5)
Directions: On the left of Adrianou St (*proceeding towards Kidathineon St*) on the junction of Adrianou and Ag Andreou Sts.

Clean, reasonably priced and popular with the younger generation, some of whom may not be entirely wholesome, but their enthusiasm is not surprising considering the inexpensively priced dishes on offer. These include moussaka special 325drs; moussaka special served with 4 kinds of vegetable 425drs; lamb special served with 4 kinds of vegetable 425drs and a vegetarian dish costing 240drs.

Plateia Agora is a lovely, elongated, chic Plaka Square formed at the junction of the bottom of Eolou and the top of Adrianou and Kapnikarea Sts. The square spawns a number of cafe-bar restaurants, including the *Posidion* and *Appollon*, the canopies, chairs and tables of which edge the street all the way round the neat, paved plateia. Don't forget that prices reflect the square's modishness with a bottle of beer at the *Posidion* costing 200drs. There is a spotless public lavatory at the top (Monastiraki) end. The *Appollon* has a particularly wide range of choice and clients can sit at the comfortable tables for an (expensive) hour or so over a coffee (120drs), a fried egg breakfast (300drs) or a full blown meal, if anyone can afford the same. On this tack it is becoming commonplace for some of the smarter places such as the *Posidion* to display unpriced menus. Hope your luck is in and the organ grinder wanders through the square.

From the little square formed by a 'junction of the ways', adjacent to the Lysikrates Monument (*Tmr* 21D5), Odhos Vironos falls towards the south Acropolis encircling avenue of Dionysiou Areopagitou.

Snackbar Odhos Vironos
Directions: As above and on the right (*Plaka behind one*) of the street.
More a small 'doorway' souvlaki pita shop but small is indeed splendid.

Restaurant Olympia 20 Dionysiou Areopagitou
Directions: Proceed along Dionysiou Areopagitou, from the junction with Odhos Vironos, in a clockwise direction. The restaurant is on the right, close to the junction with Thassilou Lane (that incidentally climbs and bends back up to the top of Odhos Thespidos) hard up against the foot of the Acropolis. Between Thassilou Lane and the sun-blind-shaded lean-to butted on to the side of the restaurant, is a small grassed area and an underground Public toilet.
The prices seem reasonable and the place appears to portend good things but....I can only report the promise was in reality, disappointing. The double Greek salad was in truth only large enough for one, the moussaka was 'inactive', the kalamares were unacceptable and the roast potatoes (yes roast potatoes) were in actuality nothing more than dumpy wedges. Oh dear! They do serve a kortaki retsina.

STADIUM (PANGRATI) AREA (*Tmr* E/F6)
Karavitis Taverna (ΚΑΡΑΒΙΤΗΣ) 4 Pafsaniou (Paysanioy).
Directions: Beyond the Stadium (*Tmr* E/F6) going east (*away from the Acropolis*) along Vassileos Konstantinou, and Pafsaniou is the 3rd turning to the right. The taverna is on the left.
A small, leafy tree shaded gravel square fronts the taverna, which is so popular that there is an extension across the street, through a pair of 'field gates'. Our friend Paul will probably berate me (if he was less of a gentleman) for listing this gem. Unknown to visitors but extremely popular with Athenians,

more especially those who, when college students, frequented this jewel in the Athens taverna crown. A meal for four of a selection of dishes including lamb, beef in clay, giant haricot beans, garlic flavoured meatballs, greens, tzatziki, 2 plates of feta cheese, aubergines, courgettes, bread and 3 jugs of retsina, from the barrel, for some 2400drs. Beat that. But some knowledge of Greek is an advantage and the taverna is only open in the evening.

Instead of turning off Vassileos Konstantinou at Odhos Pafsaniou, take the next right proceeding further eastwards.

ΜΑΓΕΜΕΝΟΣ ΑΥΛΟΣ **(The Magic Flute)** Odhos Aminda (Amynta).
Directions: As above and the restaurant is 20m up on the right.
Swiss dishes including fondue, schnitzels and salads. Despite being rather more expensive than its near neighbours it is well frequented by Athenians including the composer Hadzithakis (so I am advised).

Virinis Taverna, Archimedes St
Directions: Prior to the side-streets to the two restaurant/tavernas last detailed, the second turning to the right off Vassileos Konstantinou, beyond the Stadium (*Tmr* E/F6) proceeding in an easterly direction, is Odhos Eratosthenous. This climbs up to Plateia Plastira. To the right of the square is Archimedes Street. The taverna is about a 100m along on the left. Incidentally, if returning to the centre of Athens from hereabouts, it is possible to continue along this street and drop down Odhos Markou Moussourou back to Vassileos Konstantinou.
A good selection of bistro dishes at reasonable prices, including, for instance, beef in wine sauce at a cost of 350drs. It has been indicated that I might find the place rather 'up market' as there were no souvlaki pitas on offer. Cheeky! It's only that I have learnt through expensive experience over the years that, in Greece, gingham tablecloths and French style menus tend to double the prices!

SYNTAGMA AREA (*Tmr* D/E4/5)

Corfu Restaurant 6 Kriezotou St Tel 361 3011
Directions: North of Syntagma Sq and first turning right off Panepistimiou (El Venizelou).
Extensive Greek and European dishes in a modern, friendly restaurant.

Delphi Restaurant 15 Nikis St Tel 323 4869
Directions: From the south-west corner of Syntagma Sq, east along Mitropoleos and the first turning left.
Modern, reasonably priced food from an extensive menu and friendly service.

Sintrivani Restaurant 5 Filellinon St
Directions: South-west corner of Syntagma Sq and due south.
Garden restaurant serving a traditional menu at reasonable prices.

Vassillis Restaurant 14A Voukourestiou.
Directions: North of Syntagma Sq and the second turning off Panepistimiou St, to the right, along Odhos Smats and across Akadimias St.
Variety, in traditional surroundings.

Ideal Restaurant 46 Panepistimiou St.
Directions: Proceed up Panepistimiou from the north-east corner of Syntagma Sq and the restaurant is on the right.
Good food at moderate prices.

YWCA 11 Amerikis St.
Directions: From Syntagma Sq proceed north-west along either Stadiou or Panepistimiou St and second or third road to the right, depending which street is used.
Cafeteria serving inexpensive sandwiches.

There are many cafes in and around Syntagma Square. Recommended, but expensive, is the:-
Brazilian Coffee Cafe
Directions: Close by Syntagma Sq, in Voukourestiou St.
Serves coffee, tea, toast, butter and jam, breakfast, ice-creams and pastries.

OMONIA AREA (*Tmr* D3)
Ellinikon Taverna (*Tmr* D2/3) Dorou St.
Directions: North of Omonia Sq, along Dorou St and almost immediately on the left down some steps to a basement.
A cavernous, 'greasy spoon' well frequented by workmen and sundry officials, as well as a sprinkling of tourists. Inexpensive fare and draught retsina available.

Taverna Kostoyannus 37 Zaimi St.
Directions: Leave Omonia northwards on 28 Ikosiokto Oktovriou, turn right at Odhos Stournara to the nearside of the Polytechnic School, and Zaimi St is the second road along. The taverna is to the left approximately behind the National Archaeological Museum.
Good food, acceptable prices and comes well recommended. As in the case of many other Athenian tavernas, it is not open for lunch or on Sundays.

Snackbars
Probably the most compact, reasonably priced 'offerings' but in grubby surroundings, lurk in the arcade between Dorou St and 28 Ikosiokto Oktovriou, off Omonia Sq. Here are situated cafes and stalls selling almost every variety of Greek convenience fast food. A 'standard'* souvlaki costs 70drs and a 'spezial'*, or de luxe, 90drs BUT do not sit down unless you wish to be charged an extra 15-20drs per head. A bottle of beer costs 80drs.
**Note the 'standard' is a preheated slab of meat whilst the 'spezial'(sic) is the traditional, giro meat-sliced offering.*

Cafes
Everywhere of course, but on Omonia Sq, alongside Dorou St and adjacent to the *Hotel Carlton*, is a magnificent specimen of the traditional kafeneion.
Greek men sip coffee and tumble their worry beads, as they must have done since the turn of the century.

Bretania Cafe
Directions: Bordering Omonia Square, on the left hand side (*Acropolis behind one or more easily facing the Hotel Omonia*) of the junction with Athinas St.
An excellent, very old-fashioned, Greek, 'sticky' sweet cake shop which is more a galaktozacharoplasteion than a cafe. Renowned for its range of sweets, yoghurt and honey, cream and honey, rice puddings and so on, all served with sugar sweet bread and drinks until 0200hrs every morning. A speciality is 'Flower of the Milk', a cream and yoghurt dish costing 200drs per head.

Continuing on down Athinas St, beyond Plateia Kotzia, leads past the covered

meat market building on the left and a number of:-
'Meat Market' Tavernas
Directions: As above and towards the rear of the building. It has to be admitted that it is necessary for prospective diners to pick their way through piles of bones and general market detritus after dark.

Open 24 hours a day and a find for those who like to slum it in less expensive establishments of some note.

LYCABETTUS (LYKAVITOS) AREA (*Tmr* F/G4)
As befits a high priced area,, these listings are very expensive.
Je Reviens Restaurant 49 Xenokratous St.
Directions: North-east from Kolonaki Sq, up Patriachou Ioakim St to the junction with and left on Odhos Marasli, up a flight of steps until it crosses Xenokratous St.

French food, creditable but expensive. Open midday and evenings.

L'Abreuvoir 51 Xenokratous St
Directions: As for *Je Reviens* as are the comments, but even more expensive.

Al Convento Restaurant (*Tmr* G4) 4 Anapiron Tel 723 9163
Directions: North-east from Kolonaki Sq along Patriachou Ioakim to Marasli St. Turn left and then right along Odhos Souidias and Anapiron St is nearly at the end.

Bonanza Restaurant 14 Voukourestiou
Directions: From the north-west corner of Plateia Kolonaki, take Odhos Skoufa, which crosses Voukourestiou St.

Once known as the *Stage Coach*. Not only Wild West in decor, air-conditioned and serving American style food but very expensive with steaks as a house speciality. Why not to to the good old US of A? Lunch and evening meals, open 1200 to 1600hrs and 1900 to 0100hrs.

THE A TO Z OF USEFUL INFORMATION

AIRLINE OFFICE & TERMINUS (*Tmr* 12C6) Referred to in the introductory paragraphs, as well as under **The Accommodation**. The busy offices are to the left (*facing Syntagma Sq*) of the traffic frantic Leoforos Sygrou. As with other Olympic facilities the office doubles as a terminus for airport buses arriving from and departing to the East and West Airports. Passengers who land up here should note that the most convenient, combined bus stop to Syntagma Square, the centre of Athens, is (*with the building behind one*), across the busy thoroughfare and some 50m up the incline of Leoforos Sygrou. This 'hosts' any number of buses and trolley-buses while the stop directly across the road serves only one or two trolley-buses.

Aircraft timetables. *See* **Chapter Three** for general details of the airports serviced from Athens described in this guide and the individual chapters for details of the timetables.

BANKS (Trapeza – ΤΡΑΠΕΖΑ) Note that if a bank strike is under way (apparently becoming a natural part of the tourist season 'high jinks'), the National Bank on Syntagma Sq stays open and in business. However, in these circumstances, the place becomes even more than usually crowded. Banks include the:
National Bank of Greece (*Tmr* 3D/E4) 2 Karageorgi Servias, Syntagma Sq.

All foreign exchange services: Monday to Thursday 0800-1400hrs, Friday 0800-

1330hrs, Saturday, Sunday & holidays 0900-1600hrs; travellers cheques & foreign cash exchange services: weekdays 0800-2000hrs, Saturday, Sunday & holidays 0900-1600hrs.

Ionian & Popular Bank (*Tmr* D/E/4/5) 1 Mitropoleos St.
Only open normal banking hours.

Commercial Bank of Greece (*Tmr* E4) 11 Panepistimiou (El Venizelou).
Normal banking hours.

American Express (*Tmr* D/E4/5) 2 Ermou St, Syntagma Sq Tel 3244975/9
Carries out usual Amex office transactions and is open Monday to Thursday 0830-1400hrs, Friday 0830-1330hrs and Saturday 0820-1230hrs.

BEACHES Athens is not on a river or by the sea, so to enjoy a beach it is necessary to leave the main city and travel to the suburbs. Very often these beaches are operated under the aegis of the NTOG, or private enterprise in association with a hotel. The NTOG beaches usually have beach huts, cabins, tennis courts, a playground and catering facilities. Entrance charges vary from 25-100drs.

There are beaches and or swimming pools at:

Paleon Faliron/ Faliro	A seaside resort	Bus No. 126: Departs from Odhos Othonos, south side of Syntagma Sq (*Tmr* E5).
Alimos	NTOG beach	Bus No. 133: Departs from Odhos Othonos, south side of Syntagma Sq (*Tmr* E5).
Glyfada (Glifada)	A seaside resort	Bus No. 129: Departs from Leoforos Olgas, south side of the Zappeion Gardens (*Tmr* E5/6).
Voula	NTOG beach Class A	Bus No. 122: Departs from Leoforos Olgas, south side of the Zappeion Gardens (*Tmr* E5/6).
Voula	NTOG beach Class B	Bus No. 122: Adults 60drs, children 40drs.
Vouliagmeni	A luxury seaside resort & yacht marina. NTOG beach	Bus No. 118: Departs from Leoforos Olgas, south side of the Zappeion Gardens (*Tmr* E5/6). Adults 100drs, children 50drs.
Varkiza	A seaside resort & yacht marina. NTOG Beach	Bus No. 115: Departs from Leoforos Olgas, south side of the Zappeion Gardens (*Tmr* E5/6). Adults 100drs, children 50drs.

There are beaches all the way down to Cape Sounion (Sounio) via the coast road. *See* **Bus timetables, A To Z**.

BOOKSELLERS Apart from the second-hand bookshops in the Plaka Flea Market (*See* **Monastiraki Square, Introduction**), there are three or four on Odhos Nikis (west of Syntagma Sq) and Odhos Amerikis (north-west of Syntagma Sq) as well as one on Lysikratous St, opposite the small church (*Tmr* 21D5).

Of all the above it is perhaps invidious to select one but here goes...

The Compendium Bookshop (& Computers) 28 Nikis St Tel 322 1248
Directions: On the left of Nikis St (*facing Syntagma Sq*).

Well recommended for a wide range of English language publications. As well as new books they sell some good condition 'used' books. The owner, Rick Schulein, is happy to buy books back into stock that he has sold to a client.The *Transalpino* travel office is in the basement.

BREAD SHOPS In the more popular shopping areas. Descending along Odhos Adrianou, in the Plaka (*Tmr* D5), from the Odhos Thespidos/Kidathineon end, advances past many shops, general stores and a bread shop (or two). They make way for souvenir and gift shops on the way towards Monastiraki.

BUSES & TROLLEY-BUSES These run variously between 0500 and 0030hrs (half an hour past midnight), are usually crowded but excellent value with a 'flat rate' charge of 30drs. Travel between 0500 and 0800hrs is free, not only on the buses but the Metro as well. Also *See* **Access to the Stations, Trains, A To Z**.

Buses The buses are blue (and green) and bus stops are marked *Stasis* (ΣΤΑΣΙΣ). Some one-man-operated buses are utilised and a few have an honesty box for fares.

Trolley-Buses Yellow coloured vehicles and bus stops. Entered via a door at the front marked *Eisodos* (ΕΙΣΟΔΟΣ), with the exit at the rear, marked *Exodos* (ΕΞΟΔΟΣ). Have the correct money to put into the fare machine as there are no tickets or change disgorged.

Major city terminals & turn-round points (*See* footnote at the end of this section).
Kaningos Sq: (*Tmr* 4D2) North-east of Omonia Sq.
Stadiou/Kolokotroni junction: (*Tmr* D/E4). This has replaced the Korai Sq terminus now that Korai has been pedestrianised.
Kifissou St: West-north-west of Omonia Sq. The depot on this major highway lies between the junctions of Lenorman and Leoforos Athinon.
Liossion St: (*Tmr* C2) North-west of Omonia Sq.
Eleftherias Sq: (*Tmr* 9C3) North-west of Monastiraki Sq.
Leoforos Olgas: (*Tmr* D/E5/6) South of the National Garden.
Mavrommateon St*: (*Tmr* D/E1) West of Pedion Areos Park, north of Omonia Sq.

* *The tree shaded north-south street is lined with bus departure points.*

Egyptou Place (Aigyptou/Egiptou): (*Tmr* D1) Just below the south-west corner of Pedion Areos Park, alongside 28 Ikosiokto Oktovriou.
Ag Asomaton Square: (*Tmr* B/C4) West of Monastiraki Sq.
Koumoundourou St: (*Tmr* C2/3) West of Omonia Sq, third turning off Ag Konstantinou.

Trolley-bus timetable
Some major city routes include:

No. 1: Plateia Attikis (Metro station) (*Tmr* C1), Leoforos Amalias, **Stathmos Larissis** (railway station), Karaiskaki Place, Ag Konstantinou, **Omonia Sq, Syntagma Sq**, Kallithea suburb (SW Athens). Every 10 mins from 0505-2350hrs.

No. 2: Pangrati (*Tmr* G6), Leoforos Amalias (Central), **Syntagma Sq, Omonia Sq**, 28 Ikosiokto Oktovriou/Patission St, Kipseli (N Athens). From 0630-0020hrs.

No. 10: N. Smirni (S Athens), Leoforos Sygrou, Leoforos Amalias, **Syntagma Sq**, Panepistimiou St, Stadiou/Kolokotroni junction (*Tmr* D/E4). From 0500-2345hrs.

No. 12: Leoforos Olgas (*Tmr* D/E5/6), Leoforos Amalias, **Syntagma Sq, Omonia Sq**, 28 Ikosiokto Oktovriou/Patission St (N Athens). From 0630-2235hrs.

Other routes covered by trolley-buses include:

No. 3: Patissia to Erythrea (N to NNE Athens suburbs). from 0625-2230hrs.

No. 4: Odhos Kypselis (*Tmr* E1) (North of Pedion Areos Park), **Omonia Sq, Syntagma Sq**, Leoforos Olgas to Ag Artemios (SSE Athens suburbs). From 0630-0020hrs.

No. 5: Patissia (N Athens suburb), **Stathmos Larissis** (railway station), **Omonia Sq, Syntagma Sq**, Filellinon St, Koukaki (S Athens suburb). From 0630-0015hrs.

No. 6: Ippokratous St (*Tmr* E3), Panepistimiou St, **Omonia Sq** to N Filadelfia (N Athens suburb). Every 10mins from 0500-2320hrs.

No. 7: Panepistimiou St (*Tmr* D/E3/4), 28 Ikosiokto Oktovriou/Patission St to Leoforos Alexandras (N of Lycabettus). From 0630-0015hrs.

No. 8: Plateia Kaningos (*Tmr* 4D2), Odhos Akadimias, Vassilissis Sofias, Leoforos Alexandras, 28 Ikosiokto Oktovriou/Patission St. From 0630-0020hrs.

No. 9: Odhos Kypselis (*Tmr* E1) (North of Pedion Areos Park), 28 Ikosiokto Oktovriou/Patission St, Stadiou St, **Syntagma Sq**, Petralona (W Athens suburb – far side of Filopapou). Every 10mins from 0455-2345hrs.

No. 10: Stadiou/Koloktoroni junction (*Tmr* D/E4), Stadiou St, **Syntagma Sq**, Filellinon St, Leoforos Sygrou, Nea Smirni (S Athens suburb). Every 10mins from 0500-2345hrs.

No. 11: Koliatsou (NNE Athens suburb), **Stathmos Larissis** (railway station), 28 Ikosiokto Oktovriou/Patission St, Stadiou St, **Syntagma Sq**, Filellinon St, Plastira Sq, Eftichidou St, N Pangrati (ESE Athens suburb). Every 5mins from 0500-0010hrs.

No. 13: 28 Ikosiokto Oktovriou/Patission St, Akadimias St, Vassilissis Sofias, Papadiamantopoulou St, Leoforos Kifissias, Labrini (just beyond Galatsi suburb – NE Athens suburb). Every 10mins from 0500-2400hrs.

No. 14: Leoforos Alexandras, 28 Ikosiokto Oktovriou/Patission, Patissia (N Athens suburb).

Bus timetable
Bus numbers are subject to a certain amount of confusion, but here goes! Some of the routes are as follows:

No. 022: Kaningos Sq (*Tmr* 4D2), Akadimias, Kanari, Patriarchou Ioakim, Marasli, Genadiou St (SE Lycabettus). Every 10mins from 0520-2330hrs.
No. 023: Kaningos Sq (*Tmr* 4D2), Lycabettus.
No. 024: Leoforos Amalias (*Tmr* D/E5), **Syntagma Sq**, Panepistimiou St, **Omonia Sq**, Tritis Septemvriou, Stournara, Sourmeli, Acharnon, Liossion St. Every 20mins from 0530-2400hrs.

NB This is the bus that delivers passengers to 250 Liossion St (Tmr C2), one of the main bus terminals

No. 040: Filellinon St (close to **Syntagma Sq** – *Tmr* D/E4/5), Leoforos Amalias, Leoforos Sygrou to Vassileos Konstantinou, Piraeus. Every 10mins, 24 hours a day. Green bus.
No. 045: Kaningos Sq (*Tmr* 4D2), Akadimias St, Vassilissis Sofias, Leoforos Kifissias to Kefalari and Politia (NE Athens suburb). Every 15mins from 0600-0100hrs.
No. 047: Menandrou St (SW of **Omonia Sq), Stathmos Larissis** (railway station).
No. 049: Athinas St (*Tmr* C/D3), (S of Omonia Sq), Sofokleous, Pireos, Sotiros, Filonos St, Plateia Themistokleous, Piraeus. Every 10mins, 24 hours a day. Green bus.
No. 051: Off Ag Konstantinou (*Tmr* C2/3), W of **Omonia Sq**, Kolonou St, Lenorman St, Kifissou St. Every 10mins from 0500-2400hrs.

*NB This is the bus that connects to the 100 Kifissou St (*Tmr *A2), a main bus terminal.*

No. 115: Leoforos Olgas (*Tmr* D/E5/6), Leoforos Sygrou, Leoforos Possidonos (coast road) to Vouliagmeni & Varkiza. Every 20mins, 24 hours a day.
No. 116,117 Leoforos Olgas, Varkiza.
No. 118: Leoforos Olgas, Leoforos Sygrou, Leoforos Possidonos (coast road) to Vouliagmeni. Every 20mins from 1245-2015hrs.
No. 121, 128,129: Leoforos Olgas (*Tmr* E6), Glyfada (SSE coastal Athens suburb).
No. 122: Leoforos Olgas, Leoforos Sygrou, Leoforos Possidonos (coast road) to Voula. Every 20mins from 0530-2400hrs.
No. 132: Othonos St (B)Syntagma Sq – *Tmr* D/E4/5), Filellinon St, Leoforos Amalias, Leoforos Sygrou to Edem (SSE Athens suburb). Every 20mins from 0530-1900hrs.
No. 153: Leoforos Olgas, Vouliagmeni (SSE coastal Athens suburb).
No. 224: Polygono (N Athens suburb), 28 Ikosiokto Oktovriou/Patission St, Kaningos Sq, Vassilissis Sofias, Democratias St (Kessariani, E Athens suburb). Every 20mins from 0500-2400hrs.
No. 230: Ambelokipi (E Athens suburb), Leoforos Alexandras, Ippokratous St, Akadimias St, **Syntagma Sq**, Leoforos Amalias, Dionysiou Areopagitou, Apostolou Pavlou, Thission. Every 10 mins from 0500-2320hrs.
No. 405: Leoforos Alexandras, **Stathmos Larissis** (railway station).
No. 510: Kaningos Sq (*Tmr* 4D2), Akadimias St, Ippokratous St, Leoforos Alexandras, Leoforos Kifissias to Dionyssos (NE Athens suburb). Every 20mins from 0530-2250hrs.
No. 527: Kaningos Sq, (*Tmr* 4D2) Akadimias St, Leoforos Alexandras, Leoforos Kifissias to Amaroussion (NE Athens suburb). Every 15mins from 0615-2215hrs.
No. 538, 539: Kaningos Sq, Kifissia (NNE Athens suburb).
No. 603: Akadimias St (*Tmr* D/E 3/4) to Psychiko (NE Athens suburb).
No. 610: Akadimias St to Filothei (NE Athens suburb).
No. 853, 862, 864: Plateia Eleftherias (*Tmr* 9B/C 3/4), Elefsina (Elefsis – West of Athens, beyond Dafni).
No. 873: Plateia Eleftherias, Dafni (W Athens suburb).

Attica bus timetable (orange buses)
Athens – Rafina: 29, Mavrommateon St (*Tmr* D/E1).
Athens – Nea Makri: 29, Mavrommateon St.
Athens – Marathon: 29, Mavrommateon St.
Athens – Lavrion*: 14, Mavrommateon St.
**See* Athens – Sounion route.
All above depart every hour on the half hour between 0630-1730hrs.
One-way fare 130drs, duration 1 hour.

Athens –	Sounion – West coast road: 14 Mavrommateon St Every hour on the half hour between 0630-1730hrs.
Return	Every hour on the hour between 0600-1900hrs. One-way fare 350drs, duration 1 ¾hrs.
Athens –	Sounion – via Markopoulo & Lavrio: 14 Mavrommateon St. Every hour on the hour, 0600-1700hrs.
Return	Every hour on the half hour, 0630-1930hrs. One-way fare 310drs, duration 2hrs.
Athens –	Vravron: Take either the 0600hrs Sounion bus via Markopoulo orthe 1330hrs Lavrio bus, get off at Markopoulo & catch a local bus to Vravron.

NB The Athens-Attica bus services detailed above cover the city and its environs

The rest of Greece is served by:
1) **KTEL** A pool of bus operators working through one company from two terminals. 260 Liossion St* and 100 Kifissou St**
2) **OSE** (The State Railway Company) Their buses terminus alongside the main railway stations of Stathmos Peloponissou and Larissis. Apart from the domestic services, there is a terminal for other European capitals, including Paris, Istanbul and Munich, at Stathmos Larissis station.
***Liossion St** (*Tmr* C2) is to the east of Stathmos Peloponissou railway station. This terminus serves Halkida, Edipsos, Kimi, Delphi, Amfissa, Kamena Vourla, Larissa, Thiva, Trikala (Meteora) Livadia, Lamia. **Refer to bus route No. 024 for transport to this terminus.**
****Kifissou St** (*Tmr* A2) is to the west north-west of Omonia Sq, beyond the 'steam railway' lines, across Leoforos Konstantinoupoleos and up either Leoforos Athinon, and turn right, or Odhos Lenorman, and turn left. This terminus serves Patras, Pirgos (Olympia), Nafplio (Mikines), Adritsena (Vasses), Kalamata, Sparti (Mistras), Githio,(Diros), Tripolis, Messolongi, Igoumenitsa, Preveza, Ioanina, Corfu, Zakynthos, Cephalonia, Lefkas, Kozani, Kastoria, Florina, Grevena, Veria, Naoussa, Edessa, Seres, Kilkis, Kavala, Drama, Komotini, Korinthos, Kranidi, Xilokastro. **Refer to bus route No. 051 for transport to this terminus.**

For any bus services connecting to the islands detailed in this guide, also refer to the Mainland Ports, Chapter Ten, and the relevant Island chapters.

CAMPING *See* **The Accommodation**.

CAR HIRE As any other capital city, numerous offices, the majority of which are lined up in the smarter areas and squares, such as Syntagma Sq and Leoforos Amalias. Typical is:
Pappas, 44 Leoforos Amalias Tel 322 0087
There are any number of car hire (and travel) firms on the right of Leoforos Sygrou, descending from the 'spaghetti junction' south of the Temple of Olympian Zeus (*Tmr* D6).

CAR REPAIR Help and advice can be obtained by contacting:
The Automobile & Touring Club of Greece (ELPA), (*Tmr* I/3) 2 Messogion St Tel 779 1615
For immediate, emergency attention dial 104.

There are dozens of back street car repairers, breakers and spare part shops parallel and to the west of Leoforos Sygrou, in the area between the Olympic office and the Temple of Olympian Zeus.

CHEMIST *See* **Medical Care**

CINEMAS There are a large number of outdoor cinemas. Do not worry about a language barrier as the majority of the films have English (American) dialogue with Greek subtitles.

Aigli in the Zappeion is a must and is situated at the south end of the National Garden. Other cinemas are bunched together on the streets of Stadiou, Panepistimiou and 28 Ikosiokto Oktovriou/Patission.

Note that the cinemas in Athens, of which there are vast numbers, generally show poor quality films complete with scratches, hisses, jumps, long black gaps and or loss of sound, especially between reels. However a recommendation is the:

Radio City 240 Patission St.
Directions: North of Omonia Sq.

Large screen, good sound and knowledgeable operators.

CLUBS, BARS & DISCOS Why leave home? But if you must, there are enough to satiate the most voracious desires.

COMMERCIAL SHOPPING AREAS During daylight hours a very large street market ranges up Odhos Athinas (*Tmr* C3/4), Odhos Sokratous and the associated side streets from Ermou St, almost all the way up to Omonia Sq. After dark the shutters are drawn down, the stalls canvassed over and the 'ladies of the night' appear.

Plateia Kotzia (*Tmr* C/D3) spawns a flower market on Sundays whilst the Parliament Building side of Vassilissis Sofias (*Tmr* E4) is lined with smart flower stalls that open daily.

Monastiraki Sq (*Tmr* 5C4) and the various streets that radiate off are abuzz, specialising in widely differing aspects of the commercial and tourist trade. Odhos Areos contains a plethora of leather goods shops; the near end of Ifestou Lane is edged by stall upon stall of junk and tourist 'omit-abilia' (forgettable memorabilia); Pandrossou lane contains a better class of shop and stall selling sandals, pottery and smarter 'memorabilia', while the square itself has a number of handcart hawkers.

The smart department stores are conveniently situated in or around Syntagma Sq, and the main streets that radiate off the square, including Ermou, Stadiou and Panepistimiou.

Tapestries are an extremely good buy. A reliable shop is sited close to and on the far side (*from Syntagma Sq*) of Kapnikarea Church (*Tmr* 6 D4), on Ermou St.

In the area south of Syntagma Sq, on the junction of Apollonos and Pendelis Sts, close by Odhos Voulis, there are three small but obliging fruit and greengrocery shops. Apollonos St is useful to shoppers because, close by the junction with Odhos Nikis, on the right-hand side, is a combined fruit and butcher's shop. Next door is a stick souvlaki snackbar and across the road an ironmongers.

See **Bread Shops & Trains, A To Z** for details of other markets and shopping areas.

DENTISTS & DOCTORS *See* **Medical Care, A To Z.**

EMBASSIES

Australia: 15 Messogion Av.	Tel 775 7650
Belgium: 3 Sekeri St.	Tel 361 7886
Canada: 4 Ioannou Gennadiou St.	Tel 723 9511
Denmark: 15 Philikis Etairias Sq.	Tel 724 9315

Finland: 1 Eratosthenous & Vas. Konstantinou Sts.	Tel 751 9795
France: 7 Vassilissis Sofias	Tel 361 1663
German Federal Republic (West Germany): 3 Karaoli/Dimitriou Sts.	Tel 369 4111
Great Britain: 1 Ploutarchou & Ypsilantou Sts.	Tel 723 6211
Ireland: 7 Vassileos Konstantinou.	Tel 723 2771
Netherlands: 5-7 Vassileos Konstantinou.	Tel 723 9701
New Zealand: 15-17 Tshoa St.	Tel 641 0311
Norway: 7 Vassileos Konstantinou St.	Tel 724 6173
South Africa: 124 Kifissias/Iatridou.	Tel 692 2125
Sweden: 7 Vassileos Konstantinou St.	Tel 722 4504
USA: 91 Vassilissis Sofias.	Tel 721 2951

FERRY-BOAT & FLYING DOLPHIN TICKET OFFICES
Apart from the headquarters, most, if not all, ferry-boat ticket offices are down in Piraeus Port.

On the other hand whilst the main *Ceres Flying Dolphin* booking office is in Piraeus, there is a first floor office in the building immediately to the left of the *National Bank* (*Tmr* 3D/E4) (Syntagma Sq behind one). Despite the staff being disinterested, they are able to hand over a comprehensive timetable and prices.

HAIRDRESSERS No problems with sufficient in the main shopping areas.

HOSPITALS *See* **Medical Care, A To Z.**

LAUNDERETTES There may be others but a good, central recommendation must be:
Coin-op (*Tmr* 13D5) Angelou Geronda.
Directions: From Kidathineon St (*proceeding towards Syntagma Sq*), at the far end of Plateia Plaka turn right down Angelou Geronda, towards Odhos Dedalou, and the launderette is on the right-hand side.

A machine load costs 200drs, 9 mins of dryer time 20drs and a measure of powder 30drs. In respect of the detergent, why not pop out to Kidathineon St and purchase a small packet of Tide for 38drs. For customers who are busy and are prepared to leave the laundry behind, the staff supervise the wash and dry operation at an extra cost of 400drs. Open in the summer daily 0800-2100hrs.

The more usual Athens style is for customers to leave their washing at any one of the countless laundries, collecting it next day dry, stiff and bleached (if necessary).

Note that my lavatorial obsession would not be satisfied without mentioning the Public toilet sited on Plateia Plaka.

LOST PROPERTY The main office is situated at 33 Ag Konstantinou (Tel 523 0111), the Plateia Omonia end of Ag Konstantinou. The telephone number is that of the Transport police who are now in charge of lost property (or *Grafio Hamenon Adikimenon*). Another 'lost & found' telephone number is 770 5771. It is still true to say that you are far more likely to 'lose' personal belongings to other tourists, then to Greeks.

LUGGAGE STORE There is one at No. 26 Nikis St (*Tmr* D5) advertising the service at a cost of 50drs per day per piece, 250drs per week and 750drs per month. Many hotels, guest houses and pensions mind a clients' bags, quite a number at no charge.

MEDICAL CARE
Chemists/Pharmacies (Farmakio – ΦΑΡΜΑΚΕΙΟ) Identified by a green or red

cross on a white background. Normal opening hours and a rota operates to give a 'duty' chemist cover.

Dentists & Doctors Ask at the **First Aid Centre** for the address of the School of Dentistry where free treatment is available. Both dentists and doctors advertise widely and there is no shortage of practitioners.

First Aid Centre (KAT) (*Tmr* 14D2) 21 Tritis Septemvriou St, beyond the Chalkokondili turning and on the left. Tel 150

Hospital (*Tmr* 15G4) Do not proceed direct to a hospital but initially attend the **First Aid Centre**. When necessary they direct patients to the correct destination.

Medical Emergency: Tel 166

METRO/ELEKTRIKOS (ΗΣΑΜ) The Athens underground or subway system, which operates below ground in the heart of the city and overground for the rest of the journey. It is a simple, one track layout from Kifissia (north-east Athens suburb) to Piraeus (south-west of Athens), and represents marvellous value with two rates of fare at 30 and 60drs. Passengers must have the requisite coins to obtain a ticket from the machine, prior to gaining access to the platforms. Everyone is most helpful and will, if the ticket machine 'frightens' a chap, show how it should be operated. Take care, select the ticket value first, then put the coins in the slot and keep the ticket so as to be able to hand it in at the journey's end. The service operates every 10 mins between 0500 and 2400hrs and travel before 0800hrs is free. Keep an eye open for the old-fashioned wooden carriages.

Station Stops There are 21 which include Kifissia (NE suburb), Stathmos Attiki (for the main railway stations), Plateia Victorias (N Athens), Omonia Sq, Monastiraki Sq (Plaka), Plateia Thission (for the Acropolis) and (Piraeus) Port. From the outside, the Piraeus terminus is rather difficult to locate, the entrance being in the left-hand corner of what appears to be an oldish, waterfront building. There used to be 20 stations but the new 'Peace Stadium' has 'acquired' a stop called Irene.

MUSIC & DANCING *See* **Clubs, Bars & Discos & The Eating Out, A To Z.**

NTOG (EOT) The headquarters of the National Tourist Organisation (NTOG) or, in Greek, the EOT (Ellinikos Organismos Tourismou – ΕΛΛΗΝΙΚΟΣ ΟΡΓΑΝΙΣΜΟΣ ΤΟΥΡΙΣΜΟΥ) is on the 5th floor at 2 Amerikis St (*Tmr* E4), close by Syntagma Sq. But this office does not normally handle the usual tourist enquiries, although the commissionaires manning the desk do hand out bits and pieces of information.

The information desk, from whence the free Athens map, advice, information folders, bus and boat schedules and hotel facts may be obtained, is situated inside and on the left of the foyer of the:

National Bank of Greece (*Tmr* 3D/E4) 2 Karageorgi Servias, Syntagma Sq Tel 322 2545

Directions: As above.

Do not hope to obtain anything other than pamphlets and a snatch of guidance as it would be unrealistic to expect personal attention from staff besieged by wave upon wave of tourists of every creed, race and colour. The Athens hotel information sheets handed out now include a list of Class D & E establishments. Open Monday-Friday, 0800-2000hrs, Saturdays 0900-1400hrs.

There is now a sign requesting, if there are long queues, that enquirers use the tourist information office inside the **General Bank** situated at the corner of Ermou St, where it joins Syntagma Square.

There is also an NTOG office conveniently sited at the East Airport.

OPENING HOURS (Summer months) These are only a guideline and apply to Athens (as well as the larger cities). Note that in country and village areas, it is more likely that shops are open from Monday to Saturday inclusive for over 12 hours a day, and on Sundays, holidays and Saints days, for a few hours either side of midday. The afternoon siesta is usually taken between 1300/1400hrs and 1500/1700hrs.

Trade Stores & Chemists Monday, Wednesday and Saturday 0800-1430hrs; Tuesday, Thursday and Friday 0900-1300hrs and 1700-2000hrs.

Food Stores Monday, Wednesday and Saturday 0800-1500hrs; Tuesday, Thursday and Friday 0800-1400hrs and 1730-2030hrs.

Art & Gift shops Weekdays 0800-2100hrs and Sundays (Monastiraki area) 0930-1445hrs.

Restaurants, Pastry shops, Cafes & Dairy shops Seven days a week.

Museums *See* **Museums, Places of Interest, A To Z**

Public Services (including Banks) Refer to the relevant **A To Z** heading.

OTE There are offices at: No. 85, 28 Ikosiokto Oktovriou/Patission St (*Tmr* 16D1) (open 24hrs a day); 15 Stadiou St (*Tmr* 17D4) (open Monday to Friday 0700-2400hrs, Saturday and Sunday 0800-2400hrs); 53 Solonos (*Tmr* E3) and 7 Kratinou (Plateia Kotzia) (*Tmr* C/D3) (open between 0800 and 2400hrs). There is also an office at 45 Athinas St (*Tmr* C/D3).

PHARMACIES *See* **Medical Care, A To Z.**

PLACES OF INTEREST

Parliament Building (*Tmr* E4/5) Syntagma Sq. Here it is possible to watch the Greek equivalent of the British 'Changing the Guard at Buckingham Palace'. The special guards (*Evzones*) are spectacularly outfitted with tasselled red caps, white shirts (blouses do I hear?), coloured waistcoats, a skirt, white tights, knee-garters and boots topped off with pom-poms. The ceremony officially kicks off at 1100hrs on Sunday morning but seems to falter into action at about 1045hrs. Incidentally, there is a band thrown in for good measure.

Museums The seasons are split as follow: Winter (1st November-31st March) and Summer (1st April-31st October). Museums are closed on: 1st January, 25th March, Good Friday, Easter Day and Christmas Day. Sunday hours are kept on Epiphany, Ash Monday, Easter Saturday, Easter Monday, 1st May, Whit Sunday, Assumption Day, 28th October and Boxing Day. They are only open in the mornings on Christmas Eve, New Year's Eve, 2nd January, Easter Thursday and Easter Tuesday. Museums are closed on Tuesdays unless otherwise indicated. Students with cards will achieve a reduction in fees.

Acropolis (*Tmr* C5). The museum exhibits finds made on the site. Of special interest are the sixth century BC statues of Korai women. Entrance charges are included in the admission fee to the Acropolis, which costs 500drs per head and is open Summer weekdays 0730-1930hrs, Sunday and holidays 0800-1800hrs. The museum hours are 0730-1930hrs, Tuesdays 1200-1800hrs, Sundays and holidays 0900-1700hrs.

Benaki (*Tmr* E/F4) On the corner of Vassilissis Sofias and Koubari (Koumbari)

St, close by Plateia Kolonaki. A very interesting variety of exhibits made up from private collections. Particularly diverting is a display of national costumes. Weekday Summer hours: 0830-1400hrs, Sundays and holidays 0830-1400hrs and closed Tuesdays. Entrance 150drs.

Byzantine (*Tmr* F4/5) 22 Vassilissis Sofias. As one would deduce from the name – Byzantine art. Summer hours: daily 0900-1700hrs; Sunday and holidays, 0900-1400hrs; closed Mondays. Entrance costs 300drs.

Goulandris 13 Levidou St, Kifissia, N Athens. Natural History. Summer hours: daily 0900-1400hrs; Sunday and holidays 0900-1530hrs; closed Fridays. Entrance costs 30drs.

Goulandris (*Tmr* F4) 4 Neophitou Douka St (off Vassilissis Sofias). The second or 'other' Goulandris Museum. The situation is not helped by the little quirk of some people referring to the Natural History Museum as 'Goulandris'. Help! This Goulandris, that is the Cycladic and Ancient Greek. Art Goulandris Museum is open daily in the summer 1000-1600hrs; closed Tuesday, Sunday and holidays. Entrance costs 150drs.

Kanelloupoulos (*Tmr* C5) On the corner of Theorias and Panos Sts in the Plaka. A smaller version of the Benaki Museum and located at the foot of the northern slope of the Acropolis, at the Monastiraki end. Summer hours: daily 0845-1500hrs; Sunday and holidays 0930-1430hrs. Entrance costs 100drs (and is charged Sundays and holidays).

Keramikos (*Tmr* B4) 148 Ermou St. Finds from Keramikos cemetery. Summer hours: daily 0845-1500hrs; Sunday and holidays 0930-1430hrs and closed on Tuesdays. Entrance to the site and museum costs 200drs.

National Gallery & Alexandros Soutzos (*Tmr* G4) 46 Vassileos Konstantinou/Sofias. Mainly 19th and 20th century Greek paintings. Summer hours: 0900-1500hrs; Sunday and holidays 1000-1400hrs and closed on Mondays. Admission is free.

National Historical & Ethnological (*Tmr* D4) Kolokotroni Sq, off Stadiou St. Greek history and the War of Independence. Summer hours: 0900-1400hrs; Saturday, Sunday and holidays 0900-1300hrs and closed Mondays. Entrance costs 100drs.

National Archaeological (*Tmr* D/E2) 1 Tossitsa St, off 28 Ikosiokto Oktovriou/Patission St. The largest and possibly the most important Greek museum, covering a wide variety of exhibits. A must if you are a museum buff. Summer hours: 0800-1900hrs; Sunday and holidays 0800-1800hrs and closed on Mondays. Entrance costs 400drs, which includes entrance to the *Santorini* and *Numismatic* exhibitions (*See* below).

Numismatic In the same building as the National Archaeological and displaying, as would be imagined, a collection of Greek coins, spanning the ages. Summer hours: 0830-1330hrs; Sunday and holidays 0900-1400hrs and closed on Tuesdays. Admission is free.

Also housed in the same building are the:
Epigraphical Collection: Summer hours: 0830-1330hrs; Sunday and holidays 0900-1400hrs and closed Tuesdays.
Santorini Exhibition: Summer hours: 0930-1500hrs every day but closed on Mondays

and
The Casts and Copies Exhibition: Summer hours: 0900-1400hrs daily but closed Sunday and Mondays.

Popular (Folk) Art (*Tmr* D5) 17 Kidathineon St, The Plaka. Folk art, folklore and popular art. Summer hours: 1100-1400hrs; Sunday and holidays 1000-1400hrs and closed on Mondays. Entrance free.

War (*Tmr* F4/5) 2 Rizari St, off Leoforos Vassilissis Sofias. Warfare exhibits covering a wide variety of subjects. Summer hours: daily 0900-1400hrs and closed on Mondays. Entrance is free.

Theatres & Performances For full, up-to-date details enquire at the NTOG office (*Tmr* 3D/E4). They should be able to hand out a pamphlet giving a precise timetable for the year. As a guide the following are performed year in and year out:
Son et Lumiere. From the Pynx hillside, a *Son et Lumiere* features the Acropolis. This show is produced from early April up to the end of October. The English performance starts at 2100hrs every evening, except when the moon is full, and takes 45 minutes. There are French versions at 2215hrs daily, except Tuesdays and Fridays when a German commentary is provided at 2200hrs.

Tickets and information are available from the *Athens Festival booking office* (*See Athens Festival*) or at the Pynx, prior to the outset of the show. Tickets cost 350drs (students 120drs), and are also available at the entrance of the Church, Ag Dimitros Lombardiaris, on the way to the show. Catch a No. 230 bus along Dionysiou Areopagitou St getting off one stop beyond the Odeion (Theatre) of Herodes Atticus and follow the signposted path on the left-hand side.

Athens Festival This prestigious event takes place in the restored and beautiful Odeion of Herodes Atticus. This was built in approximately AD 160 as a Roman theatre, seating about 5000 people and situated at the foot of the south-west corner of the Acropolis. The festival lasts from early June to the middle of September, and consists of a series of plays, ballet, concerts and opera. The performances usually commence at 2100hrs and tickets, which are on sale up to 10 days before the event, are obtainable from the Theatre 1 hour prior to the commencement of the show or from the Athens Festival booking office (*Tmr* D/E4), 4 Stadiou St, Tel 322 1459.

Dora Stratou Theatre (*Tmr* A6) A short stroll away on Mouseion or Hill of Muses. On the summit stands the Monument of the Filopapou (Philopappos) and nearby the Dora Stratou Theatre, where an internationally renowned troupe of folk dancers, dressed in traditional costumes, perform a series of Greek dances and songs. The theatre group operates daily from about the middle of May to the end of September. The show starts at 2215hrs, that is except Wednesday and Sunday when they perform at 2015 & 2215hrs. Ticket prices vary from 450-750drs (students 350drs) and are available between 0900-1400hrs (Tel 324 4395) and 1830-2300hrs (Tel 921 4650).

Performances are timed to coincide with the ending of the *Son et Lumiere*, on the Pynx.

Lycabettus Theatre On the north-east side of Lycabettus Hill. Concerts and theatrical performances take place at the hillside open-air theatre, between the middle of June and the first week of September, from 2100hrs. Tickets can be purchased from the theatre box office, one hour before the event, or from the *Athens Festival booking office*, referred to previously under Athens Festival.

Wine Festival Held daily at Dafni from the middle of July to the end of August, between 1900-0030hrs. Ticket price 220drs per head. Information and tickets from the *Athens Festival booking office*.

POLICE *See* **Tourist Police, A To Z.**

POST OFFICES (Tachidromio – ΤΑΧΥΔΡΟΜΕΙΟΞ) Weekday opening hours, as a guide, are 0800 to 1300hrs. The Central Post Office at 100 Eolou St (*Tmr* 18D3), close by Omonia Sq, is open Monday-Saturday, 0730-1500hrs. Branch offices are situated on the corner of Othonos and Nikis Sts (Syntagma Sq); at the Omonia Sq underground Metro concourse and on Dionysiou Areopagitou St, at the corner of Tzireon St (*Tmr* D6).

The telephone and telegraph system is run by a separate state organisation. *See* **OTE.**

SHOPPING HOURS *See* **Opening Hours, A To Z.**

SPORTS FACILITIES

Golf. There is an 18 hole course, the *Glifida Golf Club* close by the East Airport. Changing rooms, restaurant and refreshment bar.

Swimming. There is a *Swimming (and Tennis) Club* on Leoforos Olgas (*Tmr* 19E6), across the way from the Zappeion National Gardens. *The Hilton Hotel* (*Tmr* G4) has a swimming pool but, if you are not staying there, use of it costs the price of an (expensive) meal. *See* **Beaches, A To Z.**

Tennis. There are courts at most of the NTOG beaches (*See* **Beaches, A To Z**) as well as at the *Ag Kosmas Athletics Centre*, close by the West airport.

TAXIS (ΤΑΞΙ) Used extensively and, although they seem to me to be expensive, are 'officially' the cheapest in Europe. The Athens drivers are, now, generally without scruples. The metered fares are costed at about 23drs per kilometre. But they are subject to various surcharges including 15drs for each piece of baggage, 240drs per hour of waiting time and 30drs for picking up at, or delivering to, public transport facilities. There is also an extra charge for the hours between midnight and daylight. When a prospective fare is standing at a taxi rank, drivers must pick them up, but are not obliged to do so when cruising, for which there is an extra 'flag falling' charge of 25drs. The sign ΕΛΕΥΘΕΡΟΝ indicates a cab is free for hire. The minimum fare is 110drs and sample fares include:

Syntagma/Omonia Square to the East airport 500drs and to the West airport 400drs; the East airport to Piraeus 500drs and the West airport to Piraeus 350drs. The Syntagma taxi station telephone number is 323 7942.

TELEPHONES *See* **OTE.**

TOURIST OFFICE/AGENCIES *See* **NTOG & Travel Agents & Tour Offices, A To Z.**

TOURIST POLICE (*Tmr* 20D6) I understand, despite the reorganisation of the service, that the Athens headquarters is to remain in operation. This is situated at 7 Leoforos Sygrou (Sygrou/Syngrou/Singrou Av). Open daily 0800-2200hrs. Tel 923-9224. Tourist information in English is available on the telephone number 171.

There are also Tourist police offices close by and just to the north of Larissis

Railway Station (open 0700-2400hrs, tel 821 3574) and the East airport (open 0730-2300hrs, tel 981 4093/969 9500).

TOILETS Apart from the various bus termini and the railway stations, there is a super Public toilet on the south-east corner of Syntagma Sq, as there is a pretty grim 'squatty' in the Omonia Sq Metro concourse. This latter costs 20drs. The Plaka is well 'endowed' with one at Plateia Plaka, (on Odhos Kidathineon) and another on the Plateia Agora at the other end of Odhos Adrianou. Visitors to Mt. Lycabettus will not be 'caught short' and the toilets there are spotless.

TRAINS (Illustration 6) They arrive at (or depart from) either (a) Larissis Station (Stathmos No. 1) or (b) Peloponissou Station (Stathmos No. 2).

(A) **LARISSIS STATION (STATHMOS No. 1)** (*Tmr* B/C1) Tel 821 3882
The main, more modern station of the two. Connections to the Western European services and the northern provinces of Central Greece, Thessaly, Macedonia and Thrace. The bus stop to the centre of Athens is to the right of the station (*station building behind one*). Refer to **Buses** below.

One correspondent has reminded me to reiterate that it is advisable to reserve return seats at the International 'hatch' as soon as is possible after arrival in Greece by train.

Services in and around the building include:
The National Bank of Greece. Opens Monday to Thursday 0830-1400hrs and Friday 0830-1330hrs.
Post Office. Open Monday to Saturday 0700-2000hrs and Sunday 0900-1400hrs. They transact money exchange and cash travellers cheques.
Tourist police. There is an office just to the north of the station building. *See* **Tourist Police, A To Z**.

To the front of the station is a pavement cafe-bar (a coffee 56drs) and an elongated square, well more a widening of the road.

The Accommodation Even early and late in the summer a number of the hardier stretch out on the pavements around and about the stations (and at the *Hotel Oscar's* rates I'm not surprised). Arrivals, even whilst on the train, are bombarded with offers of accommodation, so much so that the touts are a nuisance.

With the station behind one, to the right, across the concourse and on the corner, is the:
Hotel Lefkos Pirgos (*Tmr* C1) (Class E) 27 Leof.Metaxa/Deligianni Tel 821 3765
Directions: As above.

Seedy looking establishment. All rooms share the bathrooms. Singles start off at 840drs and double rooms 1380drs, which prices increase to 1050drs and 1725drs (1st July-10th Oct).

Hotel Nana (*Tmr* C1) (Class B), 29 Leof.Metaxa Tel 884 2211
Directions: Alongside the *Hotel Lefkos Pirgos*.

Smarter (well it is B class) with the charges reflecting this pre-eminence. All rooms have an en suite bathroom with a single room charged at 2290drs and a double at 3205drs rising to 3205drs and 4395drs (16th March-31st Oct).

Directly opposite the main station entrance is the:
Hotel Oscar (*Tmr* C1) (Class B), 25 Samou/Filadelfias Tel 883 4215
Directions: As above.

I hardly dare detail the room rates, which for a double room kicks off at 4415drs rising to 5195drs, en suite naturally. Breakfast costs 340drs. I must own up to staying at the Oscar. But it was at the end of a long stint on the Greek islands, added to which there were a couple of other (good) reasons. Firstly they accept payment by *Amex* which, as I have written before, may be of great assistance in eking out dwindling funds, and secondly, the hotel is conveniently close to the railway and the inter-country coach station. Thus the comforts of this hotel, or similar, can be put to good use in order to build up the bodily reserves prior to a planned long distance bus or railway journey! That is not to say that even this luxurious establishment does not escape some of the common faults oft experienced as a 'norm' when staying at its lower classified 'cousins'. The en suite bathroom of our room had a loose lavatory seat, the bath plug had no chain attached (there was a chain but it was not attached), and the small bathroom window was tied up with string. The bedroom sliding balcony window would not completely shut – there was no locking mechanism and the air conditioning didn't. Mind you I must admit to making a reservation without Rosemary, who guarded our backpacks whilst I sorted out the formalities. It may have been the sight of the two, towering, aforementioned packs reversing through the swing doors into reception that resulted in our being allocated this particular 'downtown' room, at the rear of the hotel, overlooking and overlooked by the backsides of a block of flats.

Hotel Elena (Helena) (*Tmr* B/C1) (Class C) 2 Psiloriti/Samou Tel 881 3211
Directions: Along Samou St, south from Leof. Metaxa St, and on the right.

Single rooms sharing the bathroom cost 1135drs and en suite 1670drs; double rooms sharing are charged at 1870drs and en suite 2270drs.

Hotel Louvre (*Tmr* C2) (Class D) 9 Chiou/Favierou Sts Tel 522 9891
Directions: Next street back from and parallel to Samou St, towards the south end of Chiou St.

Greek provincial in outward appearance, despite the grand and evocative name. Single rooms sharing a bathroom cost 1190drs; double rooms sharing 1720drs and en suite 2200drs.

Joy's Hotel (*Tmr* D1) 38 Feron St Tel 823 1012
Directions: Proceed up Odhos Filadelfias, almost directly opposite the main station, across Odhos Liossion continuing along Livaniou St as far as Odhos Acharnon. Turn left and then first right on to Feron St.

Reputedly a good value, busy, Youth Hostel style establishment complete with a bar/cafeteria and offering accommodation ranging from a dormitory (500drs) to quadruples. A single bed starts off at 900drs and a double 1600drs. A hot shower costs an extra 100drs.

Street Market Whilst in this area it is worth noting that Odhos Chiou, between Kritis and Favierou Sts, is host to an extensive street market where almost everything is sold from fish to meat and hardware to clothing.

Bread shop & Supermarket (*Tmr* B/C1/2) On the corner of Samou St and Eratyras St. A bit disorganised but very useful.

Snackbar (*Tmr* B/C1) Odhos Samou.
Directions: Across the street from the Park, on the stretch of Odhos Samou between Filadelfias and Leof. Metaxa Sts.

A small, convenient, souvlaki pita snackbar, run by a very friendly chap. A souvlaki and a bottle of beer costs 125drs.

Illustration 6 Athens City inset - The Railway Stations

Buses: Trolley-bus No. 1 pulls up to the right of the station, as do the No's 2 & 4. The fare to Syntagma Sq is 30drs.

(B) **PELOPONISSOU STATION (STATHMOS NO. 2)** (*Tmr* B1/2)
Tel 513 1601

The station for trains to the Peloponnese, the ferry connections for some of the Ionian islands and international ferries to Italy from Patras.

TRAINS (General)

Tickets: The concept behind the acquisition of a ticket is similar to that of a lottery. On buying one ticket a compartment seat is also allocated. In theory this is a splendid scheme, but in practice the idea breaks down in a welter of bad tempered argument over whom is occupying whose seat. Manners and quaint old-fashioned habits of giving up one's seat to older people and ladies are best avoided. I write this from the bitter experience of offering my seat to elderly Greek ladies, only for their husbands to immediately fill the vacant position. Not what one had in mind! Find your seat and stick to it like glue and if you have made a mistake feign madness, admit to being a foreigner, but do not budge.

At Peloponissou Station the mechanics of buying a ticket take place in organised bedlam. The ticket office 'traps' open half an hour prior to the train's departure. Scenes reminiscent of a Cup Final crowd develop, with prospective travellers pitching about within the barriers of the ticket hatch, and all this in the space of about 10m by 10m. To add to the difficulty, there are two hatch 'slots' and it is anybody's guess which one to select. It really is best to try and steal a march on the 'extra-curricula' activity, diving for a hatch whenever one opens up.

Travellers booking a return journey train ticket to Europe, and routing via Italy, must ensure the tickets are to and from Patras, not Athens. (Yes, Patras). Then the purchase of the separate Patras to Athens (and vice versa) ticket, ensures a seat. A voyager boarding the train with an open ticket will almost surely have to stand for almost the whole of the four hour journey. Most Athens – Patras journeys seem to attract an 'Express' surcharge of between 100-150drs which exacted by the ticket collector.

Incidentally, the general architecture of the Peloponissou building is delightful, especially the ceiling of the booking office hall, centrally located, under the main clock face. To the left, on entering the building, is a glass-fronted information box with all the train times listed on the window. The staff manning this desk are extremely helpful and speak sufficient English so pose no problems in communication (the very opposite of the disinterest shown at the NTOG desk in the National Bank of Greece, on Syntagma Sq).

Advance Booking Office. Information and advance booking for both stations is handled at:
No. 6 Sina (*Tmr* E3) off Akadimias St (Tel 363 4402/4406); No. 1 Karolou (Satovriandou) (*Tmr* C2) west of Omonia Sq. (Tel 524 0647/8) and No. 17 Filellinon (*Tmr* D/E5) (Tel 323 6747/6273).

Toilets The station toilets usually, well always, lack toilet paper.

Sustenance (on the train) An attendant brings inexpensive drinks and snacks around from time to time and hot snacks are available from platform trolleys at the major railway stations.

Railway Head Office (*Tmr* C2) Hellenic Railways Organisation (OSE) 1-3 Karolou St. Tel 522 2491
Directions: One back from the far end of Ag Konstantinou, west from Omonia Sq.

Provisions Shopping in the area of the railway stations is made easy by the presence of the Street Market on Odhos Chiou (*See* **Larissis Station, Trains**).

Access to the stations

Bus/Trolley-bus. From the Airport, travel on the Olympic bus to the terminal at 96-100 Leoforos Sygrou (which at a cost of 100drs is good value). Then catch a bus (Nos. 133, 040, 132, 155, 903 and 161 amongst others) across the street from the terminus to Syntagma Sq, after which a No. 1 or No. 5 (via Omonia Sq) or a No. 11 trolley-bus to the Stathmos Larissis railway station. Instead of making a change of bus at Syntagma Sq, it is also possible to walk west from the terminal on Leoforos Sygrou across Falirou and Odisseos and Androutsou Sts to the parallel street of Odhos Dimitrakopoulou and catch a No. 1 trolley-bus all the way to the stations.

From Piraeus Port catch the No. 40 (green) bus on Leoforos Vassileos Konstantinou (parallel to the quay) to Syntagma Sq, or the No. 049 from Plateia Themistokleous to Athinas St, close by Omonia Sq. For other possibly conflicting information *See* **Arrival by Air, Introduction; Airline offices & terminus & Buses & Trolley-buses, A To Z.**

Metro The metro station for both railway stations is Attiki, close to Plateia Attikis. From the platform, assuming a traveller has come from the south, dismount and turn right down into the underpass to come out the far or west side of the station on Odhos Liossion. Turn left and walk to the large irregular Plateia Attikis (*with the Hotel Lydia on the right*). Proceed down Domokou St (the road that exits half-right on the far side of the square), which spills into Plateia Deligianni edged by Stathmos Larissis. A more long-winded alternative is to get off the Metro at Omonia Sq, walk west along Ag Konstantinou to Karaiskaki Sq and then up Odhos Deligianni, or catch a No. 1 trolley-bus.

Taxi A reasonable indulgence, if in a hurry, although it must be noted that in the crowded traffic conditions of Athens it is often quicker to walk than catch a cab. *See* **Taxis, A To Z.**

Station to Station To get from one to the other, say Stathmos Larissis to Peloponissou, it is necessary to turn right out of the station and climb the steps over the railway line turning left at the bottom of the far side of the steps and walk some 100m to the forecourt in front of Stathmos Peloponissou. Almost, but not quite adjacent, as some guides put it, if 150m on a very hot day, laden down with cases seems contiguous.

TRAIN TIMETABLES

Peloponissou Station It is easy to read the Peloponissou timetable and come to the conclusion that a large number of trains are leaving the station at the same time. On seeing the single-line track, a newcomer cannot be blamed for feeling apprehensive that it may prove difficult to select the correct carriages. The mystification arises from the fact that the trains are detailed separately from Athens to say Korinthos, Mikines, Argos, Tripolis, Pirgos and etc, etc. There is no mention that the railway line is a circular layout, with single trains circumscribing the route and that each place name is simply a stop on the journey.

Making changes for branch lines can be 'exciting'! Stations are labelled in demotic script and there is no comprehensible announcement from the guard, thus it is easy to fail to make an exit on cue!

Peloponissou Station
Athens to Patras:
Depart 0640, 0826, 1020, 1305, 1542, 1820, 2139 hrs
Arrive 1055, 1206, 1430, 1653, 2005, 2153, 0149 hrs

Patras to Athens:
Depart 0630, 0811, 1105, 1350, 1705, 1842, 2013, 0210 hrs
Arrive 1002, 1257, 1457, 1832, 2118, 2239, 0010, 0636 hrs
One-way fare: Athens to Patras: B Class 545drs, A Class 820drs.

Larissis Station
Athens to Thessaloniki & on to Alexandroupoli:
Depart 0700, 0800, 1100, 1425, 1900, 2110, 2310 hrs
Thessaloniki
Arrive 1448, 1550, 1806, 2217, 0336, 0553, 0750 hrs
Depart 1532, - 1832, 2316, - 0617, 0924 hrs
Drama (for Kavala)
Arrive 1854, - - 0302, - 1023, 1338 hrs
Alexandroupoli
Arrive 2216, - - 0655, - 1412, 1738 hrs

One-way fares:
Athens to Thessaloniki :B Class 1265drs, A Class 1895drs.
Athens to Drama :B Class 1650drs, A Class 2475drs.
Athens to Alexandroupoli :B Class 1955drs, A Class 2930drs.
Surcharge on Express trains from 170-300drs.

TRAVEL AGENTS & TOUR OFFICES There are offices selling tickets for almost anything to almost anywhere, which include:
ABC 58 Stadiou St. Tel 321 1381
American Express 2 Ermou St, Tel 324 4975/9
On the first floor is an excellent retail travel service. Admittedly they are mainly involved in the sale of tours and excursions but the assistants are extremely efficient and helpful. They will, for instance, telephone round to locate all or any hotels that accept an Amex card, if they have a room and the cost.
CHAT 4 Stadiou St. Tel 322 2886
Key Tours 5th Floor, 2 Ermou St. Tel 323 3756
Viking 3 Filellinon St. Tel 322 9383
Probably the agency most highly regarded by students for prices and variety.
International Student & Youth Travel Service (SYTS) 11 Nikis St Tel 323 3767
For FIYTO membership. Second floor, open Monday-Friday 0900-1900hrs and Saturday from 0900-1200hrs.
Filellinon and the parallel street of Odhos Nikis (to the west of Syntagma Sq), all the way south and up as far as Nikodimou St are jam-packed with tourist agencies and student organisations. These include one or two express coach and train fare companies. A sample, going up the rise from Syntagma Square, includes:

Budget Student Travel On the right, opposite a church.
Stafford Travel On the corner of Filellinon and Kidathineon Sts.

An example of the packaged tours on offer, in this instance from **Key Tours** but representatives of most, includes:-

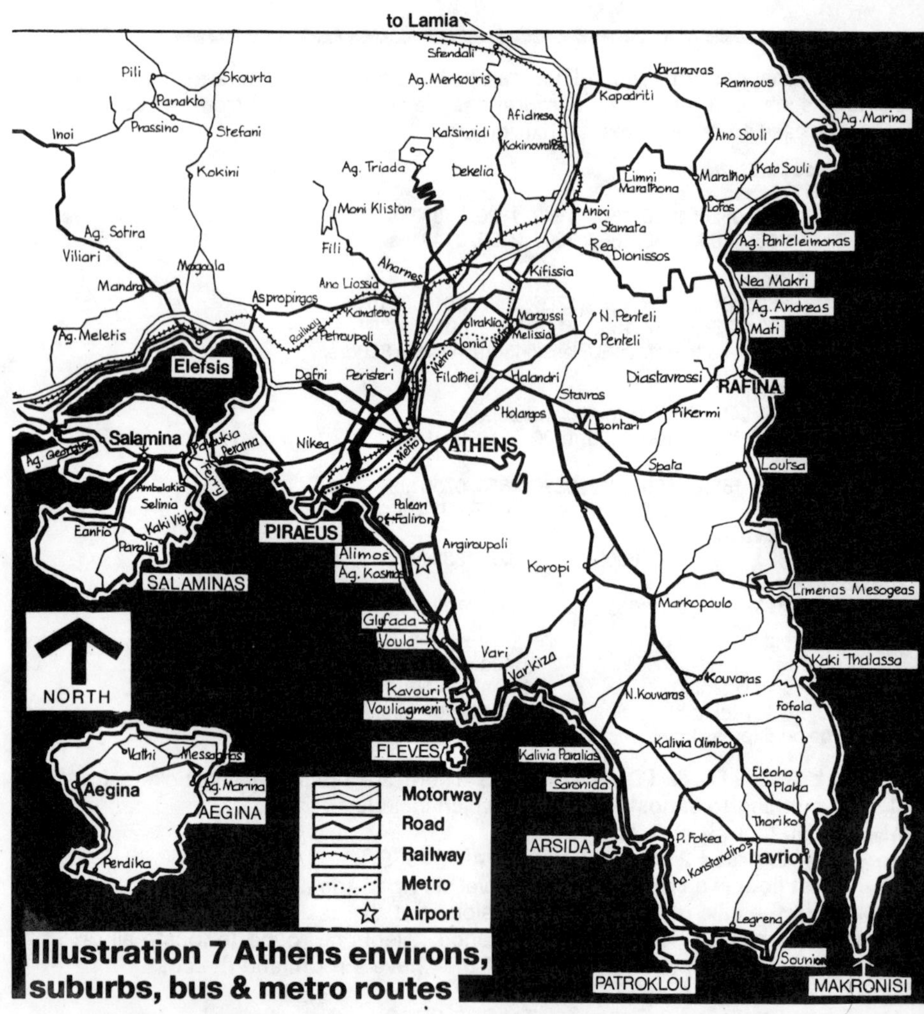

Illustration 7 Athens environs, suburbs, bus & metro routes

One day to Delphi from 4200drs; two days to Epidauras & Mycenae 10,900drs; three days to Delphi & Meteora from 26,150drs & a one day cruise to Aegina, Poros & Hydra, 4000drs.

Callers at the National Bank (*Tmr* 3D/E4/5) usually have to run the gauntlet of 'tours from touts' even if some may only be offering advice ('....I know this white woman?). They are best brushed aside otherwise the unwary might well be borne along on an unstoppable tide.

Sample 'charter' air & bus fares available from Athens to various European capitals include (as quoted by **Economy Travel**, 18 Panepistimiou St, Athens Tel 363 4045):

Air to London 25,000drs; Paris 24,000drs; Rome 17,500drs; Munich 20,000; Berlin 21,000drs; New York 40,000drs; Stockholm 29,000drs.

Bus to London 13,000drs; Paris 12,000drs; Venice 9000drs; Munich 11,000drs; Istanbul 4500drs.

YOUTH HOSTEL ASSOCIATION *See* **The Accommodation**.

10 PIREAUS (Pireas, Pireefs) & other Mainland Ports (where applicable)

Fortune and hope farewell! I've found the port you've done with me; go now with others sport. From a Greek epigram

Tel prefix 01

Piraeus is the port of Athens (Illustrations 8, 9 & 10) and the usual ferry-boat departure point for most of the Aegean islands. A confusing town on first acquaintance, but very unlike the old Piraeus portrayed in the film *Never on a Sunday*. The bawdy seaport cafes, tavernas and seedy waterfront have been replaced by smart shipping offices, respectable banks and tree planted thoroughfares, squares and parks.

Arrival at Piraeus will usually be by Metro or bus if coming from inland, or by ferry-boat if arriving by sea. (Well, it would be a long tiring swim, wouldn't it?).

ARRIVAL BY BUS

From Syntagma Sq (Athens), Bus No. 40 arrives at Plateia Korai (*Tmr* C3) but in truth that is rather an over simplification. For a start the bus is absolutely crammed early morning and it is very difficult to know one's exact whereabouts, which is germane as the bus hurtles on down to the end of the Piraeus peninsula. The first indicator that the end of the ¾ hour journey is imminent is when the bus runs parallel to the Metro lines. The second is crossing a wide avenue at right-angles (Leoforos Vassileos Georgiou) after which signs for the *Archaeological Museum* indicate that it is time to bale out.

From Plateia Korai, north-west along Leoforos Vassileos Georgiou (Yeoryiou) leads to the Main (Grand or Central) Harbour (*Tmr* D2); south-east progresses towards Limin Zeas (Pasalimani) (*Tmr* C/D4) and east towards Limin Mounikhias (Tourkolimano) (*Tmr* B5), the latter two being the marina harbours. Limin Zeas is where the Flying Dolphins dock.

From Omonia Sq (Athens) Bus No. 49 arrives at Ethniki Antistaseos (*Tmr* C2); from the East airport, (a yellow) Bus No. 19 (but often numberless), arrives at Karaiskaki Sq (*Tmr* C/D2). Karaiskaki (Akti Tzelepi) Sq is a main bus terminal. The note in brackets regarding the No. 19 bus should be expanded to point out that all the other buses are blue.

Another service (Bus No. 101) arrives at Theotoki St (*Tmr* E/F3/4) from whence head north-east towards Sakhtouri St and turn left in a northerly direction to reach the southern end of the Main Harbour quay front.

ARRIVAL BY METRO

Piraeus Metro station (*Tmr* 1C1/2), the end of the line, is hidden away in the corner of a large but rather inconspicuous building, flanked by Plateia Roosevelt. It could well be a warehouse, an empty shell of an office block, in fact almost anything but a Metro terminus. Passengers emerge opposite the quayside, at the north end of the waterfront.

If catching a ferry almost immediately, it is probably best to make a temporary headquarters by turning right out of the entrance, following the quay round to the left and 'falling' into one of the three or so cafe-bars set in the harbour-facing side of a sizeable quayside block of buildings. The importance of establishing a shore base, or bridgehead, becomes increasingly apparent whilst attempts are made to locate the particular ferry-boat departure point.

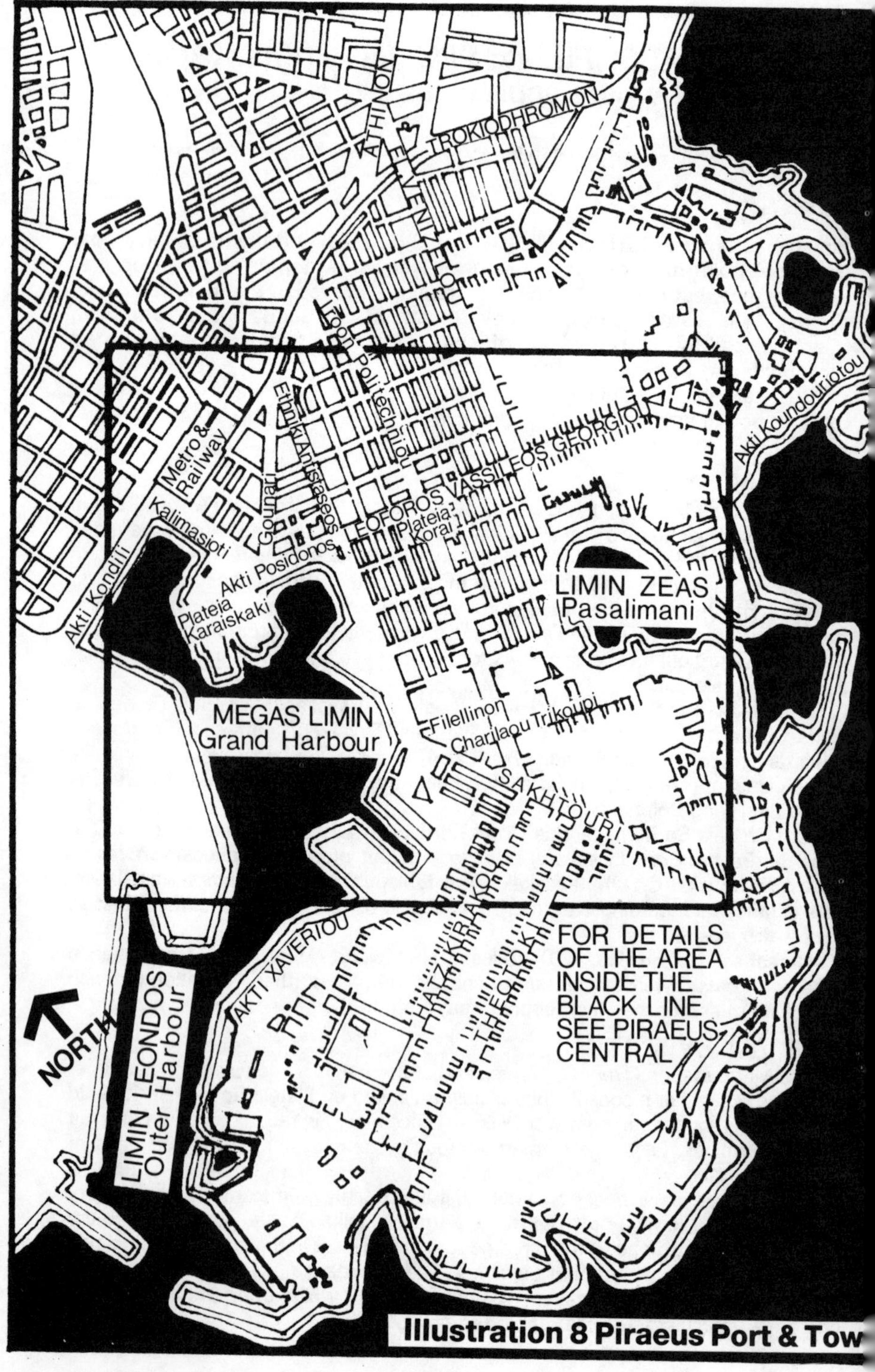

Illustration 8 Piraeus Port & Tow

To obtain tickets turn to the left (*Fsw*) out of the Metro station and follow the quayside round. One of the first major landmarks is Karaiskaki (or Akti Tzelepi) Sq (*Tmr* C/D2), fronted by large, shipping office buildings surmounted by a number of neon lit signs. These advertising slogans change from year to year but the point is that they are eye-catching. Proceed along the quay road (Akti Posidonos), between the Streets of Gounari and Ethniki Antistaseos, (*Tmr* C2), keeping the waterfront to the right. Reference to **Ferry-Boat Ticket Offices, A To Z** gives details of various ticket offices. The Port police are located in a quayside shed and must be regarded as favourites to dispense fairly accurate information about ferry-boats. Any information received though is best tucked away for future comparison with the rest of the advice acquired.

ARRIVAL BY FERRY

Reorientate using the above information, but bearing in mind that ferries dock all the way round the Grand Harbour, from the area of the Metro Station (*Tmr* 1C1/2) as far down as the Olympic office (*Tmr* 8D3).

ARRIVAL BY FLYING DOLPHIN

The hydrofoils dock at Limin Zeas Harbour. *See* **Flying Dolphins, A To Z.**

ARRIVAL BY TRAIN

If passengers have not alighted at Athens, Peloponnese trains pull up at the same terminus building as the Metro (*Tmr* 1C1/2) and the Northern Greece trains on the far (north-west) side of the Grand Harbour (*Tmr* 19D/E1/2).

THE ACCOMMODATION & EATING OUT

The Accommodation General remarks for Athens also apply here. Although I have never had to doss (or camp) out in Piraeus, I am advised that it is not to be recommended. There are just too many disparate (desperate?) characters wandering about.

Close by the Metro Station are the:

Hotel Ionion (*Tmr* 4C2) (Class C) 10 Kapodistrion Tel 417 0992
Directions: Turn left from the Metro station and or Roosevelt Sq (*Fsw*) down the quay road, Kalimasioti St, and left again at the first turning.

The hotel, halfway up on the right, is noticeable by the prominent sign promising *Family Hotel and from now on Economical Prices*. But is it, with a single room sharing a bathroom charged at 1600drs and a double room, also sharing, 2845drs (1st April-14th Oct)?

The Delfini (*Tmr* 5C2) (Class C) 7 Leoharous St Tel 412 3512
Directions: As above, but the second turning left.

Singles cost 2500drs and doubles 3500drs, both with bathroom en suite.

Hotel Helektra (*Tmr* 6C2) (Class E) 12 Navarinou Tel 417 7057
Directions: At the top of Leoharous St, turn right on to Navarinou St and the hotel is at the end of the block.

During the season a single room costs 1020drs and a double 1400drs, both sharing the bathroom.

Follow the quay road of Akti Posidonos round to the right, along the waterfront of Akti Miaouli as far as Odhos Bouboulina, the side street prior to Odhos Merarkhias. Turn up Bouboulina St.

Youth Hostel No. 1 (*Tmr* 24D3) 8 Filonos St.
Directions: As above and on the right between the 3rd and 4th lateral street, including the Esplanade.

A large, very seedy looking establishment.

Further on along the waterfront Esplanade towards the Custom's office (*Tmr* 14D/E3), and close by the Church of Ag Nikolaos, advances to the bottom of Leoforos Charilaou Trikoupi (*Tmr* D3). This street runs south-east and is amply furnished with cheaper hotels including the:

Capitol Hotel (*Tmr* 7D3) Class C) Ch. Trikoupi/147 Filonos Sts Tel 452 4911
Directions: As above.

A single room costs 1500drs and a double room 2000drs, both en suite.

Glaros Hotel (Class C) 4 Ch. Trikoupi Tel 452 7887
A breakfast costs 220drs. Single rooms are en suite and start at 1300drs while a double room sharing a bathroom cost 1500drs and en suite 1750drs. These charges rise to 1370drs for a single room and 1570/1840drs for a double room (1st July-31st Dec).

Serifos Hotel (Class C) 5 Ch. Trikoupi Tel 452 4967
A single room costs 1200drs and a double room 1750drs, both with en suite bathrooms.

Santorini Hotel (Class C) 6 Ch. Trikoupi Tel 452 2147
Prices as for the *Serifos Hotel*.

Homeridion Hotel (Class B) 32 Ch. Trikoupi Tel 451 9811
Rather expensive but all rooms have an en suite bathroom with singles costing 2700drs and a double room 3900drs.

Forming a junction with Leoforos Charilaou Trikoupi is Notara St up which turn left. On this street is sited the:

Faros Hotel (Class D) 140 Notara St Tel 452 6317
Directions: As above.

More down-to-earth prices despite which all rooms have en suite bathrooms. A single room costs 1050drs and a double 1350drs which rise respectively to 1100drs and 1450drs (1st July-31st Dec).

Again at right angles to Leoforos Charilaou Trikoupi, is Kolokotroni St on which are situated:

Park House (Class B) 103 Kolokotroni St Tel 452 4611
Directions: As above.

A single room costs 1950drs and a double 2700drs, both with en suite bathrooms increasing to 2250drs and 3100drs (16th May-31st Oct). A breakfast costs 350drs.

Aris Hotel (Class D) 117 Kolokotroni St Tel 452 0487
A single room sharing a bathroom is charged at 880drs and with an en suite bathroom 1100drs. A double room sharing costs 1200drs and en suite 1460drs.

Also leading off to the left is Iroon Politechniou (once Vassileos Konstantinou) whereon:

Noufara Hotel (Class B) 45 Iroon Politechniou Tel 411 5541
Directions: As above.

All rooms have an en suite bathroom with singles costing 2315/2845drs and doubles 3115/3915drs. (Phew!)

Savoy Hotel (Class B) 93 Iroon Politechniou Tel 413-1102
Guests will have to be 'flush' with a single room charged at 3590drs and a double room 4810drs, both with en suite bathrooms.

Continuing along Iroon Politechniou, turn right (*or south-east*) at Plateia Korai along Leoforos Vassileos Georgiou (Vassileos Yeoryiou) which proceeds, on the left, to:

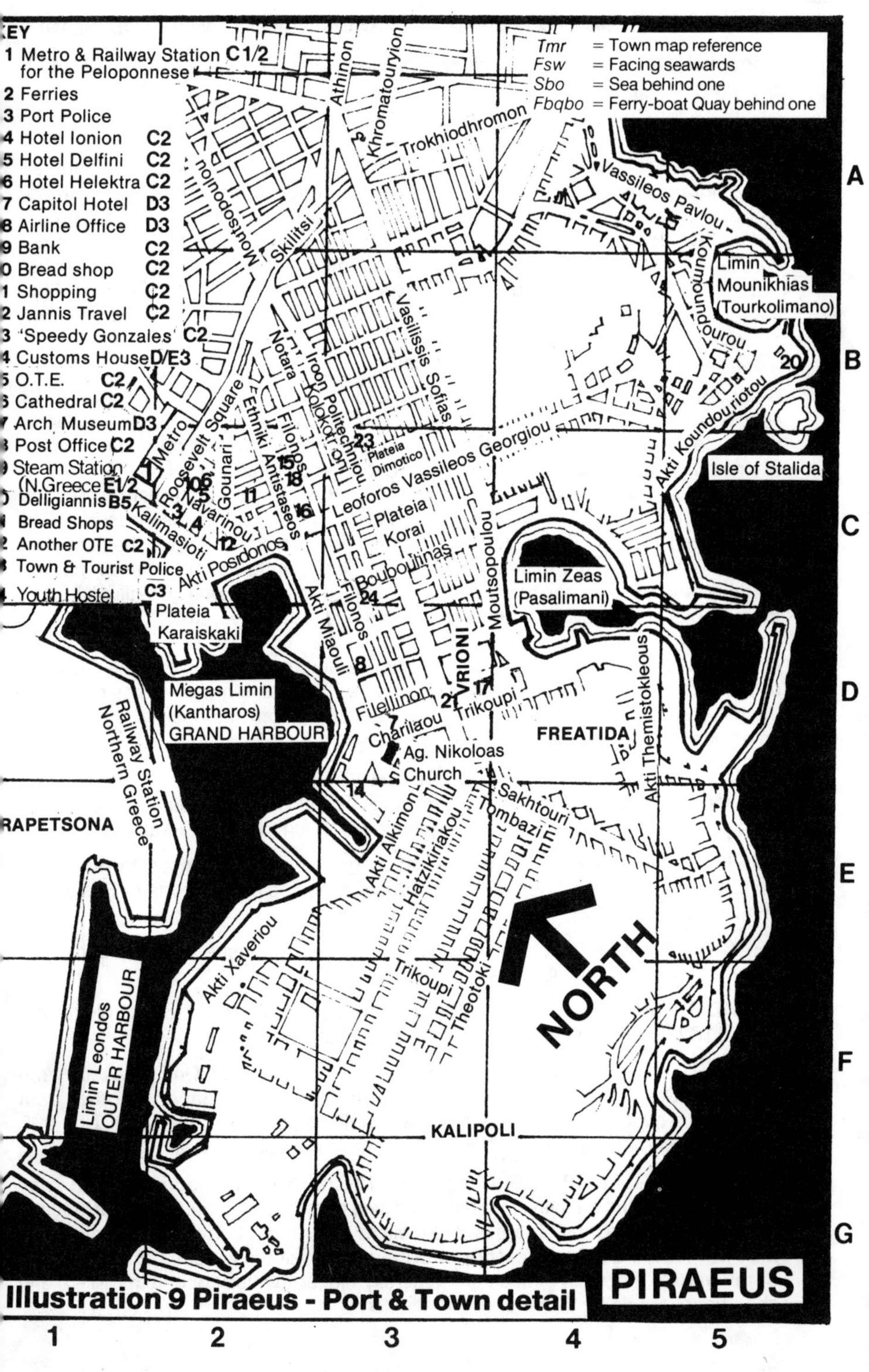

Illustration 9 Piraeus - Port & Town detail

Diogenis Hotel (Class B) 27 Leoforos Vassileos Georgiou Tel 412 5471
Directions: As above.
Within a few hundred drachmae of the Savoy.

The Eating Out For eating out read the Athens comments as a general guide. Piraeus is not noted for outstanding rendezvous around the Grand Harbour and its encircling terrain, despite the numerous restaurants, tavernas and cafes along the quayside roads. On the other hand there are some excellent eating places in the area bordering the eastern coastline of the Piraeus peninsula, bounded by Akti Moutsopoulou (*Tmr* C/D3/4) and Akti Koumoundourou (*Tmr* B5) encircling (respectively) the Zeas and Mounikhias harbours.

Especially recommended is the classy:

Delligiannis (*Tmr* 20B5) 1 Akti Koundouriotou Tel 413 2013
Directions: A very pleasant setting in the 'pretty' part of Piraeus up on the hill to the south-west of Limin Mounikhias. This overlooks a few million pounds worth of private yachts lying to anchor in the most attractive harbour.

Apart from the position, the selection of food is excellent and there is outside seating while the inside resembles a high-class saloon bar. The service is quick, friendly and honest. For instance, enquirers will be advised that the 'souvlaki flambe' is nothing more than souvlaki on fire! 'Inside information' advises that the 'birds liver in wine' is delicious, despite being listed as a starter. Costing 450drs, the portions are larger than most main courses at other tavernas.

On Plateia Karaiskaki, a number of cafe-bar/restaurants stretch along the quayside of the large building that dominates the square. A white van sometimes parks up, early in the day, on the edge of the square, selling from the back of the vehicle, small pizzas and feta cheese pies for about 80drs.

THE A TO Z OF USEFUL INFORMATION

AIRLINE OFFICE & TERMINUS (*Tmr* 8D3) The Olympic office is halfway down the Esplanade of Akti Miaouli, at the junction with Odhos II Merarkhias.

BANKS The most impressive is the vast, imposing emporium housing the *Macedonia & Thrace* situated opposite the corner of the Esplanade roads of Posidonos and Miaouli (*Tmr* 9C2).

BEACHES Between Zeas and Mounikhias harbours, opposite Stalida island. Also *See* **Beaches, A To Z, Athens**.

BREAD SHOPS One on Roosevelt Sq (*Tmr* 10C2) and others on Odhos Kolokotroni (*Tmr* 21C2/3) and Charilaou Trikoupi (*Tmr* 21D3).

BUSES Two buses circulate around the peninsula of Piraeus. One proceeds from Roosevelt Sq to Limin Mounikhias, and on to Neon Faliron, and the other from Korai Sq (*Tmr* C3) via the Naval Cadets College to Limin Zeas. Bus No. 905 connects the Metro station to the Flying Dolphin quay, Limin Zeas.

COMMERCIAL SHOPPING AREA (*Tmr* 11C2) There is a flourishing and busy Market area behind the bank mentioned above, hemmed in by the streets of Gounari and Ethniki Antistaseos. There is an excellent supermarket on the corner of Odhos Makras Stoas, if a shopper cannot be bothered to visit the various shops and stalls of the market. Prices in Piraeus are generally higher than elsewhere in Greece and shop hours are as for Athens.

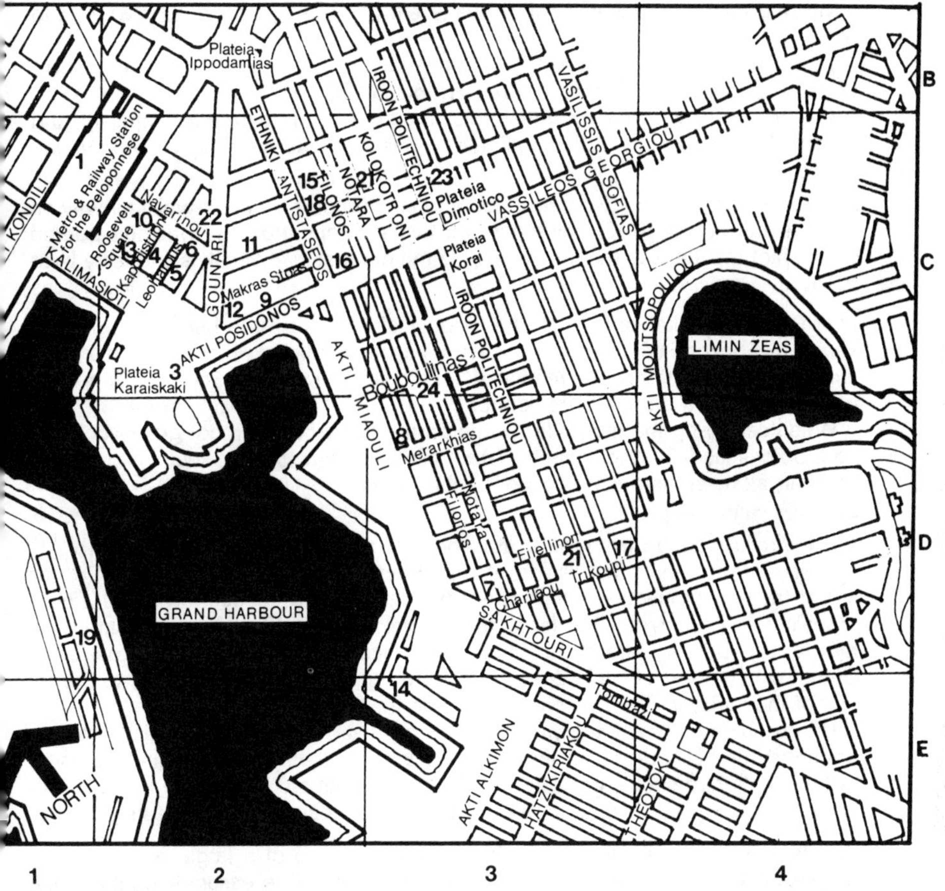

Illustration 10 Piraeus inset

FERRY-BOATS Most island ferry-boats leave from the area encompassed by Akti Kondili, to the north of the Grand Harbour, Karaiskaki Sq, Akti Posidonos and Akti Miaouli, to the west of the Grand Harbour. As a general rule the Aegean ferries depart from the area of Karaiskaki Square and International ferries leave from the south or far end of the Akti Miaouli quay road.

See **Chapter Eleven** for a synopsis of the islands and ports and the individual islands for details of the timetables.

FERRY-BOAT TICKET OFFICES Yes well, at least they lie extremely thick on the waterfront. It is probably best to make enquiries about the exact location of a particular ferry's departure point when purchasing the tickets. It has to be admitted the vendors tend to refer to a ship's point of departure with any airy wave of the hand. Ticket sellers 'lie in wait', all the way along the quayside streets of Kalimasioti and Akti Posidonos, that is from the Metro station, past the Gounari St turning to the bottom of Ethniki Antistaseos.

My two favourite offices lie at opposite ends of the spectrum, as it were, and are:

Jannis Stoulis Travel (*Tmr* 12C2) 2 Gounari St Tel 417 9491
Directions: Situated on the right (*Sbo*) of Gounari St.

The owner, who wears a rather disinterested air, is extremely efficient and speaks three languages, including English. This business is usually closed outside 'office' hours.

His fast talking, 'speedy Gonzales' counterpart occupies a wall-to-wall stairway on Kalimasioti St (*Tmr* 13C2). My regard for the latter operator may well be coloured by the fact that he was the man who sold me my first ever Greek island ferry-boat ticket.

There are two ticket offices on the harbour side of the large building on Plateia Karaiskaki, beyond the cafes, two of almost dozens of ticket offices spaced around this edifice. An enterprising vendor of tickets lurks, from early morning, amongst the ferry-boat stalls on Akti Posidonos.

When searching the quayside for the correct ferry-boat, do not go beyond the Port offices and Custom house (*Tmr* 14D/E3), towards the south end of the harbour, as these berths are for cruise ships only.

FLYING DOLPHINS

The hydrofoils depart from the south side of Limin Zeas Harbour, so allow ¾hr for the walk up and over the hillside of the streets from the Metro station. Do not forget the bus connection if time is not paramount. Foot-sloggers will find it best to walk down Akti Miaouli as far as the Olympic Airline office (*Tmr* 8D3), at which turn left up Odhos Merarkhias. This street ascends and descends to the large, almost circular port of Limin Zeas where turn right and keep right round to the far end of the harbour. The hydrofoil quay is on the left.

One problem is that the Flying Dolphins are used by package holiday firms to transport their clients to, for instance, the islands of Poros, Hydra and Spetses, but the early bird should get a seat. These hydrofoils are very well equipped with lavatories, a small snackbar, as well as a central and aft viewing platform.

The terminus is conveniently overlooked by the patio of a large, modern cafe-bar/restaurant/zacharoplasteion which is open during the essential hours of the Flying Dolphins' operation. Mind you it is not inexpensive. Two Nes meh ghala (and not a lot of ghala) cost 248drs and two toasted sandwiches 450drs. A breakfast is also served but I have never been able to save up enough to indulge this fancy... One plus point is that the ladies toilets are very clean even if the gentlemens is not so spotless.

FLYING DOLPHIN TICKET OFFICES

Main Booking Office (*Tmr* C/D4) 8 Akti Themistokleous Tel 452 7107
Directions: As above.

METRO *See* **Arrival by Metro, Introduction.**

NTOG Somewhat inconveniently situated at Limin Zeas Harbour (*Tmr* C/D4) and only open weekdays between 0700-1500hrs.

OTE The main office (*Tmr* 15C2) is north of the Post Office with another on Odhos Navarinou (*Tmr* 22C2).

PLACES OF INTEREST

Archaeological Museum (*Tmr* 17D3) Situated between Filellinon and Leoforos Charilaou Trikoupi Sts. Reopened in the last few years and reportedly well laid out, with easy to identify exhibits. Opening hours Mondays to Saturday, 0845-1500hrs, Sunday 0930-1430hrs and closed Tuesdays. Only Greeks are allowed free admission here, as elsewhere in Greece, foreigners having to pay 100drs.

Ag Triada (*Tmr* 16C2) The Cathedral was rebuilt in the early I960s, having been destroyed in 1944. Distinctive, mosaic tile finish.

Zea Theatre Adjacent to the Archaeological Museum, the remains date from about the second century BC.

Limin Zeas (Pasalimani) (*Tmr* C/D4) This semicircular harbour is of great antiquity. Now it is lined by high-rise buildings, shelters fishing boats and caiques, provides a yacht basin for larger, modern yachts, is the location for the Naval Museum of Greece, contains a Flying Dolphin (hydrofoil) terminal as well as a base for yacht charterers. Excavations have shown that, in ancient times, several hundred boat sheds radiated out around the edge of the harbour housing the triremes, the great, three-banked warships of antiquity.

The Naval Museum of Greece Adjacent to Zeas Harbour with a varied and interesting series of exhibits down through the ages.

Limin Mounikhias (Tourkolimano or Mikrolimano) (*Tmr* B5) From Limin Zeas, continue on north-east round the coast cliff road, past the bathing beach (*facing the tiny island of Stalida*), and the Royal Yacht Club of Greece, to reach this renowned, 'chatty', picturesque and again semicircular harbour of Mounikhias. From here racing yachts are believed to have departed for regattas in Saroniko Bay as far back as the 4th century BC, as they do now. The quayside is ringed with tavernas, cafes and restaurants forming a backcloth to the multi-coloured sails of the assembled yachts crowded into the harbour.

The Hill of Kastela overlooks the harbour and has a modern, open-air, marble amphitheatre, wherein theatre and dance displays are staged, more especially during the Athens Festival (*See* **Places of Interest, A To Z, Athens**).

Filonos Street (*Tmr* B/C/D2/3) The 'Soho' of Piraeus, espousing what's left of the old *Never on a Sunday* atmosphere of the town.

POLICE
Port On the quay bounded by Akti Posidonos.
Tourist & Town (*Tmr* 23C3) Dimotico Square.

POST OFFICE (*Tmr*18C2) On Filonos St, north-west of the Cathedral.

RAILWAY STATIONS *See* **Arrival by Metro & Arrival by Train, Introduction.**
Metro (Underground) (*Tmr* 1C1/2).
'Steam' Station (*Tmr* 1C1/2) The Peloponnese terminus is alongside and the far side of the Metro station.

'Steam' Station (*Tmr* 19D/E/2) The terminus for Northern Greece is situated on the far, north-west side of the Grand Harbour.

SWIMMING POOL Adjacent to Limin Zeas Harbour.

TELEPHONE NUMBERS & ADDRESSES

NTOG (*Tmr* C/D4) Zeas Marina	Tel 413 5716
Port Authorities	Tel 451 1311
Taxi station	Tel 4178138

OTHER MAINLAND PORTS
For Evia island

RAFINA (Illustration 11) Tel prefix 0294

A noisy, clamorous, smelly, busy seaport, with an excellent bus service to Athens.

ARRIVAL BY BUS

The buses park up on the dual carriageway (*Tmr* 1/C4) that curves up from the large Ferry-boat Quay (*Tmr* 2/D1/2). The Bus office is a small hut towards the top end on the right of this road (*Sbo*) with a timetable stuck up on the window.

ARRIVAL BY FERRY

There are Ferry-boat connections to Marmari & Karistos (Evia island).

The Ferry-boat Quay (*Tmr* 2/D1/2) is at the bottom of the wide dual carriageway that climbs up to the Main Square. To the left (*Sbo*), the waterfront road follows the sea round but do not be side-tracked. Passengers disembarking at night and not prepared to travel on to Athens should make directly for one of the more easily accessible hotels.

The ferry-boat ticket offices are scattered about in amongst the restaurants and tavernas lining the road from the Ferry-boat Quay.

THE ACCOMMODATION & EATING OUT

There are numerous restaurant/tavernas doing a roaring trade but accommodation is another matter.

The Accommodation

Hotel Korali (*Tmr* 3/B5/6) (Class D) 11 Plateia N Plastira Tel 22477

Directions: From the top of the dual carriageway, half-right across a small square, and the hotel is on the left-hand side of the large pedestrian square (that now blocks off the old Main Street). A couple of *Mobil petrol pumps are set on the far left corner of this square.*

A grey, urban, soulless, rather down-at-heel but clean 1920s establishment in front of which is a periptero. The high ceilinged, linoleum floored rooms share the cavernous, massively equipped bathrooms. You know, cast iron cisterns, supported on very large cast iron brackets, 25mm pipes and mahogany lavatory seats. A single room costs 1300drs and a double 2000drs. Madam does not live on the premises so if intending to leave early pay up the night before departure.

Hotel Ina Marina (*Tmr* 4/C6) (Class C) Olympionikou Chr Manlika Tel 22215

Directions: From the top of the dual carriageway, keep along the avenue to the left and the hotel is on the right.

All rooms are en suite with a single room costing 2060drs and a double room 2615drs. These rates rise to 2800drs and 3630drs (1st July-30th Sept).

Hotel Rafina (*Tmr* 5/A/B4/5) (Class E) 2 Plateia N Plastira Tel 23460

Directions: Almost directly across the pedestrian way from the Hotel Korali.

Greyer, scruffier and older than its counterpart across the way but cheaper with double rooms, only sharing the bathroom, costing 1350drs.

Hotel Kymata (*Tmr* 6/C5) (Class D) Plateia N Plastira Tel 23406

Directions: Before the Hotel Korali over a row of pizza-joints and rather difficult to spot.

Similar prices and conditions to the *Hotel Korali*.

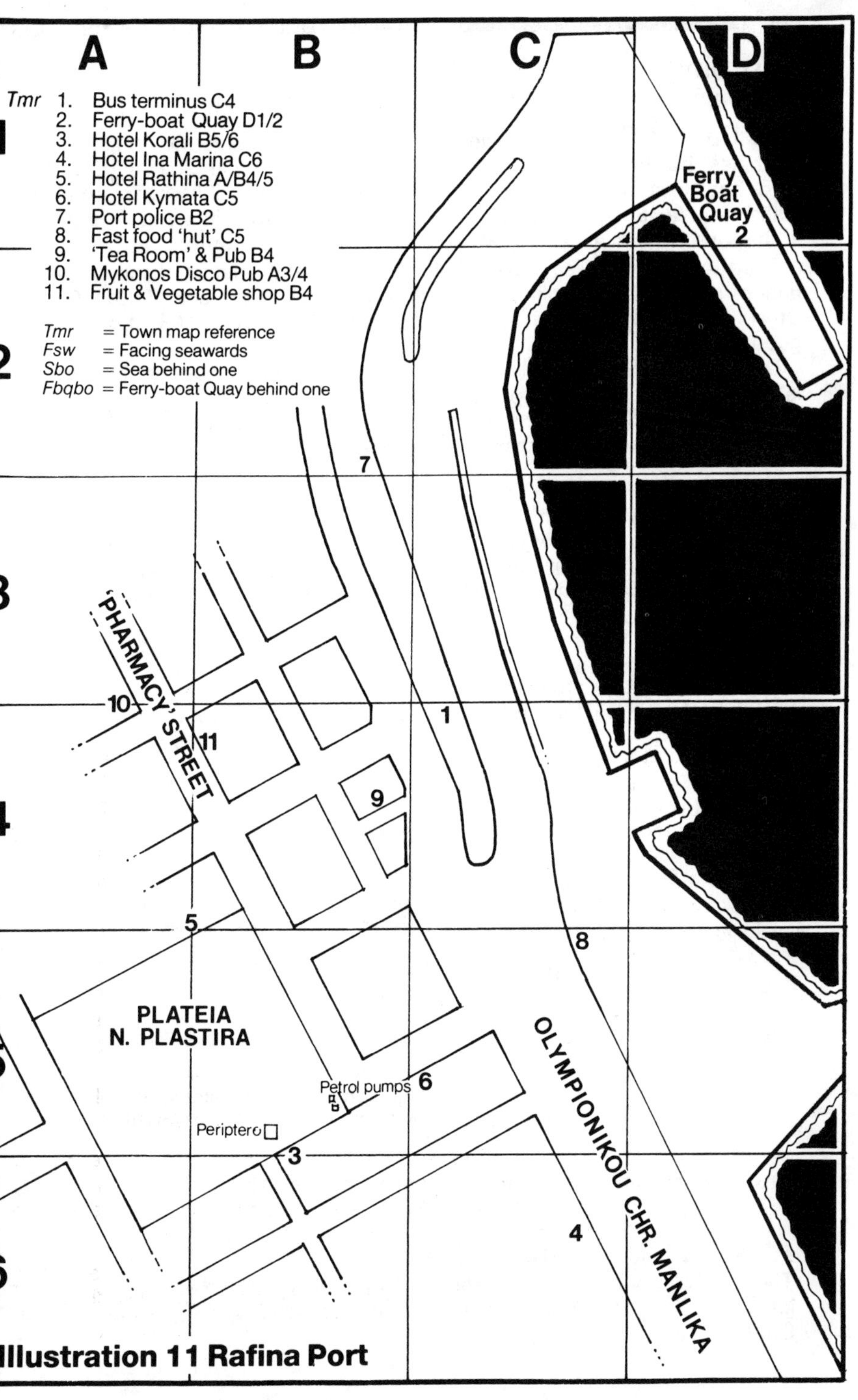

Illustration 11 Rafina Port

Camping

See **Camping, The Accommodation, Athens, Chapter Nine.**

The Eating Out Side-by-side fish restaurants and tavernas, with rooftop balconies, border the right-hand side (*Sbo*) of the dual carriageway from the Ferry-boat Quay as far as the Port police office (*Tmr* 7/B2). Apart from the mass of pizza eating places, the late night, hot-dog, soft-drink hut (*Tmr* 8/C5) at the top of the dual carriageway could fill a nook or cranny.

Some might try the Tea Room & Pub (*Tmr* 9/B4) at the outset of and on the far right of the Plateia N Plastira. Open between 0800-1200hrs and 1900-2400hrs. Others might be moved to visit the Mykonos Disco Pub (*Tmr* 10/A3/4). Oh goody, goody.

On 'Pharmacy' St (thus named due to the high proportion of these establishments) is, on the right, a *fruit and vegetable shop* (*Tmr* 11/B4).

Further along, the main avenue, or more correctly pedestrian way, of Plateia N Plastira are the banks and other public services.

Buses & timetables

Athens buses depart from 14 Mavrommateon St at:-
0600, 0620, 0645, 0715, 0800, 0845, 0915, 1010, 1045, 1115, 1145, 1215, 1245, 1315, 1345, 1415, 1445, 1515, 1545, 1615, 1645, 1715, 1800, 1845, 1930, 2015, 2100, 2200hrs.

They depart from Rafina at:
0550, 0620, 0650, 0720, 0750, 0830, 0915, 0950, 1020, 1110, 1150, 1220, 1250, 1320, 1350, 1420, 1450, 1520, 1550, 1630, 1720, 1750, 1840, 1915, 2000, 2030, 2120, 2200, 2230hrs.
The one-way cost is 140drs for the 30km journey.

Ferry-boats & timetables

Day	Departure time	Ferry-boat	Ports/Islands of Call
Daily	0830hrs	Marmari	Marmari (Evia)
	1400hrs(except Sunday)	Marmari	Marmari (Evia)
	1600hrs(except Friday & Sunday)	Papadiamantis I	Karistos (Evia)
	1715hrs(except Sunday)	Marmari	Marmari (Evia)
Friday	1630hrs	Papadiamantis I	Karistos (Evia)
Sunday	1630hrs	Marmari	Marmari (Evia)
	1915hrs	Papadiamantis I	Karistos (Evia)
	2000hrs	Marmari	Marmari (Evia)

Third class, one-way fares: Rafina to Marmari 365drs; duration 5hrs.
to Karistos 545drs;

ARKITSA for Loutra Edipsou.

There are plenty of ***Rooms*** on the road into Arkitsa which emerges at the far left of the jetty (*Fsw*). For Athens bus connections *See* **Ag Konstantinos, Chapter Ten.**

Ferry-boat timetable
Daily 0715, 0915, 1115, 1315, 1515, 1715, 1915, 2115hrs
One-way fare: 180drs; duration 50 mins.

SKALA OROPOU for Eretria.

Athens buses terminus on 14 Mavrommateon St.
Athens buses depart at:-
0610, 0640, 0800, 1000, 1100, 1215, 1300, 1400, 1530, 1700, 1830, 2000hrs.
They leave Skala at:-
0600, 0700, 0715, 0820, 0915, 1015, 1215, 1320, 1430, 1615, 1730, 1920, 2030, 2050hrs.
One-way fare: 290drs for the 55km jouney.

Ferry-boat timetable
Daily 0600-1930hrs every ½hr, 2000, 2100, 2200hrs.
One-way fare: 80drs; duration 25mins.

AG MARINA for Panaghia (Almiropotamos) & Nea Stira.

Athens buses terminus on 14 Mavrommateon St.
Athens buses depart at:0600, 0815, 1230, 1600hrs.
They leave Ag Marina at: 0730, 1030, 1430, 1600hrs.
One-way fare: 320drs.

Ferry-boat timetable
Daily 0800, 1100, 1430, 1800hrs
Sunday 0800, 1115, 1345, 1700hrs
One-way fare 215 drs; duration 50mins
and:-

GLIFAforAgio Kampos.

A small way-station on to the Esplanade of which the road spills, towards the left-hand end (*Fsw*), where the landing craft ferries dock. The tiny ferry-boat ticket office is also at the left-hand end of the village, across the road from the waterfront.

There are several ***Rooms*** as well as the Hotel Akroyali (Class C – tel 0238 51312) with a single room en suite rate of 1300drs, a double sharing 1500drs and a double room en suite 1600drs.

A baker, mini-market and several tavernas look after the inner person. The small beach is beyond the hotel.

Ferry-boat timetable
Daily 0645, 1040, 1400, 1630, 1900hrs
One-way fare 120drs; duration 30mins

For the Sporades

AG KONSTANTINOS (Constantinos, Konstandinos)

Tel prefix 0235

The town is now simply a point on the extremely fast Athens-Lamia main road along which vehicles thunder night and day.

The settlement borders the left-hand side of the road, facing west and the massive Ferry-boat/Flying Dolphin Quay is to the right.

There is a pleasantly tree shaded Town Beach to the east, back towards Athens, but it is rather gritty and polluted. There are showers spaced along its length. A very large species of unpleasant looking, dome-headed jellyfish is present in abundance all the way along this coastline and nowhere more so than here. The locals assure me they are harmless, demonstrating with gusto how to upturn them and extract any small fishes within their gelantinous form. Ugh! No thanks.

The slip road off to the left (*proceeding in a westerly direction*) is edged first by a big church after which are large formal gardens and then a wide, rectangular street (Akademias St) – more a Main Square. Most of the 'activities' of Ag Konstantinos take place on or in the side-streets branching off the west side of this square. The garden or east side of the Main Sq is dominated by the terraces of cafe-bar restaurants across the Plateia. At the north, or main road side of the square, are two tour travel agents:-

Alkyon Travel 98 Akademias St Tel 31989
Directions: As above.

The office handles and sells tickets for the Nomicos ferry-boats and excursion coaches to Athens. These tie in with ferry-boat arrivals.

Bilialis Travel Akademias St Tel 31614
Directions: Next door to *Alkyon*

They act and sell tickets for the Flying Dolphins.

Over and above the travel agents are the offices of the *Port police*.

Next, in an inland direction, is the *Bank National de Grec* which transacts every form of currency exchange imaginable.

All these businesses are interspersed by the cafe-bar restaurants.

Beyond the Square, along the highway bordering slip road, are the *OTE* (open weekdays only 0730-1510hrs) and the *Post Office*.

The first side street off the Main Square, from the Highway end, has a baker's on the right opposite which is a grocers, wherein a small girl speaks English.

At the far, or top south-west corner of the square are most of the shops.

ARRIVAL BY FERRY-BOAT/FLYING DOLPHIN

The ferry-boats connect with all the Sporades islands, except for Skyros (*See* **Kimi Port, Evia island, Chapter Nineteen**), and some other mainland ports, including distant Kavala and close to Trikeri and Volos, as well as the far-flung islands of Ag Estratios and Limnos. There is a drinking water fountain close to the passenger sheds.

THE ACCOMMODATION & EATING OUT

The Accommodation

Most travellers time arrival at the port so as to be able to make their ferry-boat journey during daylight hours. Thus accommodation is not usually on the agenda. There are a number of inexpensive hotels and pensions including the:-

Hotel Olga (Class C – tel 31766), all rooms with en suite bathroom. A single room from 1200drs and doubles 1750drs; the *Pension O Tassos* (Class C – tel 31610), double rooms only sharing the bathroom 1100drs; the *Hotel Achilles* (Class D – tel 31623), all rooms share the bathroom, singles costing 900drs and doubles 1300drs and the *Hotel Poulia* (Class D – tel 31663) with singles en suite 1150drs, doubles sharing 1200drs and en suite 1600drs, which rates rise respectively to 1400, 1600 & 2100drs (1st June-31st Aug).

The Eating Out The Main Square is well provided with a number of look-alike establishments.

Buses & timetables

The Athens buses depart from 260 Liossion St at:-
0615 and hourly thereafter to and including 1915, 2030hrs.
They depart from Ag Konstantinos at:-
0500 and hourly thereafter to and including 1700, 1815, 1930hrs.
The one-way fare: 900drs.

FERRY—BOATS & FLYING DOLPHINS

Ferry-boat timetable (Mid-season)

Day	Departure time	Ferry-boat	Ports/Islands of Call
Monday	1300hrs	Skiathos	Skiathos, Glossa (Skopelos), Skiathos, Trikeri (M), Volos (M).
Tuesday	1230hrs	Skyros	Skiathos, Glossa (Skopelos), Skiathos, Trikeri (M), Volos (M).
	1300hrs	Skopelos	Ag Estratios, Limnos.
Wednesday	1130hrs	Papadiamantis II	Glossa (Skopelos), Skiathos, Trikeri (M), Volos (M).
	1300hrs	Limnos	Skiathos, Glossa (Skopelos), Skiathos, Volos (M).
Thursday	1230hrs	Skyros	Skiathos, Glossa (Skopelos), Skiathos, Trikeri (M), Volos (M).
Friday	1300hrs	Skiathos	Skiathos, Glossa (Skopelos), Skiathos, Trikeri (M), Volos (M).
Saturday	1300hrs	Limnos	Skiathos, Glossa (Skopelos), Skopelos, Alonissos.
Sunday	1130hrs	Papadiamantis II	Skiathos, Glossa (Skopelos), Skiathos, Trikeri (M), Volos (M).
	1300hrs	Limnos	Skiathos, Glossa (Skopelos), Alonissos.

Third class, one-way fares:				
Ag Konstantinos	to Alonissos	1415drs;	duration	6hrs
	to Glossa(Skopelos)	1220drs;		4½hrs
	to Kavala (M)	2195drs;		16½hrs
	to Limnos	1739drs;		10½hrs
	to Skiathos	1070drs;		3¼hrs
	to Skopelos	1270drs;		5½hrs
	to Volos	865drs;		9½hrs

Flying Dolphins timetable

Day	Departure time	Ports/Islands of Call
Daily	1415hrs	Skiathos, Glossa (Skopelos), Skopelos, Alonissos.
additionally:-		
Friday	1845hrs	Skiathos, Glossa (Skopelos), Skopelos, Alonissos.
Sunday	1915hrs	Skiathos, Glossa (Skopelos), Skopelos, Alonissos.

One-way fares: Ag Konstantinos		
	to Alonissos	2645drs
	to Glossa(Skopelos)	2090drs
	to Skiathos	1845drs
	to Skopelos	2110drs

***Note. Due to reasons totally outside my control, it is more than likely that the above will not tie in with those detailed from the islands. It would need a large frame computer to compare the misleading 'tissue of lies' emenating from the various authorities!**

VOLOS (Illustration 12) Tel prefix 0421

A very large, soulless, concrete jungle of an industrial town and commercial port – not really a desirable point from which to depart (or disembark).

ARRIVAL BY BUS

The bus station (*Tmr* 1A/B1/2) is one row back from the waterfront Esplanade.

ARRIVAL BY FERRY/FLYING DOLPHIN

The Ferry-boat Quay (*Tmr* 2B2) is some 750m to the right or east of the International liner and cargo quays, opposite which is a **Tourist Board** office (NTOG) (*Tmr* 3A1/2 – tel 23500). This latter facility is open weekdays only and siesta's between 1430-1800hrs.

Coming from the west past the cargo quays, the signs for the ferry-boats 'conveniently' run out close to the Tourist office. Just follow the waterfront.

The ticket offices are across the Esplanade Akti Argonafton from the quayside, as is the **Olympic Office**, a taverna, kafeneion and periptero. A baker is conveniently in the side-streets off to the left (*Sbo*). A yacht marina is to the right.

ARRIVAL BY TRAIN

If a traveller must, but it seems a lengthy procedure. The station (*Tmr* 4A1) is to the west of the town.

THE ACCOMMODATION & EATING OUT

The Accommodation There are a number of inexpensive, if austere hotels in the waterfront area.

The Eating Out Plenty of eating places on the quayside Esplanade or one street back.

Buses & timetables

There are two daily Athens bus services which depart from:-

260 Liossion St: 0700, 0900, 1030, 1200, 1330, 1500, 1630, 1800, 2200hrs
Return journey 0700, 0900, 1030, 1200, 1330, 1500, 1630, 1800, 2200hrs
One-way fare 1650drs; duration 5 hrs.
or
Larissis Railway Station: 0730, 1100, 1330, 1630, 1830hrs
Return journey 0800, 1020, 1300, 1700, 2145hrs
One-way fare 1680drs; duration 5 hrs.

Note buses connect Volos to Patras.

Ferry-boats/Flying Dolphins
Ferry-boat timetable

Day	**Departure time**	**Ferry-boat**	**Ports/Islands of Call**
Monday	0800hrs	Skyros	Skiathos, Glossa (Skopelos), Skopelos, Alonissos, Kimi (Evia).
	1300hrs	Limnos	Trikeri(M), Skiathos, Skopelos, Alonissos.
	1330hrs	Papadiamantis II	Trikeri(M), Skiathos, Glossa (Skopelos), Skopelos, Alonissos.

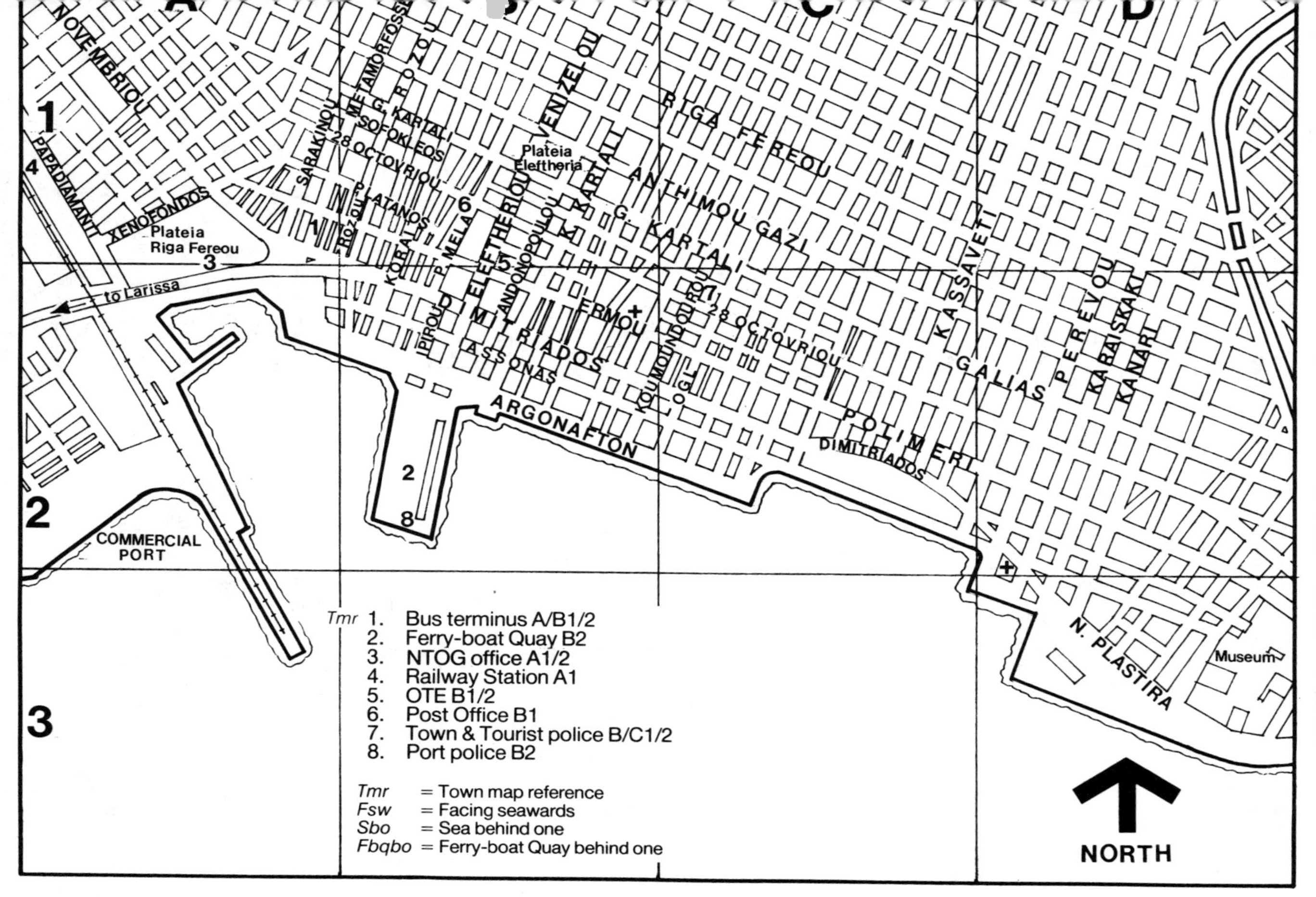

Illustration 12 Volos Port

Tuesday	0800hrs	Skiathos	Skiathos, Glossa (Skopelos), Skopelos.
	1300hrs	Limnos	Trikeri(M), Skiathos, Skopelos, Alonissos.
	1330hrs	Papadiamantis II	Trikeri(M), Skiathos, Glossa (Skopelos), Skopelos.
	1845hrs	Skiathos	Trikeri(M), Skiathos, Glossa (Skopelos), Skopelos.
Wednesday	0800hrs	Skyros	Trikeri(M), Skiathos, Skopelos, Glossa (Skopelos).
	1300hrs	Skiathos	Trikeri(M), Skiathos, Skopelos, Alonissos.
	1900hrs	Skyros	Trikeri(M), Skiathos, Glossa (Skopelos).
Thursday	0800hrs	Limnos	Skiathos, Glossa (Skopelos), Skopelos.
	1300hrs	Skiathos	Trikeri(M), Skiathos, Skopelos, Alonissos.
	1330hrs	Papadiamantis II	Trikeri(M), Skiathos, Glossa (Skopelos), Skopelos.
	1845hrs	Limnos	Trikeri(M), Skiathos, Glossa (Skopelos), Skopelos.
Friday	0800hrs	Skyros	Trikeri(M), Skiathos, Glossa (Skopelos).
	1300hrs	Limnos	Trikeri(M), Skiathos, Skopelos, Alonissos.
	1330hrs	Papadiamantis II	Trikeri(M), Skiathos, Glossa (Skopelos), Skopelos.
	1800hrs	Skyros	Trikeri(M), Skiathos, Glossa (Skopelos).
Saturday	0800hrs	Skiathos	Trikeri(M), Skiathos, Glossa (Skopelos), Skopelos.
	1300hrs	Skopelos	Skiathos, Skopelos, Alonissos, Kimi (Evia).
	1330hrs	Papadiamantis II	Trikeri(M), Skiathos, Glossa (Skopelos), Skopelos, Alonissos.
Sunday	0800hrs	Skiathos	Skiathos, Glossa (Skopelos), Skopelos, Alonissos.
	1300hrs	Skyros	Trikeri(M), Skiathos.
	2000hrs	Skiathos	Skiathos.

Third class fares:Volos	to Ag Konstantinos	865drs;duration	9½ hrs
	to Alonissos	1150drs;	5 hrs
	to Glossa (Skopelos)	945drs;	3½ hrs
	to Kimi (Evia)	2615drs;	8 hrs
	to Skiathos	805drs;	3 hrs
	to Skopelos	1010drs;	4½ hrs
	to Skyros	2265drs;	11 hrs
	to Trikeri (M)	435drs;	1½ hrs

Flying Dolphin timetable

Day	**Departure time**	**Ports/Islands of Call**
Daily	0730hrs	Skiathos, Glossa (Skopelos), Skopelos, Alonissos.
	1330hrs (except Friday)	Skiathos, Glossa (Skopelos), Skopelos, Alonissos.
	1800hrs (except Thursday & Sunday)	Skiathos, Skopelos, Alonissos.
	1900hrs (except Sunday)	Skiathos, Skopelos, Alonissos.
Wednesday, Saturday	1300hrs	Skiathos, Glossa (Skopelos), Skopelos, Alonissos, Moudania(M).
Thursday, Sunday	0730hrs	Skiathos, Glossa (Skopelos), Skopelos, Alonissos, Skyros.
Friday	1300hrs	Skiathos, Glossa (Skopelos), Skopelos, Alonissos.

One-way fares: Volos				
	to Alonissos	2370drs;	duration	2⅔hrs
	to Glossa (Skopelos)	1955drs;		1⅔hrs
	to Moudania (M)	3480drs;		5¼hrs
	to Skiathos	1675drs;		1⅓hrs
	to Skopelos	2090drs;		2¼hrs
	to Skyros			4⅓hrs

Trains & timetable

Athens:	depart		arrive	
		0700hrs		1428hrs
		0800hrs		1458hrs
		1100hrs		1737hrs
		1425hrs		2101hrs
		1530hrs		2245hrs
		2110hrs		0530hrs*
		2310hrs		0653hrs*

Return journey:

	depart		arrive	
		0609hrs		1320hrs
		0916hrs		1600hrs
		1200hrs		1802hrs
		1445hrs		2303hrs
		1627hrs		2306hrs
		2300hrs		0645hrs*

* next day
One-way fares: B Class 900drs, A Class 1350drs.

Average duration: 6½ - 8½ hrs - what an average and that depends on the train not breaking down!

One of Hydra's characters often to be found sleeping off the night before in a port alleyway.

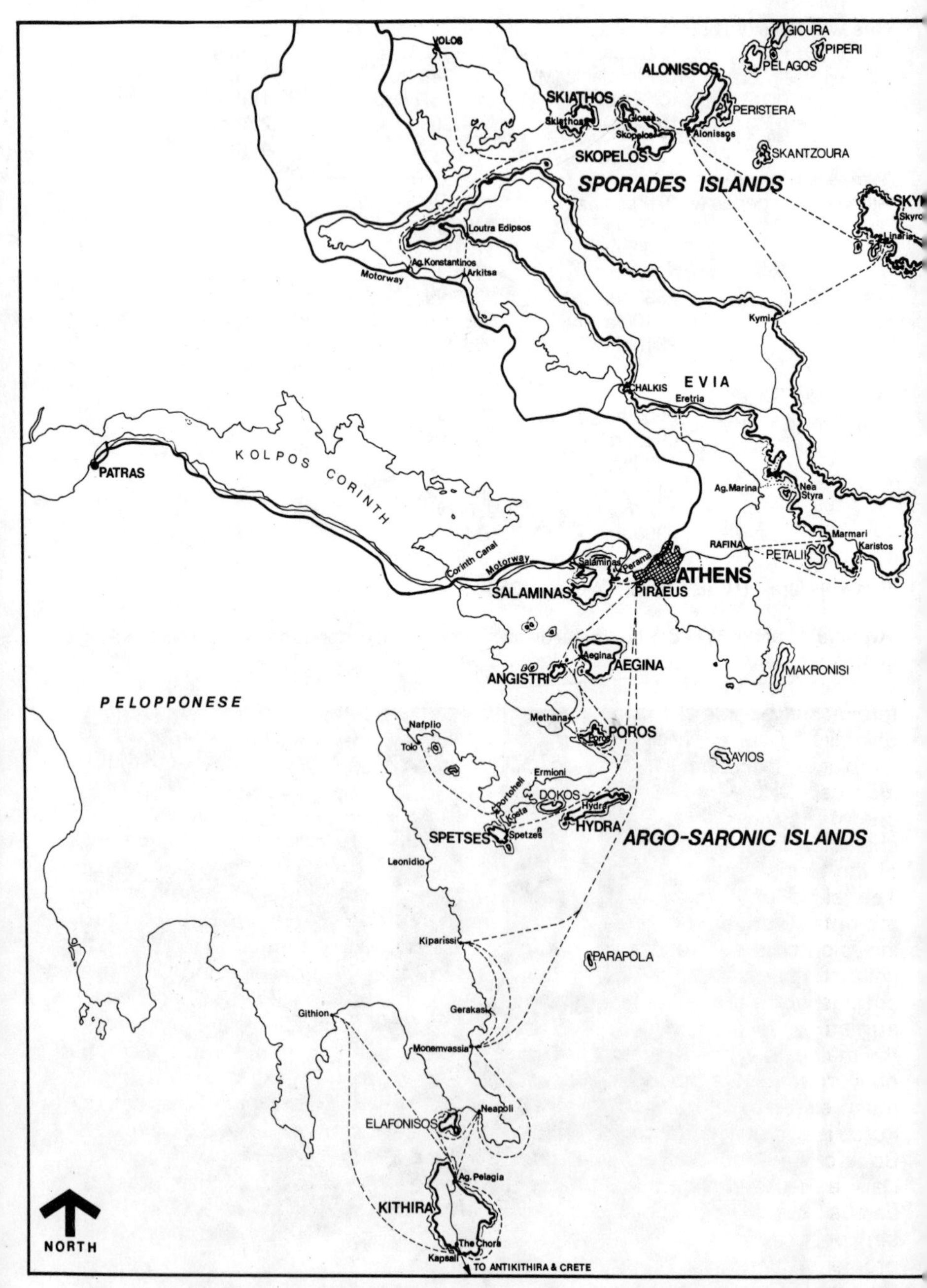

Illustration 13 Mainland islands

PART THREE

11 Introduction to the 'Mainland' Islands of the Argo-Saronic (Saronic or Argolid Gulf) & the Sporades (Aegean)

'Whoever has once seen Greece will carry forever in his heart the remembrance of a miracle of light. No blinding glare, no blazing colours, but an all-pervading, luminous brightness which bathes the foreground in a delicate glow, yet makes the furthest distances clearly visible.' Walter F Otto.

The islands included in the two clusters grouped under the title of 'Mainland' are amongst the most popular, with both Greeks and overseas tourists. Perhaps that might say it all! There are two exceptions to this wholesale onslaught, one in each group – Kithira in the Argo-Saronic and Skyros of the Sporades.

Kithira, once administratively linked to the Ionian islands, is only connected by sea with the other Saronic islands and the Peloponnese. Its far-flung position has ensured that the island remains a pleasant, relatively isolated location, but the presence of an airfield may well, eventually, alter that. Similarly Skyros, being rather further from the other Sporades islands and separated from the mainland by the bulk of Evia island, has managed to retain the old world attractions of yester-year.

The islands that go to make up the Argo-Saronic are very widely spaced out, in and around the Saronic Gulf and the Peloponnese coastline. Few, if any guides describe the island of Salaminas, and I'm not surprised. I had always assumed that Kasos, at the southern end of the Dodecanese chain, would forever hold pride of place as the most unlovely Greek island. Rest assured Salaminas (which Rosemary nicknamed Salmonella!) might cause an upset in the placings. It is best to consider Salaminas as a suburb of Piraeus and leave it at that. Of the traditionally accepted islands included in the chain, Aegina is one of the most attractive, retaining those quintessential Greek qualities and character. Possibly this is because the port and main town are not the centre of the tourist thrust, an 'honour' reserved for Ag Marina, on the east coast. The island of Angistri, just off the coast of Aegina, possess many of the attributes sought by those casting about for the Greece of old. But the inclusion of the island in some package tour brochures must destroy these characteristics, if it has not already done so, despite which winnowing and cottage looms are still to be observed. The town and port of Poros is extremely attractively located, overlooking the pretty sound separating the island from the mainland. The waterfront tavernas of the Poros waterfront are, for some obscure reason, a magnetic attraction for day-tripping Greeks but there is not much easily accessible coastline to absorb the large numbers of visitors. If Poros is somewhat cramped, Hydra could probably be accepted in the Guinness Book of Records as the single most crowded island location in the Aegean. Daily a plethora of hydrofoils, ferry-boats, trip boats and cruise ships decant an absolute glut of people on the quayside of this stunningly attractive, 'film-set' port, only to scoop them up again as the night hours approach. The problem is that there simply is nowhere for them all to go once they have filled the town. That is, apart from the very steep mountains that tower behind the port or the short east and west tracks branching out along the coast. It is also necessary to report that there is at least one A, B and C menu in Japanese (Yes, Japanese), added to which Hydra is only the third location, in some ten years and a hundred islands, where an attempt has consciously been made to overcharge us. Spetses is a very popular tourist location and rightly so. The port town is interesting, the people friendly and the countryside extremely attractive, more especially the forests of pine trees edging the track that circumscribes the island. This mainly unsurfaced route dips down, here and there, to most attractive beach locations. One Greek guide book states '... that it is hard to separate fact from fiction...' Yes, well this could not be more true of Hydra and Spetses as both islands claim to have won, almost single-handed, the naval battles of the Greek War of Independence.

Evia is fully described in its own chapter as it is too simplistic to assert that the island is only a number of ferry-boat ports, gathered together by a huge length of land! It could be said that Evia's very proximity to the mainland makes it nothing more than an adjunct to Central Greece. Certainly most of the holiday seaside locations are particularly and peculiarly Greek, added to which they are, in the main, widely separated from each other. Only the stretch of coastline between Chalkis, the capital, and Amarinthos, to the east, is being developed for package tourism. Any independent traveller, relying on public transport, faces a long task getting from one location to another. The surest method of covering the greatest distance on the island is by utilising the Athens bus, which thunders across to Kimi Port for travellers intending to go to Skyros island.

Some islanders still refer to the Sporades as The Balkans, fascinatingly a name used over the centuries. In order to achieve the greatest satisfaction, I can only advise travellers to the Sporades to visit the islands in the order of Skiathos, Skopelos, Alonissos and lastly Skyros. Skiathos, the most touristic of the group, has, depending on your viewpoint, the 'advantage' of an airport. It is occasionally difficult to assess why this or that island appears to have achieved the pinnacle of tourist desirability. Skiathos must rate as one of the imponderables. The port and main town, which on first impression appears attractive, is really rather scrubbly and the overall countryside may be pretty but is not outstanding. Skopelos, administratively the senior island, smarts under the fact that Skiathos is 'top dog' of the Sporades tourist statistics. But why they should worry, I don't know. Skopelos port and town has a stunning Chora, the countryside and scattered beaches are mainly very pretty and there is the added attraction of Glossa, the northern port and old town. Meanwhile the citizens of Alonissos dream of just a few crumbs, from any tourist table! An earthquake destroyed much of the old town, high upon the hill, and resulted in a 'New Town' ambience to the hastily erected port. This and the two adjacent bay settlements make up the sole development of any size, joined together by the only tarmacadam swathe of road on the island. Added to this, despite the serenity of countryside, none of the numerous beaches are anything but pebbly.

At the end of this chapter there is an alphabetical list of the islands included in the book, their major town and port(s), as well as a quick reference resumé of ferry-boat and hydrofoil connections.

The island chapters follow a format which has been devised and developed, over the years, to make the layout as simple to follow as is possible, without losing the informative nature of the text. Each island is treated in a similar manner, allowing the traveller easy identification of his (or her) immediate requirements. The text is faced by the relevant port and town maps, with descriptions tied into the various island routes.

Symbols, Keys & Definitions

Below are some notes in respect of the few initials and symbols used in the text, as well as an explanation of the possibly idiosyncratic nouns, adjectives and phrases that are to be found scattered throughout the book.

Where and when inserted, a star system of rating indicates my judgement of an island, and possibly its accommodation and restaurant standards, by the inclusion of one to five stars. One star signifies bad, two basic, three good, four very good and five excellent. I must admit the ratings are carried out on whimsical grounds and are based purely on personal observation. For instance, where a place, establishment or island receives a detailed 'critique' I may consider that sufficient unto the day... The absence of a star, or any mention at all, has no detrimental significance and might, for instance, indicate that I did not personally inspect this or that establishment.

Keys The key *Tmr*, in conjunction with grid references, is used as a map reference to aid easy identification of this or that location on port and town plans. Other keys used in the text include *Sbo* – 'Sea behind one'; *Fsw* – 'Facing seawards'; *Fbqbo* – 'Ferry-boat quay behind one' and *OTT* – 'Over The Top'.

GROC's definitions, 'proper' adjectives & nouns: These may require some elucidation, as most do not appear in 'official' works of reference.

Backshore: the furthest strip of beach from the sea's edge. The marginal rim edging the shore from the surrounds. *See* **Scrubbly**

Benzina: a small fishing boat.

Chatty: with pretention to grandeur or sophistication.

Dead: an establishment that appears to be 'terminally' closed, and is not about to open for business.

Donkey-droppings: as in 'two donkey-droppings', indicates a very small, 'one-eyed' hamlet. *See* **One-eyed.**

Doo-hickey: an Irish based colloquialism suggesting an extreme lack of sophistication and or rather 'daffy' (despite contrary indications in the authoritative and excellent *Partridges Dictionary of Slang!*).

Downtown: a rundown/derelict area of a settlement – the wrong side of the 'railway tracks'.

Ethnic: very unsophisticated, Greek indigenous and, as a rule, applied to hotels and pensions. *See* **Provincial**.

Gongoozle: borrowed from canal boat terminology, and is the state of very idly and leisurely, but inquisitively, staring at others who are involved in some busy activity.

Greasy spoon: a dirty, unwholesome cafe-bar, restaurant or taverna.

Great unwashed: the less attractive, modern day mutation of the 1960s hippy. They are usually Western European, inactive loafers and layabouts 'by choice', or unemployed drop-outs. Once having located a desirable location, often a splendid beach, they camp under plastic and in shabby tents, thus ensuring the spot is despoiled for others. The 'men of the tribe' tend to trail a mangy dog on a piece of string. The women, more often than not, with a grubby child or two in train, pester cafe-bar clients to purchase items of jewellery.

Note the above genre appears to be incurably penniless (but then who isn't?).

Grecocilious: necessary to describe those Greeks, usually tour office owners, who are making a lot of money from the tourists but are disdainful of the 'hand that feeds them'. They appear to consider holiday-makers as being some form of small intellect, low-browed, tree clambering and inferior relation to the Greek homo-

sapiens. They usually can converse passably in two or three foreign languages (when it suits them) and display an air of weary sophistication.
Hillbilly: another adjective or noun, similar to 'ethnic', often applied to describe countryside or a settlement, as in 'backwoods'.
Hippy: those who live outside the predictable, boring (!) mainstream of life and are frequently genuine, if sometimes impecunious travellers. The category may include students or young professionals taking a sabbatical and who are often 'negligent' of their sartorial appearance.
Icons: naturally, a religious painting of a holy person or personages, usually executed on a board. During the Middle Ages the Mediterranean would appear to have been almost awash with unmanned rowing boats and caiques mysteriously ferrying icons hither and thither.
Independents: vacationers who make their own travel and accommodation arrangements, spurning the siren calls of structured tourism, preferring to step off the package holiday carousel and make their own way.
Krifo Scholio: illegal, undercover schools operated during the Turkish occupation, generally run by the inmates of religious orders to educate Greek children in the intricacies of the Orthodox religion and the traditional ways of life.
Mr Big: a local trader or pension owner, an aspiring tycoon, a small fish trying to be a big one in a 'smaller pool'. Sometimes flashy with shady overtones, his lack of sophistication is apparent by his not being Grecocilious!
Noddies or nodders: the palpable evidence of untreated sewage discharged into the sea.
One-eyed: small. *See* **Donkey-droppings.**
Poom: a descriptive noun 'borrowed' after sighting on Crete, some years ago, a crudely written sign advertising accommodation that simply stated POOMS! This particular place was basic with low-raftered ceilings, earth-floors and windowless rooms, simply equipped with a pair of truckle beds and rickety oilcloth covered washstand – very reminiscent of typical Cycladean cubicles of the 1950/60s period.
Provincial: usually applied to accommodation and is an improvement on **Ethnic**. Not meant to indicate, say, dirty but should conjure up images of faded, rather gloomy establishments with a mausoleum atmosphere; high ceilinged Victorian rooms with worn, brown linoleum; dusty, tired aspidistras as well as bathrooms and plumbing of unbelievable antiquity.
Richter scale: borrowed from earthquake seismology and employed to indicate the (appalling) state of toilets, on an 'eye-watering' scale.
Rustic: unsophisticated, unrefined.
Schlepper: vigorous touting for customers by restaurant staff. It is said of a good schlepper, in a market, that he can 'retrieve' a passer-by from up to thirty or forty metres beyond the stall.
Scrubbly: usually applied to a beach or countryside and indicating a rather messy, shabby area.
Squatty: A Turkish or French style ablution arrangement. None of the old, familiar lavatory bowl and seat. Oh no, just two moulded footprints edging a dirty looking hole, set in a porcelain surround. Apart from the unaccustomed nature of the exercise, the Lord simply did not give us enough limbs to keep ones shirt up and control wayward trousers that constantly attempt to flap down on to the floor, which is awash with goodness knows what! All this has to be enacted whilst gripping the toilet roll in one hand and wiping one's 'botty' with the other hand. Impossible! Incidentally the ladies should perhaps substitute blouse for shirt and skirt for trousers, but then it is easier (I am told) to tuck a skirt into one's waistband!

Way-station: mainly used to refer to an office or terminus, stuck out in the sticks and cloaked with an abandoned, unwanted air.

Mainland islands described include:-

Island name(s)	Capital	Ports (at which inter-island ferry-boats & Flying Dolphins dock)	Ferry-boat/Flying Dolphin connections (FB=ferry-boat; FD=Flying Dolphin; EB=excursion boat; M=Mainland).
Aegina (Egina) Argo-Saronic	Aegina	Aegina	**FB:** Piraeus(M);Methana(M),Poros, Hydra,Ermioni(M),Spetses,Kithira; Angistri. **FD:** Piraeus(M);Zea Port(Piraeus), Methana(M),Poros,Hydra,Ermioni(M), Spetses,Portoheli(M).
		Souvala	**FB:** Piraeus(M).
Alonissos (Alonnissos, Alonnisos) Sporades	Patitiri Port	Patitiri Port	**FB:** Skopelos,Glossa(Skopelos), Skiathos,Ag Konstantinos(M);Trikeri(M), Volos(M);Kymi,Port(Evia). **FD:** Skopelos,Glossa(Skopelos), Skiathos,Skyros,Ag Konstantinos(M); Volos(M);Moundania(M).
Angistri (Agistri, Aghistri) Argo-Saronic	Skala Angistri	Skala Angistri	**FB:** Aegina,Hydra,Piraeus(M).
Evia (Evvia, Evoia, Euboea, Eyboia) Mainland island	Chalkis (Chalki, Chalkida, Khalkis, Halkida),	Paralia Kymi (Kimi)	**FB:** Linaria(Skyros),Alonissos,Skopelos, Ag Estratios,Mirina(Limnos),Kavala(M).
		Agiokampos	**FB:** Glypha(M).
		Loutra Edipsos	**FB:** Arkitsa(M).
		Eretria	**FB:** Skala Oropou(M).
		Panaghia (Almyropotamos)	**FB:** Ag Marina(M).
		Nea Styra	**FB:** Ag Marina(M).
		Marmari	**FB:** Rafina(M).
		Karistos	**FB:** Rafina(M).
Hydra (Idra, Idhra, Ydra) Argo-Saronic	Hydra	Hydra	**FB:** Spetses,Ermioni(M),Poros, Methana(M),Aegina,Piraeus(M). **FD:** Ermioni(M),Spetses,Portoheli(M), Leonidio(M),Kiparissi(M),Gerakas(M), Monemvassia(M),Neapoli(M),Kithira, Poros,Methana(M),Aegina,Zea Port(Piraeus).
Kithira (Kythira, Kythera, Cythera) Argo-Saronic	The Chora (Kithira Town)	Ag Pelagia	**FB:** Githion(M),Kapsali(Kithira),Antikithira, Kastelli(Crete),Neapoli(M), Monemvassia(M),Piraeus(M). **FD:** Neapoli(M),Monemvassia(M), Gerakas(M),Kiparissi(M),Leonidio(M), Spetses,Portoheli(M),Zea Port(Piraeus).
		Kapsali Port	**FB:** Antikithira,Kastelli(Crete), Ag Pelagia(Kithira).
Poros Argo-Saronic	Poros (Spheria, Sferia)	Poros	**FB:** Methana(M),Aegina,Hydra,Spetses, Piraeus(M).

			FD: Methana(M),Hydra,Ermioni(M), Portoheli(M),Spetses,Leonidio(M), Kiparissi(M),Gerakas(M), Monemvassia(M),Neapoli(M),Kithira, Zea Port(Piraeus).
Salaminas (Salamina, Salalaminos, Salamis) Argo-Saronic	Salamina	Selina	**FB:** Piraeus(M-passengers only)
		Paloukia	**FB:** Perama(M).
Skiathos Sporades	Skiathos	Skiathos	**FB:** Glossa(Loutraki Port,Skopelos), Skopelos,Alonissos,Skyros,Volos(M); Ag Konstantinos(M);Piraeus(M); Thessaloniki(M). **FD:** Glossa(Loutraki Port,Skopelos), Skopelos,Alonissos,Skyros, Ag Konstantinos(M);Volos(M); Moundania(M).
Skopelos (Scopelos) Sporades	Skopelos	Skopelos	**FB:** Glossa(Loutraki Port,Skopelos), Skiathos,Alonissos,Skyros,Volos(M); Ag Konstantinos(M);Piraeus(M); Thessaloniki(M). **FD:** Glossa(Loutraki Port,Skopelos), Skiathos,Alonissos,Skyros, Ag Konstantinos(M);Volos(M); Moundania(M).
		Loutraki Port	As for Skopelos.
Skyros (Skiros) Sporades	Skyros Town (The Chora)	Linaria	**FB:** Kymi Port(Evia). **FD:** Alonissos,Skopelos,Glossa (Loutraki Port,Skopelos), Skiathos,Volos(M).
Spetses (Spetsai, Spetsae) Argo-Saronic	Spetses	Spetses	**FB:** Ermioni(M),Hydra,Poros,Methana(M), Aegina,Piraeus(M);Kotsa(M). **FD:** Portoheli(M),Ermioni(M),Hydra, Poros,Methana(M),Aegina,Zea Port (Piraeus);Leonidio(M),Kiparissi(M), Gerakas(M),Monemvassia(M), Neapoli(M),Kithira.

Feeding the 5000! No an informal fish sale, Paralia Kymi, Evia.

12 SPETSES (Spetsai, Spetsae, ΣΠΕΤΣΕΣ) ***
Argo-Saronic Islands

FIRST IMPRESSIONS
Monipos (horse drawn carriages); beautiful flowers & gardens; pine forests; British tourists & 'Full English breakfasts'; rocky inlets & clear seas; baroque buildings; mosquitoes & some rubbish

SPECIALITIES
Amygdalota – a cone shaped, almond cake covered in sugar & flavoured with rosewater; Ergolavos – a macaroon like almond cake.

RELIGIOUS HOLIDAYS & FESTIVALS
include: Epiphany, 6th January – Tis Vaftisios, Ag. Nikolaos, celebrating Christ's baptism; 3rd February – Service for the Three Spetsiot Martyrs at the church alongside the Monastery of Ag. Nikolaos, The Old Harbour, Spetses Town; 23rd April – Festival of Ag. Georgios, Zogeria; Friday after Easter – Festival of Zoodochos Pighis, Monastery of Elona; 1st July – Festival, Ag. Anargyri Church; 17th July – Festival, Ag. Marina Church; 20th July – Profitis Elias Church; 26th July – Ag. Paraskevi Church; 15th August – Koimisis tis Theotokou (The Assumption of the Virgin Mary), Panaghia Church, Kastelli, Spetses Town; weekend closest to 8th September – Celebration of The Battle of the Straits of Spetses (1822), Spetses Town; 8th September – Birth of the Virgin Mary, Panaghia Armata Church, Lighthouse headland, Old Harbour, Spetses Town; 1st November – Festival of the Penniless Saints Cosmas & Damian, Ag. Anargyri Church; 6th December – Service for sailors & fishermen, Monastery Ag. Nikolaos.

VITAL STATISTICS
Tel prefix 0298. Spetses, an oval island, has an area of some 22sq km and is about 10km from side to side and 7km from top to bottom. The population is circa 3,500.

HISTORY
Not a great star performer in the annals of early Greek history. Albanian refugees arrived during the 16/17th centuries, as did Peloponnese Greeks in the 18th century. It was from their numbers that some of the prominent Spetses families originated. Support by the islanders for the Russians during their war with the Ottoman Empire (1768-1774) resulted in the Turks exacting retribution, killing many inhabitants and setting fire to Kastelli – the original settlement above the port.

The home-grown boat and ship-building industry, which established itself in the 17th century, expanded hand-in-hand with the increasing prosperity of the merchants. In company with other Aegean island opportunists, the running of the British blockade, during the Napoleonic Wars, resulted in ever increasing wealth and numbers of ships. The enlarged fleet worried the Turks. Ironically a female ship's captain, one Lascarina Bouboulina, was ordered to Constantinople to explain away the size of her own flotilla. It is postulated that the tax revenues culled from the shipowners dissuaded the Turks from pursuing the matter, which must stand as one of the great historical military gaffes of all time. At the outset of the War of Independence (1821), the Spetsiots were able to put some fifty four fighting ships, as well as other support craft, into the field (as it were) against the Turks.

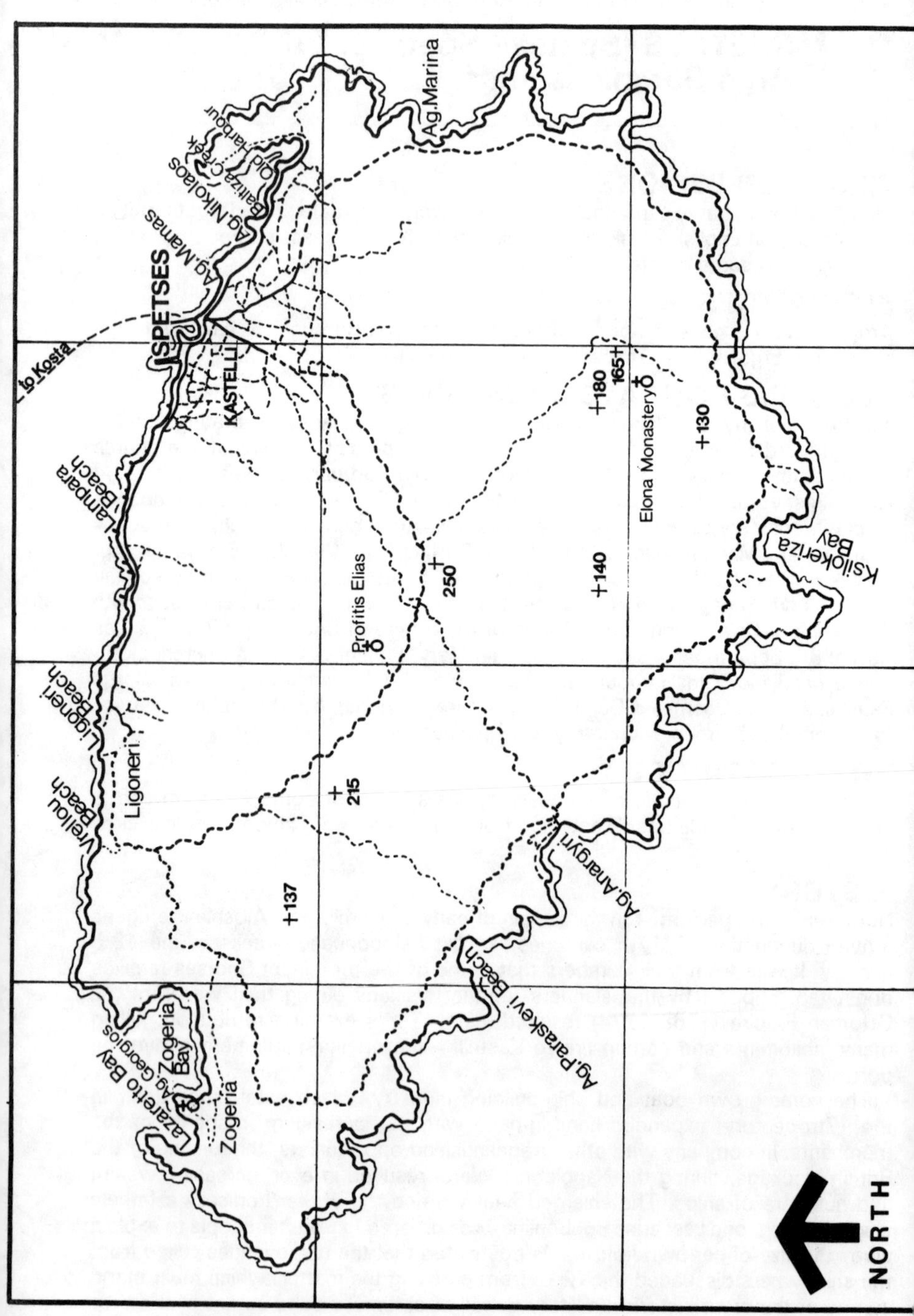

Illustration 14 Spetses island

The overall leader was Andreas Miaoulis, a native of Hydra. He commanded the combined fighting fleets of Hydra, Spetses and Psara (yes, tiny Psara, north of Chios in the North-Eastern Aegean). The aforementioned lady, Bouboulina, was one of the foremost captains – there's gratitude for you! Rumour has it that on one occasion the islanders placed their red caps on the spikes of a local plant to convince a fleet of Turkish ships that there was a large army present. Oh yes!

History is not a kindly bedfellow and, after the glories of the War of Independence, the island's fortunes declined with the rise in the commercial fortunes of Syros, and then Piraeus.

Strangely enough Spetses is no newcomer to tourism for the island became fashionable and enjoyed a resurgence of prosperity between the First and Second World Wars. There was a casino as well as the massive *Posidonion Hotel*, built by the island's great benefactor, Sotirios Anargyros. The crews of British Navy warships often visited the island during those halycon days.

GENERAL

A spacious, sunny, old and new world port/town presages well for the visitor, who will not be let down by these auguries. But, there is a big but and a big but at that – visitors must be anglophiles, for it is on the beaches and streets, as well as in the tavernas and cocktail bars, that the 'Brits' have repulsed the Continental hordes. For instance the constant ebb and flow of package holiday-makers has resulted in the eateries being rather mediocre, expensive and dominated by the English breakfast. Another manifestation is the wholesale conversion of most of the traditional kafeneions into cocktail bars throbbing to a disco beat.

The pleasant main town and port, Dapia, has the added attraction of the nearby and equally engaging Old Harbour. The small town beach is supplemented by a number of strips of acceptable foreshore, beside the very long seafront. It has to be said that these beaches become rather crowded. If it were not for the heat and constant coming and going of the fast clip-clopping *Monipos*, a blindfolded sunbather would be hard-pressed to decide whether he was on the sands of Blackpool or Southend, but there you go.....!

The independent traveller must almost exclusively rely on the efficient tourist offices for accommodation, of which the dominent 'Mr Big' is **Takis Travel** (*See* **The Accommodation**).

The road to either side of Dapia, quite surprisingly, runs out on to a sometimes extremely poor and rutted surface which circles the island some height above sea-level. Apart from the rather bare slopes of the south-east, the island is extensively forested and the journey affords wonderful glimpses of the beautiful coastline. Here and there a track branches off or the main 'highway' dips down to sea-level to this or that bay or cove. The beaches will be a disappointment to sand lovers but quite a few are made up of acceptable, fine shingle. The sea is almost entirely clear, clean and inviting.

Despite the island being water-short, the problem is efficiently handled with fresh water ferried in every day. Perhaps the Sporades islands could follow suit?

Cars are banned and the *Monipo* reigns, some thirty of them being licensed for hire. There is only one taxi but the 'necessary' vans and trucks, added to the clattering hooves and clanging bells of the *Monipos* and the countless scooters, manage to create a fairly constant cacophony of sound. As some observer put it 'As cars are not allowed, Spetses only has three problems – scooters, water & rubbish.' To this short list I could add a few more, including mosquitoes.

One thing is certain, Spetses should not be left off the schedule.

SPETSES (Dapia): capital town & main port (Illustration 15). Not a wildly attractive seafront and very spread out, especially if the Old Harbour is taken into the orbit of the town. However, there is no doubt that some of the imposing buildings are impressive, especially the *Hotel Posidonion*. This was built, incorporating the older *Goudis House*, by Sotirios Anargyrios. This remarkable philanthropist was born on Spetses in 1849 but emigrated, initially to London where he traded in sponges. He then turned to the making of cigarettes and finished up in America, where he eventually set up his own business. On the back of his resultant fortune he married, returned to Spetses and invested in the island, building roads, reservoirs and aqueducts. After the construction of the hotel, in 1914, he conceived the idea of founding an English style Public School (would you believe), complete with a fives court. Completed in 1927, the first headmaster of the *Anargyrios & Korgialenios School* was an Englishman. Anargyrios died a year later, not beloved by his fellow Spetsiots because he had felt it necessary to purchase much of the island in order to re-afforest the same. Probably an altruistic man but misjudged. One of several English teachers at the School who achieved literary fame was John Fowles, he of *The French Lieutenant's Woman* and *The Magus*. This latter novel had a Greek island as a setting for the story.

Many of the older businesses (some of which have changed 'complexion' in the meantime) still have colourful ceramic tiles on which are lettered the original name of the firm. Parts of the old streets are still made of pebble mosaics.

ARRIVAL BY FERRY & FLYING DOLPHIN

Spetses is well connected with Piraeus by both several hydrofoil services and a daily ferry-boat sailing, as well as being linked with Kosta on the Peloponnese mainland. Both the Piraeus based hydrofoils and the ferry-boat call in at other Argo-Saronic islands. For reasons detailed under **The Accommodation** owners of ***Rooms*** generally do not meet ferry-boat arrivals.

THE ACCOMMODATION & EATING OUT

The Accommodation There are a number of hotels close by the waterfront, some of which rather mar the skyline. The Pensions and ***Rooms*** are almost entirely under the control of one or two travel agents offices, the market leader being **Takis Travel** (*Tmr* 3B2/3). There are one or two 'operators' outside the 'spider's web' but this monopoly does not appear to make **Takis** rooms more expensive than the few free-booters.

Takis Travel (& Tourist Office) (*Tmr* 3B2/3).
Directions: From the bottom of the Ferry-boat/Flying Dolphin Quay (*Tmr* 1B2) turn left (*Sbo*) and the office, which stretches all the way through to the street behind, is on the right, just beyond the water pumping station (*Tmr* 2B2).

As the office acts for one or two large package tour companies, including *Thompson*, the office is always pretty busy. The accommodation desk is to the right and a young man, Babbis, handles the allocation but Mama grabs the money! Babbis 'ferries' prospects to this or that house on his scooter. A well-found, en suite double room, with a hot water shower, costs 1700drs in the mid-season.

From the bottom of the Ferry-boat Quay (*Tmr* 1B2), and within fairly easy walking distance, hotels that look out over the waterfront Esplanade and the Harbour include:-

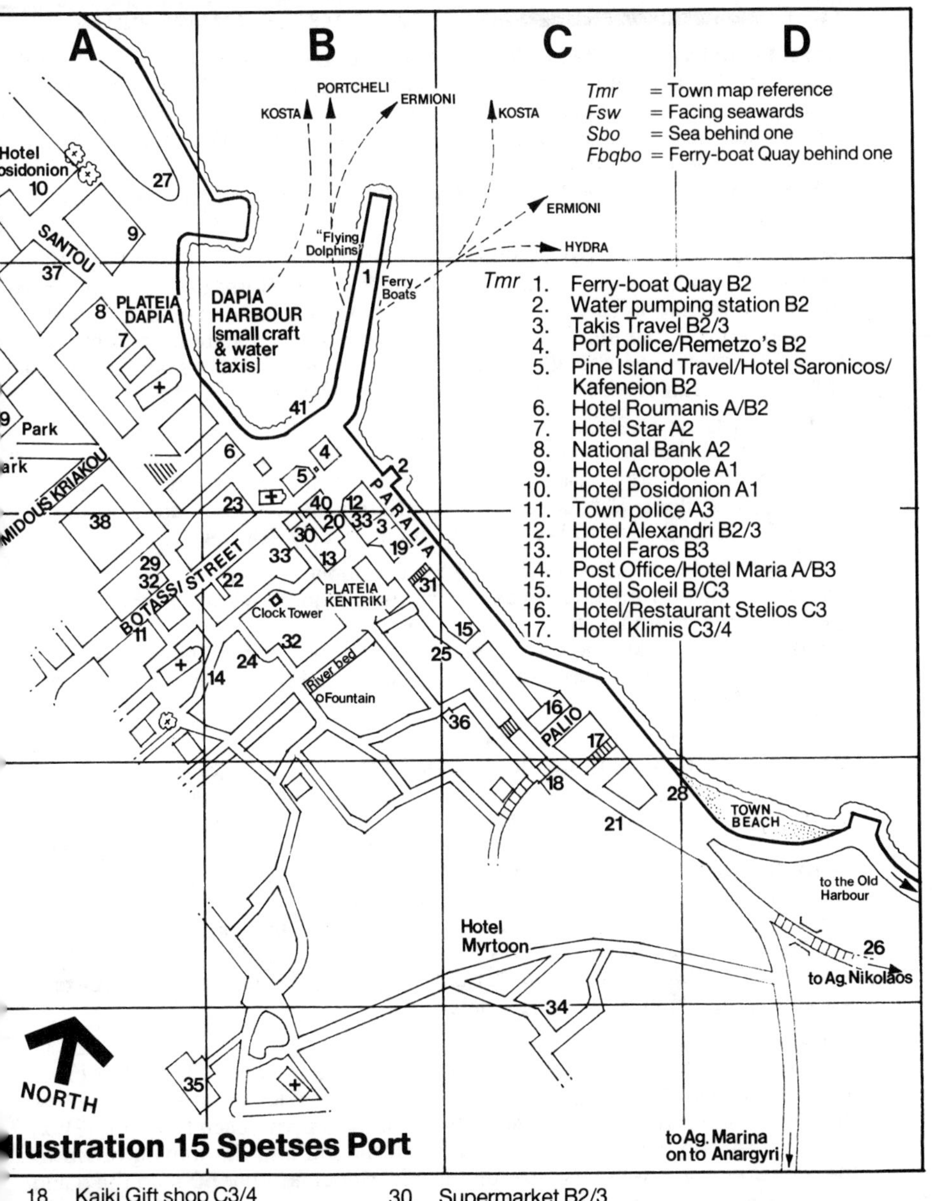

llustration 15 Spetses Port

18. Kaiki Gift shop C3/4
19. Kafeneion B/C3
20. Chicken & Chips snackbar B2/3
21. Taverna Ta Tzakia C4
22. Bakery/Patisserie A/B3
23. Ionian & Popular Bank A/B2/3
24. Moto Service B3
25. Kostas Scooter Hire B/C3
26. Motor Bikes for Rent D4
27. 'West' Bus terminus A1
28. 'East' Bus terminus C/D4
29. Cinema A3
30. Supermarket B2/3
31. Fish Market B/C3
32. Laundries (2)
33. Chemists (2)
34. Clinic C4/5
35. Museum/Mexis Mansion A/B5
36. Doctor's Clinic B/C3
37. OTE A1/2
38. Anargyros Mansion A2/3
39. Bouboulina Mansion A2
40. Bardakos Tours B2/3
41. Water Taxis *et al* B2

Hotel Saronicos (*Tmr* 5B2) (Class D) Plateia Dapia Tel 72646
Directions: To the right (*Sbo*), as if proceeding around Dapia Harbour, and in a block on the left, beyond the office of the Port police (*Tmr* 4B2). In the ground floor is Pine Island Travel, the hydrofoil ticket office, and, at the far end, a kafeneion well frequented by locals.

Previously the *Kardasi*, this is an older, two storey building and a typical D Class hotel.

Hotel Roumanis (*Tmr* 6A/B2) (Class B) Plateia Dapia Tel 72244
Directions: Continue on round the Harbour from the *Hotel Saronicos*, leaving the best periptero in town on the left. The next building contains the hotel.

A modernish, four storey building. All rooms have en suite bathrooms (and at these rates they should) with a single costing 2040drs and a double 3000drs. Breakfast may well be obligatory, in busy times, and costs 250drs.

Hotel Star (*Tmr* 7A2)(Class C) Plateia Dapia Tel 72214
Directions: Further on round the Harbour, in a clockwise direction.

Another four storey building with, in this case, the National Bank of Greece in the ground floor. Similar to the *Hotel Roumanis* but rates are 2000drs & 3200drs respectively and breakfast costs a princely 400drs.

Hotel Acropole (*Tmr* 9A1) (Class D) Plateia Dapia Tel 72219
Directions: Still on the Esplanade, which rises high above the Harbour at the back and falls down again on the far side.

Rather seedy looking and may well be 'dead' out of the height of season. Double rooms only, sharing bathrooms, start at 1800drs, rising to 2200drs (1st April-30th Sept).

Hotel Posidonion (*Tmr* 10A1) (Class A) Tel 72208
Directions: Prominent, to the right of the Ferry-boat Quay (*Sbo*).

Faded, very faded elegance. The rear of the building reveals cracked wood-work, cracked paintwork and cracked water tanks. Single rooms sharing the bathroom start at 1550drs and en suite 2550drs (1st April-14th May), rising to 1690drs and 2800drs (15th May-30th June & 16th-30th Sept) and 1900drs and 3300drs (1st July-15th Sept). Similarly double rooms start at 2535drs and 3500drs, increasing to 2800drs and 3830drs and on to 3380drs and 4650drs. Breakfast costs 400drs and dinner 1250drs, rising respectively to 480drs and 1280drs between 1st July and 15th September. *See* **Spetses Town Introduction** for historical detail.

Pension Anna Tel 72631
Directions: From the bottom of the Ferry-boat Quay (*Tmr* 1B2) turn left (*Sbo*) along the Esplanade and turn right beyond the Port police (*Tmr* 4B2) up Odhos Botassi, the nearest thing to a High St. Leave the Town police (*Tmr* 11A3) on the left. Proceed past the *Taverna Ezine* on the left and the turning down to the *Villa Christiana Xenonas*, also on the left. About another 50m up the rising street, where it narrows, is an alleyway to the left, as is the Pension.

A large house and courtyard set in a pleasant garden planted with lemon trees. Provincial, with en suite double rooms costing 1500drs in mid-season. The Greek Mama speaks no English but her son does, if he is present. Remains well booked so best to telephone ahead.

Closer to hand is the:-

Hotel Alexandri (*Tmr* 12B2/3) (Class E) Tel 73073
Directions: Borders the Square on which the Monipos park and in front of which are the town's petrol pumps.

Single rooms en suite start at 1050drs, doubles sharing the bathroom 1400drs and en suite 1500drs. These charges rise respectively to 1300drs, 1600drs and 1800drs (15th June-14th Sept).

Hotel Faros (*Tmr* 13B3) (Class C) Plateia Kentriki Tel 72613
Directions: Continue on round to the left (*Sbo*) from the *Hotel Alexandri*, on the street parallel to the Esplanade. Turn right on to the irregular shaped, large square. The hotel is on the right. Modern. All rooms have en suite bathrooms with singles costing 2000drs and a double 2700drs.

From the *Hotel Faros* wind up the lane that skirts the prominent clock tower, cross over the first lateral street and fork left at the Church. The Post Office (*Tmr* 14A/B3) is on the left, above which is the:-
Hotel Anna Maria (Class E) Tel 73035
Directions: As above.
Only double rooms, with en suite bathrooms, costing 2100drs, which rate rises to 2300drs (1st June-30th Sept).

Beyond Takis Travel (*Tmr* 3B2/3), continuing along the Esplanade to the left of the bottom of the Ferry-boat Quay (*Tmr* 1B2), passes by the:-
Hotel Soleil (*Tmr* 15B/C3) (Class C) Tel 72488
Directions: As above.
A smart, five storey hotel with a *Roof Top Cocktail Bar*. Oh goody!
A single room costs 2950drs and a double 3690drs, both en suite (1st April-30th Sept). In October the rates drop to 2215drs and 2655drs.

and the:-

Hotel Stelios (& Restaurant) (*Tmr* 16C3) (Class D) Tel 72364
Directions: As above.
Only double rooms which cost 1840drs, with or without an en suite bathroom.
Hotel Klimis (*Tmr* 17C3/4) (Class D) Tel 73777
Directions: Further on past the *Hotel Soleil*.
All rooms have en suite bathrooms with single rooms costing 1715drs and doubles 2100drs, which rates increase to 2065drs and 2400drs (1st June-30th Sept).

Behind the *Hotel Klimis* (*Tmr* 17C3/4), and across the street that runs parallel to the Esplanade, is the:-
Kaiki Gift Shop (*Tmr* 18C3/4) No. 18050 Tel 73791
Directions: As above.
A noticeboard has a sign *For Rent one house and 3 self catering studios. Rooms also available. Please ask for details inside.*
The shop itself is most interesting (for details of which *See* **Places of Interest, A To Z**) but so is the accommodation. Yani Papadimos and his fair English wife Sarah have built a small terrace of self-contained studio flats for rent by the week. These are situated on the horn of headland that frames the eastern boundary of the Old Harbour. Well worth considering when two or three people wish to spend some time on Spetses.

Beyond the *Restaurant Patralis* (*See* **The Eating Out**) is a sign off to the left *Rent Flats for Summer Tel 73664 or 01 941 8492*.

The Eating Out The predominance of English package tourists has ensured a plethora of 'English Breakfast' and cocktail bar locations. So much so that there are not many traditional kafeneions left and those that have survived tend to close fairly early, leaving the scene clear for their 'flawed' counterparts.

Kafeneion
Directions: Centrally located on the edge of the Square bordering the Harbour, and at the far end (*from the seafront*) of the building in which is situated the *Hotel Saronicos* (*Tmr* 5B2).

Consistently smiley service with 2 Nes meh ghala costing 150drs.

Kafeneion (*Tmr* 19B/C3)
Directions: Beyond Takis Travel, in a wide side-street off the Esplanade, opposite the small Fish Market.

Sleazy but reasonably priced with 2 milky coffees costing 150drs and two Henninger beers 200drs.

Kafeneion Ο ΒΑΣΙΛΗΣ (O Vasilis)
Directions: Two-thirds of the way round to the Old Harbour.

Makes a welcome watering hole with pleasantly located tables and chairs looking over the sea. Two Nes meh ghala cost 140drs.

In strict contrast, next door is the:-
Restaurant Giorgos (Exedra)
Directions: As above with a wooden patio jutting out over the waters edge. Apparently also known as *Haralambos*.

I'm not sure why this establishment has at least two names but it certainly represents the unacceptable face of eating out. Apathetic and surly service. A pre-prepared Greek salad, old, inadequate bread and a bottle of beer cost 290drs.

Another establishment that readers might consider 'avoiding' is:-
Remetzo's
Directions: Situated in the ground floor of the building in which is located the Port police (*Tmr* 4B2) and facing out over Dapia Harbour.

The position is perfect for 'gongoozling', more especially watching the antics of holiday-makers availing themselves of the water taxis and excursion craft. Once a kafeneion but now purports to be a cafe-bar and is actually a late night rip-off. For instance two Nes meh ghala and one ouzo is overcharged at 390drs. To add insult to injury the service is indolent, despite which it is best to keep criticism to a low whine as the joint appears to be a hang-out for one or two of the town's more aged Mafiosa.

Although there are no souvlaki snackbars, fast food is well catered for (oh dear) with the:-
Pie Shop
Directions: To the left (*Fsw*) of Takis Travel's (*Tmr* 3B2/3) rear door.

Excellent cheese pies (65drs) and sausage rolls (70drs). Also available are tost, hamburgers as well as strawberries and cream – not all together I hasten to add!

Chicken & Chips Snackbar & Take Away (*Tmr* 20B2/3)
Directions: On the right of a narrow lane behind the *Hotel Faros*, leading off the street that runs parallel to the waterfront Esplanade. Recognisable (as long as he lives) by the caged, white cockatoo that hangs outside – that is the cage not the cockatoo! A portion of chicken costs 180drs, a kilo of chicken 660drs and french fries 55drs.

For more pies, to the west of the Town, *See* **Bread Shops A To Z**. Also in this direction, some 400m beyond the Hotel Posidon, is:-

The Yachting Club

Directions: As above.

Not a Yacht Club, more a combined 'Rent a This or That' with water sports, cocktail lounge/breakfast bar, tourist services, excursions and a hairdresser's. The rooms are exclusively let out to *'Sun Med'* and have decent bathrooms that don't smell. There is a very nicely presented first floor balcony with detachable side screens to protect clients from the wind, when necessary.

Serious eating is on offer at:-

Patralis

Directions: Another 100m or so beyond *The Yachting Club* and about 100m before *The Hotel Spetses*.

Well attended by the *cognoscenti*, and recommended to us by Yanni, the buggy driver (*See* **Monipos, A To Z**). Admittedly famed as a fish restaurant but if treating yourselves, why not here? An enormous lobster for two (4000drs each), and a large bottle of retsina (285drs), bread (30drs) and two coffees (200drs) cost 8515drs. I have to own up, it was my birthday! More reasonably priced fish dishes are available. Incidentally, softly spoken Stefanos, the bespectacled waiter, speaks good English.

More mundane, but no less praiseworthy is:-

Stelios (*Tmr* 16C3)

Directions: In the ground floor of the Hotel of the same name, with tables and chairs set to the far side, when approaching from the Ferry-boat Quay.

Good food at fair prices. A lunchtime repast of a plate of stuffed tomatoes (190drs), spaghetti (214drs), 2 beers (81drs each) and bread (35drs for two – how much is that each please?) totals 601drs. An evening meal of a plate of tzatziki (130drs), a Greek salad (200drs), two plates of stuffed tomatoes (190drs each), 2 bottles of retsina (86drs each) and bread (35drs) cost 917drs. Friendly, efficient service.

One other 'unacceptable' establishment must be the:-

Ta Tzakia (*Tmr* 21C4)

Directions: Beyond the *Klimis Hotel (and patisserie)*.

Any query is referred to the pock-marked Manager. Questionable behaviour, that occasions his presence to 'sort the matter out', includes demanding kortaki retsina – obviously available as it is on the tables of locals but denied to tourists, who are 'encouraged' to drink more expensive tipples. The service is dismissive and unpleasant, added to which food is often served cold. A meal for two of briam (103drs), giants (190drs), spinach (frozen cold, 80drs), a plate of 'Spetsiota' fish (563drs), kalamares (cold, 318drs), a bottle of retsina (91drs) and bread (16drs each) cost 1377drs.

For a treat it is worth considering the:-

Roof Garden Bakery Restaurant

Directions: On the left of the High St, immediately prior to the Bakery (*Tmr* 22A/B3).

A rather classy menu at classy prices.

The fact is that despite there being many eateries, the presence of so many package tourists has probably blunted the chef's imaginative, culinary powers (– their what?).

THE A TO Z OF USEFUL INFORMATION

BANKS

The Ionian & Popular Bank (*Tmr* 23A/B2/3). Alongside Dapla Tours. Changes Eurocheques. Opens Monday to Friday evenings between 1800-2000hrs, in addition to the normal banking hours.

The National Bank (*Tmr* 8A2). Set in the ground floor of the *Hotel Star*.

BEACHES Despite the island being blessed with a number of excellent beaches, Spetses Town is rather poorly served. The pebble Town Beach, beyond the *Hotel Klimis* (*Tmr* 17C3/4), is not really large enough for the potential numbers of summer-time clients. The streetwise locals have christened it *Balcony Beach*, supposedly due to the massed exposure by the ladies of their upper torso... Oh well.

There are two or three smidgins of beach edging the Esplanade and 'urban' development that borders the coastline from Dapia Harbour to the west. On the other hand, fairly close by are:-

Ag Marina Bay To the east of the Town and accessed either along a lovely cliff walk from the Old Harbour, which passes a defunct Nunnery and cemetery (from which beautiful views), or a *Monipos* ride via Analypsis Church. Signed *Paradise Beach*, not because of the presence of the crowded *Restaurant & Bar Paradissos*, but after the Church set on a low headland to the north of Ag Marina Bay. A large pebble cove with pedaloes and windsurfers. The sea bottom is very pebbly and a lot of people visit here in the summer months. Beyond Ag Marina Church is a quieter cove, tucked away.

Lampara Beach To the west, beyond the *Spetses Hotel* and the other side of the road from the Anargyros School. Sometimes referred to by one or two *Monipos* drivers as the best beach on the island, but it is shingly sand and not over attractive.

Ligoneri Beach Still further to the west and in a lovely setting. The area is marked by a bridge fording a summer-dry river-bed about 50m beyond which is the 100m rough track that descends through pine and tamarisk tree covered hillsides prior to running out on a very narrow, brown sand foreshore edging the cove. This beach is backed by large pebbles and the sea-bed is also pebbly. A grove of trees, in which is set down a stone bench, crowns the backshore and makes a very pleasant, shady picnic spot. Buses allow passengers to dismount and the *Monipos* come this far.

Note that 50m beyond Ligoneri, on the main road (which is now in truth a wide, very rutted track), is a small, sun-trapped cove with a pebble shore.

It is worth noting that **Kosta**, on the Peloponnese mainland, and to which there are frequent, daily ferry-boats, possesses a fine, broad sandy beach *See* **Ferry-boat timetables, A To Z**.

BICYCLES & SCOOTER HIRE The 'going' daily hire rate for bicycles is 600drs and for scooters 2000drs. There are a number of businesses operating. There are no cars for hire.

Moto Service (*Tmr* 24B3) The cheapest scooter hire in town, at 1500drs a day, even if the machines are rather rickety. The young man running the show is rather uncommunicative. The workshop is in a lane behind the Clock Tower.

Other outfits include **Kostas**(*Tmr* 25B/C3), in the street behind the *Hotel Soleil*, and **Motor Bikes for Rent** (*Tmr* 26D4) over the hump bridge and on the left of the path that climbs up the hillside from the Town Beach, towards Ag Nikolaos

Church. This path angles off between the sea wall Esplanade round to the Old Harbour and the main road out of town to Ag Marina and Ag Anargyri.

A number of the firms offer a free map of the island to each hirer but it is best to ignore these blandishments and opt for the most competitive rates.

BOOKSELLERS In the street behind Takis Travel (*Tmr* 3B2/3) is a *Book Shop English French German Italian Books Sold Here*. A dark, high ceilinged, cavernous establishment.

BREAD SHOPS The most centrally located is in the High St (*Tmr* 22A/B3), on the left (*Sbo*). Not only a baker but also a patisserie.

There are also bakers at either end of town. One is on the right of the same path as Motor Bikes for Rent (*Tmr* 26D4). The other is to the west, opposite a smidgin of beach, beyond *Zorbas Cocktails Bar* (*sic*) and prior to the *Snack Bar Korali*. There are custard and cheese pies displayed in the latter baker's window.

BUSES Just two Town bus stops service the island's couple of destinations.

Bus timetable

1. Spetses Town, west to Ligoneri Beach past a baker, Taverna Patrali, Hotel Spetses, Anargyros School, Xenia Beach Hotel & Hotel Castelli. The bus 'terminus' (*Tmr* 27A1) is on the Esplanade, at the Dapia Harbour side of the Hotel Posidonion.
   Daily 0930, 1130, 1330, 1730, 1930, 2130hrs.
2. Spetses Town to Ag Anargyri via Ag Marina. This bus 'terminus' (*Tmr* 28C/D4) is adjacent to the Town Beach.
   Daily 1000, 1115, 1500hrs
   Return journey
   Daily 1030, 1530, 1630hrs
   Return fare 200drs, journey time approx. ½hr.

NB Bus times, especially the return schedules, must be carefully checked. The buses get very, very crowded on the return trip from Ag Anargyri at the height of the season. It is best to purchase a return ticket and avoid catching the last bus.

CINEMAS One (*Tmr* 29A3) to the right of the High St (*Sbo*). Next door, for those of a competitive frame of mind, is the *Cafe Angelos* which 'sports' a pool table or two.

COMMERCIAL SHOPPING AREA None, the individual shops being spread about the town. There are a number of general stores, mostly labelled supermarkets. An especially good example of this genre (*Tmr* 30B2/3) is in the block to the west of the *Hotel Faros*. The approach, leaving the *Chicken & Chips* establishment (*Tmr* 20B2/3) on the right, is a rich 'vein' passing a gift shop, a doctor, butcher and greengrocer, all on the right.

Opposite the back door of Takis Travel (*Tmr* 3B2/3) is a drink shop, alongside which is an excellent greengrocers. To the left (*Sbo*) of the back door of Takis Travel is a cigarette shop and to the right, beyond the *Snackbar*, is a very modern butcher with great, stainless steel topped freezer cabinets. None of your tree trunk chopping block, with chickens wandering about.

A fruit van draws up on the small square alongside the Fish Market (*Tmr* 31B/C3). To the nearside of the *Hotel Soleil* (*Tmr* 15B/C3) is a supermarket, alongside which is a shopping arcade. In the street behind the *Soleil* is a Kaba drink shop.

As I have written before, I rarely detail gift or souvenir shops as they rarely merit any more publicity. But every so often one comes across a business that is worthy of a mention, as does:-

Kaiki Gift Shop (*Tmr* 18C3/4) For details of the location *See* **The Accommodation**. Not only are the owners very interesting but so are the wares as this is not just an ordinary gift/souvenir shop. Many of the items on display are antiques and country items including a number of old, agricultural implements. But if the goods make the shop more than worth a visit, the proprietors put the gilt on the gingerbread. Yani, an urbane, quietly spoken, pleasant young man with impeccable English, is happy to chat about the shop and his island whilst his wife Sarah is as Home Counties as any 'English rose' could be. If Yani is pleased to talk, his father Dimitri Papadimos is absolutely enthusiastic. A dignified man, he is possibly most interesting when discussing his abiding passion, photography. His photographs have graced a number of books and he has also written a number himself, including an excellent photographic record of the vanishing culture of Greece, now sadly out of print.

FERRY-BOATS & FLYING DOLPHINS The options available allows a good daily selection of destinations including Piraeus and some other Argo-Saronic island connections. On the other hand, it is almost impossible to make a lateral move with another chain of islands. I should write 'it is impossible', but my hand is stayed by not only a lack of courage but the knowledge that nothing, but nothing, is definite where any form of Greek transport is concerned, especially the ferry-boats.

Having been categorical it is a fact that one of the Piraeus based ferry-boats calls in at various Peloponnese mainland ports, as well as Ag Pelagia and Kapsali, both Kithira island ports, and continues on to Kastelli, Crete. This allows 'cross pollination' where particular Argo-Saronic islands connect with the same ports. Otherwise it may be necessary to utilise the Flying Dolphins to continue on to Kithira island.

Ferry-boat timetable (Mid-season)

Day	**Departure time**	**Ferry-boat**	**Ports/Islands of Call**
Daily	0715, 1000, 1300, 1630hrs	Alexandros/ Mekalis	Kosta(M)
Return	0745, 1030, 1330, 1700hrs		

NB At the height of season craft depart every hour, on the hour

One-way fare 1000drs

Monday-Friday	1430hrs	Eytyxia	Hydra, Poros, Methana(M), Aegina, Piraeus (M-2000hrs).
Saturday & Sunday	1530hrs	Eytyxia	Ermioni(M), Hydra, Poros, Methana(M), Aegina, Piraeus (M-2100hrs).

Spetses to:					
	Ermioni(M)	one-way fare	280drs;	duration	½hr
	Hydra		300drs;		1¼hrs
	Poros		600drs;		2¼hrs
	Methana(M)		550drs;		2½hrs
	Aegina		695drs;		4hrs
	Piraeus(M)		850drs;		5½hrs

Flying Dolphin timetable (Mid-season)

Day	**Departure time**	**Arrival time**	**Ports/Islands of Call**
Daily	0615hrs	0815hrs	Hydra, Zea Port (Piraeus).
	0845hrs	1145hrs	Ermioni(M), Hydra, Poros, Methana(M), Aegina, Zea Port(Piraeus).
	1030hrs	1040hrs	Portoheli(M).
	1115hrs	1315hrs	Hydra, Zea Port(Piraeus).

	1300hrs	1540hrs	Ermioni(M), Hydra, Poros, Zea Port(Piraeus).
Tuesday, Saturday	1125hrs	1505hrs	Leonidio(M), Kiparissi(M), Monemvassia(M), Kithira, Neapoli(M).
Tuesday, Thursday	1125hrs	1255hrs	Leonidio(M), Kiparissi(M), Gerakas(M).
Tuesday, Thursday Saturday, Sunday	1125hrs	1315hrs	Leonidio(M), Kiparissi(M), Monemvassia(M).
Monday, Wednesday Friday	1125hrs	1135hrs	Portoheli(M).
Daily	1225hrs	1235hrs	Portoheli(M).
Sunday	1425hrs	1435hrs	Portoheli(M).
Monday, Wednesday, Friday	1430hrs	1650hrs	Hydra, Poros, Zea Port (Piraeus).
Saturday	1430hrs	1620hrs	Zea Port, (Piraeus).
Sunday	1515hrs	1735hrs	Hydra, Poros, Zea Port(Piraeus).
Sunday	1605hrs	1615hrs	Portoheli(M).
Thursday, Sunday	1610hrs	1830hrs	Hydra, Poros, Zea Port(Piraeus).
Monday-Saturday	1635hrs	1645hrs	Portoheli(M).
Sunday	1645hrs	1845hrs	Hydra, Zea Port(Piraeus).
Monday-Saturday	1715hrs	1915hrs	Hydra, Zea Port(Piraeus).
Sunday	1805hrs	1815hrs	Portoheli(M).
Saturday	1825hrs	1835hrs	Portoheli(M).
Tuesday, Friday, Saturday	1830hrs	2020hrs	Zea Port(Piraeus).
Sunday	1835hrs	2025hrs	Zea Port(Piraeus).
Friday	1925hrs	1935hrs	Portoheli(M).
Monday-Saturday	1935hrs	1945hrs	Portoheli(M).
Daily	2035hrs	2045hrs	Portoheli(M).

Sample one-way fares: Spetses to			
	Portoheli	250drs;duration from	10 mins
	Kithira	3100drs;	3hrs 10mins
	Hydra	490drs;	35 mins
	Poros	600drs;	1½hrs
	Aegina	1050drs;	1¼hrs
	Zea Marina (Piraeus)	1500drs;	2hrs

FERRY-BOAT & FLYING DOLPHIN TICKET OFFICES

Flying Dolphin Ticket Office

Directions: The office faces Dapia Harbour and is alongside Pine Island Travel, both beneath the *Hotel Saronicos* (*Tmr* 5B2).

Ferry-boat tickets are sold from a desk on the Ferry-boat Quay (*Tmr* 1B2). A now terminally dead ticket office beneath the Port police (*Tmr* 4B2), and behind *Remetzo's*, is now occupied by a barber.

HAIRDRESSERS Ladies please *See* **The Yachting Club, The Eating Out** and gentlemen *See* **Ferry-boat Ticket Offices, The A To Z**.

LAUNDRY There are no launderettes (despite the message of the signs) but two dry-cleaners/laundries (*Tmr* 32A3 & 32B3). The one in the High St (*Tmr* 32A3), opposite *The Palm Tree Breakfast Bar*, is the least expensive, but that is only comparatively inexpensive. Shirts/blouses cost 170/200drs and trousers/jeans 300drs.

LUGGAGE STORE Most travellers pile their belongings, on and around the steps of Takis Travel (*Tmr* 3B2/3).

MEDICAL CARE

Chemist & Pharmacies At least two (*Tmr* 33B2/3 & 33B3).

Clinic (*Tmr* 34C4/5) It is probably easiest, if not most direct, to proceed to the Town Beach, then along the Ag Marina road, after which turn right up towards the Museum (*Tmr* 35A/B5). The clinic is off to the left before, or after the *Hotel Myrtoon*. Open weekdays 1000-1200hrs & 1600-1800hrs.

Doctors Dr. Alexia Bougou resides between a gift shop and a butcher (*See* **Commercial Shopping Area, A To Z**). Another has a clinic (*Tmr* 36B/C3) situated at the end of the track that heads eastwards from Kentriki Square, on the side of which is the *Hotel Faros* (*Tmr* 13B3).

MONIPOS They line up from the Water Pumping Station (*Tmr* 2B2) all the way round to the Square on the edge of which is the *Hotel Alexandri* (*Tmr* 12B2/3). Normally not a method of travel that I would recommend but as there is only one taxi.... Extensively used by the locals. The fare to the Old Harbour is 400drs. The standard tour *Round the Island*, which only takes in Ligoneri Beach, the Old Harbour and Ag Marina Beach, costs 3000drs but at quiet times 2000drs might be negotiated.

The loquacious Yanni is one of the drivers and he speaks quite passable English (having spent 2½ years in Chicago) as well as some French. He is a larger than life character, lives on a smallholding and, when asked the age of his horse, advises 'As old as the Acropolis' – probably.

NTOG None. *See* **Police, A To Z**.

OTE (*Tmr* 37A1/2). To the west of the *Hotel Star*. Only open weekdays 0730-1510hrs.

PETROL There are a couple of pumps in front of the *Hotel Alexandri* (*Tmr* 12B2/3)

PLACES OF INTEREST

Cathedrals & Churches As would be expected any number but of interest must be:-

The Monastery of Ag Nikolaos On a low headland set between Dapia and the Old Harbour. The path that climbs from the Town Beach crosses a hump backed bridge and angles off to the left of the main road to Ag Anargyri, via Ag Marina. Conspicuous for its Ionian style campanile and large pebble mosaic courtyard, the building was erected in the 17th century and the campanile added in the early 1800s. It was here that the islanders raised their flag of Independence, on 3rd April 1821. Of interest may be that the body of a nephew of Napoleon was stored for five years at the monastery, in a barrel of rum, until removed by the French Navy. One wonders which suffered most, the body or the rum?

Mansions More commonly called *Archontika*, these were the homes of the wealthy, leading 18th & 19th century families, usually shipowners. It has to be pointed out that many of these buildings would not rate as more than manor houses in the United Kingdom. On the other hand, Spetses possesses an uncommonly large number and the families that founded them are, in many cases, worth more than a passing mention.

Anargyros Mansion (*Tmr* 38A2/3) Now signed *Cultural Office*, this imposing pile was constructed in 1904. For details of the owner *See* Spetses Town **Introduction**.

Bouboulina Mansion (*Tmr* 39A2) This edifice is across a pine tree shaded park/playground to the right (*Sbo*) of the *Anargyros House*. One of the homes of this apparently amazing, woman sea captain. Lascarina was born in 1771.

Her first husband, with whom she sailed, died at sea as did her second husband, one Dimitrios Bouboulis. By now she had amassed wealth and possessions which included a number of ships. By the time of the declaration of Independence she was master of the *Agamemnon*, reputedly the largest corvette on the Greek side, which was further supported by other, smaller craft. Fact and fiction may well have become inextricably mixed, as in the case of many folk heroes. What is indisputable is that she blockaded the Turkish forces in the town of Nafplio on the Peloponnese coast until they surrendered. Other of her exploits were used to damage Bouboulina's growing reputation. For instance, at the siege of Tripoli it is arguable whether she took or accepted the harem ladies' jewellery in order to vouchsafe their safety, when the city fell to the besieging forces. It was also voiced abroad that she seduced sexual partners at gunpoint! Well, there you go. I've dreamt of being seduced at gunpoint. It seems a great shame that after all this excitement her life was precipitately ended. On the other hand, if the stories were true about the gunpoint seductions, then the manner of her death must be considered a veritable quirk of fate. Bouboulina was shot dead, in 1825, on the balcony of another of the family houses (described later under this heading) by an enraged relative of a girl with whom one of her son's had eloped.

The Botassis family had at least three mansions that have survived to the present day:-
Botassis Mansion 1. Supposedly relatively unaltered, it is located behind the Cinema (*Tmr* 29A3). The house was used, during the Second World War, to conceal British troops on the run.
Botassis Mansion 2. On the left, towards the top of the High St. The main room of the house is said to be a look-alike of the cabin of the ship of the original owner, Ariagnostis Botassis.
Botassis Mansion 3. Overlooking Baltiza Creek, towards the Old Harbour.

In the same area as this last mansion, and just off the main road to Ag Marina Beach, is Plateia Analypsis on the side of which is Analypsis Church. On the side of the approach road to the Square is a house gateway. The ground at the entrance door is covered with a pebble mosaic and the pediment of the doorway has a carved ship in full sail with the legend KPHTH (Crete) 1867 ΑΡΚΑΔΙΟΝ (Arkadhi Monastery). It would be nice to think this celebrates Cretan resistance to the Turks at the Monastery of Arkadhi but the final (self-inflicted?) explosion there was in November 1866.
Mexis Mansion (*Tmr* 35A/B5). This imposing building, once the home of the shipowner Hadziyannis Mexis, was built about 1795 and is now the island's Museum. The rather dark courtyard is peripherally lined with busts of various Greek naval 'chappies' of the War of Independence, whilst in the centre is a bust of the erstwhile owner. Open daily 0845-1500hrs, except Sundays and holidays when it is open 0930-1430hrs and closed Tuesdays.

Going west from Dapia, the centre of the Town, the Esplanade is lined with impressive piles of this and that including the:-
Hotel Posidonion (*Tmr* 10A1) *See* **Spetses Town Introduction**.
Hadzipavlinas House Further west of the *Hotel Posidonion*, just beyond a road bridge. This 'pile' was built in the 19th century.
Daskalakis Cotton Mill Constructed by Dimitrios Daskalakis, who was a friend of Sotiros Anargyros and a Piraeus factory owner. Now abandoned, this very large

industrial building, built in 1921, also supplied the island's electricity needs up until about 1960, as well as ice for the fishing fleet. Incidentally, there is nothing so derelict as an abandoned Greek industrial site. One wonders why they are not demolished? On the other hand, sometimes apparently 'dead' premises 'leap into life' at the appropriate time and season.

The Town Hall (ΔΗΜΑΡΧΕΙΟΝ) Once the family home of Nikolaos Kyriakos, a War of Independence sea captain.

At the next jink in the sea wall is:-

Lembessis House The home of an island shipowner behind which, on the street that angles off behind the town, is another:

Bouboulina Mansion The house where Lascarina was shot, as described previously.

Economou Mansion Constructed in 1851 by the shipowner Michail Economou and graced by a visit from the Greek King, George 1. Still extant are the painted ceilings.

Altamura House About 100m prior to the *Hotel Spetses*. Famous for its longtime owner, Eleni Altamura, who was born in 1821. The house was built by her father, Yannis Boukouris, another sea captain, who was involved in the War of Independence. Eleni's father ensured her education was broad based and extensive but would appear to have been over protective towards his daughter. It wasn't until aged 27, and still a single woman, that she went to Italy to further her artistic education. Father accompanied her and insisted she dressed as a man. Still thus disguised she became a pupil of Saverio Altamura. It is postulated that at a Greek festival, staged at Naples, she became so involved in the celebrations that she clasped one of the Greek lady participants to her bosom. This act so shocked the assembled company that she had to cast off her outer clothes in order to reveal all – that she was in fact a women. For some obscure reason Saverio proposed on the spot (perhaps it was lust), they married, had three children but did not live happily ever after. Oh no! There was a serpent in their midst, a pretty companion engaged to accompany Eleni and with whom 'naughty' Saverio ran off. Eleni went to Athens and expanded her artistic activities. Here she was joined by one of her sons, Yanni, who was probably a better artist and achieved Royal Patronage. On returning to Spetses things went from bad to worse for Eleni with the death of Yanni and her daughter, after which the remaining child rejoined his father. Eleni's sorrow resulted in her destroying all her paintings and becoming a recluse, grieving until her death twenty two years later, in 1900.

Beyond the *Hotel Spetses* is the *Anargyros and Korgialenios School* for details of which *See* **Spetses Town Introduction.**

Two other 19th century buildings in a poor state of repair, but worthy of a mention, are those on the hillsides behind the *Hotel Stelios*. The larger one, on the right (*Sbo*), is a crenallated wonder that is probably the *Leonidas Lambrou House*, a casino between the two World Wars.

POLICE

Port (*Tmr* 4B2) Close by the end of the Ferry-boat Quay.

Town (*Tmr* 11A3) On the left of the High St (*Sbo*). Although available in emergencies, 24 hours a day, the normal office hours are 0800-1300hrs plus 1800-2000hrs on Monday, Thursday and Friday.

POST OFFICE (*Tmr* 14A/B3) For directions *See* **Hotel Anna Maria, The Accommodation**.

TAXIS Only one that ranks close by the Post Office (*Tmr* 14A/B3)

TAXIS, WATER Almost uniquely the Harbour 'sports', in addition to the more usual and less expensive trip boats, a number of stylish, cabin speed boats that ferry clients round the island and across to the Peloponnese. The drawback is that they are very expensive, with fees ranging from some 850drs to Kosta (Peloponnese) and 2750drs to Ag Anargyri.

TELEPHONE NUMBERS & ADDRESSES

Clinic (*Tmr* 34C4/5)	Tel 72472
Dentists	Tel 72421/73666
Doctors	Tel 72502/72879
Olympic Airways	Tel 73141/2
Police (*Tmr* 11A3)	Tel 73100/72205
Taxi Rank	Tel 72198

TRAVEL AGENTS & TOUR OFFICES I have expanded on the **Takis Travel & Tourist Office** (*Tmr* 3B2/3), *See* **The Accommodation**.

Other agencies include:-
Pine Island Travel (*Tmr* 5B2) Tel 72464
Directions: On the ground floor of the building also housing the *Hotel Saronicos*, on the left of Dapia Harbour (*Sbo*)
Bardakos Tours (*Tmr* 40B2/3) Tel 73141
Directions: The office is on the far side of 'Monipos Square'.

The tour offices and the package tour companies try to ensure the complete satisfaction of the (mainly British) holiday-makers, with a full itinerary of trips, excursions, evenings on (and off) the town, (wild) party nights and 'Round-the-Island' yachting cruises. Goody! Excursion boats and caiques moor to the Plateia Dapia quay wall (*Tmr* 41B2) and charge about 250drs for the round trip to Ag Anargyri.

WATER All the islands fresh water has to be shipped in and the pumping station (*Tmr* 2B2) is located by the sea wall, to the left (*Sbo*) of the Ferry-boat Quay.

ROUTE ONE

To Ag Anargyri & on back to Spetses Town, an almost circular route anti-clockwise round the island (about 25km). The initial section of the route westwards from Spetses Town is along the asphalted Esplanade. This stretches as far as Ligoneri Beach, much of which has already been detailed (*See* **Beaches & Places of Interest, A To Z**). To the near side of the *Hotel Spetses* is *Costas Water Sports*, followed by a waterside area known as Lampara, the other side of the road to which is the Anargyros School.

The *Castelli (Xenia) Hotel/Bungalows/Apartments* complex marks the commencement of a profusely wooded area colloquially known as Blueberry Hill, after a local taverna and selected for a smart residential development looking out over the sea. Beyond Lampara Beach the road, which is pleasantly shaded by pine and tamarisk trees, winds along the coast some 100m above the shoreline.

From Ligoneri Beach the road surface becomes dirt track, wide but very rutted.

VRELLOU BEACH (4½km from Spetses Town). A 200m, rocky track bumps down to this small, pebble cove. There is a large slab of shelving biscuit rock to the nearside. The backshore is messy and the coastline hereabouts is made up of 'aggregate' look-alike.

Back on the main road, about 200m further on and a track off to the left wanders up to Profitis Elias Church. This is more or less at the centre of the island and the highest point, only a meagre 250m above sea-level.

At about 5½km a turning to the right lurches down to:-

ZOGERIA BAY (6km from Spetses Town) This is a truly beautiful and picturesque area made up of rocky inlets set in low pine tree covered slopes. It comprises the far Lazaretto Bay and close to Zogeria Bay separated by a low headland, on which stands Ag Georgos Church. Lazaretto Bay would have almost certainly been the site of a quarantine hospital.

It is unfortunate that there are no sandy beaches but some of the pebble shores sally forth to a sandy sea-bed. Bathers should beware as sea urchins are present. Naturally enough the location is popular with the pedlars of boat trips as well as flotilla yachts. A rustic *Cantina* blossoms into life at each of the bays during the height of season.

From the Zogeria turning, the main track cuts across the western headland to rejoin the coast close to:

AG PARASKEVI (10km from Spetses Town) A lovely little bay, probably once a settlement with a small church still on the site, set in the litter strewn pine forest that almost stretches down to the beach. The backshore is made up of larger pebbles but the seashore is finer, more comfortable pebbles. At the height of season a *Cantina* opens. Naturally, this idyllic tranquillity is disturbed by both daily trip boat excursions and an enterprising local who has made it a centre for his water sports business. The delights of water skiing, wind surfing and pedaloes are supplemented by sun-beds and umbrellas. To the far right (*Fsw*) of the bay is an unofficial, nudist section.

In case anyone savouring the peaceful atmosphere were to miss the arrival of the excursion boats, they herald their arrival with blaring bouzouki music.

Between the bays of Ag Paraskevi and Ag Anargyri, on the right of the road, opposite the foot track to the centre of the island and Profitis Elias Church, is a house owned by the Botassis family (*See* **Places of Interest, A To Z Spetses Town**). Known to readers of John Fowles' novel (The Magus) as *Bourani*, or *House of the Magus*.

A wide track proceeds down from the island circling road to:-

AG ANARGYRI (11km from Spetses Town). Rather more developed than the other bays and coves so far encountered. The hillsides of the valley backing the bay, which are only sparsely covered with trees, are being built on. There is a cocktail bar and a hotel:-

The Akroyali (Class A) Tel 73695

Actually classified as an A Class pension. All rooms have en suite bathrooms and prices start at 1710drs for a single and 2700drs for a double, rising, in the season, to 2600drs and 4800drs.

Up against the backshore and close by a small church is the taverna:-

Porfyris Taverna Service is excellent and prices average. A bottle of beer costs 90drs, most mincemeat dishes 265drs, veal dishes 365drs and lamb 450drs. A moussaka costs 300drs, salads 105drs with a Greek salad charged at 210drs. Two Nes meh ghala and a brandy costs 260drs. The current bus timetable is displayed on the back wall of the taverna's patio.

The beach backshore is medium sized pebbles, the foreshore fine pebbles and the sea-bed pebble but the sea is clean and pleasant. Even out of the height of the season, the location becomes crowded and there are wind surfers, water skiing, canoes, pedaloes, sun loungers and umbrellas for one's enjoyment and pleasure. Yes, well.

To the right (*Fsw*) a track leads, after a five minute walk to:-

Bekiris Cave As is often the case, this cave will probably prove a disappointment and its oft proclaimed beauty might well be best left to the imagination. Due to rock falls it is necessary to be as sure-footed as a mountain goat and it might help to be a stunted midget. Stoicism is a personal characteristic that could help assuage any feelings of anger at the missing stalactites and stalagmites. It has to be admitted that the small beach within the cave is the sandiest on Spetses, even if it is overhung by millions of tons of rock! A torch is mandatory to enjoy all the visual aspects, as apart from the light that filters through from the sea and the tortuous entrance, it is rather dark. Still if it was more accessible, attractive and dramatic, entrance would be by admission charge and there would be row upon row of air-conditioned, excursion coaches – wouldn't there? The cave has been used, over the years, as a place of refuge in time of full scale invasions. The latter included that experienced after the islanders joined with an opportunistic Russian incursion into the Mediterranean in 1770 – an event known as the Orlov uprising, after the Russian fleet commander.

From Ag Anargyri, continuing in an anticlockwise direction, the road, although still unsurfaced, is in much better condition. After 3½km, beyond a headland on which is plonked a rather incongruously situated football pitch and prior to a sign on a tree announcing *Bus Stop*, the road surface becomes tarmacadamed. This is also the spot where a 1km path descends steeply and roughly to:-

KSILOKERIZA BAY (14km from Spetses Town) A lovely 'U' shaped cove with a shingle beach. Due to the lack of the 'Oh, so' necessary tourist facilities, and the difficulties of reaching the spot, it remains fairly deserted when other beaches are jam-packed.

On rounding the south-east corner of the island, the islet of Spetsopoula moves into view, the pine trees die out and the countryside becomes rocky granite. The hillsides once sported terraces of vines but now broom has taken over the slopes. Spetsopoula is the private preserve of the modern day, Greek shipping magnates, the Niarchos family. One wonders which malcontent decided to place the island's rubbish dump smack opposite this private retreat?

Directly across the way from the islet a horn of land and rock projects into the ½km channel from which juts a sizeable quay, obviously built to service Spetsopoula and in the lee of which is a thin, narrow strip of not very clean beach.

From hereon to Ag Marina a number of expensive properties have been constructed.

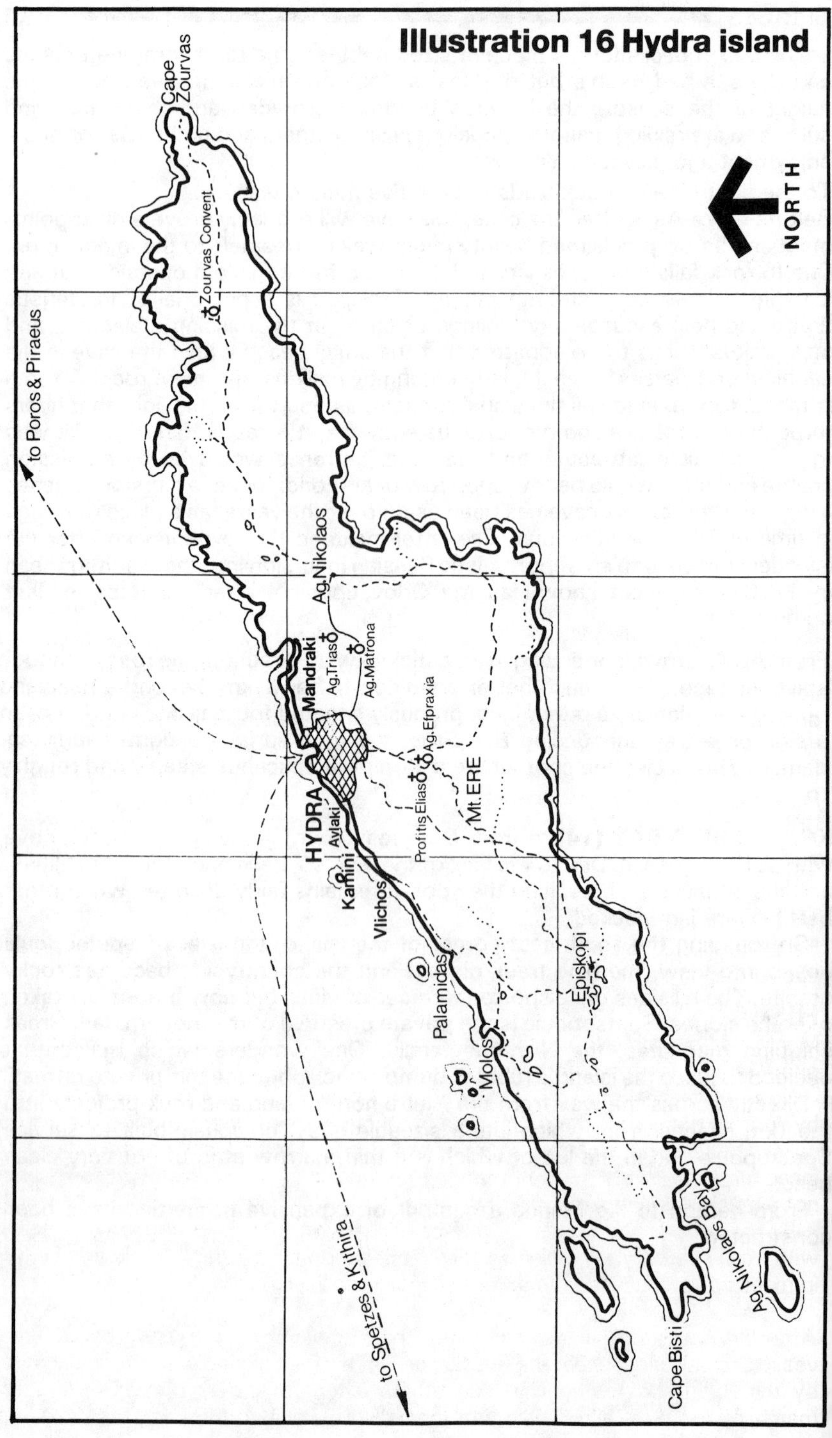

Illustration 16 Hydra island

13 HYDRA (Idra, Idhra, Ydra,)

Argo-Saronic Islands

Beauty of the port ****

The ambience *

FIRST IMPRESSIONS

Tourists, tourists and more tourists; yachts; cats; donkey trains; gold emporiums; lack of beaches; shiny marble streets and pavements; beauty of the port and photogenic quarters of the town.

SPECIALITIES

Amigdalota – Turkish delight in which is mixed chopped almonds.

RELIGIOUS HOLIDAYS & FESTIVALS

include: 30th January – Festival of the Three Hierarchs, Hydra; 2nd February – Purification of the Virgin Mary, Papandi Chapel, Hydra; 10th February – Festival of Ag Charalambos, Monastery of Panaghia, Hydra; 25th March – The Annunciation, Greek Independence Day; 30th June – Festival of the Holy Apostles, Holy Apostles Chapel, Dokos Island. (This used to be combined with the 1st July – Festival to the Saints Cosmas & Damian, Monastery Ag Anargyroi at Ermioni (M), *Anargyroi* indicating penniless, because the saints dispensed free medical advice. As one authority plaintively points out, Hydriots no longer feel able to take two days off during the tourist season. I bet not! They would not take 2 hours, let alone 2 days). Late June – Miaoulia Feast & Festival over two days to celebrate War of Independence; 8th September – The Birth of the Virgin Mary, Monastery of Panaghia, Zourvas; 14th September – Bell ringing to the Exaltation of the Holy Cross; 13-14th November – Ag Konstantinos, Patron Saint of Hydra; 6th December – Festival Ag Nikolaos, Monastery of Panaghia, Hydra and throughout the island; 12th December – Festival Ag Spyridon, Monastery of Panaghia.

VITAL STATISTICS

Tel prefix 0298. The island is up to 6km in width and 23km long, with an area of about 52sq km and a population of some 2000.

HISTORY

Mentioned by Homer (Hydrea), the island was sold once or twice, passing from one mainland town to another via Samiot exiles of the 6th BC.

Not a lot happened till the 16th century AD when this dry, arid island was settled by Albanian refugees. Mainly farmers by tradition, they slowly took to the sea for a living. Due to the location, smallness of overall size and lack of population, the inhabitants were very much left to their own devices, so much so that taxes were not extracted until the mid 1700s.

By the time of the Russo-Turkish conflict, Hydriot ships & crews were sailing with the Turkish navy as auxiliaries and support vessels – a pastime which immeasurably enhanced the sailors seagoing abilities.

After the Russian naval incursions into the Aegean Seas, a treaty allowed Greek vessels to sail under either the Russian or Turkish flag, a condition swiftly exploited by the Hydriots. Additionally, due to the extent of piracy that existed, these merchantmen were allowed to arm themselves. Running the English blockade of the Napoleonic garrisons allowed the Hydriot skippers, as well as other Greek island shipowners, to accumulate large amounts of wealth. Some of this money was used to purchase more vessels with which to make more blockade-busting runs. As an aside it would appear that the Hydriots soon formed co-operatives in which all the crew shared in the ship's earnings. Who says profit sharing and management buy-outs are a product of 20th century industrial ingenuity? Naturally enough this idyllic state of employer/employee affairs was besmirched by the small matter of a sailor's mutiny, which lasted for some years during the late 1700s.

Whatever is written in the panegyrics, the paeans of praise, the eulogies to the Hydriots wholehearted support for the War of Independence, in actuality the islanders were cautious participants... almost reluctant. For a start many of the citizens were more Albanian than Greek, added to which they were no fools and accepted they were doing very well, thank you, from the status quo. They had their own island legislature and were, to all intents and purposes, self-governing. Idealism won over though and, after an initial stutter when an upstart called Oikonomos stole the limelight, the chaps with the wealth got their hands back on the tiller. Names that have come down through the years include Jacob Tombazis, Lazaros Koundouriotis as well as Economou, Voulgaris and Andreas Miaoulis, the latter being the most famous of them all. Mind you, even then, not all was light and honey due to inter-island rivalry, especially between Hydra and Spetses – well there you go!

Unfortunately the outpouring of money and effort devastated the islands' wealth. Additionally, the centres of shipping flitted to other island ports with the progression to steam power. It was not until the tourist boom of the l970s that the island was able to commence rebuilding its resources and fortunes. To get an idea of the effect of the War of Independence, it is only necessary to realize that in 1820 the population of Hydra numbered about 30,000 but in the 1840s had fallen to some 4,000.

GENERAL

The port and town are scenically most attractive, if not beautiful, and there are no cars or scooters, there being only one rubbish truck and one small van. But those are the plus points. As distinct from most Greek islands it has been my pleasure to visit, I can only suggest that readers consider the matter of Hydra very carefully. As with Simi, in the Dodecanese, to which Hydra Town is remarkably similar in both appearance and ambience, there is not only the aura of money but the conviction that the local traders are extracting it (money that is) from visitors with an almost indecent haste and thoroughness. Nod, nod, wink, wink. Oh and here, as so very rarely elsewhere in Greece, it was necessary to award *GROC's Rip-off Badge of Demerit*. This was to a taverna that I considered would prove satisfactory, but didn't let Hydra down, overcharging some 20% on an 850drs bill. That is not to say that one or two accommodations, one taverna and one kafeneion have not deserved a meritorious mention in dispatches – but that is all out of a total of some hundreds of such establishments.

Apart from the exorbitant cost of services and supplies, there are only two or three other easily accessible settlements and the same number of generally unsatisfactory, stony coves. Despite this, seemingly as many day trippers ebb and flow into Hydra as do into St Marks Square, Venice. They spill out of Flying Dolphins, ferry-boats, excursion craft and cruise liners. This stream of fun loving visitors, which engulfs Hydra, has encouraged the shop keepers and owners of 'halls of fare' to ask for and get astronomical prices. Occasionally, in the more tourist ravaged resorts, there can be seen the occasional menu A, B, C and D but

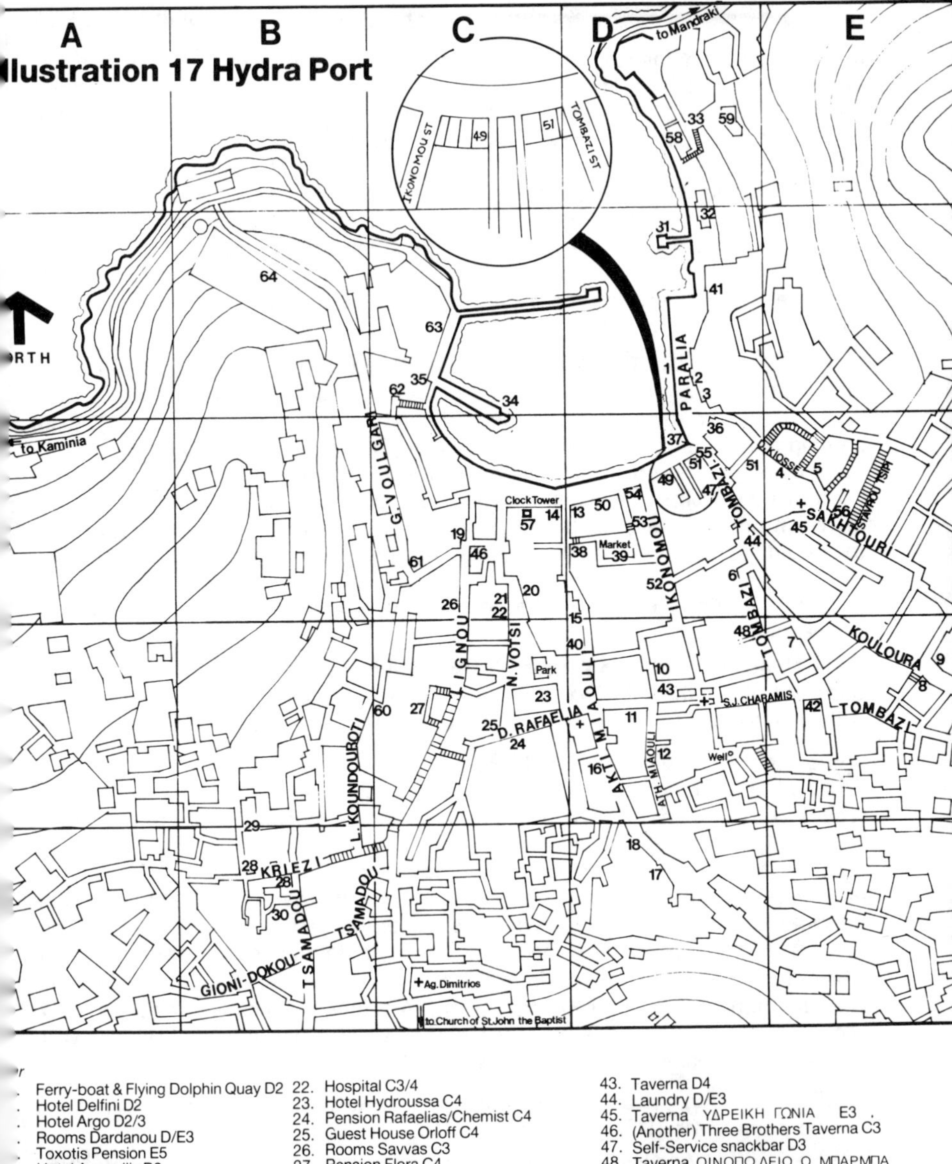

r

. Ferry-boat & Flying Dolphin Quay D2
. Hotel Delfini D2
. Hotel Argo D2/3
. Rooms Dardanou D/E3
. Toxotis Pension E5
. Hotel Amaryllis D3
. Three Brothers Taverna D/E3/4
. Pension E4
. Taverna Philipas E4
. Georges Guest House D4
. Hotel Leto D4
. Rooms D4
. Hotel Sophia C/D3
. Hotel Christina C/D3
. Pension Coral C/D3/4
. Hotel Miranda D4
. Pension Agelika D5
. Clinic/Surgery D4/5
. Rooms/snackbar Thalami C3
. OTE C3
. Town police C3/4

22. Hospital C3/4
23. Hotel Hydroussa C4
24. Pension Rafaelias/Chemist C4
25. Guest House Orloff C4
26. Rooms Savvas C3
27. Pension Flora C4
28. Stores (2)
29. Hotel Theano B4/5
30. Rooms Efstathiou B5
31. Water Ship jetty D2
32. Museum D1/2
33. Pension Stelios D1
34. Inner Harbour jetty C2/3
35. Pension Douglas C2
36. Antonios Cafe-bar D2/3
37. Water Taxis D2/3
38. Kafeneion C/D3
39. The Market D3
40. Taverna ΤΟ ΣΤΕΚΙ C/D3/4
41. Taverna Laikon/Tsamados Mansion D2
42. Taverna O Douskos E4

43. Taverna D4
44. Laundry D/E3
45. Taverna ΥΔΡΕΙΚΗ ΓΩΝΙΑ E3 .
46. (Another) Three Brothers Taverna C3
47. Self-Service snackbar D3
48. Taverna ΟΙΝΟΠΩΔΕΙΟ Ο ΜΠΑΡΜΠΑ ΔΗΜΑΣ D/E3/4
49. Commercial Bank D3
50. National Bank D3
51. Bread shops (2)
52. Cinema D3
53. Post Office/Supermarket D3
54. Cigarette shop D3
55. Pan Travel/Hydra Corner Jewellery D3
56. Chemist E3
57. Monastery Panaghia C3
58. Port police/Old Arsenal D1
59. Kriezis Mansion D1
60. Lazaros Koundouriotis Mansion B/C4
61. George Voulgaris Mansion C3
62. Tombazis Mansion B/C2/3
63. Voulgaris Mansion C2
64. George Koundouriotis Mansion B2

here on Hydra it is the rule rather than the exception, and due to the large number of men from the land of the rising Yen, one restaurant even has a Japanese translation of this Chinese menu habit! Perhaps it would not matter if the prices for these idiot proof translations were reasonable but the whole, more often than not, adds up to 50%-100% more than the individual items. The prices of accommodation are similarly stratospheric.

The overall number number of tourists are topped up by the presence of some very large private yachts that berth overnight in the small Harbour.

Early morning, prior to the mass arrivals, Hydra bears a passing resemblance to its former self but once the hordes arrive, it is almost impossible to get away from the influx.

HYDRA; capital (& only) town & port (Illustration 17). The Introduction says it all as, for all intents and purposes, the town is the island. A plus point for any traveller is the immediate compactness of the port. One striking feature is the inordinate number of gold, fine art and souvenir shops, there being even more than there are waterfront tavernas.

Due to the lack of vehicles, all goods are transported by donkeys, strings of which marshal daily on the Esplanade. It makes for a rather strange sight to behold this timeless Greek method of hauling merchandise, tied up amongst all the 'glitterati'.

Without doubt the harbour waterfront becomes rather smelly in the height of season.

ARRIVAL BY FERRY & FLYING DOLPHIN

Craft 'pull up' on the left (*Sbo*) of the inner Harbour (*Tmr* 1D2) with the 'U' shaped, wide quayside Esplanade curving away to the right.

THE ACCOMMODATION & EATING OUT

The Accommodation Passengers disembarking are not accosted by waves of room offering Mamas although one or two skulk about, carefully inspecting prospects before 'moving in'.

Due to the overall shortage of accommodation it is a very bad move to arrive on a Friday or Saturday night, and it is worth noting that generally little English is spoken. Accommodation, which is generally taken at the height of the season, is very expensive. Even the simplest double room costs 1980drs whilst a good class, en suite double room will set a client back 4000drs and a luxury double, up to 5000drs. Ouch! Another problem associated with accommodation is that the bells, the church bells, blast away every day with special efforts being made on Sundays.

On disembarking, almost immediately on the left, across the way from the landing point (*Tmr* 1D2), are the:-

Hotel Delfini (*Tmr* 2D2) (Class B) Paralia Tel 52082

Directions: As above.

Provincial and classified as a pension.

Hotel Argo (*Tmr* 3D2/3) (Class D) Tel 52452

Directions: One or two buildings towards the main quayside from the *Hotel Delfini*.

Provincial, with double rooms en suite only starting at 2100drs, rising to 2500drs (1st May-30th Sept.)

Close to the Ferry-boat Quay (*Tmr* 1D2), a narrow lane named D Kiosse, one before Odhos Tombazi, snakes off to the left (*Sbo*).

Rooms Dardanou, Danai (*Tmr* 4D/E3)(Class C) D Kiosse St Tel 52794
Directions: On the right, behind an unrevealing door set in the wall.

Almost *Cycladic Pooms*, the cubicles are ranged round the courtyard/storage tank with showers and toilets to one side. However simple, at least the rooms have a lampshade. The Mama is hard-working and the establishment is kept very clean, even if it is crudely simple. Mama and Papa keep a keen eye on proceedings, even sleeping on a truckle bed in a large windowed room that gives them a clear vision of their domain. Mid-season, double room rates are 1780drs plus 100drs a head for the use of the (admittedly hot) showers. Those forced to use the toilet facilities in the middle of the night must be careful, due to the varying levels of the yard and the pipes that crisscross the uneven steps. There are some rooms available in the large house that forms one side of the courtyard and the interior of which is a delight – matchboard ceilings, wall tapestries and old furniture.

Toxotis Pension (*Tmr* 5E5) (Class B) D Kiosse St Tel 52606/52101
Directions: Further along the lane from *Dardanou* and on the left, in a pleasant, old, large provincial house.

Better value than *Dardanou* at 1700drs, with no extras, in more salubrious accommodation.

The next major street radiating off the Quay Esplanade, Odhos Tombazi, houses the:-

Hotel Amaryllis (*Tmr* 6D3) (Class B) 15 Tombazi Tel 52249
Directions: As above and on the right, where the street forks and jinks to the right.

More modern than previously described establishments and now classified as a pension. Only double rooms, starting at 2150drs sharing the bathroom and 2750drs en suite, rising to 2500drs and 3150drs respectively (1st July-30th Sept).

At the fork, instead of following Tombazi St to the right, another lane curves away to the left past *Three Brothers Taverna* (*Tmr* 7D/E3/4) on the right side of an irregular square. A left and then a right advances to Odhos G Kouloura.

Pension (*Tmr* 8E4)
Directions: As above and on the right, across the wide street from the *Taverna* ΟΦΙΛΙΠΠΑΣ (*Philipas*) (*Tmr* 9E4)

G Kouloura is a wide, tree lined and paved avenue which is not only the route from the Town to the Eastern monasteries but the:-

Greco Hotel (Class B) Odhos G Kouloura Tel 53200
Directions: As above.

Actually classified as a pension but, as would be expected for a modernish hotel with only en suite bathrooms on Hydra, not inexpensive. At least it can offer single rooms which start at 2880drs while doubles cost 3800drs, which rates increase to 3025drs and 4140drs (16th June-30th Sept).

Back at the Harbour, and proceeding round to the right (*Sbo*), the next street branching off the Esplanade is Odhos Ikonomou. At the upper end this street divides around a large square of buildings. The right-hand choice runs along the north and then the west side of the block, on the left of which, at a zig-zag in the lane, is the:-

Georges Guest House (*Tmr* 10D4) Tel 52288
Directions: As above.
Listed as apartments but I'm fairly sure ***Rooms*** are available.

Beyond *Georges*, is a flowerpot bedecked and taverna-table filled Square. The north-south lane Ath Miaouli, advances from the right (*Sbo*), top-hand corner of the Square, off which branches the narrow Odhos D Rafaelia. To the right is the:-

Hotel Leto (*Tmr* 11D4) (Class C) D Rafaelia Tel 52280
Directions: As above and on the left.
Almost absurdly modern considering the position but does offer single rooms as well as shared and en suite bathrooms. Single room rates start at 700drs sharing a bathroom and 1670drs en suite with double rooms costing 1270drs sharing and 2040drs en suite. These charges climb to 1360/1680drs for singles and 2200/2880drs for doubles.

Further along Odhos Ath Miaouli is:-

Rooms (*Tmr* 12D4)
Directions: As above and on the left.
Shares outside toilets but more sophisticated than say *Rooms Dardanou*, with mid-season double rooms charged at 2800drs.

Back at the Esplanade, the next accommodation is the:-

Hotel Sophia (*Tmr* 13C/D3) (Class D) Paralia Tel 52313
Directions: Located above a mishmash of shops looking out over the harbour and entered from Odhos Akti Miaouli.
Ethnic but the least expensive hotel in Hydra Port. Rooms facing out over the Esplanade are very, very noisy. The bathrooms are shared, with a single charged at 1000drs and a double 1400drs.

Pension Christina (*Tmr* 14C/D3)
Directions: Across the side-street from the *Hotel Sophia*. The pension also faces out over the Harbour, with the access from Odhos Akti Miaouli.
Very ethnic.

Proceeding up Odhos Akti Miaouli advances towards:-

Pension Coral (*Tmr* 15C/D3/4)
Directions: As above and on the right.

Rooms
Directions: Next door and one up from the *Pension Coral*.

Further along Odhos Akti Miaouli, across the junction with Odhos D Rafaelia, and on the right is the:-

Hotel Miranda (*Tmr* 16D4) (Class A) Tel 52230
Directions: As above.
Recommended but, in 1987, apparently under reconstruction. Classified as a pension, rates for a single room sharing a bathroom start at 2000drs, double rooms 3000drs rising respectively to 2400drs and 3600drs (1st July-30th Sept) En suite single rooms cost 3100drs and doubles 4200drs increasing to 3700drs and 5000drs respectively.

Pension Agelika (*Tmr* 17D5) (Class A) Odhos Akti Miaouli Tel 52360
Directions: Further up Akti Miaouli St, beyond the Clinic (*Tmr* 18D4/5). Modern with en suite bathrooms. Single rooms from 1450drs and doubles 2300drs.

Almost at the far side of the bottom of the Harbour Esplanade, from the Ferry-boat Quay (*Tmr* 1D2), is Odhos N Votsi. Odhos N Votsi is a narrow and undistinguished street at the outset, being crowded in by various shops on the right (*Sbo*). In a town that is really all 'Old Quarter', this end of Hydra is more 'Old Quarter' than the rest, if you see what I mean! The first turning off to the right, an alleyway, where Odhos N Votsi breaks into a Square, leads to:-

Rooms (*Tmr* 19C3)
Directions: As above and on the right opposite a right angled corner, over the *Snackbar Thalami*.

Continuing up Odhos N Votsi, leaves the OTE (*Tmr* 20C3) on the left, and the Police station (*Tmr* 21C3/4) and Hospital (*Tmr* 22C3/4) on the right, after which the street widens out past a public garden.

Hotel Hydroussa (ΥΔΡΟΥΣΑ) (*Tmr* 23C4) (Class B) Tel 52400
Directions: As above and shuts off the south end of the park.

Once the *Xenia*, the hotel appears rather run-down, almost barrack-like at the rear. All rooms have en suite bathrooms with single rooms costing 2600drs and double rooms 3200drs, rising to 3400drs and 4200drs (16th June-30th Sept).

Pension Rafaelias (*Tmr* 24C4) Odhos D Rafaelia Tel 52584
Directions Diagonally across the road from the *Hotel Hydroussa*.

The pension is really a mansion owned by the proprietor of the Chemist shop next door. A wonderful place to stay as the house is fitted with pleasantly old fashioned furniture and hangings. A single room costs 1800drs and a double 4000drs, both including breakfast, but the accommodation is so popular that it is full, even out of season.

Guest House Orloff (ΟΡΛΩΦ) (*Tmr* 25C4) 9 N Votsi/Rafaelia Sts Tel 52564
Directions: Where the road widens out, at the junction of N Votsi and Rafaelia Sts, and indicated by a very discreet, red sign on the brick gatepost. The other side of Rafaelia St is a large carpenter's workshop.

A magnificent house – just take a 'gander' at the Reception Hall or the wooden beam supported, open cellar, rather imperiously called 'The Arcade'. The large, high ceilinged bedrooms are simply but elegantly furnished. Daily rates for the ten units, most with an en suite bathroom, vary between 3750 and 5000drs. Admittedly these fees include breakfast served in the garden. The garden courtyard becomes a bar at night.

Back at the harbour end of N Votsi St, Odhos A Lignou branches off and scales the hillside to the right of the Port (*Sbo*). This ascends steeply into the rabbit warren of lanes and alleyways that crown the outcrop.

Rooms Savvas (*Tmr* 26C3) Odhos A Lignou Tel 52259
Directions: As above and on the right, next door to the *PASOK* office.

Pension Flora (*Tmr* 27C4)
Directions: Further up Odhos A Lignou on a parallel, higher alley reached by climbing lots of steps from Odhos A Lignou.

Ethnic rooms, ethnic *Poom* toilets and an ethnic courtyard. The reception office is open between 0900-1300hrs & 1530-2030hrs.

Continuing up the seemingly ever ascending and widely spaced steps of Odhos A Lignou gives access to the steps of Kriezi St. These climb away to the right and progress to a scattered, hilltop 'village within a village'. At the first crossroads 'of the alleyways' is the lateral Tsamadou lane and a small store (*Tmr* 28B5) on the left. At the next crossroads along Odhos Kriezi, is another store (*Tmr* 28B5) on the right. Turn right and on the right is the:-

Hotel Theano (*Tmr* 29B4/5) Tel 53157
Directions: As above, tucked away down the lane.

It may be nicely appointed but the 'advert copy' that describes it as being only five minutes from the centre of Hydra may well have been written by a very fast mountain goat or a direct flying crow, especially if the centre is taken to be the waterfront.

Rooms Efstathiou (*Tmr* 30B5) Tel 52392
Directions: As for the *Hotel Theano* but turn left, not right at the 'store crossroads' and left again.

The left-hand headland, entering the port (*Sbo*), also harbours some accommodation. This is a rather smart area, with lanes and steps confusingly wandering about the contoured ramparts of the hillside, the slopes of which climb steeply from the very wide Quayside.

Pension Stelios (*Tmr*33D1)
Directions: The name of the pension is conveniently painted on the wall but the establishment is rather more difficult to actually reach. Proceed along the quay towards the sea, past the water bowser docking jetty (*Tmr* 31D2) on the left and the Museum (*Tmr* 32D1/2) on the right. A steep flight of steps clambers up the slope and turns to the left leading to the pension, again on the left.

The Esplanade follows the curve of the Harbour round to the right (*Sbo*) in a westerly direction. Across the quay from the inner harbour jetty (*Tmr* 34C2/3), which acts as a repository for various building supplies, is:-
Pension Douglas (*Tmr* 35C2) (Class C) No. 48 Paralia Tel 52597
Directions: As above.

Reputably owned and run by an Englishman, Douglas Wilson. Rooms share the bathroom with a single room costing from 1150drs and a double room from 1750drs.

See **Excursions to Kamini & Vlichos and Mandraki**.

The Eating Out As is often the case on 'day-trip islands', the number of establishments is only equalled by their overall blandness. The serried ranks of Esplanade restaurants set out their tables and chairs in the morning, after which the staff brace themselves for the hungry hordes.

Many of the restaurants offer set menus, up to six in number in one case. One establishment even has a Japanese translation.... These set menu meals range in price between 1000-2000drs per head, which charges often total more than the individual items would....

Another general point is that those eateries situated in the back streets are not more competitive than their 'waterfront cousins'. For instance a Nes meh ghala at the *Thalami Snackbar* (*Tmr* 19C3) costs 120drs whilst the average quayside cost is 110drs – added to which the area of the *Thalami* smells of lavatories. Hydra is also one of those few islands where taxes, which are by law incorporated in the right-hand menu prices, are often added to the end of the bill as a surcharge – nasty.

One of the most popular (and expensive) waterfront locations is:-
Antonios (*Tmr* 36D2/3) situated on the corner of Odhos D Kiosse and the Esplanade. Sitting here allows observation of the diverting antics in and around the water taxi section of the quay (*Tmr* 37D2/3), the ferry-boat and hydrofoil comings and goings as well as the *Volta*. Two Nes meh ghala (250drs) and a brandy with mezes (250drs) will set a couple back 500drs, so take your time.

On the other hand, all is not lost as there is one traditional establishment, even if it does lack a view:-

Kafeneion (*Tmr* 38C/D3) Odhos Akti Miaouli.
Directions: On the left of Odhos Akti Miaouli, on the far side of a spur lane to the Market (*Tmr* 39D3).

A 'real' live commonplace kafeneion with a metered phone and a hut-like kiosk selling cigarettes and camera film. Two Nes meh ghala 150drs, yes 150drs! A find.

Further up Odhos Akti Miaouli, beyond *Pension Coral* (*Tmr* 15C/D3/4) and ***Rooms***, and on the right is the *Taverna To* ΣTEKI (*Tmr* 40C/D3/4) which displays a reasonably priced bill of fare.

Taverna Laikon (ΛAIKON) (*Tmr* 41D2)
Directions: A pleasant harbour position, if somewhat outside the orbit of the main waterfront activity, which some might consider a plus point or three. The building was the Tsamados family mansion and the upper floors housed the Merchant Marine School.

A wide range of fare at less expensive prices than the more central establishments. Omelettes to lobster, coffee to whisky, the only drawback being that there doesn't seem to be a kortaki retsina on the menu. Sample prices include bacon omelette 170drs, mixed omelette 200drs, squid 224drs, liver 224drs, meatballs 250drs, pork souvlaki 500drs, pork steak 500drs, Greek salad 180drs and a bottle of beer 80drs.

Two attractively situated tavernas are:-
Taverna O Douskos (*Tmr* 42E4)
Directions: Occupying a pleasant, tree shaded Square at the top of Tombazi St.

Recommended to us but... Apart from the set dishes 1 and 2, the usual offerings are listed in a menu titled 'et alla carte' (*sic*). Greece, oh Greece where art thou....
Taverna (*Tmr* 43D4)
Directions: Occupies most of the pot-planted, irregular Square, beyond the block in which is situated *Georges Guest House*.

Only open in the evenings. Average fare at average (Hydra) prices.

Whilst walking along Tombazi St towards *Taverna O Douskos* (if you were) – Sakhtouri St branches off to the left (*Sbo*), close to a Laundry (*Tmr* 44D/E3).

Taverna ΥΔΡΕΙΚΗ ΓΩΝΙΑ (*Tmr* 45E3)
Directions: Where Sakhtouri St bends round to the right, immediately after a Church on the outside of the curve. Chairs and tables line a beflowered stone wall across the street and there is a largish charcoal BBQ unit standing to one side of the building.

The establishment appears to be a reasonably priced taverna. Notice carefully the word 'appears' because this taverna achieves a unique honour, that of joining my very small band of *Rip-off Joints*. The management have an unpleasant habit of ignoring the menu prices and overcharging. We ordered two BBQ chicken at 250drs each, a Greek salad at 150drs which was charged at 800drs instead of 650drs. After a complaint, we were informed the chicken had a special sauce, which explanation we turned down. Eventually, after alluding to the police, we received the refund! It must be admitted that a resident musical trio, who park themselves on the outside chairs, performed very well with excellent bouzouki.

A little further along Tombazi St and, at the fork adjacent to the *Hotel Amaryllis* (*Tmr* 6D3), the left-hand street curves past the garden wall entrance to a *Three Brothers Taverna* (*Tmr* 7D/E3/4) displaying menu options 1, 2, 3 and 4. (Incidentally, there is another *Three Brothers Taverna* (*Tmr* 46C3) on the corner of Odhos L Pinotsi and Odhos N Votsi, on the other side of the port. They also 'sport' menus 1, 2, 3 and 4).

On the far side of the first *Three Brothers 'Square'*, is Odhos G Kouloura.
Taverna Ο ΦΙΛΙΠΠΑΣ (Philipas) (*Tmr* 9E4) Odhos G Kouloura
Directions: As above and on the left, at the outset of a tree lined avenue.
No written menu, but 'pots' of this and that at average prices of 240drs.

Self-service Snackbar (*Tmr* 47D3)
Directions: On the right of Tombazi St, beyond Pan Travel.
A souvlaki costs 90drs.

Another snackbar is:-
'The Original Souvlaki Place'
Directions: On the right of Odhos A Miaouli, just past the entrance door to *Hotel Christina* (*Tmr* 14C/D3)

But the best buy, an absolute find must be:-
ΟΙΝΟΠΩΛΕΙΟ Ο ΜΠΑΡΜΠΑ ΔΗΜΑΣ.(*Tmr* 48D/E3/4) Odhos Tombazi
Directions: A low, small, one-time wine shop on the right (*Sbo*) of Tombazi St, beyond the fork by the *Hotel Amaryllis*.

Run by friendly, Papa Yanni. Apart from the contents of his bubbling pots and pans, which might include beef stew, fish in tomato sauce, meatballs or griddle cooked fish, there is a meal of the day. Some of these are quite exotic and include snails. A full-scale 'blow-out' for two averages 1200drs and there is retsina from the barrel. A beer (80drs), a plate of tzatziki (90drs), a Greek salad (170drs), a plate of liver with a few chips (280drs), fish (400drs), 2 jugs of retsina (50drs each) and bread (50drs – 3 helpings) costs 1170drs. Dolmades stuffed with meat are charged at 280drs and a large plate of octopus 350drs. Both kortaki and barrel retsina are available. The kitchen is tucked away in a 'mezzanine cellar' (a what?).

See **Excursions to Kamini & Vlichos and Mandraki**

THE A TO Z OF USEFUL INFORMATION

BANKS Only two, which is rather fewer than one would anticipate. (Perhaps everyone 'does very nicely' with credit cards). These are the:-
Commercial Bank of Greece (*Tmr* 49D3) 14 Paralia
and the
National Bank (*Tmr* 50D3) The Esplanade.
This bank also opens for exchange transactions early weekday evenings during the months of June to September.

BEACHES *See* **Excursions to Kamini & Vlichos and Mandraki.**

BICYCLE, SCOOTER & CAR HIRE None.

BREAD SHOPS There is one (*Tmr* 51D3) on the Esplanade in the very first block of buildings to the right (*Sbo* of Odhos Tombazi, next door to the Hydra Corner Jewellery Shop. Another (*Tmr* 51D/E3), that is also a patisserie and store, is tucked away in the narrow alleyway that connects the streets of D. Kiosse and Tombazi. Here they sell a good feta pie for 60drs. This shop not only opens Saturday evenings but Sunday mornings as well.

BOOKSELLERS Here and there, along the busiest section of the Esplanade, some foreign language newspapers are sold, as are the more popular paperbacks from swivelling racks.

BUSES None.

CINEMAS One (*Tmr* 52D3) on the right (*Sbo*) of Odhos Ikonomou.

COMMERCIAL SHOPPING AREA There is an excellent central Market (*Tmr* 39D3) behind the main section of the Quayside Esplanade. The meat and fruit stalls also open Saturday morning, as do one or two on Sunday morning.

A 'greengrocers caique' moors to the inner Harbour quay wall; there is a butcher, prior to the steps at the western entrance to the Market from Akti Miaouli St, and a supermarket (well, more a jumbled store) beneath the Post Office (*Tmr* 53D3), at the bottom of another flight of steps up to the Market. Beyond and on the same side of Odhos Akti Miaouli as the traditional Kafeneion (*Tmr* 38C/D3), is a greengrocers. Cigarettes are sold from an Esplanade edging gift shop (*Tmr* 54D3). It goes without saying that the majority of the Esplanade shops are gift or gold shops and most even open on Saturday nights.

FERRY-BOATS & FLYING DOLPHINS The island is well served, some might think too well!

Ferry-boat timetable (Mid-season)

Day	**Departure time**	**Ferry-boat**	**Ports/Islands of Call**
Monday-Friday	1215hrs		Spetses.
Monday-Friday	1545hrs		Poros, Methana(M), Aegina, Piraeus(M).
Saturday,	1215hrs		Ermioni(M), Spetses.
Sunday	1545hrs		Poros, Methana(M), Aegina, Piraeus(M).

One-way fares: Hydra to Piraeus 580drs; duration 4hrs 10mins
Spetses 300drs; 2¼hrs

Flying Dolphin timetable (Mid-season)

Day	**Departure time**	**Port/Islands of Call**
Daily	0650hrs	Poros, Zea Port, (Piraeus).
	0655hrs	Zea Port, (Piraeus).
	0945hrs	Ermioni(M).
	0945hrs	Poros, Methana(M), Aegina, Zea Port(Piraeus).
	0950hrs	Spetses, Portoheli(M).
	1045hrs	Spetses.
	1050hrs	Poros, Zea Port, (Piraeus).
	1155hrs	Zea Port (Piraeus).
	1530hrs	Ermioni(M).
	1635hrs	Poros, Zea Port (Piraeus).

	1955hrs	Spetses, Portoheli(M).
Monday-Saturday	1555hrs	Spetses, Portoheli(M).
	1755hrs	Zea Port(Piraeus).
	1835hrs	Ermioni(M), Spetses, Portoheli(M).
	1945hrs	Ermioni(M).
Tuesday, Thursday	1045hrs	Spetses, Leonidio(M), Kiparissi(M), Gerakas(M).
	1400hrs	Poros, Zea Port(Piraeus).
Friday	1825hrs	Ermioni(M), Spetses, Portoheli(M).
Sunday	1345hrs	Spetses, Portoheli(M).
	1525hrs	Spetses, Portoheli(M).
	1555hrs	Poros, Zea Port(Piraeus).
	1725hrs	Spetses, Portoheli(M).
	1725hrs	Zea Port(Piraeus).
	1750hrs	Zea Port(Piraeus).
	2025hrs	Ermioni(M).

Tuesday, Saturday	1045hrs	Spetses, Leonidio(M), Kiparissi(M), Monemvassia(M), Kithira, Neapoli(M).
Tuesday, Thursday, Saturday, Sunday	1045hrs	Spetses, Leonidio(M), Kiparissi(M), Monemvassia(M).
Monday, Wednesday Friday, Saturday, Sunday	1400hrs	Poros, Zea Port(Piraeus).
Monday, Wednesday	1045hrs	Spetses, Portoheli(M).
Friday	1510hrs	Poros, Zea Port(Piraeus).
Thursday, Sunday	1650hrs	Poros, Zea Port(Piraeus).
Saturday, Sunday	1145hrs	Spetses, Portoheli(M).
	1345hrs	Spetses.
Monday-Friday	1145hrs	Spetses, Portoheli(M).
Saturday	1745hrs	Spetses, Portoheli(M).
Friday, Saturday	1745hrs	Spetses.

Sample one-way fares: Hydra to			
	Spetses	490drs;duration from	35mins
	Kithira	3300drs;	3hrs 50mins
	Poros	360drs;	½hr
	Aegina	800drs;	1¼hrs
	Zea Port (Piraeus)	1450drs;	1hr 40mins

FERRY-BOAT & FLYING DOLPHIN TICKET OFFICE The ferry-boat tickets are sold from a table set-up, prior to a boat's departure, on the Esplanade, in the area of the National Bank (*Tmr* 50D3).

Flying Dolphin tickets are sold by:-
Pan Travel (*Tmr* 55D3) Odhos Tombazi/Paralia Tel 52019
Directions: The office is above 'Hydra Corner' – a jewellery, gold and silver shop. Access is up a flight of steps at the outset of and on the right of Odhos Tombazi.

HAIRDRESSERS There is a 'front room' ladies hairdresser at the Harbour end of Odhos A Lignou.

LAUNDRY One (*Tmr* 44D/E3), situated in Tombazi St, on the left (*Sbo*) of an irregular Square, prior to the *Hotel Amaryllis*.

MEDICAL CARE
Chemists & Pharmacies The Rafaelias family appear to dominate the medical

scene and own the large Pharmacy (*Tmr* 24C4) just beyond the *Hotel Hydroussa* on Odhos D Rafaelia. I write 'appear to dominate', because I believe there is also a related Doctor Rafaelias who can be contacted via the Chemist Shop. There is another, large Pharmacy (*Tmr* 56E3) on the left of Sakhtouri St, which angles off Tombazi St.

Clinic (*Tmr* 18D4/5). At No 38 Odhos Akti Miaouli, on the right and prior to the *Pension Agelika*. Open for business weekdays between 0800-1200hrs & 1700-1930hrs and on Saturday and Sundays between 1000-1200hrs.
Dentist Pangyiotis A Zerios whose surgery is on the right (*Sbo*) of Odhos N Votsi, prior to the Police station (*Tmr* 21C3/4).
Doctors *See* **Clinic & Chemists, Medical Care**. There is a Dr. Charalabos Coccoris in Odhos D Kiosse, on the left opposite *Rooms Dardanou* (*Tmr* 4D/E3).
Hospital (*Tmr* 22C3/4) A modern building on the right of Odhos N Votsi.

NTOG None.

OTE (*Tmr* 20C3) Across the road from the Hospital. Open weekdays between 0730-1510hrs.

PLACES OF INTEREST
Churches, Cathedrals & Monasteries
Monastery of the Panaghia (The Assumption of the Virgin Mary) (*Tmr* 57C3) Prominent due to the tall bell and clock tower which borders the central section of the Esplanade, and marks the harbour entrance to the Monastery. The site, supposedly chosen by a nun from another island, was completed in 1776 and the construction materials include ancient temple building blocks from Poros island. There is a western entrance from Odhos N Votsi via another bell tower. It may be of interest that the clocks are approximately accurate time pieces – most unusual

Monastery Profitis Elias (The Prophet Elijah) Located high above and looking down on the Port. A 1½-2hr walk starting out on Odhos Akti Miaoulis and branching off left (*Sbo*), prior to the *Goroyannis Mansion* (*See* **Mansions**). From this track another left turn leads to the cemetery and right to the Monastery.
The Church of St. John the Baptist Proceed up the steeply stepped Odhos A Lignou to the crossroads with Tsamadou lane, whereon is a general store (*Tmr* 28B5), where turn left. Another left off Tsamadou proceeds due east to the Church of Ag Dimitros around which the path divides. Take the right fork and another right-hand track to the Church. Restored in 1738, the whole interior is covered with Byzantine style murals illustrating Biblical events.

Mansions (Archontika) & other buildings Left to right (*Sbo*), some of the outstanding family houses, mainly dating from the French revolution and Napolonic blockade-running years (1789-1815), are as follows:-
Old Arsenal (*Tmr* 58D1) Now houses the Port police.
Kriezis Mansion (*Tmr* 59D1) One of two family houses, the other being to the west of the Port, in the hill village of Vlichos.
Tsamados Mansion (*Tmr* 41D2) The family gave the house to the State. The ground floor is occupied by the *Taverna Laikon* and the upper storeys housed the National Merchant Marine Academy.
Lazaros Koundouriotis Mansion (*Tmr* 60B/C4) Lazaros was brother of George Koundouriotis (*See* **George Koundouriotis Mansion**) and this house was built by their father, in the late 1700s.
George Voulgaris Mansion (*Tmr* 61C3) Now a ruin, but still displays a Moorish entrance, which betrays the fact that it was built for Voulgaris by a Turkish friend.

Tombazis Mansion (*Tmr* 62B/C2/3) Both imposing and prominent being at the foot of the western headland. Now serves as a dormitory for the Athens School of Fine Art.
Voulgaris (Economou-Merikles) Mansion (*Tmr* 63C2) Originally owned by a brother of George Voulgaris, the ground floor is taken up with shops.
George Koundouriotis Mansion (*Tmr* 64B2) George Koundouriotis was both Prime Minister (1848) and President of Greece (1822-1826).
Goroyannis Mansion Some way up the hillside backing the Port, on the route to the Monastery Profitis Elias. Not only interesting as a large house dating back to the 1700s but also because its main, western aspect faces out over Kala Pigathia Square, or sweet water wells. The plateia is so named because of the presence of two large metal capped wells. This area was where the original Albanian settlement of Kiapha was located.

Museum (*Tmr* 32D1/2) A large, modern construction that replaced an original building pulled down because it was unstable.

POLICE
Port (*Tmr* 58D1) On the left-hand (*Sbo*), eastern headland.
Town (*Tmr* 21C3/4) A large, grand, two storey building on the right (*Sbo*) of Odhos N Votsi and quite unlike any other police station. The building is labelled ΑΣΤΥΝΟΜΙΚΟ ΤΜΗΜΑ ΤΑΞΗΣ ΥΔΡΑΣ and the office is on the first floor.

POST OFFICE (*Tmr* 53D3) Confusingly the sign is over a basement 'supermarket', which a number of tourists mistakenly enter. The Post Office is up steps to the level of the Market.

TAXIS, WATER (*Tmr* 37D2/3) The speedboat variety moor in the crook of the inner Harbour, opposite the *Cafe-bar Antonios*. The one-way fare to Mandraki Beach, for instance, costs 550drs.
The more conventional excursion boats, which moor against the centre of the Harbour Esplanade, only cost 50drs per person each way.
Both water taxis and excursion boats run scheduled trips to Kamini, Vlichos and Mandraki Beaches. The excursion boats also organise a round-island trip.

TELEPHONE NUMBERS & ADDRESSES

Chemist (*Tmr* 24C4) D Rafaelia St	Tel 52059
Clinic (*Tmr* 18D4/5) 38 Akti Miaouli St	Tel 52420
Hospital (*Tmr* 22C3/4) N. Votsi St	Tel 53151
Olympic Airways	Tel 53135
Police, port (*Tmr* 58D1) Paralia	Tel. 52279
Police, town (*Tmr* 21C3/4) N. Votsi St.	Tel 52205
Town Hall	Tel 52210

TOILETS Located on the right, at the side of the steps up to the Market, diagonally across the way from the Post Office/supermarket (*Tmr* 53D3). They are very clean.

TRAVEL AGENTS & TOUR OFFICES
Pan Travel (*Tmr* 55D3) Tombazi/Paralia Sts Tel 53135
Directions: Up steps to one side of and over the precious metal shop, 'Hydra Corner'.

Information for *Rooms to Let – Hotels Boats* (*sic*) and they sell tickets for the Flying Dolphins.

WATER Drinking water has to be shipped in and the boats berth to a small quay in the outer Harbour (*Tmr* 31D2).

EXCURSIONS TO HYDRA PORT SURROUNDS

Excursion to Mandraki Beach (about 2km) The sea hugging road advances from the Port Esplanade to the right (*Fsw*), rounding the old fort on the eastern headland. The 20-30 minute walk round to Mandraki Beach highlights the lack of shade, the road traversing a moorland like, shrubbery covered granite bedrock. About 80m beyond the port is a small square shack on the sea side of the road, beyond which are steps down to the water's edge. People swim from and lie out on this boulderous shore. The hillsides sprout a number of private villas some of which are very 'sassy'. Close to Mandraki the road curves round following the contours of the coastline past a tree shaded chapel and a boatyard on the left. Across the road, on the right, is a very small boat building shed. Believe it or not, quite large boats are launched across the road and down a ramshackle runway of poles and timbers, a distance of some 50m with the necessity to swing left close to the sea's edge. The ropes used to curb a craft from thundering down out of control are wrapped around, amongst other items, the front gate posts of a nearby private villa, tree trunks and a buried cannon barrel.

MANDRAKI BEACH (about 2km from Hydra Town) The pebble beach, set in bare hillsides at the bottom of a 'U' shaped bay, is kept quite clean, even if there is some sea worn brick rubble here and there. The *Hotel Mirimar* has walled in the beach and backshore but it is only necessary for walkers to pass through a pair of highly varnished doors set in the nearside of the wall. The set-up is pleasantly laid out and Mandraki is probably the best of all the island's beach options, even if it is quite frenetically busy. The sea bottom is made up of rather slimy, big pebbles. Just so nobody gets bored, there is water skiing, wind surfing and pedaloes. Drinks at the hotel bar are, naturally, very expensive with a Nes meh ghala costing 120drs and a bottle of beer 150drs, but they do have a monopoly.

Water taxis ensure a constant stream of punters and by midday the place is damned crowded.

Excursion to Vlichos via Kamini (about 2km) There are three routes, two from the upper reaches of Hydra Town. One is along Odhos Kriezi, which emerges on the edge of the summer dry river-bed that runs down to Kamini. The other, higher path is along Odhos A Pipinou which stretches from *Goroyannis Mansion* towards Vlichos, passing between a couple of Mansions above Kamini. The easiest route, the 'main road', is that edging the coastline from beyond the western headland of the port. At the ragged inlet of Avlaki, beneath a discotheque and a snackbar, are several concrete bathing platforms accessed down steep steps. The roadway passes the *Boudouris Mansion* on the left and then proceeds to:-

KAMINI (about 1km from Hydra Town) The coastal road forms a junction with the Main St that climbs the hillside to the left. On the right of this junction are *Apartments to Let Tel 52481* whilst the Main St passes a *Pension*, with apartments, and ***Rooms***, beyond which are the *Hotel Thiano* and *Pension Kamini*.

Early arrivals at Hydra Port might consider escaping to this, admittedly, not wildly attractive but certainly quieter outpost. The hillsides edging the village are topped by at least two, now defunct, windmills.

The coastal road continues on parallel to and about 50m up from the sea, prior to dropping down to the small, rocky mole protected harbour of Kamini.

This is set in a pleasant little cove with the aforementioned river-bed forming a swathe of pebble foreshore, on which a number of small boats are beached. On the far side is a quayside on which is a taverna interestingly painted in ochre and browny yellow. A beer at the taverna costs 100drs. *George and Annas Taverna Restaurant* is further up the side of the river-bed.

Beyond the harbour, the path, which skirts round the quayside taverna, climbs the hillside leaving a napkin sized, pebble beach set amongst the rocks. Offshore is a tiny, chapel topped islet. The wide, flint track continues on quite high up until rounding a headland from which are pleasant, panoramic views extending out over the sea to a mainland and island bounded horizon. Below is the settlement of:-

VLICHOS (about 2km from Hydra Town) The prospect takes in a curved beach backed by a scrubbly, 'pylon littered' backshore bounded, on the far side, by a dwelling draped rocky outcrop behind which are the rust coloured roofs of a pleasant, small village. Beyond this are some agricultural holdings. In the far distance is the western end of Hydra, the island of Dokos and various rocky outcrops which break up the unending sea vista.

There is a tricky goat track (that is tricky even for a goat) that crabs down to the nearside of Vlichos Beach. This passes a spot on which is evidence of occasional, unofficial camping. Unofficial because camping is forbidden. Older, more decrepit walkers, such as myself, proceed round to the left past the parochially famous, ruined, humpback bridge, to cross a deep, narrow gorge on a more modern span and thence to the back of the hamlet. There is the very welcome *Lichos Taverna* on the left, half-way to the shore. The owners are of Romany appearance but very smiley. Simple fare is available and a beer costs 100drs.

The area is flyblown, and the beach, on closer inspection, is dirty with quite a lot of tar scattered about and mixed up with building rubble interspersed by pebbles. A number of craft are drawn up on the middle shore. Unfortunately the sea is also rather dirty with jellyfish, cigarette ends and (possibly) some 'noddies' floating about.

The very energetic might consider the further 4km trek to the once, agriculturally busy but now almost completely deserted village of **Episkopi** that nestles in a concealed mountain valley.

Excursion to the Eastern Monasteries (about 10km) The route commences along Odhos G Kouloura, past the *Hotel Greco*, and or the Football Ground from Hydra Town. As with most of the island, the eastern end is dry, parched and barren, so this trip should be undertaken only by the hardiest travellers.

Ag Matrona Convent About 45-60 minutes walk. Once famous for the weaving of the nuns, as were all Hydriot convents.

Ag Trias Convent Another 15 mins further on and quite possibly the most attractive of the four religious houses on this route.

Ag Nikolaos Monastery Erected in 1724 and until recently still occupied by a sole monk.

Zourvas Convent Once a monastery, but became a convent and is still inhabited. The total journey time from Hydra Town is about three hours.

14 POROS (ΠΟΡΟΣ) **
Argo-Saronic Islands

FIRST IMPRESSIONS
Friendly people; pretty countryside; snakes; saganaki (a mouth watering, small panful of scrambled eggs cum omelette with a bacon/sausage filling); ferry-boats; 'imported' beach; flotilla yachts; 'Lefkas-like' sound or channel.

SPECIALITIES
None that spring to mind.

RELIGIOUS HOLIDAYS & FESTIVALS
include: 23rd April – Festival, Cathedral of Ag Giorgios, Poros Town; 3-4th June – Flower Festival, Galatas (M); 8th June – Panaghia; Last week of June – Navy Week, Naval School, Poros Town.

VITAL STATISTICS
Tel prefix 0298. Poros island is made up of Kalavria, the large, main island, and Spheria (Sferia), the main town and port islet. The two are separated by a very narrow ditch, sorry canal! The overall island area is some 31sq km with an east to west length of 6km and a maximum top to bottom distance of 3km (excluding the Ag Paraskevis peninsula). The channel between the mainland and Poros Town is only 370m wide and up to 2km in length. The population numbers some 4000 plus.

HISTORY
The island's early history was dominated by its association with the ancient mainland city of Trizina. Poros was historically known as Calauria (Kalavria). The mythological character Theseus, who slayed the Cretan Minotaur with the aid of Ariadne, is linked with the island by his mother Aethra. The Temple of Poseidon, established about 500 BC, is the island's most famous link with early history. The Temple was well known as a sanctuary for fugitives, one of the most famous of whom was the renowned Athenian orator, Demosthenes. Hounded by his enemies he is supposed to have committed suicide in 322 BC with poison he carried in a quill pen.

From about the middle of the first century BC the island was laid waste, on a fairly regular basis, by the incursions of various invaders and pirates.

The Venetians established a castle on Bourtzi islet to the south-west of Poros Town. The island probably reached its zenith of modern day historical fame during the Greek War of Independence when the favourable anchorages hosted various allied naval fleets. These associations with ships of war continued with the establishment, for a few years, from 1828, of a Russian Naval Base in Russian Bay. This was followed by the use of Megalo Neorion Bay as a repair and building yard for the Greek Navy, immediately after Independence.

Perhaps the island's most notorious pages of history, written in 1831, also involved the sea. Admiral Miaoulis, a Hydriot, celebrated naval captain during the War of Independence and subsequently Admiral of the fleet, objected to the Government's Chief Minister, one Kapodistrias. To express this resentment he took over the island's arsenal as well as the Greek fleet at anchor, probably rattling a few anchor chains at the same time. The Government sent in the troops and the Russian fleet to demand his surrender but Miaoulis blew up a couple of ships

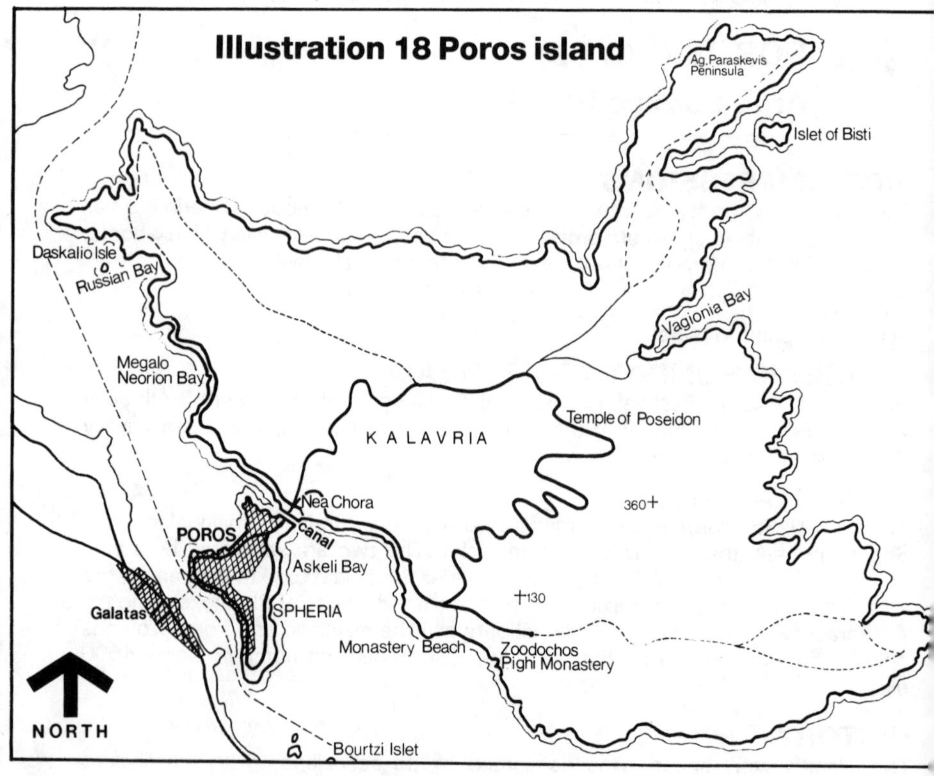

and escaped to Hydra. The victory of Kapodistrias was short-lived as he was assassinated not long afterwards.

King Otho, the first Greek King, caused the establishment of the Naval Base on Spheria island in 1846. After the transfer of these facilities to the island of Salaminas the base became a Naval School.

GENERAL

The setting is lovely, with the mountains of the Peloponnese forming an attractive backdrop to the sea passageway that beguilingly separates Poros from the mainland. Scenically the island is attractive; the town port is very interesting with enough of a hill to allow an upper village; the people are most friendly and there are adequate ***Rooms*** and tavernas. So where's the catch? Simply put, there aren't any satisfactory beaches. Those stretches of foreshore that the locals enthusiastically eulogise about are nothing more than narrow strips of pebble, many of which have been overlaid with 'imported', coarse sand. If this were not bad enough, most of the beaches are some distance from the Town, despite which they become very crowded as all but two have been 'matched' with low-rise hotels, interspersed by taverna restaurants.

The active and investigative mind might, in some measure, become a trifle apathetic. One day's hire of transport will suffice to allow all the island's attractions to be visited and still allow time to catch a ferry across to the mainland and take in at least one of the sights.

Poros is not water-short, as are many of the other Argo-Saronic islands, nor is it devoid of scooters, the fearsome noise of which are punctuated by rare moments of tranquillity in the town. But head for the countryside or the 'upper village' and you could be a million miles away from the rest of the world. But I do wish Poros had a worthwhile beach!

POROS: capital town & port (Illustration 19) The Esplanade borders the town's waterfront and requires every metre to cater for the extensive use to which it is put. These demands include those of the local fisherman, the large flotilla sailing fleet, hydrofoils, Piraeus ferries, excursion craft, so many 'islands in a day' boats, large inter-island Ro-Ro's and mini car ferrries (that connect Poros to mainland Galatas). That's quite a lot of activity. The Port and Town are absolutely 'infested' with the *Island Sailing Club*, the craft of which moor both sides of the Ferry-boat Quay headland.

A very interesting feature of the settlement is that the quayside and its development is a semicircle, radiating out from a conical hillside. This low-rise knoll is capped by a quiet 'upper village' which is in some ways remote from the frenetic Esplanade activity. Even the rubbish in the 'upper village' is gathered using pack-mules.

ARRIVAL BY FERRY & FLYING DOLPHIN

It is almost like Clapham Junction, with boats, ferries and hydrofoils docking and departing all day long. A central section of quayside, adjacent to the Main Square, Plateia Iroon (*Tmr* 1B3), caters for all the passenger craft (*Tmr* 2B2/3). At the height of summer the Esplanade is converted into a one-way street (*from left to right, Sbo*) and, due to the congestion, ferry-boats have to berth as far round the Esplanade as the *Hotel Latsi* (*Tmr* 3C1/2).

Independent travellers will be pleased to hear that the worthy citizens proposition disembarking passengers with the offer of ***Rooms***.

THE ACCOMMODATION & EATING OUT

The Accommodation The 'going' rate for a double room is between 1500-2000drs.

If a prospect is not smartly gathered up or is not prepared to search out accommodation, then it is possible to dump luggage alongside the Main Square statue, adjacent to the taxi rank, and proceed directly to:-

Takis Tours (*Tmr* 4 Inset) Tel 22048/23980

Directions: From the Main Square the office is visible above the *Cafe George*. It is necessary to climb the steps to the right of the cafe (*Sbo*) and turn left on the undulating alley that almost parallels the Esplanade below. The office is the first on the left.

For a market leader I'm sorry to report that the staff's attitude is off-hand, even 'couldn't care less', if not bordering on the ill-mannered. Any enquiry about the type of accommodation being offered is met with disinterest or, worse, a demeanour indicating that the enquirer has a damned nerve to make any query. I dared to ask how far from the office some rooms were, after being advised to catch a taxi. The dark, tanned male, who struck me as being a Cypriot Welshman (but I don't wish to insult either nation), shot back, 'Near the Naval Base – maybe 4½mins by taxi – Is that too far?' Never having, at that time, set foot 'in anger' on Poros before, that piece of gratuitous information meant absolutely nothing. I mean to say some Greek taxi drivers can frighteningly cover quite a lot of ground in 4½ minutes!

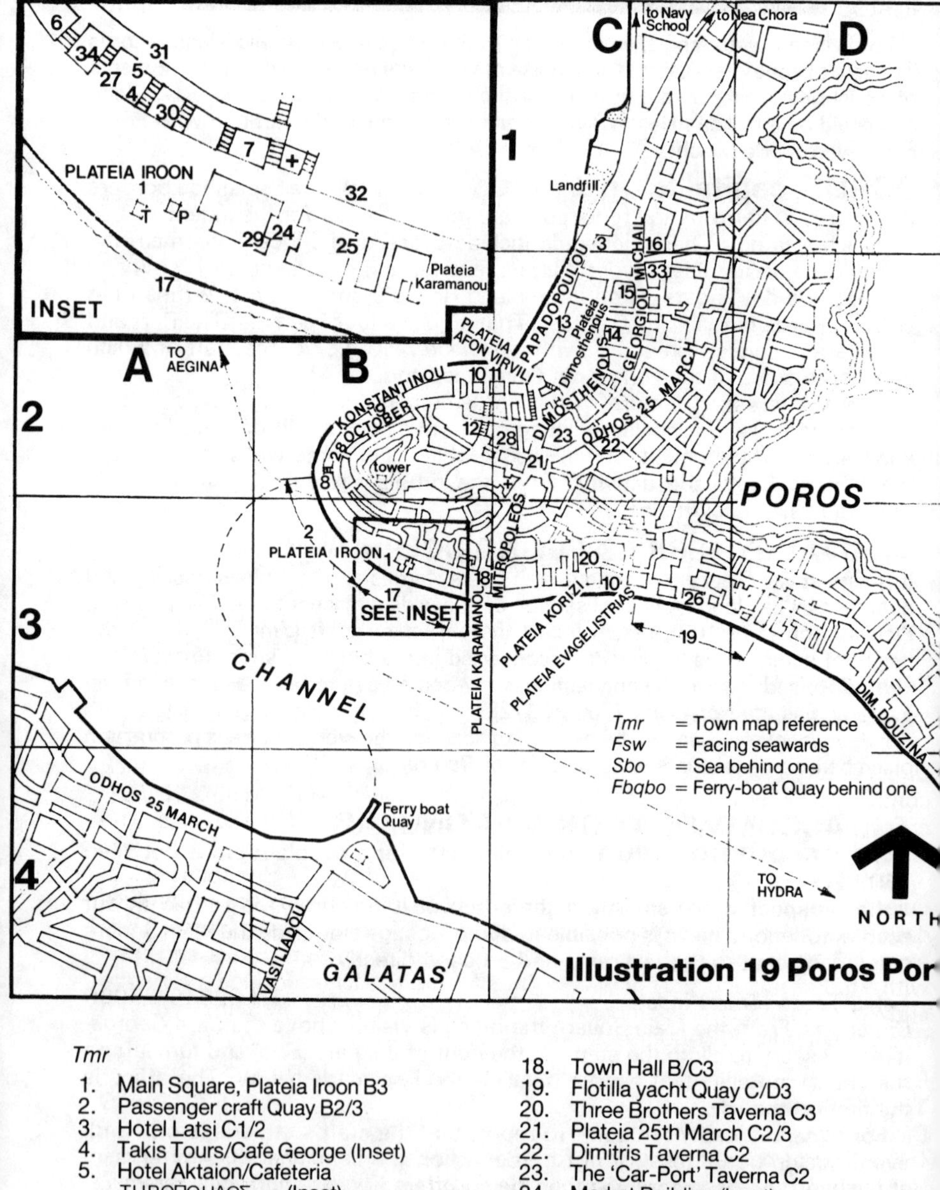

Illustration 19 Poros Por

Tmr

1. Main Square, Plateia Iroon B3
2. Passenger craft Quay B2/3
3. Hotel Latsi C1/2
4. Takis Tours/Cafe George (Inset)
5. Hotel Aktaion/Cafeteria ΤΥΡΟΠΟΥΛΟΣ (Inset)
6. Hotel Saron (Inset)
7. Hotel/Restaurant Seven Brothers (Inset)
8. Hotel Manessi/Askeli Travel Agency B2/3
9. OTE B2/3
10. Pharmacy (2)
11. Cinema DIANA B/C2
12. Maria's Rooms B/C2
13. ('Dead') Petrol Station C2
14. Rooms Nicos Douros C2
15. George's Rooms C2
16. Villa Dimitra C1/2
17. Water taxis Quay B3
18. Town Hall B/C3
19. Flotilla yacht Quay C/D3
20. Three Brothers Taverna C3
21. Plateia 25th March C2/3
22. Dimitris Taverna C2
23. The 'Car-Port' Taverna C2
24. Market Building (Inset)
25. Taverna Ο ΠΑΝΤΕΛΗΣ (Inset)
26. National Bank C3
27. Bookseller/Newsagents (Inset)
28. Baker B/C2
29. Greengrocer-cum-bread shop (Inset)
30. Flying Dolphin ticket office (Inset)
31. Ladies & Mens Hairdresser (Inset)
32. Laundry & Dry Cleaners (Inset)
33. Clinic C1/2
34. Port police (Inset)

P = Periptero
T = Taxi rank

Generally most ***Rooms*** are to the left (*Sbo*) along the Esplanade. Those who wish to only walk a few paces, can consider the:-

Hotel Aktaion (*Tmr* 5 Inset) (Class C) 6 Plateia Iroon Tel 22281

Directions: Over the *Cafeteria* Τμποπομλοξ, to the left of the Main Sq (*Sbo*).

Hotel Saron (*Tmr* 6 Inset) (Class B) Paralia Tel 22279

Directions: Further round to the left, in front of which is a periptero.

Smart. A single room with en suite bathroom costs 2200drs and an en suite double room 2500drs with a possibly mandatory breakfast charged at 250drs.

Hotel Seven Brothers (*Tmr* 7 Inset) (Class B) Tel 22412

Directions: From the Main Sq (*Sbo*), proceed right along the narrow lane that runs parallel to the waterfront and behind the Market (*Tmr* 24 Inset). The building is on the left, prior to a small Church, above the expensive *Restaurant Seven Brothers*.

Smart, expensive and tour operator booked.

After the Lord Mayors show...... continuing on along the Esplanade towards the Naval School (*left from the Main Square, Sbo*) advances past the:-

Hotel Manessi (*Tmr* 9B2/3) (Class C) Paralia Tel 27273

Directions: Where the road narrows down as it curves round the bluff and above the Askeli Travel Agency.

Single rooms sharing the bathroom cost 2460drs and en suite 2750drs, double rooms 2750drs and 3020drs respectively.

Beyond a flight of wide steps is the office of **Family Tours** advertising ***Rooms*** and close to the OTE (*Tmr* 9B2) there is accommodation at the *Villa Maria Kourmoulakis* (Tel 22548).

'Maria's' Rooms & Studio Apartments (*Tmr* 12B/C2) 10 Christou Mexi Tel 22309

Directions: From the Esplanade, a lane, that makes off between a block containing a Pharmacy (*Tmr* 10B/C2) and the Cinema DIANA (*Tmr* 11B/C2), crosses one lateral street and then climbs steps to Odhos Christou Mexi. The accommodation is diagonally across the street.

Maria is the daughter of Nicos Douros (*See Nicos Rooms*). Her house is in a quiet situation. The nomenclature 'Rooms' is a misnomer as the accommodation consists of four studio apartments in the basement of the house. They have 2/3 beds each and are very nicely finished. A kitchen area is equipped with a fridge and endless hot water. The bathroom facilities include a separate shower room. A two bed apartment is charged at 2500 drs per day and a three bed studio at 3000drs.

Back on the Esplanade, to the nearside of the Cinema DIANA is:-

Tourist Bureau Lela Tel 22532/24439

Directions: As above.

Lela Douros has run the agency for twenty five years and she speaks English. Her husband, who is Nicos' brother (*See Maria's Rooms* and *Nicos Rooms*), owns a pension (*See George's Rooms*). Naturally, she steers clients to their accommodation first but they have other rooms, apartments, villas and hotels on the books. Incidentally, Lela also hires out small boats and there are usually a few English paperbacks languishing on a rack, towards the rear of the office.

Beyond yet another motorbike outfit, is the irregular Plateia Afon Virvili off which steps climb to Odhos Dimosthenous. There are ***Rooms*** at No. 4 on the right, telephone 22342.

Back on the waterfront and the Esplanade is now a wide thoroughfare leaving a school and a 'dead' petrol station (*Tmr* 13C2) on the right. A side-street leads up to Plateia Dimosthenous, and Dimosthenous St. On the right of this Square is the *KTM Pension*, but it displays a *Sunmed* sticker, and is therefore probably full of package tourists.

Along Dimosthenous St to the right and on the left is:-

Nicos Rooms (*Tmr* 14C2) 9 Dimosthenous St Tel 22633
Directions: As above.

A clean, well-run house owned and run by Nicos Douros and his wife. They have ten rooms to let, three of which have 3 beds. A double room, mid-season, costs 1800drs. There is a rather higgledy-piggledy verandah with a sea view where washing can be hung out to dry. Incidentally, Nicos reckons he is a pretty ace dancer, a titbit of information I cannot vouch for. On the other hand, I can guarantee his kindliness.

Back on the Esplanade again, prior to the area of sea-shore that has been landfilled and the *Hotel Latsi* (*Tmr* 3C1/2), a lane climbs to Georgiou Michail St. Note that it is possible to proceed on Odhos Dimosthenous from south to north and join up with this selfsame lane.

George's Rooms (*Tmr* 15C2) Georgiou Michail St Tel 22532
Directions: As above and on the right-hand corner (*Sbo*) of the junction of the lane with Georgiou Michail St.

A nice double room sharing the modern bathroom costs 1500drs mid-season. George is married to Lela of the Tourist Bureau Lela (alongside the Cinema DIANA – *Tmr* 11B/C2) and brother of Nicos, he of *Nicos Rooms* which all seems a bit incestuous, but there you go.

Rooms Christos Georgiou Michail St Tel 23228
Directions: Across the lane from *George's Rooms*, on the left-hand corner (*Sbo*) of the junction of the lane with Georgiou Michail St.

Similar to *George's Rooms*.

North along Georgiou Michail St from the accommodation above and the first lane up the hill to the right and first left leads to:-
Villa Dimitra (*Tmr* 16C1/2) Tel 22697
Directions: As above and on the left.

A modern block titled *Reasonable Prices* but now a stronghold of *Grecian Holidays*, so is probably tour company block booked.

Back on the Esplanade is the:-
Hotel Latsi (*Tmr* 3C1/2) (Class B) 74, Akti Papadopoulou Tel 22392
Directions: Opposite the landfilled area of the quay, on the west Esplanade road proceeding towards the Naval School.

A modern hotel with single rooms sharing a bathroom costing 1760drs, single rooms with an en suite bathroom 2700drs and double rooms en suite 3900drs.

Camping Close by the water taxis section of the quay (*Tmr* 17B3), across the Esplanade from the Market, is a sign advising *Camping. 500m to the west of this point Tel 24520/21*. (This may be one of my deliberate errors). The campsite, if there is one, will be to the right (*or east, Sbo*) round the port islet. I did not see the location so cannot report.

The Eating Out The Main Square (*Tmr* 1B3) is edged by a bank of cafe-bars and restaurants. To the right (*Sbo*) along the Esplanade from the Main Square, proceeds past the Market, the 'Town Hall Square' (*Tmr* 18B/C3), Odhos Mitropoleos and continues towards Plateia Korizi passing a number of, inexpensive fast food breakfast places. These have prolificated to cater (sorry) for the large flotilla of charter sailing yachts that moor alongside this section of the Quay (*Tmr* 19C/D3).

Plateia Korizi (*Tmr* C3) hosts three (widely) differing establishments including the:-

Kafeneion/Cafe-bar Plateia Korizi

Directions: At the back of the small gardens that make up the Square. The occasional chunk of antique column and masonry lie about, which must be an overflow from the Museum, the building shutting off the left-hand (*Sbo*) side of the Square.

Probably once a hotel, the toilets are kept spotlessly clean and have built-in showers. Rose is of the opinion that the ladies lavatory is 'Harrods' standard, which must be pitching it a bit strong but I did not have the nerve to check on her hyperbole. Apart from the more usual Nes meh ghala (75drs), they serve limon – not Fanta, but the real stuff. A very appetising line in breakfasts is supplemented by *saganaki*. This latter is a cross between an omelette and scrambled eggs with a bacon and or sausage filler, cooked in olive oil in a small (6") frying pan. Very, very tasty. A breakfast for two of 2 eggs and bacon and coffee was charged at 375drs. Set in the same facade, and to one side, is a boutique, on the first floor of which resides a Mama. When she requires anything she simply lowers a bucket on a length of string. How sensible. An evening brandy costs 80drs, but they close at midnightish so late night revellers might have to migrate to the:-

Yachting Club Remezzo Plateia Korizi

Directions: On the far, Esplanade corner of the Square.

Not really a Yacht Club, more a cafe-bar, but there you go! The establishment is smack opposite a wide trot of quayside moored, *Island Sailing Club* charter yachts which rarely appear to go anywhere. The balding owner is appropriately obsequious and thus stays busy and popular, although his prices are much higher than those of the previously detailed *Kafeneion*. For instance his Nes meh ghala is charged at 90drs, a brandy at 120drs and a breakfast costs 395drs. Perhaps fawning pays off?

Also in this area, in fact just round the corner from the right-hand, bottom corner of the Plateia Korizi (*Sbo*), is the:-

Three Brothers Taverna (*Tmr* 20C3)

Directions: As above. The rustic building occupies a corner site and the tables and chairs stretch along the narrow lane to the right.

Absurdly popular as it unashamedly caters for the migrant charter yacht crews. When I write migrant, that is a comparative description as they appear pretty static to me, if only for one or two weeks! Wall-to-wall tourists are served reasonable fare at less than moderate prices. Naturally the menu includes a rich vein of (expensive) fish as well as fresh strawberries – well it would wouldn't it! The final seal of 'disapproval' must be the absence of kortaki retsina from the far-from-cheap wine list. A tzatziki costs 140drs, kalamares 350drs, stuffed eggplant 1800drs, a Greek salad 180drs, patatas 80drs, pork chops or souvlakia 430drs, lamb chops 480drs and an average fish dish 450/550drs. The cheapest bottle of wine, a 'Cambas' retsina, is charged at 230drs and a bottle of 'Demestica' 250drs. Incidentally the waiters appear groomed and attentive.

Further east along the Esplanade are a number of rather incongruous cocktail bars advertising hot showers.

Above the port lurks the 'upper village'. One clearly defined route to this hilltop, 'inner sanctum', and Plateia Ag Georgiou, is by climbing the steeply ascending Odhos Mitropoleos from the Esplanade, just beyond the Town Hall (*Tmr* 18B/C3). To the left of Mitropoleos St, prior to the ascent, is a 'Taverna Corner' and two-thirds of the way to the top, on the right, is *Taverna The Dolphins*. At the top, the Cathedral of St George is surrounded by a paved Square. A lane from the far, right-hand side proceeds to the small, irregular, sloping Plateia 25th March (*Tmr* 21C2/3).

This Square is dominated by a Church and edged by a grocer, greengrocers, a general store, butcher, drink shop and a hardware shop. A tiny, model chapel is incongruously mounted on the top of a truncated column. There is a periptero and, filling the north side of the area, a domed roof, tall chimnied building built on to the side of the Church. From the far side of the Plateia 25th March, on the other side of the Church, a downward sloping street angles and winds off to the right. Some 100m along on the right, opposite a junction with a side-street that connects with Odhos Georgiou Michail, is the:-

Dimitris Taverna (*Tmr* 22C2)
Directions: As above.

Dimitris, a pleasant, neat, moustachioed young man of careful appearance masterminds this 'squeaky clean' and correctly embellished restaurant. I'm surprised he uses the appellation taverna – it indicates a so much less refined joint than restaurant. Dimitris really should be running a facsimile Greek taverna, in Woking perhaps? There perhaps the colourful table covers, flowers and wooden platters would be so much more authentic! I felt distinctly under-dressed and remember vainly trying to polish the uppers of my sandals against the back of one of my trouser legs. Despite the excellence of the service, it is a pity that the measure of decor to which he aspires is unmatched by the easily forgettable standards of the comestibles. I hasten to point out that the not inexpensive offerings aren't substandard but the ambience surely leads a client to expect the best. For instance, the moussaka, which is fortunately not labelled 'Special', has the consistency of bread pudding and is served with over-salted chips. A meal of taramosalata (150drs), gigantic beans (120drs), fassolakia freska (beans – 170drs), two helpings, of moussaka (300drs each) 2 beers (80drs each) and bread (10drs each) cost 1220drs. I made the mistake of requesting a kortaki retsina to accompany the repast and received the possibly to be expected look of disdain that I should possibly think that his cellars would be sullied by such a lowly 'amber nectar'. The meat should be good as the family appears to own the butcher's shop next door, wherein they constantly edge for more supplies as the evening progresses.

My nomination for the 'Golden Moussaka' award must be the:-

'Car Port' Taverna(*Tmr* 23C2)No. 4
Directions: On the same street as the *Dimitris Taverna* but back towards Plateia 25th March and on the right.

An old, cavernous building that spills out on to a sort of mezzanine in a skeletal building alongside. The occasional car is often parked to one side of the tables that are spaced out on the concrete patio. A redoubtable meal of two plates of beef, in a 'gravy' of lemon sauce, with chips (340drs each), briam (200drs), a Greek salad (200drs), two carafe's of draught retsina (50drs each) bread and tax (30drs each) cost 1240drs. It has to be admitted that the fastidious may find the kitchen rather ethnic.

Before leaving the subject of eateries, the Esplanade does sport a cafe-bar that offers a *Special Four Course Chinese Meal – Every Thursday Night*. To accompany this culinary delight the management thoughtfully provide tomato ketchup, no doubt for the further delectation of their discriminating clientele.

ΟΠΑΝΤΕΛΗΣ **Restaurant** (*Tmr* 25 Inset)
Directions: On a corner of the street that runs parallel to the Esplanade, behind the Market (*Tmr* 24 Inset) and opposite a Laundry and Dry Cleaners.

Really a taverna and the province of market folk, but good value if clients can put up with the shouting.

THE A TO Z OF USEFUL INFORMATION

BANKS Only one active establishment, the:-
National Bank (*Tmr* 26C3) The Esplanade.
Directions: Towards the far end of the eastern Esplanade, beyond Plateia Evagelistrias.

Usual hours. The services include changing Eurocheques and the staff are very smiley.

The only other bank, **The Trapeeza**, situated above the office of Family Tours on the Esplanade, is not a tourist facility.

BEACHES The port and main town islet of Spheria has none. There are even signs, on the way round to the Naval School, advising against swimming (off the Quayside). For the closest stretch of sand it is necessary to cross the Canal and turn sharp right to 'Canal Beach' (*See* **Route One**.)

BICYCLE, SCOOTER & CAR HIRE The island's size is such that only one day's hire of a scooter is required to see most of the sights. The 'quick' will also be able to pay a fleeting visit to the Peloponnese mainland port and town of Galatas. A general point here is to note that scooter operators 'frown on' their 'steeds' crossing the water (even by ferry!) Hirers who experience a malfunction on the mainland are advised to get back on to the island prior to reporting the matter. Scooters are only hired by the day, between 0900 – 1900hrs. Keeping the machine overnight costs an extra 300drs. A Honda is charged at 1400drs a day and a Vespa/trials bike 1800drs.

There are a number of scooter hire firms mustered on the Esplanade round to the left (*Sbo*) from the Ferry-boat Quay (*Tmr* 1B3). These include:-

Stelios Bikes
Directions: In the vicinity of the Cinema DIANA (*Tmr* 11B/C2), on the nearside of Saronic Gulf Travel.

The rather disinterested and off-hand owner only requires a driving licence.

and:-

Stelios Bikes & Motorbikes
Directions: Also in the area of the Cinema DIANA (*Tmr* 11B/C2), in this case on the nearside of the Pharmacy (*Tmr* 10B/C2), just a few metres along the Esplanade from the previously mentioned Stelios.

Both the above outfits also hire bicycles.

Note that the BP petrol station, across the Canal Bridge and at the outset of Nea Chora, is closed on Sunday. It might seem superfluous to mention but it is best to ensure that there is a full tank of fuel with any machine hired on that day.

BOOKSELLERS There is an excellent overseas language book and paper shop (*Tmr* 27 Inset), across a flight of steps from the Port police. Mitropoleos St widens out not far from the Esplanade and on the left (*Sbo*), at the junction with a side lane, is a foreign language bookshop.

'Out of town' but appropriate to list here is:-
Anita's Books No. 17 Nea Chora
Directions: The 'shop' is in the ground floor of a house, some 150m beyond the BP petrol station, on the left of the Temple Poseidon road from the 'Canal junction'.

This excellent facility, run by an English lady, swops, buys and sells second-hand books. The shop is open weekdays 0900-1430hrs and weekends 0900-1230hrs.

Note that further on from Anita's, also on the left, is a bread shop.

BREAD SHOPS One old time Baker (*Tmr* 28B/C2) hides away on the right of a lane that tumbles down from the hilltop Plateia 25th March. On the Esplanade, beyond Korizi Square, is a Chemist's (*Tmr* 10C3) at the far side of which is an alley and on the left (*Sbo*) of which is another Baker. Alongside the Esplanade entrance to the 'Market' (*Tmr* 24 Inset) is an excellent greengrocer-cum-bread-shop (*Tmr* 29 Inset). *See* **Anita's, Booksellers, A To Z.**

BUSES A daily bus service runs from Plateia Iroon, the Main Square (*Tmr* 1B3), to the Monastery Zoodochos Pighi. The journey time is 15 minutes, the buses start running at 0700hrs and stop at 2200hrs all for a one-way cost of 40drs. A bus leaves every 15-20 minutes and can be hailed anywhere along the route. A bus service also shuttles to and from Megalo Neorion Bay.

CAMPING *See* **The Accommodation**.

CINEMA (*Tmr* 11B/C2) Cinema DIANA borders the Esplanade, round to the left (*Sbo*) from the Ferry-boat Quay.

COMMERCIAL SHOPPING AREA There is a 'good news', but small Market building (*Tmr* 24 Inset) around the outside of which are a number of greengrocers, grocers, a supermarket (well more a narrow fronted, deep, general store), a butchers with four more butchers inside the Market building. Gift shops line the street that stretches behind the Market building, from the Main Square to Plateia Karamanou.

Odhos Mitropoleos is edged by various emporiums including a video shop, a tailor's and a sportswear shop.

Up on the hilltop, approaching *Dimitris Taverna* (*Tmr* 22C2) along Odhos 25th March, is a small, 'front room' greengrocer's which incidentally displays a ***Rooms*** sign. As described, adjacent to *Dimitris Taverna* is a butcher.

FERRY-BOATS & FLYING DOLPHINS An extensive service of scheduled connections is supplemented by various express craft. The plethora of Piraeus passenger boats, that include majestic ferries and sleek, purposeful hydrofoils, are augmented by the 'chain ferry' to Galatas, various Ro-Ro's and constantly scurrying water taxis. All these craft, that constantly ply the channel, results in a lasting impression of a very busy river crossing, a sensation heightened by the length and narrowness of the sound combined with the juxtaposition of the Poros port and town islet, Spheria, to the mainland.

Ferry-boat timetable (Mid-season)

Day	Departure time	Ferry-boat	Ports/Islands of Call
Daily	Up to 4 ferries a day		Methana(M), Aegina, Piraeus(M). Hydra, Spetses.
	1100hrs	Aegina	Aegina.
	1830hrs	Aegina	Aegina.

One-way fares: Poros to Aegina 280drs;
Piraeus 525drs; duration 3hrs 40mins.

Flying Dolphin timetable (Mid-season)

Day	Departure time	Ports/Islands of Call
Daily	0725hrs	Zea Port (Piraeus).
	0910hrs	Hydra, Ermioni(M).
	1010hrs	Hydra, Spetses.
	1020hrs	Methana(M), Aegina, Zea Port (Piraeus).
	1110hrs	Hydra, Spetses, Portoheli(M).
	1125hrs	Zea Port (Piraeus).
	1455hrs	Hydra, Ermioni(M).
	1710hrs	Zea Port (Piraeus).
Tuesday, Saturday	1010hrs	Hydra, Spetses, Leonidio(M),Kiparissi(M), Monemvassia(M), Kithira, Neapoli(M).
Tuesday, Thursday	1010hrs	Hydra, Spetses, Leonidio(M), Kiparissi(M), Gerakas(M).
	1435hrs	Zea Port (Piraeus).
Tuesday, Thursday Saturday, Sunday	1010hrs	Hydra, Spetses, Leonidio(M), Kiparissi(M), Monemvassia(M).
Monday, Wednesday	1010hrs	Hydra, Spetses, Portoheli(M).
Friday	1545hrs	Zea Port (Piraeus).
Saturday, Sunday	1310hrs	Hydra, Spetses, Portoheli(M).
Sunday	1310hrs	Hydra, Spetses, Portoheli(M).
	1610hrs	Spetses.
	1945hrs	Zea Port (Piraeus).
Monday, Wednesday Friday, Saturday, Sunday	1435hrs	Zea Port (Piraeus).
Friday, Saturday	1710hrs	Hydra, Ermioni(M), Spetses.
Saturday	1710hrs	Hydra, Spetses, Portoheli(M).
Thursday, Sunday	1725hrs	Zea Port (Piraeus).
Monday-Saturday	1800hrs	Hydra, Ermioni(M), Spetses, Portoheli(M).
	1910hrs	Hydra, Ermioni(M).

One-way fares: Poros to			
Methana	415drs;	duration	15mins
Hydra	345drs;		20mins
Ermioni	400drs;		1hr
Spetses	580drs;		1hr 10mins
Portoheli	620drs;		1hr 45mins
Aegina	650drs;		40mins
Leonidio	1065drs;		1hr 50mins
Zea Port (Piraeus)	1015drs;		1hr 5mins
Kiparissi	1345drs;		2hrs 20mins
Gerakas	1345drs;		2hrs 45mins
Monemvassia	1715drs;		3hrs 5mins
Kithira	3500drs;		4hrs 25mins
Neapoli	3500drs;		2hrs 55mins

FERRY-BOAT & FLYING DOLPHIN TICKET OFFICES

Ferry-boat office EYTYXIA Squashed in between a foreign language bookshop (*Tmr* 27 Inset) and the *Cafeteria* Τυροπουλοξ,(*Tmr* 5 Inset) towards the far, left-hand end of the Main Square (*Sbo*). Does not open until 0900hrs.

Delfini Express office Let into the left side (*Sbo*) of the *Cafe George*, over which is Takis Tours (*Tmr* 4 Inset).

Flying Dolphin office (*Tmr* 30 Inset) Sandwiched between the *Cafe-bar New Astoria* and Tan Tours.

Tickets for various ferry-boats are sold from temporary desks set up close to the particular embarkation point. For instance, the last boat to Aegina island, the FB ΑΙΓΙΝΑ, departs at 1830hrs and the tickets are available from the quay, close by where the Galatas 'chain ferry' docks, beyond the *Cafe-bar Asteria*, on the way round to the OTE (*Tmr* 9B2/3). Incidentally, the *Asteria* is a very useful spot at which to while away any time spent waiting for a ferry-boat, having a good field of vision. Admittedly drinks are not cheap (a Nes meh ghala costs 120drs and a beer 130drs) but nobody is hustled, so a drink can be made to last a very long time indeed.

HAIRDRESSERS There is a men's hairdresser on the right of Odhos Mitropoleos (*Tmr* B/C) and another close to Tan Tours, going left (*Sbo*) past the OTE (*Tmr* 9B2/3).

Ladies & Men's Hairdresser (*Tmr* 31 Inset) In the lane to the rear of Takis Tours (*Tmr* 4 Inset).

LAUNDRY There is an expensive facility tucked away on the left of a short alleyway off the Esplanade, immediately prior to the OTE (*Tmr* 9B2/3). The laundry opens 0930-1400hrs Monday-Saturday and 0930-1200hrs on Sunday during the summer season. They charge some 800drs per machine load (Phew!).

Laundry & Dry Cleaners (*Tmr* 32 Inset) On the left of the narrow lane, behind the Market (*Tmr* 24 Inset) that runs parallel to the Esplanade and connects the Main Square and Karamanou Square.

LUGGAGE STORE No official facility. Most travellers pile their bags around the statue on Plateia Iroon, close to the Taxi rank.

MEDICAL CARE

Chemists & Pharmacies There are at least two (*Tmr* 10B/C2 & 10C3), one at each end (almost – that is almost at each end of the Esplanade.

Clinic (*Tmr* 33C1/2) Proceed left (*Sbo*) along the Esplanade beyond the 'dead' petrol station (*Tmr* 13C2), almost as far as the *Hotel Latsi* (*Tmr* 3C1/2). A narrow lane climbs to Odhos Georgiou Michail. Turn left and the two storey building is on the right. Incidentally, the Naval School has a hospital but admission might prove difficult!

NTOG None.

OTE (*Tmr* 9B2/3) Bordering the Esplanade on the way round to the Naval School. Open weekdays 0730-2200hrs.

PETROL Across the Canal separating Spheria islet from the main island and close to the four-way junction, on the left of the road to the Temple of Poseidon. Note this station is closed Sundays. One other contender (*Tmr* 13C2) has obviously given up, but hires out bicycles.

PLACES OF INTEREST

Museum, Plateia Korizi (*Tmr* C3) On the edge of Plateia Korizi. Not very large but entrance is (to date) free. Open weekdays between 0900-1500hrs and Sundays and holidays between 0930-1430hrs. Closed Tuesdays.

Naval School The antecedents are sketched in the **History**. The base is ever so smart and clean but there are no ships which seem's a pity. The legendary *Battleship Averoff* had been moored alongside the school as a floating exhibit but was certainly absent in 1987. The Averoff and its fame perhaps helps to illustrate the Greeks' need for tangible proof of their comparatively modern military might. The Italian built warship was purchased, in 1911, with the help of a bequest from the philanthropist George Averoff. He had made his money from the British in Egypt. Frankly, the vessel was rather out of date by the First World War but joined in sea battles against the Turks, between 1912-13, at Eli and Limnos. During the Second World War the ship was loaned to the Allies and carried out escort duty in the Indian Ocean. In 1945 it was retired and finally berthed at Poros. I wonder what the Greeks would have done with, say, the *Hood* or the *Ark Royal*?

POLICE

Port (*Tmr* 34 Inset) Facing the Esplanade at the far, left-hand (*Sbo*) end of the Main Square.

Town On the right of narrow Ag Nikolaos lane. This branches off the Esplanade prior to the Museum, which edges Korizi Sq (*Tmr* C3).

POST OFFICE At the right-hand corner (*Sbo*) of Karamanou Square (*Tmr* B/C3), which edges the Esplanade to the right (*Sbo*) of the Ferry-boat Quay.

TAXIS Rank on the Main Square.

TELEPHONE NUMBERS & ADDRESSES

Clinic (*Tmr* 33C1/2)	Tel 22600
Police, port (*Tmr* 34 Inset)	Tel 22274
Police, town	Tel 22462
Taxi Rank (*Tmr* T Inset)	Tel 23003

TOILETS The Market (*Tmr* 24 Inset) 'hosts' some smelly ones on either side of the rear entrance. There are Public Lavatories, hidden behind some small trees and electricity poles, round the Esplanade, going towards the Naval School and prior to the OTE (*Tmr* 9B2/3).

TRAVEL AGENTS & TOUR OFFICES There are any number including:-

Takis Tours (*Tmr* 4 Inset). *See* **The Accommodation**.Note the office closes for the midday siesta.

Tan Tours 36 Konstantinou/Papadopoulou St Tel 22112

Directions: Borders the Esplanade, beyond the OTE (*Tmr* 9B2/3).

Offers a wide choice of Excursions which include *Greek Night* 1500drs; *Round the Island* 1500drs; *Classical Tour* 2700drs; *Spetses & Hydra* 1800drs; *Aegina & Angristri* 1500drs; *Evening BBQ* 1700drs – ...a boat trip... to a setting far from the madding crowd (you know, apart from the hundreds of other people who are on the fun-packed night out) for a feast (!) of scrumptious barbecued meat (chicken, I'll be bound), Greek salad and unlimited wine. And for those who wish to join in, there are organised games with fun prizes and surprises for everybody (It sounds absolutely idyllic, doesn't it?). Other tours take in the *Lemon Groves*; *Hydra By Night*; *Epidavros Festival*; *Athens By Night* and *Athens By Day* 4100drs. Mind you, anybody can indulge these whims at half the cost by organising their own outing, but there you go.

On the way round to the **Tan Tours** the Esplanade passes **Family Tours 'Rooms to Let'**, **Greek Island Tours** and **Askeli Travel Agency**, the latter in the ground floor of the *Hotel Manessi*(*Tmr* 8B2/3).

WATER TAXIS These are more small, water-borne char-a-bancs, most of them motorised but some powered by oars, which tie up alongside the Esplanade, across the way from the Market (*Tmr* 24 Inset). They depart for Galatas when they have sufficient passengers and also ferry passengers round to the (Zoodochos Pighi) Monastery Beach for some 40drs.

EXCURSIONS TO POROS TOWN SURROUNDS

Excursion to Galatas, Lemonodassos (the lemon groves) & beyond. Small Ro-Ro's make the short crossing to the Peloponnese mainland port as detailed under **Ferry Boats, A To Z.**

GALATAS If Poros Town gets too busy and crowded, it might be an idea to migrate to Galatas, which is immeasurably quieter. The High St and Esplanade, Odhos 25th March, which is one back from the waterfront, opposite the Ferry-boat Quay, has been laid out as if the planners once expected a far greater volume of traffic than has been actually generated.

The bus stop and ticket office are adjacent to the Ferry-boat Quay. Buses depart for Trizina, Epidavros and Nafplio (for an Athens bus connection) along Odhos 25th March to the right (*Sbo*) and for Lemonodassos and Ermioni to the left.

Across the waterfront from the Ferry-boat Quay is a friendly taverna where a saganaki of eggs, bacon and sausage is on the menu. A filling meal for two of saganaki (250drs), bread (20drs) and an Amstel beer (80drs) costs 350drs.

There are plenty of ***Rooms*** spread along the waterfront road in the direction of Lemonodassos. Galatas seems to have everything including taxis, bicycles and scooters for hire as well as two discos, to the east of the town (the Cavos and the Sirocco).

About a kilometre out of Galatas, on the road to Lemonodassos, is Plaka Beach. There are some offshore islets, the beach is pebbly and the place is a bit of a dump – which is a pity as Poros Town boats run trips here. Some scrawny, moth-eaten donkeys are 'encouraged', by their rather piratical owners, to carry punters to the lemon groves for 100drs each way. Around the spit is a much larger but exposed bay with another pebble beach. Let into the nearside of the far promontory of this bay is a small beach.

Lemonodassos A large, well irrigated area (some 180 acres) of lemon tree groves. The wise stick to the main road that angles off the coastal highway whilst the foolish (like myself), who wish to make the final assault on foot, can take the signed track to the right of the main road. This bimbles off on the apex of a left-hand curve, alongside a small chapel just before the village of Lemonodassos. Signposts pointing along the track indicate *No Parking* & *To Kadassi Inn*. It takes about twenty minutes to walk this dry, dusty footpath, edged by concrete water conduits, for the most part now dry, but once used to irrigate the groves. A rather ramshackle taverna marks the end of the trail. Here the friendly owner serves a glass of pressed lemon juice at a cost of 65drs. The sound of running water fills the air and round the corner, beyond the taverna, is a 'real live' waterfall. I must say it all seems a lot of 'to do' about little.... Certainly the views are pleasant but I can't do more than gently enthuse.

Further along the coastal route, the road dips down to edge the very narrow shore of Aliki Bay. There are smidgins of sand here and there but most of the shore is pebble, covered in kelp and bits of rubbish. The greatest concentration of sand is clustered round a broad flight of concrete steps down to the backshore. The sea-bed is almost entirely big pebbles and the nearside of the bay is nothing more than a rocky cove.

Two Brothers Caique This ties up alongside the Esplanade Quay, almost opposite the Town Hall (*Tmr* 18B/C3) to the right of the Ferry-boat Quay (*Tmr* 1B3). Various trips here and there in rollicking good company!

ROUTE ONE

To Russian Bay (approx. 2km) The main coastal road off Spheria islet passes by a caique lined foreshore on the left-hand side and low rise hotels and the occasional ***Rooms*** on the right, prior to leaving the spacious Naval School to the left. The western (& eastern) Spheria circling road passes over a low bridge that spans the Canal (Kanali). This is more a high fenced, irrigation ditch.... Once across the bridge, a path to the right. proceeds to the:-

Canal Beach A dirty, shingly, dusty, scrubbly stretch of pebble with a pebble sea-bed. On the edge of the backshore is a single storey, concrete 'prefab' adorned with crudely handwritten signs indicating that this is the *Canal Tavern* serving *ice-coffee, drinks, toasts, ice-creams,* but do not get too excited, it is abandoned and wired off.

On the main island (Kalavria) side of the Canal is the satellite suburb of **Nea Chora**, a modern development of new buildings, supermarkets and large stores. At the outset of Nea Chora is a three-way junction. Straight on leads along the east coast to **Zoodochos Pighi Monastery**.The road, half-left climbs past the BP petrol station towards **The Temple of Poseidon** and left, along the west coast, proceeds to the:

Russian Bay The view to the left from the first stretch of this sea-level, backshore hugging road is across an inlet to the Naval School, overlooked by hill-topping Poros Town with a mainland backcloth. Towards the end of this stretch, in the lee of a hotel capped headland, Cape Voudouri, is a very small patch of beach. The shore is pebble, finished off with coarse sand. There is a beach bar at far side. The road, prettily edged with pines and tamarisk trees, rises behind the fairly large, *Hotel Xenia* (Class B) before dropping down to:-

MEGALO NEORION BAY (approx 1¼km from Poros Town) The road rims the backshore of this pleasant and pretty location. The gentle, tree planted hillsides to the right fringes the long bay and the Peloponnese mountains continue to form a beautiful backdrop. Surprise, surprise, the sea-bed to the nearside is sand. A triangle of beach is tree shaded and a sign nailed to one of the tree trunk's proclaims the presence of *Anita's Book opposite the Gas Station*. In the main the beach is made up of pebbles overlaid by imported, coarse sand, which is particularly gritty at the backshore.

On the right of the road are three hotels including the *Pavlou* (Class B – tel 22734) and the *Angyra* (Class C – tel 22368). At the far end are one or two ***Rooms***, the last of which advises that it is necessary to ask for details at the adjacent taverna – the telephone number is 22371. A water ski school operates here and there are some pedaloes.

Proceeding westwards, around the corner from Neorion Bay is a lovely little cove with a fine pebble beach, set in pine trees that grow right down to the backshore, providing welcome shade to the alluring, cool-looking sea-water.

Hereabouts the road becomes an unmade, wide track that winds some 30m from and above the boulderous waters edge, through abundant tree growth. The track continues on round to:-

RUSSIAN BAY (approx 2km from Poros Town) This is more a large inlet with small coves spread round the periphery. The setting is lovely, even if the beaches of the coves are nothing more than shingle and pebble. Understandably the location is popular with pleasure craft that randomly anchor in the bay. The surrounding hillsides are sparsely vegetated, the cover being reminiscent of moorland country. Close to the shores' edge are the remains of some once substantial, stone built buildings. They were probably part of the infrastructure constructed at the time when the bay was a Russian Naval Base. The views of the sound between the island and the mainland are enhanced by the chapel topped, tiny islet of Daskalio.

The track towards the far western end of the island degenerates into nothing more than a goat path.

ROUTE TWO
To the Temple of Poseidon, Monastery Zoodochos Pighi, Monastery & Askeli Bays & back to Poros Town – a circular route (circa 9km).

Take **Route One** to **Nea Chora,** where proceed up the angled road past the BP petrol station and Anita's Book Exchange.

The climb towards the Temple passes through lovely countryside. The small plains are subject to intensive agriculture and the hillsides support both olive and pine trees, rather reminiscent of Thassos (NE Aegean), if not so verdant.

At about 2km an unsigned, rough path angles off the main road down to the left, in the general direction of the north coast and in particular:-

ORMOS VAGIONIA (approx 5½km from Poros Town) After leaving the main road there is a divergence of the ways, now signposted with the right-hand fork running down the hillsides on an increasingly rough track to the backshore of the bay. From the hilltops, in the region of the Temple, this area appears outstandingly beautiful but not all that looks lovely ... (– to misquote a line or two). The beach is very narrow and almost entirely made up of big pebbles. An appalling amount of rubbish is evenly distributed about the high water mark and the gorse surrounds, which are also littered with old plastic. The detritus includes tar as well as sea and wind blown junk and tins. Attempts have obviously been made to clean the area because there are signs of a bonfire some twenty metres from the backshore. If all this were not enough there is no taverna. Oh dear!

Temple of Poseidon (approx 5km from Poros Town) Back on the 'high sierra' it is only 300 or 400m prior to the rather pathetic, fenced piles of rubble – all that remains of this once mighty edifice. It is only too easy to flash past without realising the site has been reached. One unquestionable fact is that the views are magnificent, especially down towards Ormos Vagionia!

The road continues on past the Temple and back down to the coastline where there is a junction with the coast road. Left (*Fsw*) passes the swanky *Hotel Sirene* (Class B), complete with two swimming pools, a turning down to the *Taverna O Nikolas – Sea Sports, Monastery Beach* before ending up at:-

Zoodochos Pighi Monastery (approx 3km from Poros Town) A large, whitewashed, square building originally erected in the 18th century, but which had to be rebuilt after a fire in the 19th century. It is prettily located close by a summer-dry river gorge and set amongst tall pine trees with excellent sea views. Pighi means The Virgin of the Life Giving Spring or more simply the Virgin Mary. Those buried here include two Admirals of the Hydra born Tombazi family, famous for their War of Independence exploits. Entrance is permitted to those who are properly dressed daily between 0800-1900hrs.

Close by the gorge is a taverna alongside a Byzantine chapel and there are footpaths that go on towards the east coast.

MONASTERY BEACH The beach cove is semicircular and clean with a pebble beach and sea-bed. Three beach tavernas slug it out, the most colourful of which must be the red painted *Taverna O Nikolaos* to the left (*Fsw*). No monastery beach would be complete without water sports (would it?). These activities include pedaloes and wind surfers. A couple of outfits compete for the clients.

Back at the road junction with the road down from the Temple, the road towards Poros Town is edged by pine trees until:-

ASKELI BEACH (approx 1km from Poros Town) This is the major (British) package tourist centre. I cannot but help wonder what are the attractions? On either side of the very narrow, curved beach is a stretch of foreshore the whole, rather shadeless sweep, being edged by a large number of hotels and some ***Rooms***. The sea-bed is pebble and the beach has been overlaid with an unpleasantly coarse, gritty sand. On the Poros Town side is the *Pub Rendevous* (Oh goody!) and more hotels, none of which are, as the Americans would put it, supported by a 'sea-shore facility'.

Kamina Harbour, Hydra.

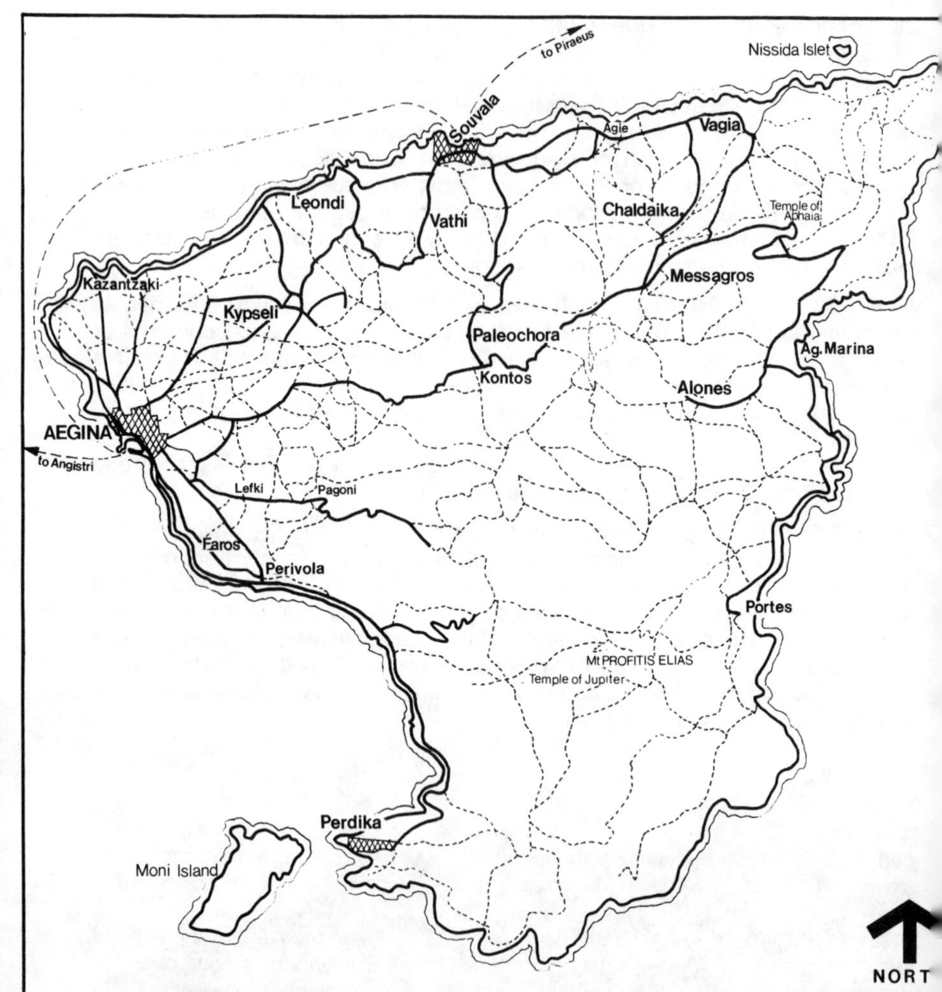

Illustration 20 Aegina island

15 AEGINA (EGINA, ΑΙΓΙΝΑ)

Argo-Saronic Islands

Aegina Port ****

The island **

FIRST IMPRESSIONS
Few cats; busy port; boats; unattractive countryside; the Temple; a (few) sandy beaches; inexpensive; possibly saline drinking water.

SPECIALITIES
Pistachio nuts; ravani – a sponge made with semolina and soused with cognac and orange syrup.

RELIGIOUS HOLIDAYS & FESTIVALS
include: None out of the ordinary.

VITAL STATISTICS
Tel prefix 0297. The almost triangular island is some 11km from top to bottom and up to 14km from side to side, with a total area of about 86sqkm. Out of a population of circa 10,000, at least 5,000 live in Aegina, the main town and port.

HISTORY
Aegina is steeped in historical and mythological connections. The mythology was recorded by the famous poet of the ancients, Pindar, and the author Pausanias. The island was renamed Aegina, from that of Oinone (or wine island) by Aeacus, a son of Zeus, after his mother.

The island has at least three archaeological sites of repute – Kolona, alongside the present town and port; the Temple of Aphaia, built in 480 BC and close by Ag Marina, and the Sanctuary of Zeus, located on Mt Profitis Elias (or Mt Oros).

Aegina became extremely powerful and prosperous during the 7th and 6th centuries BC, a pre-eminence reflected in the establishment of a mint famous for silver tortoise coins. The island sculptors of this period achieved considerable fame.

After the final battle, in 455 BC, for supremacy between the Aegina and Athens, which Aegina lost, the island was sacked and the islanders driven out. The Romans were given the place in 133 BC. Due to constant piratical plunderings, the inhabitants founded an inland capital, Paleochora, sometime in AD 800/900.

The Franks, Venetians, and Catalan overlords were followed by the Venetians, rulers between the middle 1450s and 1715, after which the Turks established supremacy. Following the War of Independence, the island achieved its apotheosis of modern day fame when it was made, albeit temporarily, the capital for the first Greek Government.

GENERAL
Closest of the (official) Argo-Saronic islands to Piraeus, Aegina hosts any number of ferries, express craft, excursion boats and Flying Dolphins. The island is a weekend resort for many Athenians and a holiday destination for (mainly) Austrian and German tourists. Overseas tourism naturally plays a significant role in the well-being of the island, but the lure of Aegina for mainland Greeks ensures its prosperity. This fact is reflected in the friendly but relaxed style of the inhabitants and the ambience of quiet affluence.

Although ***Rooms*** are in short supply, due to many pensions giving over part of their accommodation to tour companies, most supplies and services are less expensive than elsewhere else in the Argo-Saronic.

Of all the islands in the group, the main town and port is blessed with the only adjacent, quality beaches of any consequence. Conversely the island is not very pretty and the coastline is mainly unattractive.

Despite the promise hinted at by the town's small but sandy beaches there is only one other, that at Ag Marina. Consequently this location has become an over-developed 'Costa' resort, the sandy beach of which is swamped by sun seeking holiday-makers.

For my money, and you probably have more of it at Aegina to spend than elsewhere, one of the choice islands of the group, but Kithira must run it close.

AEGINA (Egina): capital town & port (Illustration 21). The town and port is probably the most *typic* of all the Argo-Saronic locations. Despite this, the waterfront is rather spread out and may well prove directionally confusing to first time visitors, especially as the outline is more of a bulge than the usual 'U'.

There are a few Monipos and a number of large vegetable and greengrocers' caiques that moor to the harbour quayside.

ARRIVAL BY FERRY & FLYING DOLPHINS

The Ferry-boat Quay (*Tmr* 1B3) is a very large, exposed sheet of concrete with an extensive pier projection to the right (*Sbo*). Flying Dolphins conveniently dock inside the Harbour (*Tmr* 2B3).

THE ACCOMMODATION & EATING OUT

The Accommodation Here, as on a number of other islands in the group, visitors are not met by owners of ***Rooms***. In fact lodgings are difficult to come by, due to the mainland Greeks who enjoy the island's attractions and the number of accommodation owners who cater for package tourists.

Hotel Togias (Toghia) (*Tmr* 3B2) (Class E) Odhos Apolonos Tel 24242
Directions: From the left-hand end (*Sbo*) of the Ferry-boat Quay (*Tmr* 1B3) across the wide Esplanade, Akti Kazantzaki, is a bus office shed, some way behind which is the hotel.

Double rooms with en suite bathrooms start off at 1750drs, which charges rise to 2275drs (16th June-15th Sept).

Further to the left (*Sbo*) along the Esplanade are two other smart hotels, the:-
Hotel Avra (*Tmr* 4B2) (Class C) 2 Kazantzaki St Tel 22303
Directions: As above and on the right.

Single rooms with an en suite bathroom start off at 2180drs and doubles en suite 2850drs, rising respectively to 2620drs and 3420drs (1st June-30th Sept). At the height of season breakfast (300drs) and one other meal (700drs) may be mandatory.

Hotel Plaza (Class E) 4 Kazantzaki Tel 25600
Directions: All as for *Hotel Avra*, but one along. En suite double rooms only which start at 2200drs rising to 3500drs (1st June-30th Sept).

Hotel Artemis (*Tmr* 5B2) (Class D) 20 Kanari Tel 22523
Directions: It is possible to cross over the wasteland to Kanari St from the area of the Ferry-boat Quay (*Tmr* 1B3) or walk up Pan Irioti lane to Odhos

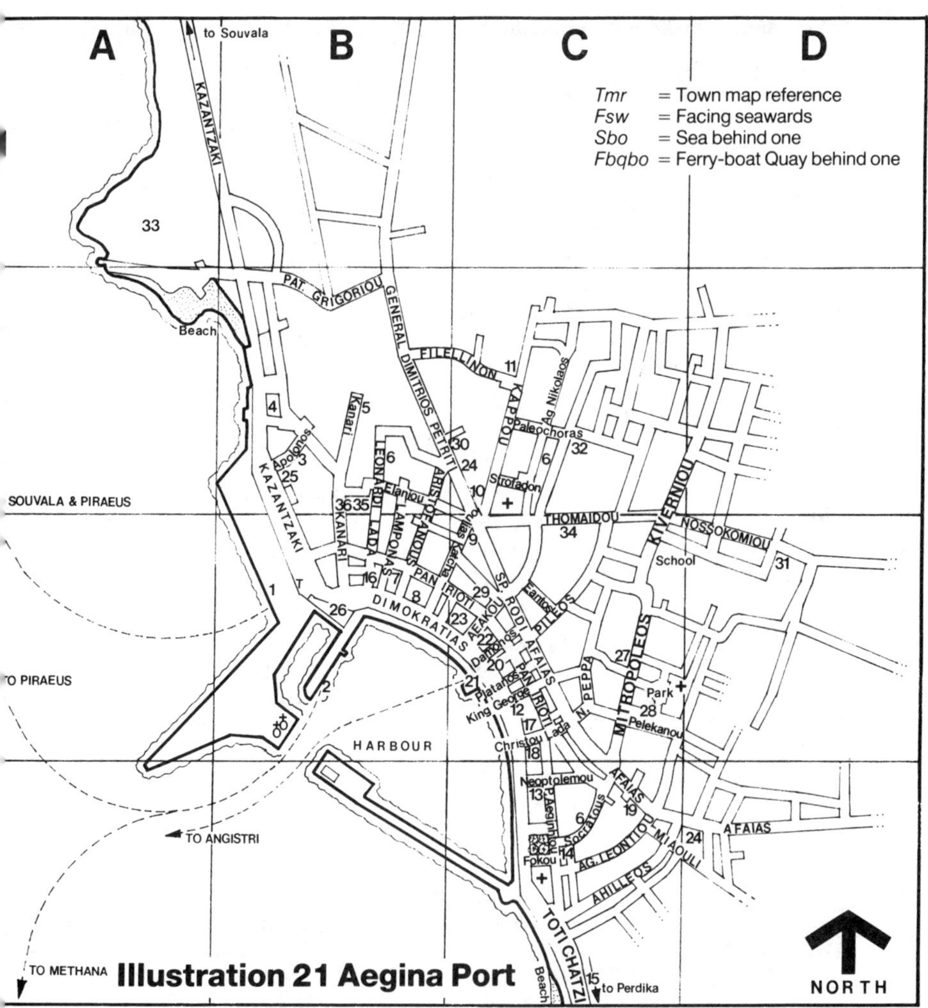

Illustration 21 Aegina Port

Tmr 1. Ferry-boat Quay B3
2. Flying Dolphin Quay B3
3. Hotel Togias B2
4. Hotel Avra B2
5. Hotel Artemis B2
6. Rooms
7. Pension Romios B3
8. Ionian & Popular Bank B/C3
9. ΚΑΠΠΟΣ Cafe-bar B/C2/3
10. Supermarket B/C2/3
11. Antoniou's House C2
12. Fish Market/Taverna C3
13. Tourist office C4
14. Hotel Guest House Pavlou C4
15. Hotel Brown C4
16. Leoussis Tours B3
17. 'Town Hall' Kafeneion C3
18. House of the Fisherman C3/4
19. Ouzerie ΤΑ ΠΕΡΔΙΚΩΤΙΚΑ C4
20. National Bank B/C3
21. Angistri Ferry-boat Quay B/C3
22. Book/Papershop B/C3
23. General store B/C3
24. Bakers (2)
25. Bus office B2/3
26. Port police/Ferry-boat & hydrofoil ticket offices B3
27. Dry Cleaners C3
28. Museum C3
29. Chemist (2)
30. Clinic B/C2
31. Hospital D3
32. OTE C2
33. Colona A1
34. Medieval Castle Keep C2/3
35. Town police B2/3
36. Post Office B2/3

T = Taxi rank

Kanari, turn left and proceed to the upper end. The hotel is on the right.

Single rooms sharing the bathroom cost 930drs and with an en suite bathroom 1300drs. Double rooms sharing cost 1485drs and en suite 1860drs. These rates rise to 1450/1860drs for single rooms and 2180/2775drs for double rooms (11th April-14th June & 16th Sept-31st Oct) and to 1820/2600drs and 2600/3650drs (15th June-15th Sept).

One block over is Odhos Leonardi Lada (ΛΕΟΝΑΡΔΗ ΛΑΔΑ), at the top of which are:-

Rooms (*Tmr* 6B2) Leonardi Lada St.
Directions: As above and on the right. The house stretches between Lada and the next street. A large double room costs 2000drs in mid-season,
and the:-

Hotel Marmarinos (Class D) 24 Leonardi Lada St. Tel 23510
Directions: Beyond the ***Rooms*** (*Tmr* 6B2) above and on the same side of the street.

A single room sharing the bathroom costs 980drs and with an en suite bathroom 1340drs. A double room sharing the bathroom is charged at 1340drs and en suite 1600drs. These rates rise for a single room sharing to 1120drs and en suite 1560drs and for a double room to 1600drs and 1960drs respectively (1st June-30th Sept).

Pension Romios (*Tmr* 7B3) Pan Irioti St Tel 22597
Directions: A first floor sign is visible from the outset of the Esplanade, approaching from the Ferry-boat Quay (*Tmr* 1B3). Admittedly the name board, sited above a tourist gift shop, is almost obscured by an *Inter-American* placard.

This is a 'sleazy', the entrance to which is in the next street back that runs parallel to the Esplanade. A single bed in a dormitory costs an average 550/700drs and a double room sharing a basic and dirty bathroom costs 1000-1400drs.

Antoniou's House (*Tmr* 11C2) 25 Kappou St Tel 23560
Directions: From the direction of the Ferry-boat Quay, proceed along the Esplanade to the right (*Sbo*), as far as Odhos Ioulias Katcha. This is the street beyond the Ionian & Popular Bank (*Tmr* 8B/C3). Walk up the slightly rising street to a five-way junction alongside the ΛΑΠΠΟΣ *Cafe-bar* (*Tmr* 9B/C2/3). Across the way is a supermarket (*Tmr* 10B/C2/3). Jink right and then left along Kappou St, leaving a large church on the right. The modernish house is on the left, beyond the lateral Filellinon St.

The *patron* is a pleasant man (incidentally related to the lady owner of Lela's Tours, Poros island). A small, clean cell (sorry, double room), sharing the bathroom costs 1600drs per night. There is a communal fridge on the landing.

In the vicinity of *Antoniou's* is:-

Rooms (*Tmr* 6C2) Ag Nikolaos St Tel 23072
Directions: On the way to *Rooms Antoniou's*, beyond the large church turn right along Odhos Strofadon and then left on Odhos Ag Nikolaos. The accommodation is on the right.

Tourist office (*Tmr* 13C4)
Directions: Beyond both the Fish Market (*Tmr* 12C3), which borders the Esplanade, and the side turnings of Odhos Christou Lada and Neoptolemou.

The office advertises ***Rooms***.

Continue along the Esplanade to the next side-street, which edges a small, rectangular tree planted park. Here turn left into Odhos P Aeginhtou for:-

Hotel Guest-House Pavlou (*Tmr* 14C4) (Class B) 21 P Aeginhtou Tel 22795

Directions: As above, turn right along Odhos Aeginhtou and the pension (for that is what the accommodation is licensed) is the far side of Odhos Socratous.

Single rooms sharing the bathroom start at 1300drs, double rooms sharing 2000drs and double rooms en suite 2200drs. These rates rise respectively to 1500drs, 2300drs and 2650drs (1st July-15th Sept). Note that the owners of this rather Edwardian 'pile' tend to request 200drs or so over the odds. The proprietors also own the *Hotel Athina* (Class D – tel 23091) on 42a Telamonos, which they proffer to prospective punters who blanch at the *Pension Pavlou* prices. Those at the *Athina* are some 300drs less per night.

Rooms (*Tmr* 6C4) Odhos Socratous

Directions: Up the street from the *Pension Pavlou*, but on the other side of the road.

Ethnic.

Hotel Brown (*Tmr* 15C4) (Class C) 4 Toti Chatzi St Tel 22271

Directions: At the far right-hand end (*Sbo*) of the Esplanade, from the Ferry-boat Quay, and overlooking a sandy beach.

A single room sharing a bathroom costs 970drs, whilst double rooms sharing are charged at 1265drs and en suite 2040drs. These rates rise respectively to 1355drs, 1670drs and 2880drs (1st July-30th Sept).

The Eating Out Naturally enough the Harbour Esplanade is lined with cafe-bars, tavernas and restaurants but outstanding kafeneions and eateries are not so easy to locate. Worry not – all is not lost. For a start there is the *'Fish Market' Kafeneion* (*Tmr* 12C3), in the street behind the Market and opposite the 'arcade' that runs through the building. A mite of a 'greasy spoon' but, if it is necessary to keep costs down, this is the place. Octopus is a 'house' speciality and the Kafeneion is well patronised by the locals.

Incidentally, at the entrance to the Fish Market arcade, on the right, is a traditional souvlaki pita stall. They serve 'giro' meat, as distinct from the more usual stick souvlaki available elsewhere in the Town. Only pies are available in the mornings, it being necessary to wait for the evening shift for a souvlaki pita.

Elsewhere, in fact up the side-street from the entrance to Leoussis Tours (*Tmr* 16B3), is a rather greasy, narrow fronted cafe-bar that sells an excellent stick souvlaki for 80drs and a bottle of beer at 80drs.

Kafeneion (*Tmr* 17C3)

Directions: Beyond the Fish Market (*Tmr* 12C3) and beneath the Town Hall. This particular kafeneion is the nearside, left-hand one (*Sbo*). There is another kafeneion next door.

The owner is a quiet, rather dignified man. A Nes meh ghala costs 70drs, an ouzo 60drs, a 'limon' 40drs and a bottle of Amstel beer 77drs.

The House of the Fisherman (*Tmr* 18C3/4)

Directions: On the far side of the Fish Market from the Ferry-boat Quay, across the side-street of Odhos Christou Lada and on the left.

One dish worth ordering is the fish soup. Not only is the soup served but also a plate with the remnants of the fish and vegetables that went towards making the dish. As the fish bits weigh about a 1lb that is quite a tummy-full.

A meal for two of fish soup (480drs), a souvlaki and chips (480drs), Greek salad (180drs), bread (30drs) and 2 bottles of 'open' retsina (75drs each) cost a total of 1320drs. Mind you, the souvlaki was not great shakes, even if it was two 'stickfulls'.

We had an intriguing experience here one night when we were accosted by a smiling Greek who took our order. He advised us which dishes were unavailable – only to observe them being served later – and then clattered off, never to be seen again. Furthermore, the meal that was served to us did not bear much resemblance to that ordered, but there you go! Even if you are fortunate enough to avoid this gentleman it may be that a local father and his demented child take a seat. If so, the young boy, who occasionally slavers at the mouth, can be a bit of a nuisance as he is a noisy, fractious brute who charges up and down the Esplanade.

Restaurant Maridaki *Directions*: Next door but one to the *House of the Fisherman* (*Tmr* 18C3/4), in between them being a baker.

The dishes on offer are preprepared but not unduly unacceptable for all that – in fact the standard is not too bad. A meal for two of a salad (95drs), a tzatziki (90drs), a plate of kalamares (360drs), keftades (meat balls) for one (260drs), a plate of chips (58drs), a bottle of beer (77drs), a bottle of retsina (48drs) bread and tax (28drs) all for 1016drs.

An establishment worth mentioning, if only for the eye-catching building it occupies is the:-

Ouzerie ΤΑ ΠΕΡΔΙΚΩΤΙΚΑ (*Tmr* 19C4)

Directions: Towards the far south-eastern end of Odhos ΑΓΑΙΑΣ and on the right of the street, from the direction of the Ferry-boat Quay.

For two hundred odd years this was a store incorporating a money changer's office, but now a very old-fashioned, high-bar top ouzerie. Fascinating.

The baker in between the *House of the Fisherman* (*Tmr* 18C3/4) and the *Restaurant Maridaki* sells feta cheese pies for 50drs.

THE A TO Z OF USEFUL INFORMATION

BANKS

National Bank (*Tmr* 20B/C3) Faces on to the Esplanade, across the way from the Angistri ferry docking point (*Tmr* 21B/C3).

BEACHES Yes. Not one but two, one at each end of the Esplanade.

Beach 1 To the left (*Sbo*) of the Ferry-boat Quay. This beach is bordered by a small park and edged, on the right (*Fsw*), by a patch of shore on to which some local boats are beached. This spot is probably the site of the ancient city's 'Hidden Port'. The tiny, sandy beach becomes crowded. The sea-bed gently shelves.

Beach 2 At the far right end of the Esplanade (*Sbo*), almost opposite the *Hotel Brown* (*Tmr* 15C4). The sandy beach has a pebbly shoreline and the sandy sea-bed also slowly shelves.

BICYCLE, SCOOTER & CAR HIRE As mentioned, hire firms are infrequent in Aegina. In fact, apart from a sign on a periptero close by a church towards the far (south) end of the Esplanade, there is only:-

Miras (*Tmr* B3)

Directions: The office is in the side-street of Lamponos, which branches off the Ferry-boat Quay end of the Esplanade.

The slow, but ambitious young man displays his wares (oh yes!) on the broad

Esplanade edging pavement, in the vicinity of Odhos Lamponos. 'Very famous here. No problem'! He charges 1600drs a day for an automatic Honda which includes a full fuel tank.

BOOKSELLERS (*Tmr* 22B/C3) Only one vendor of foreign language books and newspapers exists. The shaded shop is located on the edge of the wide Esplanade pavement, between the side-streets of Aeakou and Damonos.

BREAD SHOPS Any number including the General Store (*Tmr* 23B/C3), located towards the centre of the Esplanade, which sells bread. Also on the Esplanade is the Baker tucked in between the *House of the Fisherman* taverna (*Tmr* 18C3/4) and *Restaurant Maridaki*. There is a Baker (*Tmr* 24B/C2) on Odhos General Dim Petriti, to the left of the supermarket (*Tmr* 10B/C2/3) located at the junction with Ioulias Katcha. Another Baker (*Tmr* 24C/D4) is situated at the far, south-east end of the same street, which is here named Odhos Afaias.

BUSES The service is both widespread and frequent, so much so that rental firms are 'thin on the ground'. The Bus office (*Tmr* 25B2/3) and adjacent terminals, from which the buses emerge, are towards the left-hand end (*Sbo*) of the Ferry-boat Quay. The Bus terminal 'lean-to's' are usually full of parked cars 'sheltering' from the sun.

The timetables list two times, which certainly adds to the confusion! I have detailed the first stated.

Bus timetable
Aegina Town to Souvala, Agie, Vagia
Daily: 0515 (to Vagia), 0645 (to Agie), 0745 (to Agie), 0900 (to Agie), 0930 (to Vagia), 1100 (to Agie), 1215 (to Vagia), 1335 (to Agie), 1430 (to Agie), 1530 (to Vagia), 1715 (to Agie), 1900 (to Vagia), 1025hrs (to Vagia).

NB Note the time difference is 25 minutes.

Aegina Town to Ag Marina, Alones, Portes
Daily: 0515 (to Ag Marina), 0615 (to Alones & Portes), 0745 (to Ag Marina), 0900 (to Ag Marina), 0930 (to Alones), 1000 (to Alones), 1100 (to Ag Marina), 1215 (to Ag Marina), 1333 (to Alones), 1430 (to Portes), 1530 (to Alones), 1715 (to Ag Marina), 1900 (to Alones), 2015hrs (to Ag Marina).

NB Note the time difference is 25 minutes.

Aegina Town to Perdika
Daily:0530, 0630, 0750, 0900, 0930, 1015, 1100, 1200, 1230, 1335, 1430, 1530, 1715, 1900, 2015hrs.

NB Note the time difference is 20 minutes.

There are also 3 daily services between Vagia and Chaldaika as well as Aegina Town, Lefki and Pagoni.

COMMERCIAL SHOPPING AREA Naturally enough the Fish Market (*Tmr* 12C3) must take pride of place. Through the arcade of the building is Odhos Pan Irioti (ΠΑΝ ΗΡΕΙΟΤΗ), a 'Commercial Street' that runs more or less parallel to the Esplanade. In this and its associated side lanes are almost every type, shape and size of shop that sell everything from haberdashery to hardware. The greatest concentration of shops in the area of the Fish Market. Damonos St has a small greengrocer's.

Continuing along the Esplanade towards the Ferry-boat Quay passes a splendid

General Store (*Tmr* 23B/C3) on the left (*Sbo*) of which is a drink section. Bread is sold and out front is a greengrocer's stall. The shop is a bit of a muddle with mysterious tins of this and that propped and propping up other containers with contents that, on occasions, defy both description and identification. From hereon the buildings are increasingly taken up by gift and souvenir shops. The Esplanade swings round the bottom of the large pier that shuts off the north of the inner Harbour. This pier broadens out to accommodate a most picturesque, eye-catching double chapel. At the outset of the pier are a row of huts amongst which is a Pistachio Co-operative counter.

At least two or three greengrocery caiques moor to the Harbour Quay, almost opposite the *House of the Fisherman* taverna (*Tmr* 18C3/4).

FERRY-BOATS & FLYING DOLPHINS In common with other islands in this group, the service supplied by scheduled ferry-boats, excursion craft and the *Ceres* hydrofoils is excellent. It will perhaps amuse readers to realise that not so many years ago there were only three boats a week, not three in a morning. Note that a number of the Piraeus-bound ferries also call in to Souvala port on the north coast of Aegina.

The large inter-island ferry-boats dock at the enormous Quay (*Tmr* 1B3) to the left of the Harbour (*Sbo*), whilst the Flying Dolphins glide into the Harbour and pull up alongside a finger pier (*Tmr* 2B3).

The large cabin caiques that connect with Angistri island also dock (*Tmr* 21B/C3) in the Harbour, almost opposite the National Bank.

Ferry-boat timetable

Day	**Departure time**	**Ports/Islands of Call**
Daily	Nine boats a day (except Sunday when there are seven)	Piraeus(M).
	1400hrs	Methana(M), Poros.
Monday-Saturday	1100hrs	Souvala(Aegina), Piraeus(M).
Monday-Thursday	1545hrs	Methana(M), Poros.
Friday	1630hrs	Methana(M).
	1700hrs	Methana(M), Poros.
Saturday	0930hrs	Methana(M), Poros, Hydra, Ermioni(M), Spetses.
	1630hrs	Methana(M), Poros.
Sunday	0915hrs	Methana(M), Poros.
	0930hrs	Methana(M), Poros, Hydra, Ermioni(M), Spetses.
	1030hrs	Souvala(Aegina), Piraeus(M).
	1330hrs	Methana(M), Poros.
	1830hrs	Methana(M), Poros.

One-way fares: Aegina to			
	Piraeus	345drs;duration	1½hrs
	Methana(M)	;	1hr 50mins
	Poros	;	2hrs 10mins
	Ermioni(M)	;	2½hrs

Note that alongside the Port police office (*Tmr* 26B3) is an easily comprehensible notice board detailing all the scheduled ferry-boat departure times.

Flying Dolphin timetable (Mid-season)
Note there is both a Piraeus and Zea Port (Piraeus) service.

Day	**Departure time**	**Ports/Islands of Call**
Daily	0800, 1100, 1300, 1500, 1800, 1900hrs	Piraeus(M).
Return journey		
Daily	0700, 1100, 1300, 1500, 1800hrs.	Piraeus(M).
Monday-Friday	0930hrs	Piraeus(M).
Monday-Thursday	1630hrs	Piraeus(M).
Friday-Sunday	1600, 1700hrs	Piraeus(M).
Saturday & Sunday	0900, 1000, 1200hrs	Piraeus(M).
Daily	1105hrs	Zea Port (Piraeus).
Monday-Saturday	1715hrs	Methana(M), Poros, Hydra, Ermioni(M), Spetses, Portoheli(M).

One-way fare: Aegina to			
	Piraeus	540drs;duration	40mins
	Methana(M)	450drs;	20mins
	Poros	650drs;	40mins
	Hydra	780drs;	1¼hrs
	Ermioni(M)	940drs;	1¾hrs
	Spetses	1030drs;	2¼hrs
	Portoheli(M)	1130drs;	2½hrs

FERRY-BOAT & FLYING DOLPHIN TICKET OFFICES The ticket boat offices for both ferries and hydrofoils, as well as the timetables, are in the block of huts (*Tmr* 26B3) that range along the bottom of the large Quay edging the north of the Harbour. The ferry-boat tickets are to the left (*Fsw*) and the Flying Dolphin tickets to the right. There is another office behind a periptero bordering the Esplanade, close to the Fish Market (*Tmr* 12C3).

LAUNDRY There is a Dry Cleaners (*Tmr* 27C3) in Mitropoleos St on the other side of the road to the Park, just beyond the Museum (*Tmr* 28C3).

MEDICAL CARE
Chemists & Pharmacies There are two (*Tmr* 29B/C3) on the left (*Sbo*) of Odhos Aeakou that branches off the Esplanade, two blocks prior to the National Bank (*Tmr* 20B/C3). There is a shop on the right of Odhos Pan Irioti (*Fbqbo*), prior to the Fish Market (*Tmr* 12C3) and another (*Tmr* 29C3/4) at the south-east end of Odhos ΑΓΑΙΑΣ, on the left, opposite the *Ouzerie Ta* ΠΕΡΔΙΚΟΤΙΚΑ.
Clinic There is a Medical Centre (*Tmr* 30B/C2) on the right of Odhos General Dim Petriti, beyond the baker's.

On the corner of Odhos Aiakoy and ΣΠΥΡ ΡΟΔΗ is the first floor office of a combined Neurologist/Psychiatrist/Dermatologist & Venereologist – just in case.
Hospital (*Tmr* 31D3) Located beyond the School (*Tmr* C/D3), on Odhos Kiverniou, soon after which turn right (*Sbo*) on to Nossokomiou St.

MONIPOS There are a few that line up close to the Ferry-boat ticket offices (*Tmr* 26B3).

NTOG None.

OTE (*Tmr* 32C2) The building is towards the back of the Town on the right of a broad street, Odhos Paleochora. The office is only open weekdays between 0730-1510hrs.

On the right (*Sbo*) of the Esplanade entrance to the Fish Market arcade (*Tmr* 12C3) is a periptero announcing a *world-wide call* – obviously a metered, overseas telephone.

PETROL A pair of Mobil petrol pumps are situated on the right (*Sbo*) of Odhos Christou Lada.

PLACES OF INTEREST
Cathedrals & Churches
The Cathedral (*Tmr* C/D3) Behind a Park, close by the Museum and built in 1806.

Colona (*Tmr* 33A1) A single column and all that is easily visible of the remains of the ancient Temple of Apollo. Further north, occupying a pleasant headland, are remnants of the rest of the ancient city.

Medieval Castle Keep (*Tmr* 34C2/3) A rather 'Toytown' structure about which there is a conspiracy of silence! Probably dates back to the Venetians. I suppose if one was fortunate enough to possess the outstanding Temple Aphaia a rather boring, blog, squat, if whimsical castle remnant must be a 'teeny-weeny' bit uninspiring?

Museum (*Tmr* 28C3) Close by the Cathedral and containing some fine island finds.

POLICE
Port (*Tmr* 26B3) The office is in the row of huts and offices at the bottom of the large pier that edges the north end of the Harbour.
Town (*Tmr* 35B2/3) On the left (*Sbo*) of Leonardi Lada St.

POST OFFICE (*Tmr* 36B2/3) On the right (*Sbo*) of Kanari St.

TAXIS Queue on the Ferry-boat Quay (*Tmr* T.B3).

TELEPHONE NUMBERS & ADDRESSES

Bus office(*Tmr*25B2/3)	Tel 22787
Hospital (*Tmr* 31D3)	Tel 22209
Medical Centre (*Tmr* 30B/C2)	Tel 25546
Police (*Tmr* 35B2/3)	Tel 22391/22260
Taxis	Tel 22635

TRAVEL AGENTS & TOUR OFFICES
Leoussis Tours (*Tmr* 16B3) Tel 22334
Directions: The first floor office is visible from the Esplanade but the access steps are in Odhos Leonardi Lada, the lane to the left (*Sbo*).

Run by a friendly, roundish man who presides over a rather 'shambolic' set-up.

ROUTE ONE
To Portes via Souvala, Vagia, the Temple of Aphaia, Ag Marina and back via Messagros & Paleochora (about 47km round trip)

The northern coast road continues on along Kazantzaki Avenue from the Ferry-boat Quay (*Tmr* 1B3), past the upper town beach. The road rises to some 50m above sea-level, with the hill slopes on the coast side nurturing pine trees, and leaving the promontory topping Temple of Apollo on the left. This is followed by bits of shore here and there, which are not very sandy but the steep slopes to which can be scrambled down.

The countryside becomes even less vegetated, with a marked lack of trees but the occasional villa dotted about, some of which are quite distinctive. The route curves away from the rather unusual, featureless north-west coast where a lighthouse, 'coupled' with a chapel, is set down on a low bluff.

The sea-level road hugs the rocky, undulating coast through unattractive, scrubbly countryside in which is scattered various indeterminate, skeletal building frameworks. The shoreline is made up of a series of mucky coves with the occasional fishing boat mole jutting into the sea. The general unloveliness is not helped by there being absolutely no tree cover although there are signs of a tree planting programme in progress. This tract is within the 'parish boundaries' of Kypseli and as the road progresses along the north coast, in an almost due west direction, the coves get bigger and muckier and rockier... but there are smidgins of sand. A *Texaco* petrol station is followed, after another kilometre, by a very large, ugly, 'dead' factory. On the other side of the road is a shoreside boatyard with a number of yachts, caiques and motorboats in various states of repair, drawn up on the hardstanding. The road winds through the middle of an extremely ugly, concrete block-making works in the grounds of which is located the *Disco Aphrodite*. Yes, a disco here... the mind boggles!

LEONDI (Leonti) (5km from Aegina Town) ***Rooms***, apartments, the occasional taverna and the *Hotel Galaxy* but the locality is extremely dank, despite which there is much building development in hand.

Another 3km on advances to the outskirts of:-

SOUVALA (Suvala) (8km from Aegina Town):- port A quite pretty centre to the settlement, with the main road bordering a comparatively large cove (or small bay) which has an almost disproportionately large Ferry-boat Quay to the right (*Fsw*). On the left-hand side of the cove is a very, very small, pebbly bathing beach.

There is a 1960s 'Costa' ambience to the location, with a surprisingly numerous quantity of package tourists 'dumped' here. There is certainly the necessary infrastructure of hotels, tavernas, as well as a Supermarket Katerina, but it is not a location at which I would like to find myself stuck for two weeks.

There are ***Rooms*** and hotels include the:-

Hotel Ephi (Class C) Tel 52214

Directions: On the approach to Souvala, beside the coast road from Aegina Town.

All rooms have en suite bathrooms with singles starting at 1940drs and doubles 2665drs, which rates rise to 2565drs and 3375drs (21st June-15th Sept).

Less expensive accommodation is available at the:-

Hotel Saronikos (Class D) Tel 52224

Down-market but a single room sharing the bathroom costs 1000drs, a double room sharing 1500drs and a double room with en suite bathroom is charged at 1700drs. These charges rise, respectively, to 1200drs and 1650/1850drs (16th June-15th Sept).

Beyond the Market Square, and still on the main front, is a small, clean cove. The tiny beach is shingle and fine and coarse sand.

The scenery appears prettier if only, and probably because, there is now some tree cover, even on the hillsides.

On the far, east outskirts is:-

AGIOUS (Agie) (10km from Aegina Town) Here is a nucleus of package tourists centred in the area of the *Hotel Golden Beach*. The observant, noting the large numbers of holiday-makers clutching beach mats that are to be seen queuing for the buses, may well surmise that the shore is not so much a 'Golden Beach', more 'Golden Rocks' and they will be 'dead right'. There are ***Rooms*** if you must! Incidentally, the *Hotel Golden Beach* is strictly apartments for tour companies.

VAGIA (13½km from Aegina Town) A small, straggly, unattractive and older hamlet than Souvala, with a modest cove. Unfortunately, the shingly, sandy beach has a lot of kelp but is clean to the left (*Fsw*). Alongside this section, to the right, is a little harbour inlet and mole for small fishing boats. Most of the development is new with a few, older buildings spread about.

To the west of Vagia a coastal track runs out, up against a gate signed *Hellenic Navy – Forbitten* (*sic*) area. Offshore is the islet of Nissida.

South of Vagia the distant outline of the Temple of Aphaia can now be seen atop the distant hillside, even if the far view is rather blemished by a large radio mast that has been plonked down alongside the Temple. The road surface so far has been acceptable but from hereon becomes moth-eaten in patches, as the route commences on the steady climb through groves of pistachio and olive trees. In addition, pine trees pleasantly shade the road. There is a rather confusing triangulation of roads close to the Temple but keep right for the hilltop,which is magnificently surmounted by the:-

Temple of Aphaia (17km from Aegina Town, along the coastal road) A truly majestic pile, with an impressive amount of frieze still in position, and erected on the remains of a previous temple. There are memorable views over the Saronic Sea. The firm knowledge that the temple was not dedicated to Athena but to Aphaia (Aphaea) is all due to a German chappie with the unlikely name of Adolf Furtwangler. (One does wonder, doesn't one?) Legend has it that a lively Cretan lass, one Dictynna, who is reputed to have invented hunting nets, was fancied by King Minos. To escape his lustful advances she is reputed to have jumped into the sea only to become entangled in the nets of a fisherman. This unfortunate fell in love with her, whereon Dictynna re-launched herself into the sea and was washed up on the shores of Aegina. In order to escape from all the fellows she became invisible and vanished – thus Aphaia.

Entrance to the site (and museum) costs 250drs and is open weekdays between 1000-1600hrs, Sundays and holidays 1000-1500hrs. It is a pity that despite being an inspiring experience, the Temple is roped off and that the site gets very crowded. I advise visitors to arrive on the dot of 1000hrs as, in mid-season, the first tour bus arrives at 1015hrs, the third at 1016hrs the fifth at 1017hrs and so on until 1035hrs, by which time some twenty air-conditioned conveyances will have spewed out their eager, chattering passengers.

To seaward of the Temple, on the side of a cliff-edge layby, is a neat, pine tree shaded, discreet cafe and gift shop. I suppose I wouldn't have minded the exorbitant 120drs charged for a cup of coffee if it wasn't the old, familiar 'acorn brand'.

AG MARINA (23km from Aegina Town, along the coastal road – 14½km via Paleochora) Chips and sun-tan oil with everything and everybody – and is there or is there not a lot of everybody? In order to titillate the jaded palates of these sun loving hedonists, the main drag, a modern High St has been thoughtfully provided with such fun diversions as *The (air conditioned) Red Cock, Jimmy's Pub, Sunny-Burgers,* pub-cafes and bistros (almost all apparently with roof gardens), *UFO games, Pizza for Two* and more, much more. Naturally, most of the drinking establishments, necessary to assuage the combined thirsts of the English, German, Swedish, Dutch *et alii* tourists, variously promote 'happy/doubles/cocktail and or sundowner hours'. Almost every meal or drink is 'Special' – well it would be wouldn't it? The rest of the building plots are taken up by several *Rent A Bike* firms, and a mass of hotels and ***Rooms***, of which there are almost as many as there are hotels, an absolute cornucopia. The *raison d'etre* for all this, it must be admitted not unpleasant development, is a small bay with a sandy beach. By midday this is blanketed by sun-beds and sun-tan oil soaked people. There is a small amount of pebble in the first metre or so of the sea-bed but the beach is a natural for children as it gently shelves beneath the surface of the sea. So as to preclude anybody expressing displeasure at the absence of the trappings absolutely vital to the enjoyment of a holiday-maker, there are pedaloes, canoes, rowboats (300drs per hour), water skiing, wind surfers (800drs per hour), peddle boats (400drs per hour), sun-beds (400drs per session) and umbrellas (300drs a session).

In case there are not enough people here already, daily excursion boats make the voyage. As if to underline the authorities' knowledge that Ag Marina can take much more punishment – sorry tourists – on the right-hand horn of the headland (*Fsw*), that overlooks the seaside resort, are literally thousands of square metres of yet uncompleted development Oh, dear!

Proceeding south beyond Ag Marina, towards Portes, is a startling contrast to the seaside resort. The next sandless cove is rather pretty, in a rural way, even if it is only a small fishing boat hamlet, backed by plain hillsides entirely devoted to agricultural matters. A sign pointing along the track winding down to the cove indicates something about there being a taverna specialising in some fish dish or other. Rest assured the location is as dusty as it appears from the roadside. Inside the tiny mole enclosed harbour are incongruously tethered a couple of 'exhausted' pedaloes. One wonders if they have 'strayed' from Ag Marina and been salvaged?

Around the headland from the 'taverna cove' is a reasonably pretty, quiet inlet with a stony little foreshore. The road climbs steeply through increasingly attractive, if rather dry countryside, to overlook yet another pebbly cove, in this case hemmed in by substantial, terraced but now vineless hillsides. From these heights the route then wanders down to:-

PORTES (circa 28km from Aegina Town) The approaches overlook this small settlement that almost dips its 'toes' into the sea of the bay. The hamlet, which is experiencing a modest development programme, is backed by an agricultural plain edged by sparsely vegetated, substantial hills. A small, rocky mole encircles a tiny fishing boat harbour. It is straddled by a large, grey pebble foreshore to the nearside and on the far side, beyond a jumble of rocks, another stretch of pebble shore. The clean looking sea-bed is also pebbly.

On the return journey it is necessary to back-track all the way beyond the Temple of Aphaia to the junction of the Vagia and Messagros turnings. The cross island road, that almost parallels the north coast, is much prettier, passing through more verdant countryside.

It is worth pointing out that the island signposting, as well as the bus stops, are clearly indicated.

MESSAGROS (Mesagros) (8½km from Aegina Town) There is a petrol station here. The area was once famed for the number of potters who specialised in producing pitchers.

PALEOCHORA (5½km from Aegina Town) The island's capital for some 900 years, up until about 1800, and lauded for the number of churches that were supposedly built over and around the almost conical hill. There are very few of the rumoured three hundred and sixty five churches left, in fact only thirty or forty. The place forcibly reminds me of one of those Belgian First World War battlegrounds. One or two of the churches date back to the 12th century, including Ag Ekaterini built in 1225. It seems to me that Paleochora would look so much better if the buildings were whitewashed, as elsewhere in Greece.

KONTOS (5km from Aegina Town) The most notable religious building in the proximity of Paleochora is the Church of Saint Nektarios. It is named after an almost modern day Saint who spent the last year of his life in the Monastery of Ag Trias, dying in 1924. The magnificent Church is supposed to be a replica of St Sofia in Constantinople (modern day Istanbul). It might be, if it had a tower.

The road wanders back down to Aegina Town.

ROUTE TWO

To Perdika (9km) The west coast road proceeds south of Aegina Town from the Esplanade Toti Chatzi, around a headland, and along the backshore of a series of tiny coves. Most of these are unattractive, being rocky, dirty and filled with kelp. After about 1km there is a spot with a smidgin of sandy sea-bed, where the locals swim.

The road passes by a small settlement, with a little harbour, created by a mole on three sides, and a couple of disco bars.

The road then closes with the still rocky coast from which the occasional small quay juts into the sea, after which the shore becomes marshy and definitely scrubbly. A long concrete quay has been built and an attempt made to create a sandy beach but it is not particularly attractive.

A small, palm tree shaded chapel tops a bluff followed by a small harbour and the Disco Asteria close to which a thin sliver of shore encourages a few locals to swim.

The road hereabouts is edged by pistachio nut trees and, in the far distance, the view of a large promontory off which is an island. This protuberance hides the fishing boat village of Perdika.

Back on the route an 'actual' beach is encountered. Admittedly it is small but it is sandy, as is the sea-bed. There are ***Rooms***, a cafe and tavernas set in low hills. This first 'sensible' piece of sand on this route is followed by yet another sandy beach which is scraped to keep it clean. There are bits of boulder scattered about and biscuit rock at the water's edge.

After a sign proclaiming that the limits of Aegina Town have been left behind, the road passes a smart Nautical Club on a headland with a swimming pool, tennis court and a lighted quay. Beyond the bluff is a pleasant bay, even if it only has a rocky shore. The far side is subject to a lot of kelp set down on a dirty bit of seashore. At least here lovely great gum trees provide welcome shade.

The road continues to hug the contours of the hillside advancing past the chalet bungalow, hotel complex, *Aegina Maris*, draped around a small cove.

PERDIKA (9km from Aegina Town) This fishing boat port is set in low, level land bordered by shallow hills. A fair amount of development is taking place on the outskirts of the settlement.

The older part of the village parallels the surprisingly long quay of the port. In actual fact the concrete quay, which hosts a surprising number of fishing boats, is edged by a higher level Esplanade lined, to seawards, by awning covered patios and on the other side by tavernas, behind which is the village proper. The Quay and Esplanade form a one-way road system and any amount of signs proclaim the presence of a supermarket, tucked away somewhere. It really is a rather strange place with, for instance, an old kafeneion 'table by napkin' with a 'smarty' cocktail bar followed by the *Pub/Snackbar Belle Epoque*. Accommodation includes ***Rooms*** and a Pension. The port is very popular with day-tripping scooterists.

To the far left (*Fsw*) of the bay is a tree lined slice of sandy shore, even if a number of craft are scattered untidily about the backshore. A path along the waterfront to the right, towards the looming, offshore island of Moni, is edged by a boulderous shoreline on which the locals have created concrete patios for swimmers and sunbathers to lie out. During the height-of-season months excursion craft ferry the inquisitive out to the craggy, uninhabited island of Moni, but it is necessary to take a supply of drinking water if planning to visit this barren lump.

A 'Barrat' home! No The Temple of Aphaia, Aegina.

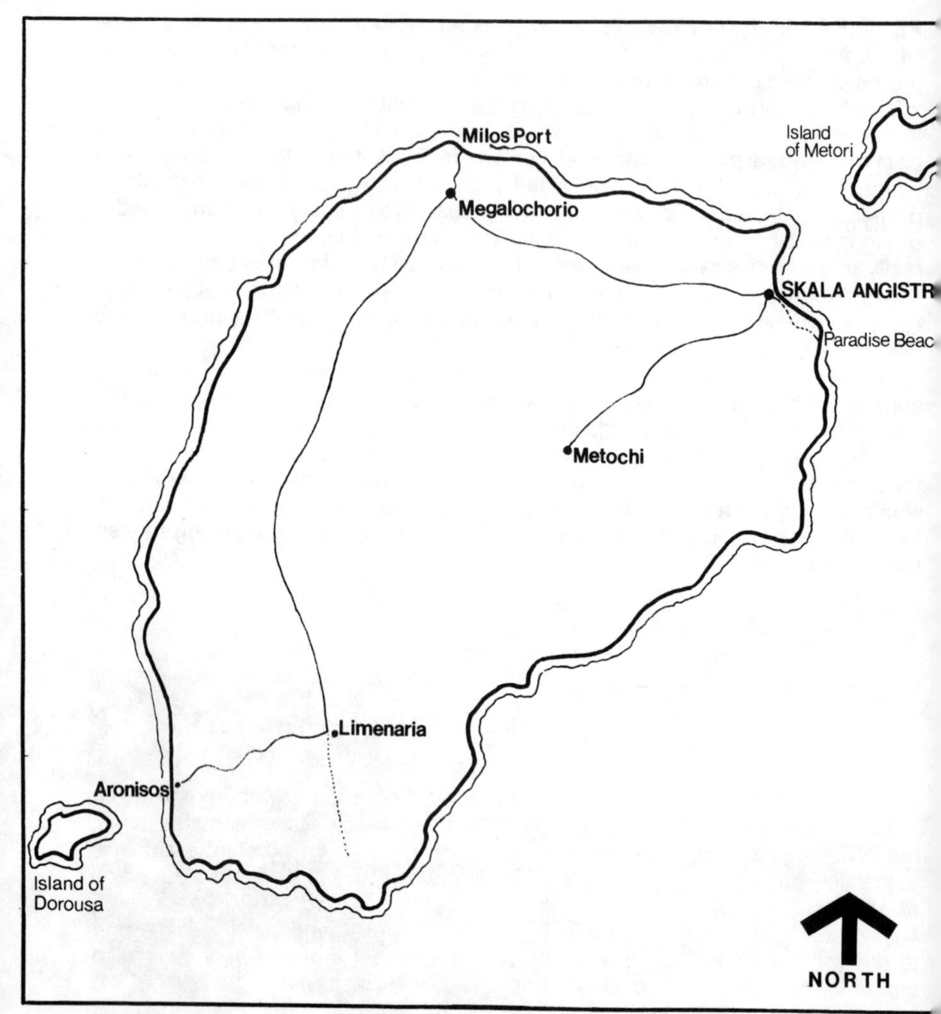

Illustration 22 Angistri island

16 ANGISTRI (Agistri, Aghistri) **
Argo-Saronic islands

FIRST IMPRESSIONS
A sandy beach; clear seas; flies ^{x10}; ***Rooms***; comparative inexpensiveness; new buildings; English package tourists – despite which the island is still a 'way station'.

SPECIALITIES
Until recent times a local wine received approbation but I am not sure if it is still available. Women wear a traditional headgear, which looks rather South American in style. This is a black square of material placed over the head on which is perched a hat.

RELIGIOUS HOLIDAYS & FESTIVALS
include: First Friday after Easter – Zoodochos Pighi; 30th June – Ag Anargyroi Church; 7th July – Ag Kiriaki Church.

VITAL STATISTICS
Tel prefix 0297. The island is approximately 5km from north to south and 3¼km from east to west with an area of 14 sqkm.

HISTORY
The island's name, in ancient times, was Cecryphalea and, as such, it was mentioned as being close to where an Athenian fleet defeated a Peloponnese navy. It was also referred to by Homer.

GENERAL
The date when tourism 'officially' commenced was 1957. A Piraeus ferry-boat connection was inaugurated in 1960 and in 1971 water and power were piped in.

Preconceived notions are, at the best of times, an unsatisfactory mental exercise, but in Greece it can ruin a long anticipated island sojourn. An excellent example is to imagine that Milos, of Venus de Milo fame, would prove to be a visit to an island of great beauty. Nothing could be further from the truth. So with Angistri, rarely commented upon except to laud its beaches. It is understandable if visitors were to develop the distinct impression that Angistri should prove to be a voyage to one of the 'off-the-beaten-track' islands. An island with frequent glimpses of the past, a refresher course well away from the clamour and bustle of its neighbours in the Argo-Saronic chain.

This dream may well persist even after taking the crowded Aegina passenger ferry-boat to Angistri. Surely the passengers are locals returning from a day out or natives of the island making a visit to the place of their birth. But any lingering dreams must dissolve, crumble and crash at the sight of the large sign facing disembarking passengers after some metres walk from the small Ferry-boat Quay (*Tmr* 1E4). This proclaims *Agistri Tours welcomes you. Call at the office for details of excursions, tours, BBQ's... et al, ad nauseam*.

On the other hand it is important not to over react. Despite the presence of a few package holiday companies, an almost continuous flow of excursion craft, low-key motorbike hire, a bus service and an almost immeasurable number of ***Rooms*** to rent, Angistri is, after all, a 'doo-hickey' destination, especially when the surface is more than scratched. Naturally the tour operators have spawned a smart hotel or three, one or two discos and the occasional cocktail bar but these are unquestionably out of character and well balanced by the rustic and provincial drawbacks, – no, no hush my mouth – charms of the island. Do not call at a weekend when the mainlanders almost outnumber the flies, a difficult task, believe me!

SKALA ANGISTRI: main settlement & port (Illustration 23)

A rather spread out, straggling but strangely attractive location. It has to be admitted that the juxtaposition of old Greece and modern-day package tourism uneasily rubs shoulders with each other. For instance the way-station ambience has to compete with a couple of signboards advertising just about every tourist temptation imaginable. These blandishments include *Traditional Greek dinner with retsina; B-B-Q'd chicken and lamb on the spit; excursions; the Copa Cabana pub (!); the Agistri Dance Club with cash prizes, trophies, champagne this Saturday at two* – Oh I can't wait till then.

Certainly the port must possess one of the most attractive stretches of sandy beach in the Argo-Saronic. The location and one or two of the hotels are very reminiscent of, say, Ag Roumeli, Crete.

ARRIVAL BY FERRY

A surprisingly regular and abundant daily service connects Angistri directly to the Piraeus. Some craft go on to Hydra, which can fool the unwary who might be deluded into thinking they were travelling back to Piraeus! Those travelling from Aegina island pass by Metori island.

Package tourists must arrive by ferry. Naturally to many it is their first visit to Greece, let alone the island of Angistri. Long stay visitors and locals gather round to watch the new arrivals being corralled and marshalled by the guides for the trek to their accommodation. The tourists, for their part, usually watch the separation and departure of their baggage, on the luggage truck, with a certain amount of trepidation. And who could blame them?

THE ACCOMMODATION & EATING OUT

The Accommodation The location is littered with ***Rooms*** and some hotels. A couple of these are of the 1960s variety, built in the inimitable Greek style of that period. The quintessential construction is a pre-stressed concrete barn-like place, with a total lack of atmosphere and support pillars dotted about. These latter seemingly placed with no regard to guests prerequisites or people's usual directional movement. Quite often the columns are located in the middle of a bedroom or on the direct approach path to the restaurant door. I remember one 'five star' example on Serifos where one column was situated in such a manner as to make it necessary to wriggle past it to gain access to the bedroom. In buildings of this era the stairs to the first floor are, without exception, unfinished raw concrete, rarely with any railings. The doors are made in such a manner as to be the envy of any loudspeaker manufacturer. Why? Because they have the ability to magnify sound in such a way that would appear, to the uninitiated, to be unachievable.

Hotel (& Taverna) Aktaion (*Tmr* 3D4) (Class E) Tel 91222
Directions: From the Ferry-boat Quay (*Tmr* 1E4) turn right (*Sbo*) and follow the shoreline round to the right. The track passes the *Agistri Tours* notice board and then branches left and right leaving the *Rooms/Hotel* ΙΚΑΡΣΟΝΙΕΡΕ (*Tmr* 2D4) in the fork.

The *Aktaion* appears to be inseparably twinned with the nearside *Hotel* ΑΛΕΞΑΝΔΡΑ (*Alexandra*), the old-fashioned, ground floor taverna terraces of the pair only being separated from each other by a low division. Dogs and cats.

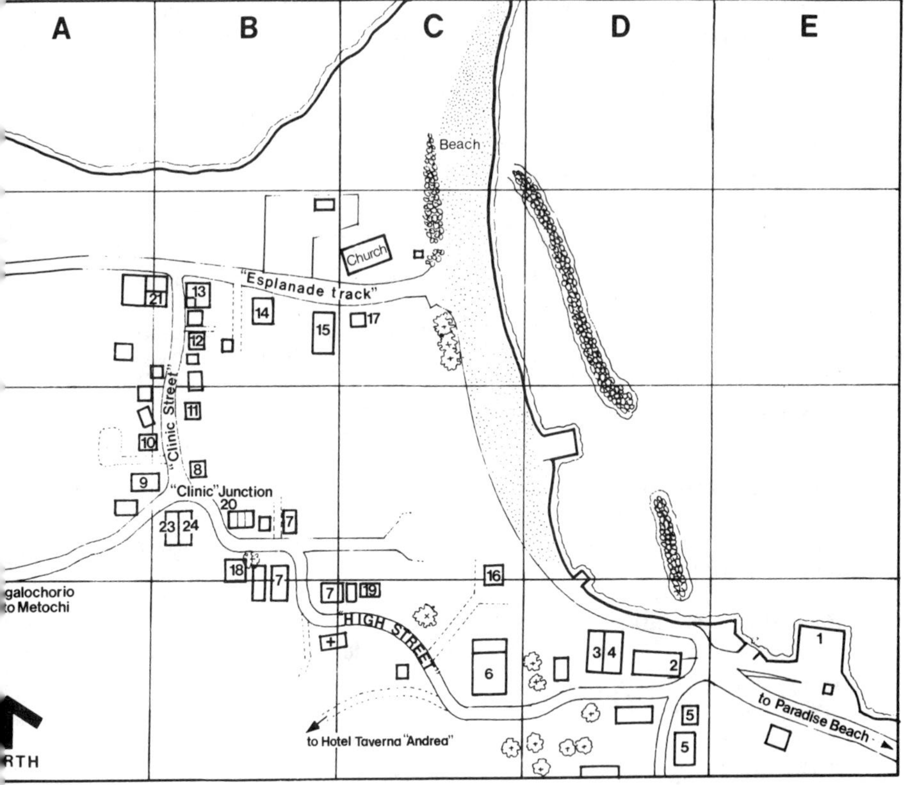

Illustration 23 Skala Angistri

Tmr = Town map reference
Fsw = Facing seawards
Sbo = Sea behind one
Fbqbo = Ferry-boat Quay behind one

Tmr
1. Ferry-boat Quay E4
2. Hotel ΙΚΑΡΣΟΝΙΕΡΕΣ D4
3. Hotel & Taverna Aktaion D4
4. Hotel& Restaurant Alexandra D4
5. Rooms (side by side) D4
6. Hotel Yanna C4
7. Rooms (3)
8. Clinic B3
9. Toxotis Snackbar & Rooms A/B3
10. Hotel Pagona A/B3
11. Rooms A/B2/3
12. Hotel Manaras B2
13. Hotel Aghistri/Skala Tours B2
14. Hotel Galini B2
15. Hotel Saronis B/C2
16. Mini-Mam Taverna C3/4
17. Kafeneion B/C2
18. Quatro's Snackbar B3/4
19. Scooter hire C3/4
20. Baker B3
21. General store A/B2
22. Mini-Market A3/4
23. Chemist A/B3
24. Angistri Tours B3

jump back and forth over this as they are desultorily chased from one or other of the establishments. The *Aktaion* is one of the hotels that the introductory accommodation observations are based on, so no more need be said. The taverna part of the business is on the cavernous, open fronted ground floor and the steps to the first floor accommodation are towards the rear. Despite the officially listed prices of 1600drs for a single and 1900drs for a double room, both with en suite bathrooms, a mid-season enquirer will be offered a double room for 1500drs which includes a breakfast. Of the 'management team', Mary, who is more Jewish looking than an archetypal Greek, speaks excellent English. Most bedrooms have a narrow balcony from which a squint of the beach can be seen. It is a pity that the bedrooms are spaced out along the side of the building because the view from the few rooms that face out over the front is really super. This takes in the bush clad headland spit with a lovely, domed, white church to the left and, on the right, a sweep of sand separated into two curves. The first of these edges a rock circled fishing boat mooring and the far one is the beach 'proper'.

Also *See* **The Eating Out**.

Hotel (& Restaurant) Alexandra (*Tmr* 4D4) (Class E) Tel 91251
Directions: As above.

All as for the *Hotel Aktaion*, but the high season's rates might be 300drs more expensive.

Back at the *Hotel* ΙΚΑΡΣΟΝΙΕΡΕΣ (*Tmr* 2D4) fork in the road, there are smart ***Rooms*** (*Tmr* 5D4), two side by side, on the left of the steep path to the left.

Hotel Yanna (*Tmr* 6C4) (Class E) Tel 91356
Directions: From the Ferry-boat Quay branch left along the 'High St' (the what?), the surfaced road that constitutes the Main Street.

All rooms have an en suite bathroom with singles starting off at 1500drs and a double room 1800drs, rising, respectively, to 1700drs and 2000drs (16th June-15th Sept).

The Hotel Taverna Andrea, a package tour location, is off across a field to the left of the 'High St'.

Continuing along the road, in the general direction of Megalochorio, there are ***Rooms*** (*Tmr* 7B/C3/4) on the right (*Fbqbo*), opposite a Church, and, after the 'chicane', more ***Rooms*** on the left (*Tmr* 7B3/4) and right (*Tmr* 7B3, tel 91228*).

* The observant will note that this telephone number is shared by the *Hotel Aghistri* and **Skala Tours** – probably because they share the same family and or booking agency.

At the junction of the Megalochorio road, and the street down to the waterfront, alongside the Clinic (*Tmr* 8B3), is, on the far side, the *Toxotis Snackbar & Rooms* (*Tmr* 9A/B3).

Hotel Pagona (*Tmr* 10A/B3) (Class E) Tel 91327
Directions: As above and on the left of 'Clinic St', proceeding towards the waterfront.

Only double rooms with en suite bathrooms at a cost of 1800drs.

Further on down the street, on the right, are ***Rooms*** (*Tmr* 11A/B2/3, tel 91293) and the:-

Hotel Manaras (*Tmr* 12B2) (Class D) Tel 91312
Directions: As above.

Calls itself a pension, but is categorised as a hotel, and only has double rooms. Those sharing a bathroom are listed at 1700drs and those with an en suite bathroom 2100drs.

Hotel Aghistri (*Tmr* 13B2)(Class E) Tel 91228
Directions: On the junction of the street above and the 'Esplanade track', from the direction of the beach.

Smart, despite it's rating, and booked by tour companies. All rooms have en suite bathrooms with a single room being charged at 1300drs and a double room 1600drs. These rates rise to 1500drs and 1900drs (16 June-15th Sept).

Hotel ΓΑΛΗΝΗ (Galini) (*Tmr* 14B2) (Class D) Tel 91219
Directions: Along the 'Esplanade track' towards the Church and the beach.

En suite rooms with singles costing 1600drs and doubles 2000drs.

Hotel Saronis (*Tmr* 15B/C2) (Class D) Tel 91394
Directions: Almost opposite the Church, across the 'Esplanade track' and behind the *Taverna Mochos*.

All rooms have en suite bathrooms, with a single room listed at 1400drs and a double room 1800drs. These rates rise to 1600drs for a single room and 2000drs for a double (1st June-31st Aug).

Before leaving the subject of accommodation, if the surnames of the hotel owners are anything to go by *Panou* must be the most common island name. Nine out of a total of some nineteen hotels are owned by a Panou.

The Eating Out Rather limited in Skala Angistri, which can be a little restricting as the only alternative is to walk to Megalochorio.

Restaurant (Hotel) Aktaion (*Tmr* 3D4)
Directions: *See* **The Accommodation.**

The all pervasive cooking smells and constant presence of cats and dogs, which sometimes fight when they are ineffectually expelled, can be wearisome. The television is usually blaring away, which might help distract diners from the omnipresent flies, but the food is very good and helpings are plentiful.

A dinner for two of spaghetti and meatballs (300drs), local kalamares (300drs), spinach (150drs), courgettes (120drs), 2 bottles of retsina (60drs each), bread and tax (20drs each) and 2 Nes meh ghala (80drs each) cost 1190drs. A plate of veal (450drs), a moussaka (300drs), a Greek salad (200drs), a tzatziki (100drs), a bottle of retsina (60drs) and bread will set a couple back 1150drs. On the other hand it is not necessary to sit down to a full blow-out. A plain omelette, a potato omelette, a salad, 2 beers and bread costs 670drs.

In respect of the adjacent *Restaurant (Hotel) Alexandra* (*Tmr* 4D4) re-read the *Restaurant Aktaion*.

Mini-Mam Taverna (*Tmr* 16C3/4)
Directions: The path to the taverna, which is more a smart hut, is either through a wilderness from the beach backshore or over a 'bombsite' from the 'High St'.

An extensive and very reasonably priced menu which includes saganaki. Its a pity that the taverna is rather screened off from its surroundings. The neat patio is rather small but makes for a good coffee stop. Two fluffy Nes meh ghala and a stiff brandy costs 200drs and a bottle of beer 85drs. Service can be rather slow at times.

Kafeneion (*Tmr* 17B/C2)
Directions: The old-world, single storey kafeneion, housed in an elderly building, edges the 'Esplanade track' close to the beach, opposite the Church.
A bottle of beer costs 80drs, which isn't too bad considering the logistics of supply and bearing in mind that the same costs 77drs on Aegina.

Taverna Mochos
Directions: Further along the 'Esplanade track', away from the beach and to the front of the *Hotel Saronis* (*Tmr* 15B/C2).
Expensive and the target for excursion boat passengers and their midday 'troughing'. The craft dock and tour leaders 'pied piper' their flock – if that is not mixing to many metaphors – making straight for this place where tummies are replenished. I couldn't bring myself to pay the prices requested with a Greek salad costing 220drs and a bottle of beer 105drs.

Quatro's Snackbar (*Tmr* 18B3/4)
Directions: Close to 'Clinic Junction', on the Ferry-boat Quay side of the 'High St'.
A 'smarty', cocktail bar type of establishment but advertises loukoumades, which are only available every other day. The trick is to find out the day... One of the only late night spots and a preserve of the young but the coffee is good and hot and, considering the establishment's style, is not outrageous at 100drs.

The patisserie/baker (*Tmr* 20B3), almost opposite *Quatro's*, stays open late in the evening and sells tripotika for 50drs and cakes, which might help fill a gap after an early evening meal.

THE A TO Z OF USEFUL INFORMATION

BANKS None, nor are there any exchange offices or a Post Office so bring enough drachmae. The various travel offices may effect travellers cheque transactions for their clients (*See* **Travel Agents & Tour Offices, A To Z**).

BEACHES The main beach, that runs the length of the headland spit, is very sandy and the sea-bed gently shelving. This is ideal for children but adults have to walk so far out to reach deep water that a swimmer is very nearly into a weedy section of sea bottom. Pedaloes cost 250drs, canoes 150drs, wind surfers 350drs and a parasol 60drs (all per hour).

See **Excursions to Skala Angistri Surrounds**.

BICYCLE, SCOOTER & CAR HIRE Despite the excellent bus service and the few roads, there is a scooter hire firm (*Tmr* 19C3/4) bordering the side of the 'High St'. The scooters only take one person and cost 1300drs a day, complete with a full tank of petrol. Bicycles are also available for 500drs a day, but it is a long, steep climb to Limenaria.

BREAD SHOPS One, a baker/patisserie/store (*Tmr* 20B3) on the 'High St', close to 'Clinic Junction'. The shop stays open fairly late in the evenings, including Saturdays. (*See* **The Eating Out**).

BUSES The very small bus parks in front of the Church (*Tmr* B/C2). The route takes in Megalochorio (Milos Port) and Limenaria. In places the ride is very bumpy and in others it is a 'finger-licking' tight fight.

Bus timetable
Skala Angistri to Limenaria via Megalochorio

Monday to Friday	0800, 1100, 1520, 1620, 1930hrs
Saturday	0800, 1000, 1220, 1520, 1620, 1930hrs
Sunday/holidays	0800, 1030, 1315, 1520, 1620, 1930hrs.

Departure from Limenaria is about 40 minutes after the Skala times.
One-way fare from Skala to Limenaria costs 120drs.

CAMPING Despite being officially frowned upon, a point reinforced by signs to that effect, there are a number of tents scattered about the hills on the way to **Paradise Beach** (*See* **Excursions to Skala/Angistri Surrounds**).

COMMERCIAL SHOPPING AREA Naturally, in such a small, scattered development, none but there are a few, all-purpose stores. These include one General Store (*Tmr* 21A/B2) that appears to sell almost everything, sited close to the junction of 'Clinic Street' with the 'Esplanade track', and a Mini-Market (*Tmr* 22A3/4), at the outset of the road to Megalochorio. Those who are desperate to take home a few gifts need not despair as there are quite a number of souvenir shops.

DISCOS There is a rather smart looking one about five minutes along the Megalochorio road, on the left, and in 1987, named **Zorba's**.

FERRY-BOATS As indicated in the Introduction to Skala, there is almost an over-abundance of craft available. The Aegina connection is to be expected, but the Piraeus service is a surprise and accounts for the large amount of mainland Greeks that 'hit' the island, more especially over the weekend.

The island bus meets most ferry-boats arrivals.

Ferry-boat timetable (Mid-season)

Day	Departure time	Ferry-boat	Ports/Islands of Call
Monday to Saturday	0700, 1410, 1710hrs	Mochlos Express or Kapetan Davelis	Aegina
Sunday	0730, 1010, 1500hrs.	Mochlos Express or Kapetan Davelis	Aegina

NB There is a rather mysterious listing of a '5' & '10' Piraeus departure but I have not managed to sort out whether this is a.m. or p.m. and even if they run! If so they must be at 1700 & 2200hrs.
The **Kapetan Davelis** is the older of the two small craft.

One-way fare 100drs; duration 20 mins.

Monday	0550hrs*	Manaras Express+	Piraeus(M).
	1000hrs	Manaras Express	Piraeus(M).
Tuesday, Wednesday	0600hrs	Manaras Express	Piraeus(M).
Thursday	0600hrs	Manaras Express	Piraeus(M).
	1610hrs	Manaras Express	Piraeus(M).
Friday	1010hrs	Manaras Express	Piraeus(M)
	1610hrs	Manaras Express	Piraeus(M).

	2015hrs	Manaras Express	Piraeus(M).
Saturday	1010hrs	Manaras Express	Piraeus(M).
	1645hrs	Manaras Express	Piraeus(M).
Sunday	1430hrs	Manaras Express	Piraeus(M).
	1830hrs	Manaras Express	Piraeus(M).

Journey duration 2 hours.

*Rumour has it that this craft sometimes departs on Sunday night.

+ The Manaras Express quite often continues on to Hydra island, after stopping at Angistri, and before returning to Piraeus. Unless a traveller wants a pleasant sea voyage or, of course, wishes to go to Hydra, check carefully the next port of docking!
A largish Ro-Ro, the **CF Aias,** also drops in to Angistri, but on what basis I do not know.

FERRY-BOAT TICKET OFFICES Tickets are purchased on board the relevant craft.

MEDICAL CARE
Chemists & Pharmacies (*Tmr* 23A/B3) One conveniently close to 'Clinic Junction'.
Clinic (*Tmr* 8B3) Bordering 'Clinic Junction'. The surgery is open between 1030-1230hrs & 1830-2000hrs on Tuesday, Wednesday, Friday and Saturday. Thursdays it opens 1830-2000hrs. There is also a doctor's surgery in Megalochorio with the doors open between 0830-1030hrs & 1700-1830hrs, from Tuesday to Saturday.

NTOG, OTE, PETROL, PLACES OF INTEREST, POLICE, POST OFFICE, TAXIS, TOILETS None.

TRAVEL AGENTS & TOUR OFFICES
Angistri Tours (*Tmr* 24B3) Tel 91307/91255
Directions: Conveniently situated edging 'Clinic Junction'.
The staff speak English (well they would, wouldn't they?) and one, at least, is English. Not very helpful to' Independents', who stand out like 'sore backpacks' from their package holiday compatriots.
Skala Tours Tel 91228
Directions: The office is let into the ground floor of the *Hotel Aghistri*, situated on the junction of 'Clinic St' and the 'Esplanade track'.

EXCURSIONS TO SKALA ANGISTRI SURROUNDS
Excursion to Paradise Beach (about 15 minutes walk)

It is advisable to wear some strong shoes as the track is rather rough. The path leads off from the vicinity of the Ferry-boat Quay (*Tmr* 1E4), in fact to the left (*Sbo*). The route passes by:-

Katerina's Inn (Tel 23814) on the right. Advertised 'pleasures' include wind surfing, pedaloes, water skiing, a beach bar and disco. I presume most of these 'wonderful delights' are down to the left, on the beach shoreline.

Hotel Alkyoni (Class D – tel 91377). Mainly occupied by package holiday-makers,
and the:-
Angistri Club on the left. Host to a darts competition evening.

The route now becomes nothing more than a narrow path running along a cliff which edges a rocky shore some way below. The clear sea-water shows up the rocky nature of the sea-bed.

Despite any impressions that the destination should be named 'Paradise Rocks', press on to the right, round a little headland, take the track down to the point, then walk along the rocks on to the whitish pebbles of the rock cliff edged, narrow but rather pleasant:-

Paradise Beach It is a pity that there is no sand on either the beach or the sea-bed, which is also almost entirely made up of pebbles. The sea is very clear and clean.

As observed in the **A To Z, Skala Angistri**, despite signs forbidding the same, there are tents in the hillsides.

Excursion to Metochi (about 30 minute walk) Too close to the port to be considered a quiet backwater. The road to Metochi angles off left from the Megalochorio route, almost opposite the Mini-Market (*Tmr* 22A3/4). There is only one taverna.

ONE (& ONLY) ROUTE

To Aronisos via Megalochorio & Limenaria (about 3¼hrs walk) The road out of Skala makes off from the 'Clinic Junction', passing the Mini-Market (*Tmr* 22A3/4) on the right, the turning off to the left to Metochi and, after some five minutes, a disco on the left. There are only a few trucks on the island, in addition to the bicycles and scooters that are hired, thus the road is not exactly crowded. Unfortunately it is also without any shade all the way to:-

MEGALOCHORIO (Milos Port) (About ¾hr walk from Skala Angistri) The approach to the village and port passes the *Hotel Flisvos*. At the fork in the road, by a house with a 'Mickey Mouse' painted on the wall, a sign points right towards the *Taverna Three Brothers*. The outskirts indicate a steady (Greek) suburban development which includes holiday homes and a scattering of ***Rooms***.

The core of Megalochorio is centred on the old, fly-blown village whilst the package tour industry (which embraces *SunMed*) has caused a certain amount of development in the area of the port. This includes the *Hotel Milos* that overlooks the port, and in the ground floor of which is Marousa Tours. This latter travel and tourist office opens daily between 0900-1230hrs & 1730-1930hrs. Close by the hotel is a snackbar and from hereabouts, walking towards the harbour, there is a lovely view back along the coast towards Skala. There is also the very smart *Hotel Akti*. The harbour is open ended with a large rocky mole closing in the seaward side. The main beach isn't very good, in fact it is a series of very, very small inlets set in a largish bay with biscuit rock, weed and very little sand. To compensate for this the quayside *Cafe-bar Ul*, which appears to double up as a disco in the evenings, has contained some sand within a concrete rim on the sea's edge. It seems a pity that the sea-bed is large pebbles followed by rock. There are a few wind surfers about.

Back in the village proper, from the direction of Skala, there is the *Taverna Boulas*, just beyond the Church to the right. Straight ahead is the *Taverna Three Brothers*, a package tourist hot-spot probably inflated for the summer, being deflated and stowed away out of season! But not all is lost for there is the *Taverna O Setis* and, beyond the small village store on the left, the:-

Restaurant/Taverna Yiannis

Directions: Next door to a sign attached to an oldish house that announces

Cellar choose your own wine home made.

The interior is large, clean, airy and pleasant and at the rear is a nice, if small, balcony that looks out over an old olive grove. The owner speaks English. The menu is not extensive but the food is well presented if some of the portions are rather small. A tzatziki costs 120drs, a (small) Greek salad 179drs, dishes of moussaka, meatballs, stuffed tomatoes, spaghetti bolognese and kalamares are charged at 210drs. A ½ pint glass of beer costs 50drs, an Amstel beer 85drs and a carafe of house retsina 50drs. Omelettes are also available.

On the way out of the village, towards the road on to Limenaria, there is the *Kouros Pub-cafe*, opposite a very, very smart, but tiny, public square with seats.

If you are walking, the road becomes pine tree shaded after about ten minutes. There is evidence of resin collection and that the hillsides were once extensively used for the cultivation of grapes. The extensive terracing is now almost overgrown by pine tree groves which supply patchy cover all the way to:-

LIMENARI (about 2¾hrs walk from Skala Angistri) The road funnels through a narrow but short cutting prior to emerging above and to one side of the village. To the left is a large, paved, winnowing circle which is still in use. It has to be admitted that this super, old-world, 'hillbilly' little village is fly-blown but it has not yet been ravaged by the package tourists. There are a couple of tavernas, one close to where the bus stops, the:-

Supermarket Taverna O Tasos The word supermarket in the title alludes to the small store activities of this delightfully 'doo-hickey' establishment. A family concern with a spacious lean-to on the side of the main building. Hanging on the walls of this are a number of large tapestries and, on one side and hemmed in by tables and chairs, an old fashioned loom, often with a number of tapestries under 'construction'. Drinks and simple meals are available as are ice-creams. A beer costs 80drs and they stay open well into normal siesta time, closing for the afternoon at about 1430hrs.

There are two signs in the village, one round to the left to a beach. But do not get too excited. Those who venture down this path end up on a concrete platform set in the rocks of a plunging cliff edged bay. To get into the 'briny' it is necessary to either jump or scramble over the edge on the left (*Fsw*). The water is lovely but there a quite a lot of large jellyfish flopping about on occasions.

Back in the village another sign announces *Aronisos Taverna, fresh fish every day, little harbour, beautiful place, safe swimming*. This route leads past the other small taverna bordering what could be called, in an expansive mood, the village square.

After quarter of an hour's walk on a concrete path (laid in January 1986 according to the scrawled marks) the surfaced area runs out and reverts to a track. The route descends a hillside through groves of mature olive trees passing a wall encircled water well on the left. The thirsty might like to know this is still operational.

Where the stony track levels out there is a very large *Alikes* (or salting) edging the route, now set in low hills. After another five to ten minutes the trail peters out on the backshore of:-

ARONISOS (about 3¼ hours walk) A small, 'donkey-dropping' harbour, at first sight apparently set in the nearside of a rocky bay. I write at first sight because it becomes apparent that the land plonked down in the sea, very close to the water's edge, is a tree crowned islet that actually divides the shoreline. Beyond this islet is the offshore island of Dorousa.

Aronisos is a delightfully attractive if rather messy spot with a rocky mole forming a small, benzina harbour to the right (*Fsw*). There is a small quay, almost directly ahead, and, to the right, a rustic, hut-like taverna. Despite the allure of the sign 'the beachcomber' management are very laid back and the service slow to indolent. A warm bottle of beer costs 100drs.

The other side of the harbour mole is a pocket handkerchief of shingle beach. The first metre or so of the sea-bed is pebble, followed by some sand, then seaweedy stones after which a large area of sand, so it is a fine place to have a swim.

The beach, Skala Angistri, Angistri.

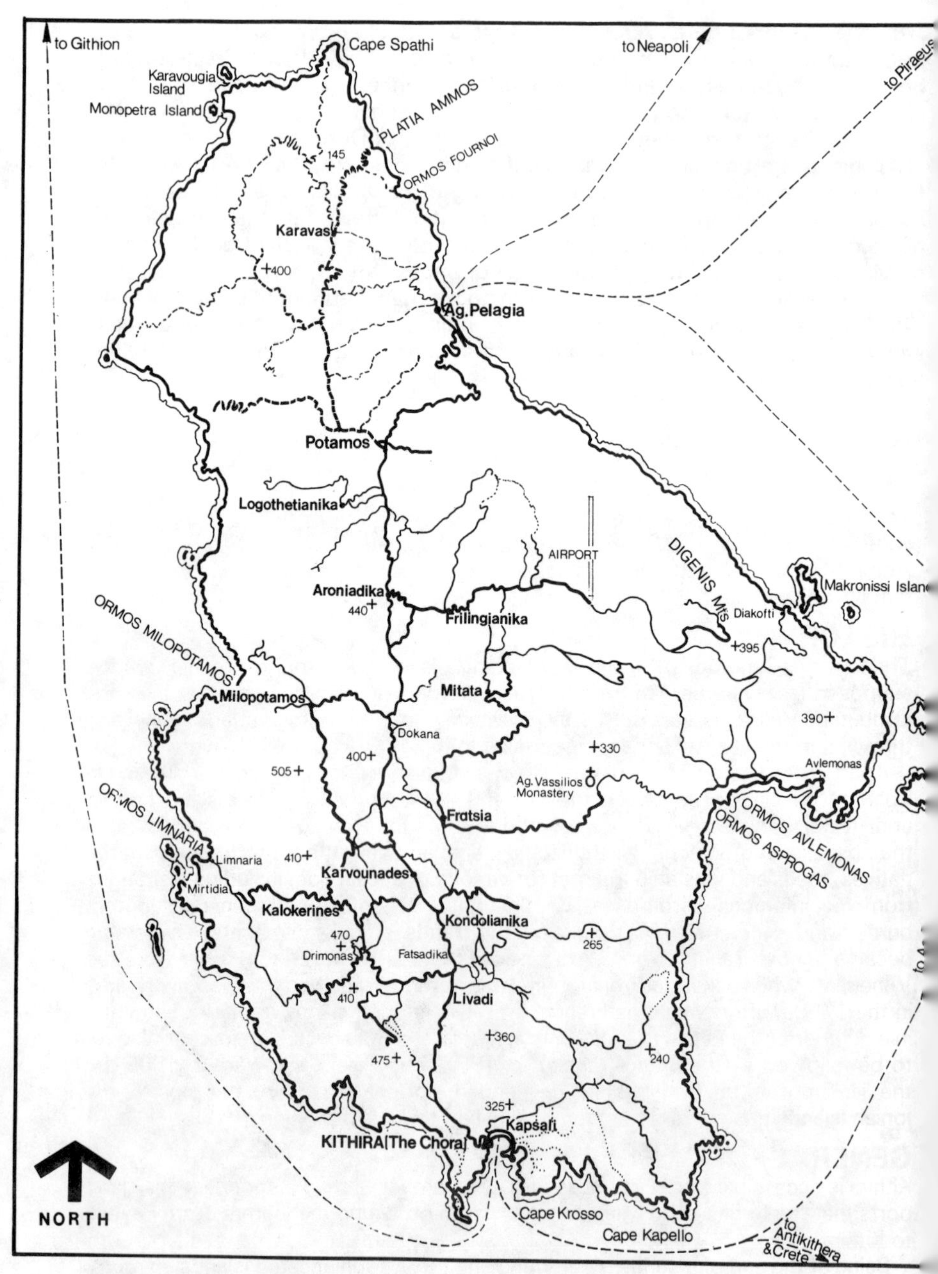

Illustration 24 Kithira island

17 KITHIRA (Kythira, Kythera, Cythera) ****
Argo-Saronic islands

FIRST IMPRESSIONS
Lovely countryside, greens & yellows; wild flowers; birds; a couple of dramatic views; friendly people; wind; lack of kafeneions; tractors (but in the countryside, donkeys); farming communities; churches, some with barrel roofs and a few with wide, tiled roofs; a unique Sunday market; some snakes; lack of public transport.

SPECIALITIES
No disco's

RELIGIOUS HOLIDAYS & FESTIVALS
include: 29-30th May – Festival Ag Trias Church, Mitata; 24th September – Festivals throughout the island.

VITAL STATISTICS
Tel prefix 0733. The island is about 25km from top to bottom and up to 16km in width with an area of 280sqkm. The population is 'rumoured' to be about 3500. Administratively now linked to Piraeus, which seems more sensible than the 'idiocy' that linked the island with the Ionian islands, in years gone by.

HISTORY
The island is reputed to be the first landing place of Aphrodite (Venus), who is supposed to have emerged from the foam of the sea. I am not sure that I like the attributation that she was born after Zeus had chopped off his father's 'willy' and thrown it in the sea, whence the goddess. It makes you go cold all over.

Apart from Cretan Minoan associations and being involved in the Athenian-Spartan 'punch-ups', between the 6th and 4th centuries BC, the island had an undistinguished history. After the withdrawal of the Romans, the island became the possession of various Byzantine and Venetian overlords. Unfortunately for the natives, the island was also a target for various piratical raids, including visitations from the infamous Barbarossa. He, 'naughty, vengeful boy', generally looted, burned and sacked Kithira, selling off thousands of the inhabitants. Ownership became almost frenetic from 1715 onwards when the Turks took over from the Venetians, who took it back only three years later. Pirates had another 'away-day' in the 1750s, after which the French, in 1797, imprinted their authority here, and in a number of the Ionian islands. Only a year later a Russo-Turkish force took over to be followed by the French (again), in 1807. They were followed, in 1809, by the 'jackboot' of the British which descended, not only on Kithira, but most of the Ionian islands. The United Kingdom finally had to cede dominion in 1864.

GENERAL
Kithira is accessible from Piraeus as well as a number of the Peloponnese mainland ports that the ferries and Flying Dolphins call in on during the journey from Piraeus to Kithira.

Being at the end of a series of tempting and more sophisticated islands en route, Kithira remained remote and comparatively unfashionable even with 'Independent' travellers. In the meantime the building of the airport enabled the more adventurous package holiday companies to exploit Kithira's advantages. Thus the island's development, as a holiday resort, has been lopsided, not progressing smoothly through discovery by the *cognescent* and then a gradual exposure to an ever increasing number of holiday-makers. No, with little infrastructure of suitable accommodation, the tour operators have 'snaffled' most of that available, leaving a very thin layer for unheralded visitors.

Further difficulties are caused by the main port of Ag Pelagia being a rather small, straggling, dusty way-station of a development and 28km distant from the Chora (Kithira Town), and its associated, small port of Kapsali. Perhaps not unexpectedly Ag Pelagia has the lion's share of the available ***Rooms***. Accommodation and tavernas may be few and far between but, even more unusually, so are kafeneions of which there are very, very few. On the other hand, one or two of the tavernas adequately compensate for their lack of numbers.

Even more annoying and inconveniently unusual, is the lack of any bus service, so travel is in the hands of the taxi drivers! This hampers easy movement between centres. A retired Greek couple (met on Spetses one night when we were celebrating my birthday) assured us that buses used to run, but that was after the Second World War. They also told us that the islanders speak with phrases and intonations common with the other Ionian islands and that the reason for the chapel-like looking dwelling houses was that the owners wished to deceive maurauding Christian pirates – cunning. It may be that a bus is put on at the height of the season – I say might, but do not bank on it. There is also a 'rumour' of a Sunday service to tie in with the market day at Potamos.

The island's countryside is immensely attractive with any number of delightful farming villages dotted about the landscape. There are no dramatic mountain elevations but there is plentiful wildlife and flora. In respect of Natural History matters, the bird life is extensive, with a profusion of hawks and a bird with a yellow neck ring. Donkeys and derivations are in short supply, tractors having very largely supplanted them.

The Chora (Kithira Town) is almost Cycladean in layout, being overlooked by a ruined castle. One or two of the coastal and inland hamlets are truly very interesting. Incidentally, the inhabitants regard the tourist season to commence on the 20th June (and no sooner!) and to end in mid-September (and no later!).

If Kithira has a 'first', it must be almost one of the only islands that I have visited that does not possess a disco. Not an island to be missed off an *aficionados* schedule, under any circumstances.

AG PELAGIA: the main port Really rather shabby, 'doo-hickey', scrubbly and one-eyed, considering it is the main port of the island. The settlement spreads along the sea-shore to the right (*Sbo*) from the bottom of the Ferry-boat Quay.

The first, and perhaps second, impulse is to depart 'poste-haste' for the Chora. Reflection and more considered counsel might result in the decision to stay on at Ag Pelagia. The reason is that at least the port has some accommodation, which is in very short supply at the Chora. Naturally enough(!) the airfield is neither convenient to Ag Pelagia or the Chora, but there you go...

ARRIVAL BY AIR

The airfield is situated out in the wilds of the low hills to the east of the island. Taxis are the only form of public transport, that is apart from 'Shanks pony', but remember the nearest settlement of Aroniadika is about 5km distant. Fares are variable but travellers must expect to be asked 1500/1600drs to the Chora. It is best to cram four in a vehicle, thus considerably reducing the unit cost.

Back at Ag Pelagia:-

ARRIVAL BY FERRY & FLYING DOLPHIN

The Ferry-boat Quay is truly very large, strangely curved and unevenly surfaced with street lamps supported on tall poles. Incidentally, the other island port is Kapsali (the Chora's port), at the south end of the island. The sea's around Kithira island can become very rough, which state causes ferry-boats to dock at Kapsali rather than Ag Pelagia. The Flying Dolphins only dock at Ag Pelagia. Arrivals are not generally met with offers of accommodation. For schedules *See* **Ferry-boat & Flying Dolphin timetables, A To Z, The Chora**.

Note that the only transport out of Ag Pelagia is by taxi. The bus that parks on the main road is only for school children. The taxi fare to The Chora or Kapsali is 1500/1600drs, so its best to share.

Travellers must be very, very careful not to disembark at a mainland Peloponnese port in error for Kithira. There are many ports of call on the way down, some not always the same as those listed on the timetable, which means it is not good enough to count them off. I certainly have nearly disembarked at Monemvassia, in error for Ag Pelagia. So beware.

At the bottom of the Ferry-boat Quay, on the left (*Sbo*), is an abandoned toilet-block, the roadside of which is 'a little block of a building' in which there was once a pharmacy. Across the road is the:-

Hotel Kythereia(Class B) Tel 33321
Directions: As above.

Actually classified as a Pension, this square, two-story building, sporting a lifebuoy on the first floor balcony, has rooms with en suite bathrooms. A single room costs 1520 drs and a double room 1930 drs.

Let into the ground floor of the Hotel is the **Souvenir Centre**. The girl who looks after the shop speaks excellent English.

Next door to the Hotel, on the right (*Sbo*), is the:-

Taverna Pharos
Directions: As above.

Across the road are set out some tree shaded tables and chairs bordering the rather dirty backshore of the sandy beach .

The pleasant, thirty year old Greek owner is married to Donna, a Canadian lass. She is a mine of helpful information and they are a hard working couple, serving a good repast. A meal for two of 'fresh' tiropites (175 drs), an excellent Greek salad (180 drs), bread for two (30 drs) and two beers (75 drs each) costs 535 drs.

The **Ferry-boat Ticket Office** is let into the right-hand side (*Sbo*) of the *Taverna Pharos* and opens prior to a craft's arrival. Off the alley between the hotel and the taverna is a spotlessly clean toilet.

Continuing to the right (*Sbo*) from the bottom of the Ferry-boat Quay, the beach is sandy. The backshore, which is edged by heavily pollarded arethemusa trees, is rather scrubbly but it does support a lovely spread of plants, prominent amongst which are sun daisies.

The Esplanade road widens out to form, in effect, an informal square. The outwardly rather smart *Restaurant/Taverna Kavorce*, with a bamboo shaded patio across the road and edging the beach backshore, serves Continental and English breakfasts. This establishment is followed by a couple of small kafeneion-cum-tavernas. Beyond these a building bears the sign *We rent bicycles and motorcycles* but there is little evidence of continuing activity. A small store is grandly labelled *Super Market*, after which the Esplanade narrows down to accommodate a small caique building yard on the right. A sweep of fine shingle and pebble beach hosts some fishing boats drawn up on the shore, beyond which the foreshore becomes rocky. The road, now edged by various unfinished and dilapidated buildings, becomes unsurfaced before climbing past a stony little beach towards the horn of land at this side of the large bay and the, as yet, (possibly) unfinished *Hotel Apartments Marou*.

Beneath the hotel and towards the port is:-

Papa 'Dia's' Rooms
Directions: As above. The house, that is identifiable by its blue painted doors, is reached around the bottom of the bluff on which it sits.

The spinster who owns the accommodation nicknamed it thus because her father was a priest.

Back at the bottom of the Ferry-boat Quay, towards the left (*Sbo*) leads along the Potamos/Chora main road off which a left-hand fork tracks along the edge of a fairly narrow beach. From a distance this, appears to be white shingle. Actually the backshore is made up of gritty sand, the middle is pebbles and kelp and the foreshore fine pebbles with a pebbly sea bottom. Further on is a cove of reddish shingle beach with a spotting of villas being constructed on the slopes of the hills.

Rooms Fotis Gerakitis Tel 33462
Directions: About 200/250m along the track and pleasantly situated against the edge of the beach.

A three storey, white building with green shutters, probably built in the 1960/70s. The accommodation is run by a smiley lady who speaks English. A double room with en suite bathroom and use of a kitchen is a very reasonable 1500 drs. It must be said that this does seem an ideal, get-away-from-it-all spot.

The main Chora road climbs out of the port up the steep sided hills in a series of long, serpentine loops. On the third bend from the seafront Esplanade, close by where the school bus parks, is a most eye-catching building with some eleven round columns spaced along the front of the house, the:-

Rooms Kalogridi Tel 33371
Directions: As above and almost directly above *Rooms Gerakitis*. The house is most distinctive with red shutters, windows and balcony rails and appears well constructed.

The en suite double rooms are very nice indeed and cost 2000 drs a night. Neither of the owner brothers, Panayotis or Nikos speaks any English.

Those who spurn the blandishments of Ag Pelagia will, in all probability, make for the main town:-

THE CHORA (Kithira) capital (Illustration 25). A slow drive takes about ½hour. One of the most 'active' taxi drivers, a middle-aged, swarthy, small, neat, moustachioed gentleman has a link with an owner of apartments located in Kapsali Port. His taxi registration plate number is E2747 which I mention because he has a tendency to take 'prospects' straight there. Everyone is careful not to talk price until the punters are in place. It's a bit like a 'Time Share' hard sell but, at last, the figure is rolled out at 4000 drs. By this time the taxi has gone!

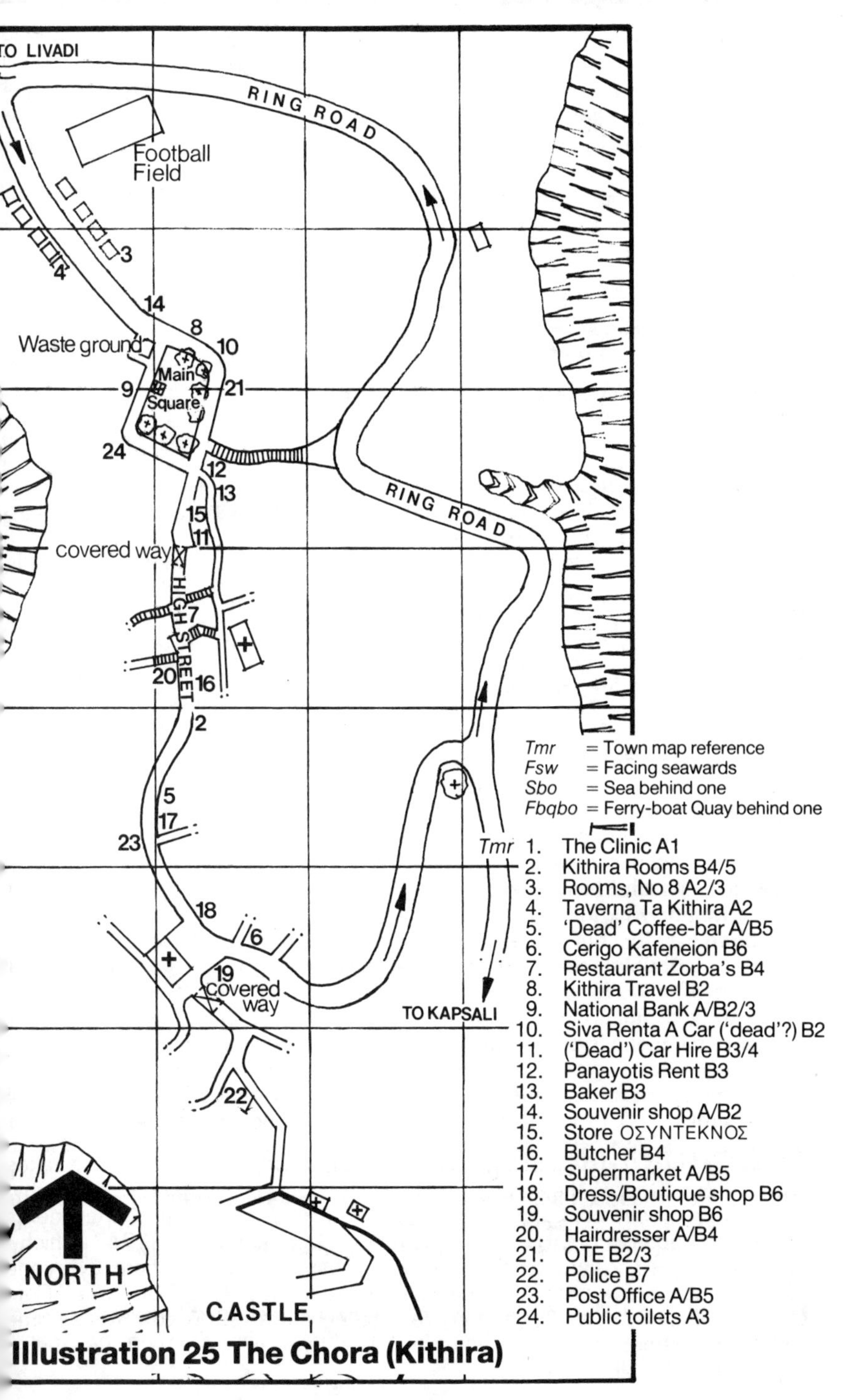

Illustration 25 The Chora (Kithira)

Not all is lost for there is some other accommodation in the Port (*See* **The Accommodation**) and the Chora (*See* **The Accommodation**).

The Chora is a most attractive development ranged either side of the hill climbing, winding High Street. It is very similar to an archetypal Cycladean town, even down to the detail of being overlooked by a ruined, Venetian Castle.

The authorities have sensibly made the High St a one-way system. The up-side traffic is routed via a 'ring road' that branches off at the outset of the southern side of the town and rejoins the High St, almost opposite the Clinic (*Tmr* 1A1).

Whilst wandering the streets an upward glance reveals the richness and variety of the well crafted chimneys and pots. I don't think I have seen such diversity, other than on the island of Siphnos (Cyclades).

THE ACCOMMODATION & EATING OUT

The Accommodation Attractive as the town may be there is very little accommodation, in fact only two outlets:

Kithira Rooms (*Tmr* 2B4/5) Tel 31026

Directions: From the Main Square follow the High St down the hillside through the covered way section. The rooms are on the left.

More a pension, it is run by a pretty young lady who speaks reasonable English and is most welcoming. But, as Eleni Kalligeroy's accommodation is 'the best in town', it fills up very quickly. Mind you, that is not to say it is luxurious or anything more than basically acceptable. However, when compared to the only other alternative it is 'Ritz like'. A double room en suite costs 2000drs, rising to 2200drs in the high season.

Rooms (*Tmr* 3A1/2) No. 8 Odhos ΚΑΘΗΓΗΤΟΥ ΕΜΜ ΚΟΝΤΟΛΕΟΝΤΟΣ.

Directions: On the left of the High St as it drops towards the Main Square (*coming from the direction of Livadi and Ag Pelagia*). The entrance is in a stepped alleyway. The proprietors are the owners of the *Taverna Ta Kithira* at No 5, almost directly across the street.

If the taverna is sleazy, the accommodation is probably the most ethnically appalling in which I have ever stayed. (Rosemary only entered the bathroom and her bed fully clothed!) Initially, enquirers who call at the taverna may well be 'shooed away' but travellers who are desperate for a room should be insistent. A double bed in this most decrepit lodging is charged at 1000drs per night. The beds are in danger of breaking up; the uneven floors are inexpertly patched, and are not even covered with the ubiquitous brown linoleum; the wiring is pre-Edison and these rooms are genuinely described by the all encompassing noun – 'a pit'. The sole bathroom, approached through an ethnic washroom, is an eye-watering, rather cavernous facility. The toilet lacks a seat, the bin for the toilet papers remains unemptied, the sink waste pipe requires a tin positioned to catch the water leaks, there is no hot water and the pipe that fills the lavatory cistern is adjusted so that it takes about an hour to fill the header tank. A number of the rooms equipped with beds are nothing more than boxes constructed within the shell of the building. A double room costs 1000drs mid-season, but the accommodation is only for those of a strong constitution.

The Eating Out The island evinces a distinct lack of kafeneions, if not a dearth, nowhere more so than here in the Chora, where there are not many eating places either.

Taverna Ta Kithira (*Tmr* 4A2) No 5 Odhos ΚΑΘΗΓΗΤΟΥ ΕΜΜ ΚΟΝΤΟΛΕΟΝΤΟΣ. *Directions*: *See* **The Accommodation**.

As one would expect of a family that owns the accommodation described previously, an insalubrious little establishment but they do serve a 'meal of the night' which I have not been able to bring myself to sample. Mark you, this may well be a bony lamb stew lurking in the recesses of a big pot or a pan of spaghetti and some old beans. Two Nes meh ghala costs 140drs.

Apart from a 'dead' coffee-bar (*Tmr* 5A/B5) and the *Cerigo Kafeneion/ breakfast bar* (*Tmr* 6B6), both of which may spring to life at the height of season, there is the:-

Restaurant ΖΟΡΜΠΑΣ (Zorba's) (*Tmr* 7B4) No. 34 'High St'
Directions: From the Main Square walkdown Odhos ΣΠΥΡΣΤΑΗ (the High St) in the direction of Kapsali Port, through the covered way. The restaurant is on the left.

Everything is relative, and no more so than when commenting on eateries. There are islands where the fact that some dishes were preprepared and others were rather small would result in their not receiving even a mention. But here, in the Chora, *Zorba's* is a culinary delight in an absolute desert (dessert did I hear?), added to which the quality is good. There is no doubt that this 'chatty' establishment is spotlessly clean and mine host, Georgio, a high school professor out of season, is an attentive and pleasant host. He speaks English, which is rather useful as the menu is written in indecipherable Greek. A meal of two souvlaki pita without any souvlaki (yes, I know without souvlaki – that is the meat, at 60drs the pair), 2 souvlaki pitas (160drs the pair) a poor Greek salad with plenty of feta (150drs), patatas, an Amstel beer and a bottle of retsina costs 555drs. A splendidly prepared chicken (246drs and we were asked 'leg or breast'), a plate of Kithira meatballs (super and rather like smoked pork sausages, 4 in number and served with tzatziki at 340drs), a tomato, cucumber and onion salad, an Amstel beer (78drs) and 2 bottles of retsina costs 849drs. Oddly enough the price of a bottle of retsina spiralled from 77 to 104drs during our last visit. A house speciality is the delicious *Zorba's* bread, an organic, wholemeal loaf soaked in olive oil and served with tomatoes. It is important to order as late as possible to be served freshly prepared salad, but early enough to beat the evening rush. The crucial time depends upon the time of year, but 2000hrs is a watershed.

THE A TO Z OF USEFUL INFORMATION

AIRLINE OFFICE & TERMINUS No terminus but tickets from:-
Kithira Travel (*Tmr* 8B2) No. 12 Tel 31390
Directions: The office edges the rather attractive, large, paved, palm tree circumscribed Main Square. They act for Olympic Airways as well as Ceres, the Flying Dolphin business, and the ferry-boat company Karageorgis Lines.

Aircraft timetable (Mid-season)

Kithira to Athens (& vice-versa)

Monday, Wednesday, Friday & Sunday 1020hrs
Tuesday, Thursday & Saturday 1325hrs

Return

Monday, Wednesday, Friday & Sunday 0910hrs

Tuesday, Thursday 1215hrs
& Saturday
One-way fare 4500drs; duration 50 mins.

BANKS One, the:-
National Bank of Greece (*Tmr* 9A/B2/3) An imposing building, also overlooking the Main Square.

BEACHES *See* **Kapsali Port**

BICYCLE, SCOOTER & CAR HIRE There are two apparently 'dead' businesses. One is **Siva Rent A Car** (*Tmr* 10B2), at No. 10 on the Main Square, and the other, a car hire firm (*Tmr* 11B3/4), is close to the covered way part of the High St. But not all is 'dead' for there is:-

Panayotis Rent (*Tmr* 12B3) Tel 31004
Directions: Conveniently situated on the Kapsali side of the Main Square.
Panayotis is an engaging young man who hires out scooters from the Chora, as well as canoes, pedaloes, surfboards and water skis down in Kapsali Port. Engaging yes, but no pushover. His steeds are not particularly inexpensive with a Puch moped costing 800drs and a scooter 1700 drs. Despite an impression gained that these are inclusive rates, petrol is an additional cost.

BREAD SHOPS Only one, a Baker (*Tmr* 13B3) in the small alleyway that angles off to the left from between Panayotis Rent (*Tmr* 12B3) and the Kapsali High St exit from the Main Square.

COMMERCIAL SHOPPING AREA No central market building but the length of the High St houses any number of shops that make up for this omission. Starting at the top, Livadi end of the High St, close by the Main Square, on the left opposite some waste ground, is a Souvenir shop (*Tmr* 14A/B2 – at No. 2) that sells island maps. On the left of the High St, below the Main Square, is a Tailor followed by, at No. 58, ΠΑΝΤΟΠΩΛΕΙΟΝ ΟΣΥΝΤΕΚΝΟΣ. This latter is a very good shop which sells *Frigid Products* (*sic*). 'Mr Frigid Products' speaks Australian and runs a very clean shop with an excellently stocked delicatessen counter.

Beyond the covered way and *Zorba's* is a Hairdresser (KOYPEION), on the right of the High St, opposite which is a Butcher (ΚΡΕΟΠΩΛΕΙΟΝ (*Tmr* 16B4). Further on down the High St, at No. 14, is an inexpensive, traditional, narrow fronted store run by an elderly man and distinguishable by the old, enamel advertising sign for a sewing machine company that is screwed to the wall. In total contrast, some metres further on is a 'Super Market' (*Tmr* 17A/B5), which is actually a very large, high ceilinged Aladdins' cave full of shelves piled high with all sorts of goods. Supplies here though are more expensive than at the old man's shop, back up the High St. For example there is a 100drs difference in the price of a pot of honey (350/450drs). Still descending the High St, close by a small, 'Church Square' is a Dress/boutique shop (*Tmr* 18B6) on the left, and at No. 1, a 'superior' Souvenir shop (*Tmr* 19B6) with good quality products.

Siesta is strictly observed between 1400-1700hrs but most shops open on Sunday's, some even in the evening.

FERRY-BOATS & FLYING DOLPHINS
See **Airline Office, A To Z and Arrival by Ferry & Flying Dolphin, Ag Pelagia**

Ferry-boat timetable (Mid-season)

Day	**Departure time**	**Ferry-boat**	**Ports/Islands of Call**
Monday	2000hrs	Ionian	Ag Pelagia (Kithira), Githion (Gythion)(M).
Tuesday	0300hrs	Ionian	Kapsali (Kithira), Antikithira, Kastelli (Crete).
Tuesday	1630hrs	Ionian	Ag Pelagia (Kithira), Monemvassia(M), Piraeus(M).
Thursday	1800hrs	Ionian	Ag Pelagia (Kithira), Githion(M).
Friday	0200hrs	Ionian	Kapsali (Kithira),Antikithira, Kastelli (Crete).
Friday	1800hrs	Ionian	Ag Pelagia (Kithira), Neapoli(M), Monemvassia(M), Piraeus(M).

Flying Dolphin timetable (Mid-season)

Day	**Departure time**	**Ports/Islands of Call**
Tuesday	1445hrs	Neapoli(M), Monemvassia(M), Gerakas(M), Kiparissi(M), Leonidio (M), Spetses, Portoheli(M), Zea Port(Piraeus).
Saturday	1445hrs	Neapoli(M), Monemvassia(M), Kiparissi(M), Leonidio(M),Portoheli(M),Zea Port(Piraeus).

FERRY-BOAT & FLYING DOLPHIN TICKET OFFICES *See* **Airline Office**

HAIRDRESSERS (*Tmr* 20A/B4) On the High St.

LAUNDRY *See* Potamos village.

MEDICAL CARE
Chemist & Pharmacy *See* Potamos village.
Clinic (*Tmr* 1A1) There is a facility at the top end of the High St.

OTE (*Tmr* 21B2/3) No 6 Main Square. Open weekdays 0730-1510hrs.

PETROL Despite the presence of an upper High St garage, the pumps are no longer in use, it being necessary for those requiring petrol to go to the village of Livadi. The garage office is now a drink and trinket shop, but never appears to open.

PLACES OF INTEREST
Castle (*Tmr* B8) Access to the building is along the path that branches off the High St at the small Church. This direction passes the Police station (*Tmr* 22B7). Imposing from a distance this Venetian Castle is rather uninteresting once inside the walls. There are masses of summer flowers and a cluster of English manufactured cannons scattered about.
Museum A few metres up the Livadi road from the Chora and on the right. Displays some of the archaeological finds of the island. Opens weekdays between 0845-1500hrs, but is closed on Tuesdays. On Sundays and holidays the doors are open between 0930-1430 hrs.

POLICE
Town (*Tmr* 22B7) On the right of the lane that leads to the Castle.

POST OFFICE (*Tmr* 23A/B5) Situated at the Kapsali end of the High St. There is a post box and stamp machine bolted to the wall of the Electricity Company (ATE) building on the Main Square.

TAXIS There is a taxi rank (*Tmr* T) on the Main Square but there is very rarely one there, especially when needed. There is a taxi driver who lives at No. 22 Main Sq, next door to the souvenir shop (*Tmr* 14A/B2). He comes recommended by Panayotis of Scooter hire 'fame' and quotes 1400drs to Ag Palagia. Whoopee a saving of 200drs over other charges. No, he jacks the price up to 1500drs on arrival at the destination. *See* **Introduction, The Chora**.

TOILETS There are some 'underground' toilets (*Tmr* 24A3) conveniently sited down steps from the Main Sq. They are 'squatties' and measure 7 on the 'Richter scale'.

TRAVEL AGENTS & TOUR OFFICES *See* **Airline Offices, A To Z.**

WATER The Main Sq sports a working tap close by steps from the road to the paved area, almost opposite the National Bank (*Tmr* 9A/B2/3).

ROUTE ONE

To Kapsali (2km) This is a very steeply descending road that serpentines down the hillside past a most extraordinary and 'kitsch' dwelling, Harbour View No. 999. It is not difficult to deduce that it has been built by a successful sea captain as the concrete and brick building is constructed in the shape and outline of a white ship with red appurtenances – Oh dear! There's even a sign on the surrounding wall *Keep Clear of Propeller*. Other notices include *Departure 9pm to Cyprus-Haifa; Blue Sea Line Ltd; Ship Details... Speed 22 knots... Gross Ton 2200... Radio Signal... Built in Japan.* Yes well! As this house is close to top of the tall hill (or low mountainside, depending on your point of view) on which The Chora is built, does the owner know something we don't? I did look round for pairs of animals... The ship is close to the junction with the 'Ring road', which climbs to the left (*The Chora behind one*) back round to the top (Livadi) end of the High St. Incidentally on the side of this road, overlooking a deep, picturesque gorge, is an unusual, old-fashioned, railway carriage style, wooden Romany caravan. The European occupant advises that it was once a circus ring-master's wagon.

KAPSALI (2km from The Chora): second port (Illustration 26) Visitors might well consider Kapsali to be the best of the three alternatives at which to base themselves. The location is attractive, the beaches good and there is possibly more accommodation and eating place options than The Chora. I write, possibly because 'out-of-the-Kithira-season' this may well not be so.

The large Gulf of Kapsali is split into two by a rather large headland made up of two rocky outcrops, the far right-hand (*Sbo*), eastern one is topped by a chapel. The settlement lies across the neck linking the larger nearside bay and the further, almost circular, fishing boat cove.

The Esplanade of the nearside bay is neat, sparsely planted with small trees, edged by spaced out, tidy buildings circumscribed by hills and dramatically overlooked by the Castle topped Chora peak to the west of the sea's sweep. The beach is narrow and stony but widens out in a sweep of stony backshore and sandy foreshore as it curves round in the neck of the headland promontory. The rest of this central side of the headland is an extensive concrete quayside that includes the Ferry-boat Quay (*Tmr* 1B1). Prior to the outset of the long quay, in a crook of the hillside headland, is (or certainly was in 1987) the remains of the public lavatory block (*Tmr* 2B/C2/3). In common with other Aegean island

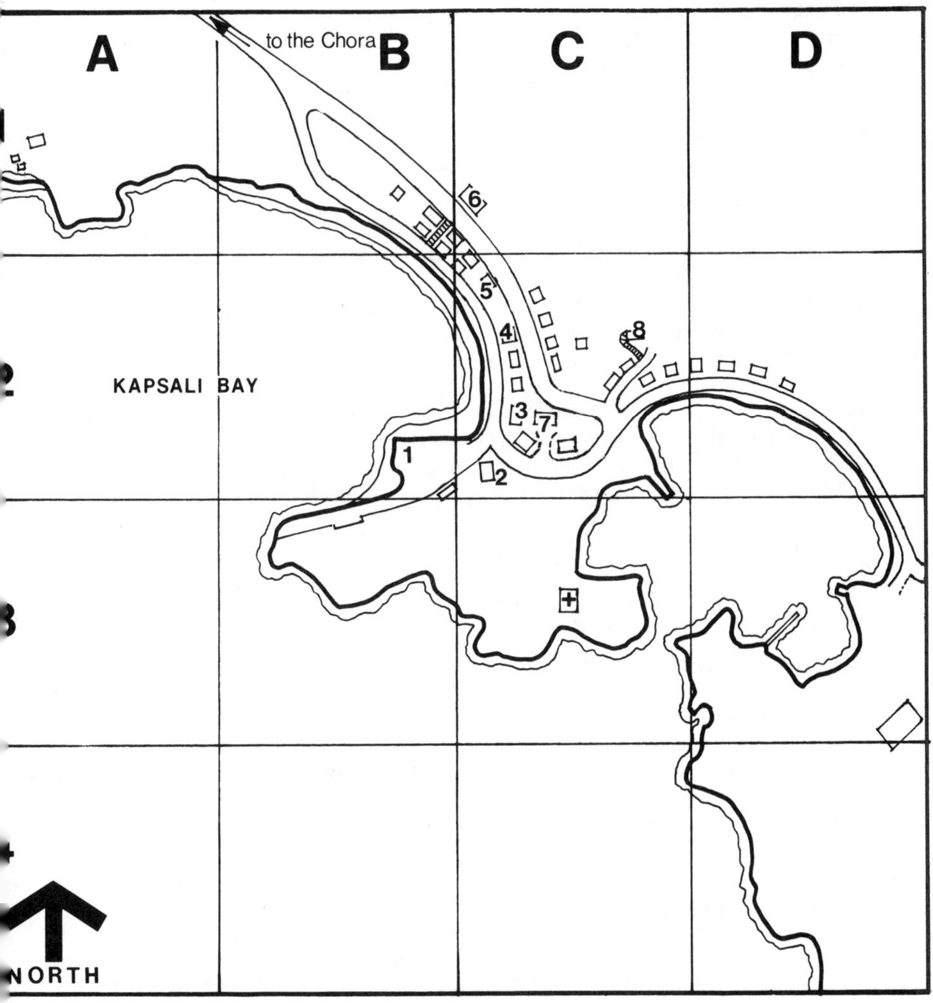

Illustration 26 Kapsali Port

Tmr

1. Ferry-boat Quay B1
2. ('Dead') Toilet block B/C2/3
3. Taverna/Pension C2
4. Port police C2
5. Panayotis Rent B/C1/2
6. Rooms B/C1
7. Mike's Bikes C2
8. Furnished Apartments C2

Tmr = Town map reference
Fsw = Facing seawards
Sbo = Sea behind one
Fbqbo = Ferry-boat Quay behind one

'squatties' that have become 'topped up', this has been dynamited. The island ports possess an increasing number of these defunct toilets.

At this end of the bay, prior to the aforementioned toilet block, and across the Esplanade from the beach is a *Taverna Pension* (*Tmr* 3C2) with accommodation and a small store. The food is wholesome, even if the menu is restricted to a 'take it or leave it' diet of chicken or fish. A meal for two of 2 substantial patata omelettes, a 'greens' salad (yes, greens), a plate of feta and 2 bottles of beer cost 710drs. A double room en suite costs 1500drs.

Going the left (*Sbo*) along the large bay bordering Esplanade is a wall mounted post box, the Port police (*Tmr* 4C2) and, alongside the *Taverna Kapsali*, the neatly whitewashed, breeze block enclosed yard in which are enclosed the marine activities of Panayotis Rent (*Tmr* 5B/C1/2). A pedal boat for 4 costs 350drs for one hour, and the day hire (0800-1900hrs) of a fishing boat, complete with a 10hp Johnson outboard motor, is charged at 6000drs. For more details of this operation *See* **Bicycle, Scooter & Car Hire, A To Z, The Chora**. About half-way round this waterfront road are steps that climb to the main road and up which can be sighted ***Rooms*** (*Tmr* 6B/C1 – tel 31247). The Esplanade follows the curving backshore wall all the way round to a very steep, paved track up to the main road.

The main road enters Kapsali Port at the back of the settlement, about opposite the neck of the headland. On the right (*Fsw*) is Mike's Bikes (*Tmr* 7C2). To the left, the seafront road curves round the almost circular backshore of the fishing boat anchorage, set in a cove that is almost, but not entirely, landlocked by the horns of the land. The sea-shore is narrow and comprised of scrubbly pebble. To the left, one street behind the waterfront, are the:-

Furnished Apartments of A & M PHFA (*Tmr* 8C2).
The office and rooms are up steep steps to the left of the road, but even in early season they want 4000drs for a double room. Whow! (*See* **Introduction, The Chora**).

At the far side of the cove are a group of grey stone, barrel roofed buildings which are worth exploring. They enclose a now overgrown courtyard and, by the look of the few cells still extant, may have housed a religious order at some time or other. Entrance is through a pair of large, dressed stone gateposts.

There is a sign to a *Campsite* from the main road between Kapsali Port and The Chora. This points up a track into the pine tree covered foothills. This prettily situated campsite only opens at the height of season. By proceeding left, on past the campsite, the very rough, wide path advances to a deserted, white painted Monastery that can be clearly seen from the Port and dramatically clings to the perpendicular cliff-face. To the far side of the buildings, close to the top of the cliffs, are a couple of white Lorraine crosses. This Monastery is startlingly similar to Hozoviotizza Monastery on Amorgos Island in the Cyclades.

The road from Kapsali Port to The Chora crosses a small bridge that spans a ravine, flanked by paths that track down to the sea, with the coastline obscured by a rocky outcrop. At the bottom of the summer-dry river gorge, just round the corner from the large Kapsali Bay, is a small, shingle beach popular with nudists. Incidentally, the paths referred to above do not lead down to the beach. The hillsides between the road and the sea are built on with grey stone walls and square, cell-like buildings which almost meld into their surroundings of stone and heather clad outcrops. It is possible to get to the beach by taking the first path before the ravine, from the direction of Kapsali, walking up the hillside towards a house – despite the 'Private' sign, and then tramping down the steep hillside path.

ROUTE TWO
To Platia Ammos via Livadi, Potamos & Karavas (about 37km) with excursions to Limnaria, Milopotamos, Avlemonas & Diakofti

The road climbs out of The Chora through gently undulating countryside to:

LIVADI (6km from The Chora) This village is simply strung along the broad main road. Apart from a shop or two there is a 'Super Market' that opens on Sunday. So does the Shell petrol station, on the left of the High St, which sells two-stroke fuel.

There are ***Rooms*** on the left (*The Chora behind one*) and on the right, at the Mirtidia/Ag Pelagia end of the village, the friendly Kafeneion/Taverna ΤΟ ΠΙΕΤΚΑΚΙ ΙΩΑΝΛΟΥΡΑΝΤΟΥ. The outside is unprepossessing, as is the large interior which is laid out similarly to a European restaurant. The place is (understandably) very popular with the locals who eat here in numbers. The menu is varied with locally caught fish and lobster available. This is not to say that diners cannot eat reasonably with, for instance, a meal of briam for two (150drs each), a green salad (70drs), two beers (75drs each), bread (30drs) costing 550drs.

The road to the next village is 'enlivened' by an imposing, square, cut stone, neo-Georgian building to the left, set in fields on a hilltop. This is reputed to have been an English School in the days of Colonial rule. Reference to this remnant of the British Empire reminds me to draw readers' attention to 'The Bridge' so proudly signposted. This spans a wide river-bed but would not rate much attention other than on a Greek island, which are generally pretty short of any, let alone outstanding, architectural works of the 18th/19th century.

At the hamlet of **Fatsadika** is a petrol station but they close on Sundays and do not sell two-stroke fuel. The countryside hereabouts is pleasant and rolling, supporting small, stunted groves of olive trees set in a spread of gorse, amongst which goats and sheep graze, as does the occasional 'sacred' cow with the impressively worked, rope noseband. Fatsadika nearly straggles all the way to **Kondolianika**.

From either of the villages of Livadi or Kondolianika it is possible to advance westward through **Kalokerines**. Beyond this hamlet the heights of the winding road provide dramatic views of the coastline, off which are a speckling of offshore islets, prior to descending to:-

Panaghia Mirtidiotissa (Approx 18km from The Chora) A prominent, not very 'old-world-attractive', 17th century nunnery. The large car and coach park gives an indication of the size of the congregation that gathers on the 24th September. Flanking the track that proceeds towards Ormos Limnaria are a row of cells that closely resemble stables.

Despite one of the popular tourist maps detailing a hamlet at **Limnaria**, there is only a tiny quay in amongst a tumble of rocks. The almost circular, tiny natural harbour can contain half a dozen small boats and is edged by a number of small stone sheds. High up a hillside overlooking the rocky bay is what appears to be a statue but which, on closer examination, turns out to be a tailor's dummy, capped with a crash hat. *C'est la vie*.

KARVOUNADES (12km from The Chora) A rather ramshackle village but possessing a magnificent, blue domed church complete with a colour matched pair of campaniles.

All round, in the low hillsides, are small hamlets and villages nestling in the folds of the rolling ground. Two kilometres beyond Karvounades, a turning off to the right makes towards the village of **Fratsia**, after which the road is surfaced all the way to Ag Vassilios Church, despite one of the tourist maps indications to the contrary. The countryside is exceptionally pretty and verdant, especially on the last stretch to the wildly lovely Ormos Asprogas. The usually deserted bay is edged by a vast expanse of coarse sand and pebbly beach. The first metre or so of the sea-bed is also pebbly.

AVLEMONAS (32km from The Chora) An almost obsessively neat, whitewashed fishing village built around the rocky, volcanic inlets that indent the coastline. At the centre of the settlement is a chapel, unusually mounted on an outcrop of rock, and alongside which is a prominent water well. The occasional palm trees flourish. Unfortunately, the one restaurant only opens at the height of the season.

The main, north-south road, now coursing along the gorse and thyme scattered, rock strewn spine of the island, leads to **Dokana** (16km from The Chora. Now only a hamlet straddling a road junction, from the footings and foundations in the vicinity, it appears that the settlement was once a much larger development.

At Dokana the turning to the left advances to:-

MILOPOTAMOS (18km from The Chora) This is a lovely, old, country village set in very lush countryside. A summer running stream flows through an engineered, profusely shaded river-bed. There are similarities to Spili on Crete, even if there is only one lion's mouth here, and it doesn't spout water. Ducks float on the pools close by the Church and its impressive campanile. The village square, close by the river, is shaded, on one side, by three large plane trees and bounded on another flank, by a low chapel with a prominent, double bell arch.

Across the road is the *Taverna O Platanos* owned by a nice, round, nut brown faced, English speaking (well, Tasmanian really) Greek. A couple of Nes meh ghala cost 140drs.

Close to Milopotamos are the ruins of a medieval town, a 13th century castle, a 17th century church and a limestone cave complete with a chapel. Naturally both church and chapel have icons.

The main road surface is generally fair but absolutely appalling in places with crater-like depressions scattered evenly along the way. Considering the windswept nature of the island there are a lot of mature cypress and maritime pines. In fact, in places, the pines grow in spinneys and copses. The surface of the rolling hills is scattered with bee hives, from whence obviously the island honey. There is also a lot of stone walling and, here and there, threshing floors peek through the undergrowth.

Back at the main road junction, the next village to the north is:-

ARONIADIKA (19km from The Chora) An unexceptional, sprawling place with a lot of new buildings mixed in with the old. Aroniadika is where the road to the airport branches off in an easterly direction.

Drivers heading off towards Diakofti must be very, very careful as at the end of a temptingly straight stretch, the road is diverted from the path of the airport runway by the simple, rustic solution of throwing up earthworks. Enough to say these are not easy to see until almost on top of them.

The scenery is lovely, rolling mountain slopes across which the rough track scrabbles. Soon after a fork, at which the right-hand turning makes off to **Avlemonas**, the left-hand turning snakes round a bluff, high up on the slopes to look distantly down over:-

DIAKOFTI (some 33km from The Chora) The sparse hamlet is set on the edge of the sea, backed by a rather barren, wide plain which is flanked by the foothills of the Digenis Mountain. Offshore is the elongated islet of Makronissi that almost connects to the shoreline. On the way down to the settlement are a comparatively large number of long, 'semi-detached', barrel roofed buildings grouped together in 'batches' of three or four.

At the outset of the once-upon-a-time fishing hamlet, which is a look-alike for a sun drenched Yukon frontier settlement (if such a simile is possible), is a sign *No Camping*. Perhaps the sandy beach has, in the past, attracted the great unwashed? I write 'once fishing hamlet' as an expansion of the original settlement is evidenced by the scattered erection of a number of skeletal concrete frameworks. Where these buildings are unfinished they serve as covered areas for the goats and sheep which are to be found grazing throughout the village, in amongst the rubbish strewn, cropped grass precincts, bounded by lava-like concrete oversites.

The road runs out opposite a prominent quay which dominates the water-front. Some of the buildings and their waste area backyards spill on to the backshore. To the left (*Fsw*) the sea-shore is rocky and covered with sea driven rubbish. Beyond an ethnic taverna, identifiable by the stacked Amstel crates, is a 'smarty' *Seafood Restaurant*. To the right of the quay is a lovely, sandy beach cove and clear sea unfortunately set in fairly squalid surrounds and spotted with tar. Further to the right are outcrops of lava rock dotted about in the sea and on the foreshore, all the way to the spit that almost connects the mainland to Makronissi islet. Around the corner from this spit, and beyond a small concrete quay, the rocky outcrops disappear but the kelpy and rubbish strewn shore is 'cliffed' by the action of the sea.

Returning to the main north-south road, beyond Aroniadika, the next major village is:-

POTAMOS (22km from The Chora) On the approach from the south, for once the signposting is uncharacteristically missing. The Ag Pelagia turning is not signposted and travellers heading there, but passing a BP petrol station have missed the correct route. This, incidentally, is straight on, crosses over an Imperialistic bridge and swings past a large, two storey building, possibly a sanatorium. For Potamos it is necessary to fork left.

Really more of a town than The Chora with a chemist, in addition to any number of stores and shops. The bank, which cashes Eurocheques, is on the left, traversing the length of the High St from the south after which, on the same side, is a small, triangular Main Square - if that is not too much of a contradiction of terms! Beyond the Square, on the right of the High St, is a Post Office and Money Exchange side by side with a butchers as well as an Olympic office. The lady in charge of the latter is most helpful. It was she who attempted to explain the 'difficulty' of the island's buses. Yes, well! Across the road from the Olympic office is an agent for the **FB Ionian**, with an indecipherable timetable in the window, and next door to which is the baker.

Incidentally another sign in the ferry-boat ticket office advises that the Ag Pelagia office opens whenever the ferry-boat is due to dock. There are several (kava) wine shops with some of the local 'juice' available, in bulk. But whatever else Potamos is famous for in the past, the modern day wonder is that there is a Sunday morning market, as a result of which all the shops and the bank are open. On this day the streets are awash with people and locals displaying their agricultural produce on every available space. This type of Sunday market is, as far as I am aware, absolutely unique in Greece.

Proceeding northwards, very soon after leaving Potamos, the road surface 'goes' unmetalled. Mind you, this is, in the main, better than some sections of the metalled road! The unspoilt countryside becomes Greek moorland in character, with the sides of the hills liberally covered in gorse and bushes where grass is not growing. From a Karavas/Ag Pelagia road junction, the views are pleasant. These include a sight through the hills down towards the northern tip of the island as well as to a promontory mounted, tree surrounded, red roofed chapel overlooking the sea, way down to the right. After the junction this 'interesting little proposition' of a road becomes metalled again.

The entrance to the village of **Karavas** (34km from The Chora) is marked by a rather unusual gateway, but there is no evidence of an accompanying encircling wall.

The road reverts to the familiarly, that is a wide swathe of deeply rivuletted, pot-holed rock and loose scree. Prior to Platia Ammos a narrow track makes off to the totally deserted **Ormos Fournoi**, which has a shingle cove backed by scrub.

The route then advances to:-

PLATIA AMMOS (36km from The Chora) This is a pleasant fishing port/ hamlet with a sweeping bay bordered by a broad beach made up of small shingle. The backshore is, oddly enough, almost wholly sand in composition.

There are two ethnic tavernas, one overlooking the quay. This latter is a 'doo-hickey' but friendly establishment with a generator clattering away in the background. Two good, large coffees and a quality brandy, served with a mezes of nuts, cost a very reasonable 200drs.

The short-cut route from Karavas to Ag Pelagia very soon becomes an unmade, red coloured track. The countryside is thickly covered with shrubs and passes down a ravine all the way to the coastal plain. There is visual evidence of much vineyard terracing, now in disuse and growing olive trees.

The inviting little track that makes off to the left of this route runs out at a small cove. It is unfortunate that this is covered with a lot of sea driven and windblown rubbish, including dollops of tar, old shoes, plastic bottles, under which is a smidgin of sand, but is mainly very large pebbles mixed with small stones.

18 SALAMINAS (Salamina, Salalaminos, Salamis)

(yes, minuses!) - - - -

Argo-Saronic

FIRST IMPRESSIONS
Ramshackle, shanty town development; filthy beaches & dirty seas; moth-eaten, messy countryside; swarms of cars and people.

SPECIALITIES
A Salaminas bread.

RELIGIOUS HOLIDAYS & FESTIVALS
include: 4th September – Festival at Faneromeni (Phaneromeni) Monastery.

VITAL STATISTICS
Tel prefix 01 – as for Athens. Up to 15km from side to side and 15km from top to bottom, with an area of some 93sqkm. The population numbers some 22,00 with about 17,500 living in the main town of Salamina. The Police telephone number is 4653100 and Paloukia Taxis 4650293.

HISTORY
Somehow it comes as a surprise, bearing in mind the general unattractiveness of the island, to realise how pivotal Salaminas was in historical times. It was here that the Greeks sprung the trap that allowed their Triremes to smash the overwhelming, all-conquering Persian Navy of Xerxes in 480 BC. It is adjudged that this victory saved the Western European nations from the all-embracing, and until then, unstoppable advance of the Persians. It is written that the Persian King sat on his silver or gold throne, depending on whom you believe, high on Mt Aegalus to watch the battle. Little did he expect to observe his fleet being destroyed.

Over the next two or three hundred years the island slid into the cloak of obscurity, which it was to wear with consummate ease up to modern times.

GENERAL
Every so often a particular island intrigues and beckons. None more so than Salaminas, that is to the uninformed. For instance, why is the island not officially grouped with the other islands of the Argo-Saronic? Why does it appear on the maps in a curious isolation? Most peculiar of all, why is Salaminas not included in the comprehensive system of ferry-boats and incredibly efficient Flying Dolphins that comb this group of islands? The answer is simply that Salaminas is a suburb, for all intents and purposes, of Athens and Piraeus. Over the years the worthy citizens of the 'mega-metropolis', desperate to escape the smog, human, car and garbage polluted capital, have escaped to the 'attractions' of Salaminas for not only *Le Weekend* but, as it is so conveniently close, even a night out. In so doing the good burghers of Athens have created a home from home! That is a human, car and garbage polluted holiday environment. Even to the supposed 'Litter Kings of Europe', the English, the sight of the massed ranks of mainlanders disporting themselves on and in the thoroughly polluted surrounds of the filthy, narrow, pebbly foreshores and the very dirty seas, must come as a surprise. Incidentally, tourist office inspired literature referring to golden beaches must have been written by shortsighted liars!

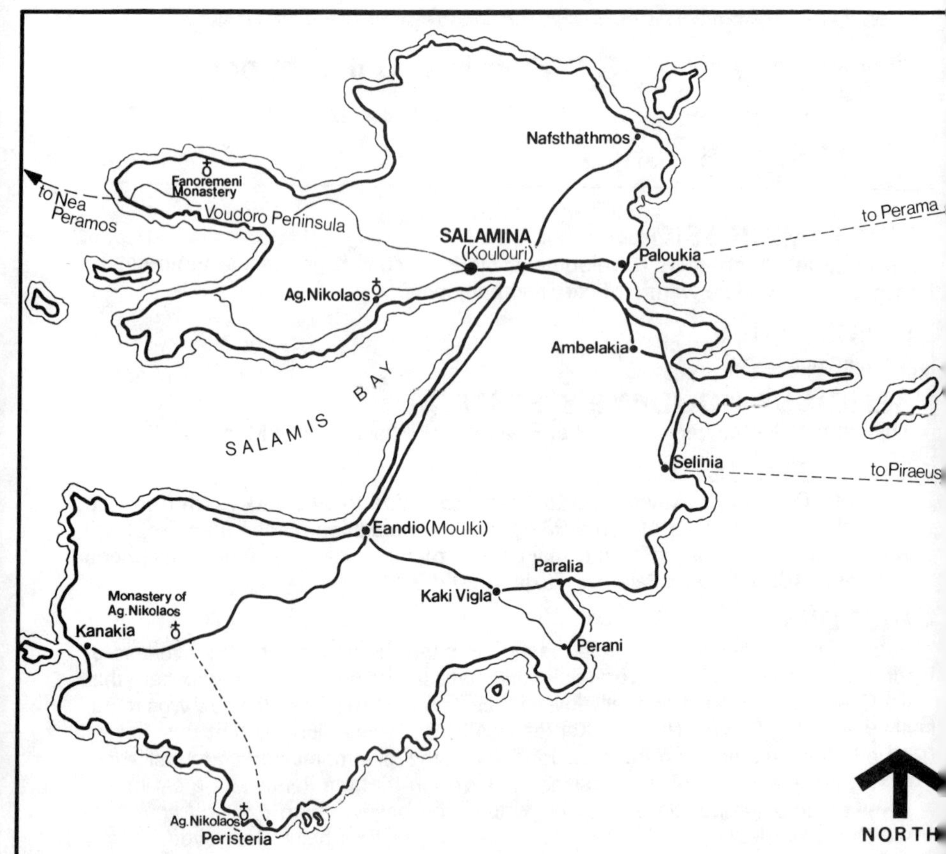

Illustration 27 Salaminas island

To add to the drawback of the massive weekend invasion and a chronic lack of suitable bathing, there are only one or three hotels. There are none at the main port of entry, Paloukia, two at the subsidiary passenger ferry port of Selinia, and supposedly two in Salamina Town, where no ferries dock, and which must be avoided like the plague! For the purist who must add the island to the 'bag', head for Eandio for reasons that will be made plain later.

Incidentally, apart from the south-west, the one area of Salaminas not served by the island's excellent bus service, the north-east houses the Navy and or is being thoroughly mauled by ore extraction machinery. Most of the rest of the island is covered in a higgledy-piggledy of urban sprawl, at its worst. No wonder the ferry-boat planners left it off their itineraries!

SELINIA (7km from Salamina): passenger ferry-boat port. A neat place, especially when considering the rest of the island.

There are two hotels listed, the:-

Akoyali (Class D) 92 Akti Themistocleous Tel 465 3341

and the:-

Votsalakia (Class D) 64 Akti Themistocleous Tel 465 3494
Here a single room costs 800drs and a double 1100drs, sharing the bathroom, whilst a single room en suite is charged at 1010drs and a double room en suite 1400drs.

ARRIVAL BY FERRY

The passenger ferries **FB Aggelikh** and **Aypa** are simply large, decrepit river boats. They depart from the Piraeus waterfront to the left (*Fsw*) of the Aegina ferry-boat docking point, in the angle of the quay. This is the other side of the Esplanade from the monstrous, high-rise **Macedonia and Thrace Bank (Piraeus**, *Tmr* 9C2) and a 'dead' information office. There is no formal ticket office, the fares being paid on board. The fare costs 75drs, the voyage duration is ½hr and one of the last boats departs from Piraeus at 1430hrs. The sea route leaves the rocky islet of Psytaleia and a stranded liner wreck to the right-hand.

The craft dock at a small quay beyond which is the Main Square and from whence there is an excellent bus service to the island's main town of Salamina. Buses appear to run every ½hr, including Sundays, at a standard fare of 55/65drs. Taxis are plentiful and charge 350drs for the same trip. The route edges the coastline and the town of Ambelakia, both of which are despoiled, being engulfed by shipbreaking yards.

SALAMINA: capital town A rather squalid town and not a place in which to be stranded. Despite being at the end of the large Bay of Salamis, there are no ferry-boats and thus no reception facilities.

The main, east-west, dual carriageway borders a very wide quay edging the Gulf. A substantial fishing fleet operates from close by the major 'Five-Ways' road junction at the east end of Salamina Town and there is a large, single storey Fish Market.

Almost opposite the Fish Market, close to the main 'Five-Ways' junction at the bottom of the Bay, is the not very noticeable OTE with a couple of phones outside.

The High St angles off the Esplanade to the right in a west-north-west direction and is signposted as being the direction of the Fanoremeni Monastery – which it is. The High St climbs upwards past an amazing cross-section of smart (and not-so-smart shops) and stores. On the left, about 200m from the junction with the waterfront, is the National Bank of Greece. As if to stress the lack of foreign tourists, changing money here is back to the old days of being sent from one desk to another, each asking for passports, place of accommodation, a 'hair count', 'toenail clippings' and etc... A few metres further up the street, on the right, is the Commercial Bank of Greece, just beyond which is a (firmly closed) Tourist Office.

Tucked away in the area enclosed by the Esplanade and the affluent, modern High St are a number of old buildings and dwellings, some garishly painted and still a fascinating glimpse of yester-year. Apart from the more conventional shops there is an early morning market that blossoms on the Esplanade quayside, close to the Fish Market.

Apart from the bus stops sprinkled the length of the High St and along the Esplanade, perhaps the best one to use is that at the 'Five-Ways' junction. Here one turning, alongside a 'metal bashing' works, makes off along the east, bottom end of the Bay of Salamis to Eandio and others to **Paloukia** and **Ambelakia/Selinia**. Despite the bus service being excellent, for some extra-ordinary reason, there is no connection with **Kanakia** on the west coast. As a guide, Bus No. 8 goes in the direction of Faneromeni Monastery, No. 11 to Eandio and No. 12 to the (Salamina) Ag Nikolaos. Buses run about every ½hr and commence operation very early in the morning. They are the most inexpensive way to see the island, as there are no scooter or car hire firms. The drivers are friendly and very soon recognise 'regular foreigners' – regular in a bus-catching mode you understand....! And do keep the ticket stubs as inspectors occasionally board a bus.

EXCURSIONS TO SALAMINAS TOWN SURROUNDS

Excursion to the north-west Almost at the far, west end of the Esplanade highway, it narrows down, after a mile or two, on the approach to Ag Nikolaos (the Salamina Town Ag Nikolaos to distinguish it from the island's three other Ag Nikolaos!). Hereabouts is the *Hotel Akroyali*, a smart E Class establishment (Tel 465 1136) at the 'lido' end of town, beyond which the surroundings degenerate. The ramshackle waters edge is a mishmash of rickety, wooden piers, fishing boats and a boatyard. From here the track climbs into 'scabby' countryside, prior to breasting a saddle in the hillside and descending to yet another moth-eaten, unattractive, large bay facing the mainland coastline.

Excursion to Voudoro peninsula via Ag Georgios Proceeding up the High St of Salamina Town, in the direction of Faneromeni Monastery, gives access to the north-west ferry-boat port on Voudoro peninsula. The countryside is rather more agricultural and not so despoiled by urban blight, although the islanders have not entirely missed the opportunity to deface even this corner of the island. Naturally enough there is another Ag Nikolaos Church. The bus turns round, close by a pretty, small cove with a shingly, fine grit beach which would be pleasant if it were not for the amounts of kelp and the weedy sea-bed. There are three or four dead tavernas and the air of desolation is increased by the number of 'Ro-Ro', landing craft style ferries laid up in the sound.

Excursion to Paloukia Port

PALOUKIA (3km from Salamina Town): ferry-boat port This truly is an amazing 'way-station' of a place with a Naval Base blocking off the northern end of the port, and the island. The main road widens out to 'M1' proportions alongside the quay. This is to cater for the enormous number of cars that zip on and off the island. On the waterfront side is the busy Bus 'pavement terminus' and the Taxi rank. The quay is edged by dozens of Ro-Ro ferries and large passenger boats. At times, especially Friday and Sunday nights, there is an air of absolute bedlam and the traffic volume is unbelievable. There are no hotels but opposite the kerbside Bus office is a friendly taverna where two beers and a frappe coffee cost 190drs, octopus mezes are served and helpful advice is free.

About 200m along the road towards Salamina Town, is a Post Office, which does not change money but exhorts enquirers to go to Salamina Town. Further on is a turning down to a Clinic, across the road from which is a Calpac/BP petrol station.

The ferry-boat journey to the appalling, unlovely, ship-building and repair port of Perama takes fifteen minutes and costs 40drs. The boats run every quarter of an hour between 0500-2400hrs and then every half-hour until 0300hrs. To make matters worse the Perama ferry-boat dock is at the far, west end of the Port, making it necessary to take in, and enjoy to the full, all of the waterfront's scenic delights.

Excursion to Eandio (about 5km) A backshore bordering road edges the most incredibly filthy, narrow shoreline that runs all the way along the bottom of Salamis Bay. There are a number of restaurants and tavernas lining the route. Two-thirds of the way to Eandio is the shambles of a fresh water pumping station at which water lorries constantly arrive and depart. A small dinghy is incongruously slung in some davits.

EANDIO (Eantio, Eantion, Moulki, Mouliki) (5km from Salamina Town) There is a bus stop at the outset of Eandio, close to where the main road begins to angle away from the shoreline, between the *Cafe Holiday Music Pub* and the *Snackbar Eupho-Surfing*. Road signs indicate that the road divides, swinging left to Kaki Vigla and right to Kanakia, whilst sharp right along the shore of the bay leads, after 100m, to the:-

Hotel Gabriel (Class C) Tel 466 2275
Directions As above.

The most renowned hotel on the island overlooking the bay with a sea-edging, awning covered patio. It should be idyllic shouldn't it? Yes, well it isn't. There is some pebbly beach but it is the state of the sea that totally lets the side down. It is similar to swimming in a thin pea soup with fronds of underwater matter floating about on the surface and a distinctive aroma of, I know not what. Enough to say my usual 150 strokes had to be cut down to 40 or so, after which it was necessary to have a thorough, a very thorough shower.

Mine host, the middle-aged, myopic Georges or his 'Melina Mecouri' look-alike daughter, welcomes clients. All rooms have an en suite shower/bathroom, even if it is so small that it is necessary to place one's feet in the shower whilst sitting on the toilet. The plumbing is left exposed. On the other hand the sheets are ironed, the pillows soft and the rooms have nice balcony looking out over the Bay. A single room costs 1600drs and a double room 2000drs, which rates rise to 2000drs and 2300drs (1st July-31st Oct). Don't arrive at the weekend as mainlanders fill all the available accommodation. The hotel sports a large dining/reception room on the ground floor. Drinks and meals are available. A cup of Nes meh ghala cost 95drs but, with the amount of hot water served, it is possible to squeeze 1½ cups. One potato omelette and one plain omelette, a beer (100drs) and bread cost 380drs.

Across the way from the *Hotel Gabriel* is a 'doo-hickey', but lively, taverna that reeks of fish most nights. From the waterfront a path, to the side of the hotel, ascends steeply to join the main Kanakia road, close by a large petrol station. This road has curved round behind the *Hotel Gabriel* and then straightened out to climb through the village of Eandio before swinging off to cross over the mountain between Eandio and Kanakia. Proceeding up the High St hillside passes a building materials shop and souvlaki snackbar, on the right. Beyond that, again on the right, is the *Taverna* Η ΣΥΝΑΝΤΗΣΗ (of which more... much more later), a butcher and another souvlaki snackbar. Further on, still ascending, is a shop and a small supermarket, where a daughter speaks excellent, if slow, English. At the top of the rise is a small Main Square with a periptero on the left, and around the edge, a baker, hairdresser, bar, butcher and a drink shop. Now back to the:-

Restaurant/Taverna ΗΣΥΝΑΝΤΗΣΗ
This is not just the best taverna on the island (which would not be particularly difficult) but might well be the best value for money in the Argo-Saronic. The

establishment, and its owner Dimitri, is meticulously clean, the food excellent and reasonably priced. Once 'mine host' has taken the measure of a dedicated client I am fairly certain that he serves what he thinks will be good for him, her or them. I only postulate this because I am not sure I have always been served that which I have ordered! A meal for two of very good tzatziki (80drs), two sticks of souvlaki, each served on a bed of pita bread (400drs per person), a plate of splendid patatas (57drs), an excellent Greek salad with an enormous slab of feta (80-87drs), beautifully prepared with just the right amount of olive oil, courgettes in a batter (96drs each), bread (15-30drs each) and a kilo of open retsina (89drs) cost 1245drs. Not only do I think that Dimitri serves up that which he wishes, but I am fairly sure he bills a flat rate, give or take a drachmae or ten. Certainly charges for the same dish vary from night to night so only regard the price information as even more of a guide than usual! Don't misunderstand me, he does not overcharge, just evens out the costs. Also available are liver (300drs) and mouth watering meatballs on a bed of pita (300drs). Meals are often followed by a plate of 'on the house' fruit.

EXCURSIONS TO EANDIO SURROUNDS

From Eandio there is a road that edges this south side of the Bay of Salamis but it runs out after about 3km In the far distance is a prominent shore mounted hose arrangement that must be used for pumping from or to something, mustn't it?

Excursion to Paralia & Perani (about 4km) From Eandio it is possible to travel by bus through the usual, generally messy, moth-eaten countryside, in which are scattered outcrops of ramshackle, shanty huts and sprawl, to the undistinguished village of:-

PARALIA (Also called Kaki Vigla) (4km from Eandio) A grey, sandy, pebble beach set in 'hillbilly' surrounds
or to:-

PERANI (4km from Eandio) A small cove with a slate coloured beach, weedy sea and a dusty taverna.

Excursion to Kanakia (about 7km) Perhaps the loveliest area of the island is covered by the route from Eandio to Kanakia. It may be nothing remarkable where other, 'normal' islands are concerned but here on Salaminas...! This is a 2½ hour walk up and over the mountain, or a taxi ride, as the buses do not operate a service. If walking, purchase a couple of bottles of water from the baker prior to setting out. The route leads off, parallel to the sea-shore of Salamis Bay below, from the top of Eandio village. The road passes, on the left, a small Byzantine church with lovely roofs, on the far side of which is a most unsympathetic, modern archway, after which the ascent commences in a series of long, slow serpentine bends. The slopes of the pine tree and olive grove covered mountain are scattered with holiday homes and nice gardens, which are, in the main, of a better quality than most of the beach huts and prefabs littering the rest of the countryside. This *ad hoc* development quickly peters out, as does the surface of the road at the crest of the mountain. On the reverse side is an unsigned, three-way junction. The right-hand track wanders off into the hilltops and the left-hand track descends to **Peristeria** and (another) Ag Nikolaos Church.

Keep to the centre track, on the right of which is the rather pretty Ag Nikolaos Monastery, set in the folds of the hillsides. It is easy to become confused with some four island religious establishments all named Ag Nikolaos.

Prior to reaching Kanakia, there is a pleasant picnic area set amongst a pine tree forest, after which the stony track emerges on the outskirts of:-

KANAKIA (Karakiani) (8km from Eandio) What could have been, is not, if you follow me. No, well read on. It really is a most awful place, a parody of a Greek seaside settlement. The hamlet is laid out on a grid basis with a number of parallel, stony roads running down towards the sea-shore and criss-crossed by other, parallel, stony flint roads. The building plots of this 'Soweto-style', jerry-built development are divided from each by chain link fencing. Some houses have been in position long enough to develop lush, verdant gardens but they are interspersed by overgrown, parched, unsold or undeveloped backyards. Most of the 'streets' have been grandly titled with names. This shanty town is set some way back from the pebble foreshore that circles the bay, in which is set down a rather bare, granite surfaced islet. It certainly could be absolutely super and it is obviously one of the main destinations of the 'M1' sized traffic flow that streams on and off the island at weekends. Unfortunately it is most definitely not 'super'. The indescribable filth and litter that was the narrow shore, is unbelievable. Small boats are pulled up on the beach. To the left (*Fsw*), the pine trees that cover the low foothills grow to within 100m of the water's edge, but even the backshore, the land backing the bay and the forest are all littered with piles of rubbish. At the far, left-hand end of the shore is a very small stretch of sand but the rubbish is so thick as to be repugnant. It would be a help if the sea was clean and clear but even that is unattractive due to the weed covered nature of the pebble sea-bed. To the right (*Fsw*) is a large, ugly, single storey taverna with an extensive, covered patio in front. The owner is an elderly, bad tempered man who serves clients, if they insist. It helps if it is made plain that one is not a German! A cold beer and Fanta orange costs 130drs. The inside of the building matches the general unattractiveness of the exterior. Piles of crates are littered about and an unlovely, prominent stove and its stack pipe rather spoil the decor!

A ringmaster's circus caravan overlooking the heights, The Chora, Kithira.

Illustration 28 Evia island

19 EVIA (Evvia, Evoia, Euboea, Eyboia)

Selected areas ****

A Mainland Island

The rest *

FIRST IMPRESSIONS
With an island that is almost mainland sized and second only in proportions to Crete, it is impossible to impart overall impressions.

SPECIALITIES
Timber and forests; agriculture; stock and poultry raising; fishing; petrol stations; Evia wine (which is what all the backshore barrels are about).

RELIGIOUS HOLIDAYS & FESTIVALS
include: Lent – Wedding Feast, Ag Anna (North island); 27th May – St John, the Russians Feast Day – Prokopion (North island); 24th June – 'Klidona' (or folk celebrations), St John's Day, at various Evia locations; 15th August – Dormition of the Virgin, Church of the Virgin Chatirianon, Oxylithos (East island) – I know this is the most widespread feast day but the Oxylithos ceremony is worth a mention for the exuberance of the celebrations and meal served to the celebrators; 12th November – Feast of St David Geronta, (East-north-east) Rovies (North-east island).

VITAL STATISTICS
Tel prefix. *See* individual areas, ports and towns. Evia, once joined to the mainland from which it was probably sundered by prehistoric movement of the tectonic plates, is 175km long and between 6 and 50km wide with an area of some 3800sqkm (compared to the 8200sqkm of Crete) and a population of about 160,000.

HISTORY
Chalkis, Eretria and Kymi were important City States between the 8-6th century BC, with colonies as far away as Southern Italy. But that was that, for from then on, give or take the occasional historical hiccup, Evia followed the general course of overall Greek history. Ownership passed from the Athenians to the Romans (194 BC), after which it fell under the Byzantine mantle. The Franks (AD 1207) were followed by the Venetians (1306-1470), then the Turks took over for the next 351 years until the island was incorporated into the new Greek nation. The Venetian presence is amply evidenced by the prominent, large, square watchtowers sprinkled about the island on various hilltops. It is perhaps worth mentioning that Phylla, close to Chalkis Town, was the birthplace of Andreas Miaoulis, one of the most famed fighters for Greek freedom from the Turks.

GENERAL
Before discussing generalities, the first time visitor may well be puzzled by the barrels, new and old, that appear on the backshore of beaches all over the island in late summer. These barrels are for wine but it may seem peculiar to observe them being washed out with sea-water. This is the first of several stages in the preparation of the containers prior to their being filled. After the first sea-water cleansing they are washed out with hot water, followed by more sea-water and lastly by a forest herb drench. Okay!

As would be expected on such a large island, Evia is a land of wildly contrasting locations and scenery, despite which, compared to, say, Crete there are few large ports or towns. The stretch of coast due east from Chalkis Town, all the way to Amarinthos, has and is being seriously developed, based on a number of well-established seaside towns. These include Vasilikon, Eretria and, naturally, Amarinthos. For those seeking the best of unspoilt Evia it must be said this spread represents the worst. On the other hand, general areas worth investigation include the top north-west (Ag Georgios), the top north-east, without doubt the middle-west coast around Kymi and Paralia Kymi and the southern neck, perhaps the most typically island portion of Evia island.

Certainly a revelation is the capital:-

CHALKIS (Chalcis, Chalki, Chalkida, Khalkis, Halkida): capital town (Illustration 29). Tel prefix 0221. Due to the narrowness of the channel between the mainland (about 37m), which was bridged as early as 410-411BC, Chalkis is not a ferry-boat port. The only shipping is confined to that handled by the commercial port to the south of the present, comparatively modern turntable bridge. The straits between Evia island and the mainland are subject to a rare phenomenon in the Mediterranean – a tidal flow. This gives a metre rise and fall in the sea-level which results in an even stranger occurrence in the channel bordering the Esplanade – a current rip which changes direction some four times a day. This, I believe, still unexplained peculiarity is supposed to have so puzzled and taxed Aristotle's powers that he drowned himself in the straits.

The modern-day development is adjacent to the Ancient City of Chalcis and straddles the narrows. The Town has an air of prosperity and the Esplanade that borders the north island side of the channel is amazingly chic, almost Parisian in character. This wide Esplanade, Akti Voudouri, is lined, end to end, with smart cafe-bars and restaurants on the one side and their awning covered patios on the other (water) side. Considering the establishment's location their prices are not unreasonable, but more of that in the appropriate section.

As is often the case in Greece, the stylishness of this cafe-bar society is pleasantly and unbelievably contrasted by a couple of cockerels dancing around on the sawdust scattered floor of a butcher's shop not far distant, in Ermou St. Naturally this ideal thoroughfare is the main *volta* for the residents.

The shop and municipal building bordered Leoforos Eleftheriou Venizelou branches off the Esplanade, rising up the hillside beyond the amazing, covered Market.

ARRIVAL BY BUS

Buses from Athens thunder over the turntable bridge either to stop at the main terminal (*Tmr* 1D3) or career on to Kymi Port, on the east coast, stopping at Eretria and Amarinthos.

ARRIVAL BY FERRY

See the various coastal ports including (from top to bottom, in an anticlockwise direction):- Agiokampos, Ag Georgios, Loutra Edipsos, Eretria, Panaghia, Nea Styra, Marmari, Karistos and Kimi.

ARRIVAL BY ROAD

The last stretch of the mainland approach to the capital passes through an extremely industrial area. Once over the bridge, and in need of somewhere to park and a stretch, it is probably favourite to swing right on to Akti Liaska and slip into one of the parking bays beyond the Taxi rank (*Tmr* T4/5).

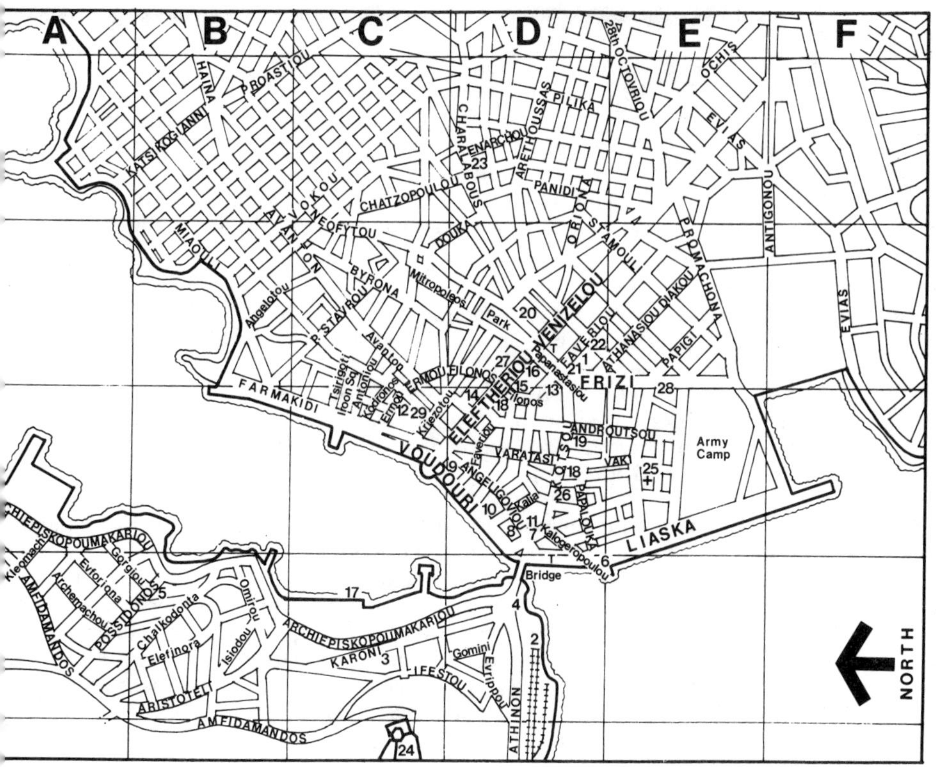

lustration 29 Chalkis Town

Tmr = Town map reference
Fsw = Facing seawards
Sbo = Sea behind one
Fbqbo = Ferry-boat Quay behind one

nr 1. Main Bus terminal D3
2. Railway Station D5
3. Hotel Chara C5
4. Port police D5
5. Hotel Morfeus B5
6. Town Bus terminal D/E4/5
7. Plateia Gefyras D4/5
8. Hotel Kentrikon D4
9. Hotel Hilda C/D4
10. Hotel Lucy D4
11. Cafe-bar D4
12. Restaurant ΜΟΥΧΡΙΤΣΑΣ C3/4
13. Souvlaki snackbar D3/4
14. National Bank D3/4
15. Tourist/Town police D3/4
16. OTE D3
17. Asteria Lido C5
18. Bakers (2)
19. Baker-cum-shop D4
20. The Market D3
21. 'All purpose' shop/store D3
22. Dry Cleaners D/E3
23. Hospital D2
24. Castle C6
25. Ag Paraskevi Church E4
26. Mosque D4
27. Archaeological Museum D3
28. Folklore Museum E3/4
29. Post Office C4

T = Taxi ranks

ARRIVAL BY TRAIN

The trains from Athens pull into the Railway Station (*Tmr* 2D5), on the mainland side of the town.

THE ACCOMMODATION & EATING OUT

The Accommodation There are quite a number of hotels but few, if any *Rooms*.

On the mainland side there are the:-

Hotel Chara (*Tmr* 3C5) 21 L Karoni Tel 25541

Directions: From the Port police office (*Tmr* 4D5) proceed north along the Esplanade road, A Makariou, turn left on the far side of the first square along Odhos Karoni and the hotel is on the left.

All rooms have en suite bathrooms. Single rooms are charged at 1750drs and double rooms 2625drs, rising respectively to 2100drs and 3150drs (16th March-15th Sept).

and the:-

Hotel Morfeus (*Tmr* 5B5) 3 Possidonos Tel 24703

Directions: Keeping to the Esplanade, advance as far as Odhos Possidonos. The hotel is on the left.

Single rooms sharing a bathroom start at 980drs and with an en suite bathroom 1070drs whilst double rooms sharing cost 1150drs and en suite 1460drs. These charges rise, respectively, to 1160/1245drs and 1340/1690drs (1st April-30th Sept).

On the island side of the channel, in Chalkis Town proper, a number of hotels radiate out from the area of the turntable bridge, including the:-

Hotel Kymata (*Tmr* D4/5) (Class E) 21 Liaska Tel 21317

Directions: Turn right (*bridge behind one*) along Akti Liaska and advance past the Taxi rank. The hotel is in the block edged by Kalogeropoulou and Papalouka Sts, almost opposite the Town Bus terminal (*Tmr* 6D/E4/5).

Ethnic, provincial accommodation with single rooms sharing the bathroom charged at 900drs. Double rooms sharing a bathroom cost 1100drs and with an en suite bathroom 1400drs.

Hotel Iris (*Tmr* D4/5) (Class E) 3 Plateia Gefyras Tel 22246

Directions: Immediately across from the bridge.

A noisy location and another provincial hotel, with rates about the same as the *Kymata*.

From Plateia Gefyras (*Tmr* 7D4/5) the narrow street of Angeli Goviou branches off to the left (*bridge behind one*).

Hotel Kentrikon (*Tmr* 8D4) (Class C) 5 Angeli Goviou Tel 22375

Directions: As above and on the left.

Singles share the bathrooms and cost 990drs per night whilst double rooms sharing are available for 1250drs and with an en suite bathroom 2090drs. These rates rise, respectively, to 1790drs and 1500/2500drs (1st June-30th Sept).

A metre or so beyond the *Hotel Kentrikon* and on the left is:-

Hotel Johns (*Tmr* D4) (Class B) 9 Angeli Goviou Tel 22496

Directions: As above.

All rooms have en suite bathrooms, a single costing 1800drs and a double 2600drs.

Hotel Evripos (*Tmr* D4) (Class D) 5 S Kalia Tel 22956

Directions: Further along Odhos Angeli Goviou and the first street branching off to the right is Odhos S Kalia. The hotel is on the left.

Rates averagely the same as *The Morfeus*.

Hotel Hilda (*Tmr* 9C/D4) (Class B) Angeli Goviou/Favierou Sts. Tel 28111
Directions: Almost at the north end of Odhos Angeli Goviou, on the left, at the junction with Favierou St.

There are two more hotels overlooking the Esplanade Akti Voudouri, the luxury *Hotel Lucy* (*Tmr* 10D4, tel 23831) and the B Class *Paliria* (*Tmr* C/D4, tel 28001).

Camping *See Evia Camping,* **Malakonda, Route One.**

The Eating Out As indicated there are any number of establishments along Akti Voudouri. Despite the excellent position looking out over the 'river', prices are not too exorbitant with, for instance, a tzatziki costing 120drs, a Greek salad 180drs and a moussaka 330drs. That is not to say prices aren't on the high side with a Nes meh ghala costing 150drs at one of the smarter cafe-bar restaurants.

For more reasonable refreshment try the:-

Cafe-bar (*Tmr* 11D4)
Directions: On the edge of Plateia Gefyras, close to the bridge.

One of those locations where there are chairs and tables on the adjacent pavement as well as some across the very busy, main dual carriageway. The waiters 'interview' with the Almighty must be only a matter of time! A Nes meh ghala is reasonably priced at 77drs, a beer and orange drink costs 135drs and they serve a very nice line in fish mezes. Another attraction for 'gongoozlers' is the almost frenetic activity in the locality. This includes the bustle of the traffic crossing the bridge, passengers that mount and dismount from the Town buses, that stop in the Square, and the comings and goings at the amazing, extensive, rambling periptero on the *Hotel Iris* side of the cafe-bar.

Restaurant ΜΟΥΧΡΙΤΣΑΣ (*Tmr* 12C3/4) Ermou St.
Directions: From the bridge proceed north along Akti Voudouri beyond the outset of Eleftheriou Venizelou to Ermou St. Turn right up the curving crescent of a street (that makes round to the middle of the Main Avenue, Leoforos Eleftheriou Venizelou) and the restaurant is on the right.

Popular with the locals which is no wonder as it is a reasonably priced establishment.

In the area of the main Bus terminal (*Tmr* 1D3) are a number of options. These include an inexpensive, if somewhat 'greasy spoon', the *Roumeli Taverna* and a souvlaki pita snackbar, both on Odhos Favierou and almost opposite the Bus terminal; a stick souvlaki snackbar at the rear of the terminus and an excellent souvlaki snackbar (*Tmr* 13D3/4) at the junction of Odhos Papanastasiou and Kotsou St. At this latter an appetising souvlaki cost 75drs.

THE A TO Z OF USEFUL INFORMATION

BANKS An abundance, mainly lining Leoforos Eleftheriou Venizelou, including the **National Bank** (*Tmr* 14D3/4) which changes Eurocheques. Further up Eleftheriou Venizelou, between the Tourist police office (*Tmr* 15D3/4) and the OTE (*Tmr* 16D3) and on the same side of the street is a Change/Bank.

BEACHES It is necessary to either proceed to the north-eastern suburbs (*See* **Route Two**) or cross the bridge to the mainland side for the Asteria Lido (*Tmr* 17C5). Further on round the coast is a beach at **Ag Minas**.

BICYCLE, SCOOTER & CAR HIRE No scooters for hire. Cars can be hired from the office of **Evia Tours** (*Tmr* D4), Kalogeropoulou St that edges the small Gefyras Park, close to the bridge. They are agents for Budget Rent A Car.

BREAD SHOPS There is a Baker (*Tmr* 18D3/4) on the right (*Sbo*) of Leoforos Eleftheriou Venizelou, at the corner of Odhos Filonos. There is another (*Tmr* 18D4) on the right (*Sbo*) about half-way up Kotsou St. Still in Odhos Kotsou, again on the right, and further up this steeply rising street, at the junction with Odhos Ioustinianou, is a Baker-cum-small shop (*Tmr* 19D4).

BUSES The chaotic, main terminus is in a hanger-like building (*Tmr* 1D3) that spans Favierou and Athanasiou Diakou Sts. The ticket office and waiting rooms are on the Favierou side. Some bus timetable information is available but the 'pundits' are of the opinion that many of the far-flung locations on Evia are best reached by catching a bus back to Athens and then out to the nearest mainland port! An example is that to reach, say, Loutra Edipsos, it is probably best to catch an Athens bus to Arkitsa and take the local ferry. Well, there you go.

The Town Bus terminal (*Tmr* 6DE4/5) is on Akti Liaska. As with much else Evian it is very difficult to find out any information, let alone the complete scenario.

Bus timetable
Before proceeding I must draw attention to the impossibility of 'carving out' any facts.

Chalkis Town to Athens
Daily 0600-2000hrs (every half-hour), 2030hrs.

Return journey (260, Liossion St, Athens)
Daily 0600-2000hrs (every half-hour), 2115hrs.

Chalkis Town to Paralia Kymi (Kymi Port) via Vasilikon, Eretria, Amarinthos, Velos, Monodrion & Kymi.
Daily 0600, 0730, 1000, 1115, 1330, 1430, 1515, 1800, 2000hrs.
Return journey
Daily 0530, 0630, 0730, 0830, 0945, 1030, 1130, 1230, 1330,
1430, 1530, 1630, 1730, 1830hrs.

Note there are Chalkis Town buses individually to Eretria & Amarinthos. *See* Amarinthos for some local bus routes.

Chalkis Town to Karistos via Eretria & Amarinthos
Daily 0615, 1315, 1715hrs.
Details of buses to the northern part of the island may be obtainable (by the use of torture) but.....!

COMMERCIAL SHOPPING AREA Chalkis Town is fortunate to possess one of the best and most interesting, if 'shambolic', covered markets I have come across on the islands.

The Market (*Tmr* 20D3) Similar to Odhos 1866, Iraklion (Crete), but that is a street market and this is the genuine Marseilles-type set-up. The very large building is situated close to the top of the rise half-way up Leoforos Eleftheriou Venizelou and faces over a small park. Most of the stalls are on 'a first floor level' reached up a flight of stone steps. There's a 'mess' of vegetables, fruit, fish, meat and poultry. The market should rate as a tourist attraction under the A To Z heading – Places of Interest.

Convenient to the Main Bus terminus is an all purpose shop/store (*Tmr* 21D3) on Plateia Papanastasiou. There is an excellent cake shop on the corner of Plateia Gefyras (*Tmr* 7D4/5) and Angeli Goviou St.

DISCOS In the northern suburbs are such exotic delights as **Castello Sex Show** (and other similar blandishments).

ELPA (*Tmr* D4) On the right and about half-way up Kotsou St. The staff are very helpful indeed and if their English fails somebody will translate, probably from the first balcony of a nearby block of flats.

LAUNDRY No launderette, only a Dry Cleaners (*Tmr* 22D/E3) on Odhos Velissariou, beyond the Main Bus terminus (*Tmr* 1D3).

MEDICAL CARE
Chemists & Pharmacies One (*Tmr* D3/4) on the right (*Sbo*) of the Main Avenue.
Hospital (*Tmr* 23D2) A large, modern facility, well signposted from all directions until just out of reach. Then the signs completely disappear in an old town warren of back streets. The maps quaintly refer to the hospital as a First Aid Centre, which nomenclature rather fails to conjure up the actuality.

OTE (*Tmr* 16D3) On the right (*Sbo*) of the Main Avenue, prior to Plateia Papanastasiou. Open for business weekdays only between 0730-1510hrs.

PETROL There are so many petrol stations (an actual glut), all over the island, that it is unnecessary to highlight their existence.

PLACES OF INTEREST
Castle (*Tmr* 24C6) Built by the Turks in the 1680s and named Karababa. From the battlements there are fine views out over Chalkis Town and the surrounds.
Churches & Cathedrals
Ag Paraskevi Church (*Tmr* 25E4) A 14th century church based on a very early Christian building and quite possibly the site of a Greek temple.
Mosque (*Tmr* 26D4) An imposing building that can be sighted, across a park, whilst ascending Kotsou St. As was often the case, the Turks took over and converted a church – the Venetian *San Marco di Negroponte*. Incidentally, the name Negroponte, or black bridge, was that assigned by the Venetians to both the bridge and the island. Beyond the Mosque, to the south, is the area of the Old City or Kastro.
Museums
Archaeological (*Tmr* 27D3) On the left (*Sbo*) of Eleftheriou Venizelou Avenue, prior to the Market. Naturally displays island finds, including some sculptures from the Temple of Apollo at Eretria.
Museum of Folklore (*Tmr* 28E3/4) South of the rear of the Main Bus terminal, where Odhos Frizi starts to narrow down.

Incidentally the large, imposing building on the left-hand side of Eleftheriou Venizelou Avenue, with an inner courtyard and 'labelled' *Themides Melathron*, is the Law Courts.

POLICE
Port (*Tmr* 4D5) On the mainland side.
Tourist (*Tmr* 15D3/4) In the same building as the Town police, which is on the right (*Sbo*) of the Main Avenue. The Tourist police office is on the 4th floor and is open daily between 0800-1400hrs. Unfortunately their English is limited, as is their interest!

Town *See* **Tourist police**. The building cannot be missed as police motorbikes litter the wide pavement, on which orders of the day appear to be issued, à la *Hill Street Blues*.

POST OFFICE (*Tmr* 29C4) On narrow Karamourtzouni St, which branches left (*Sbo*) off the Main Avenue, at the Esplanade end.

TAXIS There are ranks (*Tmr* T) to the right of the bridge (*Tmr* TD4/5) on Akti Liaska as well as on Plateia Papanastasiou (*Tmr* TD3).

TELEPHONE NUMBERS & ADDRESSES

Hospital (*Tmr* 23D2) ΗΡΑΚΛΕΩΣ ΓΑΖΕΠΗ	Tel 22282
Police, tourist (*Tmr* 15D3/4) Eleftheriou Venizelou	Tel 24662

TOILETS The most convenient (whoops) facility is on the edge of the small park adjacent to Plateia Gefyras (*Tmr* 7D4/5). It appears to be permanently locked. There are also public toilets beneath the main, central steps up to the Market (*Tmr* 20D3), on the park side. If taken short (very short indeed) there are also some at the rear of the Main Bus office waiting room (*Tmr* 1D3)

TRAINS A surprisingly frequent service.

Train timetable

Chalkis Town to Athens via Inoi junction
Daily 0500, 0602, 0718, 0820, 0930, 1100, 1215, 1310, 1410, 1530, 1725, 1820, 1906, 2117, 2115, 2155, 2245hrs.

Return
Daily 0420, 0520, 0542, 0635, 0735, 0900, 1030, 1200, 1340, 1455, 1550, 1646, 1800, 1912, 2005, 2050, 2205hrs.
One-way fare: B class 225drs, A class 340drs; duration: average 1½hrs.

TRAVEL AGENTS & TOUR OFFICES
Evia Tours (*Tmr* D4) in Odhos Kalogeropoulou that edges Plateia Gefyras. A sister (or brother) company of **Eretria Tours**.

ROUTE ONE (Eastern island)

To Paralia Kymi (Kymi Port) (97km) via Vasilikon, Eretria, Amarinthos, Aliverion & Kimi The main road out of Chalkis Town is signposted to lead vehicles 'round the houses' and, for that matter, the outskirts of the suburbs. Unfortunately on the new, smart main road there is an unsignposted major junction. It is necessary to take the right-hand fork, between the messy industrial surrounds of repair workshops, a petrol station and a tyre depot. The bypass leads back to the route to the northern portion of the island (*See* **Route Two**).

The countryside for about 12km from Chalkis Town is olive tree planted, which groves are subject, more's the pity, to outbreaks of industrial buildings and a fair scattering of petrol stations.

N. LAMPSAKOS (6km from Chalkis Town) At this junction a road off to the right advances on to the flat, 'East Anglian like', Ag Nikolaos promontory. This is also, and more correctly, known as *Bourtzia* after a, now long eradicated tower. **Ag Nikolaos** village has a couple of large stores, a fish shop, a butcher's as well as a kafeneion or three. Continuing eastwards, a road follows the shoreline edged by a dusty, agricultural landscape with an ethnic fishing village flowing along the undulating coastline and beside which are scattered any number of fish tavernas. The weedy, gently shelving sea-bed is bordered by a narrow strip of foreshore on which are spaced smart, white painted beach showers and bamboo umbrellas. It's quite amazing really because this is a scrubbly dump.

Rather than return to N. Lampsakos, a road from the route that encircles the promontory rejoins the main road close by:-

VASILIKON (11km from Chalkis Town) The outset of this unattractive, sprawling industrial town is marked by a broad, summer-dry, stony river-bed. Most notable is the widespread building activity, especially on the outskirts, and the numerous petrol stations.

From Vasilikon a road sallies forth to the south a kilometre or two as far as **Lefkandi Beach**. Here is an 'infrastructure' of eating and drinking spots.

North of Vasilikon, a road proceeds to the once countryside village of:-

PHYLLA (12km from Chalkis Town) Famed as the birthplace of Admiral Miaoulis, a hero of the War of Independence. Close by and to the north of Phylla is the hamlet of **Aphrati**, above which towers the ruins of Kastelli Castle from whence are marvellous views. The village has a couple of Byzantine churches, one with well preserved murals and the almost 'Welsh language, railway station length name' of **Rizokastelliotissa**. This signifies that it is the Church at the foot of the Castle on the Hill (I am reliably informed). From Phylla village a track to the east leads, after 11km, to The Monastery Ag Georgiou Arma, wherein are carvings and murals of note.

Bags of signposting off the main road to the right, guide the intrepid traveller along a stony track to:-

LOULI BEACH (14km from Chalkis Town The path swings back on itself, paralleling the shore, and progresses past the *Louli Beach Development*, a once rather pleasant set-up that might now have 'died'. Beyond this group of buildings, the track becomes narrower before terminating at the nearside of a shallow, curved length of large pebble beach, which is stopped off at the far end by a timber yard. Floating at anchor and visible 'round the corner' are a number of merchant ships. If there had not been such a 'hullabaloo' it may all have appeared more attractive....

At about 15km from Chalkis town, in a comparatively pleasant outbreak of olive groves and on the right, is the pleasantly situated *Via Camping* which is backed by a coastal strip of gritty beach.

From here onwards, for the next 5km or so, the Greek 'look-alike' for the 1960s Spanish Costa coastal countryside is increasingly encroached on by various unlovely, scattered developments. These include ***Rooms***, tavernas, restaurants, the *Vogue Hotel*, agricultural holdings, a restaurant on the left, with a reconstruction of a Trireme on the forecourt, the *Olympic Holiday Club Hotel*, with a pebbly, dank beach, the *Eretria Beach Hotel* complex on the right, more restaurants, hotels and petrol stations, all on the left and in the area of **Malakonda**.

Hard up against the sea is the *Malakonta Beach Hotel and Bungalows*, villas and then a narrow band of polluted foreshore (21km from Chalkis Town). You know, just an everyday description of a typical Greek coastal strip! Bicycle and scooter hire firms have sprung up in the area of the more isolated, very big hotel developments. This is understandable as some form of transport may well be a necessity on this last section of the route.

ERETRIA (22km from Chalkis Town) (Illustration 30) Tel prefix 0221. A very widespread, spaced out, rather dusty development set in treeless, seemingly arid, flat countryside. From the main road bypass, yes bypass, it is not possible to deduce the size of the place which fans out in a grid layout of streets from the centre of the town.

Of all the traditional, package holiday locations on Evia I consider Eretria to be the most ideal with a combination of one fine beach (and two other not so good), enjoyable swimming, a regular bus service to the capital, a ferry-boat connection to the mainland and the infrastructure necessary to support holiday-makers' various requirements including extensive and interesting archaeological remains.

To aid visitors, the authorities have erected a number of town maps. On the other hand it seems inevitable that one is not to hand when most urgently required, but there you go! The Town has a number of public gardens or parks.

HISTORY

In days of yore, well actually between the 8-6th century BC, Eretria was a very important City State with colonies on Corfu, Sicily and Southern Italy.

The town's alternative name is Nea Psara. This derives from the mass exodus of islanders from Psara (NE Aegean), who fled their small island, settling on Evia, in 1824 to escape devastating, punitive Turkish retribution.

THE ACCOMMODATION & EATING OUT

The Accommodation A number of ***Rooms*** and package tourist hotels which include the expensive B Class *Hotel Perigiali Eretrias* (*Tmr* 1E5, tel 62439) and the C Class *Hotel Delfis* (*Tmr* 2D/E4/5, tel 62380) with en suite single rooms costing 3000drs and a double room 3600drs. The C Class *Hotel Xenia* (*Tmr* 3D6, tel 61202) occupies the islet-like blob at the end of the narrow neck of land that projects into the sea. Despite the 'favoured' position a double room en suite is not outrageously expensive at 2500drs, that is if a room is available. The islet is known as *Pezonisi* or the 'island of the dreams'.

There are a number of ***Rooms*** available throughout the Town.

The Eating Out There are a row of smart restaurants (*Tmr* 4D4), but with nondescript offerings, lined out along the north-south down leg of the Harbour. There are one or two traditional kafeneion/tavernas that 'bubble away' at night, in the streets stretching down towards the Ferry-boat Quay (*Tmr* 5C4) from the High St. This is a stick-souvlaki town.

THE A TO Z OF USEFUL INFORMATION

BANKS None but *See* **Travel Agents & Tour Offices, A To Z** and do not forget the Post Office (*Tmr* 6C2).

BEACHES

Beach 1 (*Tmr* D5) Almost in front of the *Hotel Delfis*. The small, long, gritty sand and pebble beach and pebbly sea-bed, with some biscuit rock on the sea's edge, is bordered by very clear sea-water and the swimming is excellent. The backshore,

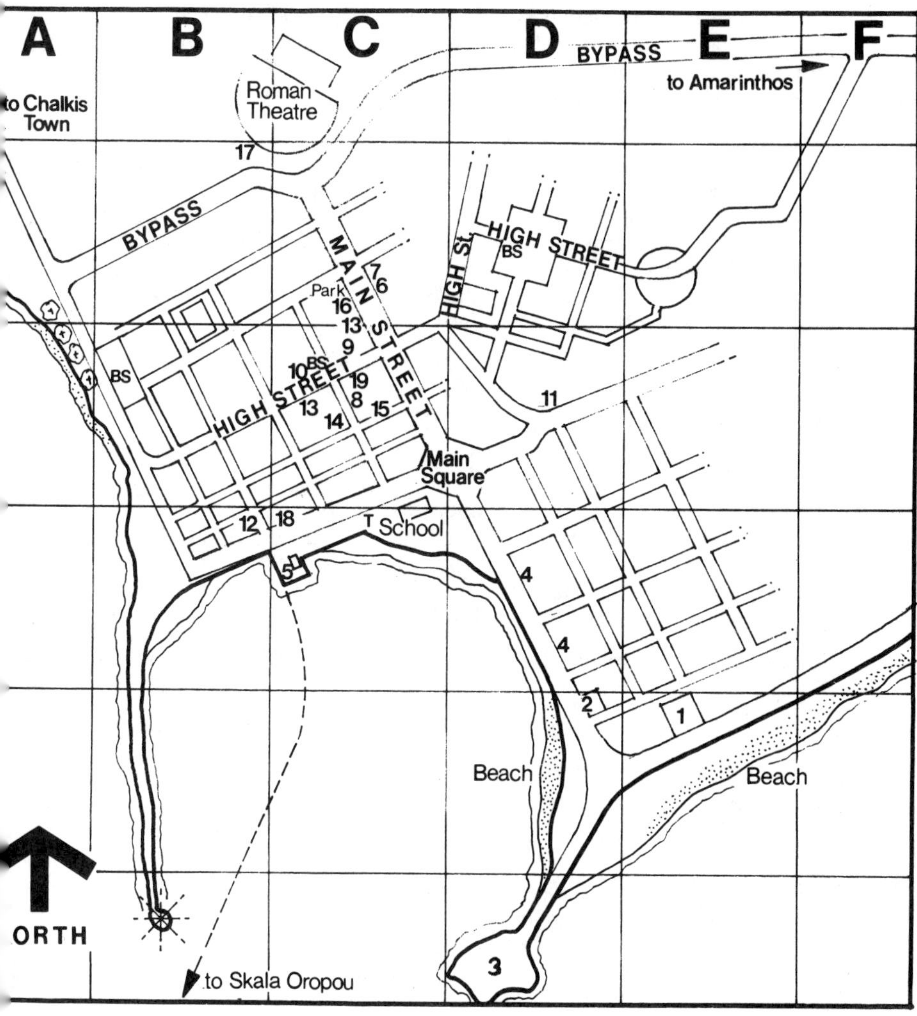

Illustration 30 Eretria Port

Tmr = Town map reference
Fsw = Facing seawards
Sbo = Sea behind one
Fbqbo = Ferry-boat Quay behind one

Tmr
1. Hotel Perigiali Eretrias E5
2. Hotel Delfis D/E4/5
3. Hotel Xenia D6
4. 'Row of Restaurants' D4
5. Ferry-boat Quay C4
6. Post Office C2
7. Scooter Hire Sakis C2
8. Scooter hire C3
9. Eretria Tours C3
10. Newspaper shop C3
11. Baker D3
12. Bread shop B/C3/4
13. Chemists (2)
14. Clinic/Surgery C3
15. Dentist C3
16. OTE C2
17. Museum B/C1/2
18. Port police C3/4
19. Town police C3

T = Taxi rank
BS = Bus Stops

edged by a neat, green hedge (not privet but similar), is almost manicured grass in which are planted some small palm trees. The beach shower water remains fairly warm due to the supply pipe being close to the surface. The few beach umbrellas are free and a large plane tree, to the right (*Fsw*), provides ample shade.

Beach 2 (*Tmr* E/F5) Around the corner from **Beach 1**. The narrow strip of foreshore stretches away eastwards from about the proximity of the *Hotel Perigiali Eretrias*. The shore is windswept and kelpy, somewhat offset by an eye-catching, offshore islet. The sea-bed is somewhat muddy. This foreshore, backed by a dusty track, continues eastwards for some 1½km past a large, flat, dry area that has been fenced off for various, still unbuilt, villa plots. The now kelpy shoreline runs out alongside the fence of a hotel's grounds that stretch down to and across the narrow, dirty, pebbly beach.

Beach 3 (*Tmr* A/B2/3) This kilometre long, narrow, pebbly, dirty foreshore borders the Chalkis main road from about opposite a bus stop.

BICYCLE, SCOOTER & CAR HIRE

Scooter Hire Sakis (*Tmr* 7C2) The firm is alongside the Post Office. Honda type scooters for hire.

There is another outfit (*Tmr* 8C3), opposite the Doctor's Surgery, in a side street stretching from the High St down to the Ferry-boat Quay (*Tmr* 5C4). 'Budget Rent A Car's' are available by courtesy of **Eretria Tours** (*Tmr* 9C3), situated on the High St, across the road from the Police station. The usual, now very high rates and almost crippling daily deposit, as outlined in the introductory chapters of the book.

BOOKSELLERS Well at least a newspaper shop (*Tmr* 10C3) in the High St.

BREAD SHOPS There is a Baker (*Tmr* 11D3) to the east of the Main 'School' Square and a Bread shop (*Tmr* 12B/C3/4), close to the Ferry-boat Quay.

BUSES There are a number of Bus stops (*Tmr* BS) along the length of the High St.

Bus timetable

See **Bus timetable, Buses, A To Z, Chalkis Town.**

Eretria to Chalkis Town

Daily 0640 (except Sunday), 0740, 0840, 0940, 1010, 1140, 1240, 1340, 1440, 1540, 1640, 1740, 1840, 1940hrs.

Eretria to Kymi

Daily 0630, 0800, 1030, 1145, 1400, 1500, 1545, 1830, 2030hrs.

Eretria to Karistos via Styra

Daily 0630 (stopping at Aliverion), 1330 (except Sunday), 1730hrs.

Eretria to Gymnon via Amarinthos

Daily 1045, 1500, 1545, 1945hrs (except Sunday).

COMMERCIAL SHOPPING AREA Gift shops line the water frontage to the right (*Sbo*) of the Ferry-boat Quay (*Tmr* 5C4) and stores line the left-hand side of the street, running up from Main 'School' Square to the High St. The High St is lined with shops of 'every description'.

DISCOS Worry not, attractions include the **Disco Pub Oh La La** – every night 'happy hours' and the **Dancing Pub Amnesia** – do they really mean Amnesia? Probably.

FERRY-BOATS Eretria connects, with landing craft type boats, to Skala Oropou on the mainland, some 52km from Athens. The channel here is about 8km wide.

Ferry-boat timetable
Daily 0500-1900hrs (every half-hour), 2000, 2115hrs.
Return
Daily 0600-1930hrs (every half-hour), 2000, 2100, 2200hrs.
One-way fares:passenger 80drs; duration 25mins vehicle 480drs.

FERRY-BOAT TICKET OFFICES The ticket hut is on the outset of the Ferry-boat Quay (*Tmr* 5C4).

MEDICAL CARE
Chemists & Pharmacies One shop (*Tmr* 13C3) is in the High St and another (*Tmr* 13C2/3), just before the OTE.
Clinic/Surgery (*Tmr* 14C3).
Dentist (*Tmr* 15C3).

OTE (*Tmr* 16C2) On the left of the street, north of the High St crossroads and prior to a garden park. Open weekdays only between 0730-1510hrs.

PETROL At least three in the High St.

PLACES OF INTEREST
Archaeological Site (*Tmr* C1) North of the main road bypass. The remains include an ancient 4th century BC Theatre, a 5th century BC Doric building and a 6th century BC Temple. Much of the fenced-off site is rather overgrown with grass and looks rather forlorn. The lack of trees to shade the area doesn't help.

Museum (*Tmr* 17B/C1/2). Naturally enough displays finds from the site. Well it would, wouldn't it? It goes without saying that the National Archaeological Museum in Athens has 'half-inched' some of the prize exhibits.

POLICE
Port (*Tmr* 18C3/4) The office is close to the Ferry-boat Quay.
Town (*Tmr* 19C3) Located in the High St.

POST OFFICE (*Tmr* 6C2).

TAXIS (*Tmr* T.C3/4) Rank on both sides of the road between the Ferry-boat Quay and the School.

TELEPHONE NUMBER & ADDRESSES
Doctor Tel 62203
Police, town Tel 62204

TRAVEL AGENTS & TOUR OFFICES
Eretria Tours (*Tmr* 9C3) The High St. Tel 62909/61909
Apart from car hire, the office offers a number of the to-be-expected tours and cruises including a one-day cruise to Aegina, Poros and Hydra (2000drs); sightseeing Athens & Piraeus (900drs); Athens by Night (3200drs) and a one-day tour to the Corinth Canal, Epidaurus and Mycenae (1900drs). The firm transacts travellers cheque and money exchange.

WATER There is a water tap on the edge of the small public garden, opposite the Post Office (*Tmr* 6C2). There is a fountain on the side of the eastern end of the main road bypass.

Continuing eastwards from Eretria the scrubbly bypass is bordered by the remnants of a tall, graceful avenue of plane trees. At the 24km milestone (!) the route passes, on the right, the *Golden Beach Hotel and Bungalows* complete with disco. One thing is for certain and that is that the beach is definitely not golden sand. The foreshore, with which the road now closes, is still pebble and rock. At 25km, alongside the seashore, is a graceful, old hacienda on the right, the more noticeable for its elegance, especially when compared to the modern-day buildings that 'blot' the landscape. As if to make up for this lapse of architectural desirability, in the general area of **Magoula**, the modern day *Hotel Miramare* is surrounded and followed by various shops, tavernas, restaurants, villas, holiday-makers diversions and then the *Hotel Holidays in Evia*, a vast hotel and bungalow complex. This latter hosts wind surfers, beach boards and all the other necessary paraphernalia, despite which I'm fairly certain that the beach is man-made! To complete the 'rinky-dinky' picture, there is a taverna, disco and a few small coves as the route continues eastwards.

The not unattractive valley beyond Eretria is planted with fenced off olive groves and pistachio tree orchards. Despite the continuing villa construction the scenery is much prettier here. The direction of the road swings back to skirt the sea's edge, which is a series of small coves, unfortunately quite a few of them fenced in. These are followed by the *Hotel Stefania* bordering a pebbly beach. The Disco Welcome, a marble works and an outcrop of hotels presages the approaches to the Greek tourist resort of:-

AMARINTHOS (30km from Chalkis Town) Tel prefix 0221. The present day settlement is that of an ancient site. Six kilometres to the north-east, via the pretty village of **Ano Vathia**, is the Monastery of Ag Nikolaos, built in about 1560.

At the outset to the one time port and now seaside resort, is the *Hotel Flisvos* (C Class – tel 72385). The main road borders the waterfront and the small harbour, in which are moored caiques and benzinas. The other side of the road is the Main Square. ***Rooms*** tend to be advertised as *Zimmer* and there is a D Class hotel, *The Artemis* (Tel 72255). The far end of the Esplanade, across the way from the waterfront, is lined with tavernas. There are lashings of chemists shops, a number of peripteros, petrol stations, an OTE, a Post Office, Police station, doctor, clinic and a cinema. The main road to the east of Amarinthos runs parallel to and some 50-100m back from the rubbish littered seafront. This is a series of tiny beach coves with foreshores of grey, fine sand and shingle, biscuit rock and pebble sea-beds. A diving board completes the bathing essentials. At the far end is a Restaurant that offers ***Rooms***.

The buses park on the edge of the Esplanade High St and Amarinthos is an important bus 'way-station'.

Bus timetable
Amarinthos to Chalkis Town

Daily 0545 (except Sunday), 0630, 0730, 0830, 0930, 1045, 1130, 1230, 1330, 1430, 1530, 1630, 1730, 1830, 1930hrs.

Amarinthos to Kymi

Daily 0645, 0815, 1045, 1430, 1600, 1845, 2045hrs.

Amarinthos to Karistos

Daily 0645 (with a stop at Aliverion, except Sunday), 1340 (except Sunday), 1745hrs.

Amarinthos to Gymnon
Daily 1100, 1530, 1600hrs (except Sunday).

Amarinthos to Ano Vathia (NE of Amarinthos)
Daily 1400hrs (except Sunday)

Amarinthos to Manikia via Seta & Makrychori (N of Amarinthos)
Daily 1400hrs (except Sunday).

Beyond the eastern outskirts of Amarinthos is some messy development. Smallholdings, allotments and villas are followed by a straight stretch of road alongside which are some ***Rooms***. The route becomes more island-like in character, (meaning it becomes narrow and twisting) rejoining the sea's edge and a pebble beach, only to wind away with villas spotted about and more ***Rooms*** (35km from Chalkis Town). A pebble strip set in pretty surrounds is followed by a straggly development and an area in which caravans and camper-vans park. This is followed by the *Face to Face Pub*, ***Rooms***, the *Dionysos Taverna* and the *Olympic Star Hotel* (37km from Chalkis Town), which is the other side of the road from a smidgin of lido-like beach and a disco. Pedaloes are available for hire.

The route once again skirts the coastline, for some 4km, in an attractive setting of low, gorse covered hills, after which the rocks at the sea's edge are intermittently dotted with outbreaks of pebbly beach and low pine trees until the outskirts of:-

ALIVERION (49km from Chalkis Town) The few pebble beach inlets set in low, rocky surrounds and pleasant groves of trees, disappear. The new scenery of mangy, sparsely vegetated hills is soon punctuated by marble works, but that is nothing to that which is to come. It will not require a keen observer to have sighted the refinery complex towers at the far, east end of the town. Aliverion houses a bank, hotel, plenty of chemists, a Post Office, a Police station, innumerable petrol stations and shops, after which the full industrial nature of the settlement is revealed. The unremitting ugliness of the refinery is 'enhanced' by a concrete works and other industrial enterprises, including the mandatory marble works. It is the type of treeless, sparsely vegetated Mediterranean scenery that is thoroughly 'rogered' when this type of blanket, industrial development is allowed to take place.

The main road continues eastward leaving, to the right, a hill on which there are castle ruins. The countryside is now lowland, planted with spaced out olive trees, many of which are old – maybe so are the olives! The road climbs through much more traditional island scenery to the small 'Garden-City' development of **Velos** (54km from Chalkis Town), which is not short of a petrol station or two, nor of marble works. To the right is another low hill, topped by a Venetian square tower, beyond which is the village of **Lepoura** (57km from Chalkis Town). Most of the women here wear straw hats, underneath which are neck tied scarves.

The right-hand fork leads to the southern portion of the island (*See* **Route Three**) while the left-hand road continues on, now in a northerly direction towards Kymi.

Beyond the turning off to **Avlonarion**, which leads to the very old Monastery of Lefkon, rebuilt in the 11th century, there is a pleasant little village with a lovely old church and, of course, several petrol stations. Fourteen kilometres on from Lepoura, the road forks. Only the (fool) hardy would consider the right-hand choice through **Oxilithos** village. Not only does the road all but disappear at some obscure hamlet, but the surface from there on will ruin a tank, let alone a car or scooter. Those foolish enough to pursue this course pass through Oxilithos to **Paralia (Stomio)**, where the road borders the seafront and a fine pebble, quite wide beach before 'corniching' along the rocky sea's edge. A small pebble beach is followed by another beach with large boulders plonked down on it. The road hereabouts is subject to a certain amount of erosion, in fact it appears to have been gobbled by a big fish in places. This goes on for a kilometre or two as far as **Platana**, a pleasant seaside village with some fishing boats, some holiday industry, a waterfront planted out with young tamarisk trees, some tavernas, a dry river-bed and a quay that juts into the sea.

Back at the main road fork, the left-hand, prettier route, with some stunning views of the distant mountain ranges, proceeds the climb via **Monodrio**, to **Konistres**. This latter is a rather industrial town compared to the other hillside villages, possessing an OTE, Post Office and a Bank. Beyond Konistres the ascent continues on to **Taxiarchi** and **Mendulis**, from whence a road descends to **Platana**, and the main road advances all the way to:-

KYMI TOWN (Kimi) (93km from Chalkis Town) Tel prefix 0222. A 'country town', red roofed settlement, high above the port, Paralia Kymi. The approach road to the centre descends, passing, on the right, the:-

Hotel Kimi (Class D) 20 L. Athinon Tel 22408
Directions: As above.

A single room sharing a bathroom costs 900drs and a double room 1400drs with an en suite double room charged at 1600drs
and the:-

Hotel Halkidis (Class D) 15 L. Athinon Tel 22202
Directions: As above, proclaiming *Rooms With Bath*.

Only double rooms are available. Those sharing a bathroom are charged at 1400drs and en suite 1800drs.

The narrow High St contains the Post Office, on the right, beyond which is the junction with the road off to the right down to the Port, then a Bank and the:

Main Square, Plateia G. Papanicolaou.

This is bordered by the attractive looking, but E Class, *Hotel Krinion* (Tel 22287), with double rooms only, sharing a bathroom, charged at 1300drs, and another Bank. The taxis rank on the Square.

Beyond the Square, bordering the continuation of the High St, is a baker and the OTE (weekdays only between 0730-1510hrs), both on the left, and opposite which are ***Rooms***.

Kymi Town is the site of an Ancient City state which was at its most powerful in the 8th and 4th centuries BC.

A path due north from the town advances some 6km to a wooded mountain-side on which is built the 16th century Monastery Sotiros (or the Saviour), overlooked by a Venetian Fort. The views, if not the setting, are worth the walk.

Back at the High St of Kymi Town, a 'B' Class road serpentines the 4km steeply down towards the sea, past a Folklore Museum, a once grand, now ruined house, a brace of church bells and a campanile, and groves of olives to:-

PARALIA KYMI (Kimi Port) (97km from Chalkis Town)

(Illustration 31). Despite the name, more the port of Kymi Town than the beach, which is not to decry the splendid, sandy beach to the south of the enormous Harbour. The attractions of Kymi Port are such that many intending to visit the islands may well decide to stay on here. One cannot say more, can one? The location presents a most pleasing combination of typical island charm and commercial activity, even if some of the natives appear to have a rather 'couldn't care less attitude' and the number of places in which to lay 'one's head' is severely limited. The waterfront Esplanade, that runs the length of the village, is pleasantly bordered by mature trees. For those not prepared to subject themselves to the rigours of the walk up to the Town both buses and taxis ply the route.

The Esplanade (Odhos ΑΓ ΓΕΩΡΓΙΟΥ) to the right (*Sbo*) of the Ferry-boat Quay (*Tmr* 1C/D4) peters out beyond the *Hotel Beis* (*Tmr* 2A/B2/3) but an unsurfaced road continues on, hemmed in by a rock face and following the curves and sweeps of the rocky sea's edge. Alluring as the exploration might seem, especially taking account of the number of people and cars that wander off in that direction, it is a bore that the track peters out on the backshore of a pebble and rocky seashore, close by which are a few dwellings and a small church.

The Harbour, which not only 'hosts' the ferry-boats but a fishing boat fleet, is enormous, as is the quay, for such a 'way-station' of a place. Despite the present size, the main sea wall is still being extended. The 'bit' of harbour foreshore, hemmed in by the Esplanade wall, is rather scrubbly, with grass growing, rubbish a-gathering and a few small boats quietly rotting. The south Harbour wall sprouts an enormous piece of 'meccano' which must have been used for cargo handling in the past.

The cliff-face on the inland side of the Esplanade, approximately behind one of the general stores, has a section of rather strange, dam-type concrete wall with the inevitable graffiti scrawled across the surface.

ARRIVAL BY BUS

Buses connect with Chalkis Town and directly to Athens.

ARRIVAL BY FERRY

The port is the main jumping-off point for Skyros island. There is also a weekly ferry-boat service to the Sporades islands of Alonissos and Skopelos as well as the far flung NE Aegean islands of Ag Estratios, Limnos and mainland Kavala.

THE ACCOMMODATION & EATING OUT

The Accommodation If Kymi Port has a drawback, apart from the downright ignorance of a few of its inhabitants, of which more later, it is the lack of accommodation.

Rooms (*Tmr* 3B3) No. 59 Tel 22638

Directions: From the bottom of the Ferry-boat Quay (*Tmr* B4) and or the Bus stop (*Tmr* 4B5), turn right (*Sbo*) along the waterfront.

A double room sharing the bathroom in this rather basic but very clean and pleasant house, costs 1000-1200drs mid-season. Also available is a double room with en suite bathroom. This latter includes the use of a kitchen complete with a 1930s fridge (about the size of a bank vault), a gas ring and the usual rickety little table, covered with an oilcloth, and chairs – also rickety. The landlady is a nice, smiley lady but has no English.

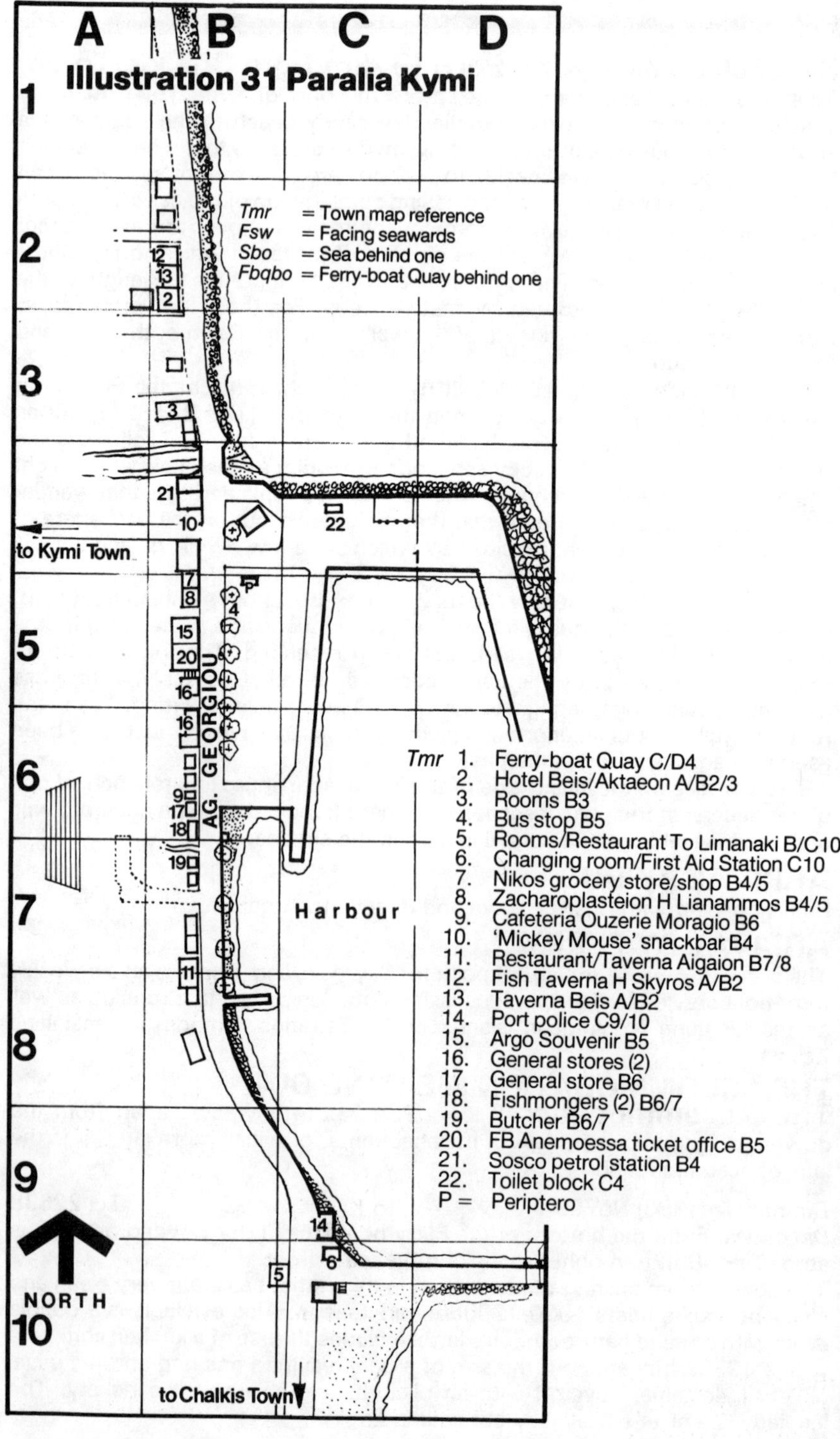
A
B
C
D
Illustration 31 Paralia Kymi
1
2
3
4
5
6
7
8
9
10
Tmr = Town map reference
Fsw = Facing seawards
Sbo = Sea behind one
Fbqbo = Ferry-boat Quay behind one
to Kymi Town
AG. GEORGIOU
Harbour
to Chalkis Town
NORTH
Tmr 1. Ferry-boat Quay C/D4
2. Hotel Beis/Aktaeon A/B2/3
3. Rooms B3
4. Bus stop B5
5. Rooms/Restaurant To Limanaki B/C10
6. Changing room/First Aid Station C10
7. Nikos grocery store/shop B4/5
8. Zacharoplasteion H Lianammos B4/5
9. Cafeteria Ouzerie Moragio B6
10. 'Mickey Mouse' snackbar B4
11. Restaurant/Taverna Aigaion B7/8
12. Fish Taverna H Skyros A/B2
13. Taverna Beis A/B2
14. Port police C9/10
15. Argo Souvenir B5
16. General stores (2)
17. General store B6
18. Fishmongers (2) B6/7
19. Butcher B6/7
20. FB Anemoessa ticket office B5
21. Sosco petrol station B4
22. Toilet block C4
P = Periptero

Rooms (Restaurant) To Limanaki (*Tmr* 5B/C10) Tel 22732
Directions: At the far left-hand end (*Sbo*) of the waterfront, from the Ferry-boat Quay, across the road from the changing room/First Aid station (*Tmr* 6C10) and overlooking the outset of the main beach.

Hotels Beis/Aktaeon (*Tmr* 2A/B2/3) (C Class) Tel 22604
Directions: From the bottom of the Ferry-boat Quay turn right (*Sbo*) and the hotel is on the left. The D Class *Hotel Aktaeon* is under the same ownership and management. At the modern *Hotel Beis* all rooms have an en suite bathroom with a single room charged at 1700drs and a double room 2365drs.

If stuck, Nikos or his smiley mother, the owners of the grocery store/shop (*Tmr* 7B4/5), close to the bottom of the Ferry-boat Quay, may well be able to help with advice. Nikos speaks excellent English, his mother none.

See **Babis Spanos, Restaurant/Taverna Aigaion, The Eating Out**

The Eating Out It is whilst indulging the delights of Kymi Port kafeneions that visitors may well be unfortunate enough to experience the not so pleasant, couldn't care less character of one or two of the locals.

Zacharoplasteion H Lianammos (*Tmr* 8B4/5)
Directions: Across the wide Esplanade from the Bus stop, close to the bottom of the Ferry-boat Quay.

Considering its prime position, convenient to the Bus stop and Ferry-boat Quay, it is a great pity that the patron is in dire danger of winning the *Golden Surly* award. This well merited decoration is only considered for the management of accommodation and eating places who register an extraordinarily consistent degree of surliness and unpleasantness. Once he tore a ferry-boat timetable off the inside of his window as we were reading the details thereon. On another occasion he declined to serve us, advising it was too early at 0900hrs, he was closed and that we must return later, after which he waited on a number of locals...! This is despite advertising a breakfast and opening hours between 0700-0200hrs (next day)... If a client can obtain service, the prices are not unreasonable with a bottle of beer or a glass of 3 star Metaxa charged at 80drs and nuts mezes 20drs. It may be difficult to get served but the quietest request for the bill results in immediate attention.

Despite the prominent sign over the awning, 'another elsewhere' is agent for the **FB Anemoessa** (*See* **Ferry-boat Ticket Offices, A To Z**).

Cafeteria Ouzerie Moragio (*Tmr* 9B6).
Directions: Further to the left (*Sbo*) from the Ferry-boat Quay with green chairs.

The service here is 'iffy' – they may or may not serve a client. If a customer accepts the more expensive *Kaiser* bottled beer, fine, if not it is necessary to state the choice, say an Amstel, but they only serve the stubby 330gm bottles

The Mickey-Mouse Snackbar (*Tmr* 10B4)
Directions: On the corner of the road up to Kymi Town.

There are seats on the narrow pavement in front of the snackbar as well as across the Esplanade, close to a small church and in the shade of the trees. The owner, bearded and in his middle 30s, prefers clients to sit across the road due, he graphically explains, to the smell emanating from the storm drains. A large Nes meh ghala, without saucer, costs 80drs.

Restaurant/Taverna Aigaion (*Tmr* 11B7/8) Tel 22641
Directions: Two-thirds of the way along the Esplanade, towards the left (*Sbo*) from the Ferry-boat Quay.

This barn-like establishment may have been known by another name. A garish sign over the entrance proclaims *Spanos*, the owners surname. To further confuse matters there is a sign advertising the *Xenodoxeion (Hotel) Cafe-bar To Korali* (Tel 0228 22212). Now, despite the fact that there is no doubt that this restaurant has accommodation, which appears to be redundant at the present, the sign is for a hotel 100m or so further on down the road – so why the Politicha telephone exchange?

If Babis Spanos is not present it may well be that his American Greek friend Athonasos, or Tom for short, is running the place. Tom is a ship's captain in the USA and an American citizen, due to his Suez pilot father opting to emigrate to the New World. Being a good Greek, and because he keeps his yacht in the harbour, Tom returns to Kymi Port every year. Most evenings the high ceilinged interior. with an enormous walk-in fridge fascia blanking off the back wall, fills with locals. The kitchen is to the right and the toilets are through a door 'in the fridge'. The management thoughtfully provide a massive bolt on both the ladies and gentleman's toilet doors. It just seems a pity there is no keep in which the bolt can locate, thus locking out incomers! There are also some pleasantly sited, tree shaded taverna tables and chairs across the Esplanade, edging the Harbour quay wall. From here it is fun to watch the minnows 'hurricane' about the messy shallows after bits and pieces of bread.

The meals may well be on the 'cool side' but the food is extremely good and plentiful, the menu varied and the prices very reasonable, especially when compared to other Sporades offerings. A meal for two of a very large Greek salad, a plate of green beans, a helping of pistachio, a dish of stuffed tomatoes (160drs), 2 bottles of retsina and bread cost 920drs. A lunch time 'snack' for two of tasty, minced beef steak meatballs and potatoes (200drs each), a large Greek salad, two beers and bread cost 720drs. An enormous Greek salad (180drs), a plate of 'giants' (beans – 180drs), a splendid moussaka (250drs), beef with potatoes (very tasty indeed – 380drs), a bottle of retsina (80drs) and bread (20drs each) costs 1110drs, rounded down to 1100drs. The charge for bread at 20drs may seem a little expensive but there is plenty of it. To those who have been to, say, Skiathos a meal here will represent amazing value in money, quantity and quality. No need to say any more really except that it is possible to simply order a drink in the quieter hours and that the taverna is open midday and evenings. A beer and a bottle of *Sprite* cost 120drs.

Fish taverna H Skyros (*Tmr* 12A/B2)
Directions: To the right (*Sbo*) from the bottom of the Ferry-boat Quay, beyond the *Hotel Beis*. Looks interesting but lacks 'throughput' out of the height of season.

There is also the *Restaurant (Rooms) To Limanaki* (*Tmr* 5B/C10), to the far left (*Sbo*) and the *Taverna Beis* (*Tmr* 13A/B2) to the right from the bottom of the Ferry-boat Quay.

THE A TO Z OF USEFUL INFORMATION

BANKS It is necessary to go to Kymi Town.

BEACHES There is a splendid, sandy beach (*Tmr* C10) at the south, far left-hand end (*Sbo*) of the Esplanade, that is on the other side of the Harbour protection wall. An onshore wind tends to make the shallows rather kelpy.

On the north side of the main Ferry-boat Quay is a pebbly, triangular smidgin of foreshore (*Tmr* B3/4), on to the back of which is 'culverted' a summer-dry river-bed.

BREAD SHOPS Nikos Grocery Store/Shop (*Tmr* 7B4/5) sells bread. There is a baker in Kymi Town. A daily bread van, with the sign *CERA* on the windscreen, parks at various spots along the Esplanade, including adjacent to the ***Rooms*** at No. 59 (*Tmr* 3B3) at about 1145hrs.

BUSES One bus stop (*Tmr* 4B5) is close to the bottom of the Ferry-boat Quay and another by the office of the Port police (*Tmr* 14C9/10). Buses, in the main, meet the ferries, as do taxis, even if owners of accommodation don't.

Buses dash up and down between the Port and Town and to and from the Port and Chalkis Town, every hour.

COMMERCIAL SHOPPING AREA The Esplanade is lined with businesses some of which include, from the bottom of the Ferry-boat Quay (*Tmr* B4) and to the left (*Sbo*):-

Nikos Grocery Store/Shop (*Tmr* 7B4/5); Argo Souvenir (*Tmr* 15B5); General Stores (*Tmr* 16B5 & 16B6); a General Store (*Tmr* 17B6), in an old roofed building, advertising car insurance (ΑΣΦΑΛΕΙΑΙ ΑΥΤΟΚΙΝΗΤΟΝ) and with a tuna tail nailed to the door; a couple of fishmongers side by side (ΙΧΘΥΟΜΟΛΕΙΟ) (*Tmr* 18B6/7) and a Butcher (*Tmr* 19B6/7).

A periptero (*Tmr* P.B4/5) stands on the harbour side of the Esplanade, opposite Nikos Store.

FERRY-BOATS The small **CF Anemoessa** connects daily with Skyros island, even if the 1700hrs departure doesn't leave much time to land at Linaria Port, catch the bus to Skyros Town, find accommodation, take one's bearings and grab a meal. Once a week (at least) there is a Kymi connection to the NE Aegean and another to other Sporades islands, but it must be stressed that detailed information is extremely difficult to ascertain. For instance, even on the same timetable a particular NE Aegean ferry is listed as sailing, variously, on Saturday or Friday, whilst on another schedule the same boat is detailed as sailing on Sunday!

Ferry-boat timetable (Mid-season)
Please note most of the following is subject to even more checking than usual!

Day	Departure time	Ferry-boat	Ports/Islands of Call
Daily	1700hrs	Anemoessa	Linaria (Skyros).
NB At the height of season (July & August) there is also an 1100hrs boat.			
Thursday	1700hrs		Alonissos, Skopelos.
Saturday	2300hrs	Skopelos	Ag Estratios (0615+),Limnos,Kavala(M).

+ Next day

For up to date information in respect of the **CF Anemoessa** telephone (0222) 22020; for other craft telephone Athens 3632575 or Piraeus 4172415.

Kymi to Skyros: One-way fare 720drs; duration 2½hrs
(despite some 'official' indications of 1¾hrs)
Kymi to Alonissos: One-way fare 1400drs; duration 3hrs
Kymi to Skopelos: One-way fare 1520drs; duration 3½hrs.

FERRY-BOAT TICKET OFFICES Tickets for the **FB Anemoessa** are sold from an office (*Tmr* 20B5), to the left (*Sbo*) of Argo Souvenir shop. The Sosco petrol station (*Tmr* 21B4), across the Esplanade from the bottom of the Ferry-boat Quay, is the agent for Loucas Nomicos, owners of the **FB Skiathos, Skopelos, Aegeus, Skyros and Thira**. Both ticket offices open prior to a ship's departure.

MEDICAL CARE
Chemists & Pharmacies None although some of the stores sell proprietary medicines.

OTE The official office is at Kymi Town, but Nikos store (*Tmr* 7B4/5) has a metered phone from which international calls can be made – in amongst the cans and customers. A local telephone kiosk lurks near the Church at the bottom of the Ferry-boat Quay.

PETROL There is the Sosco Petrol Station and Garage (*Tmr* 21B4) on the Esplanade, close to the Kymi Town turning. The garage has a water tap by the pumps. The taciturn owner's son has married an English girl, so he (the son) speaks good English. A repair workshop (ΓΚΑΡΑΖ) is sited further along the Esplanade, to the left (*Sbo*).

POLICE
Port (*Tmr* 14C9/10).

POST OFFICE None, but Nikos Store (*Tmr* 7B4/5) sells stamps and there is a post box on the outside wall. Otherwise it is necessary to visit Kymi Town.

TAXIS Any number park on the Esplanade, in the area of the Ferry-boat Quay.

TOILETS There is a toilet block (*Tmr* 22C4) at the outset of the Ferry-boat Quay.

ROUTE TWO (Northern island) To Agiokampos via Psachna, Strofilia, Vassilika, Istiaea & back via Loutra Edipsos, Ilia, Rovies & Limni (272km) with excursions to Politika & Ag Georgios

On the way out of Chalkis Town for the north of the island, the coast edging road passes a large, beautiful expanse of tide exposed, sandy beach. There is a rocky harbour mole at the far end which the tides leave high and dry at low tide. Across the road from the beach is the *Kastello Sex Show*. Oh yes!

The northern urban outskirts of Chalkis Town are a complete mishmash of houses, gardens, backyards, edifices, incomplete buildings, scrapyards, boat sales outfits, hotels, smart apartment blocks, marble works, concrete block makers, (another) sex show, petrol stations, lorry repair workshops, the occasional olive grove, an out of town supermarket, porcelain factory, reinforcing bar cutting yards, fields of rubble, the occasional combine harvester standing in a ½ acre field, tyre shops, service stations, the inevitable closed factory and dead buses *et al*.

NEA ARTAKI (8km from Chalkis Town) This development, which is almost a suburb of Chalkis Town, has a smartish look from a distance but in actuality is nothing more than a conglomeration of the rag-bag sprawl so far detailed from Chalkis Town to Nea Artaki. The hillbilly kernel of the settlement is still evident.

The B Class *Hotel/Motel Bel Air* (Tel 422643) has single rooms with en suite bathrooms from 1700drs and double rooms en suite from 2500drs.

A turning off, in an easterly, inland direction leads to **Katheni**, the outset of a water abundant area, and on to **Kato Steni** and **Steni Dirphos** (35km from Chalkis Town). The Stenis' are rather Alpine in nature, similar to Spili on Crete, with freshwater springs and backed by the Dirphys mountain range which rises to 1743m (Mt Dirphys). There are two C Class hotels, the *Dirphys* (Tel 51217) and the *Steni* (Tel 51221). Taking the tracks to the various mountain villages and crossing over to the eastern coastline provides marvellous and varied walks, views, natural habitat, flora, fauna and, for the very energetic, a visit to the Chiliadon Monastery, close to the shoreline. The authorities, for some extraordinary reason, wish to open up this comparatively secluded countryside by constructing a metalled link road with Kymi. Oh dear!

Back at the main road the route passes between 50 and 100m of the seafront. The north end of Nea Artaki has a fishing port set in tidal sand flats. Commerce appears to sprawl unchecked into the surrounding countryside.

PSACHNA (16km from Chalkis Town) At the road junction to the left of the dusty town, which is set in scrubbly surrounds, the main road continues in a north-easterly direction.

The left-hand fork makes off towards the west coast across flat, rather dirty market garden scenery. Close to the sea's edge is a structure that looks horribly like a refinery of some sort. The road here runs along the sea's edge past a number of old and now disused, stone built, windowless and often roofless industrial buildings, before passing beneath a conveyor belt system carrying ore. The shore is mainly rock with some pebble here and there. The road now turns inland through improving, but still flat countryside and narrows down over a flat plain of fields and old olive groves until the outskirts of:-

POLITIKA (20km from Chalkis Town) A not very pretty, commercial village with a narrow, winding High St that is edged by old buildings, a petrol station, a police station and a doctor's surgery.

A turning to the left, in the middle of the village, is tarmacadamed and slowly descends, through olive groves and pastureland to:-

PARALIA POLITIKA (21km from Chalkis Town) The road joins the long, flat waterfront opposite a quay jutting into the sea and around which cluster fishing boats.

To the right (*Fsw*), the 'Esplanade' runs along the boring, arrow-straight backshore which edges a narrow band of pebble beach all the way to a navigation light marked, pebble spit. Here the road turns inland whilst a wide track continues along the barren coastline, now bordered by a mishmash of holiday homes and villas, some patrolled by guard dogs, only to abruptly come to an end in this presumably exclusive, but rather unattractive cul-de-sac.

Back at Politika, the road climbs steeply up fire ravaged hillsides through the mountainside, winding, friendly village of **Nerotrivia**(23km from Chalkis Town), which possesses a store and taverna. From Nerotrivia the country lane 'roller coasters' over the lovely countryside of the foothills of the massive mountains to the right, all the way down to:-

DAPHNI (27km from Chalkis Town) This sea-level hamlet possesses a pebble beach, despite some maps indicating that Daphni is located in the hills or that there is no seashore of any consequence. Admittedly the beach is only some 3m wide but the sea is clear. In fact I am of the opinion that the location is far more attractive than Paralia Politika – not that this comparison means a lot. Unfortunately there is no accommodation available, and the track runs out on the seashore, alongside a private caravan site. At the height of summer the owners of the caravans result in the location being both noisy and crowded. The few original buildings are being supplemented by a scattering of holiday homes and villas. The Ormos Politika fishing fleet motors round to this sweep of coast to fish.

Back at Psachna, the main road has to climb across a mountain range. This serpentine route is attractive, if continuously ascending through pine covered slopes 'turns you on'. The reverse side of the hillsides are covered with a pleasant mix of deciduous trees, a lot of which are mature, large holm oaks. At about 42km from Chalkis Town is a veritable 'bee farm' of different coloured hives covering some acres of parched meadowland hemmed in by the forest. An extensive, summer-dry river gorge edges one side of the road, which is bordered with beehives for several kilometres, in almost alpine scenery. The tree cover becomes predominately pine but is still interspersed with a variety of deciduous trees. At about 46km from Chalkis Town the lower slopes of the mountains give way to a fertile plain of fields and copses amply planted with trees, some of which have substantial boles. The gorge now widens out, on the right-hand side, to become a wide, still summer-dry river-bed and the road surface, good until hereabouts, commences to evince signs of a deteriorating surface.

PROKOPION (50km from Chalkis Town) A smallish, spread out but pleasant country village set in extremely lush countryside. In the area ferns grow to 2-3m in height, the roadside is densely tree lined and the river-bed, still on the right-hand side, is water bearing. The pleasant farmland, picturesquely spaced out amongst trees and orchards, supports grazing sheep. The winding road snakes across the plain which is edged by steep hillsides. It almost could be England. This is not such a wide-of-the-mark comment as it may appear as Prokipion is the area in which was located the 12,000 acre woodland estate of the English Noel-Baker family. Francis Noel-Baker, a former Labour MP, inherited the land and a mansion, as well as a host of problems. The original purchase, by his great grandfather in 1832, increasingly became the focal point for local dissent. This exploded in a 'spot of bother', in 1975, after which the ownership issue developed into a point of principle of the Socialist Government in Athens. They appropriated the land after which the matter fell into the hands of the lawyers. My last notes relate to 1984 – but I hope all has worked out well for the family.

Some 4km from the next large centre of population, the thick vegetation finally begins to thin out, despite which the river-bed holds an appreciable amount of slow flowing water. A petrol station heralds the approach to:-

MANDOULION (60km from Chalkis Town) A dusty, working township off to the right of the main roadway, across a bridge spanning the river. Mandoulion possesses an OTE.

The main road is signposted Istiaea.

At **Kirinthos** (61km from Chalkis Town) a vicious, rutted track, extensively plane tree lined on one side, makes off to the right. The trees are probably succoured by the running stream that the main road bridges. Another right again, at the the unsigned fork, advances to:-

KRIA VRYSI (66km from Chalkis Town) A small hamlet laying back and separated from the shore by some quite large, scrubbly, grass growing dunes. Over the crest of the sand hills reveals a very long, pebble and dark sand beach. The right-hand end (*Fsw*) of this long, flat bay is terminated by a quite pretty, small headland and pinnacle of rock. On the island of Skiathos this location would undoubtedly be a day trip outing! The hamlet sports an almost grand, old manor house and, close by, an 'English parish', hand operated water pump. These are to be observed here and there on Evia. There is evidence of a height of summer taverna.

Back at Kirinthos the main road commences to gently climb through pleasantly wooded hillsides, mainly pine trees which are being tapped for resin, prior to descending towards the village of:-

STROFILIA (66km from Chalkis Town) This is the main junction of a westerly road to Limni (and the clockwise route round the north Evian coastal road) and the northern road to Ag Anna (the counter clockwise direction round the top of the island).

From Strofilia, in the right-hand northern direction, the road once again climbs a well vegetated hillside, mainly supporting olive groves with outbreaks of pine trees, towards the hilltop. These trees are tapped for their resin. At 68km from Chalkis Town, the road is still ascending countryside which is almost pastoral with fields and trees, prior to:-

AG ANNA (71km from Chalkis Town) A rather 'mangy' village, strangely hosting a museum and, not so strangely, a petrol station.

Beyond Ag Anna the route continues to rise, but now across less tree covered but still well grassed meadows past the right-hand turning to **Beach Frigani**.

The road surface has deteriorated sufficiently in spots to prompt all sorts of signs including exclamation marks! The route now switchbacks through scenery which is mostly fields, divided by banks of ferns and low shrubs as well as a scattering of woodland copses.

Prior to **Pappades** village (82km from Chalkis Town), through which the main road narrows down, is a woodyard, a very rare sight on a Greek island but essential due to the extensive Evian forests. I can only remember seeing a similar enterprise on Thassos island (NE Aegean).

At last the road commences to gently descend through pine trees which thinly cover the hillsides. There are lovely views over the surrounding hills and countryside towards:-

VASSILIKA (91km From Chalkis Town) A long, hillside village, the upper portion of which is typically Greek with vistas over the magnificent looking, 3-5km stretch of **Vassilika (Psaropuli) Beach**. Both the beach and the Port police are signposted off to the right.

Beyond Vassilika the landscape is a mix of hill-topping pines, olive groves and fields, amongst which are spread out batches of beehives.

ELLINIKA (99km from Chalkis Town) There is another sign to a beach. The villages of Ellinika and Vassilika are supposedly so titled in connection with the sea battle of Artemisium. This was named after the nearby Artemision headland, is so called from the presence of a Temple to the Greek goddess Artemis. The Naval engagement between the fleets of Xerxes, the Persian King, and the Greeks took place close to the headland, in about 480 BC.

The landscape is still hills covered with pine trees, beneath the branches of which are 'droves' of beehives which are painted in the individual colours of their owners. A woodyard heralds the outskirts of the village of **Agriovotano** (105km from Chalkis Town), from whence the road descends through fields, some of which support grapevines, and continues through pine tree covered hillsides crossing and recrossing a dry river-bed, prior to levelling out and leaving a large restaurant/ taverna on the left, close to **Gouves**. From now on the route is bordered by cultivated fields and olive groves.

ARTEMISION (114km from Chalkis Town) A 'donkey-dropping' of a settlement with a petrol station.

To the right of the road between Artemision and the next village, is *Pefki Beach and Camping Pefki*, a facility frequently signposted from as far away as 100km. Spread about in the fields are a number of smart houses, as well as the occasional skeletal framework of a yet-to-be-completed dwelling, in the basements of which families appear to favour camping out.

ASMINION (121km from Chalkis Town) This pleasant, small village is approached through two very tall plane trees bordering the road and groves of lofty pine trees. There are least three houses offering ***Rooms***, a bakery and, beyond the village, a *Shell* petrol station.

The road, which edges the sea, traverses the coastal plain, itself bordered by distant hills. The fields are planted out with maize, which seems to grow as 'high as an elephant's eye', in addition to which there are neat orchards and occasional, large groves of deciduous and olive trees, throughout which are dotted the occasional homestead. What is so pleasant is the total lack of factory and junk development that the Greeks seem unable to resist 'planting out' in otherwise pleasing vistas. The coastal plain narrows down as the low hills inexorably close in on the sea's edge. The road swings inland past a cement works, running along the edge of a very wide, summer-dry river bed, which it crosses on the untidy approaches to:-

ISTIAEA (131km from Chalkis Town) Tel prefix 0226. Despite Istiaea's distinguished ancient history, the modern, large town is not particularly attractive and the signposting is non-existent. To continue it is necessary to turn right at the main square road junction, after which take the next major road to the left. There are at least two hotels which include the D Class *Hermes* (Tel 52245) and the E Class *Neon* (Tel 52226).

OREI (137km from Chalkis Town) Tel prefix 0226. Beyond a rise, the road shoots into the small fishing port, where drivers would be deposited in the sea, if the road did not veer sharply to the left along the waterfront. There are some ***Rooms*** and three hotels, the C Class *Evia* (Tel 71263), the C Class *Corali* (Tel 71217) and the E Class *Kentrikon* (Tel 71525).

NEOS PIRGOS (137km from Chalkis Town) Tel prefix 0226. Another fishing boat village with a beach and a fairly new, small harbour at the north end. Close to the Harbour are several houses offering ***Rooms*** and three hotels, the C Class *Vyzantion* (Tel 71600) and two D Class hotels, the *Akroyali* (Tel 71435) and the *Oasis* (Tel 71422).

As the road rounds the headland of Ag Sostis, the narrow channel between Evia and the mainland hoves into sight, as does an inshore, ruined castle capped islet, beyond which is a mid-channel buoy. There is a kelp and rubbish covered beach.

From the main road a turning to the right advances through olive and broad leafed trees to:-

AGIOKAMPOS (141km from Chalkis Town) Set on a very large, flat bay. The road junctions with the backshore of the tiny, pleasant port at the far left-hand end (*Fsw*). To the right the pleasantly tree planted, gently curving, shingle waterfront bordering road edges the sea, finishing up on the Ferry-boat Quay. The 'Esplanade' is lined by small, low, old, stone wall houses capped with red roofs, in amongst which are a number of villas, a taverna, a kafeneion and, at the outset of the Ferry-boat Quay, a restaurant.

Beyond the Ferry-boat Quay, the pebbly foreshore carries on to a spit beyond which is a headland. An unmade backshore track appears to go on 'for ever', following the curves of the shore's edge.

The 'landing craft' ferries depart for the mainland village of **Glypha** daily at: 0730, 1130, 1500, 1730 & 1930hrs. The ferries from Glypha depart daily at: 0645, 1040, 1400, 1630 & 1900hrs. The one-way passenger fare costs 120drs, a car 775drs and the voyage duration is 30 minutes.

Taxis park on the quay, which is a good thing as there aren't any ***Rooms*** are in evidence.

Back on the main road, the route rises through olive groves and verdant countryside, set in low hills, prior to dropping down to:-

AGIOS (141km from Chalkis Town) A big, agricultural village with a large church, two or three kafeneions and tavernas and a petrol station.

The 'B Class', narrow road from Agios winds on through more olive groves and small vineyards to a ridiculously wide sweep of road, whereon surprise, surprise, a petrol station, adjacent to the large 'High St' village of **Edipsos (Aedipsos)**.

This bypass continues to advance past a muddle of agricultural holdings, in amongst which are a number of smart new buildings under construction, descending to the Esplanade backing waterfront of:-

LOUTRA EDIPSOS (Lutra Aedipsos, Edipsou) (153km from Chalkis Town anticlockwise or 119km clockwise) Tel prefix 0226. A classy health spa and Greek holiday resort that dates back to ancient times. Legend has it that even Hercules partook of the restorative powers of these cure-all springs.

On the approach a sign affixed to one of the trees that line the water's edge proclaims *No Camping*. On my last visit, just beneath this injunction, a lone tent was strung between a couple of tree trunks. The Esplanade is bordered by swish restaurants, their patios, and shops. On the right is the large Ferry-boat Quay, beyond which vehicles are diverted to the left into the grid street structure of the well laid out, prosperous town. One or two of the major streets have flower and shrub planted central islands. The Esplanade, now a very wide, tree shaded pedestrian way, proceeds on with fishing boats moored to the quayside.

Many ***Rooms*** are scattered throughout the town, as are literally dozens and dozens of hotels. There is an OTE, Post Office and several banks. On the Ferry-boat Quay a sign has been erected by *The Ministry of Mercantile Harbour Corps Headquarters* entitled:-

'Instructions to Bathers'
No. 1 Do not get into sea being tired or perspired.
No. 2 Do not swim with a full stomach.
No. 3 Do not exaggerate in long divings.
No. 6 If you perceive a swimmer asking for help and you do not know how to help (him) call immediately for help (– 'or both sink'?).
No. 7 Submarine fishing among bathers is forbidden as well as with diving apparatus.

Loutra Edipsos connects to mainland **Arkitsa** by ferry and these landing craft style boats depart daily at: 0600, 0800, 1000, 1200, 1400, 1600, 1800 & 2015hrs. The Arkitsa ferries depart daily at: 0715, 0915, 1115, 1315, 1515, 1715, 1915 & 2115hrs. The trip takes 50mins and costs 180drs for passengers and 920drs for vehicles.

There are Athens buses which catch the ferries (well they would get very wet if they didn't) but to confuse matters, the Loutra Edipsos departure times are listed as 0815, 1400 & 1630hrs. Now I don't profess to quite understand the time discrepancies... Athens (260 Liossion St, tel 8317153) bus departures are listed daily at: 0645, 1245 & 1445hrs. The journey time is 3½hrs and the cost is 715drs, plus the ferry fare.

Note that at the height of the season a passenger boat connects Loutra to Ag Georgios (at the north-west tip of Evia) and then proceeds to Kamena Vourla, on the mainland. Kamena Vourla has a scheduled Athens bus connection which departs from Kamena daily: every ½hr between 0530-2000hrs & 2100hrs. Buses depart from Athens (260 Liossion St, tel 8317158) daily at: 0615, then every ½hr between 0700-1900hrs & 2030hrs.

EXCURSION TO LOUTRA EDIPSOS SURROUNDS

Excursion To Ag Georgios This is a five star region of Evia (for others *See* **Kymi, Route One & Route Two**). From Loutra Edipsos it is possible to make a well worthwhile foray to Ag Georgios by proceeding westwards along a coastal track. This borders a gritty beach edging a biscuit rock sea's edge. Initially there is a pleasant grove of trees on the inland side. The shore is messy and not very attractive, becoming large pebble and finally rocky at the far end.

From Edipsos village there is the more conventional road, leading to:-

AG NIKOLAOS (3km from Loutra Edipsos) A small, Greek tourist, seaside resort with a very long, road edged – but narrow beach. The backshore is gritty sand, the middleshore is sandy and the sea's edge (at low tide) is made up of biscuit rock lying at the angle of the beach. There are four pensions, the *Ag Nikolaos* (Tel 22494), the *Chryssi Ammoudia* (Tel 22685), the *Kastoria* (Tel 23044) and the *Park* (Tel 22714). They are all B Class and charge almost the same rates of 1000drs for a single room sharing the bathroom, 1250drs for a double room sharing and 1750drs for a double room with en suite bathroom.

The road climbs out of Ag Nikolaos into pleasant, agricultural countryside 'sprinkled' with olive groves and the occasional villa, running parallel to the undulating coastline. Back at sea-level enough land is left between the road and the backshore to allow olive trees on both sides of the road. There is a narrow, sea-blown rubbish strewn and kelpy shore before it becomes apparent that the route is bordering the large, almost fjord like Ormos Edipsos. The inland side of the road is low-lying and marshy with the occasional, inland, salt water lake and pond. Where the road commences to follow the curve of the bottom of the bay there is a pleasantly wide, tree and shrub growing swathe of land to the left of the highway bordered, on the far side, by a delightful, wide crescent of yellow, gritty sand edging a steeply shelving sea bottom and very clear, clean sea, even if it is weedy in patches. The rise and fall of the tide exposes a fine sweep of still gritty sand at low tide. There is a chapel, a portion of the shore which is used as an *ad hoc* boatyard and, on the inland side of the road, a disco. All the way round the sweep of the bay are sporadic, unofficial camping sites. At the far side of the bay the road climbs steeply away from the shoreline into the hills towards:-

GIALTRA (Jialtra) (16km from Loutra Edipsos) A large, 'bubbling', ethnic mountain village, way above the coast, and through which the road undulates. There is a shop here and there and, obviously, a kafeneion or three which encourage the locals to sit out, sprawled across the 'High Street'.

The road drops quickly away from the village, winding through attractive, spacious scenery. One blot on the landscape is a large factory building set in the middle of nowhere and for no apparent reason.

LOUTRA GIALTRON (18km from Loutra Edipsos) The shambling, but attractive backwoods fishing port (of Gialtra) is spread along the tamarisk tree planted seafront with the occasional kafeneion and taverna dotted about. The narrow seashore is pebbly.

The road continues westwards following the contours of the coastline, through an area spotted with villas and ***Rooms***, on to a coastal plain scattered with habitations and bordered by the cliffs of a mountain spine on the inland side. Further on, to the left, in a thickly wooded area, is the long perimeter fence of a *Club Mediterranee* complex. The trees are mainly pines, beyond which is a football pitch, followed by more dwellings and:-

AG GEORGIOS (29km from Loutra Edipsos) The road into the 'village proper' passes a water fountain on the right, ***Rooms***, an olive grove, a small petrol station and a village store before turning left on to the waterfront 'Esplanade', close to a Ferry-boat Quay. The waterfront road to the right proceeds on and on and on, following the jinks, curves and contours of this busy, sometimes bustling, small fishing boat village.

Ag Georgios is an absolute find as long as the lack of a sandy beach is of no concern.

From where the main road joins with the waterfront, to the left is a not overlong, backshore track bordering which are a baker and ***Rooms***, prior to the *San Antonio Taverna*. The shore is pebbly but there are beach showers.

To the right, the road stretches the full length of the tree planted waterfront Esplanade. Various, small, short rickety piers jut into the sea. Across the road are a scattering of kafeneions, a couple of tavernas, a periptero and two B Class pensions. They are the *Vachos* and the nice looking *Alexandros* (Tel 33208), which is close to the little store that sells loukoumades, with en suite double rooms only, costing 1850drs a night.

The women folk help the men prepare the nets and sort the catch. The presence of *Club Mediterranee* has resulted in some quirkish deviations from the quiet, rural nature of the village, as evidenced by a number of signs in French, one of which proclaims *We speak French and Italian*, and the presence of the Boutique Stratos.

At the height of season a passenger boat connects with Loutra Edipsos and Kamena Vourla on the mainland (*See* **Loutra Edipsos**).

The delights of this place are not yet exhausted. The road continues on beyond the village, only to curve inland but off which a rough track hugs the coastline for another 4 or more kilometres. The first section of foreshore is messy, pebbly and kelpy but the countryside becomes increasingly attractive, as do the vistas. There is the occasional pebbly patch of shore. Away to the left is the mainland and offshore is Monolia islet. The track, either side of which are randomly scattered, tiny plots on which are jacked up single room, portable prefabs, peters out in neat countryside on a pebble and sand spit past which glide the Ag Konstantinos(M) to Skiathos ferry-boats.

Back at the far, east end of **Loutra Edipsos**, and continuing on the anticlockwise **Route Two**, a steep road winds past more ***Rooms*** and the *Grand Hotel*, which is set in lovely, formal flower-planted gardens. The road then joins a dramatic highway. In 1987 this was still in the process of being completed but is passable as long as drivers are prepared to wait while bulldozers clear the path. The wide road majestically sweeps along the coastline some third of the way up the mountain face. To the right is a bare, precipitous slope into the sea and on the left towering cliff-faces. Whatever the maps show, this 'Evia corniche' proceeds all the way along to join the existing coastal road at Rovies.

ILIA (110km from Chalkis Town) A small, exposed fishing village stretched along the waterfront and probably not accessible to motor vehicles until recent years. The position is rather exposed because there is no bay, only the bare, steep mountainside which steeply slides into the long coastline. A summer-dry river-bed tumbles down through the settlement. There's a cafe-bar/-kafeneion and a taverna. The shore is made up of grit and large pebbles and the sea-bed, of rounded stones, shelves very steeply beneath the delightfully clear water. The best swimming is to the left (*Fsw*), just beyond the main quay where the small pebbles of the shore extend into the sea.

At present (1987) the route through Rovies is still under construction but it is possible to get through as long as the construction engineers are not dynamiting. Where the new highway joins the existing coastal road, there are, between the road and the shore, a number of strange, unfinished precast concrete buildings, possibly of a planned holiday complex.

The road climbs and veers away from the continuous foreshore of pebble and low tide grit before dropping back to both sea-level and the backshore. The main road sweeps past the turning down to the seaside village of:-

ROVIES (98km from Chalkis Town) Tel prefix 0227. A spread out, 'way-station' of a Greek holiday resort. The settlement appears remote from the shore, which is not surprising as the main band of the development is about 80m back from and runs parallel to the long stretch of seashore. The beach is not overly attractive, despite being wide and very long, with a pebble shore and a low water strip of sand and grit. The sea is very clean but... Perhaps it is the almost total lack of tree cover (although the authorities are planting out some saplings) and the fact that Rovies does not snuggle in a bay but stands on a long stretch of bare coast.

There appear to be the ruins of a medieval castle, close by the Church, there is a petrol station (naturally), ***Rooms*** and the E Class *Hotel Rovies* (Tel 71213).

About 8km to the east-north-east of Rovies is the:-

Monastery of David Geronta A 15th century order famed, not only for its founder but due to a Turkish reprisal when all the monks were murdered for supporting the Independence struggle. A panayia is held here on 12th November. The Church possesses some excellent murals.

From Rovies an excellent coastal road (despite what the maps may indicate), connects with Limni but does not hug the shore, leaving plenty of room for olive groves between the highway and the sea. The New road separates from the Old to leave the small village of **Kronia** to the right. There are some ***Rooms*** and a pebble foreshore.

SIPIAS (91km from Chalkis Town) A red roofed village on a promontory which is somewhat out of sight of the main road. On the approach road from the bypass there are at least three houses that offer ***Rooms***.

Opposite the junction of the side road down to Sipias is a track leading inland to the village of **Retsinolakkos**, my interest in which should be obvious to any reader of **The Eating (and Drinking) Out** sections.

At the end of the Sipias bypass is a large olive grove planted on the plain to the right, between the road and sea. After the route has passed over a wide river-bed, the road runs along the backshore of a pebble beach and gritty foreshore before rising to a junction high above:-

LIMNI (87km from Chalkis Town) Tel prefix 0227. From the heights above Limni, a pine tree edged road descends steeply to the centre of this clean, attractive, red roofed old town and seaside resort. The layout is a pleasantly tree lined Esplanade, off which climbs the Main St, as well as various other side streets all interconnected in a loose, widespread grid layout. A drawback is that, in common with other settlements on the north-east coast, Limni is not set in a bay but on the edge of a rather featureless coastline.

To describe the layout it is best to approach the task from an inland direction, as if arriving from Strofilia. The steeply descending main road into the Town runs into the equally steep High St from the right (*Fsw*) and at an acute angle. In the upper High St, ascending to the left and beyond the Church, is a baker, plenty of shops, a laundry and dental surgery. Back at the junction of the main road and the High St, close to the Church is a Taxi rank. Proceeding on the way down to the Esplanade passes more shops, a petrol station and the Post Office which is situated on a pretty, tree planted Main Square to the right of the High St and some 30m before the waterfront. At the right angled 'T' junction of the High St and the Esplanade is the National Bank of Greece. Across the Esplanade is a wide, wooden slatted, steel-banded quay To the right (*Fsw*), along the Esplanade, is the *Hotel Avra* (C Class, tel 31220). Beyond the *Avra* is the *Ilion* (E Class, tel 31768) followed by the *Hotel Plaza* (C Class, tel 31235). Room rates average out at about 1250drs for a single room with en suite bathroom, 1250drs for a double room sharing a bathroom and 1750drs for a double room with an en suite bathroom.

Buses park on the Esplanade and further along, to the right (*Fsw*), is a shingle, unshaded, 100m long beach, on which are drawn up a number of boats.

Most of the kafeneions, cafe-bars and tavernas edge the Esplanade to the left (*Fsw*) which, from the junction with the High St, 'chicanes' around a kafeneion. There is a chemist the far side of the *Restaurant Avra*. To the far left of the town is a 'Main Street' which runs parallel to the High St, the two being connected by a lateral lane. The OTE, which is well signposted from the other side of the town, is in a side-street off to the right (*Sbo*) of this 'Main Street' and on the right. The office is open weekdays only between 0730-1510hrs. Across the road is a school and gymnasium.

The attractive waterfront continues along to the left at sea-level, edging a narrow, fine shingle, pebble and sandy shore. The metalled road runs out, becoming a rutted track which continues to hug the contours of the clean, pebble shoreline. There is a scattering of large, but now deserted and forlorn buildings of abandoned industries. By persevering for a total of 8km the traveller can attain the:-

Monastery of St Nicholas (Galataki) Built in the 10th century AD on the lower slopes of a mountain range, close to a 5th century BC Temple dedicated to Poseidon. The monastery was destroyed on several occasions. It is rumoured that a merchant navy captain, in danger of floundering in nearby seas, prayed (probably very, very hard) and was saved, whereon he rebuilt the monastery from which act originates the alternative name. Another seaman saved from the perils of the sea is supposed to have organised the murals.

Returning to Limni, the main road climbs steeply past forests of pine trees which are tapped for resin. It is noteworthy that the collectors do not 'muck about' with galvanised hoppers – they use large plastic bags. The highway becomes a more usual, 'cross island road' all the way back to Strofilia.

ROUTE THREE (Southern island)

To Karistos (133km) via Krieza & Styra. Follow **Route One** as far as **Lepoura** (57km from Chalkis Town), where take the right-hand fork for:-

KRIEZA (60km from Chalkis Town) A not very attractive, widespread and mainly modern, if agricultural village.

What's left of the old settlement is evident on the branch road excursion to Ag Apostoli. This climbs steeply out of Krieza on a tarmacadamed surface over moorland countryside, from which there are splendid views, These include, to the south, a plain with an isolated, conical hill – probably the centre of a very old volcano. The road continues all the way to the pretty moorland village of **Petries (Petriae)** where the women wear a distinctive head-dress

This route forks close to and high above the coastline, of which there are glimpses. The left-hand, metalled road drops down to the attractive, large, fishing boat harbour and modern village of:-

AG APOSTOLI (69km from Chalkis Town) The road runs out on the backshore with, to the left, a harbour which hosts a number of medium sized fishing boats and, curving away to the right, a sandy beach. Edging the backshore of the beach is the D Class *Hotel Xenon Roudy*, in the ground floor of which is a taverna. There are a couple more tavernas but very few other concessions to modern tourism – a delightful spot.

The right-hand fork is only a track, off which a left-hand turning tumbles down to a couple of small coves, with shingle and sand beaches edging the clean sea. Any number of little coves are dotted along this attractive, 'Cornish' look-alike coast.

Back on the main road and continuing south from Krieza, the route descends on to a very large, agricultural plain with the strange, conical hill which is topped off by a Venetian watch-tower.

A turning off to the left advances through the village of **Koskina** on a tarmacadamed road which peters out some way from the backshore of:-

PARALIA KOSKINON (71km from Chalkis Town) This is a rather strange setting, a ghost town of a place with a number of not so old but ruined buildings and unfinished, newer constructions. The backshore of the cove, set in a wild landscape of moorland hillsides, is scraped level and the foreshore is almost entirely rocky.

Back on the main road, another 4km south of the Koskina turning and a road makes off to the right, towards Argiro, across simply magnificent countryside. The route passes round the back of another very large, isolated, conical hillside set down on this great plain. Once round this 'stack', an amazing vista opens up to the right over an immense, flat green pasture. In the winter-time this becomes a lake (as it is marked on the maps) which drains off in the summer. To the north of this was the site of the Ancient City of Distos.

Continuing towards **Argiro** leaves a stony, granite hillside, again to the right, the sides of which are covered with a large number of stone enclosed fields. This rather unusual sight is followed by a view out over an enormous, treeless plain of pasture which, in the autumn, has many hues of browns and golden colours. At least half a dozen separate shepherds and their flocks graze this expanse.

As the road advances towards the coast there are clumps of olive trees. A fork in the route allows the traveller to proceed right to **Buphalon Harbour** (75km from Chalkis Town) and the attractive inshore islet of Buphalo on which are medieval remains. The left-hand fork leads to the hillside settlement of **Pyrgaki** (78km from Chalkis Town), beyond which the surface becomes unmade, only to be crudely concreted for a further section. Breasting the crest of the hillside reveals a beautiful outlook over a marvellous fjord-like vista, on which the port of Panaghia shows up, very clearly to the left. In the neck of the deep inlet is an island and some islets set in the sea, beyond which is the mainland backdrop.

The winding, now unsurfaced track sets out on the abrupt descent down the extremely steep, granite mountainsides, crudely fashioned in the form of an amphitheatre. Way, way down below is the wide sweep of a tree lined beach edging Ormos Almyropotamou. The track, which is a busy thoroughfare for friendly donkey and mule drivers, despite its fearsome gradient, is concreted here and there. The last length of the approach is very rough going, prior to running out on the lovely crescent of fine shingle and hard sand beach at the right of the bay. The hamlet of **Ag Dimitrios** is further to the right and possesses one taverna. The very wide backshore, stretching away to the left, generates a 'crop' of spiky sea-grass and is lined by a fine grove of trees through which the locals have fashioned a dirt 'dual carriageway'. It is not so horrific as it sounds. It is obvious from the fire blackened, stone cairns and the occasional caravan parked in areas outlined by boundary stones that the Greeks have not been slow to appreciate the idyllic charms of the location. There are one or two villas dotted about the foothills backing the bay. If there is a drawback, it is that the sea-bed is rather weedy. At the far end, going south, or right to left (*Fsw*), there is a taverna. Fortuitously a way through to the next settlement has fairly recently been blasted. I write fortuitously because the thought of backtracking up the mountainside is daunting, to say the least. Mark you, the very rough, stony track that jinks from the shoreline inland and edges a dirt surfaced football pitch must be negotiated with care, as there are some extremely deep pot-holes concealed by the constant presence of surface water. The football pitch and the filthy ditch of a stream mark the outskirts of:-

PANAGHIA (84km from Chalkis Town) Tel prefix 0223. It has to be borne in mind that there are two approaches to this splendidly 'doo-hickey' fishing and ferry-boat village port, but I am 'zeroing in' from the direction of Ag Dimitrios.

Close by the football pitch are ***Rooms*** (Tel 644715) in a very nice looking house. The track passes the back entrance of an Ordnance depot which stretches through to the waterfront. Perhaps 'Ordnance depot' is a bit 'high faluting' for a field full of a variety of buoys and great long strops of wire rope. The track then curves to the right and disgorges, along with the filth laden stream, on to the waterfront.

The pleasantly tree lined sweep of backshore, which edges a very narrow, rather scrubbly shore, is bordered by a concreted road. This stretches away and runs out to the right (*Fsw*). To the left it crosses the stream's discharge into the sea and then advances a few metres to the village 'proper'. Landing craft style ferries are moored to the foreshore, to the right, roughly opposite the main gates of the depot. The village supermarket (more a store really)-cum-kafeneion conveniently possesses a metered phone, to which the OTE signs refer. The booth hides away behind an antique switchboard.

To the left is the ferry-boat ramp. The main road decants close by the small harbour, across the road from which is the surprisingly smart looking *Hotel Galazio Delfini* (D Class, tel 22177) in the ground floor of which is a restaurant.

At the outset of the main road, on the left, are freshwater taps and on the right (*Sbo*) is a baker followed by another supermarket and a couple of restaurants.

The ferry-boat link is with mainland **Ag Marina**, from whence ferries also connect with Nea Styra, further down the western Evia coast. Official time-tables tend to detail Panaghia as Almyropotamos, just to confuse matters! There is only a once a week sailing, out of the height of season, and this is on Saturday from Ag Marina at 1600hrs. The one-way fare costs 210drs for passengers and from 700drs for cars. The duration of the crossing is 50 mins. *See* **Nea Styra** (this **Route**) for details of Athens bus connections.

Before departing one wonders how long it will be before the quaint, old-fashioned charm of both Ag Dimitrios and Panaghia villages and the surrounding area is ruined by an excess of development? How long before the waterfronts are joined by a sweep of tarmacadam Esplanade and the olive trees have been uprooted to make way for hotels, apartments and villas? How long before the almost unearthly quiet of the night is shattered by more than one truck, a barking dog and the dusk and dawn thud of a distant fishing boat engine?

The road out of Panaghia makes a steep ascent to the attractive, cut stone buildings of the village of **Almyropotamos** (79km from Chalkis Town).

Back on the main north-south island road, the countryside is attractive, mountainous moorland with olive groves scattered about.

Four kilometres south of Almyropotamos a turning off to the left progresses towards:-

MESOCHORIA (84km from Chalkis Town) A nice, working agricultural village of grey slate and stone roofs. The maps do not 'tell a lie' as the route down to **Ormos Karalides** is not only unsurfaced but extremely rough in places, especially the last section.

The small bay is a surprise, or should be, as there is a very large, dune-like expanse of fine grit and pebble beach. This borders a beautifully clear sea in which largish, rounded rocks are scattered about but they are not obtrusive enough to hinder a fine swim. A number of small fishing boats are pulled up on the backshore and there are two unobtrusive tavernas. Why two? Well, one Greek won't allow another to get on with it without any competition, that's for certain. A lovely spot. Incidentally, the two tracks down to Ormos Karalides drawn on some maps do not connect (not that the referred to maps show them so doing).

The well maintained main road is surprisingly arrow-straight for quite a length (after which it reverts to island serpentine). It runs through a scenery attractively sprinkled with groves of cypress trees, that is in addition to the more usual plants and trees. There are some fine views out over the south of the island before the road commences on a long, slow descent to lower hillsides. The most reliable turning off the main road to Nea Styra is in:-

STYRA (100km from Chalkis Town) A pleasant village with at least two chemists, a petrol station and a one-way roundabout at the far south end of the settlement. The unusual nature of this traffic control system (in Greece that is) may well have prompted the police to position their office on the periphery of the small square, sorry roundabout, from whence the hawk-eyed officers watch over motorists antics.

Incidentally, signposting from hereon is poor to non-existent, many of the signs having fallen over or become obscured by adjacent vegetation.

At the outset of the village, a very acute angled, backward facing turning to the right proceeds down to:-

NEA STYRA (105km from Chalkis Town) A delightful Greek and overseas tourist, seaside holiday location. Mind you the signpost only indicates the direction as a ferry-boat destination. On the approach is *Venus Beach Bungalows*, advertising tennis and water sports, a bus stop, a petrol station, several discos and *Rola Computer & Billiard* (*sic*) & *spaghetti...* One wonders!

The road slants past several hotels on to the tree planted Esplanade of this pleasant resort. The Ferry-boat Quay is situated about central of the waterfront. Between the hotels, at the left-hand side (*Fsw*), and the quay is a nice, wide if not overlong, coarse sand beach lapped by clear seas and bordered by the Esplanade. The inland side of the Esplanade is lined with cafe-bars, shops, tavernas and several supermarkets About 150m beyond the Ferry-boat Quay, going right (*Fsw*), and the waterfront road turns away from the seafront alongside a garage. Beyond this turning are a couple of little coves and another long beach stretching all the way to a small headland. The backshore of this far beach is simply a track, informally edged by hotels and apartments which are interspersed by the occasional taverna.

There is a restrained approach even to tourists. For instance the office of Styra Tours, across the road from the Ferry-boat Quay and which sells ferry-boat tickets, in common with the other tour offices, is low-key. No garish, neon lit, smartly staffed emporiums here. There is a Rent A Car office but no scooters for hire. The baker is on a street that runs parallel to the Esplanade, located roughly in line with the Ferry-boat Quay.

Cafe-bar and taverna prices are reasonable with, for instance, two Nes meh ghala and a local brandy costing 190drs. There are a surprising number of hotels, all C Class, with rates averaging out as follows: single room sharing a bathroom 1000drs; a single room with an en suite bathroom 1000-1600drs; a double room sharing 1300drs and a double room with en suite bathroom 1700-2100drs. In July and August these nightly charges rise respectively to 1200drs; 1300-1850drs; 1700drs; 2200-2500drs. The hotels include the *Aegilion* (Tel 41204), *Aktaeon* (Tel 41261), Delfini (Tel 41210), *Evoikon* (Tel 41218), *Nektarios* (Tel 41544), *Plaza* (Tel 41429), *Styra Beach* (Tel 41271) and *Sunday*(Tel 41308).

Ferry-boats connect with Ag Marina on the mainland every day. The ferries depart daily (except Sundays) at: 0600, 0945, 1315, 1700hrs. Sunday sailings are at: 0630, 1000, 1230, 1500, 1600, 1830hrs. Ag Marina sailings depart daily (except Sundays) at: 0800, 1100, 1430, 1800hrs. Sunday departures are at: 0800, 1115, 1345, 1700hrs. The one-way passenger fare costs 215drs and cars from 800drs. The duration of the crossing is 50mins.

Buses depart from Ag Marina (M) for Athens daily at: 0730, 1030, 1430, 1600hrs. Buses depart from Athens for Ag Marina daily at: 0600, 0815, 1230, 1600hrs. The one-way fare costs 320drs.

The road inland from Styra southwards climbs steeply to the village of **Kapsala** (103km from Chalkis Town), from whence there are super views, to the right, out over a plain and low hills. Beehives litter the mountainside and a turn in the road offers wonderful vistas over a vast archipelago of islands, islets and coves in and around Ormos Marmariou.

The road is now a clearly defined, having been blasted across the granite surface of the mountain. The junction with the Marmari Port road (120km from Chalkis Town) is set in a saucer-like, moorland depression. This is a bit of a 'way-station' with ruined buildings scattered about, in amongst which are one or two tavernas.

The right hand turning descends to:-

MARMARI PORT (125km from Chalkis Town) A much larger, more important Ferry-boat Port than Nea Styra, but a much less attractive location. This is not to say that the community has not made an effort with formal gardens edging the Esplanade in places, as well as trees pleasantly spaced out along its length. The settlement spreads along and out from the Esplanade, the quayside of which borders the curved bay. The road down to Marmari enters at the south, left-hand end (*Fsw*) of the waterfront.

The Ferry-boat Quay shuts off the far, right-hand end of the Esplanade. On the side of this quay is a small hut-like ticket office and proceeding south along the Esplanade, advances past the usual mix of cafe-bars, supermarkets, mini-markets, and ouzeries. To the left, opposite the seafront Main Square, climbs Odhos Elefetherious Venizelou, in which are to be found the Post Office, ***Rooms*** and a baker. Further along the Esplanade is the main fishing boat quay, around which are gathered a large fleet, and on the left, a modern Church, beyond which is a pharmacy in a side-street. There are most shapes, sizes and types of hotel, a fish shop or two, a Texaco garage and, beyond the main road junction, a sign to the *Disco Amore*.

Continuing southwards, the waterfront road edges a narrow stretch of pebbly beach, on which a number of small fishing boats are pulled up, after which the track becomes unsurfaced. The narrow, pebbly, kelpy, town beach (if that is not too grand a description) is backed by spindly arethemusa trees. Not so much a beach, more a bit of shore, but not all is lost – read on. About 2½km beyond a messy hamlet to the left, and keeping to the coastal track which ascends some slopes, leads to a view down over a super, wide sand bar jutting into the sea. A path descends down to this splendid, but unsheltered spot. Small fishing boats chug round the coastline and some of the Ormos Marmariou archipelago forms a pleasing backcloth.

Ferry-boats connect Marmari to mainland Rafina three times daily. The departures from Rafina are daily (except Sundays) at: 0830, 1400, 1715hrs. The one-way fare for passengers costs 365drs and cars from 1315drs. The duration is listed at five hours (which I don't believe, reckoning it to be two hours, at the most). *See* **Karistos for Rafina to Athens bus timetables**.

Back at the main road, and continuing towards Karistos, the countryside of this last, southern section of the island is expansive, sweeping moorland hills. The road then cuts through the mountain range to overlook a very large fertile plain to which the route slowly descends and on the sea's edge of which is:-

KARISTOS (Karystos – 133km from Chalkis Town) Tel prefix 0224. The outskirts of this large town and Ferry-boat port have plenty of petrol stations, marble works and extensive industry. Peripteros are plentiful.

The main road/High St makes a 'T' junction with the very broad Esplanade and to the right (*Fsw*), almost centre of the waterfront, is the large Ferry-boat Quay. The inland side of the Esplanade from the waterfront is lined with cafe-bars, restaurant/tavernas and the occasional hotel, in tall buildings some five or six storeys high.

The taverna directly across the way from the Ferry-boat Quay is owned by the fellow with the big, bushy moustache. A meal for two of a good sized and well cooked chicken (probably prepared much earlier in the day – 270drs each), a helping of giant beans (a full plateful – 180drs), a plate of patatas (60drs), 2 carafes of local wine (50drs each), bread and service (20drs each) costs 920drs.

The ferry-boats dock in the angle formed by the quay and the waterfront. Continuing to the right (*Fsw*), the fairly short length of harbour wall leads round to a large boatyard. Opposite the point at which the boatyard foreshore angles away from the Esplanade, are ***Rooms*** (Tel 22597). The road continues on to the Town Beach which is a lovely stretch of fine shingle with a sandy foreshore. There are beach showers and, across the road, a couple of tavernas. The road continues on as a track to another, not nearly so attractive, wide sweep of shingle beach. Unfortunately it is bordered by the town's tip for messy building materials and rubble.

Back at the centre of the Esplanade, the Harbour contains some large fishing vessels and the quay wall is occupied by smaller fishing craft. Keeping to the left (*Fsw*), and on the left, is an extensive Main Square where taxis rank and around which are sufficient pharmacies to the day thereof.... The hospital is signposted off the rear of the Main Square, from whence a wide street, Odhos Ioankotsika, runs parallel to the High St (which is to the left now – *Sbo*). Odhos Ioankotsika is flanked by businesses, shops, an excellent fruit and vegetable shop and a baker. The top of this street makes a 'T' junction with a wide thoroughfare that parallels the Esplanade. Across the road is the imposing Town Hall and Square. To the right (*Sbo*) is the OTE, open weekdays between 0730-2200hrs and closed at weekends. By turning left the roadway at the termination of the Town Hall Square becomes a dual carriageway (yes a dual carriageway). This makes a junction with the top of the High St, which descends left to the Esplanade (thus squaring the square). On the way down the High St passes, on the right, a bank that carries out all transactions, plenty of butchers, a drink shop or two, a dry cleaners followed by an ethnic taverna, a pharmacy, a bakers and another pharmacy, all on the right. On the left is another baker and some archaeological ruins (probably Roman from their abandoned air). These are followed by a couple of fish shops and, in the last side-street to the right, a cafe that advertises a meal of eggs, bacon, and *Wimpey* sausages! On the left is a gentleman's outfitters and, across the road, a couple of good, if rather ethnic, tavernas followed by the Esplanade bordered waterfront.

To the left (*Fsw*), beyond the Main Square, the Esplanade rises past the remnants of a Castle and down to another nice, but small, beach in front of the smart, expensive *Hotel Appolan Resort* (B Class – tel 22045). Other hotels in the town include the *Als* (C Class – tel 22202), *Galaxy* (Tel 22600), *Hironia* (Tel 23239), *Karystion* (Tel 22391) and the *Plaza* (Tel 22337). Prices are on the high side. Single rooms with an en suite bathroom start off at between 1200/1745drs and en suite double rooms 1750/2400drs, which rates increase, respectively, to 1400/2125drs and 2400/2890drs.

Ferry-boats connect Karistos to mainland Rafina. A ferry departs from Rafina at 1600hrs every day, except Sunday when departure is at 1915hrs. The one-way passenger fare costs 550drs and a car from 1600drs. The crossing takes about 2½hrs. The ticket office is let into the corner of a restaurant, almost directly across the Esplanade from the Ferry-boat berth.

Before finishing with Karistos and Evia, a possible excursion is to follow the road and track to Bouros, to the south-east of Karistos. This is generally an attractive, wild, if arid, and shadeless route that winds round the coast (well, for most of its duration it follows the coast). Quite a lot of the countryside in this direction has a quarried look without it having been mined.

To start out it is necessary to proceed left (*Fsw*) along the Esplanade, past the Castle and *Hotel Appolan Resort*. The main road to and beyond **Metochi**, which is surfaced well past Metochi, snakes up into the mountains. The coastal track, which branches off to the right, borders the sea for a kilometre or two, prior to briefly rejoining the Metochi road, after which the track swings back to and along the coast. The route progresses past fine shingle coves here and there and the *Aetos*, a cubist bungalow condominium development plonked down in a most unattractive setting. In the nearside of a promontory is a sandy little cove. On the far side of this promontory is a great, long sweep of broad beach, mainly composed of fine shingle but with a sandy foreshore. To the back of this beach is a concrete blockhouse on which is scrawled *Cantina*.

Beyond 'Cantina Beach' are a few more, gritty, sandy, small coves in lovely but treeless locations prior to the *Bouros (or Karystos) Beach Club* (7km from Karistos). This whacking great hotel development is close to the point of the islands most southerly headland with another hotel tucked in the cleft of the bay. There is a beach to the side of the hotel but I will never be able to understand the creative motives for building a luxury complex in such a desolate position, miles from anywhere.

Kounistra Monastery, Skiathos.

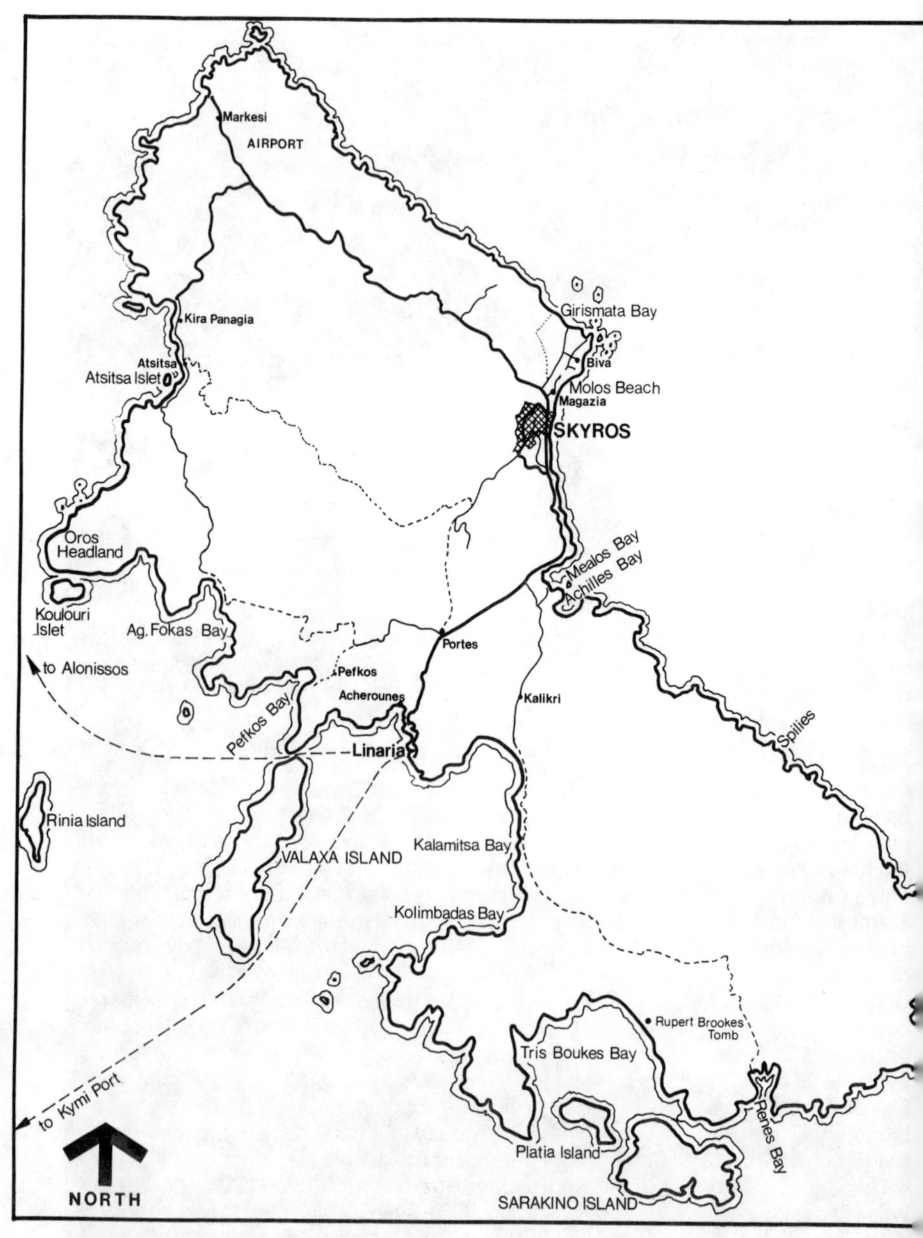

Illustration 32 Skyros island

20 SKYROS (Skiros, ΣΚΡΟΣ) ****

Sporades Islands

FIRST IMPRESSIONS
Fig trees; the army; friendly people; lovely beaches; older mens distinctive apparel; 'bubbling' Chora with a night-time lit High St; few package tourists; a scarcity of 'proper' hotels; cats; not a flotilla, nor a package holiday island, thus prices are lower, as yet.

SPECIALITIES
Rupert Brooke; homes decorated with plates; fig trees.

RELIGIOUS HOLIDAYS & FESTIVALS
include: February/March prior to Easter - Carnival/Panaghia*, Chora; 23rd April - Festival for island's patron saint; Monastery Ag Georgios, Chora; 2nd September - Festival, Ag Mamas, close by Kalikri/Kalamitsa. * *See* **General**.

VITAL STATISTICS
Tel prefix 0222. The island is approximately 40km from the north-west to south-east, up to 19km wide and some 215sqkm in area. The population is approximately 2700 most of whom (2200) live in The Chora (Skyros Town). The highest mountain is about 740m above sea level.

HISTORY
Famed as a hiding place of mythological Achilles, whose mother is supposed to have dressed him as girl. Odysseus persuaded Achilles to join in the Trojan War, only for the prophesy of his death in battle to come true when he was struck on the heel by an arrow. This was the heel by which his mother held him and was the only portion of Achilles' body not immersed in the magical waters of the Styx.

Another famous, part historical, part mythological resident was the warrior king of Athens, Theseus. He escaped from and killed the Cretan Minotaur with the aid of Ariadne, daughter of King Minos, only to abandon her on the island of Naxos. Ungrateful fellow and so typical of the older generation! Despite (or perhaps because of) all these exploits the old boy finished up exiled under the care and protection of Lycomedes, King of Skyros. His friendship proved fatal because Lycomedes is supposed to have pushed Theseus over a cliff-edge. Whoops! Very few of these mythological fellows proved to be entirely 'chappish', if their complete biography is perused. In 475 BC an Athenian called Kimon declared he had found the tomb of Theseus and returned the remains to Athens.

Ownership of the island followed the average historical course, even if Skyros was almost considered a suburb of Athens (469-340 BC). Occupying Macedonians were booted out by the Romans after which the island followed the star of the Byzantine Empire, interrupted by a brief, fifty year period of Frankish suzerainty. After the demise of Byzantium, the Venetians were in occupation. The Turks muscled them out in 1538, until they were finally ousted during the War of Independence.

Another famous, adopted son of Skyros was Rupert Brooke who tragically fell ill and died on 23rd April 1915, probably due to an infected mosquito bite. He was on board a British ship bound for the First World War campaign at Gallipoli. Ironically a year previously he had penned some of the most famous lines of comparatively modern poetry.

If I should die, think only this of me:
That there's some corner of a foreign field
That is forever England *The Soldier*.

Did he have a presentiment that he would be laid to rest on a Greek hillside? Whatever, his tomb is situated close by the Bay of Tris Boukes (or Three Entrances) at the south of the island. This bay, sheltered by inshore islets, and once a pirate's lair, was used during the First World War by Allied Navies as a safe anchorage.

GENERAL

The island forcibly reminds me, in many ways, of its Argo-Saronic 'cousin' Kithira, probably because of a similar, rather medieval or old world ambience. These welcome signs of yester-year are evinced by the conspicuous and distinctive peasants' dress and the, at first less noticeable, but equally singular house interiors and wall decorations of copper, brass and ceramic plates. The medieval, even pre-christian, milieu is manifested by the Chora Carnival held before the Greek Orthodox Easter. During these partially religious, but mostly pagan celebrations, groups of at least three men put on fancy dress, two of whom wear a face mask made of a goatskin. The older lead is called *Geros* and wears a belt, from which are draped numerous goat and sheep bells. His younger, goat skin masked partner, *Korela*, is dressed in traditional Skyriot women's dress whilst the third man, *Frangos*, is costumed in the clothes of a 17th century European, that is with the addition of a face mask and a large bell tied behind his back. They all make their way through the winding lanes to the Monastery Ag Georgios.

The Chora possesses many typic houses, old 16/18th century homes often of small dimensions filled with wooden furniture. Some are almost doll's house sized, with walls festooned with brass, ceramic, copper, pottery and wooden bowls, dishes and plates. These plates originated, not only in Rhodes and Europe, but as far away as Korea and China and were probably brought home by seamen. At one time they were traded as a commodity. These traditional Skyriot houses bring to mind those of Simi island and Lindos (Rhodes island).

Perhaps the greatest drawback to Skyros is getting there. Apart from a flight, the most direct approach is via Kymi on Evia island. This makes for a long bus journey from Athens to catch the daily Kymi-Linaria ferry-boat. Admittedly it is possible to connect from Skopelos by Flying Dolphin but out of the high season – July & August – these schedules are very limited.

The port of Linaria augers well as it is small and pretty but there are no ***Rooms*** available. This does not particularly matter as the (sole) bus route and timetables are geared to the Linaria – Chora journey. Despite the 'entrails', the final approaches to the capital, Skyros Town, (or more informally The Chora) are not entirely satisfactory. The hillsides are scrubbly and the coastline rather rocky, but fear not.

The bus stops at the outset to The Chora to disgorge its passengers who usually will be engulfed with offers of accommodation by smiling children. Either accept unseen, cards blind, or join the trails of people climbing through the lively, attractive High St that pierces the jumble of hill clinging buildings. Enough to say that the Skyros 'main drag', in the hours of darkness, made as much impression on me as Mykonos or Limnos – and that is praise indeed. To arrive at nightfall is a magic experience. All the lights are on and the grocers, ironmongers, cafes, bars, tavernas, restaurants, chemists and numerous other shops are lit up in an orgy of neon. The steeply climbing concourse is a constant *ramblas* night and day, that is apart from the siesta, which is strictly observed.

For those 'who dare', a wander through the back streets will elicit countless offers of accommodation. If a traveller is lucky it may well be in a traditional house, with the family 'out to pasture' for the summer season. The lack of package tourists ensures Skyros is a backpackers/Independent traveller's delight, apart from which, or maybe because of which, prices are comparatively low for eating and drinking out, if not for the actual nights stay.

A further pleasure is that many of the older men wear their traditional clothes as an every day dress and not for the titillation of visitors. If that were not enough, the town beach of Molos is exceptional and there are so many other sandy destinations scattered around the island that I don't have to list them here, in the preliminaries.

ARRIVAL BY AIR

Usually an airport is 'death' to the purity of an island but, as in other matters, Skyros defies conventional wisdom. Despite a flight a day connecting with Athens, the island is the least touristic of the Sporades group, nor has its presence (yet) resulted in a rash of hotels and package tourists. Certainly the location of the airfield, to the north of the island, coupled to the lack of a bus service tends to mitigate its presence.

The Greek Airforce utilise the airport, the Greek Navy berth at Linaria Port and the Army are in evidence. Maybe their presence is another reason for the slow rate of tourist development.

See **Route Two** for the location and **The Chora** for the timetables.

LINARIA: main (& only) port (Illustration 33). A small, clean, pretty, classic Greek port in the shape of a 'U'. A drawback is that the sea is rather dirty.

Due to the (total?) lack of accommodation it is difficult for visitors to go no further. This is a pity because the port is well equipped with the other facilities to support a stop-over.

ARRIVAL BY FERRY & FLYING DOLPHIN

Skyros is not connected by ferry with the other Sporades islands but, fortunately for the 'island hopper', a Flying Dolphin does make link on Thursdays and Sundays.

THE ACCOMMODATION & EATING OUT

The Accommodation The new, smart block along the circular Esplanade from the Ferry-boat Quay (*Tmr* 1B3), signed *KING LIKOMIDES* (*Tmr* 2B4), and over empty, ground floor offices, might be holiday apartments. Apart from these there are no signs of ***Rooms***.

The Eating Out The most convenient place is:-

Taverna H Kalikadia (*Tmr* 3A/B3)
Directions: On the right of the Esplanade (*Sbo*), bordering the large expanse of the Ferry-boat Quay.

Considering the prime position of the taverna and its convenience to the bus, ferry and hydrofoils, a Nes meh ghala at 75drs is jolly cheap. Despite this the snackbar style meals are rather expensive. A beer, an orange drink, two plates of spaghetti bolognese (a lot of bolognese mind you) and bread cost 650drs. The service is quick and efficient.

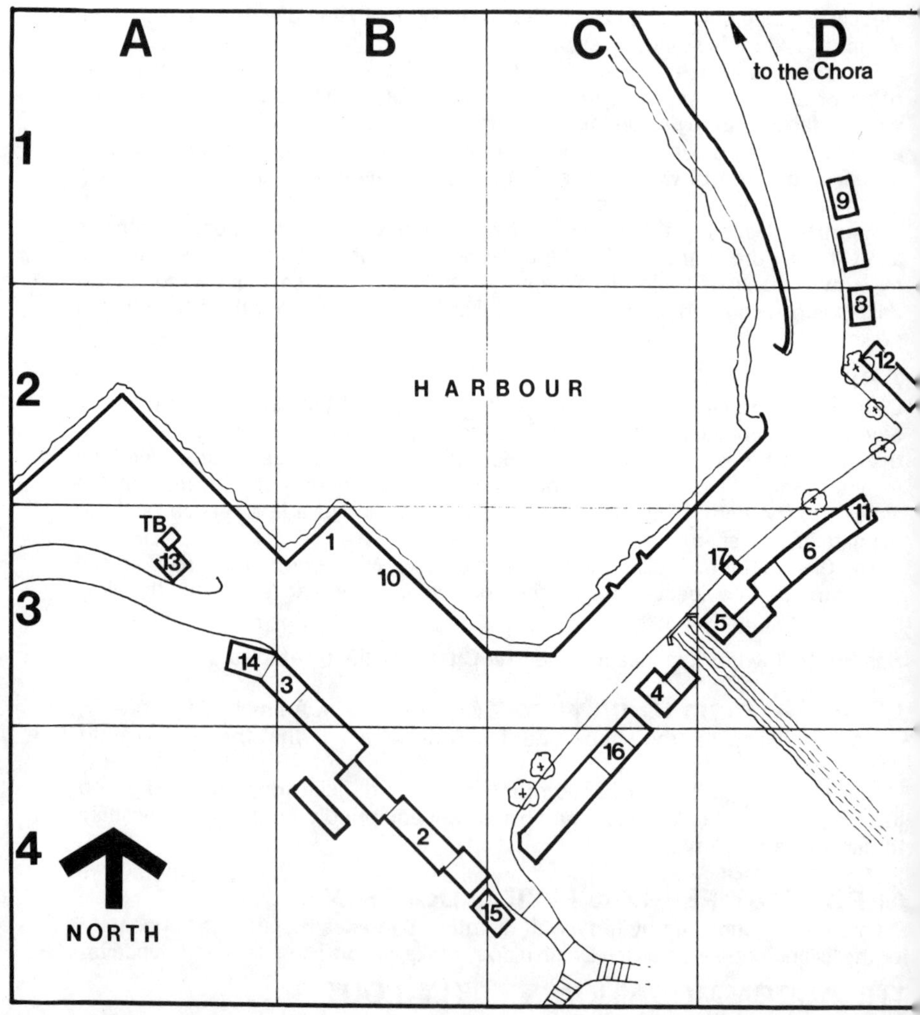

Illustration 33 Linaria Port

Tmr = Town map reference
Fsw = Facing seawards
Sbo = Sea behind one
Fbqbo = Ferry-boat Quay behind

Tmr

1. Ferry-boat Quay B3
2. Smart, new building B4
3. Taverna H Kalikadia A/B3
4. Restaurant/Cafe-bar C3
5. Cafe D3
6. Restaurant Anemoessa D3
7. Kafeneion D2
8. Cafe Ouzerie D2
9. Taverna D1
10. Bus 'pull-up' B3
11. General store D2/3
12. Grocery store D2
13. FB Anemoessa ticket office A3
14. 'I' Travel office A3
15. Petrol station B/C4
16. Port police C4
17. Taxi rank D3

There are other establishments (*Tmr* 4C3 & 5D3) as well as the *Restaurant Anemoessa* (*Tmr* 6D3), a *Kafeneion* (*Tmr* 7D2), *Cafe-ouzerie* (*Tmr* 8D2) and a taverna (*Tmr* 9D1).

THE A TO Z OF USEFUL INFORMATION

BEACHES *See* **Route Two** for the nearest locations.

BUSES Pull up on the generously proportioned Ferry-boat Quay (*Tmr* 10B3). The buses connect with the ferry-boat and flying dolphin arrivals. Rumour has it that, at the height of season, a second bus is laid on which proceeds direct to (Skala) Molos, the sweep of beach to the north of The Chora. If two buses are present, or to be seen 'lurking', ask once, ask twice and ask once again whither each proposes to travel.

Bus timetable *See* **Ferry-boat timetables**. The fare to The Chora costs 60drs.

COMMERCIAL SHOPPING AREA There is a General store (*Tmr* 11D2/3) and a Grocery store (*Tmr* 12D2).

FERRY-BOATS The **FB Anemoessa**, a mini ferry-boat, sails daily to and from Kymi Port, Evia.

Ferry-boat timetable (Mid-Season)

Day	Departure time	Ports/Islands of Call
Daily	1100hrs, return 1830hrs.	Kymi Port

Note on Wednesday, for instance, a second boat is put in the schedule!
See Kymi Port for more and possibly contradictory details.
One-way fare 650drs (from Linaria) or 690drs from Skyros; duration 2½hrs.

There is a timetable on the wall of the *Restaurant Anemoessa* (*Tmr* 6D3). This not only lists the **FB Anemoessa's** daily sailings to Kymi Port but 'pencils in' a Friday trip to Ag Fokas on Ormos Tris Boukes and Sarakino islet, both at the southern end of the island, as well as the sea caves at Spilies on the east coast. (*See* **Skyros Travel, Travel Agents & Tour Offices, A To Z, The Chora**).

FLYING DOLPHINS The hydrofoils provide a welcome, if only bi-weekly link with the other islands in the group.

Flying Dolphin timetable (Mid-Season)

Day	Departure time	Ports/Island of Call
Thursday	1245hrs	Alonissos, Skopelos, Glossa (Skopelos), Skiathos, Volos(M).
Sunday	1630hrs	Alonissos, Skopelos, Glossa (Skopelos), Skiathos, Volos(M).

FERRY BOAT & FLYING DOLPHIN TICKET OFFICES

Anemoessa Ticket Office (*Tmr* 13A3) Tel 91790

Directions: Across the quay from where the ferry-boat docks.

Open for the sale of tickets between 0630-0800hrs, 1230-1400hrs and 1800-1930hrs. They also sell Kymi Port to Athens bus tickets.

I Travel Tourist Office (*Tmr* 14A3) Tel 91944

Directions: On the right of the Esplanade (*Sbo*), close to the the Ferry-boat Quay (*Tmr* 1B3), and in the angle of the track that climbs off behind the **Anemoessa Ticket office**.

The office is labelled *Flying Dolphin Skyros Agency*

OTE Not surprisingly none but there is a telephone box, adjacent to the Anemoessa Ticket Office (*Tmr* 13A3).

PETROL (*Tmr* 15B/C4) This petrol station, that observes the siesta, is tucked away on the right of a lane off the right-hand corner of the Esplanade (*Sbo*).

POLICE

Port (*Tmr* 16C4) Bordering the bottom of the Esplanade.

TAXIS Rank (*Tmr* 17D3) on the Esplanade, half-way round the quayside

ROUTE ONE

To Skyros Town (The Chora – 8km) About a kilometre along the road to The Chora, after curling round the island generating station, the road leaves a pleasant sweep of sand and fine grit beach to the left. This is Ormos Acherounes. The beach 'hosts' informal beach parties, if the occasional pile of blackened stones are a reliable indicator. About middle backshore is a small taverna that only comes to life during the 'height of season' months. This lack of dedication is understandable considering that the average beach head-count is six. There is small, more secluded beach to the left (*Sbo*).

The route then crosses the neck of land that, as it were, joins the north and south of the island. The road advances between pleasant hills, passing a turning off to the left, signposted Pefkos, at about 3km. This junction is close by a 'pile' of quarry works building.

On the approach to the east coast, and the fjord-like indent of Mealos Bay, the countryside becomes pleasant well tree'd and pastoral with a number of farms scattered about. Close to the bottom of Mealos Bay a turning off to the right is signposted Kalamitsa Beatch (*sic*) (*See* **Route Three**).

At the outset of Mealos Bay is a sandy, pebbly cove and a taverna with accommodation. To the right (*Fsw*) is Ormos Achilles with some rather strange looking rocks breaking through the surface of the sea. They resemble semi-submerged whales.

The road runs along the north flank of Mealos Bay and then along a coastline indented with small inlets, coves and a bay edged by shelving biscuit rock with a sandy section to the south side. The whole section is set in unattractive countryside. To the right, the sea side of the road is mainly larva type rock and to the left are thyme covered, scrubbly hillsides.

Alongside a small, nice looking cove with a sandy beach, the road divides around a cliff faced hill. Incidentally, this pleasant looking cove is at the end of a grubby, narrow river gorge along which I am fairly certain some of The Chora's sewage might be piped! Oh well. I just hope the prevailing currents sweep the stuff to the south...

The right-hand fork of the road runs along the coast with the heights of The Chora (Skyros Town) flanking the inland side. The sea edge is bordered by a long sandy beach and 'accommodates' some 'wild' camping.

The left-hand fork winds up a narrowing road, through rather bare, fenced fields supporting a few olive trees, to the southern outskirts of:-

THE CHORA (SKYROS TOWN): capital (Illustration 34). A most attractive, hill-climbing, Cycladean style Chora in the class of Mykonos or Ios for looks. I stress for looks because there is none or little of the unacceptable tourist razzamatazz that is to be associated with the aforementioned towns. On the other hand this is not to say that the High St is not

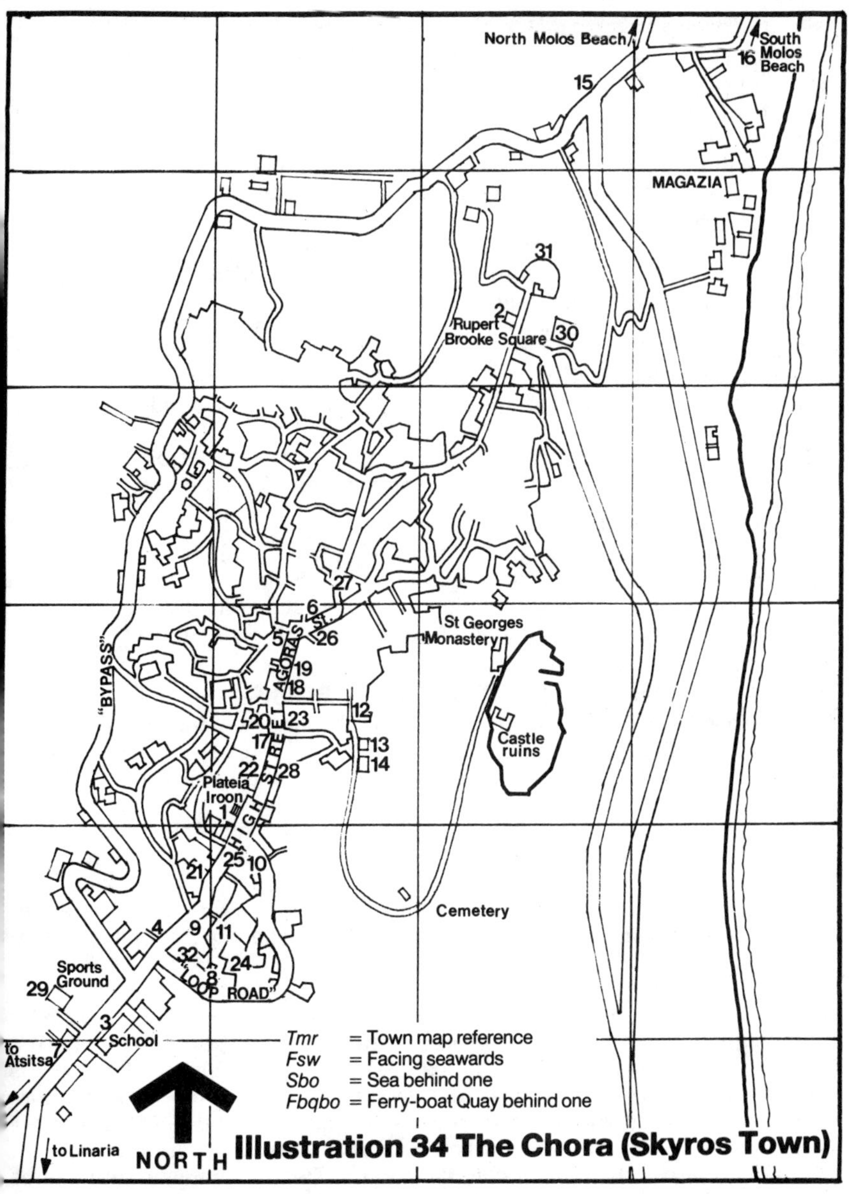

Illustration 34 The Chora (Skyros Town)

Main Square A/B4
Rupert Brook's Square C2
Bus 'terminus' A5
National Bank A5
Cathedral B4
Travel Tourist/Skyros Agency B3/4
OTE A5/6
Hotel Elena A/B5
Rooms A5
Chicken/Souvlaki Restaurant B5

11. Rooms Maria Florous A/B5
12. Skyros Motorbikes B4
13. Baker B4
14. Police station B4
15. Camping Skyros C1
16. Xenia Hotel D1
17. Taverna Dimkatsarelia B4
18. Cafe-bar (No 868) B4
19. Zacharoplasteion (No 865) B4
20. Laundry/cigarette shop/'OTE' B4
21. Trattoria Restaurant Bistro A/B5
22. Skyros Travel & Tourism B4
23. Stamati Paper & bookshop B4
24. Rent A Moto B5
25. Tourist office B5
26. Chemist B4
27. Sandal cobbler B3
28. Chemist B4
29. Clinic A5
30. Archaeological Museum C2
31. Museum Faltaitz C2
32. Post Office A/B5

incredibly lively, an impression reinforced by the well-lit, night-time *ramblas* that surges up and down Odhos Agoras. This sets out near to the junctions of the town bypass and the one-way 'loop' road that spills out close to the Main Square, Plateia Iroon (*Tmr* 1A/B4). Plateia Iroon is pleasantly gum tree shaded and dominated, on the left-hand side (*High St behind one*), by The Town Hall and a cafe-bar. The tables and chairs of the latter are spread out over the flagstones of the Square.

The vehicle-free, cobble and paved High St climbs the Chora hillside, with lanes and alleyways stepping off to either side and bordered by dwellings all the way to Rupert Brooke's Square (*Tmr* 2C2).

There are even the remains of a brown, crag topping Castle below which, and hugging the cliff-face, are the splash of whitewashed buildings of the Monastery Ag Georgios. Both Castle and Monastery overlook the Chora. Incidentally, this hill clambering Chora is probably best viewed from Molos Beach.

The presence of Armed Forces personnel results in a lot of unattached, young men, many in mufti, who swell the numbers of the evening *ramblas*.

ARRIVAL BY BUS

The town bus decants passengers (*Tmr* 3A5) below The Chora, on a stretch of the main road straddled by a football ground and a School. The High St 'proper' starts beyond the bypass to the left, alongside the junction with the one-way 'loop' road to the right. From hereon Odhos Agora constantly climbs to the far, top end of the town.

THE ACCOMMODATION & EATING OUT

The Accommodation Travellers disembarking from the bus will almost certainly be mobbed by families 'working the buses'. Those who are of a mind to seek out their own digs, in an older house in the upper Chora, should doggedly climb the High St, past the National Bank (*Tmr* 4A5) the Main Sq (*Tmr* 1A/B4), and the Cathedral (*Tmr* 5B4), all on the left. This latter is really rather more a small church, beyond which the High St turns half-right past the office of Travel Tourist/Skyros Agency (*Tmr* 6B3/4). From hereon ask. Enquirers may well be led to *Maria* who owns a lot of ***Rooms*** in the upper town, which in mid-season cost from 1000drs (sharing the bathroom) to 1400drs (en suite bathroom).

Back at the Bus stop (*Tmr* 3A5), turning south leaves the OTE (*Tmr* 7A5/6) on the right beyond which is a fork in the road. Here a right-hand track makes off to Atsitsa hamlet, on the west coast, and on the right-hand of which is a 'proper' supermarket. The main road swings to the left, and about 150m further on along, on the right, is *The Hotel Evgenikou* (Tel 91374). These are really holiday apartments and booked by mainlanders for most of the season. On the left, across the road, are some ***Rooms***. Two hundred and fifty metres further on down the road is a Petrol Station on the right and, on the left, the:-

Pension Eleni Atherini
Directions: As above.

Swish rooms with an en suite bathroom and balcony cost 2000drs (2500drs in 1988).

Beyond the Petrol Station, and on the same side of the road, are more ***Rooms*** (Tel 91752). This stretch may prove very fruitful to the 'fleet of foot' when the Chora becomes booked up.

To return to the outset of the High St and the junction of the one-way roads. The road to the right loops round to rejoin the High St across the way from the Main Square (*Tmr* 1A/B4). Walking up this 'loop' road leads to the:-

Hotel Elena (*Tmr* 8A/B5) (Class E) Tel 91738
Directions: As above.
A typical E Class establishment with a single room sharing a bathroom charged at 650drs, a double room sharing 1250drs and with an en suite bathroom 1500drs. The rates rise, respectively, to 750, 1450 & 1700drs.

Back on the steeply climbing High St, on the right, is a house with ***Rooms*** (*Tmr* 9A5, tel 255291) above a cafe-bar.

Further up the High St, turn right back down the 'loop' road past a *Chicken/ Souvlaki Restaurant* (*Tmr* 10B5) and, from the back of a piece of 'waste land car park', on the right, a path leads to:-

Rooms Maria Florous (*Tmr* 11A/B5) Tel 91294
Directions: As above and on the left, at the end of the path.
A pleasant private house, from which the owners move for the summer months. Possibly due to the value of the wall hanging plates, one member of Maria's family 'stakes out' the shaded patio, around the clock. Maria speaks no English but one of her two daughters, Anna can converse very well. The bathroom is one of those within the walls of which are crammed the mandatory washing machines (yes machines, one 'dead', one 'alive') as well as other fascinating household bits and pieces. Ventilation is provided by a ragged ½m hole in the ceiling. Well, why not? It is worthwhile writing down the rate quoted at the bus stop where they gather in prospects. Failure to so do may well result in 'confusion' about the price at a later date. We were quoted 1200drs per night but an attempt was made to charge 1500drs.
As quite a number of ***Rooms*** do not display an official price list, 'misunderstandings' can easily occur.
In the street hosting a scooter hire firm (*Tmr* 12B4), a baker (*Tmr* 13B4) and the Police (*Tmr* 14B4), there are ***Rooms*** to the north of the scooter firm.

Proceed along the bypass to the west of The Chora or south along the main road from The Chora. This latter route sallies forth to the junction of the Linaria Port road and the coastal road, angled north along the eastern flank of The Chora's craggy outcrop. Turning left, to the north, progresses past Disco Skiropolou, some ***Rooms***, a restaurant followed by more ***Rooms*** after which is:-

Camping Skyros (*Tmr* 15C1) Tel 91955
Directions: As above, north of The Chora, almost at sea-level and adjacent to the junction of the bypass and the coastal road that divide round the town's rocky outcrop. The campsite is some 30-40mins walk from The Chora Bus stop (*Tmr* 3A5).
Rather ethnic. Some of the bivouac tents have an aura of long term residency. To add to the 'attractions' the management offer the almost 'unresistable' goody of traditional Greek dancing on Wednesday and Friday nights and a 'dish-of-the-day' menu. Despite all these blandishments I don't think this is 'your actual' NTOG show site!

Hotel Xenia (*Tmr* 16D1) (Class B) Magazia village Tel 91209
Directions: Beyond *Camping Skyros* and right at the next fork, where the road diverges. (The right-hand turning advances to the nearside of Molos Beach and the left progresses to the far, north end of the same beach). The hotel is on the right of a left-hand corner.

Rather old and provincial for an Xenia but the charges do not reflect these 'attributes'. A single room sharing the bathrooms is charged at 1850drs and en suite costs 3650drs. A double room sharing a bathroom is charged at 3500drs and with an en suite bathroom 4600drs.

See **Molos Beach, Excursion to Skyros Town Surrounds** for other accommodation details.

The Eating Out A varied selection of establishments, even if the smarter taverna or two tend to 'get a bit above themselves' and use names such as 'Trattoria'.

A 'local character', rather ethnic establishment is the:-

Taverna Dimkatsarelia (*Tmr* 17B4) No. 226 Odhos Agoras
Directions: On the left of the High St.

Frankly rather squalid, and certainly cramped, despite which it hums with activity and is very popular with the locals. A large portion of the main room is occupied by the souvlaki-cum-BBQ apparatus and food preparation area which is divided off by a counter. It is to be hoped that an 'English Food Inspector' does not wander out this way as he (or she) would have to close down this little 'den of iniquity'. Best to dine out in overalls. On the other hand, these trifling drawbacks are more than overcome by the excellence and inexpensiveness of the limited menu. Six large sticks of souvlaki (60drs each), a very large Greek salad (180drs), a plate of excellent patatas (70drs) and a carafe of open retsina (50drs) cost 660drs. Alternatives include chicken (880drs per kilo), shish-kebabs (pure meat thru' and thru', 500drs for a ½ kilo) and 'take-away' souvlaki pita. Bread is very reasonably priced at 10drs, especially as most other establishments charge up to 40drs. It has to be admitted the air is rent by a cacophony of sound including discordant, wailing Turkish 'muzak', the screams of children and the buzz of the rotisserie extractor fan. The management team consists of a rather emaciated, chain smoking Papa, crippled by one leg being shorter than the other and who operates the rotisserie, an enormous Mama, who presides over the kitchen and also smokes while preparing the grub, and a bespectacled, nice daughter who serves the tables. Despite the hubbub and the children, who appear to wander about at will, all orders appear to be efficiently executed.

Further along the High St are a clutch (or would 'tablecloth' be a better 'collective noun') of establishments which include:-

Cafe-bar (*Tmr* 18B4) No. 868
Directions: As above and on the right.

Run by an old lady who can be smiley and a bit of a wit – did I say witch? Yes, maybe. Popular with some. A couple of small, plain omelettes, bread and a bottle of retsina costs 320drs.

Taverna (*Tmr* B4)
Directions: A pace or so further on up the High St from the previously detailed Cafe-bar (*Tmr* 18B4). The building almost faces down the street, which has

not only widened out but veers a little to the right (*Facing north*) leaving the building, which appears to be dug into the hillside, on the left.

The taverna is in the basement, as it were, and is popular with the locals. Service is haphazard and getting a bill impossible. A meal for two of stifado (a stew), chicken, Greek salad, bread and two ½ litres of open retsina costs 920drs.

Across the road is:-

Zacharoplasteion (*Tmr* 19B4) No. 865
Directions: As above.

Run by a quite old but delightful couple. The value is very good with a 'thick' morning brew – okay, a Nes meh ghala, served in a big cup on a plate, costing 65drs. An evening coffee and a local brandy cost 140drs.

Another Kafeneion, in the High St, that offers equally good value is on the left (*Main Sq behind one*). It is next door to and one up from the *Skiros Pizza*, itself next but one beyond the Laundry-cum-cigarette-shop-cum-'OTE' (*Tmr* 20B4). The owner manages to perch a few tables and chairs on the very narrow pavement. Two large Nes meh ghala, served in glasses, and a brandy costs 170drs.

Chicken/Souvlaki Restaurant (*Tmr* 10B5)
Directions: From the Main Sq (*Tmr* 1A/B4) proceed down the 'loop' road and the restaurant is twenty or so paces along, on the right.

The owner doesn't mean to indicate that he serves up chicken souvlaki! Perhaps the insertion of an indefinite article might have helped. He does include both chicken and souvlakia on the menu.

Trattoria Restaurant Bistro (*Tmr* 21A/B5)
Directions: From the Main Sq (*Tmr* 1A/B4) proceed south down the High St and the establishment is on the right, up some steps to a balcony.

Rather smart and pretentious.

THE A TO Z OF USEFUL INFORMATION

AIRLINE OFFICE & TERMINUS

Skyros Travel & Tourism Center ((*Tmr* 22B4) Tel 91123/91600
Directions: In a large building, on the left and set back from the High St.
See **Travel Agents & Tour Offices, A To Z**.

Aircraft timetable (April to September)
Skyros to Athens

Daily 1250hrs.
Return
Daily 1140hrs.

One-way fare 6400drs; duration 50mins.

BANKS

National Bank (*Tmr* 4A5) On the left of the High St, half-way between the Bus stop and Plateia Iroon
and
Stamati Sarri Paper & Bookshop (*Tmr* 23B4) On the right of the High St (*Main Sq behind one*). An agent for the Commercial Bank and open between 0800-1300hrs & 1600-2100hrs.

BEACHES

Gialos Beach Proceeding up the High St, which dwindles to the width of a lane, half-way (plus) between the Main Sq and Rupert Brooke's statue and the route forks. This is indicated by a wooden off-cut, nailed to a green window shuttered house, and crudely arrowed to the right *Brooke*, and to the left ΓΙΑΛΟΣ. The left-hand alley, Odhos Ag Ioannoy, descends to the bypass round to Magazia village (or Gialos) and a beach.

Molos Beach From the heights occupied by Rupert Brooke's statue (*Tmr* 2C2), steps and a path ascend to the south of the long sweep of beach, that continues all the way to the far, north end of Molos Beach. This south end is an unofficial nudist beach.

BICYCLE, SCOOTER & CAR HIRE No car or bicycles for hire but there are three scooter and motorbike outfits which include:-

Rent A Bike

Directions: Across the lower High St from the National Bank (*Tmr* 4A5).

Certainly the next two described firms don't exactly 'fight it out', more they 'sleep it out' as neither appears to consider rising from their truckle beds, prior to mid-morning. Nor do either hire out machines that are at the 'pinnacle' of mechanical perfection. Mid-season rates average 700drs for the smaller Honda's and 1200drs a day for the bigger bikes.

Rent A Moto (*Tmr* 24B5)

Directions: From the Main Sq proceed along the 'loop' road past the *Chicken/Souvlaki Restaurant* (*Tmr* 10B5) and a laundry. A path angles off to the right.

Skyros Motorbikes (*Tmr* 12B4) Tel 91115

Directions: Proceed up the High St from the Main Sq, beyond the paper and book shop (*Tmr* 23B4), and turn down the next lane to the right. This is very straight and descends to a junction with a lane to the right that roughly parallels the High St. Turn right and the scooter hire outfit is located, almost immediately across the way, in a large backyard alongside a private house. Mr Trachanas is ably assisted by a leggy German lass called Matina, who is 'all about'.

A 'useful street' this with a baker, the police and ***Rooms***.

Before setting out on sorties to the more far-flung parts of the island, more especially those described in **Routes Two and Three**, hirers should consider whether their chosen transport will be able to survive the rigours of the trip. For instant, on the northern circuit **(Route Two)**, going anticlockwise, beyond the seaside hamlet of Atsitsa the road becomes very rugged in places. On the southern route **(Route Three)**, beyond Kalamitsa the road deteriorates to a rough track which becomes progressively worse on the way round to Ormos Tris Boukes.

BOOKSELLERS

Stamati Sarri Paper & Bookshop (*Tmr* 23B4) Odhos Agoras

Not only a goal for bibliophiles but offers stationery, operates an agency for the Commercial Bank and, at the rear, has a food store... how very diverse. Open for long hours, apart from a 'not to be put aside' siesta.

BREAD SHOPS (*Tmr* 13B4). For directions *See* **Skyros Motorbikes, Bicycle, Scooter & Car Hire, A To Z**.

There is a cake shop tucked away between a Tourist office (*Tmr* 25B5) and the *Chicken/Souvlaki Restaurant* (*Tmr* 10B5) on the right-hand of the 'loop' road round from the Main Sq end of the High St.

BUSES They park on the Main Road (*Tmr* 3A5) below The Chora flanked by a School and football ground. At about bus departure time a mixed horde of worthy locals and backpackers gathers in that uncertain frame of mind engendered by any Greek travel facility. The scene is reminiscent of the galloping herd of cattle as portrayed in American 'soap' westerns after the stampede has been halted. In this case the passengers aimlessly but menacingly mill about the waiting bus in a state we British laughingly refer to as a queue. Here the doubt factor is refined by the operators deeming that the baggage must only be loaded on one side of the bus, but nobody appears able to advise which side. A hint is that the drover, sorry driver, usually selects the hatches that are tight up against the School wall, thus maximising the difficulties in the ensuing crush. At exactly the moment that the lottery of the baggage trap is decided, the bus doors are thrown open. The whole procedure is designed to ensure maximum damage to both bus and passengers – the little old, black clothed ladies come off best!

Bus timetable

Difficult to ascertain but there is inevitably one setting out to connect with the Linaria ferry-boat's arrival and departure. For example the Chora – Linaria bus struggles into life at 0700hrs for the 0800hrs boat. The evening bus departs at 1830hrs for the arrival of the ferry at 1930hrs.

CAMPING *See Camping Skyros*, **The Accommodation**.

COMMERCIAL SHOPPING AREA No actual market building but the High St is flanked, along it's length, by all the necessary shops. These include, from the outset of the High St and proceeding in a northerly direction, a Butcher, beyond *Taverna Dimkatsarelia* (*Tmr* 17B4) and on the left, followed by a rather strange Cigarette shop-cum-laundry-cum-informal OTE (*Tmr* 20B4), the sign of which proclaims *Here you can phone abroad*; a drinks shop, Cava Porton, across the road from the upper Chora chemist (*Tmr* 26B4) and a Shoe shop (*Tmr* 27B3) that still cobbles the traditional Skyriot sandals (trohadia). These rather medieval, leather fabrications were brought up to date during the Second World War when the leather sole was and remains replaced by a section of tyre tread.

Grocers, greengrocers and general stores are too numerous to mention. Many enticingly display their wares in tiers of pavement mounted boxes. Worthy of note is a 'genuine' Supermarket to the south of the OTE (*Tmr* 7A5/6), just off the main road. This is the real McCoy with tills, counters and turnstiles.

I don't often mention souvenir type shops, but should Mike Themelidis continue to run his gift shop then it is worth a visit and a chat. The shop is located one up from and next door to the *Taverna Dimkatsarelia* (*Tmr* 17B4). But don't stop for a chin-wag if soft hearted, for he has had a harrowing personal life, including six years in hospital as well as the death of his wife and his son in a car crash. Mike's excellent English is due to his mother hailing from Newcastle and his father being a Greek Canadian. In amongst the array of ceramics, silver, dresses, gifts and popular art, there are camera films and island maps.

There are a sufficient number of peripteros ranged along the High St.

HAIRDRESSERS There is a barber on the right (*Main Sq behind one*) towards the top end of the High St, just prior to a Chemist (*Tmr* 28B4).

LAUNDRY (*Tmr* 20B4) On the left of the High St (*Main Sq behind one*). This rather unique business also sells cigarettes and provides the use of a metered international telephone – *Here you can phone abroad*.

MEDICAL CARE

Chemists & Pharmacies At least two (*Tmr* 28B4 & 26B4). Note the lady assistant in the uppermost shop speaks English.
Clinic (*Tmr* 29A5) On the edge of the far side of the sports/football ground. Perhaps they just play rough!

NTOG *See* **Travel Agents & Tour Offices, A To Z.**

OTE (*Tmr* 7A5/6) Open weekdays only between 0730-1510hrs. Also *See* **Laundry, A To Z.**

PETROL There is a petrol station on the main road south of The Chora.

PLACES OF INTEREST

Castle (*Tmr* C4) The best route is a rough but wide track that climbs to the walls via the cemetery from the 'Police station' street. On the way up there are fascinating views out over the huddled, flat roofed dwellings of The Chora. The Castle was probably built at the end of the 13th century AD, on the site of earlier fortifications, and is supposed to be from whence Theseus was pushed. Entrance to the Castle is not always possible.

Monastery (*Tmr* C4) The Monastery of Ag Georgios, founded in the 9th Century AD, typically hangs on to the rock face, to the west of the Castle cliffs. Within the whitewashed walls of the monastery is Ag Georgios Church, built in 1680 and possessing some murals of note.

Museums
Archaeological (*Tmr* 30C2) To the right of and overlooked by the Rupert Brooke statue. Probably more interesting exhibits than displayed in many other island museums. Closed on Tuesdays.
Museum Faltaitz (*Tmr* 31C2) To the north of the Rupert Brooke statue Square. A most interesting, if rather ethnic establishment, housing an unrivalled collection of Skyriot artefacts and memorabilia based on collections of the Faltaitz family. They were one of the island's autocrats, the upper ruling class or *Megali Strata*. The donor, Manos Faltaitz, is still in residence and is author of the definitive book of the island, which is on sale here at a cost of 650drs. A guide shows visitors round the various rooms crammed with ceramics, wall coverings, embroidery, pictures, drawings, prints, photographs, pottery, copper and brassware, display cases, hundreds of books and magazines, wood carvings and antique furniture. One or two rooms depict typical Skyriot house interiors of years gone by. These displays not only include furniture and implements but various costumes and clothing. I was lucky enough to be shown round by the Director of Historical Research at the Museum who speaks excellent English. She explained that the smallness of the chairs and seats displayed was not that Skyriots were unusually diminutive, simply that the houses, and consequently the rooms, were tiny. Makes sense doesn't it. The guides are historians or local artists and designers who also display their modern wares. Admission is free but visitors are expected to make a donation. An informal teaching class also appears to take place with a kaftan clothed, Papa-like figure in charge. His hippy looking class of young men (or acolytes?) might well let the curious into the museum. I felt rather uneasy about the set-up but perhaps that was due to the robed lady who appeared to be 'bombed out of her mind'.

Rupert Brooke Statue A bronze nude dominating not so much a square, more a threshing circle. From these heights are dramatic views out over the surrounding countryside and seascape.

Local Dress Any number of the older men dress in the traditional Skyriot costume. This consists of a straw hat or black cap, a check shirt and blue or black baggy pantaloon trousers tucked into black woollen stockings with their feet shod in the (medieval) leather sandals.

POLICE
Town (*Tmr* 14B4).

POST OFFICE (*Tmr* 32A/B5) From the south outset to the High St, turn up the 'loop' road. The building is on the left, prior to the *Hotel Elena*.

TAXIS Rank on the edge of Plateia Iroon (*Tmr* 1A/B4).

TELEPHONE NUMBERS & ADDRESSES

Clinic (*Tmr* 29A5)	Tel 91207
Olympic Airways (*Tmr* 22B4)	Tel 91600
Police (*Tmr* 14B4)	Tel 91247

TRAVEL AGENTS & TOUR OFFICES A surprising number, considering that Skyros is the least visited tourist resort of the Sporades. These include:-

Tourist Office Information (*Tmr* 25B5) No. 827
Directions: Across the High St from the Main Sq, on the corner of the junction of the High St and the 'loop' road.

Across the road, on the opposite corner, is the:-

Skyros Shipping Co
Directions: As above

Not a lot of use to the usual traveller as it is a commercial shipping company, as should be deduced from the title, but there you go.

Skyros Travel & Tourism (*Tmr* 22B4) Tel 91123/91600
Directions: On the left of the High St, north of the Main Sq beyond a periptero.

Rather 'Grecocilous' to male enquirers and 'oily' to females. Not only an Olympic Airline agent but handles apartment and villa lets as well as boat trips to the various island attractions. The latter include the Sea Caves at Spilies (east coast, south part of the island); Rupert Brookes Tomb and Ag Fokas at Ormos Tris Boukes and Sarakino islet off Tris Boukes Bay (on the south coast). The average cost of an excursion by boat to Ormos Tris Boukes is 1100drs.

Travel Tourist & Flying Dolphin Skyros Agency (*Tmr* 6B3/4) Tel 91828
Directions: Scale the High St from the Main Sq, past the Cathedral (*Tmr* 5B4) and fork right. The office is on the left.

EXCURSION TO THE CHORA (SKYROS TOWN) SURROUNDS

Excursion to Girismata via Molos & Magazia (3km) The coastal and bypass roads junction alongside the site of *Camping Skyros*. From the campsite the road falls towards the coastline, passing the left turning to the far, north end of Molos Beach, the lane to the right down to Magazia hamlet and continues on to the *Xenia Hotel*, where the road angles sharply left to the near, south end of Molos Beach.

MAGAZIA The lane to the hamlet drifts down past oldish housing to a sturdy sea wall some 6m above a sandy, narrow beach. At this end are a supermarket as well as a pleasantly situated taverna and ***Rooms***. Out of the height of season months the beach, which is really a continuation of Molos Beach, is almost empty.

At the south end of Molos Beach are a few shops.

The main road to the north end of Molos Beach curves to run inland, but parallel to the sea-shore, passing through rather scrubbly, 'small holding countryside' on which a number of single storey villas are being constructed. Accommodation is scattered about in the shape of a couple of quaintly named *Motels* (somebody must have been to America) and a plethora of ***Rooms***. The road then curves to the right almost back the way it came and ends up on the northern end of:-

MOLOS BEACH (3km from Skyros Town) The road terminates on a small, irregular square edged by a kiddies playground up against the backshore of the beach. To the left (*Fsw*), beyond a bamboo and grass shaded taverna patio, is a rocky mole enclosing a fishing boat harbour. A wide sweep of beautifully sandy beach stretches away to the right past Magazia hamlet to some low cliffs on the eastern flanks of The Chora. The Castle topped, rocky outcrop and the whitewashed buildings of Skyros Town, which are draped over the hillside, forms a magnificent backdrop.

Admittedly the backshore of the beach is a bit scrubbly, there being bits of old tin, yoghurt cartons and goodness knows what littered about. But it is a wide expanse and, once over the thin, winter seaweed line, the sand is absolutely splendid and the sea clear. There are rubbish bins spaced along the middleshore but it should come as no surprise that these are not emptied. Apart from the months of July and August, this pleasant paradise is comparatively free of all but a quite acceptable number of people, even at the height of the day. Mid-morning there might well only be half a dozen people and, perhaps, a dog. Wind surfers are in evidence. In conclusion a splendid spot.

Backtracking from the north of Molos Beach and a turning north, to the right progresses to:-

GIRISMATA BAY (3km from Skyros Town) A series of long, slow, narrow beaches curve to form the main bay. Unfortunately the winter seaweed, middleshore is very dirty with a lot of trash in addition to which some of the sea-bed is made up of biscuit rock and seaweedy boulders. If only it was clean it would be a delightful spot.

To the left (*Fsw*) a sandy track, at a discernable height above the backshore, runs parallel to the beach only to dip and peter out in a look-alike for a rubbish dump on the beach. The landward side is speckled with straggly homestead development. Oh dear!

To the right is a low headland, with a solitary, sailess windmill prettily located above a dwelling on the edge of a small cove. The sea-bed is biscuit rock and the shore is unfortunately rubbish strewn. Off the headland are a series of low, rocky islets ranged from left to right. It would not surprise me to learn that Girismata bay and the headland are hedged in by a ring of underwater rock. To the right (*Fsw*) of the windmill is a small chapel interestingly, if not unusually, chiselled out of a squared off pillar of rock. The rock hereabouts is a sort of basalt, much of which appears to have been cut out and trued up with trenching tools. Is this the site of early vertical graves? A simple open fronted rock house is quaintly labelled *WC*.

ROUTE TWO

Round the north of the island via Atsitsa, Pefkos Bay & Portes (29km) Before setting out on either this or **Route Three**, scooter hirers must check they have a full tank of petrol. Due to the nature of the terrain between Ag Fokas and Pefkos bays it is urged that riders proceed in an anticlockwise direction. The Chora bypass loops round the town past *Skyros Camping* and, after ½km, the main road to the north of the island branches off (from Girismata bay) to the left. The route passes over rocky scenery, gently climbing past an extensive, ruined village, possibly **Krini**, almost a 'ringer' for a 'North Wales Deserted Medieval Village'. At the far end of this jumble of stone ruins and foundations, a crest in the hills overlooks the flat expanse of a plain that almost entirely fills the northern end of the island. The rather uninteresting vista is broken up by the tarmacademed sweep of the airport runway and an adjacent military base.

The road drops down on to the plain, sweeps past the Airfield and a *No Entry* sign barring access to the road to Markesi. The road continually curves round to the left into wooded countryside, joining the north-east coastline on the edge of a small cove at the top of a large bay.

This has a sandy beach but is not absolutely idyllic due to the local authorities having scarred the right-hand side (*Fsw*) of the hillside with an unsympathetically engineered track. Further along the route, close to the shore are some ships' buoys and a small, Army outpost. Hereabouts the road edges the sea and the third cove is pebbly with indications of semi-permanent, summer-time camping beneath the trees that edge the beach. You do not have to be a detective - somebody has laid down some paving slabs. The south end of this cove sports a little chapel, **Kira Panaghia**.

The road is surfaced all the way to:-

ATSITSA (16km from Skyros Town) Prior to dropping down to the hamlet, the road passes through stone masonry pillars which extend into the sea and may have carried a conduit or duct. Alongside a pair of these, on the left, is a rustic cafe-bar across the road from a tree covered, fenced promontory forming the right-hand (*Fsw*) horn of the bay. A dear old lady runs the kafeneion for her son. The out-of-the-way position does not result in low prices though, with a couple of milky coffees and a brandy costing 230drs. Mind you the presence of a metered international phone might alert travellers to the fact that there is something unusual present here. And they would be correct.

A prominent, square, solid, pleasant looking, three storey house dominates and overlooks the lovely indented bay in which is set a conical, rocky islet. To the right (*Fsw*) of the the bay, almost as far over as the cafe-bar, is a very small beach with a sandy shore bordering crystal clear seas covering a stony, seaweed covered sea-bed. Kayaks and pedaloes are in evidence. But back to the house. Ah yes! This is the premises of *a holistic and fitness holiday centre* which promotes a healthy body and mind, amongst other worthy pursuits. No wonder I felt uneasy! I must admit that I perceived the atmosphere engendered as that of an avant-garde Youth Hostel or Butlins! You know the sort of thing, up and about residents, don't forget to clean your mind in time for classes... However I may well be ever so mistaken. What is indisputable is that the originators of *The Skyros Centre* would be hard pressed to have chosen a more idyllic situation. The *habitues* escape to the 'local' when they get the chance, which explains the metered telephone in the cafe-bar. Mind you the presence of all these 'return to nature chaps' (and chapesses) rather ruins the situation for other away-from-it-all travellers.

At the south end of the hamlet, across a summer-dry river-bed, is a taverna/restaurant. Only one blot occasionally disturbs the peace. For some reason when the Greek Airforce have saved up enough 'coupons' for the fuel, their pilots (just) overfly the location.

The track out of Atsitsa fords the river-bed and climbs round to another small, very pretty cove backed by a flat area enclosed in the folds of the verdant, tree planted, encircling hills. Unfortunately, not only is the shore pebbly and rather slimy at the water's edge, but there is also some rubbish littered about.

The route now cuts across the wide neck of the Oros headland. At the signpost to a *Restaurant & Zimmer* is the turning off to the right to the 'hillbilly' backyard of:-

AG FOKAS (22km from Skyros Town) The path leads down to the centre of the bay, the curving shore of which is pebbly. The agricultural, fenced backshore is stony with clumps of couch grass growing. To the immediate right is a single storey block that may (or may not) offer ***Rooms*** at the height of the season. To the far left, edging the seashore, is a 'doo-hickey' taverna which also only opens, if at all, in July and August. Beyond the taverna, in the crook of the sweep of the land encircling the bay, are a few fishing boats and caiques. Sheep, chickens and turkeys randomly 'graze' here but beware because the turkeys are man-eaters. I mean it, they are prepared to attack!

From Ag Fokas Bay the track rises into the tree covered hillsides, the going gets rough and the signposting is non-existent. Nowhere on the island are directions even adequate but hereabouts they cease. Fortunately the route to take is fairly obvious but the climb is a long, slow haul. At the 'coll' the road runs through a large, tree shaded quarry and the required direction can be very, very difficult to determine. Take the left-hand exit. The view out over the almost enclosed bay below is lovely with the far side closed off by a sparsely vegetated, rounded headland that stretches out into the sea and off which is the long, soft, whaleback-like island of Valaxa.

On the reverse side of the heights, the descent is extremely steep, hence my recommendation to travel in an anticlockwise direction. From the other direction this steep section would probably defeat most scooters, with two up, in the heat of the midday sun, if only due to overheating. The track starts to level out in the tree covered hillsides above the centre of:-

PEFKOS BAY (27km from Skyros Town) A rough vehicle access descends to the attractively situated *Restaurant/Taverna Pefkos* set on the slopes.

Despite the prettiness of the location, the immediate backyard surrounds to the not-so-neat establishment are messy rural. Goats graze, chickens peck, all to the background throb of the diesel generator necessary to power the establishment's electrics. From the restaurant/taverna a path falls down between a pair of large fig trees to the sandy backshore of a glorious sweep of wide beach that stretches away to the right (*Fsw*). The middleshore is made up of tiny pebbles and the foreshore sand and small pebbles. As elsewhere on Skyros there are rubbish bins which, it hardly needs mentioning, are rarely emptied. The first five or six metres of the sea bottom are uncluttered, after which are patches of seaweed. It is not surprising that this location is popular with the local, young, 'body beautiful' Greeks and their girlfriends or wives.

Continuing on round the bay, towards the far, south side is a concrete quay nestling in the angled crook of the hills. Fishing boats moor to the wall and on the back edge is the:-

Taverna Mitszos A simple establishment set in the shade of some large fig trees. The owner is rather 'tired and disinterested'. There is a suggestion that ***Rooms*** are available, but it might prove to be a struggle to be allocated one.

From Pefkos the road climbs over the uninteresting, barren hillsides passing through a jumble of dusty quarry workings before joining the main road between Skyros Town and Linaria Port.

ROUTE THREE
To Tris Boukes Bay & beyond (24km)

Take the Linaria Port road beyond Mealos Bay (where the route turns inland), as far as the signpost indicating a turning to the left to *Kalamista Beatch* (*sic*). Other signs announce *We sell honey* and *We rent Rooms*. This road runs up a wide valley set between two hill ranges and is bordered by agricultural pursuits. The road is metalled all the way to the widespread hamlet of:-

KALAMITSA (8km from Skyros Town) A quite large bay, bordered by a large pebble shore with smidgins of sand here and there. To the left is a *Pension*.

South of Kalamitsa, the fairly wide but now unsurfaced track contours round high up the mountainside. There are lovely views out over the large sweep of sea enclosed by Kalamitsa bay and in the direction of the smaller:-

KOLIMBADAS BAY (12km from Skyros Town) A gated track falls down to a beautifully situated dwelling sited smack in the middle, and on the backshore of this splendid sweep of fine pebble and sandy beach, backed by an olive grove.

The track, which switchbacks up and down the foothills of the mountainside, now cuts across the neck of a massive headland to the right, prior to the rolling hills revealing:-

TRIS BOUKES BAY (15km from Skyros Town) In the mouth of this wide bay are the large, low islets of Platia and Sarakino. Rupert Brooke's tree shaded tomb is on the left-hand horn (*Fsw*) of the curve of the bay, some 10 mins walk from the shore. Frankly to visit the spot it is probably best to take a boat excursion, which may be signed for the adjacent area of Ag Fokas (the southern Ag Fokas).

The surface of the still wide track becomes progressively worse, descending steeply and swinging down towards:-

RENES BAY (24km from Skyros Town) The small inlet has a pebble shore with a water trough set on the backshore.

This mountainous, barren, southern lump of the island was the home of a Shetland-like pony, the *Pikermic* which has probably now all but disappeared. I certainly have never seen one.

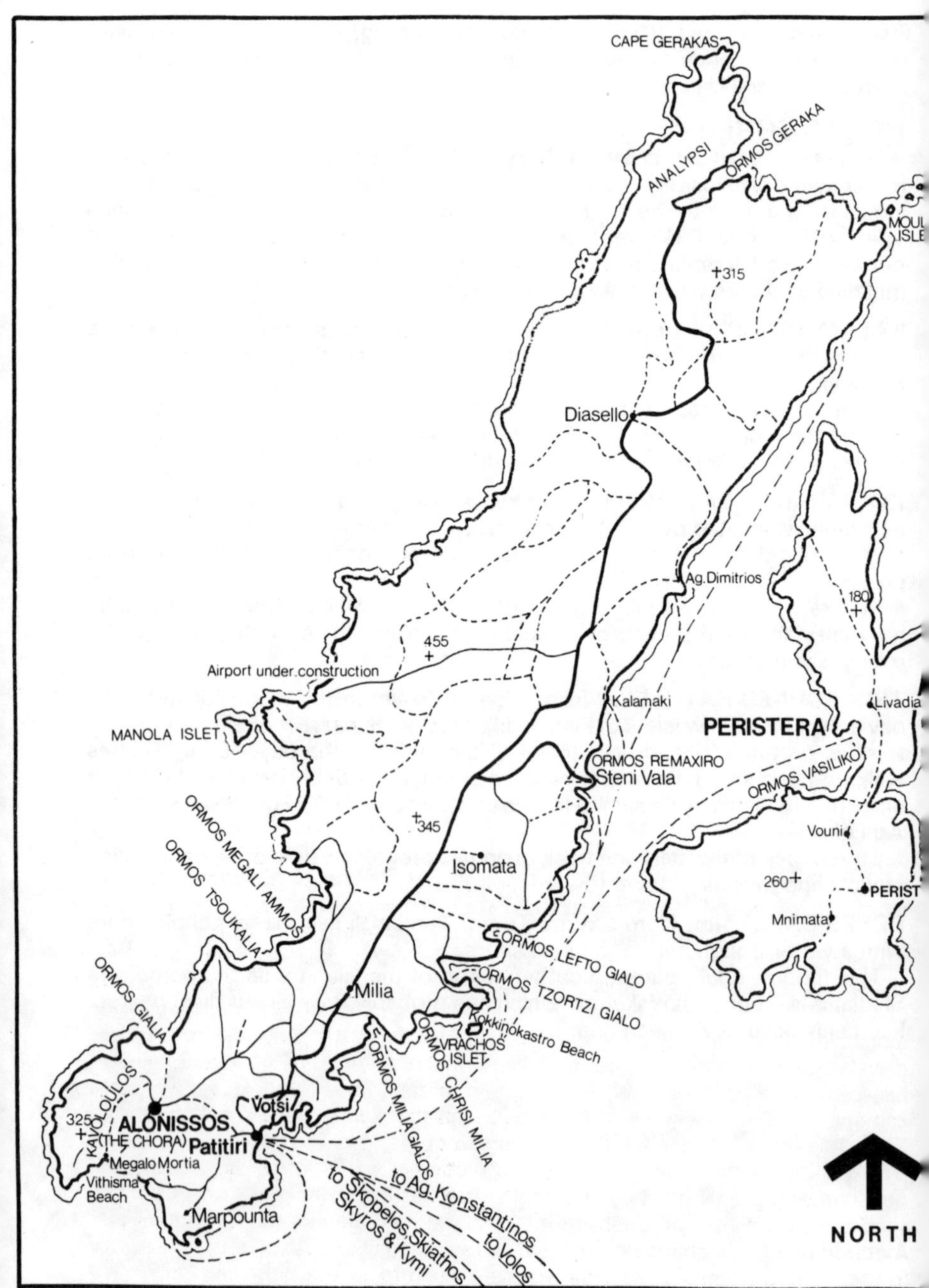

Illustration 35 Alonissos island

21 ALONISSOS (Alonnissos, Alonnisos, ΑΛΟΝΝΗΣΟΣ) **

Sporades Islands

FIRST IMPRESSIONS
Pretty countryside; untidy port; lack of villages; multiplicity of pebble bays; beautifully clean sea; unmade roads; green and profusely vegetated; women's head-dress; dogs; thin, small cats; rustic squalor; trip boats and flotilla yachts; lack of church bells on Sunday; 'suspect' drinking water; flies

SPECIALITIES
Boat trips

RELIGIOUS HOLIDAYS & FESTIVALS
include: None on Alonissos. This lack of religious fervour may account for the lack of church bells (Also *See* **History**). 8th September – Panaghia at the Monastery (on the nearby island of) Kyra Panaya (Pelagonissi).

VITAL STATISTICS
Tel prefix 0424. Alonissos lies approximately north, north-east to south, south-east, is 20km from top to bottom, is up to 5½km wide and has an area of 64sqkm. The population totals about 1400.

HISTORY
Undistinguished perhaps covers the subject. Even the name, or more correctly to which island the ancient name Alonissos referred, is in some doubt. To expand, over the thousands of years historians have been able to follow the various changes of nomenclature attributed to this or that island by the various rulers, be they Ancient Greeks, Persians, Macedonians, Athenians, Romans, Saracens, Byzantiums, Franks, Venetians or Turks. Alonissos was probably the Ikos of ancient days, Alonissos possibly being the name of the adjacent, small island of Kyra Panaya (Pelagonissi) or even Psathouria islet. Attribution of historical events is difficult unless the various names can be assigned with certainty.

In more recent years the island has suffered two catastrophies. In the 1950s the island's vines were devastated. If this were not enough, in 1965 the island was shaken by an earthquake which was sufficiently powerful to devastate the old Chora, Alonissos Town, prettily perched, high on the side of the Kalovoulos mountain range. The Greek government, faced with the enormity of this last disaster, had to instantly create a new settlement and chose the then small port based around *Paralia ton Linon*, or 'The Beach of the Wine Press'. This lovely name can still be seen on the walls of the buildings that line the 'alley' section of the Esplanade that backs the beach, to the south of the bay. The hastily constructed, jerry-built township, similar to the reconstruction at Ag Estratios (NE Aegean), is, not surprisingly, a bit of a hotchpotch. Rumour has it that the government encouraged the citizens of The Chora to move to the new development, Patitiri Port. A condition of this change of address was that they should give up any rights to their Chora homes. This was readily agreed to at the time. But, in recent years, various Europeans and Americans, seeking an escape from the evil of high pressure living, have eagerly purchased, from the Government, houses in the Chora in order to renovate them. The privations that the pampered westerners are more than happy to cope with, in order to seek their Shangri-

La, would certainly be condemned by both Greeks and slum dwellers. Despite this the former inhabitants now regard themselves as cheated and dispossessed. Well they would, wouldn't they?

A reminder of the earthquake is the Architect's office on Leoforos Ikion Doloron, established to ensure new construction is 'earthquake proof'.

GENERAL

To visitors approaching from the west, the mountain topping, old Chora is clearly visible and conjures up a promise of possible delights to come. Sadly no. The haste in the development of Patitiri Port resulted in some behind the scenes, 'rural' squalor.

In order to lengthen the pitifully short summer season, Alonissos was promised an airfield. This 'threat' lost its way, it is rumoured, in a welter of political intrigue, but more probably due to nothing more prosaic than a lack of money. The construction commenced in 1984 and so far 1000m of the incredibly unyielding rock has been roughly flattened. Certainly it would seem uneconomic to spend vast amounts of resources on an island with so little ability to take full advantage of any benefits that might accrue from an airport. Despite this, many locals are convinced that the completion of the facility would solve all the island's ills, imagined and actual. This, despite the fact that the supply of drinking water is extremely uncertain, even for the level of tourism now in existence. In fact, it is only in the last year or two that the island's elders, no doubt in desperation, topped up the system with untreated, polluted water. Visitors are strongly recommended here, as elsewhere in the Sporades apart from Skyros, to purchase bottled mineral water.

The island is a one-settlement location. There simply are no other centres of population than Patitiri Port, that is apart from the still largely deserted Chora and the very small, fishing boat hamlet of Steni Vala. All the island roads are unmade apart from those which encompass the port and two adjacent, 'suburban' bays of Rsoum Gialo and Votsi.

The main, 'up island' track heads off for the northern Ormos Geraka, with 'feeder' tracks to the lovely, but pebbly beaches that crop up with startling regularity along the length of the eastern coastline. To service these an efficient system of water taxis, based at Patitiri Port, has developed. Despite its apparent charm, it is hard to escape the conclusion that, for the moment, Alonissos has fallen between two tourist camps. The apparent promise of the package holiday-maker and flotilla fleets fulfils the wildest dreams of the islanders, but only during the months of July and August. On the other hand, their very presence tends to divert the independent traveller to other, more promising pastures. Oh dear!

The women wear a distinctive shawl head-dress as an everyday item of apparel, maybe to keep the all-pervading dust out of their hair.

Despite all the signs beseeching visitors to keep the island tidy, Alonissos remains rather scrubbly – and the Greeks ensure it stays that way!

PATITIRI PORT: capital (& only) town & (only) port

(Illustration 36) As has been outlined in the Introduction, the original, small settlement of Patitiri was rapidly expanded at the instigation of the government. This development, that stretches up the slopes surrounding the port, is an ugly blight of concrete boxes. One main road was included in the redevelopment and this wide splash of concrete circles Patitiri Port to incorporate the hamlets on Ormos Votsi Bay and Rsoum Gialo, the small bay between the two.

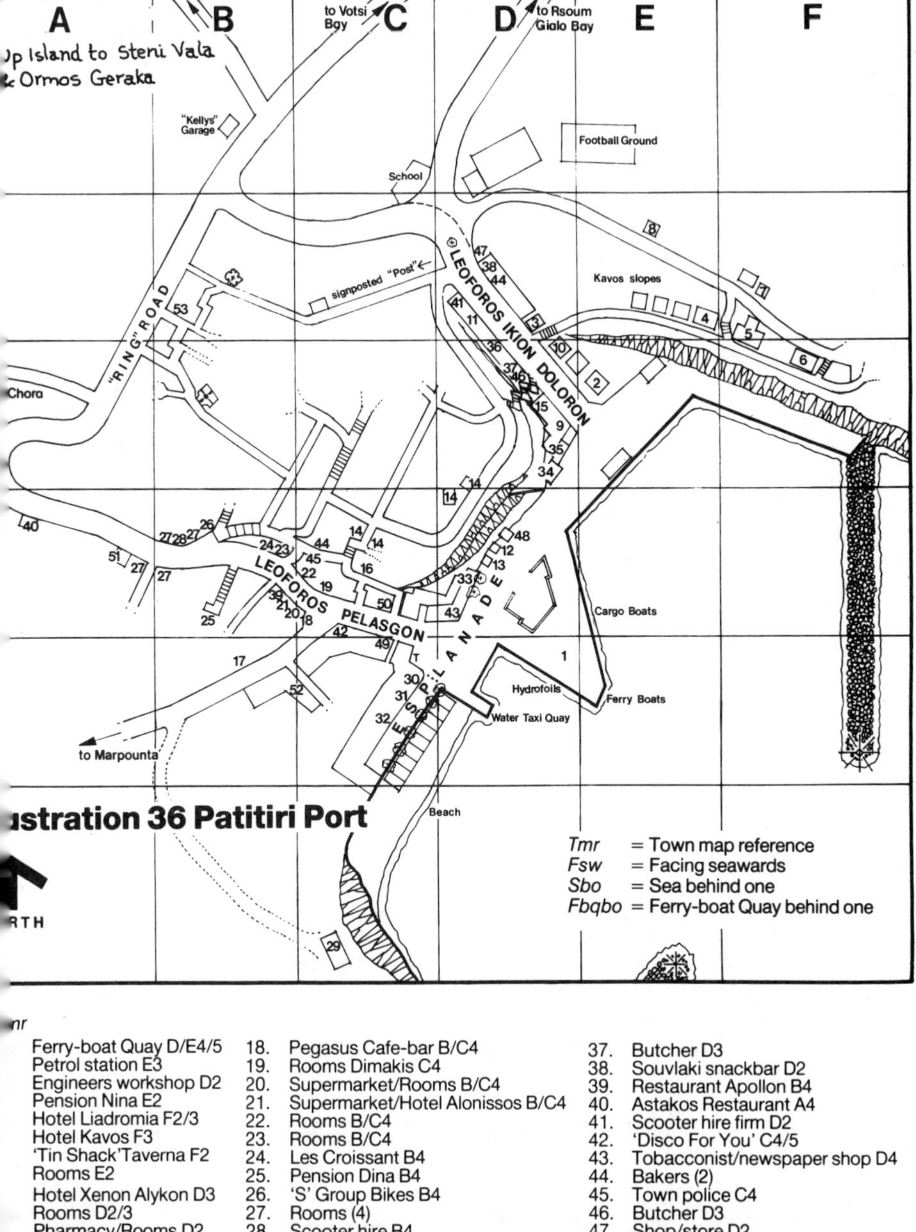

ıstration 36 Patitiri Port

nr

Ferry-boat Quay D/E4/5
Petrol station E3
Engineers workshop D2
Pension Nina E2
Hotel Liadromia F2/3
Hotel Kavos F3
'Tin Shack' Taverna F2
Rooms E2
Hotel Xenon Alykon D3
Rooms D2/3
Pharmacy/Rooms D2
'Rooms To Let' hut D4
Ikos Tours D4
Rooms (4)
Port police D3
Rooms C4
Pension Bougainvillea B5
18. Pegasus Cafe-bar B/C4
19. Rooms Dimakis C4
20. Supermarket/Rooms B/C4
21. Supermarket/Hotel Alonissos B/C4
22. Rooms B/C4
23. Rooms B/C4
24. Les Croissant B4
25. Pension Dina B4
26. 'S' Group Bikes B4
27. Rooms (4)
28. Scooter hire B4
29. Hotel Galaxy C6
30. Cafe-bar Metoikos C5
31. Taverna To Dixty C5
32. To Akrogiali C5
33. O Giannakis Kafeneion D4
34. Cafe Zacharoplasteion D3
35. Apostolos Vlaikos Ticket Agency D3
36. Ouzerie To Kamaki D2/3
37. Butcher D3
38. Souvlaki snackbar D2
39. Restaurant Apollon B4
40. Astakos Restaurant A4
41. Scooter hire firm D2
42. 'Disco For You' C4/5
43. Tobacconist/newspaper shop D4
44. Bakers (2)
45. Town police C4
46. Butcher D3
47. Shop/store D2
48. Fruit shop D4
49. 'Front Room' Fruit shop C4/5
50. Supermarket C4
51. Orpheus Laundry A4
52. Clinic B/C5
53. Post Office B2
T = Taxi rank

At night the waterfront Esplanade irresistibly reminds me of Pythagorion Port (Samos island), although the inhabitants of the latter might not fancy the comparison. This impression is heightened by the harbour hosting a large flotilla fleet.

ARRIVAL BY FERRY & FLYING DOLPHIN

Well connected into the various Sporades timetables although the Flying Dolphin schedules do not tie up with aircraft arrivals on Skiathos. This causes long delays for package tourists, for whom the Skiathos airport is pivotal.

The first impression of the Port is that of being about to dock at a cliff-face, but closer inspection reveals that this is not so.

THE ACCOMMODATION & EATING OUT

The Accommodation Arrivals are met on the quayside. Those offered accommodation at Votsi Bay must bear in mind it is a good twenty minutes walk back to the Port. This inconvenience is well compensated by the additional quietness but note the stress is on human quietude as the animal life is actively noisy.

The right-hand (*Sbo*), Harbour encircling (Kavos), slopes are thickly 'planted out' with low-rise, respectable hotels, pleasantly screened by mature pine trees. Respectable indicates that the patio tables are covered by chintz print oilcloth. And ignore their E classification, these are not Athens' flea-pits, but smart, well constructed establishments which include:-

Pension Nina (*Tmr* 4E2) Tel 65242
Directions: Turn right (*Fbqbo*) along the Esplanade and turn left up Leoforos Ikion Doloron. There is a rough path to the right that clambers off this wide street, beyond the Petrol Station (*Tmr* 2E3) and immediately prior to an Engineers workshop (*Tmr* 3D2). This climbs to the track that fronts this row of buildings lining Kavos slopes.

Comes well recommended and is owned by a very pleasant lady. A double room with en suite bathroom and balcony costs 2000drs a night, which rate rises to 2400drs in July and August.

Adjacent to *Pension Nina* are other *Rooms For Rent* owned by N Anagnostou (Tel 65339), who also has another *Pension* (*Tmr* 7E2). *See* following copy.

Next along, across the road that ascends to the School (*Tmr* C1/2), is the:-
Hotel Liadromia (*Tmr* 5F2/3) (Class E) Tel 65521
Directions: As above.

En suite double rooms only, starting off at 2000drs and rising to 2650drs (1st July-10th Sept).

Beyond the *Liadromia* are ***Rooms*** (Tel 65597) and then a waste lot, after which is the:-

Hotel Kavos (*Tmr* 6F3) (Class E) Tel. 65216
Directions: As above.

Again en suite double rooms only, costing 1550drs, which daily rate rises to 1900drs. This establishment is used by *Thompsons* package holiday-makers. There is a drinking water machine on the patio – useful to know when hot and bothered.

An old acquaintance, re-met on Alonissos after many years, and who has returned to accommodation on the Kavos slopes year after year, pointed out that the owners of the **FB Limnos** were using the Port for the first time, in 1987. So what you may ask? This change in scheduling is causing problems because Alonissos is the overnight base for the craft. The early morning departure is between 0545hrs and 0600hrs, which would not be too bad but, as befits a well-run craft, the refrigeration plant and auxiliary engines throb into life at about 0230hrs. The resultant reverberating din tends to disturb 'sleepies' at an unacceptable hour.

Incidentally, this Kavos slope path advances past a smart restaurant, overlooking the rocky mole that shelters the harbour from easterly seas and winds, and rounds the headland, only to peter out on a large, water lapped outcrop of rock. This is a favoured spot with sun worshippers who lie out here during the day. The rock continues on round the apex of the promontory for a metre or ten but unfortunately, unless a mountain goat, it is not possible to scramble onwards to Rsoum Gialo Bay.

A slip road behind the *Hotel Kavos* climbs past a pine tree shaded, rustic, tin shack taverna (*Tmr* 7F2) with a concrete patio. This appears to be a popular breakfast 'emplacement' with residents of the nearby hotels, who no doubt while away the mornings swopping reminiscences about Marks & Spencers or whatever. There is the hint of an informal book-swop, if the paperbacks stacked on the window ledge are an indication.

Next, ascending the slope is the *Pension Paradisos* (*Tmr* F2), after which the slip road joins the other street heading towards the School (*Tmr* C1/2). Still amongst the trees, to the rear of this smart accommodation, are a couple of prefabricated buildings constructed of corrugated iron, cardboard and breeze blocks. They appear uninhabited but who knows? Maybe ***Rooms*** next year?

About half-way towards to the School and to the right, on the crest of the hill, set in fields is:-

Rent Rooms (*Tmr* 8E2) Tel 65221

Directions: As above.

A nice looking house owned by (another) Nina, who is also proprietor of the accommodation (*Tmr* 4E2) on Kavos slopes. The mid-season rate for an en suite double room is 1800drs a night.

Avenue Ikion Doloron, which rises from the right-hand end of the waterfront Esplanade (*Sbo*), 'houses' some widely disparate accommodation including the:-

Xenon Alykon (*Tmr* 9D3) (Class B) Leoforos Ikion Doloron Tel 65450

Directions: As above and on the left.

Very, very smart and discreet. All rooms are en suite, singles starting off at 1400drs and doubles 1500drs which rates rise, respectively, to 1800drs and 2200drs (21st June-10th July & 21st Aug-10th Sept) and 2500drs and 3500drs (11th July-20th Aug). Yes, well.

At the other end of the scale is the:-

Rooms (*Tmr* 10D2/3) Leoforos Ikion Doloron Tel 65229

Directions: On the right (*Sbo*).

Further up the street, on the left, is a Pharmacy (*Tmr* 11D2) above which are ***Rooms***.

Standing on the Ferry-boat/Flying Dolphin Quay (*Tmr* 1D/E4/5), looking in the direction of the vertical rock face across the waterfront Esplanade (*Sbo*), and, at the foot of the cliff, are, amongst other business premises, a **Rooms To Let** hut (*Tmr* 12D4). This is closed outside of the height of the summer months but Ikos Tourist office (*Tmr* 13D4) is not. This latter specialises in 'accommodating' enquirers seeking a bed but their services are not as indispensable as is sometimes indicated by other sources of information. For more details *See* **Ferry-boat & Flying Dolphin Ticket Offices, A To Z**.

Looking down from the heights of the cliff-face are one or two delightfully situated establishments (*Tmr* 14D3/4). To get to these Pensions and other nearby ***Rooms*** (*Tmr* 14C4), proceed to Leoforos Ikion Doloron. On the left (*Sbo*) are a zig-zag flight of steps that ascend the steep hillside from a point beyond the Port police office (*Tmr* 15D3). At the top, keep left along the cliff edging street and the Pensions are on the right. This street continues, curving away from the cliff. To the left, on the first lateral lane, are two other ***Rooms*** (*Tmr* 14C4), on opposite sides of the passageway.

From the left-hand of the waterfront Esplanade (*Sbo*), the High St loop road, Avenue Pelasgon, climbs and circles the town. Off this branch the various roads to Marpounta, The Chora, Rsoum Gialo Bay (the middle bay), the 'up' island route and Votsi Bay. Proceeding up the High St, and the second lane on the right leads to ***Rooms*** (*Tmr* 16C4). The other side of the street is the steeply climbing Marpounta road, on the right of which is the very pretty, bougainvillea clad exterior of the:-

Pension Bougainvillea (*Tmr* 17B5) (Class E) Tel 65222
Directions: As above.

Single rooms are only available sharing a bathroom and cost 700drs. Double rooms sharing a bathroom cost 1000drs and with an en suite bathroom 1300drs. These rates rise, respectively, to 800drs and 1200/1600drs (1st July-31st Aug).

Back on the High St, on the junction of Leoforos Pelasgon and the Marpounta road, is the *Pegasus Cafe-bar* (*Tmr* 18B/C4) over which are ***Rooms***.

Still climbing Leoforos Pelasgon from the Esplanade and, on the right, approximately opposite the Marpounta turning, is:-

Rooms (*Tmr* 19C4) Tel 65294
Directions: As above.

Owned by Nikolaos Dimakis.

Further up the street are more ***Rooms***, on the left above a supermarket (*Tmr* 20B/C4) which also advertises, in the window, *Apartments, Rooms as well as a furnished house for rent in The Chora – '2 rooms sleep 4/5 persons. Information here*!

As to be expected there is another supermarket next door, above which is the:-

Hotel Alonissos (*Tmr* 21B/C4) (Class E) Tel 65210
Directions: As above.

Average room rate charges, as this is an older, archetypal E Class hotel.

Across the road, on the right, are ***Rooms*** (*Tmr* 22B/C4). Again on the right are ***Rooms*** (*Tmr* 23B/C4) in a house immediately prior to *Les Croissants* snackbar (*Tmr* 24B4).

Pension Dina (*Tmr* 25B4) Tel 65266
Directions: The pension is at the end of a short alley, the second turning off the High St to the left, beyond the Marpounta road.
A neat looking establishment. A sign on the wall proclaims *Breakfast refreshines* (*sic*), *water, drinks, beer.*

Still on Leoforos Pelasgon, beyond S Bikes (*Tmr* 26B4), are, on the right, more ***Rooms*** (*Tmr* 27B4) as there are ***Rooms*** on the left of the road (*Tmr* 27B4). Beyond another Scooter hire firm (*Tmr* 28B4), on the right of the High St, is accommodation (*Tmr* 27A/B4) with some more ***Rooms*** (*Tmr* 27A/B4, tel 65396) across the street, on the left.

Hotel Galaxy (*Tmr* 29C6) (Class C) Tel 65251
Directions: On the low cliffs that constitute the left-hand horn of the harbour bay (*Sbo*) and reached from the Marpounta road.
All rooms have en suite bathrooms. Single rooms are charged from 1800drs and double rooms 2600drs, which rates rise to 2600drs for a single room and 3200drs for a double room (16th June-14th Sept).

See (the 'suburbs' of) **Rsoum Gialo** and **Votsi Bays, Excursions to Patitiri Port Surrounds**.

Camping *See* **Steni Vala, Route One**. Note the sign that greets those disembarking from the ferries or hydrofoils advising that *free-camping* is not allowed.

The Eating Out

The restaurants and tavernas, especially those lining 'Beach Esplanade', experience a lot of pressure from the 'yellow wellie' brigade of yachties that crew the fleet of flotilla yachts moored in the Harbour. Additionally some tourists are demi-pension, so they have to seek an evening meal and possibly some of the *Hotel Galaxy* guests 'come over the wall'! The presence of the British yachtsman and package holiday-makers probably accounts for the number of breakfasts on offer. A continental breakfast of coffee, toast and jam averagely costs 180drs and an English breakfast 300drs. They may well also have 'encouraged' the onset of the various cocktail and rock-music bars. Oh Goody!
A to-be-recommended, if smart, 'art-deco, rinky-dinky', cafe-bar is the:-

Pegasus Cafe-bar (*Tmr* 18B/C4)
Directions: On the corner of Leoforos Pelasgon and the Marpounta road.
This is a 'Wimpy Bar' look-alike with yellow covered seats. The owner, Stimatis, when encouraged to converse, has surprisingly good English.

The pleasantly tree planted, 'Beach Esplanade' pedestrian way cul-de-sac is lined by various businesses. These include a number of restaurant/tavernas, the canopy covered patios of which border the sea wall. At the outset is the smart *Cafe-bar Metoikos* (*Tmr* 30C5) where a Nes meh ghala costs 100drs and 5 star brandy 180drs (Ouch!).

Taverna To Dixty (*Tmr* 31C5)
Directions: As above.
On the 'greasy' side but the least expensive and pushy of the eateries that line this stretch. A beer (77drs), a tzatziki (120drs), 2 plates of kalamares (230drs each), a plate of large, white beans (gigantes – 250drs), a plate of chips (58drs) and bread for two (20drs each) totals 1005drs, rounded down to 1000drs.

The *To Dixty* is followed by a smart souvenir shop, another shop, a cafe-bar/cocktail drinks place, another souvenir shop and then by two look-alike tavernas. The first, owned by Agili Ioannis, offers goat's meat and potatoes cooked in oil, and has blue check, oilcloth covered tables. He is less aggressive than the next door establishment, which has floral patterned, oilcloth clothed tables, the:-

To Akrogiali (*Tmr* 32C5)
Directions:- As above.

A harder sell, in fact a 'hustle'. The wife speaks English and almost hypnotizes customers into ordering. Unfortunately they have a habit of charging for all extras, including bottled water, and tend to adjust prices upwards. A plate of tzatziki (good), a plate of patatas (old), briam (especially nice), 2 helpings of tuna (plentiful and good value, which didn't make up for the fact that we were quoted 250drs but an attempt was made to charge 300drs – an effort that was resisted), a Greek salad, a bottle of retsina, bread and water cost 1200drs.

The *To Akrogiali* is followed by the La Vie Pub, a rock cocktail bar, the *Cafe-restaurant H Moypia* and, at the end, the Pub Ix Muses, cafe rock-bar.

Back on the waterfront Esplanade (in a more Greek environment) is the:-
O Giannakis (Ο ΓΙΑΝΝΑΚΙΣ Kafeneion (*Tmr* 33D4)
Directions: Across the road from the left-hand side (*Sbo*) of the large, wide Ferry-boat and Flying Dolphin Quay (*Tmr* 1D/E4/5).

A traditional, 'local popular' kafeneion, with a tree shaded terrace, charging reasonable prices, that is reasonable compared to the 'Beach Esplanade' fellows. When busy the service becomes abysmally slow but that's a small price to pay with two large, very hot, good Nes meh ghala and a large ouzo costing 240drs. The water is served cold as well. Prices can fluctuate. For instance, a milky Nescafé varies between 72drs and 80drs.

Cafe Zacharoplasteion (*Tmr* 34D3)
Directions: At the right-hand end (*Sbo*) of the Esplanade. Above the cafe and up some steps to the side is the Pub Paradise, which 'dies' out of the height of season. To the right is the Apostolos Vlaikos Ticket Agency (*Tmr* 35D3).

On offer are saganaki, as well as kalamares and fish dishes. They also sell cigarettes alongside the international metered telephone counter. When required the telephone is pushed through the window on to a wide ledge. Across the Esplanade, hard against the quayside, is a small canopy covered terrace. The cafe closes for siesta.

Ouzerie To Kamaki (*Tmr* 36D2/3)
Directions: On the left of Leoforos Ikion Doloron, climbing from the Esplanade, beyond a butcher (*Tmr* 37D3) and prior to a Chemist (*Tmr* 11D2).

An establishment with rare fare – plate upon plate of mezes, some of them almost unique. Invariably, in English Greek restaurants, diners are served diverse plates of slush. At the *To Kamaki* are available the 'real McCoy'. Sample offerings include egg and tomato, hot pepper and mussel mezes, salad, cold gigantic bean salad, Alonissos sausage with green or yellow peppers and a scallop of some description. Naturally tzatziki is on the menu as are grilled fishes, all served with tost (*sic*).

A meal for two of an egg dish (150drs), mussels (400drs), Alonissos sausages (300drs), gigantic beans (180drs), tzatziki (120drs) two bottles of retsina (92drs each) and toast costs 1354drs. Perhaps not inexpensive but certainly a most enjoyable as well as very unusual meal. More popular with locals than the 'grotty yachties', who tend to prefer the more conventional offerings.

Further up the street, on the right (*Sbo*), is a *Souvlaki snackbar* (*Tmr* 38D2).

On Leoforos Pelasgon are situated the *Restaurant Apollon* (*Tmr* 39B4), which is a popular breakfast place and sells pancakes, and *Les Croissant* (*Tmr* 24B4). This latter is a rather pretentious establishment selling a range of pies, with fancy contents at fancy prices, which look very nice but cost double that of the more traditional pies. Much further up the road, on the left, is the *Astakos Restaurant, The Lobster Fish Taverna* (*Tmr* 40A4) with a large terrace. Even if I could afford such luxuries as lobster, the establishment is rather a long way from the Esplanade to easily attract custom.

See the 'suburbs' of **Rsoum Gialo** & **Votsi Bay, Excursions to Patitiri Port Surrounds**.

THE A TO Z OF USEFUL INFORMATION

BANKS None. The two travel offices, **Ikos Tourist** (*Tmr* 13D4) and **Apostolos Vlaikos** (*Tmr* 35D3) effect transactions, even on Sundays (*See* **Ferry-boat & Flying Dolphin Ticket Offices, A To Z**). Do not forget the less costly alternative of the Post Office (*Tmr* 53B2).

BEACHES There is the small, not very wide, town beach at the left-hand side (*Sbo*) of the Esplanade, but it is made up of small pebbles and rather dirty. The state of the beach is not helped by the fishermen pulling their craft on to the shore to carry out repairs, despite the sign *Please do not pollute our beaches*! On the other hand, it has the evocative name, *The Beach of the Wine Press*. I would have loved to see the port's shoreline years ago.

An alternative within walking distance, apart from nearby Rsoum Gialo & Votsi Bays, is the:-

Rope Beach The water taxis and trip boats have an agreement not to stop here, so it is necessary to 'scale' the Marpounta road and turn off to the left, after about ten minutes. A certain amount of nudism here, despite the shore being pebbly. Oh, the final descent is by abseiling down with the aid of a rope, thus the name.

See **Water Taxis, Places of Interest, A To Z**

BICYCLE, SCOOTER & CAR HIRE No car hire but a number of scooter and motorbike firms. There is one (*Tmr* 41D2) on the left and towards the top of Leoforos Ikion Doloron, but the majority are on Leoforos Pelasgon.

Malamatenios Rent A Bike Tel 65371

Directions: The office is on the left of Leoforos Pelasgon, at the junction with the Marpounta road. The scooters are 'displayed' on the pavement outside Disco For You (*Tmr* 42C4/5)

Theodorou Nikos, a very pleasant and interesting fellow with good English, is the 'frontman' for the owner. Scooters of uncertain condition cost 1300drs a day.

Incidentally, the average quoted prices, mid-season, are 1200drs a day for the smaller Hondas and 1400drs for larger scooters.

Further up the street, on the right is:-

Bikes of Alonissos/S Group (*Tmr* 26B4) No.24 Leoforos Pelasgon Tel 65578
Directions: As above.

Activities incorporate tourism and travel, Estate agency, licensed pubs, tavernas, discos, outboard engine repairs, motorboat (Sting Ray Boats) as well as motor cycle rental. Well that's what their card says. Oh I nearly forgot to mention that the two partners, Elias Papanikolaou and Michael Savvides, both good London boys with Cypriot parents, are also consultants to the Airport development. Well, there you go. Need one say any more other than to take along a bag of salt, let alone a pinch. Perhaps the self-publicity owes much to the fact that Michael Savvides ('say he') was once a rock group manager and 'best friend' of Richard Branson (of Virgin fame), despite which he refers to a dastardly deal which denied him of some enormous managerial gems... They plan to take over Disco on The Rocks, fly out lighting groups etc., etc., etc....

One thing they do well is probably what they originally set out to do, that is hire motorbikes. They have some well maintained Simpson bikes and charge between 800 and 1800drs a day, depending on the time of year. They represent a good, if possibly more expensive choice than their competitors.

They also represent the horse riding outfit up in the Chora. Well, they say they do, but admit that 'your actual' proprietor is not as active as he might be.

A few metres further up the road, separated by a house with accommodation – possibly 'dead', is yet another **Rent A Bike** outfit (*Tmr* 28B4). Typical!

BOOKSELLERS (*Tmr* 43D4) More a tobacconist and foreign language paper shop.

BREAD SHOPS There is a Bakery (*Tmr* 44D2) on the right, towards the top of Leoforos Ikion Doloron. They sell the special Alonissos bread, which is sold in slabs. It is a 'solidish', cooked dough sprinkled with feta – very intriguing and makes most interesting 'K' rations. There is another Baker (*Tmr* 44C4) opposite the Police station.

BUSES None.

COMMERCIAL SHOPPING AREA No central market but plenty of shops spread along the two main streets and the Esplanade. These include, in Leoforos Ikion Doloron, a Butcher (*Tmr* 46D3), a Drink shop in the Petrol Station kiosk (*Tmr* 2E3) and a Shop/store (*Tmr* 47D2). There is an excellent Fruit shop (*Tmr* 48D4) let into the cliff-face of the Esplanade and, on Leoforos Pelasgon, a 'Front Room' Fruit shop (*Tmr* 49C4/5), a Supermarket (*Tmr* 50C4) on the right, flanked by a boutique and another store. Back across the road, on the left (*Sbo*), is a Supermarket (*Tmr* 20B/C4). Next door is yet another Supermarket (*Tmr* 21B/C4), a good one with a cold meats counter as well as a selection of cheeses and drink. Tucked alongside is an alleyway paper-cum-stationery shed strictly for the Greeks. Two doors further on up the street is a shop followed by Kastanis Market – a general store.

Even the butcher opens on Sunday but there is evidence of a locals and tourist price differential. Often suspected, but here definitely established.

Note there are no Peripteros but the Tobacconist/paper shop (*Tmr* 43D4) and the Kafeneion (*Tmr* 34D3) fill the role. The Souvenir shop to the left (*Sbo*) of *Kafeneion O Giannakis* (*Tmr* 33D4) is owned by a forgetful old lady but she sells the most inexpensive, if dusty, maps and postcards.

One other, 'out of town shopping centre' may merit a mention, (*See* **Excursions to Patitiri Port Surrounds**). More seriously there are also two large Supermarkets on the approach to Votsi Bay (*See* **Excursions to Patitiri Port Surrounds**.)

DISCOS Disco For You (*Tmr* 42C4/5) lingers close to the junction of the Marpounta road and Leoforos Pelasgon. **Disco On The Rocks** is west of the Port, to the left of the Marpounta road, beyond the turning to the *Hotel Galaxy*. Readers may remember what delights the 'S' Group boys intend to inflict on this establishment! **Beach on the Balcony** is a snazzy cocktail bar sited on the pretty street at the top of the cliff that edges the Esplanade. There is no fear of missing the establishment as the owners have placed signs even in places that a certain well known lager wouldn't reach.

FERRY-BOATS & FLYING DOLPHINS At least one ferry-boat sailing a day via the other Sporades islands to the mainland, which ports of connection include Ag Konstantinos and Kymi Port (Evia). There are several hydrofoil flights a day, again via other Sporades islands, to various mainland ports which include Moundania (Nr Thessaloniki), Volos and Ag Konstantinos.

Prior to 1988 the **CF Limnos** was engaged on NE Aegean sailings, but now plies the Sporades. This 'thoughtless' chopping and changing can make exact ferry-boat identification difficult.

Ferry-boat timetable (Mid-Season)

Day	**Departure time**	**Ferry-boat**	**Ports/Islands of Call**
Monday	0545hrs	Limnos	Skopelos (0615hrs), Glossa (Skopelos-0730hrs),Skiathos(0805hrs) Ag Konstantinos(M-1115hrs).
Tuesday	0545hrs	Skiathos	Skopelos (0615hrs), Glossa (Skopelos-0720hrs), Skiathos(0800hrs), Trikeri (M-0940hrs), Volos (M-1115hrs).
Wednesday	0545hrs	Limnos	Skopelos(0615hrs), Glossa (Skopelos-0730hrs),Skiathos(0805hrs), Ag Konstantinos(M-1115hrs).
Thursday	0545hrs	Skiathos	Skopelos(0615hrs), Glossa (Skopelos-0720hrs), Skiathos(0800hrs),Trikeri (M-0940hrs), Volos(M-1115hrs).
	1945hrs	Skopelos	Skopelos(2030hrs).
Friday	0545hrs	Limnos	Glossa (Skopelos 0715hrs), Skiathos (0750hrs), Ag Konstantinos (M-1115hrs).
	1245hrs	Skiathos	Skopelos(1330hrs), Glossa (Skopelos-1440hrs), Skiathos(1515hrs), Volos (M-1830hrs).
	1815hrs	Skopelos	Kymi Port (Evia 2130hrs & departs for Ag Estratios, NE Aegean, 0615hrs next day).
Sunday	0545hrs	Limnos	Skopelos(0615hrs), Glossa (Skopelos 0720hrs), Skiathos(0800hrs), Ag Konstantinos(M-1145hrs).
	1330hrs	Skiathos	Skopelos(1415hrs), Glossa (Skopelos 1525hrs), Skiathos(1600hrs), Trikeri (M-1740hrs), Volos(M-1915hrs).

One-way fares Alonissos to Ag Konstantinos 1415drs.
to Kymi Port 1390drs.
to Volos 1150drs.

Flying Dolphin timetable (Mid-Season)

Day	Departure time	Ports/Islands of Call
Monday	0700hrs	Skopelos, Glossa (Skopelos), Skiathos, Volos(M-0940hrs).
	1040hrs	Skopelos, Glossa (Skopelos), Skiathos, Ag Konstantinos(M-1330hrs).
	1415hrs	Skopelos, Glossa (Skopelos), Skiathos, Volos(M-1700hrs).
	1730hrs	Skopelos, Skiathos, Volos(M-1955hrs).
Tuesday	0700hrs	Skopelos, Glossa (Skopelos), Skiathos, Volos(M-0940hrs).
	1040hrs	Skopelos, Glossa (Skopelos), Skiathos, Ag Konstantinos(M-1330hrs).
	1415hrs	Skopelos, Glossa (Skopelos), Skiathos, Volos(M-1700hrs).
	1730hrs	Skopelos, Skiathos, Volos(M-1955hrs).
Wednesday	0700hrs	Skopelos, Glossa (Skopelos),Skiathos, Volos(M-0940hrs).
	1040hrs	Skopelos, Glossa (Skopelos), Skiathos, Ag Konstantinos(M-1330hrs).
	1415hrs	Skopelos, Glossa (Skopelos), Skiathos, Volos(M-1700hrs).
	1625hrs	(Non-stop) Moundania(M-1845hrs).
	1730hrs	Skopelos, Skiathos, Volos(M-1955hrs).
Thursday	0700hrs	Skopelos, Glossa (Skopelos), Skiathos, Volos(M-0940hrs).
	0815hrs	Skopelos, Skiathos.
	1030hrs	(Non-stop) Skyros.
	1040hrs	Skopelos, Glossa (Skopelos), Skiathos, Ag Konstantinos(M-1330hrs).
	1415hrs	Skopelos, Glossa (Skopelos), Skiathos, Volos(M-1700hrs).
	1730hrs	Skopelos, Skiathos, Volos(M-1955hrs).
Friday	0700hrs	Skopelos, Glossa (Skopelos), Skiathos, Volos(M-0940hrs).
	1040hrs	Skopelos, Glossa (Skopelos), Skiathos, Ag Konstantinos(M-1330hrs).
	1415hrs	Skopelos, Glossa (Skopelos), Skiathos, Volos(M-1700hrs).
	1550hrs	Skopelos, Skiathos, Ag Konstantinos(M-1825hrs).
	1730hrs	Skopelos, Skiathos, Volos(M-1955hrs).
Saturday	0700hrs	Skopelos, Glossa (Skopelos),Skiathos, Volos(M-0940hrs).
	1040hrs	Skopelos, Glossa (Skopelos), Skiathos, Ag Konstantinos (M—1330hrs).
	1415hrs	Skopelos, Glossa(Skopelos), Skiathos, Volos(M-1700hrs).
	1625hrs	(Non-stop) Moundania(M-1845hrs).
	1730hrs	Skopelos, Skiathos, Volos(M-1955hrs).
Sunday	0700hrs	Skopelos, Glossa (Skopelos), Skiathos, Volos(M-0940hrs).
	1040hrs	Skopelos, Glossa (Skopelos), Skiathos, Ag Konstantinos (M-1330hrs).
	1040hrs	(Non-stop) Skyros.
	1630hrs	Skopelos, Skiathos, Ag Konstantinos(M-1905hrs).
	1755hrs	Skopelos, Glossa (Skopelos), Skiathos, Volos(M-2035hrs).

One-way fare: Alonissos		
	to Skopelos	405drs
	to Glossa (Skopelos)	605drs
	to Skiathos	740drs
	to Volos (M)	2265drs
	to Ag Konstantinos (M)	2265drs
	to Moundania (M)	2530drs

FERRY-BOAT & FLYING DOLPHIN TICKET OFFICES

Ferry-boat tickets

Apostolos Vlaikos Ticket Agency (*Tmr* 35D3)
Directions: Close to the junction of The Esplanade and Leoforos Ikion Doloron, at the right-hand end of the waterfront (*Sbo*).

The old boy and his wife are abrupt and rather 'boot faced'. Enquiries that don't immediately concern them are dismissed and they quickly lose interest. A more than usually unintelligible ferry-boat timetable is propped on the verandah. The agency opens seven days a week, all hours, apart from siesta. They are agents for the National Bank of Greece.

Flying Dolphin tickets
Ikos (Travel & Tourist Office) (*Tmr* 13D4) Tel 65320
Directions: Conveniently situated in a hut which is tucked up against the cliff-face, across the way from the Ferry-boat Quay.

Agents for the Commercial Bank of Greece, Olympic Airline, the various package holiday operators and the hydrofoils. The owner, Panayotis Athanassiou, speaks excellent English and can be very helpful, if rather 'zap, zap'. I stress 'can' as he has contracted a serious case of 'Grecociliousness'. Females experience the 'charm bank'! Requests for ferry-boat details are countered with a curt 'Only Flying Dolphins', when only a little more conversational effort could direct people to the correct office. On the other hand, the charming, smiley, young lady assistant, Stephanie, makes up for any inconsistencies. I have observed her quite voluntarily taking somebody off to the Clinic rather than point vaguely in the general direction of the place. I believe she represents *Laskarina Holidays*. She speaks excellent English and, taking account of her Greek, may well be Cypriot English.

LAUNDRY
Orpheus Tourist Laundry (*Tmr* 51A4)
Directions: Quite a way up Leoforos Palasgon, on the left.

Clothes washed/dry one day service. Open *8.30am to 8pm. Mon thru' Sat. Closed Sunday. Clothes washed 5 kilos or less 800drs. Clothes dried 200drs each piece, pressed 100drs and clothes dried by machine 400drs*. I'm not sure I understand all this information, but there you go!

**but not out of the height of season*

MEDICAL CARE
Chemists & Pharmacies (*Tmr* 11D2) One on the left (*Sbo*) of Leoforos Ikion Doloron, above which are ***Rooms***.
Clinic (*Tmr* 52B/C5) The clinic is indicated by a sign *To the doctor's surgery* on the telegraph pole alongside *Pegasus Cafe-bar* (*Tmr* 18B/C4) and is on the right of the lane that branches left off the road to Marpounta. 'Throws' the doors open weekdays between 0900-1200hrs & 1800-2000hrs, but is closed on Saturdays and Sundays.

OTE Ah, well! Despite authoritative looking signposting up the slopes of Leoforos Ikion Doloron, the OTE either never happened or has closed. The locals display a mixed bag of emotions when questioned about the missing office. These vary from shy disbelief to outright belly-laughs. When I referred to the 'ghost OTE', he who was questioned simply 'fell about'.

On the other hand all is not lost. *See Cafe Zacharoplasteion* (*Tmr* 34DE), **The Eating Out**.

PETROL The Harbour petrol station (*Tmr* 2E3), at the junction of the Esplanade and Leoforos Ikion Doloron, has a drink store in the large kiosk office. The middle-aged couple, who own the place, slobbishly squat on stools whilst allowing their rather backward son to serve the clients. Mama and Papa ignorantly shout instructions to their offspring who tries his best.

The friendlier facility, 'Kellys Garage' (*Tmr* B1), is located on the 'ring' road that loops round from the Leoforos Pelasgon towards Votsi Bay.

PLACES OF INTEREST Not surprisingly, considering the recent history, there are no churches, Museums or Public Gardens of any note. The mention of Churches reminds me to comment that Alonissos is one of the only Greek islands where I have not heard church bells on a Sunday, nor, for that matter, at all. Perhaps the earthly disasters have driven spiritual thoughts out of the inhabitants' minds. That is not to say that there is no priest. In fact the incumbent's reputation is such that he is probably a lot more intriguing and interesting than any number of Byzantine churches. It is said, and its quite possibly only a rumour, that the reverend gentleman enjoys gaming, wining and dining, has 'four hands', is a bit of a swinger and has a penchant for blondes. It is also rumoured that he annually seeks a replacement lady friend with whom he skips off to an overseas retreat. Naturally this 'pilgrimage' is to restore the spiritual tissues! Whatever rumour says, he is, without doubt, well respected by the locals.

Water Taxis The small trip boats line up alongside the Esplanade, centred on the small quay (*Tmr* D5) to the left (*Sbo*) of the Harbour. They run morning and afternoon shuttle services to the various beaches scattered along the eastern coastline of the island. Departures from the Port start about 1000hrs, returning between 1500 & 1700hrs. Destinations include:-

Marpounta Beach, Vithisma Beach and Megalo Mortia, to the south, and, to the north, Chrisi Milia, Kokkinokastro, Steni Vala, Kalamaki and Ag Dimitrios (600drs). Prices vary for a return trip from 250drs to 2000drs – the latter being the cost of a Round-The-Island-Trip. Considering the state of the 'up island' roads the water taxis give surprisingly good value. The pity is that most of the beaches, which are set in pleasant surroundings, are generally only pebble.

Caique Excursions These include a 'fun evening' trip to Steni Vala at a cost of about 2000drs which includes (I have been reliably informed) a very indifferent meal and Greek dancing. A BBQ voyage to Peristera island cost approximately 2500drs. The 'head' office for these delights is Ikos Travel (*Tmr* 12D4). Mind you I would prefer to plump for the caique owned by Nikos (Nikolaos Karakatsanis). This is moored between the Ferry-boat Quay (*Tmr* 1D/E4/5) and the fishing/trip boat quay (*Tmr* D5), close to where the Marpounta Club boat moors. Nikos owns a very pleasant Pension round on Votsi Bay (*See* **Votsi Bay, Excursion to Patitiri Port Surrounds**) and, either side of the height-of-season months, skippers a tuna boat. His eye-catching, neat cabin boat is 9m in length and has a galley and toilet. A sign in the rigging advertises the fact that the craft is for hire. A day's rental cost 10,000drs but the boat can accommodate at least two families. Nikos is a most pleasant young man and works in co-operation with Ikos Travel, which, I suppose, can come as no surprise. He is often to be found having a Turkish coffee at *O Giannakis Kafeneion*, from whence he can 'sweep' the Esplanade with a nervous gaze, ever on the look out for possible clients for his boat or guests for his accommodation.

POLICE
Port (*Tmr* 15D3) On the left (*Sbo*) of Leoforos Ikion Doloron.
Town (*Tmr* 45C4) Tucked away at No. 3, opposite a baker in the 'Old Quarter'. Well more accurately an old street or two, presumably left more or less intact after the earthquake.

POST OFFICE (*Tmr* 53B2) Very close to the 'ring' road but interestingly signposted from the upper end of Leoforos Ikion Doloron. This latter track is nothing more than an arduous goat path through scrubbly backyards. The office is located at the rear and in the basement of a villa that fronts the Port to Votsi Bay loop road. The usual transactions including money exchange.

TAXIS There are a number which park (*Tmr* TC5) close to the junction of the Esplanade and Leoforos Pelasgon. They venture 'up island' but don't forget the Water Taxis.

TELEPHONE NUMBERS & ADDRESSES

Clinic (*Tmr* 52B/C5)	Tel 65470
Police, town (*Tmr* 45C4)	Tel 65205

TRAVEL AGENTS & TOUR OFFICES *See* **Ferry-boat & Flying Dolphin Ticket Offices, A To Z.**

WATER Despite being detailed in the Introduction, I cannot stress too strongly the possibility that, the main's drinking water might be contaminated. This is a common comment for all the other islands in the Sporades group (apart from Skyros). You have been warned! Bottled water costs, on average, 65drs.

EXCURSIONS TO PATITIRI PORT SURROUNDS

Excursion to Rsoum Gialo & Votsi Bays (2km, if that)

Rather than utilising the 'ring' road, Leoforos Pelasgon, proceed up the 'OTE' St, Leoforos Ikion Doloron. Towards the upper end,the street divides round a tree,in the middle of the road,and then bends round to the right,past a rather forlorn shop with most of the goods piled around the edges of the floor. The road widens out to become a featureless junction of the ways, almost as large as the nearby football pitch. Round to the right is a road that curves back and narrows down to peter out on the slopes of Kavos (*See* **The Accommodation**).

In the neck of land encompassed by this, and the road down to Rsoum Gialo Bay, is a small development that appears to have come to a standstill. The building was probably planned, in some measure, as a shopping precinct but only the cafe-bar has continued to trade. Behind the block is an erstwhile football pitch. Across the way is a large School whilst the main thrust of the swathe of concrete proceeds on to join the 'ring' road.

Taking the second turning, the road serpentines down past two houses with ***Rooms*** to the left-hand side (*Fsw*) of the seemingly hand chiselled, 'U' shaped:-

RSOUM GIALO BAY (1km from Patitiri Port) A concrete, waterfront road to the right (*Fsw*) edges the rather dirty, large pebble beach on which are drawn up the occasional benzina and caique. On the right-hand corner is the *Pub Agnanti*, over which are ***Rooms***. Lining the waterfront road are several tavernas, *Rooms To Rent* (Tel 65334), a dry river-bed and, at the southern end, a *Cafe-bar Restaurant* followed by a carpenter's workshop which is situated in the last building at the right-hand end of the bay. Steps ascend the hillside between houses with ***Rooms*** on the left and right – one in the ownership of K M Agalo (Tel 65365) and the other, the family Kastanis (Tel 65317). This path 'puffingly' climbs to rejoin the road down to the Bay.

The advantage of this spot is that few, if any, publications mention its existence. In addition the bay is rather too exposed and small to take many of the flotilla yachts, thus remaining just that little bit quieter and secluded. To appreciate the disadvantage of a fleet of charter yachts, consider the impact of dozens and dozens of 'yellow wellies' descending on the sparse facilities. It is certainly a thought to wander round here.

A very steep flight of steps climbs from the left (*Sbo*) of the road down to Rsoum Gialo Bay over to Votsi Bay southern headland. In addition, the 'ring road' progresses past Kelly's Garage and the 'up island' turning, both on the left, before curving round to the right and commencing to wind down the hillsides edging:-

VOTSI BAY (2km from Patitiri Port) Despite any owner of accommodation assuring prospective clients, 'on his mother's grave', that it is only a five to ten minute walk, take it from me, it is a good twenty minutes.

Prior to the road descending to the waterfront there are two supermarkets on the left. Both are cavernous, warehouse-like stores. The pick of the two is the first one which happens to have a metered international phone and stays open seven days a week, only closing for the siesta. On the way down there are dozens of ***Rooms***. A slip road to the right wanders on to the southern headland of Votsi Bay and from which very steep steps descend to the bay. Meanwhile the road narrows to wind through a scattering of houses and, on the left, the *Restaurant/Taverna Mouria*, which has ***Rooms***, a *Cafe Restaurant*, owned by Nikolaos Karakatsanis, and lastly the *Ilias Pub*, alongside which the road peters out on the quayside. To the right (*Fsw*) is a (at the moment) 'dead' building beyond which are the aforementioned steps up to the top of the south headland.

The most highly recommended of eateries is the *Restaurant Mouria*, which has a sign *To Toilets* pointing to the rear of the building. *Nikos*, the next taverna towards the waterfront, is rather expensive with 2 beers (100drs each) and an orange drink (50drs) costing 250drs. On the other hand, he stays open afternoons whilst there is any chance of custom. The owner of the *Ilias Pub* has jazzed the place up. This is, no doubt, to exploit the business potential of the flotilla yacht clientele, that is those who have exposed themselves to the dangers of passage making all the way round from the Port! The 'chic' has rather 'withered on the patio', having fallen foul of a muddle of competing cultures which include 'culture club', 'folk' and 'cocktail bar'. Despite, or because of this, it is very popular, apart from which it is the first establishment from the quayside. Need one say more!

Proceeding up the steps to the right (*Fsw*), clambers past the:-

Cafe-bar Taverna ΤΑΠΕΤΚΑ

Directions: As above or from the headland down the steps – what goes up must come down.

A limited, not very outstanding nor very cheap menu. A tzatziki cost 100drs, a Greek salad 180drs, a beef steak 250drs, a bottle of beer 80drs, a bottle of retsina 100drs and an orange drink 40drs. Bread is charged at 15drs.

Further up the steps, on the right, are:-

Rent Rooms Kologiannis Tel 65280

Directions: As above.

A large pension owned by a cousin of our favourite landlord, the aforementioned Nikos, who owns the:-

Pension Nikos Tel 65316

Directions: To the right, beyond *Rent Rooms Kologiannis* from the steps. Alternatively from the road down to the bay, angle right along a rubble track as far as an unfinished building and clamber down the fire stairs to the left.

A large building in good condition with curly headed, compact, young Nikos, his wife and family living in the basement. The spotlessly clean rooms are complete with bedside lamps (yes bedside lamps), an en suite bathroom and a balcony, even if views of the bay are now rather obscured by other buildings. Nikos' self-taught English is basic. Light, jocular, throw away remarks concerning the possibility of 'hot and cold running, blond Swedish nymphomaniacs' tend to fall flat – well so they should. Double room rates, that vary between 1500-2500drs, include the use of a small, separate hut-like kitchen at the rear of the building. This facility includes a fridge. It is worth 'negotiating' with Nikos for the best rate available. (In respect of other family activities *See* **Caique Excursions, Places of Interest, A To Z, Patitiri Port**).

Nikos, as indicated, tends to minimise the distance to Votsi Bay, which incidentally, does not guarantee a quiet ambiance. Nothing could be further from the truth. The deafening rural sounds include dogs barking, donkeys braying in addition to the appropriate noises made by sheep, goats and roosters. These background sound effects reach a crescendo between 0200 & 0600hrs in the morning. The northern headland hillside still supports a small holding or two, the animals of which form part of this delightful chorus. I once watched acted out a sunset drama of the slaying of the family goat. The Mama bungled the job of cutting its throat, her little girl screamed and screamed and the goat winnied pitifully until the arrival of a male to finish off the job. Quite a performance!

Round to the left (*Fsw*) of the quayside, from close by the *Ilias Pub* patio, is a pebbly, not very clean beach, tucked into the cliff-face that borders the backshore. To gain access it is necessary to clamber a metre or five over smooth rocks. The bay is understandably popular with splinter groups of the main flotilla fleet moored round at Patitiri Port.

Excursion to Marpounta Hotel and Coves (2km) The lane climbs very steeply for a 100m or so to the left (*Sbo*) off Leoforos Pelasgon, from between the Disco For You (*Tmr* 42C4/5) and the *Pegasus Cafe-bar* (*Tmr* 18B/C4). At the top of the road fork right, as left leads to the *Hotel Galaxy* (C Class, tel 652514).

Back on the now unsurfaced, rather tricky, rutted surface of the track and, to the left, is Disco On The Rocks, after which the tree shaded route sallies forth past one or two smart gateways. After about 1½km a track to the right is indicated, with masses of signs advertising 'surfing, beach and taverna' which, if followed, leads to:-

VITHISMA BEACH (circa 1½km from Patitiri Port) The path terminates above the cove. It is necessary to clamber the last 20-30m down to the nearside of the large, pebbly beach, which edges a beautifully clean sea. The pebbles of the beach continue into the water for a little way, after which the shelving sea-bed is clean sand, making for a lovely swim.

A backshore rubbish bin is promoted by a sign requesting visitors *please do not pollute our beaches*. The island's power supply emerges from the depths of the sea at the far end of the beach. The landward side is pleasantly planted with olive trees, in amongst which three tavernas are scattered. A lunchtime snack for two of a Greek salad, bread, a bottle of beer and an orange drink costs, on average, 330drs.

Back on the main route and the track advances through a gateway to run out in the grounds of the:-

MARPOUNTA HOTEL & COVES (2km from Patitiri Port) A rather shabby, tawdry hotel set in unkempt surrounds and bordered by a rocky coastline, offshore of which is a tiny islet. The premises include chalets, a hotel taverna, a swimming pool as well as a basket, volley ball and tennis court. Incidentally, if the pool's present condition is anything to go by, it won't be in action for a considerable time. This may upset the French, from whom the clientele is mainly drawn.

To the right (*Fsw*) of the hotel, a track advances to a tiny, pebbly cove bordered by an interesting rock strata and lapped by clear seas. To the left of the hotel is a small, not very attractive cove edged by a pebble beach with a smidgin of foreshore sand.

Excursion to Alonissos Town (The Chora – 2½-3km) The rough road that serpentines up to The Chora takes off from the 'ring' road.

For those who intend to walk to The Chora and stay to watch the dramatic sunset, a word of warning may not go amiss. At night the only chance of getting back to the Port, in some comfort, is to be lucky enough to flag down one of the taxis that connect the two. Incidentally the return taxi fare costs 1000drs. Otherwise don't forget to take along a torch, there are no street lights!

The buildings of The Chora, which was severely shaken by an earthquake, attractively undulate over the hillside and are prettily covered with grey, stone slate roofs. Disappointingly the outset of the town is spattered with a maze of indications to different bars, ceramic workshops and goodness only know's what. I can advise that these include *Mina's Bar* as well as *Astrofegia Bar* and *Astrofegia Taverna Bar*, selling, apart from drinks, ice-creams, sweets, cocktails and fruit-juices. There is another sign (to which I object on a number of grounds) that advocates *No Parking Here*. It has to be admitted that these establishments are not themselves intrusive, but I cannot see the necessity for the multiplicity of signs. On the right is a restaurant with a smart patio dominated by a stone tower and situated to take full advantage of the views out over the island and surrounding sea.

Proceeding to the left, not sharp-left but in a left direction, rises past ***Rooms*** after fifty metres. Another twenty metres on are signs indicating apartments, ***Rooms*** and small flats. A few, small cafe-bar/tavernas open for the height-of-season months, seemingly having the summer life-span of a May-fly. One of these is well worth locating, a cafe-bar run by two Greek ladies, one middle-aged and one rather ancient, who dresses in local costume.

Despite the great number of still abandoned dwellings, some have been purchased by overseas 'chappies'. They appear to have, if not a death wish, at least a desire to punish themselves beyond the call of duty, by engaging in the reconstruction of dwellings which locals, on probably a 1000th of the income, were only too happy to relinquish, as fast as they could. Allowing for the number of Choras I have seen, which may well prejudice the decision making, I consider this one rather scrubbly and disappointing.

ROUTE ONE (& only)

To Ormos Geraka (approx 23km) The 'up-island' road branches off the Port 'ring' road, just beyond Kelly's Garage (*Tmr* B1), from whence it is an unmetalled track with every imaginable state of surface finish. There are a number of signs for *Camping Ikaros* and a banner across the road states *Protect me from the fire – The Forest*, on one side, and, on the other *And I am also expecting you to protect me tomorrow*. This is situated where a track turns off to the right to:-

MILIA GIALOS BEACH (Some 4km from Patitiri Port) The profusely pine tree studded approach is subject to some uncertainty, apart from the bad surface, with a path to the left signed *Dead End*. Keep right to the next fork, where keep straight on.

The big pebble, quite pretty beach is set in a very large, 'U' shaped bay that has every appearance of being chiselled out of the coastline. The surrounds are rather scrubbly. At the height of season the blockhouse to the right (*Fsw*) doubles up as a taverna, if the empty beer crates piled high are any indication.

This bottom half of Alonissos is well wooded with resin collection an active pursuit. The 'main' road runs along the spine of the island. The surface is reasonable enough, even if the authorities have an irritating habit of dropping 300m of scalpings, in irregular piles along the length of the road.

The next turning off to the right is to:-

CHRISI MILIA BEACH (Some 6km from Patitiri Port) The track advances through a fire damaged section of wood. At the unsignposted fork proceed along the right-hand track which runs out on the nearside end of another, if shallower, 'U' shaped bay. Where the track merges with the backshore, there is a small, neat taverna on the right with oilcloth covered tables dotted about the patio.

From this right-hand end of the narrow, large pebble beach is a stretch of sand which borders the sea's edge all the way along to the far headland bluff, off which is a small islet.

The 'main' road now progresses through pleasant countryside, with olive groves planted along the route. At a tri-way are signs to the:-

(Alonissos Beach Bungalow Hotel), Kokkinokastro & Chrisi Milia (Some 7km from Patitiri Port) The sharp right turning divides. Right advances to the *Alonissos Hotel* (Tel 65281). This is a smart development, with signs instructing casual callers to stay away and keep out, to which I vigorously object. The hotel overlooks the north end of Chrisi Milia Beach. The left fork, keeping left, and not forking right, branches off to:-

KOKKINOKASTRO BEACH (Some 8km from Patitiri Port) The track runs out above the bay and the path down to the middle of the beach leaves a 'doo-hickey' *Cantina* caravan set in trees, to the left. The left-hand end (*Fsw*) of the clean, fine pebble beach is dramatically bounded by a sandstone headland that angles down into the water. There are a few boulders in the sea and the middle and backshore are made up of large pebbles, as is the seashore to the right. Also to that side is a new house in construction, with a sign *Work – No Enter*. From the general lack of activity I imagine this includes the workmen! A few tired pedaloes recline on the water's edge and a sign proclaims *No Rubbish* and yet another *In 20m there is a Caravan Cantina selling refreshments, hamburgers, beer, steaks, Greek salad and the famous cheese pie.*

This was the site of early settlements and there are supposedly sunken remains of city walls and an Agora.

TZORTZI GIALO BAY (Some 8km from Patitiri Port) This turning is the middle, slightly right route, of the 'tri-way' which almost immediately forks. The right-hand choice progresses towards the bottom of the bay and a beach. This is pebbly with a fine pebble sea's edge, as is the first 6-10m of sea-bed. On the hillside to the left (*Fsw*) are a couple of red roofed houses. The land backing the bay is planted out with olives but is not overly attractive. On the other hand, the isthmus of the peninsula bordering the far, southern portion of the bay, and in which is tucked a curved beach cove, is appealing. A range of buildings, set in fir trees, caps the headland that obscures a view of this cove from the bottom of the bay.

The left-hand fork, not taken above, leads around to the northern horn of Tzortzi Gialo Bay, where the track forks again. The right-hand turning doubles back to parallel with the coastline of the bay, allowing superb views around the inlet, only to terminate up against a concrete blockhouse, some 150m above sea-level. The left-hand turning continues round to the north of the headland to reveal the beautiful sight below of:-

LEFTO GIALO BAY (some 9km from Patitiri Port) Another 'U' shaped inlet, bordered by an almost white pebble beach, edging a crystal clear, turquoise sea, the only track to which is some of the roughest motoring on the island. This is a quite remarkable spot and still (just) the sole domain of the shepherds. It is approached through a backcloth of olive groves. Close to the backshore. a stone edged well containing rather murky looking water is complemented by a rustic log hollowed out to form a water trough. As elsewhere on the island, the beaches are now kept clean, a fact evidenced by the plastic bags stowed beneath one of the mature olive trees that border the backshore. To the right (*Fsw*) of this expansive stretch of small, round pebble beach is a 20m length of fine shingle foreshore. At the far right-hand end the sea-bed is made up of great slabs of biscuit rock. A scene of idyllic desertion as it continues to escape the 'Beach BBQ circus'.

Back at the tri-way, the left-hand route is the 'up-island', 'main' road, still signposted *Camping Ikarios*.

At approximately 8km a junction indicates **Gerakas** and **Finvikis** along the left, northerly direction and right to **Isomata** and **Steni Vala**. Taking the latter gives an impressive and unexpected view out over the coastline below with, in the middle distance, Peristera island. A right-hand track is signed to Isomata, a coastal, 'donkey-dropping' of a hamlet. The other, left-hand track branches down a good surface to the comparatively large, broad, peninsula of land jutting out into the sea and along the southern side of which spreads the unexpected:-

STENI VALA (12km from Patitiri Port) I write unexpected because the island maps give no idea of the size of the place. Let's face it, usually the smallest location, even a broken down hovel, is indicated, often by a 'mega blob'! On at least two maps, the roads aren't drawn anywhere near the location and as for an idea of the magnitude of the place, 'forget it'. Be that as it may Steni Vala has a surprisingly large fishing boat quayside, hosted by the small hamlet which spreads over the slope backing the waterfront. The place has had to adapt to the requirements of modern day tourism. The fishing boat caiques and benzinas, the traditional habitues that once lorded over the scene, are now interspersed with and outnumbered by the massed flotilla yachts.

Camping Ikaros (Category C, tel 65258) This oft advertised campsite is indicated off to the left, about 150m before reaching the Steni Vala 'proper', but I'm not sure that the site, which lies close to the shore of the adjacent Rema Xiro Bay, is open except in the height of season months.

The quayside is bordered by a taverna or four, the central one of which has a picture of Icarus on the wall. Interestingly this is the second allusion to Icarus

– the other is vis-a-vis *Camping Ikaros* but I cannot make a connection between Steni Vala and Icarus. More importantly this taverna has an international phone and is the one that *Michael Carroll*, in his book *Gates of the Wind*, wrote about so evocatively. During the flotilla season, meals are not particularly inexpensive. No prizes for the why! A couple of large, hot, milky coffees cost 140drs. A sign close to the waterfront advises *You can find Rooms for Rent. Market. Bread, Cigarettes, fruit, telephone. Showers (cold, hot). Informatios* (sic) *for transport to Patitiri through car and boat. Excursions* (sic) *to Cyclops Cave Sunken City. Round island Alonissos*. The shop in question is some 40m from the waterfront and the young girl who serves speaks excellent English. Apart from the signboard indications, there are a number of ***Rooms***.

In amongst the massed ranks of 'awfully nice' yachties, who are all 'terribly friendly' to each other, there are thinly spread one or two locals.

Continuing on past the port around to the left (*Fsw*), past the tiny church topped headland, progresses to the lovely sweep of **Rema Xiro Bay**. At the nearside end is a small, backshore boatyard, complete with winches with which to beach craft. The boatyard is followed by a pebble shore and there is another shingly, pebbly beach at the far side of the bay. The track follows the coastline round from Steni Vala, through pretty countryside, passing over a dry river-bed of olives (as distinct from one of oleanders). Around the headland, at the far, north side of Rema Xiro Bay is:-

KALAMAKIA (14km from Patitiri Port) A comparatively large settlement with a taverna, a small concrete quay and no concessions at all to tourism.

The route swings inland from Kalamakia, past an orange tree planted, dry river gorge, turns back towards the coast and then inland again after which there is an unsigned fork. Ah, well there you go! Take the left turning and proceed past another right-hand turning in order to rejoin the 'main', 'up island' road. This is close to a junction with yet another track that shambles off down to a large coastal plain criss-crossed with tracks. This area is worth exploration, if time is available.

Some maps indicate an inland village, Mourtero, at this junction but it is easy, very easy to miss – that is there isn't a settlement of any size.

The 'main' road surface varies from bad-to-awful-to-adequate and the inland side hereabouts is close to a low range of jagged topped mountains.

DIASELLO (18km from Patitiri Port) To the right of the road are a few inhabited houses and ruins, but not much else. The road is well surfaced and amazingly wide for a route that is really going nowhere, much!

A right at the next fork swings through a pass and round a rocky bluff to reveal a magnificent panorama spread out to the north. To the left is the towering headland of Analypsi and Cape Gerakas whilst to the forefront the road descends through countryside that sweeps down a wide, slow valley all the way to the distant:-

GERAKA BAY (some 23km from Patitiri Port) The large building in the lee of the headland is, for a change, not the site of a hotel but is the Institute of Marine Biology, with especial responsibility for the protection of the Mediterranean Monk seal.

The scooter ride from top to bottom of the island takes about one hour.

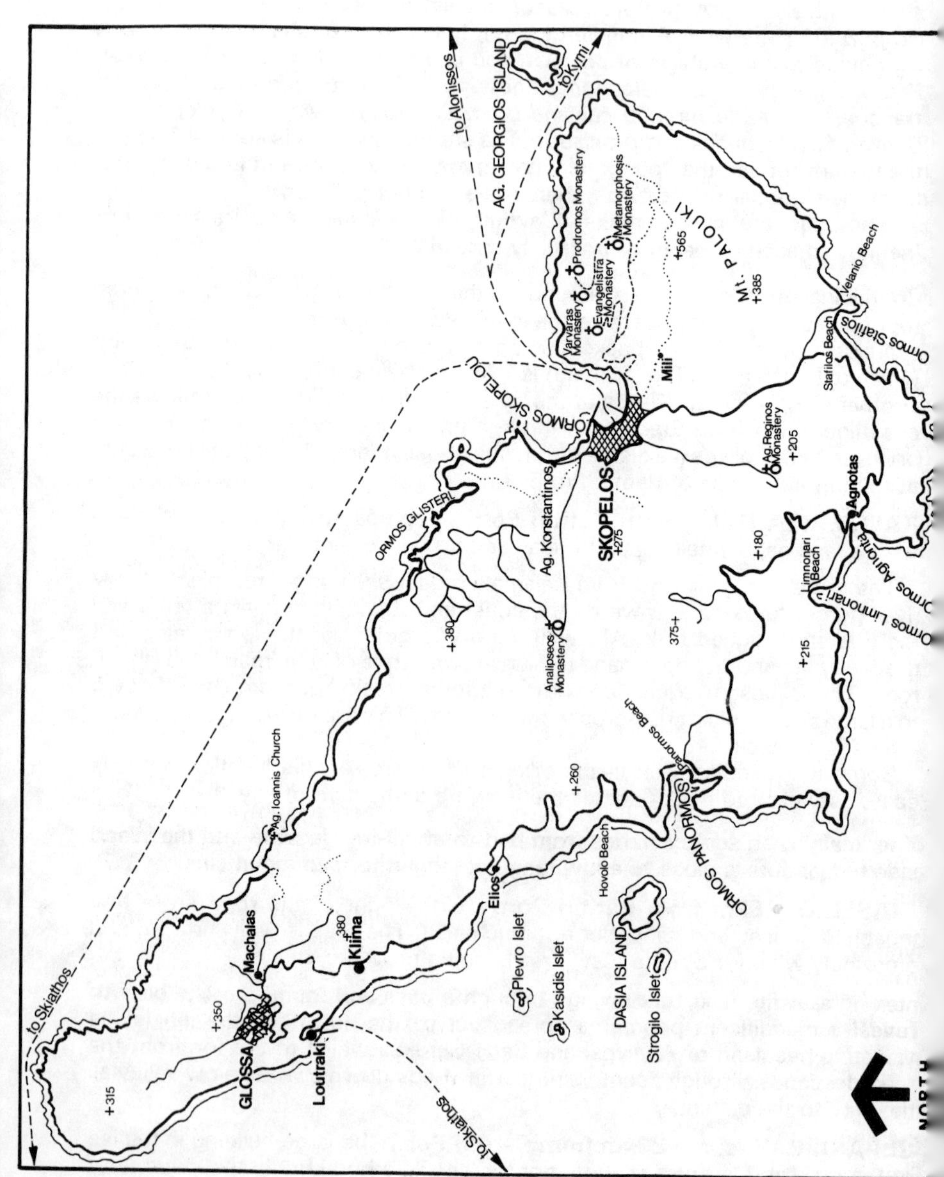

Illustration 37 Skopelos island

22 SKOPELOS (Scopelos, ΣΚΟΠΕΛΟΣ) ***

Sporades Islands

FIRST IMPRESSIONS
Picture postcard prettiness; grey slate roofs; distinctive churches; port/town/Chora maze of streets, lanes & alleys; blocked drains, so everything flows down the street surfaces; harbour pong; tourists; lovely countryside; pine trees; a damp island.

SPECIALITIES
Chora slate roofs.

RELIGIOUS HOLIDAYS & FESTIVALS
include: 25th February – Festival of St Reginos, Monastery Ag Reginos; 6th August – Festival of Transfiguration of the Saviour, Monastery of Metamorphosis.

VITAL STATISTICS
Tel prefix 0424. A cross-section of the information available reveals that Skopelos is 20km from north-west to south-east, up to 12km across at the widest point, with a total area of 95sqkm and a population of 5,000.

HISTORY
Named Peparethus by the ancient Greeks, the island was a colony of Minoan Crete. The name was a natural enough association as some mythology asserts that Peparethus (as well as Staphylus, Thoas and Oenopion) was a son of the alliance of the god Dionysus and Ariadne. Ariadne was the daughter of the King of Minos and helped the Athenian Theseus 'cheat' the intricacies of the labyrinth and its predator, the Minotaur.

Legend has it that Staphylus was both the founder and ruler of the island, an association recognised in the name of Stafilos Bay on the south coast. This affiliation was brought vividly to life by archaeological finds of a Minoan settlement discovered at Stafilos, in 1936. The dig revealed a well enriched grave, the artifacts of which included a gold handled sword worthy of a king. Naturally the popularists assumed the sword belonged to Staphylus. Well, fact is more often stranger than fiction, especially where Greek legends are concerned.

The island was terrorised by pirates for thousands of years. Their wayward tyranny was interrupted by various periods of more legitimate overrule by, for instance, the Athenians and Romans. There was also a spell as a Byzantine internment camp. This unhappy coalition climaxed, in 1538, with the fearsome Turkish Admiral and pirate Babarossa's sacking of the island, a devastation coupled with the wholesale slaughter of all the inhabitants.

The eventual re-population coincided with the War of Independence, in which the islanders took an active part.

GENERAL
First impressions cannot be denied and The Chora and port of Skopelos look absolutely stunning as a traveller approaches. The multitude of tumbling buildings, many with the old, grey slate roofs, are spread over and up three distinct hillsides, much in the manner of a Cycladean Chora. The valley in which the town is built is reputedly the most fertile of this comparatively lush island. A paradise island? Well, that rather depends from which direction a visitor approaches. If he or she has fled

the unreasonably high priced, commercial horrors of Skiathos, then Skopelos may well appear to be an Elysian land. But if the voyager has progressed from, say, Skyros, or even Alonissos, then the level of tourism and its consequent ills may well sully even this attractive island. For be assured the dazzling attractions of the Port and Chora are matched by the beauty of the island's countryside and the numerous beaches. On the other hand the town beach, which appears so magnificent at first sight, is not only smaller in actuality but inevitably 'attracts' some of the adjacent Harbour's pollution – one of the worst cases I have seen in the Greek islands.

The islanders envy the apparent success of Skiathos in attracting tourists and thus try to emulate their neighbours (Oh dear!). Happily Skopelos continues to remain a step or so behind the first division leaders in the package holiday role of horror, sorry honour. On the other hand, it was on my last visit to Skopelos that the unattractive, usually subliminal, consideration that the tourist is an 'animal to be milked and then skinned' was forcibly and vocally expressed, if only by one erudite inhabitant (of whom more later). One of the most noticeable of the unacceptable results of tourism is that the towns people no longer operate any more than a token number of fishing boats, preferring now to 'trawl' for excursion boat day trippers.

The independent traveller might well consider foregoing the 'delights' of Skopelos Town to stay in the mountainside village of Glossa or the adjacent port, Loutraki both, at the north-west end of the island. This latter is well served by both ferry-boat & hydrofoil, and the overall ambience is much more that dreamed of by those who seek the grail of the traditional, unspoilt Greek island. It's a thought!

SKOPELOS (Scopelos): capital town & main port (Illustration 38). Probably one of the most photogenic of the Greek island towns. The upper Chora is an absolute delight. The balconies, cats, jumble of differing architectural styles, donkeys, people, streets, lanes, alleys, steps and flowers combine to give the photographer a year's work, even if he (or she) laboured every day. Mind you, the complexity of the ever ascending passageways would require quite a lot of that time to be able to work out the position of this or that location, with any certainty.

ARRIVAL BY FERRY & FLYING DOLPHIN

An excellent daily network of connections with the other islands in the Sporades, as well as a number of mainland ports. The Skiathos link allows fairly easy access to an airport. But, typically, the ferry-boat and hydrofoil schedules are not co-ordinated with the aircraft flights.

It is interesting to gauge the overall growth of tourism by referring to *Michael Carroll's* book *The Gates of the Wind*. He describes the summer-time ferries of the early 1960s only calling three days a week. This must compare favourably (yes favourably) with the present day two or more ferry-boats and three or more hydrofoils that dock daily.

THE ACCOMMODATION & EATING OUT

The Accommodation Arrivals are met by owners of accommodation, including a little old lady dressed with a black headdress and a grey 'pinny' frock. This attention is a good thing as there aren't many hotels or pensions in the port or town. On the other hand there are any number of package holiday hotels in the far, eastern suburbs bordering the roads round to the Palouki Mountain monasteries and Stafilos Bay. Referring to this latter, there are also a number of small hotels, pensions and ***Rooms*** spread out along the road to Stafilos Bay (*See* **Route One**).

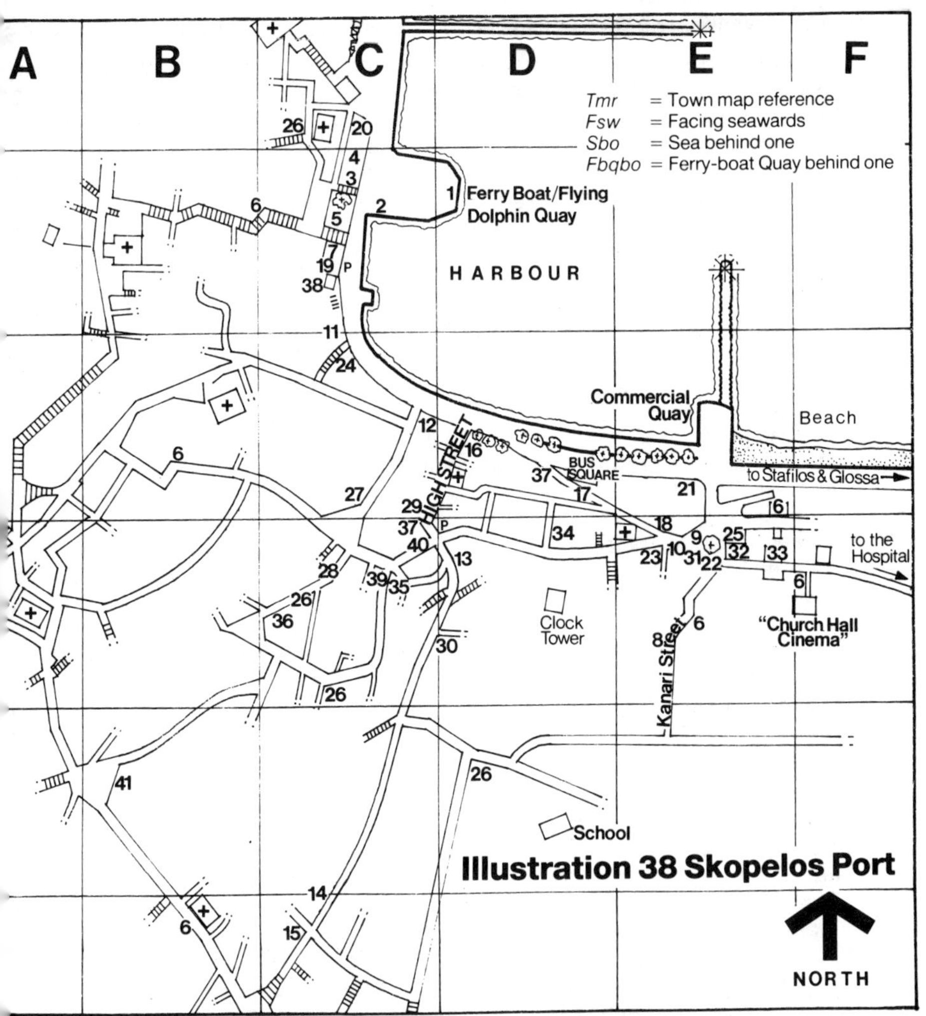

Illustration 38 Skopelos Port

1. Ferry-boat Quay C/D1/2
2. Tourist Accommodation hut C2
3. Skopelos Tours & Travel C2
4. Madro Travel/Rooms C1/2
5. Plateia 'Pantalon'/Pantalon Jazz Club C2
6. Rooms
7. The Captain's Tourist Information office C2
8. Hotel Captain E4
9. 'Five Ways' Square E3/4
10. Self-Service Laundry/Rooms E4
11. Lemonis Travel C2/3
12. Commercial Bank C/D3
13. Dry Cleaners C/D4
14. Alexandra Bar C5/6
15. Leather/Shoe repair shed C6
16. Taverna/Pension Sotos D3
17. Post Office D/E3/4
18. Hotel Adonis E3/4
19. 'Promenade' of Eateries C2
20. Taverna KYMATA C1
21. Cafeteria Skopelos E3
22. Souvlaki snackbar E4
23. Creperie Greca E4
24. National Bank/Town police/Doctor C2/3
25. Nikos Scooter Hire E4
26. Bakers (3)
27. 'Rock Market' C3/4
28. Market C4
29. Store C/D3/4
30. Greengrocers C/D4
31. Shop E4
32. Fruit shop E4
33. Shop E/F4
34. Fish shop D3/4
35. Ladies Hairdresser C4
36. Laundry B/C4
37. Chemists (2)
38. Town Hall C2
39. OTE C4
40. Spyros Tours C4
41. Water fountain B5

Room prices are on the high side compared to Skyros, Alonissos and even Skiathos. A mid-season single room averages out at between 800-1000drs and a double room at about 1500-2000drs per night. Another point to bear in mind is that Skopelos is a popular destination for weekending mainlanders, which causes problems for other travellers.

For the convenience of height of season visitors, there is a small 'Tourist Accommodation' hut (*Tmr* 2C2), set down on the Ferry-boat Quay (*Tmr* 1C/D1/2). Across the Esplanade is a row of Tourist & Travel offices including, left to right (*Sbo*), Skopelos Tours & Travel Bureau (*Tmr* 3C2) and Madro Travel (*Tmr* 4C1/2), which also appears to include the adjacent Theofanidis Ellas Travel. All offer to help find accommodation.

Rooms
Directions: Above Madro Travel (*Tmr* 4C1/2).

Rooms (*Tmr* 6B/C2).
Directions: Up the very steep steps from the tree shaded Plateia 'Pantalon' (*Tmr* 5C2)

Parked close to the retaining wall of Plateia 'Pantalon' may well be a Volkswagen 'beetle' car signwritten *Hotel Captain*. This belongs to Costas Siskos, a classic 'Mr. Big'. His *Hotel Captain* is at the far east end of the town. To overcome this niggling difficulty the apparently convivial Captain Siskos not only parks his vehicle close to the Ferry-boat Quay, from which to 'schlep', but owns a Tourist Information office (*Tmr* 7C2) and the adjacent *Kafeneion* Ο ΚΑΠΕΤΑΙΟΣ, on the left (*Sbo*) of Plateia 'Pantalon'. These act as forward base facilities for the Captain's efforts to fill his hotel. The kafeneion certainly saves him purchasing a coffee anywhere else! The chap engaged to run the place also has to 'pimp' for the Hotel, and why not?

Hotel Captain (*Tmr* 8E4) (Class C) Odhos Kanari Tel 22110
Directions: If 'scooped' by the Captain then a prospect may well be given a lift. If not... proceed all the way round the waterfront Esplanade to the left (*Sbo*) of the Ferry-boat Quay as far as the base of the far, eastern Harbour mole. Here a side-street advances to the small, irregular 'Five Ways' Square in the middle of which is plonked a tree. On the far side of this a narrow, pedestrian only lane, Odhos KANAPH (Kanari), progresses up the gentle slope. I write 'pedestrian' only but note that motor bikes do run up and down. The establishment is on the right-hand side, set in a garden of fruit trees in an almost suburban area.

More an averagely priced pension than a hotel. A mid-season, double room with a balcony, sharing a bathroom (constant running hot water) and the use of a kitchen, costs either 1500drs in the outer block or 2000drs in the main building. It must be noted that the good Captain has a 'naughty little' habit of quoting the availability of a 1200drs double room which, on arrival at the premises, is dismissed with a wave of the hand, as being in the basement and beneath discussion! Show me the basement. The rates rise to 3000drs for the peak summer months. The rooms are cleaned daily and the place is generally well cared for.

Costas' mother is always present, daily feeding a remarkable retinue of cats (for Greece that is). Mother often collects the dues and it is important to be very clear about the amount owing. There is no doubt that the accommodation is good value, so it saddens me that much more that Costas, when engaged in 'meaningful discussions', is of the opinion that tourists are mere 'marks'. Need one say more.

There are also ***Rooms*** (*Tmr* 6E4, tel 22662) in a house fronting Odhos Kanari. They cost a hundred drachmae more than *Hotel Captain*, at 1600drs for a double room, and the accommodation is not as good.
Also in the area are:-

Rooms (*Tmr* 6E/F3/4) Tel 22369
Directions: Prior to 'Five Ways' Sq (*Tmr* 9E3/4) from the Esplanade, turn down the first side-street to the left (*Sbo*) that runs parallel to the waterfront. The house is on the left.
The very smiley, youthful looking lady called Eli, 'parks herself' on the Esplanade watching out for prospects. The house is clean, and she charges 1500drs in mid-season for a double room. The rates are variable, she says!

There is accommodation (*Tmr* 6E/F4) in the next street up from the waterfront that makes off from 'Five Ways' Sq in an easterly direction. The house is on the right, close to the alleyway to the 'Church Hall Cinema' (*Tmr* E/F4).
To the west, or right (*Sbo*) of 'Five Ways' Sq (*Tmr* 9E3/4) is a Self-Service Laundry (*Tmr* 10E4), over which are ***Rooms***.

Back at the Ferry-boat Quay (*Tmr* 1C/D1/2), and proceeding south (*or to the left, Sbo*) along the Esplanade, the road advances past a *Pension*, prior to the office of Lemonis Travel (*Tmr* 11C2/3).
The next side-street off the Esplanade climbs the steep hillside from alongside the Commercial Bank (*Tmr* 12C/D3). The street runs into a triangular shaped Square, from the right (*Sbo*) of which is a lateral lane. On the right, immediately prior to a jink in the street's progress, is:-

Rooms (*Tmr* 6B3) No. 30 (No telephone)
Directions: As above.
Provincial, ethnic accommodation in an attractive, rickety old house owned by Christina Kamatopoulou. Rooms share the bathroom. A single room costs 800drs and a double room 1400drs. One room at the back has a large balcony with a view out over the roof of a church and the harbour scene below. Incidentally, the Church possesses a tiny garden, to one side, and has a natural stone finish, not the usual Skopelot whitewash.

Back on the Esplanade and proceeding eastwards, the next street climbing off the waterfront is the High St, ΥΠΕΡ ΑΠΟΠΕΡΑΤΟΣΕΟΣ. This crosses a lateral street, by a periptero on the left (*Sbo*), veers left, past a Dry Cleaners (*Tmr* 13C/D4), and then right. After leaving the shopping area, the street continues to ascend the hill towards the top of the town, past Alexandra Bar (*Tmr* 14C5/6) on the right. Over the next minor crossroad, with a tiny leather and shoe repair shed (*Tmr* 15C6) close to the junction, and the street finally runs out at the bottom of an angled and widening flight of steps. Turn right at the top for:-

Rooms (*Tmr* 6B6)
Directions: As above and on the left, is a 'grocery' Mini-Market over which is the accommodation. (Phew!). Across the alley is a modern Church complete with campanile and stained glass windows.
Quiet and in the old Chora with glorious views out over the harbour. A single room costs 800drs and a double 1500drs, all rooms sharing a bathroom.

Back at the Esplanade, on the east corner of the High St is the *Cocktail Rock-bar Opolafsis*, alongside which is the:-

Pension Sotos (*Tmr* 16D3) (Class A) Tel. 22549

Directions: As above and over a taverna.

A smart place but in a noisy location, facing a busy section of the Esplanade. The establishment's 'glittering' classification is reflected in the prices. Only double rooms with en suite bathrooms are available,starting at 2700drs and rising to 3900drs (1st July-31st Aug). Breakfast may well be mandatory in the busy months at a cost of 200drs.

Proceeding eastwards leads to the 'Bus Sq' (*Tmr* D3), behind which rises an angled street on the side of which is the Post Office (*Tmr* 17D/E3/4). To the right (*Sbo*) of the Post Office is a *Guest House*.

Continuing along the 'Post Office' street leads to the:-

Hotel Adonis (*Tmr* 18E3/4) (Class D) Tel 22231

Directions: As above, on the left and in the ground floor of which is a Grill Restaurant. Previously named the Hotel America.

Despite the classification, the en suite double rooms start at 3000drs (come back Captain Costas, all is forgiven). These (extortionate) rates rise to 4000drs (1st-30th Sept) and 5000drs (1st July-31st Aug). Breakfast hovers between 350drs and 400drs.

For other accommodation, at the far eastern end of the town, *See* **Excursions to Skopelos Town Surrounds**.

The Eating Out Not a town in which it is possible to duck into the Old Quarter and find an inexpensive, back street bijou. Meals are generally expensive with an ordinary omelette costing 230drs and pizzas start at 450drs. Salads are ridiculous things served in sweet bowls at an average cost of 150drs. In many establishments the only beer available is a bottled lager, *Kaiser*, costing a fearsome 110drs, compared to an *Amstel* or *Henninger* at 90drs. *Kaiser* is served unless otherwise stipulated. Another drink peculiarity is for establishments to serve an acceptably priced, day-time bottle of beer and an expensive night-time lager. A prime example of this retrograde habit is the otherwise excellent *Pantalon Jazz Club* (*Tmr* 5C2). During the day a bottle of *Amstel* costs 113drs whilst in the evening a *Tuborg* is charged at 240drs (Ouch!) I must point out that the menu advises clients of this day/night-time aberration.

Mind you, even bottled water on Skopelos is expensive at 73drs, compared to the average 65drs.

The Esplanade, from about the Commercial Bank (*Tmr* 12C/D3), all the way round to the far, eastern harbour protection wall, is lined with restaurants and tavernas. In the main these serve 'average fare' at 'above average' prices.

Bearing in mind the Harbour pollution, I would want to be assured that any whitebait or fish served did not originate in its murky waters.

There are a number of 'nut' handcarts that 'stake out' the Esplanade in the evenings, one of which is 'all lit up'. Their offerings are not cheap nowadays, with a small packet of pistachios nuts costing 100drs.

Despite the large number of establishments there is little 'schlepping'.

Pantalon Jazz Club (*Tmr* 5C2)

Directions: Very close to the Ferry-boat Quay, edging an attractive, flagstoned

Square (which I have nicknamed 'Pantalon' Sq) bordering the Esplanade. The Square is above the roadway, supported by a retaining wall and shaded by a very large tree, the base of which is squared off by formal railings and a brick wall.

Do not be put off by the nomenclature 'Jazz Club' or the pink decor as the establishment is a hybrid breakfast/cafe/cocktail bar advertising *Morning genuine breakfast, night jazz and blues*. A pleasant mixed repertoire of musical gramophone background. Prices are pasted on a pink blackboard (yes I know, Irish...). The excellently situated bar is run by Rikke, a very attractive young Danish lady, and her bearded Greek 'friend'. The value is good as long as one sticks to certain items such as the reasonably priced Continental breakfast. Filter coffee (yes, filter coffee) with milk costs 80drs, but ask for *filter* otherwise Nescafe is served. A straightforward bread, butter and jam (or honey) repast cost 120drs, and that includes splendidly fresh rolls and three pats of butter. On the other hand consider steering clear of the fresh fruit juice at 200drs or a grapefruit charged at 250drs. The price of bottled beers has been 'churned over' and an ouzo costs 210drs, which is pretty steep. A minor drawback of the location is the rubbish that gathers at the foot of the retaining wall. This is worse at the weekends, when it is not always collected, and, combined with the occasional harbour effluvium, can cause quite a pong.

Across the steps, to the left (*Sbo*) of 'Pantalon' Sq, is a promenade of drinking and eating places starting with, right to left (*Sbo*), the:-

Kafeneion Ο ΚΑΠΕΤΑΝΙΟΣ (*Tmr* 19C2)
Directions: As above.

Owned by our 'old friend' Captain Costas (*See Hotel Captain*, **The Accommodation**).

Depending on the manager's whim, a coffee and a beer can cost 160drs or 200drs. Captain 'Birdseye', sorry Costas, explains this away as the necessity for his protegé to live. I did enquire why the brave Captain could not pay his employees a living wage, but was obviously considered insane.

The Captain's Kafeneion is followed by the *Restaurant/Taverna* Ο ΓΙΑΝΝΗ, the *Restaurant/Taverna* ΔΙΧΤΥ and the *Restaurant* Η ΚΔΗΜΑΤΑΡΙΑ, which appear much of a muchness, with the ΔΙΧΤΥ allegedly the better of the three.

Restaurant/Taverna KYMATA (*Tmr* 20C1)
Directions: From the bottom of the Ferry-boat Quay (*Tmr* 1C/D1/2) turn right (*Sbo*). The *Kymata* is not far along the waterfront road, which comes to a circular dead-end close to the northern Harbour wall. In fact, the taverna is the last business in this direction and named Kymata, despite the blinds bearing the name Taverna Angel.

. A very popular establishment with rows of tables and chairs ranged along the Esplanade and run by a vast man who quite often operates at a 'perspiring' trot. This incongruous effort is necessary as the service is some of the fastest in Greece. To keep up this pace requires customers not to dilly-dally and, despite mine host being pleasant enough, orders have to be placed NOW. The urchin-looking child labour pressed into service are two of Papa's offspring. They are endlessly urged into greater efforts by father's constant verbal 'encouragement'. The popularity of the taverna requires clients to arrive early if they particularly want a specific dish. A meal for two of stuffed tomatoes (250drs), spaghetti bolognese (250drs), giant beans (130drs), green beans (150drs), a kortaki retsina (115drs) and bread (14drs each) cost 923drs. A plate of kalamari (very good, fresh and plentiful) cost 296drs and a Greek salad 116drs.

In amongst the businesses, restaurants and other miscellanea of eating houses and their canopied terraces that stretch along the Esplanade between the High St and the 'Bus' Sq, is the:-

Pizza Snackbar Sirene

Directions: As above, and close to the *Taverna/Pension Sotos* (*Tmr* 16D3).

Sells pizza by the slice for 150drs. A complete pizza, large enough for two and a mealful, costs 715drs. A sizeable Greek salad (sizeable for this island that is) costs 131drs, an Amstel beer (for which it is necessary 'to fight') costs 90 drs and bread (a small portion) is charged at 10drs each. The food is freshly prepared and also served at a trot, incredible to say. An enormous spaghetti bolognese costs 220drs.

Just around the corner from the *Snackbar Sirene*, beyond the *Cocktail Rock-bar Opolafisis*, and on the left of the High St, is *The Melissa*, one of the only traditional kafeneions in the town.

The furthest eating place in the stretch of three ranged at the eastern end of the Esplanade, is the:-

Zacharoplasteion Cafeteria Skopelos (*Tmr* 21E3)

Directions: As above.

Not only a sticky cake shop, that serves loukoumades (200drs), but a restaurant. A magnificent, freshly made, 'rinky-dinky', all-inclusive pizza sufficient to feed two cost 750drs, but less expensive versions are available. An ice-cream bowl sized Greek salad (as is usual on Skopelos) is charged at 120drs, beer 90drs and bread 10drs.

Souvlaki Snackbar (*Tmr* 22E4)

Directions: From the eastern end of the Harbour, opposite the harbour mole, proceed to 'Five Ways' Sq. The snackbar is on the far side, alongside the junction with Odhos Kanari.

A 'sit down' or 'take-away' 'greasy spoon', which is very popular with locals. It is almost a look-alike for the great British chippie, perhaps? Oddly enough the snackbar does not open until about 1500hrs. A number of souvlaki options available in a number of guises. A stick of souvlaki costs 60drs, a souvlaki pita 70drs, a helping of chips 68drs, a Greek salad 120drs and a 'Skopelos special pie' costs 220drs – it must be very special.

Nearby establishments, in the street that connects 'Five Ways' Sq and the 'Bus' Sq, include the *Creperie Greca* (*Tmr* 23E4), which seems a brave but hardly Greek venture, and a smart *Grill Restaurant* in the ground floor of the *Hotel Adonis* (*Tmr* 18E3/4). Despite this latter exhibiting a self-service sign it isn't, added to which the charges are very expensive, especially bearing in minding the fast food nature of the food's preparation and service. For example a moussaka costs 400drs.

For further eateries in the far-flung, eastern suburbs *See* **Excursions To Skopelos Town Surrounds**.

THE A TO Z OF USEFUL INFORMATION

BANKS

Commercial Bank (*Tmr* 12C/D3)

Directions: About half-way round the Esplanade from the Ferry-boat Quay.

A star performer when measured on the 'couldn't care less' scale of service. In fact, I am not sure that this branch has not won the *Golden drachmae*, the ultimate award for the worst customer attention at a bank or more simply the worst of a bad bunch. The teller who was serving me (or wasn't serving me) left the counter in mid-transaction to use the photostat machine, which broke down. He ended up attempting to repair the copier without excusing himself, never to serve me again. I remained speechless until, eventually, another clerk, gracelessly and wordlessly, took over. Incidentally, the bank opens weekday evenings, in addition to the usual daily hours, between 1800-2000hrs for exchange purposes only.

There is also the **National Bank** (*Tmr* 24C2/3) about midway between the Commercial Bank and the Ferry-boat Quay. Note the *Agricultural Bank*, at the eastern end of the Esplanade, only deals with, surprise, surprise, agricultural business.

BEACHES The town beach is sandy, broad at the Harbour end and pleasantly bordered by a line of pollarded trees. Furthermore the sea-bed shelves very slowly, so what's the snag? That is, apart from the usual sunbathers detritus to be found littered about popular beaches. The drawback is the adjacent Harbour which really is most unpleasant. Apart from the appearance of the grey, murky emulsion that makes up the solution enclosed by the Harbour walls, the odour is unpleasant, often pungent. It is a frequent sight to observe small fry leap out of the 'primeval soup' in an absolute frenzy. Perhaps there are some giant monsters lurking in the depths. Readers may well be thrumming the tabletop by now. What is the chap getting at? Well, simply the adjacency of the Harbour to the beach. Frankly I can't believe some of the Harbour's contents don't seep into the bay. If it is thought I may be 'OTT' in my description, it is interesting that a pleasant crowd of 'yachties' we met on Alonissos declared they wouldn't, in any circumstances, handle the boats' anchor chain after mooring in Skopelos Harbour. They were of the opinion that 'noddies' were floating around and I can only conclude that the town's sewage outfall drains into the Harbour. Enough said?

Note that as the authorities officially allow nudism on **Velanio Beach**, adjacent to **Stafilos Beach**, it is strictly prohibited elsewhere (*See* **Route One (& Only)**.

BICYCLE, SCOOTER & CAR HIRE

Nikos Scooter Hire (*Tmr* 25E4)
Directions: Close to 'Five Ways' Sq.

The owner is a nice, quiet, taciturn but friendly man. He hires out well maintained Hondas and Yamahas which, in mid-season, cost 1200drs a day. A three day hire may well reduce the daily rate to 1000drs a day.

Madro Travel/Theofanidis Ellas (*Tmr* 4C1/2)
Directions: In the row of Travel and Tour offices across the Esplanade from the bottom of the Ferry-boat Quay.

Offer scooter/motorbike hire, but probably only act as agents.

BREAD SHOPS Probably the most convenient Baker (*Tmr* 26C1) is in a lane to the right (*Sbo*) of 'Pantalon' Sq. Other Bakers 'lurk' in the upper reaches of the town (*Tmr* 26C4 & 26D5), as does a cake shop (*Tmr* 26C4/5).

BUSES The area designated as a Terminus (*Tmr* D3), and shared with the taxis, is to the side of the Esplanade overlooked by the Post Office (*Tmr* 17D/E3/4).

Bus timetable Indecipherable details are nailed to a convenient tree, adjacent to where the buses pull in. Several times a day buses serve the west coast, seaside locations all the way to Glossa Town and down to Loutraki Port (*See* **Route One (& Only)**. The best course is to ask the bus drivers.

CINEMAS (*Tmr* E/F4) A 'Church Hall' cinema, at the east end of town.

COMMERCIAL SHOPPING AREA No central market now, although I think there was one close to 'Five Ways' Sq. Certainly the boarded-up building is still there. There are an abundance of shops and stores as well as a number of Peripteros (P). The greatest concentration of shops are spread up the two main streets that climb off the Esplanade. One is the High St and the other runs approximately parallel to the High St, from alongside the Commercial Bank (*Tmr* 12C/D3). Interesting and useful stores include a Butcher almost opposite the Rock Market-store-fruit-groceries (*Tmr* 27C3/4), with a ***Rooms*** sign in the window; a Mini-Market (*Tmr* 28C4) across the road from which is a Store with a drinks cabinet on the pavement; a Shop 'trying to be a supermarket' (*Tmr* 31E4); a Fruit shop (*Tmr* 32E4); a Shop (*Tmr* 33E/F4); a Fish shop (*Tmr* 34D3/4) and a Grocery store across the side street from the Commercial Bank (*Tmr* 12C/D3). Siesta commences fairly early, at about 1230hrs. Even one of the two petrol stations closes for the afternoon, but naturally the souvenir and tourist shops stay open all and every day.

FERRY-BOATS & FLYING DOLPHINS It must be stressed that people wishing to avail themselves of the Flying Dolphins from Skopelos, via or to Skiathos, are best advised to book a ticket in advance during the height of season months. This is due to their use by package tourist companies for clients who have been flown into Skiathos and are shipped to Skopelos on the hydrofoils, or vice versa.

Ferry-boat timetable (Mid-season)

Day	Departure time	Ferry-boat	Ports/Islands of Call
Monday	0725hrs		Skiathos, Volos(M).
	0950hrs		Alonissos.
	1050hrs		Piraeus(M).
	1105hrs		Skiathos.
	1550hrs		Alonissos.
	1645hrs		Alonissos.
	1645hrs		Skiathos, Volos(M).
	1825hrs		Skiathos, Volos(M).
	2100hrs		Alonissos.
Tuesday	0600hrs	Papadiamentis II	Glossa (Loutraki Port, Skopelos), Skiathos, Volos(M).
	0725hrs		Skiathos, Volos(M).
	0940hrs		Alonissos.
	1105hrs		Skiathos.
	1550hrs		Alonissos.
	1645hrs		Alonissos.
	1825hrs		Skiathos, Volos(M).
Wednesday	0600hrs	Papadiamentis II	Glossa (Loutraki Port, Skopelos), Skiathos, Ag Konstantinos(M).
	0725hrs		Skiathos, Volos(M).
	0725hrs		Thessaloniki(M).
	0950hrs		Alonissos.
	1050hrs		Piraeus(M).
	1105hrs		Skiathos.
	1550hrs		Alonissos.
	1645hrs		Alonissos.
	1825hrs		Skiathos, Volos(M).

	2100hrs		Alonissos.
Thursday	0725hrs		Skiathos, Volos(M).
	0950hrs		Alonissos, Skyros.
	1010hrs		Alonissos.
	1105hrs		Skiathos, Piraeus(M).
	1440hrs		Skiathos, Volos(M).
	1550hrs		Alonissos.
	1645hrs		Alonissos.
	1825hrs		Skiathos, Volos(M).
	2100hrs		Alonissos.
Friday	0600hrs	Papadiamentis II	Glossa (Loutraki Port, Skopelos), Skiathos, Volos(M).
	0725hrs		Skiathos, Volos(M).
	0725hrs		Piraeus(M).
	0950hrs		Alonissos.
	1400hrs		Alonissos.
	1520hrs		Alonissos.
	1615hrs		Skiathos, Piraeus(M).
	1645hrs		Alonissos.
	1645hrs		Skiathos, Volos(M).
	1825hrs		Skiathos, Volos(M).
	2100hrs		Alonissos.
Saturday	0600hrs	Papadiamentis II	Glossa (Loutraki Port, Skopelos), Skiathos, Volos(M).
	0725hrs		Thessaloniki(M).
	0725hrs		Skiathos, Volos(M).
	0950hrs		Alonissos.
	1050hrs		Skiathos, Piraeus(M).
	1550hrs		Alonissos.
	1645hrs		Alonissos.
	1825hrs		Skiathos, Volos(M).
	1830hrs	Papadiamentis II	Alonissos.
	2100hrs		Alonissos.
Sunday	0610hrs	Papadiamentis II	Glossa (Loutraki Port, Skopelos), Skiathos, Ag Konstantinos(M).
	0725hrs		Skiathos, Volos(M).
	0725hrs		Piraeus(M).
	0950hrs		Alonissos, Skyros.
	1400hrs		Alonissos.
	1550hrs		Alonissos.
	1655hrs		Skiathos.
	1820hrs		Skiathos, Volos(M).
	2130hrs		Alonissos.

One-way fares: Skopelos			
	to Ag Konstantinos	1270hrs;duration	5¼hrs
	to Skiathos	;	1¾hrs
	to Alonissos	;	¾hrs

Flying Dolphin timetable (Mid-season)

Day	Departure time	Ports/Islands of Call
Monday	0725hrs	Glossa (Loutraki Port, Skopelos), Skiathos, Volos(M).
	0950hrs	Alonissos.
	1105hrs	Glossa (Loutraki Port, Skopelos), Skiathos, Ag Konstantinos(M).
	1440hrs	Glossa (Loutraki Port, Skopelos), Skiathos, Volos(M).
	1550hrs	Alonissos.
	1645hrs	Alonissos.
	1755hrs	Skiathos, Volos(M).
	2005hrs	Alonissos.
	2105hrs	Alonissos.
Tuesday	0725hrs	Glossa (Loutraki Port, Skopelos), Skiathos, Volos(M).
	0950hrs	Alonissos.
	1105hrs	Glossa (Loutraki Port, Skopelos), Skiathos, Ag Konstantinos(M).
	1440hrs	Glossa (Loutraki Port, Skopelos), Skiathos, Volos(M).
	1550hrs	Alonissos.
	1645hrs	Alonissos.
	1755hrs	Skiathos, Volos(M).
	2005hrs	Alonissos.
	2105hrs	Alonissos.
Wednesday	0725hrs	Glossa (Loutraki Port, Skopelos), Skiathos, Volos(M).
	0950hrs	Alonissos.
	1105hrs	Glossa (Loutraki Port, Skopelos), Skiathos, Ag Konstantinos(M).
	1440hrs	Glossa (Loutraki Port, Skopelos), Skiathos, Volos(M).
	1550hrs	Alonissos, Moundania(M).
	1645hrs	Alonissos.
	1755hrs	Skiathos, Volos(M).
	2005hrs	Alonissos.
	2105hrs	Alonissos.
	2215hrs	Alonissos.
Thursday	0725hrs	Glossa (Loutraki Port, Skopelos), Skiathos, Volos(M).
	0840hrs	Skiathos.
	0950hrs	Alonissos, Skyros.
	1105hrs	Glossa (Loutraki Port, Skopelos), Skiathos, Ag Konstantinos(M).
	1440hrs	Glossa (Loutraki Port, Skopelos), Skiathos, Volos(M).
	1550hrs	Alonissos.
	1645hrs	Alonissos.
	1755hrs	Skiathos, Volos(M).
	2105hrs	Alonissos.
Friday	0725hrs	Glossa (Loutraki Port, Skopelos), Skiathos, Volos(M).
	0950hrs	Alonissos.

	1105hrs	Glossa (Loutraki Port, Skopelos), Skiathos, Ag Konstantinos(M).
	1440hrs	Glossa (Loutraki Port, Skopelos), Skiathos, Volos(M).
	1520hrs	Alonissos.
	1615hrs	Skiathos, Ag Konstantinos(M).
	1645hrs	Alonissos.
	1755hrs	Skiathos, Volos(M).
	2005hrs	Alonissos.
	2105hrs	Alonissos.
Saturday	0725hrs	Glossa (Loutraki Port, Skopelos), Skiathos, Volos(M).
	0950hrs	Alonissos.
	1105hrs	Glossa (Loutraki Port, Skopelos), Skiathos, Ag Konstantinos(M).
	1440hrs	Glossa (Loutraki Port, Skopelos), Skiathos, Volos(M).
	1550hrs	Alonissos, Moundania(M).
	1645hrs	Alonissos.
	1755hrs	Skiathos, Volos(M).
	2005hrs	Alonissos.
	2105hrs	Alonissos.
	2215hrs	Alonissos.
Sunday	0725hrs	Glossa (Loutraki Port, Skopelos), Skiathos, Volos(M).
	0950hrs	Alonissos, Skyros.
	1105hrs	Glossa (Loutraki Port, Skopelos), Skiathos, Ag Konstantinos(M).
	1550hrs	Alonissos.
	1645hrs	Alonissos.
	1655hrs	Skiathos, Ag Konstantinos(M).
	1820hrs	Glossa(Loutraki Port,Skopelos),Skiathos,Volos(M).
	2005hrs	Alonissos.
	2130hrs	Alonissos.

One-way fares:Skopelos to	Glossa	405drs;duration	½hr
	Skiathos	540drs;	¾hr
	Alonissos	405drs;	20mins
	Ag Konstantinos	2400drs;	2½hrs
	Volos	2000drs;	2¼hrs
	Skyros	;	1hr 10mins
	Moundania	2530drs;	2hrs

There is also a high summer season Express boat to Alonissos, the **Ag Nikolaos**, which departs daily at 1000hrs and 'slips' Alonissos at 1830hrs. Some package tour companies offer day trip excursions to Alonissos for 2650drs, which seems a bit 'rich' when a hydrofoil return ticket costs 810drs. Perhaps a six course meal is included!

FERRY-BOAT & FLYING DOLPHIN TICKET OFFICES
Apart from other offices,both ferry-boat and Flying Dolphin tickets are available

from the two Travel Agents across the road from the Ferry-boat Quay (*Tmr* 1C/D1/2), more particularly:-

Skopelos Tours & Travel Bureau (*Tmr* 3C2, tel 22622) for ferry-boat tickets and **Madro Travel** (*Tmr* 4C1/2, tel 22145) for Flying Dolphin tickets. For other ticket offices *See* **Travel Agents & Tour Offices, A To Z**.

HAIRDRESSERS There is a Ladies Hairdresser (*Tmr* 35C4) on a side road connecting the two 'Main' streets.

LAUNDRY It is often feast or famine in Greece, that is plenty or none. On Skopelos there are at least three laundries. One, more a Dry Cleaners, is on the left (*Sbo*) of the High St (*Tmr* 13C/D4) and another (*Tmr* 36B/C4) is on a continuation of the 'other' Main St (open 1000-1300hrs & 1700-2000hrs). The most useful, a 'Self-Service' Laundry (launderette to you and I – *Tmr* 10E4), is close to 'Five Ways' Sq. This latter, a basement business with ***Rooms*** in the upper floors, is open between 0900-1300hrs and 1700-2100hrs, every day. There is a price list on the wall but a wash costs 600-800drs and drying (2½ kilos) another 150drs.

MEDICAL CARE

Chemists & Pharmacies Several including one (*Tmr* 37C/D3/4) on the right (*Sbo*) of the High St and another (*Tmr* 37D3), on the angled road off from the Esplanade, advancing towards the Post Office.

Doctor A doctor's surgery is located above the Police offices, which are themselves over the National Bank (*Tmr* 24C3).

Hospital A comparatively new facility completed in 1987. Walk from 'Five Ways' Sq past the 'Church Hall' Cinema for about 400m, at which point the street joins the main island road. Turn right and proceed another 50m and there is the hospital.

NTOG None, and even the Tourist Office, that was let into the ground floor of the Town Hall (*Tmr* 38C2), appears to be 'dead'.

OTE (*Tmr* 39C4) A 'retiring' little office, signposted throughout the town and only open weekdays between 0730-1510hrs.

PETROL Two filling stations on the outskirts of Skopelos Town, one of which observes the siesta.

PLACES OF INTEREST

Castle A ruined Venetian structure at the very top of The Chora and within the walls of which is an early church. It goes without saying that the views are magnificent.

Churches There are reputably some 125 churches in the Town alone, but it is not the number of them but their proportions and glorious blue/grey/green slate roofs that are so eye-catching. The archetypal Skopelot church has whitewashed walls and slate roofs topped off with a flattish, conical slate dome. Similarly to English thatched houses, eyebrow dormers are incorporated in the tiling to accommodate small windows. These churches help to frame those beautiful postcard pictures of the north end of the harbour where there is a model example situated exactly in the correct spot. For my money though the Church and campanile (*Tmr* B2), reached up the old flight of steps from 'Pantalon' Sq, is one of the loveliest examples.

Monasteries *See* **Excursions To Skopelos Town Surrounds**

Museums The Town Hall (*Tmr* 38C2) is the repository for various archaeological finds from island sites, that is those that have not been pirated by mainland museums. These remains include some from the Asclepeion at Ambeliki, now a suburb of Skopelos Town. This site has unfortunately been washed away and covered by the sea.

Apart from counting flies or making sharp asides about other tourists, it is worth popping down to the Commercial Quay (*Tmr* E3) to watch the local merchant ship **Skopelos** berth and unload its incredible cargo of everyday Greek necessities. These tend to be left piled on the unfenced quay, day in day out.

POLICE
Port & Town Their offices are grouped above the National Bank (*Tmr* 24C3). The entrance is from the alley behind the building, reached by climbing the steep steps alongside the Bank.

POST OFFICE (*Tmr* 17D/E3/4) Bordering the street angling up behind the Bus terminal and flanked by souvenir shops.

TAXIS Rank on the same Sq as the Buses (*Tmr* D3).

TELEPHONE NUMBERS & ADDRESSES

Hospital	Tel 22220
Police, town (*Tmr* D24C3)	Tel 22235
Taxi Rank (*Tmr* D3)	Tel 22566

TRAVEL AGENTS & TOUR OFFICES In the block of buildings across the Esplanade from the bottom of the Ferry-boat Quay (*Tmr* 1C/D1/2) are three offices. Ranging from left to right (*Sbo*) they are:-
Skopelos Tours & Travel Bureau (*Tmr* 3C2) Tel 22622
Directions: As above.
Car hire, ferry-boat tickets, hotel rooms, excursions and etc., etc.

Madro Travel (*Tmr* 4C1/2).
Directions: As above and separated from Skopelos Tours by a souvenir shop.
Rooms and Flying Dolphin tickets. Opening hours: Monday-Wednesday 0630-1300hrs & 1530-2100hrs, Thursday 0630-1300hrs & 1430-2100hrs; Friday 0630-1230hrs & 1330-2130hrs; Saturday 0630-1300hrs & 1530hrs and Sunday 0630-1430hrs & 1630-2130hrs.
and
Theofanidis Ellas Tel 22602
Directions: As above and appears to be part of Madro Travel
Motorbike and car hire as well as various excursions.

Continuing on round the Esplanade from the Ferry-boat Quay (*Tmr* 1C/D1/2) passes both:-
Lemonis Travel (*Tmr* 11C2/3)
Directions: As above.
Rents cars and acts as an agent for the Nomicos Shipping Company

and:-

Alkyon Travel

Directions: This office is to the left (*Sbo*) of the National Bank (*Tmr* 24C3).

Spyros Tours (*Tmr* 40C4)

Directions: On a dark side-street, off to the right (*Sbo*) of the High St.

Apart from the usual 'offices', this firm rents cars, probably on an agency basis.

WATER The admonishment not to imbibe the drinking water must not be forgotten. Most of the Town's fountains are switched off in the summer months, apart from one (*Tmr* 41B5) tucked away in the upper Chora.

EXCURSIONS TO SKOPELOS TOWN SURROUNDS

Excursion to Monastery Prodromos (via the Monasteries of Evangelistria, Metamorphosis and Varvaras (8km). Note this is the north-eastern Monastery Prodromos as some maps also detail a Prodromos Monastery close by Mili hamlet. It is wise to 'pack' some drinking water for this trip, which is dusty and has little tree cover.

The Esplanade follows the beach backshore and then angles off to the right past the *Hotel Eleni* (smart D class, tel 22393 with en suite single rooms starting off at 1900drs and doubles 2800drs). There is a concrete lined river-bed, to the left, with a small pedestrian bridge giving access to ***Rooms*** and a supermarket. The summer-dry water course passes under the road to parallel the right-hand side of the carriageway after which, on the left, is the very large, brassy *Hotel Amalia* (Class B, tel 22688). This hotel caters for, amongst other package tour companies, *Intasun, Horizon* and *Thompson*. To further the holiday-makers interests there is a swimming pool as well as the office of Hurricane Tours, let into the ground floor of the hotel.

Beyond the *Hotel Amalia*, the road continues on to the main Glossa road junction.

To the left is the route that leads into the slopes of Mt Palouki and the Monasteries. The narrow lane winds past the *Hotel Rania* (Class E – tel 22486) with double rooms en suite from 1300drs, *Thompson's* tourists), the *Restaurant Pantyboy*, *Villa Silivos*, with apartments to rent, a *House for Rent*, a Rent A Motorbike outfit, *Thompson Holiday Villas*, another Rent A Motorbike firm, *Sporades Rooms to Rent*, more *Thompsons' Apartments* and a *Restaurant/taverna*. Much of the low-lying roadside is lined with bamboo and other thick vegetation, all indicative of the likely presence of mosquitoes. In amongst the above premises is the occasional old private house with the usual accompaniment of tethered goats, donkeys and dogs.

The route borders the sea's edge for a stretch and, alongside the first section, is a tiny bit of beach squeezed in between a mole and an embankment. Fortunately the locals have not found it opportune to dump their rubbish, yet. Further on the ravages of the sea have caused the retaining wall of the road to collapse, so night-time drivers should beware, they might get a teeth rattling and a dunking.

Spaced out on the right, and interspersed by scrub, bamboo and waste ground, are the *Hotels Aelos* (Class C – tel 22233 with single rooms en suite from 2250drs and doubles 2700drs), the *Agnanti* (Class C – tel 22722) with singles and double rooms en suite from 3000drs), off the driveway down to the *Hotel Prince Stafilos* (Class B, tel 22775 – I won't even dream of listing the rates!)

At the far end of the bay is *Skopelos Villas* after which the now dusty, unsurfaced track starts the ascent of the foothills. I really don't understand how the planners of these package tourist paradises can corral their clients in these backwood areas. Any hotel out here should have a swimming pool, for it is a lengthy trudge to the town beach. On the right of the powdery, chalky slopes is the *Hotel Aegeon* (classified as Pension, Class B, tel 22619 with single rooms en suite from 1900drs and doubles 2400drs) which is in the *Grecian Holiday* brochure.

The views out over Skopelos Town are absolutely super. After about 2½km is a fork in the road, alongside which is a small taverna. The left-hand turning crosses over to the far, north, rocky valley slopes and winds up to:-

The Monastery Evangelistria (4km from Skopelos Town) Rebuilt in 1712 and now a nunnery. The altar screen, which is gold plated, has a picture reputed to date back to the 14th century. Open mornings and afternoons (0900-1300hrs & 1600-1830hrs).

A goat track does connect Evangelistria Monastery with the other mountain top monasteries but....

Back at the fork, the bulldozed track that 'scars' its way up the right-hand side of the valley ravine, winds round:-

The Monastery Metamorphosis (5km from Skopelos Town) The building is cypress tree shaded and is set down on a small, bare, almost circular plateau that the road loops round. The monastery dates back to the 16th century and also possesses a fine altar screen but is uninhabited, so the opening times listed (the same as Evangelistria) must be viewed with caution. Rather ordinary and farmhouse in appearance.

Once over the brow of the climb the countryside is much softer and more agricultural. On the left is:-

The Monastery Varvaras (Babara) (6½km from Skopelos Town) The pretty looking monastery, surrounded by a high wall, is of the fortified genre and may have been constructed as early as the 15th century. The altar screen is of a similar vintage.

Across a depression in the land, a kilometre or so further to the east, is:-

The Monastery Prodromos (7½km from Skopelos Town) Large, magnificent and 'all up together'. Rebuilt in 1721, but may date back to the 14th century as the altar screen has portions from that period. Now a nunnery, it is open the same hours as Evangelistria.

It should go without saying that those planning to look around the Monasteries must pack a skirt or trousers, blouses or shirts with long sleeves and that females should have a headscarf. These Monasteries can loan suitable apparel as the dress rules are strictly applied.

A path circles Prodromos Monastery and, on the far side, edges some cliffs. From this vantage point are marvellous views looking out over the islets of Georgios and Mikro Nisi all the way to Alonissos island. On a clear day... many of the small islands beyond Alonissos are also visible, as is Skantzoura to the south-west.

Incidentally, the steep climb to Monastery Prodomos and back takes about 3 hours.

Excursion to Ag Konstantinos (2½km) Proceed out of Skopelos Town, past the turning to the previously described Monastery Excursion, to the main road junction. Left leads to Glossa and right circles round the town, back to the coast. On the way round, after about a kilometre, a 2½km track progresses in a southerly direction to Monastery Ag Reginos.

At the far, north-western side of Skopelos Town, after another 1½km, and a westerly track leads the 3km to Monastery Analipseos and a north-westerly track meanders off in the direction of the isolated shingle beach at the bottom of Ormos Glisteri, but the route is unclear.

ROUTE ONE (& ONLY)
To Glossa & Loutraki Port via Stafilos Beach, Agnotas, Panormos, Milia Beach, Elios & Klima (circa 35km)

Proceeding along the Esplanade, which borders the beach backshore, leads to a road junction whence swing left, past two petrol stations, into pretty, olive tree planted countryside. Despite the distance from Skopelos Port, the roadside is scattered with ***Rooms***, a sample of which are as follows:-

On the right is a nice looking house (Tel 22613), followed by a bakery on the left (circa 3km from Skopelos Town), *Rooms With Toilet* (Tel 22087 & 22780), beyond which is a laundry, and on the left ***Rooms*** (Tel 22174). Despite possible transport difficulties, there is no doubt that this accommodation presents a more than acceptable alternative to the hurly-burly of Skopelos Town. Just a thought.

At about 4km, the road swings right to follow the southern coastline, past the turning down to:-

STAFILOS & VELANIO BEACHES (5km from Skopelos Town) The rough track descends the hillside, past a *House To Let* (Tel 22604/22742) on the left, to an irregular car park approximately half-way down to sea level. On the right is a rustic taverna and there are ***Rooms*** (Tel 22948) in a building to the left. Horrific piles of smelly rubbish are allowed to accumulate in mounds of plastic bags. The goat track down to the beach passes a small, low mounted fountain head on the left and a bush covered bluff on the right. This latter promontory is used as an informal, open air, latrine, presumably by those who avail themselves of the delights of both Stafilos and Velanio. Ugh! Incidentally, those who cannot resist the hedonistic delights of the two beaches, arrive by taxi and bus as the day wears on.

Stafilos Beach is attractively located on the edge of a curving crescent of a bay stopped off by a jumble of rocks on the nearside and, at the far end, by a blob of headland. The sea is clean. The fairly narrow, fine grit beach is hemmed in by a vegetated cliff-face.

No popular beach would be complete without rows of beach beds (200drs per day) and umbrellas (400drs per day). Canoes are also available for hire at 300drs per hour. To cater for the inner person, at about dead centre of the backshore, there is a *Cantina* hut. Towards the far end, in amongst the pebbles, are actually smidgins of sand.

Velanio Beach is reached from the far, east end of Stafilos Beach by climbing the well-worn, rubbish littered path over the coll of the neck of land connecting the bulbous headland to the rest of the landmass. On the other side of the promontory, and stretching away to the left (*Fsw*), is a sweep of gritty sand beach. This is interrupted by a rockfall about half-way along its length, to the nearside of which is a small *Cantina* hut. The enterprising owner hires boats, umbrellas and surfboards as well as selling sun-tan lotion and cans of drink. Apart from the extremely pleasant location, Velanio's claim to fame is that it is the island's officially approved nude beach. The extra distance and or the nudity tends to keep the place clear of 'kiddy-winkies'. Due to the aspect of the beach any wind not only causes the sea to gently break on the foreshore but provides a welcome breeze.

Back on the main road, once beyond the turning down to Stafilos Beach, the route climbs out of countryside supporting olive grooves into an area of pine trees, before descending to:-

AGNOTAS PORT (8km from Skopelos Town) A small but deep 'U' shaped bay with a disproportionately large concrete Ferry-boat Quay edging the south side of the inlet. Despite the incongruity of the structure, the *raison d'etre* is that if, in adverse weather conditions, the Skopelos Town Harbour becomes unsafe for use by ferry-boats they divert here.

On the side of the concrete road to the quay is a quite delightful fisherman's shack. I wonder what the inhabitants thought about these metres of concrete being laid down? Day trips depart from the quay for Limnonari Beach, at a return cost of 150drs, but this is not now an essential service as a track has been blasted down to that beach.

The middle of the bay's backshore is taken up by a very large building, in the ground floor of which is an extensive taverna. A pebble foreshore, which stretches all the way round the foot of the bay, widens out into a pebble beach on the north side. The occasional fishing boat is beached on the foreshore, close to the quay. There is one of the blue, steel 'watchtower' changing rooms unique to Skopelos, and a few swings adjacent to the roadside The sea is clear, the sea-bed pebbly and Agnotas is very much a Greek seaside resort.

Prior to the main road commencing to climb into the mountains, a new track to the left decants on to the nearside of:-

LIMNONARI BEACH (9½km from Skopelos Town) A lovely location, the pleasant, circular bay of which is enclosed by olive tree and brush covered hills slightly set back from the shore. Even the row of colourful pedaloes, beached on the middle of the shore, don't detract from the prospect. The beach is a splendid sweep of almost white sand with a few large pebbles dotted about and the foreshore is made up of very, very fine grit. The first metre or so of the sea-bed is sand and pebbles, becoming larger stones, despite which the middle section is mostly sand.

The (only) two storey *Pension/Taverna* (Tel 22242/22044) is owned by Georgios Lemonis, a quaint, interesting and unsophisticated character. The grounds of the building are on the scrubbly side but the interior is quite satisfactory. A sign in the taverna proclaims *Nudism is not allowed, don't light fires – police*. Double rooms with en suite bathroom cost 2100drs in mid-season. What a super place to stay and must rate as a find.

A mature, well shaped, if slightly stunted pine tree doubles up as the 'office' for the 'beach activity entrepreneur'. This sign advises *Please pay in advance, pedal boat 400drs per hour, canoe 200drs per hour, umbrella 400drs per day*.

The countryside hereabouts is very lovely, similar to the south coast of Thassos. On the approach to Panormos, the route is bordered by lots of heather and beehives but the road surface gets a little 'irregular' in places, which could prove especially tricky for night-time drivers of scooters.

PANORMOS BEACH (16km from Skopelos Town) The main road swings to the right on a corner overlooking the gentle curve of the fine shingle backshore and small pebble surface of the beach, prior to dropping down to sea-level. The sea is clean and clear and the sea-bed pebble.

Various enterprises are spread out along the road, which parallels the flat bay, rather unusually leaving a swathe of land between the road and backshore. What was once an olive grove, on the edge of the beach, is, as yet, relatively sparsely developed. Immediately to the left is the pleasantly situated, cloister-like *Psarrianos Apartment Studios*.

Amongst the various buildings are ***Rooms*** and *Restaurant Asterias*, on the left, sea side of the road, across from which is the somewhat squalid *Rent Rooms*, followed by more ***Rooms***. Towards the north side of the bay is the fully air-conditioned *Panormos Beach Hotel*, with bar and restaurant. Oh, Michael Carroll (author of *Gates of the Wind* – much of which was written round and about Panormos) where are you now?

Somehow not as an attractive location as it should be. Maybe the land backing the bay is too uninteresting.

Prior to the main road reaching the point at which the road overlooks the south end of Panormos Beach, a track meanders off to the wooded surrounds of a lovely looking inlet to the side of the main bay. Around the shores of this 'U' shaped, rocky cove are a number of private homes and small concrete quays with a number of boats anchored.

In advance of Milia Beach, two goat tracks descend the tree covered hillsides, at the side of the main road, to tracts of pebble and shingle foreshore. The first is a smidgin of pebble beach, hemmed in by rock, and the second a larger, fine shingle shore. Neither are idyllic locations but may remain more isolated than other choices. There is pleasant swimming off the rocks between the two spots. The position is usually evident by both the number of cars, parked alongside the edge of the road, and the presence of more rubbish than usual.

MILIA BEACH (18km from Skopelos Town) Signposted off the main road on a left-hand bend, distinguishable by a concentration of conspicious beehives. Riders of two wheeled transport should be very careful when turning back down the lorry wide, dusty track to the beach, as there is a sudden drop of about 23cms. Nasty!

The track divides round a taverna and informal vehicle park, located close to where the sweep of shore is interrupted by an outcrop of rock. The reverse side of the backshore dunes of the long, wide, slow crescent of fine pebble and gritty sand to the left (*Fsw*) is edged by a large swamp. The inland low slopes are pine tree covered, whilst not far offshore is the quite large, densely wooded and pretty Dasia islet. The sea is very clean and clear and is delightful for bathing. The sea's edge is paralleled by a row of beach umbrellas which are more than welcome as the beach lacks any shade.

Less than 1km beyond Milia Beach is the gritty and fine pebble Hovolo Beach, only accessible by a footpath.

This western stretch of island road, routed quite high up on the pine tree covered mountainside, is most attractive. There is plenty of visual evidence of very active resin collection on these forested slopes.

ELIOS (circa 24km from Skopelos Town) The reason for this very scrubbly, 'Greek unlovely' development is that the mountain clinging town of Klima was badly damaged by an earthquake. Elios was hastily constructed to rehouse the inhabitants. The main thrust of the settlement is bypassed, which is no bad thing. From the south side of the slip road into Elios, a road crosses a vast, unedifying, backyard-backshore. This was once a swamp but is now filled and levelled off with scalpings. Most of the unused, broken down construction plant of the island appears to have been dumped hereabouts. Incidentally, I often wonder how the Greeks are able to abandon these expensive machines without seemingly a care or second thought. Back to Elios. On the southern side is the *Motel Delphi*, which is more furnished apartments than a hotel, alongside which is the road down to the beach. On the edge of the pebble shore is a forlorn, small chapel which appears to have been in position for hundreds of years. At the south end of the bay it is possible to walk round a promontory to a quite long, narrow stretch of beach hemmed in by a cliff-face. The far end is blocked off by a rocky outcrop.

That development that makes up the village parallels the shoreline, from which it is separated by the aforementioned wasteland. Proceeding from south to north, the village 'High St' houses a grocery store, above which are ***Rooms***, a taxi service, a supermarket, the *Cafe/restaurant/bar Manolis – fresh fish*, and ***Rooms*** (Tel 33647) after which the slip road rejoins the bypass. Perhaps in twenty years time Elios will be a full-blown tourist development? Perhaps not!

The lack of a beach side taverna is, to some extent, balanced by the existence of the *Restaurant/Bar Hovolo*, which stands back from the sea's edge. The sea is clear and free from rubbish. Towards the north end of the shore are a pair of rocky moles forming a small harbour.

Some 3km beyond Elios is the narrow, slip road down to:-

KLIMA (27km from Skopelos Town) An eerily attractive,ghost town of a village made uninhabitable by the 1965 earthquake which caused severe slippage. Many of the houses that line the weed strewn lanes still possess their Turkish style, first floor balconies, complete with the toilet compartment. In a strange way some of the premises appear not to have been abandoned, only temporarily left by owners who have just slipped out for a minute or two. The green shuttered periptero is a good example. A few of the less badly damaged houses are now being renovated, a fact usually proclaimed by their new coat of whitewash and repaired roofs. It is difficult to say who is more surprised on rounding a corner of this or that street and bumping into a quietly grazing donkey.

From Klima the road continues to climb, serpentining in and around the folds of the mountain range. At first, only the seaward loops allow glimpses of distant Glossa, which finally comes into full view, across the other side of a mountain valley, where the road flattens out.

GLOSSA (30km from Skopelos Town) This very nice, very Greek, northern village clings to the side of the mountain. It is a fairly large settlement with quite a lot of new buildings being erected and an air of quiet affluence.

At the outskirts of Glossa is the junction of the road from Skopelos Town, the Glossa High St and the road down to Loutraki Port. This latter almost doubles back on the road from Skopelos Town, prior to the very steep descent to the Port. The junction is edged by a cafe-bar, wherein the local lads hang out, and respectable ***Rooms*** owned by Ilias Tsoykalas.

The very narrow High St winds through Glossa village towards the clock tower (that doesn't tell the correct time). About 30m along its length, on the right, are ethnic ***Rooms*** (Tel 33262) owned by an old lady with no English. The double rooms share a shower, simply curtained off, and are charged at between 1000drs and 1500drs.

A pharmacy is followed by a baker, a small store, that possesses an international metered telephone, and, keeping left, the *Taverna Agnanti*. In this old section of Glossa are several more stores and a grocery. The shop with the international telephone displays the Flying Dolphin and Ferry-boat timetables in the window (*See* **Ferry-Boat & Flying Dolphin timetables, A To Z, Loutraki Port**). The telephone is located in a separate booth, jammed inside the store, which resembles a *Dr Who Tardis*.

To the north and east of Glossa is a dirt road to a Military installation. About 100m along this and a donkey track makes off due east for a rewarding 3km trek across the ridged landscape to a cove, from which a flight of steps climbs to the cliff-topping Ag Ioannis Church. Don't forget to take some drinking water.

Back at Glossa village there are splendid views out over the sea to Skiathos. The Loutraki Port road snakes some 2½km down past a petrol station, a sign to the *Magic View Taverna* and, half-way down, tucked under the spreading branches of a pomegranate tree, a welcome drinking water fountain.

LOUTRAKI PORT (32½km from Skopelos Town) (Illustration 39) Once upon a time a simple fishing boat hamlet port... Now, the spaced out settlement has had 'hung on it' a very large harbour.

ARRIVAL BY FERRY & FLYING DOLPHIN

Ferry-boats and hydrofoils dock at the large quay (*Tmr* 1B4/5) on the left (*Sbo*) of the Harbour. In the main, buses coincide with the seaborne arrivals.

THE ACCOMMODATION & EATING OUT

The Accommodation Quite plentiful considering the comparatively small size of the settlement, which spreads out to the left and right of the bottom of the quay.

Rooms/Cafe/Restaurant (*Tmr* 2B3)
Directions: Just to the right, across the broad Esplanade from the bottom of the Ferry-boat Quay (*Tmr* 1B4/5).

Owned by Nikolaos Pallas and pleasantly fronted by a row of mature trees.

In the narrow street that climbs between the previous accommodation and the Church round to the main road, that descends to the Port from Glossa, are ***Rooms*** (*Tmr* 3B2) on the right (*Sbo*) and ***Rooms*** (*Tmr* 4B2) on the left, the latter owned by Maria Kaliakatsou.

Where this street joins the main road, turn left towards Glossa and, on the right, is the:-
Hotel Valentina (*Tmr* 5C1) (Class E) Tel 33694
Directions: As above.

Further along the Glossa road is the:-
Pension/Restaurant Rania (Class E) Tel 33710
Directions: As above.

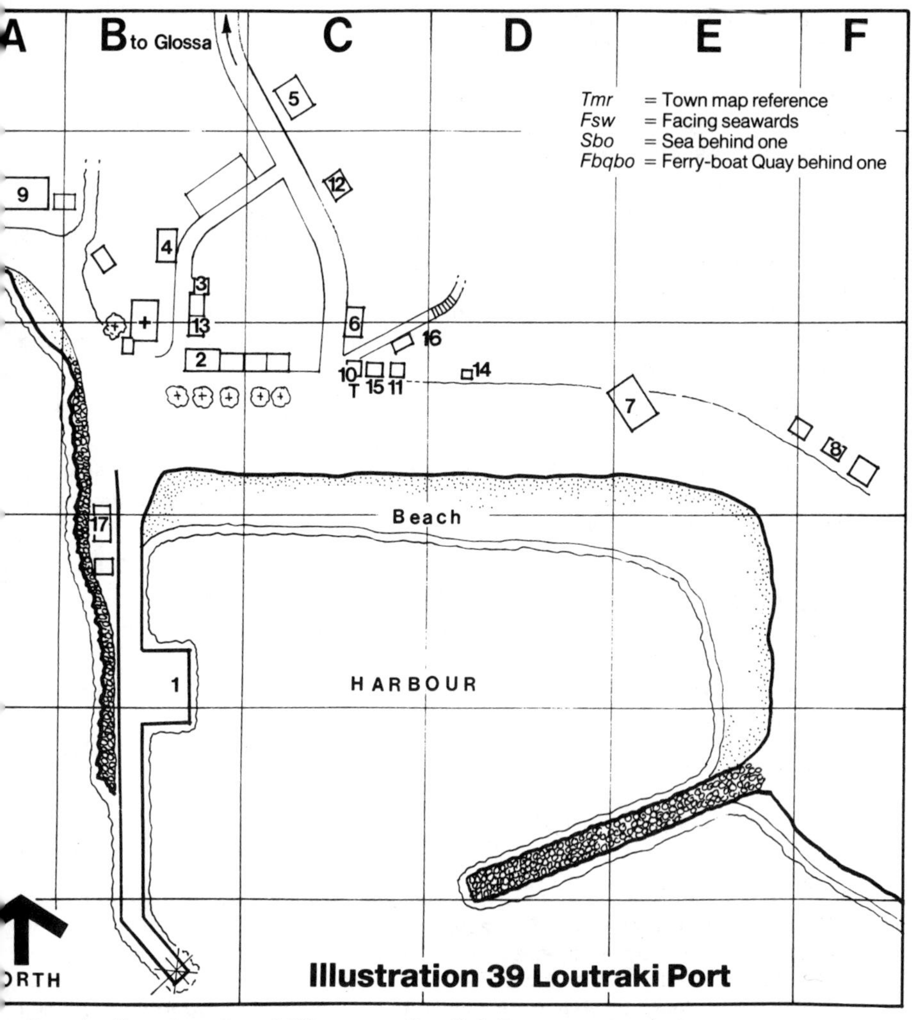

Illustration 39 Loutraki Port

Tmr
1. Ferry-boat Quay B4/5
2. Rooms/Restaurant B3
3. Rooms B2
4. Rooms B2
5. Hotel Valentina C1
6. Store/Rooms C2/3
7. Hotel Avra D/E3
8. Pension F3
9. Hotel/Restaurant Flisvos A2
10. Cafe Restaurant Aramis C3
11. Cafeteria/Pizzeria Maracana C3
12. Snackbar/Cafe Theresa C2
13. 'Market, Fruit, Bread' store B2/3
14. Souvenir shop D3
15. Ferry-boat ticket office C3
16. Glossa Tours C/D2/3
17. Fish Co-operative shack B3/4

T = Taxi rank

Double rooms only with en suite bathrooms charged at 1300drs, which rates rise to 1600drs (1st July-31st Aug).

Descending back to the Esplanade and, on the left (*Fsw*), is:-
Rooms (*Tmr* 6C2/3)
Directions: As above, over a store.

Back at the bottom of the Ferry-boat Quay and proceeding to the right (*Sbo*), with the beach foreshore on the right, advances towards the:-
Hotel Avra (*Tmr* 7D/E3) (Class C) Tel 33550
Directions: As above and on the left.
All rooms have en suite bathrooms. A single room costs 1400drs a night and a double room 1880drs, which rates rise, respectively, to 1600drs and 2280drs (21st June-10th Sept).

Further on, beyond the *Hotel Avra*, and still on the left in amongst a clutch of buildings and trees, is a *Pension* (*Tmr* 8F3).

Back at the bottom of the Ferry-boat Quay and following the line of the shore round to the left (*Sbo*), past the small beach on the left and the Church on the right, leads to the:-

Hotel (& Restaurant) Flisvos (*Tmr* 9A2) Tel 33526
Directions: As above, with the canopy covered terrace separated from the building by the street which peters out on the forecourt of the hotel.
Provincial Greek, with double rooms from 2000drs.

The Eating Out From the bottom of the Ferry-boat Quay, diagonally across the Esplanade (a grand word for a swathe of finely packed and crushed scalpings), there are at least two tavernas, side by side, with extensive, tree shaded terraces:-

Cafe Restaurant Aramis (*Tmr* 10C3)
Directions: The first on the right (*Sbo*) from the bottom of the Glossa main road.
A couple of small omelettes with bacon (220drs each), 2 bottles of beer (90drs each) and bread (10drs each) cost 640drs. Mind you, Sporades omelettes are rather pathetic, expensive substitutes for the large, potato filled articles, cooked in oil, that are still served elsewhere in the Aegean. (Mind you, it is perhaps necessary to watch these comparisons – I'll soon be swanning on about how they used to only cost 110drs...)

To the right (*Sbo*) is the:-
Cafeteria/Pizzeria Maracana (*Tmr* 11C3)
Directions: As above, and next door but one to the *Cafe Restaurant Aramis*.
Worthy of a mention, if only for it's effusive sign which proclaims ... *Taste our Special pizza, Fantastic spaghetti, Delicious ice-cream. Every kind of coffee, Skopelos cheese pie, omelettes varieties. Soft music, Free smile, we speak English, wir sprechen Deutsch*.
Apart from the other establishments mentioned under The Accommodation, there is the *Snackbar/cafe Theresa* (*Tmr* 12C2).

THE A TO Z OF USEFUL INFORMATION
BANKS None but *See* **Ferry-boat & Flying Dolphin Ticket Offices**

BEACHES The sea is, as elsewhere around Skopelos, very clean.

Enclosed by the Harbour is a splendid sweep of sandy shore but the local caiques, benzinas and other craft are beached and moored in the shallows along its length.

There is another small, pebbly and kelpy 'pocket handkerchief' of a beach across the way from the Church. Whilst mentioning the latter, it is interesting to note that an ancient column capital has been cemented into the foot of the building. Even more 'riveting' is that I have observed on this beach a section of classical column, simply lying on the shore. Perhaps it is still there.

Further on, beyond the *Hotel & Restaurant Flisvos*, are some small coves edged by fallen rocks.

BREAD *See* **Commercial Shopping Area**

BUSES Connect with Glossa and Skopelos Town, tying in with ferry-boat and Flying Dolphin arrivals. They pull up on the Esplanade, close to the Taxi rank (*Tmr* TC3).

COMMERCIAL SHOPPING AREA A sign points the way along the street on the right of the Church (*Sbo*) to *Market, fruit, bread* (*Tmr* 13B2/3). Next door is another small Store.

To the right (*Sbo*), across the Esplanade from the Harbour Beach, are one or two souvenir shops, one (*Tmr* 14D3) of which accepts credit cards. There is a Butcher on the main Glossa road.

DISCO One on the way up to Glossa.

FERRY-BOATS/FLYING DOLPHINS Almost a disproportionately fulsome service for such a 'way-station' of a place.

Ferry-boat & Flying Dolphin timetables *See* **Ferry-boat & Flying-Dolphin timetables, A To Z, Skopelos Town**. In addition to those listings are the following:-

Ferry-boats

Sunday	1520hrs	Skiathos, Volos(M).
Wednesday	1520hrs	Skiathos, Volos(M).

FERRY-BOAT & FLYING DOLPHIN TICKET OFFICES Ferry-boat tickets are sold from 'counter wheelbarrows' pulled out prior to a craft's arrival. There is also a Ferry-boat Ticket Office cum-Souvenir Shop (*Tmr* 15C3), tucked in between the tavernas bordering the Esplanade.:-

Glossa Tours (*Tmr* 16C/D2/3) Tel 33377

Directions: On the right of the alley that angles off the Glossa road.

Sells Flying-Dolphin tickets and would appear to be a local 'Mr Fixit'. He exchanges money, arranges excursions '... a Greek night in Faros'. 'Ke'?

TAXIS (*Tmr* TC3) Rank close to the junction of Glossa road and the Esplanade.

TOILETS Close to the Fish Co-operative's shack (*Tmr* 17B3/4), at the bottom of the Ferry-boat Quay, is a toilet block that has been bricked up. Perhaps it just filled up!

TRAVEL AGENTS & TOUR OFFICES *See* **Ferry-boat & Flying Dolphin Ticket Offices**.

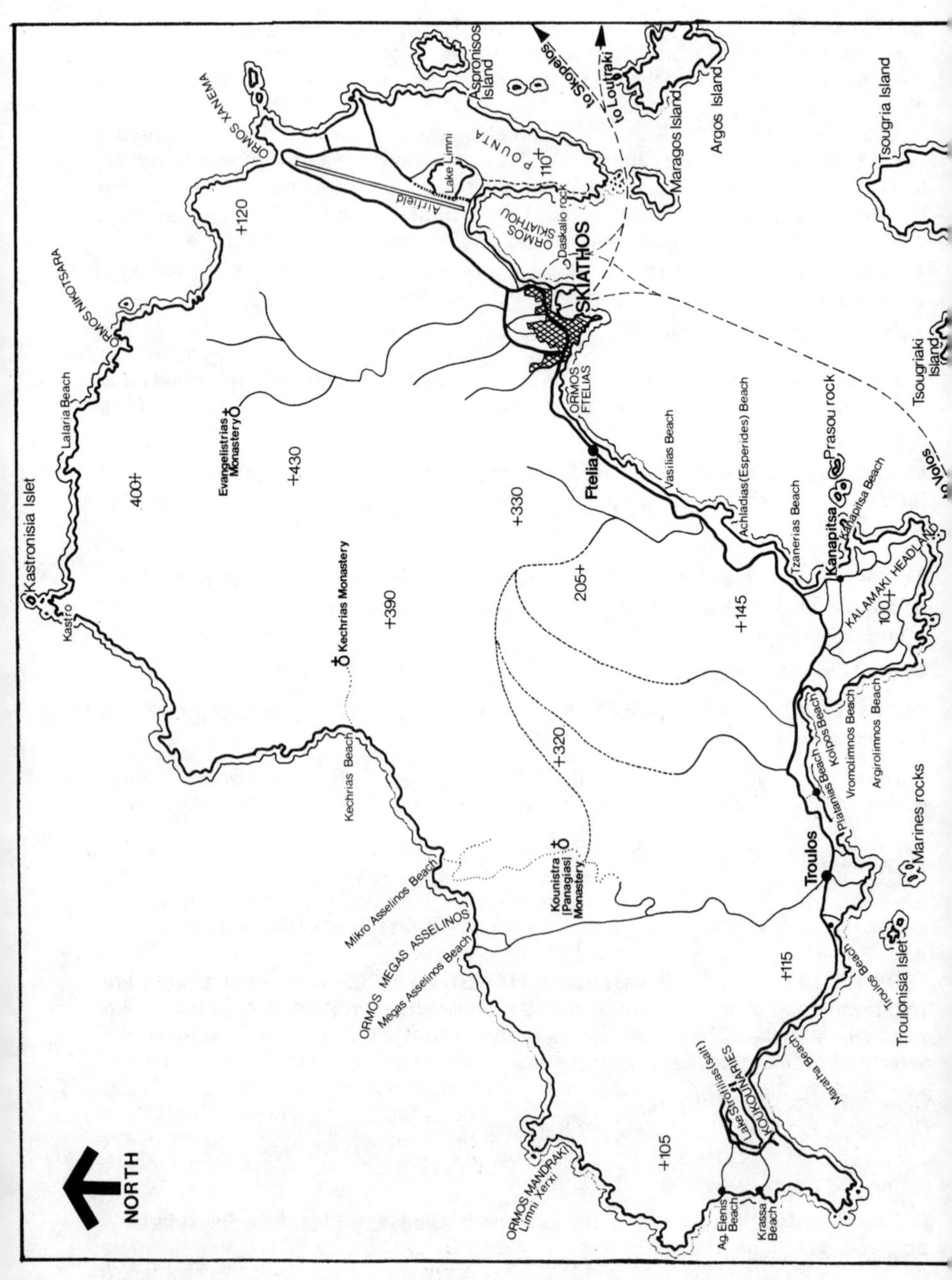

Illustration 40 Skiathos island

23 SKIATHOS (ΣΚΙΑΘΟΣ)

Sporades Islands

Skiathos Port **

The Countryside ****

FIRST IMPRESSIONS

Initial impression of a picturesque harbour; uninteresting town; appalling state of the town's streets; mass tourism; expensive; credit cards acceptable almost everywhere; sandy beaches; green, attractive countryside and forests; mule rides; a once sophisticated veneer that has slipped – like that of of an old whore's complexion.

SPECIALITIES

Trees; holiday industry; water sports.

RELIGIOUS HOLIDAYS & FESTIVALS

include: 15th August – Panaghia (The sacred burial of the Madonna), Evangelistrias Monastery; 20th November – Religious festival, Kounistra Monastery.

VITAL STATISTICS

Tel prefix 0427. The island is some 12km from side to side, 9km from top to bottom, with an area of approximately 77sqkm and a resident population of 4,000.

HISTORY

It is perhaps strange that nearby Skopelos, now living in the shadow of Skiathos in the holiday league table, was historically much wealthier.

During the Persian Naval incursion of 480 BC, under the leadership of the legendary King Xerxes, battle was engaged with the Greek fleet off Cape Artemisium (Evia island). The Persian tactical deployment was interrupted, legend has it, by foul weather forcing King Xerxes to seek refuge in a Skiathos bay still named after him (Limni Xerxi or Ormos Mandraki). Whilst holed up here, the king is supposed to have caused the construction of the first lighthouse in the world, on a reef situated between Skiathos and the Mainland.

Constant harrying by pirates, despite (or perhaps because of) the sporadic presence of the Venetians, encouraged the islanders to construct a Kastro, on the northernmost tip of the island, and to fortify the tiny inshore islet of Kastronisia. It was to this remote citadel that the islanders fled when threatened. The Castle was besieged by the Turks in 1538 in an effort to dislodge the Venetians. During the battle the commander was wounded. The islanders, hoping for sympathetic consideration, killed the injured man and threw themselves at the mercy of the blockading forces. Being Turks they 'topped' the soldiers and enslaved the locals. There's gratitude for you.

Considering its natural attributes, it seems inconceivable that the new town and port was only constructed as late as 1829/30, to coincide with Greek Independence. The inexorable growth of the development resulted in the disintegration of Kastro.

The renowned Greek writer Alexandros Papadiamantis was a native of the island, a fact recorded for posterity, not only by a commemorative statue at the outset of the Bourtzi promontory, but more prosaically by the local ferry-boat that bears his name. Papadiamantis (1851-1911) returned to the island and died in his Skiathos town house.

During the Second World War the occupying German forces destroyed a number of houses in an act of retaliatory punishment. Needless to say estimates of the damage vary from about thirty houses to the whole town being razed to the ground!

GENERAL

To 'appreciate and savour' Skiathos, and visiting a number of Sporades islands, it is probably best to call here first and follow up with Skopelos, Alonissos and Skyros – in that order! Only then will the next be compared more favourably with the last, for Skiathos holds the (dubious) honour of being one of the most tourist 'polluted' islands in the Aegean. The indefatigable hordes of Greeks and foreigners, who now swamp this once idyllic and sophisticated island, have managed to induce that which I once believed impossible in Greece, namely the Spanish 'Costa Bomba' ambience. Prices are at an almost unacceptable level; accommodation, except at the beginning and end of the season, is almost impossible to obtain and it is standing room only on most of the easily accessible beaches.

The town and port, after beguiling a seaborne visitor with an initially favourable impression, must be rather a disappointment. Package tourism and its inevitable demands predominate. As an example, most of the side-streets and lanes close to the hub of the town have at least one or three night spots. Additionally, there must be almost as many tourist offices as there are restaurants. The net result is a lack of traditional kafeneions and tavernas. And, why oh why, was the airport built prior to sorting out the condition of the town's streets?

On the other hand, Skiathos has one or two undeniable attractions. There are a number of sandy beaches, one long if narrow one adjacent to the town; there are superb countryside forest tracks; the Kalamaki headland is attractive and Koukounaries beach is a lovely location, if jam-packed. Hints to those who (still) intend to visit Skiathos must include not to do so between July and middle September (due to the total overcrowding), and not to have a room on the road towards the airport or anywhere close by the town's widespread night-time hot spots – the noise will be just too much. Oh, and don't visit Skiathos to rub shoulders with the wealthy, influential, famous or infamous – they have moved on to leave others to follow in their despoiling footsteps.

SKIATHOS: capital town & port (Illustration 41). New seaborne arrivals can only be impressed by the attractive appearance of Skiathos. The Bourtzi promontory pleasantly intrudes to divide the waterfront into two unequal lengths. Round to the left (*Sbo*) is a smallish, almost circular, natural harbour wherein berth the fishermen and trip boats. The backdrop is the houses of the Chora rising steeply up behind this Esplanade. To the right stretches the large commercial quay whereon dock the ferry-boats and merchant ships, this stretch with a backdrop of the Old Quarter's steepling lanes and alleys edged by a tumble of housing. Skiathos Bay runs out in the shallows, away to the right.

The twin hillocks, over which the town is draped, are separated by a flattish section up which the High St drives, parting a mishmash of dwellings divided by streets and lanes. Despite the massive influx of tourist pounds, dollars, marks, francs, guilders and lira (to name but a few of the available currencies) the town's infrastructure is shabby and the state of the streets is a disgrace.

Naturally beauty and attractiveness are in the eye of the beholder but I fervently hope that no visitor, for whom Skiathos is their first island, will be

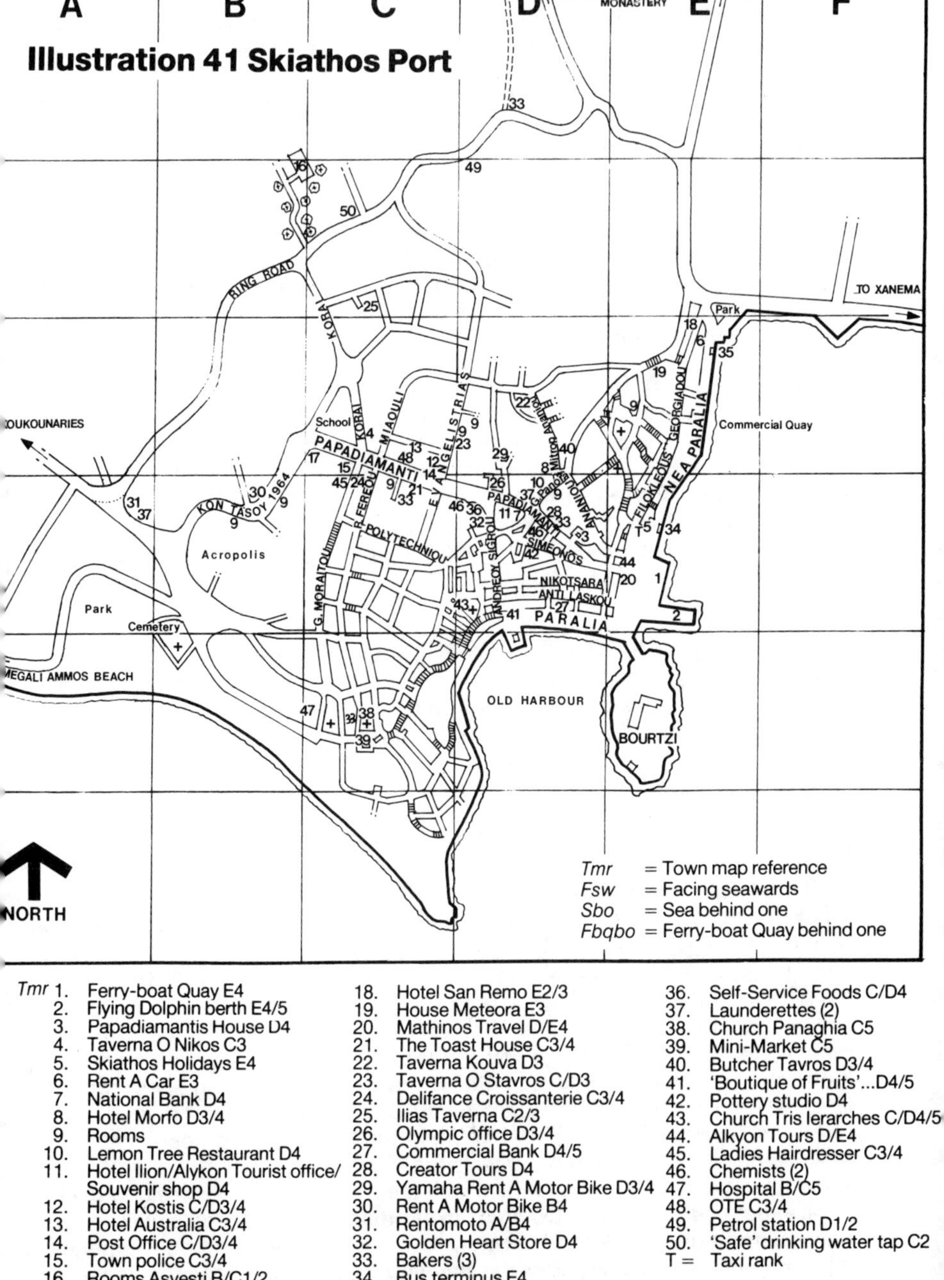

Tmr 1. Ferry-boat Quay E4
2. Flying Dolphin berth E4/5
3. Papadiamantis House D4
4. Taverna O Nikos C3
5. Skiathos Holidays E4
6. Rent A Car E3
7. National Bank D4
8. Hotel Morfo D3/4
9. Rooms
10. Lemon Tree Restaurant D4
11. Hotel Ilion/Alykon Tourist office/ Souvenir shop D4
12. Hotel Kostis C/D3/4
13. Hotel Australia C3/4
14. Post Office C/D3/4
15. Town police C3/4
16. Rooms Asvesti B/C1/2
17. Supermarket B/C3/4
18. Hotel San Remo E2/3
19. House Meteora E3
20. Mathinos Travel D/E4
21. The Toast House C3/4
22. Taverna Kouva D3
23. Taverna O Stavros C/D3
24. Delifance Croissanterie C3/4
25. Ilias Taverna C2/3
26. Olympic office D3/4
27. Commercial Bank D4/5
28. Creator Tours D4
29. Yamaha Rent A Motor Bike D3/4
30. Rent A Motor Bike B4
31. Rentomoto A/B4
32. Golden Heart Store D4
33. Bakers (3)
34. Bus terminus E4
35. Asselinos Bus 'park up' E3
36. Self-Service Foods C/D4
37. Launderettes (2)
38. Church Panaghia C5
39. Mini-Market C5
40. Butcher Tavros D3/4
41. 'Boutique of Fruits'...D4/5
42. Pottery studio D4
43. Church Tris Ierarches C/D4/5
44. Alkyon Tours D/E4
45. Ladies Hairdresser C3/4
46. Chemists (2)
47. Hospital B/C5
48. OTE C3/4
49. Petrol station D1/2
50. 'Safe' drinking water tap C2
T = Taxi rank

under the erroneous impression that this island is archetypal. The dilemma of a guide book author, in making these 'informed' judgements, is best exemplified by an extract from a letter of a 'friend of a friend' who, in thanking me for loaning him and his family a Skiathos guide, had the following to write..."what a lovely place Skiathos is, better than we even imagined ... it appears not much has changed so far as the book and map are concerned, not even the road goes any further!" And there am I going on about the unacceptable face of this and that.

I certainly do not understand the authorities reconstructing the airport terminal buildings before rebuilding the streets and their drains. The state of these are so bad that some streets run with fetid water in places. The grids close to the junction of Odhos Papadiamanti (the High St) and Paralia (the Esplanade) are so large and uneven that the unwary could experience a nasty accident. The local shopkeepers place mats over them, not only to save water splashing about but to damp down the smells and to ensure that the occasional scooter doesn't disappear through the bars!

ARRIVAL BY AIR

The runway only just squeezes into a neck of land close to the town. The planes appear to line up for their final approach by descending along a flight path that bisects Skiathos Bay – thundering over the navigation light topped, rock outcrop of Daskalio. (*See* **Places of Interest, A To Z** for an unusual Skiathos sporting activity associated with the incoming planes).

A new airport terminal building is under construction to replace the old, more familiar and friendlier huts. The vehicle journey time to the town is measured in minutes.

ARRIVAL BY FERRY & FLYING DOLPHIN

There is an extensive service that ties in with various mainland ports and the other islands in the Sporades chain of islands. The Ferry-boat Quay (*Tmr* 1E4) and Flying Dolphin docking point (*Tmr* 2E4/5) could not be more conveniently located. Owners of accommodation meet arrivals.

Ferry-boat travellers should note that the **FB Papadiamantis II** is a much slower craft than the **CF Limnos** and, despite the former departing ¼hr earlier than the latter, it docks at Ag Konstantinos(M) some twenty minutes later.

THE ACCOMMODATION & EATING OUT

The Accommodation As advised, arrivals by sea are met at the gates of the Esplanade edging quayside. It goes without saying that the various Travel Agents & Tour offices can offer accommodation (*See* **A To Z**). Don't forget that hotels are expensive, with very few exceptions.

A fair number of package holiday tourists are accommodated in the first floor apartments of buildings lining the busy Main St. This is a very noisy situation, exacerbated by the countless souvenir shops staying open extremely late, at least until 2230-2300hrs every night. Some relief for those sited between Taverna O Nikos (*Tmr* 4C3) and the Esplanade, is bestowed by the Main St being closed to traffic during the night hours.

Another concentration of tourists is in the heights that stretch along the Nea Paralia, between the Flying Dolphin ticket office (*Tmr* 5E4) and a vehicle rental outfit (*Tmr* 6E3). Those rooms looking out over the Harbour could experience a lot of noise from the commercial shipping that docks across the Esplanade.

Following Odhos Papadiamanti (the High St) from whence it sets off from the Esplanade, almost opposite the Ferry-boat Quay (*Tmr* 1E4), not only leads past various options but will result in a number of approaches from owners of accommodation.

Hotel Morfo (*Tmr* 8D3/4) Odhos Mitrop Ananiou
Directions: Turn right off the High St along Odhos G Panora, about opposite the National Bank (*Tmr* 7D4). Where the street divides, keep left and the hotel is on the left of Odhos Mitrop Ananiou.
Smart and dominated by the clients of package companies.

Rooms (*Tmr* 9D4) Tel 22364
Directions: On the right of the far end of Odhos G Panora, diagonally across the street from *The Lemon Tree Restaurant* (*Tmr* 10D4).
A double room sharing the bathroom costs about 1800drs, with a three bed room available from 2400drs.

Hotel Ilion (*Tmr* 11D4) (Class E) Tel 21193
Directions: Above the Alykon Tourist office and a stationers, on the left of the High St. A noisy location, as will be any other accommodation on this main thoroughfare. The entrance is from the street behind and one back from the High St.
All rooms have en suite bathrooms with single rooms costing 2500drs and doubles 2500drs. These charges rise, respectively, to 2500drs & 3000drs (1st-30th June & 16th Sept-31st Oct) and to 3200drs and 3800drs (1st July-15th Sept).

The High St makes a crossroads with Odhos Evangelistrias.
Hotel Kostis (*Tmr* 12C/D3/4) (Class D) 5 Evangelistrias Tel 22909
Directions: Turn right (*Sbo*) off the High St and the hotel is on the left of Odhos Evangelistrias.
All rooms with en suite bathrooms, the single room rate starts at 1900drs and a double room 2700drs. These prices rise to 2600drs and 3600drs (16th June-15th Sept).

There are also ***Rooms*** (*Tmr* 9C/D3 & 9D3) further along the same street, Odhos Evangelistrias, on the right, beyond *Taverna O Stavros*. Rates mid-season cost 2000drs for a double room. The furthest ***Rooms***, in the cul-de-sac, has singles for 1400drs.

Hotel Australia (*Tmr* 13C3/4) (Class E) Parados Evangelistrias St Tel 22488
Directions: From the High St, turn right (*Sbo*) along Evangelistrias St and left at the first lane. The *Australia* is about half-way down on the left.
The hotel now takes package clients. Only double rooms with en suite bathrooms which are charged at 1800drs. This rate rises to 2800drs (16th June-15th Sept).

Taverna Skiathos
Directions: On the right of the High St (*Sbo*), just beyond the Post Office (*Tmr* 14C/D3/4).
Certainly advertises ***Rooms***, with private bathroom, during the height of season months.

Rooms (*Tmr* 9C3/4)
Directions: On the first floor of a building edging the High St, in the ground floor of which are a number of souvenir shops. The entrance is from the 'Bakery' cul-de-sac.

At the fork in the High St, just before the Town Police station (*Tmr* 15C3/4),

Korai St angles off to the right to junction with the Skiathos Town ring road, alongside a breakers yard. To the right, and across the road by a small shrine, a winding track makes off to the left through some backyard small holdings. In this rather 'doo-hickey', but idyllic, olive grove setting is:-

Rooms Asvesti (*Tmr* 16B/C1/2) Tel 21185
Directions: As above. A number of single storey buildings form an informal square, nicely planted out with flowers. The family live in one of the buildings to the right (*Town behind one*).

Filistra and her girls are amongst those that 'trap' arrivals. She quotes 1500drs a night for a double room but this charge, cum-settlement, is upped by 100drs a head for use of the shower. This is an unnecessary subterfuge as other, comparable, accommodation is charged at 2000drs. Another 'naughty' is to describe the walk as only a few minutes.... it takes about twenty minutes. The clean, simple but pleasant double rooms share a bathroom with three or four others. The water is hot and there is a communal refrigerator.

Back at the High St, continuing on beyond the Police station (*Tmr* 15C3/4) and the School playground (on the other side of the road) and the road curves to the left past, on the left, a largish supermarket (*Tmr* 17B/C3/4), with a large display of fruit and vegetables racked outside.

Hotel Karafelas (Class E) Tel 21235
Directions: As above and just beyond the supermarket (*Tmr* 17B/C3/4).

All rooms have en suite bathrooms. A single room costs 1800drs and a double room 2200drs. These charges rise, respectively, to 2000drs and 2700drs (1st June-31st Aug).

Continuing on round the bend and, on the left, is *Rooms to Rent with Private Bathroom* (*Tmr* 9B/C4).

Rooms (*Tmr* 9B4) Odhos Kon Tasoy 1964 Tel 22573
Directions: Continue along and up the (one-way) street, against the traffic flow, from the High St and on the left – *Rooms for rent with private bath*.

Owned by Annie Magdalini, her double rooms, with an en suite bathroom, cost 2000drs in mid-season.

Back at the Ferry-boat Quay (*Tmr* 1E4), the wide Esplanade stretches away to the right (*Sbo*).

Hotel San Remo (*Tmr* 18E2/3) (Class D) 5 Filokleous GeorgiadouTel 22078
Directions: At the far end of the Esplanade advance around to the left, prior to a small park, on to the narrow street that runs parallel to the Esplanade, stretching all the way from the area of the Ferry-boat Quay.

The hotel is very expensive and all rooms have en suite bathrooms. A single room starts at 2845drs and a double room 3200drs. These rise, respectively, to 3560drs and 4000drs (1st June-9th July & 1st-30th Sept) and 4980drs and 4980drs (yes 4980drs for either) between 10th July-31st August.

The *Pension Christina*, which is on the same side of Odhos Filokleous Georgiadou as the *Hotel San Remo* but a few metres back towards the Ferry-boat Quay, only has furnished apartments.

House Meteora (*Tmr* 19E3)
Directions: Ascend the steps that rise from the north-east end of Filokleous

Georgiadou St and the building is on the left (*Sbo*).

Rooms with Private Bathrooms & Toilet for Rent. How much the *Toilet*?

Rooms (*Tmr* 9E3) Odhos Ag Nikolaos, The Old Quarter.
Directions: A number of approaches are possible up the steep steps from Odhos Filokleous Georgiadou to Odhos Ag Nikolaos. This latter is the lane that 'totters' along the crest of the Old Quarter hillside. New arrivals should turn diagonally right (*Fbqbo*) past the taxi rank (*Tmr* T) and walk up and along Odhos Filokleous Georgiadou. Opposite the house, in which is located the office of Skiathos Tourist Agency, turn left up the steps, beneath an overhanging first floor balcony. These steps zig-zag past a small chapel, after which turn right at a bigger church and proceed along Odhos Ag Nickolaos. This narrow lane runs parallel to the Esplanade down below and the house is on the left. Those approaching from the area of the *House Meteora* (*Tmr* 19E3) should climb to the far, north end of Odhos Ag Nikolaos.

An ethnic, old house in the Old Quarter. The 'Papa 'scoops up' arrivals from the quayside.

Once again back at the Ferry-boat Quay (*Tmr* 1E4)
Hotel AYPA (Avra) (*Tmr* D/E4/5) (Class D) Anti Laskou Tel 22044
Directions: From the Ferry-boat Quay start out along the High St, Odhos Papadiamanti, turn first left along the narrow lane Odhos Nifonos and take the second right on to Odhos Anti Laskou. The hotel entrance is on the left. It is equally possible to proceed left (*Sbo*) along the Esplanade and turn into Odhos Anti Laskou from between the serried ranks of canopy covered restaurant tables and chairs.

Only double rooms are available, sharing bathrooms, at a cost of 3500drs.

See **Beaches, A To Z** and **Excursions To Skiathos Town Surrounds**, for further details of accommodation.

The Eating Out Similarly to accommodation, comestibles and beverages are expensive, that is apart from Greek salads which are generally charged at 120drs for a typical helping. Perhaps it is 'a loss leader'. Bottled beer is a rarity at the waterfront bars, ½ litre mugs being the 'norm', at a cost of 150drs for a lager – Whow!

Average quayside prices include Nes meh ghala 90drs, an ouzo 150drs, a three star brandy 220drs, a three star Metaxa 450drs, a bottle of orange or lemonade 57drs, a *Full English breakfast* 360drs, a small omelette 220drs, and a Greek salad 130drs. To overcome the inadequacy of this latter dish, Skiathos offers a 'Special' Greek salad, which, in size and contents, constitutes that which a 'normal' Greek salad should be, at a cost of 300drs.

The attractive, Malta-like situation of the cafe-bars, that line the Esplanade and look out over the picturesque Harbour and Bourtzi headland, does not ease the pain of the jolly nearly extortionate prices charged. If this were not enough to bear, the waiters employed on this stretch tend to round up bills (if being forgiving) or overcharge, in truth.

The Zacharoplasteion to the left (*Sbo*) of Mathinos Travel (*Tmr* 20D/E4) serves acceptably priced coffee with little pots of hot water (which gives 1½ cups) for 70drs. This is amazing value and extremely useful to know when waiting for an early morning ferry-boat. The establishment is, understandably, popular with locals up and about in the early morning hours.

The Esplanade Paralia, Nea Paralia and the steps, Al Moraitidou, are, at night, a throbbing mess, sorry mass, of brightly lit restaurants, tavernas and cafe-bars, the terraces and patios of which are stuffed to the brim with eating and drinking clients, all overlaid by a pulsating musical 'discord'.

Every so often, glance up at the third storey of the old residences and observe the maturer residents looking down at the 'comings and goings' of the tourists with what one can only describe as utter amazement.

Many of the restaurants in the town are restaurants (Irish I know), with smartly dressed waiters and tablecloths which augers ill for the back pocket. Another bad omen is the presence of at least one Croissant shop. This manifestation (did I hear infestation?) is also visible on Alonissos, and indicates that the prices will be astronomical. Bottled water is charged for almost everywhere. A plus point is that the traditional, non-fizzy, portokaladha (orangeade) is available in pear shaped bottles.

The preponderance of expensive establishments has encouraged a plethora of souvlaki snackbars, around which crowds of tourists gather. These include a pair of 'greasy spoons', either side of the outset of the High St, another on the right (*Fbqbo*) of Odhos Anti Laskou and yet another on the side-street off to the left (*Fbqbo*) of the High St, immediately prior to the National Bank (*Tmr* 7D4). This latter snackbar, across the road from a chemist (*Tmr* 46D4), has a few stools and is quieter and cleaner than its High St counterparts. Souvlaki pita are averagely charged at 100drs.

Another High St establishment popular with tourists is:-

The Toast House (*Tmr* 21C3/4)
Directions: On the left of the High St, beyond the Evangelistrias/High St crossroads and distinguishable by the few stools set down on the narrow pavement.

A snackbar serving a Continental breakfast, sandwiches, hot dogs, hamburgers, eggs & bacon (180drs), an omelette (180drs) and, unfortunately, lager in ½ litre glasses.

Prior to the National Bank (*Tmr* 7D4), Odhos G Panora curves off to the right (*Sbo*). On the left, beyond a launderette, is the:-

Lemon Tree Restaurant (*Tmr* 10D4)
Directions: As above.

Owned by a pleasant, if lacklustre English couple, 'Buzz' from Kent and Maureen from Nottingham. The menu of this bistro-like cafe appears interesting and not expensive in comparison to other Skiathos establishments. There are various breakfast options. Salads include carrot and raisin, apple and nut, aubergine, coleslaw, rice, potato, fish roe (all costing 100drs), whilst a Greek salad, indicated as large, is charged at 200drs. Main dishes take in shepherds pie (a Greek shepherd I hope – 225drs), omelettes (250drs) and a Greek omelette 'special' (300drs). Vegetables listed embrace potatoes (53drs), peas (50drs) and Greek beans (100drs). An Amstel beer costs 77drs, an orange juice 50 or 100drs, a kortaki retsina 100drs and a Nes meh ghala 58drs, but... I have in the past postulated that Greek food does not easily cross its frontiers. A meal at the Lemon Tree convinces me that foreign cooks should also not try to traverse the Greek border. The ambience here is, without doubt, that of a clean *Last of the Summer Wine* cafe or, if the reader has been to Northern Ireland, high tea in one of that unhappy provinces restaurants. Nice and homely but definitely not Greek.

Amongst the English clientele, diners may include some attired in vests and those who request brown sauce and mustard – I must own up to enjoying brown sauce on a shepherds pie... but not in Greece! A meal of zucchini for two (150drs each), carrot and raisin salad (100drs), steak 'special' (800drs), steak and baked potato (400drs for the steak and 200drs for the baked potato), a bottle of retsina (100drs) and bottled water (no charge) totalled 1900drs. The steak was enjoyable, the meal wholesome and workmanlike (and one of us enjoyed it) but I have to admit that when in Greece I delight in most things Greek in a Greek atmosphere, not cosy 'Northern counties', but there you go.

From the Lemon Tree Restaurant, turning left along Odhos Mitropoleos Ananiou meanders towards the:-

Taverna Kouva (*Tmr* 22D3)

Directions: As above and on the left (*Sbo*), almost opposite, another new hotel in the course of construction.

A chicken on the spit establishment that is Skiathos in aspect and price.

Opposite the National Bank (*Tmr* 7D4) is the very swish *Bonaparte Restaurant* where dishes include chef's special, tournedos flambé and lamb Bonaparte. Well, well... how very Greek. I shall not enlarge.

Continue along Odhos Papadiamanti, the High St, from the National Bank to the Evangelistrias crossroads, whereon turn right (*Sbo*) for the:-

Taverna O Stavros (*Tmr* 23C/D3)

Directions: As above and on the right.

Recommended, but it has become smart, so is really a restaurant in all but name. The bill of fare is enclosed in a smart menu folder. Oh dear! The food looks good but there isn't a 500gm retsina listed.

Proceeding along the High St, beyond the crossroads, passes *Taverna Skiathos* on the right (*Sbo*), after which turn left into Odhos R Fereou.

Delifrance Croissanterie (*Tmr* 24C3/4) R Fereou St.

Directions: As above, and on the right of Odhos R Fereou.

I only draw attention to this style of eatery with much the same emotions as experienced by a snake that has spotted a mongoose – I am, as it were, fascinated by the unrepresentative nature of the 'beast' as well as the horrifying implications. The Sporades appear to be capable of spawning one or two of these chic, sandwich bar, American ice-cream parlour type of smart establishments. There is one on Alonissos. They purvey hot croissants and a range of sandwiches, pies, tarts, coffee, tea, beer, breakfast, and much more, but at a price. Sandwiches, for instance, start at 200drs. Open daily between 0830-1430hrs and 1800hrs until trade determines the doors close. Perhaps the Germans can afford to eat here?

Towards the top end of the High St, Odhos Korai angles off to the right (*Sbo*). Close to the junction, on the right, are:-

Taverna O Nikos (*Tmr* 4C3)

Directions: As above.

A conventional, to be recommended taverna which serves a reasonably priced and varied menu, reasonably priced that is for Skiathos. Meals on offer include a Greek salad (110drs), tzatziki (124drs), patatas (65drs), gigantes

beans (200drs), chicken (279drs), pork souvlaki (433drs), veal with everything (and anything) (375drs), kalamares (282drs), stuffed tomatoes and moussaka (347drs). Kortaki retsina is available (100drs) and bread (which might be stale) costs 20drs a head.
and the:-

Cafe Serano
Directions: As above and next door to *O Nikos*.

A good value, friendly cafe-bar. A Nes meh ghala costs 75drs and a 'stiff' ouzo 100drs. Compare this to the Esplanade prices of 90drs and 150drs. Open from morning to night.

Pretentiousness is not the sole preserve of the aforementioned *Restaurant Bonaparte*, as there is the:-
Ilias (ΗΛΙΑΣ) Taverna (*Tmr* 25C2/3)
Directions: From the top of the High St, turn right along Odhos Korai, past *Nikos Taverna* (*Tmr* 4C3), right at the first right-hand turning and then first left. The restaurant building is on the left and its patio is across the road.

The popularity of the establishment with smart tourists, who don't mind spending large sums of money, deems it necessary to arrive early. Latecomers will have to queue beside the wall bordering the open air 'dining room'. A tip is to order absolutely everything required at the outset. The friendly but 'Grecocilious' behaviour of the staff precludes their being able to take any amendments to a client's requirements, once stated.

A meal for two including an excellent Greek salad (110drs), a very good, if expensive bean soup (250drs), an acceptable tzatziki (180drs), a moussaka 'in the pot' (400drs – why can't it be 'outside a pot', when it would hopefully cost 100drs less), the *Ilias special*, a shrimp and ham salad (short of shrimps and long on tomatoes – overpriced at 640drs), a bottle of beer (77drs), a lemonade (41drs), a bottle of water (76drs) and bread (26drs per head) totalled 1826drs. Other dishes available include kalamari (285drs), veal or pork goulash ('special' – 480drs), chicken orloff (special – 420drs), meatballs (225drs), liver (veal-220drs). Strangely, drinks are comparatively reasonably priced with a 500gm retsina being listed, but often not available (94drs). Wines start off at about 195-212drs. This restaurant is only open in the evenings, between 1800 to 2300hrs daily.

The other quarter, with almost a superfluity of eating houses, ranges up the steps climbing the hillside to the left (*Sbo*) of the port, from the Esplanade bordering the local craft quayside. The steps, Odhos Al Moratidou, are lined with 'on-the-expensive-side' restaurants, some of which appear to cater for the very affluent. Position, as well as decor, decrees which are the costliest and those with them proclaim their sea views.

One particularly recommended by a reader is the *Kon Tiki*, a pizza house with a rather limited menu but a splendid outlook over the Old Harbour. Across the steps is *Chez Julien*, a French cuisine restaurant owned by a Frenchman, who (so he says) has all the food flown in from France. Why?

THE A TO Z OF USEFUL INFORMATION

AIRLINE OFFICE & TERMINUS (*Tmr* 26D3/4). On the right (*Sbo*) of Odhos Papadiamanti, the High St. The office is open seven days a week, between 0700-1930hrs.

The 'Mickey Mouse' airport terminal huts are being replaced by a 'super-duper', new facility.

Aircraft timetable (Summer months)
Skiathos to Athens (& vice versa)
Daily 0810, 1320, 1945hrs.

In addition to which are:-
Tuesday, Thursday & Sunday 1700hrs
Return
Daily 0650, 1210, 1825hrs

In addition to which are:-
Monday, Wednesday & Friday 0700hrs

One-way fare: 5020drs; duration 50mins.

Skiathos to Thessaloniki
Monday, Wednesday & Friday 0810, 0900hrs.

Return
Tuesday, Thursday & Sunday 1550, 1640hrs.

One-way fare 5370drs; duration 50mins.

BANKS
National Bank (*Tmr* 7D4) Odhos Papadiamanti.
Directions: On the left (*Sbo*) of the High St.
The usual hours plus evening shifts for exchange transactions. The evening opening hours are Monday-Friday between 1830-2030hrs. There is also a Saturday morning 'slot', between 0900-1200hrs. Whatever time of day a 'punter' might choose, there will be queues, even out of the height of the season.
Commercial Bank (*Tmr* 27D4/5) Paralia.
Directions: On the local boat Esplanade.

Due to the pressure on the banks, do not forget the **Post Office.**

BEACHES
Megali Ammos A road curves round and down from the west, top end of town, alongside a Church and cemetery and through a park. It then loops to the right past a scrubbly boatyard (on some maps quaintly referred to as a shipyard) and narrows down to become nothing more than a wide path. A steep track climbs up to another, higher street that runs parallel to the waterfront. This latter is a cul-de-sac on the sea side of which are:-

Rooms Tel 22249
Directions: As above and the first blue house on the left of the street.
Very ethnic, very clean with a communal shower. Single rooms cost from 700drs and double rooms from 1200drs.

The 'Megali Ammos' path finally runs out on a taverna patio, prior to steps down to the nearside of the beach. The taverna, the *Ackroyali*, serves breakfast.

Megali Ammos Beach is narrow, edging a long, gentle crescent of a bay. The inland side is bordered by vine covered, trellis shaded terraces of spaced out, single storey buildings on the right which are screened by a profusion of bushes and low trees. The beach extends for some 400m and, at the outset, is very sandy, gently sloping beneath the sea. At about two metres into the sea the sand is grown over by seaweed. Even out of the height of the season the beach becomes quite crowded at the town end, which bodes ill for the busy months. The rubbish is not always cleaned away.

About 50m along the beach, up some steps, is:-

Rooms for Rend (*sic*) Tel 21859/22637

Directions: As above.

Dimitrios Feretzelis is a kindly man, with a mouth full of gold capped teeth. His English owes much to his years in the Merchant Navy. A double room sharing the bathroom and with a shower, actually situated close by the steps, costs 2000drs. Dimitrios advises against anyone visiting Skiathos in July or August, under any circumstances. "It's all noisy Greeks with noisy children and every accommodation is full". A nod is as good as a wink, isn't it?

A few paces further on, again overlooking the beach, is the:-

Cafe-bar Taverna Aselinos (or Elias?)

Directions: As above.

A very small, pleasantly tree and vine shaded terrace edges the small hut-like building. The business is run by a hard-working couple. A bottle of Amstel beer and a lemonade cost 130drs. They serve Greek salad, omelettes, kalamari, fish and stick souvlaki. A meal for two of omelettes, a beer and fresh bread costs 660drs.

Other ethnic ***Rooms*** set in beautiful gardens, are owned by Eleni (Tel 22767). She charges from 2300drs for a double room, but her accommodation has to be booked through one of the Town's travel offices.

Hereabouts a beach based enterprise hires out wind surfers (700drs per hour), canoes (300drs ph), pedaloes (400drs ph) and parasols (beach umbrellas – 400drs per day). Another 50m or so further along the beach are more pedaloes for hire and, the terraces of a couple of side-by-side, backshore-bordering tavernas. The first is the *Taverna Thessaloniki, We serve breakfast, lunch and dinner*, and next door is the *Taverna Monika*. At about this point the sea-bed becomes rather weedy with some shelving rock, after which the beach widens out and the sea-bed clears, opposite a track connecting with the Koukounaries main road. A sign proclaims *Rooms to Let with private bathroom and apartments*. The beach proceeds on for another 50/75m whereon a small outcrop of rock divides it from the next, narrow, gritty section of about 150m of shoreline with a rather shingly middleshore and a biscuit rock foreshore. This latter length is that edged by most of the rented villas.

Certainly it is a thought, for those wishing to escape the excesses of Skiathos Town, to come out here for both accommodation and 'victualling'. On the other hand, the beach is very popular even in the quieter months, admittedly not stuffed-to-standing-room-only, but very busy.

Bourtzi promontory Beneath the *Bourtzi Dance Bar* is a flattened area suitable for sun bathing, but beware if paddling as sea urchins are present. *See* **Excursions To Skiathos Town Surrounds**.

BICYCLE, SCOOTER & CAR HIRE There is a plethora of outfits including:- **Sporades Rent A Car** and **Safeway Rent A Motorbike** (*Tmr* D4) on Odhos Nikotsara; **Rent A Car Skiathos** and **Rent A Car Motorcycle** (*Tmr* 6E3), both on Nea Paralia; **Creator Tours** (*Tmr* 28D4), who hire scooters from the High St; **Yamaha Rent A Motor Bike** (*Tmr* 29D3/4) and another **Rent A Motor Bike** (*Tmr* 30B4).

My favourite scooter hire firm is:-

Rentomoto (*Tmr* 31A/B4). PO 36, Ag Fanouriou, Acropolis Tel 21711
Directions: The 'front-room' office is located close by the junction of the town ring road and the Koukounaries road, at the western end of town.

The proprietor is the engaging and personable, if roguish, Georgios Siderados. Out of season, he lives in mainland Volos with his French wife and three children. His English is acceptable, his French very good and he can be an absolute fund of amusing anecdotes. The scooters are in extremely good condition and cost a-more-than-reasonable 1000drs a day. Georgios professes to be adding buggies and cars to his fleet for 1988.

BOOKSELLERS Beneath the *Hotel Ilion* (*Tmr* 11D4) is a souvenir shop that sells English newspapers and paperbacks, as well as *Press, Film, Suvenirs* (*sic*), *Sunoils, Books*. There is a newsagent on Odhos Andreoy Sigrou, diagonally across the street from the Golden Heart store (*Tmr* 32D4) and another in Odhos Anti Askou, the narrow street that runs parallel to the Paralia Esplanade.

BREAD SHOPS There are a number including the High St *Bread from the Village* (*Tmr* 33D4), another (*Tmr* 33C4) in a cul-de-sac off to the left (*Sbo*) of the High St, which also opens in the evenings, and a Baker (*Tmr* 33C5) on the 'western heights'. There is yet another Baker (*Tmr* 33D1) towards the eastern end of the ring road.

BUSES The island buses 'terminus' (*Tmr* 34E4) close to the Ferry-boat Quay and the private **Asselinos Bus** parks (*Tmr* 35E3) at the extreme right-hand end (*Sbo*) of the Commercial Quay.

Bus timetable
Skiathos Town to Koukounaries via the coastal villages en route, (*See* **Route One)**

Daily 0715, 0900, 0930, 1000, 1030, 1100, 1130, 1200, 1230, 1300, 1330, 1430, 1530, 1600, 1630, 1700, 1730, 1800, 1830, 1900, 1930, 2030, 2130, 2230, 2330hrs.

Return journey
Daily 0745, 0930, 1000, 1030, 1100, 1130, 1200, 1230, 1300, 1330, 1400, 1500, 1600, 1630, 1700, 1730, 1800, 1830, 1900, 1930, 2000, 2100, 2200, 2300, 2400hrs.

Skiathos Town to Camping Asselinos Beach
Daily 1030, 1200, 1700, 2300hrs.

Return journey
Daily 0915, 1100, 1500, 1800hrs.

CAMPING *See* **Asselinos & Kolpos Beaches, Route One**.

COMMERCIAL SHOPPING AREA There is no central market. On the other hand there are plenty of shops spread throughout the town but it is necessary to 'shop' around (sorry). The lunch time siesta starts early and prices vary from the acceptable to the damned expensive for exactly the same item. Another strange phenomena, for such a touristic island, is that it is very difficult to locate provision shops that are open on Sundays. Naturally the boutiques and souvenir outlets are open all hours. The High St is awash with gift and grocery shops, mini-markets and supermarkets. One of the most unusual of the general stores is the:-

Golden Heart (*Tmr* 32D4)
Directions: On the right of narrow Odhos Andreoy Sigrou, which branches left (*Sbo*) off Odhos Papadiamanti, the High St.

An extraordinary, old-fashioned, ramshackle, dirty store presided over by a friendly but astute old boy. The bottled water, cheeses and meats are stored in probably the oldest refrigeration cabinets in existence. Customers slide the glass doors back, remove their requirements and cut them to size on an antiquated slicer or with a rusty, blunt hacksaw left lying around. (Oh, Common Market shop regulators, cry your heart out here). The rest of the goods are piled up on deep racking but prices are on the high side. An example is a bottle of three star Metaxa brandy which he sells for 580drs but only costs 405drs at **Self Service Foods** (*Tmr* 36C/D4), round the corner on the High St. The Golden Heart opens Sundays and in the evenings, when many other places are closed. Worth a visit if only to observe.

The previously referred to **Self Service Foods** store displays a reasonable selection of drinks.

On the right of Odhos G Panora, a side-street to the right (*Sbo*) of the High St, is a well stocked **Super Market** (*Butchers – sheep cot*!), across the road from a launderette (*Tmr* 37D4). This looks like, and operates similarly to, its other European counterparts, rather than being a store simply labelled supermarket.

In the same street is a Fruit and Vegetable Store. On the right (*Sbo*) of Odhos Mitrop Ananiou is Butcher Tavros (*Tmr* 40D3/4).

There is another largish Supermarket (*Tmr* 17B/C3/4) at the top end of the High St, beyond the Police station. The store is noticeable for the extensive display of fruit and vegetables piled on racks outside.

There are two interesting shops located towards the far, western end of the local boat Quay. One is the Boutique of Fruits – George Vegetables (*Tmr* 41D4/5), if for the name only, and the other is the nearby Athanasios Vlahopoulos. The latter, a tiny business, sells records, cassette tapes, films, video tapes, books, cards and stamps – *We have every kind of batteries, we change watches, batteries at one hour*. Yes, well. The proprietor also has a metered international telephone.

At the top of the steps that climb from the local boat quay are a number of 'corner shops' grouped around the Church Panaghia (*Tmr* 38C5). These include a Mini-Market (*Tmr* 39C5), opposite which is a large periptero, with an international metered phone, and alongside which is a Butcher (or *Meat Market*). Around the corner, next door to a Baker (*Tmr* 33C5), is a shop which opens on Sundays.

An informal roadside market operates on the Acropolis heights of the town, close to the cemetery (*Tmr* A/B4/5). There is a periptero to one side and lorries park on this wide sweep of road.

The streets are absolutely littered with rinky-dinky boutiques catering for both men and women. As usual, I rarely list any souvenir shops, but there is an outstanding handicraft, jewellery and pottery shop, the Pottery Studio (*Tmr* 42D4), located on Odhos Simeonos. At the end of season they offer some worthwhile discounts. An interesting phenomenon is the presence of a number of arty-crafty Antique shops. One of the most prominent has a stylized exterior and edges the square to the east side of the Church Tris Ierarches (*Tmr* 43C/D4/5).

DISCOS I arrived too late, in 1987, to join in the 'G-string show' at the Disco Charlio, but will try not to miss it next year! Odhos Polytechniou is one of the richest seams of Skiathos nightlife and from the west to the east end includes such delights as the Skala Live Piano Music Bar, the Bourzoi Bar, the Banana Bar, The Admiral Benbow Inn, The Spartacus Club and, at a four-way junction, the Kirki Bar.

FERRY-BOATS & FLYING DOLPHINS In common with Skopelos island, an excellent daily service linking Skiathos with the other islands in the group and various mainland ports. The Nomicos ferry-boat **CF Limnos** ties in, at mainland Ag Konstantinos,, with an Alkyon Tours coach connection to Athens, a useful tip for those who do not want to hang about for bus connections.

Passengers should beware of the squat, bullet headed fellow, dressed in a dark blue shirt, denims and lace-up boots, who may well, unasked, grab a travellers bags, scurry on or off the boat and, for the porterage, demand a tip. He is probably a local simpleton and certainly is a butt for local bully-boys.

A daily excursion to both Skopelos and Alonissos islands departs at 1000hrs, the round trip costing 1700drs. It's cheaper on the ferries folks! A 'Round the Island' boat trip also departs at 1000hrs at a cost of 1200drs.

Ferry-boat & Flying Dolphin timetables
See **Ferry-boat & Flying Dolphin timetables, A To Z, Skopelos Town, Skopelos island.**

FERRY-BOAT & FLYING DOLPHIN TICKET OFFICES
Ferry-boats:
Alkyon Tours (*Tmr* 44D/E4) Papadiamanti/Filokleous Georgiadou Sts Tel 22029
Directions: Immediately across the Esplanade from the Ferry-boat Quay, on the right-hand corner (*Sbo*) of the High St.

Agent for Loucas Nomicos, ferry-boat owners whose fleet includes the **FB Aegeus, Skyros, Limnos, Skiathos** and **Skopelos**.

Mathinos Travel Agency (*Tmr* 20D/E4) Papadiamanti/Filokleous Georgiadou Sts.
Directions: Across the High St from Alkyon Tours.

Sells ferry-boat tickets for other craft than those owned by Loucas Nomicos.

Papadiamantis II Ticket Office Nea Paralia.
Directions: Three doors north (or further to the right (*Sbo*) of Skiathos Holidays (*Tmr* 5E4).

Naturally, sells tickets for the **FB Papadiamantis II**.

Flying Dolphins:
Skiathos Holidays (*Tmr* 5E4) Nea Paralia Tel 22018
Directions: To the right (*Fbqbo*) along the Esplanade, Nea Paralia, and on the left.

The vendors of Flying Dolphin tickets.

HAIRDRESSERS There is a ladies hairdresser in one of the side-streets between Odhos Anti Laskou and Odhos Nikotsara approximately behind the Commercial Bank (*Tmr* 27D4/5)on the Paralia Esplanade. There is another (*Tmr* 45C3/4) at the outset of Odhos G Moraitou, which branches off the High St, close to the Police station.

LAUNDRY

Automatic Laudry (*sic*) **Self Service** (*Tmr* 37D4) G Panora St.
Directions: In the street off to the right (*Sbo*) of the High St, prior to the National Bank (*Tmr* 7D4). The launderette is on the left.

Information and change is available from the supermarket across the street. A wash in one of the large number of machines costs 600drs, the drier 200drs and the use of an iron 200drs. The place is open daily between 0800-2300hrs.

A more ethnic, but markedly less expensive facility is the:-
Lavomatic (*Tmr* 37A/B4)
Directions: On the western outskirts of the town, close to the junction of the ring road and the Koukounaries road.

Signed as a *Self-service Laundry* and cheaper than its centre of town, 'smarty-pants, Miele machine' rival. A machine load is charged at 400drs, detergent 70drs and the drier 200drs. *Press is extra. Do not overload. Thank you.*

There is a Dry Cleaner at the Paralia Esplanade end of Odhos Andreoy Sigrou.

MEDICAL CARE

Chemists & Pharmacies There is one (*Tmr* 46C/D4) on the left (*Sbo*) of the High St and another (*Tmr* 46D4) in a side-street to the left (*Sbo*) of the High St. This latter pharmacy is run by a chemist with good English who is remarkably forthright about the appalling state of the Sporades island's drinking water. He forcibly expressed the seemingly irrefutable argument that, considering the excellent water available throughout Greece, it was disgusting and shameful that the islanders had to purchase bottled water. Hear, hear!
Clinic *See* **Hospital**
Dentist (& Microbiologist) Located on the first floor of a building fronting the High St, in the ground floor of which is the Self Service Foods store (*Tmr* 36C/D4).
Doctor *See* **Hospital**
Hospital (*Tmr* 47B/C5) A modern facility at the top of the steps that climb from the local boat quay.

NTOG None.

OTE (*Tmr* 48C3/4) Towards the top end, and on the right (*Sbo*) of the High St. Open Monday to Friday only, between 0730-2100hrs. Incidentally, the provision of metered telephones is almost a private industry throughout the town. I have already featured a periptero with one, in the vicinity of Church Panaghia (*Tmr* 38C5). At weekends an enterprising gentleman sets up an international telephone 'market stall' on the Paralia Esplanade, *Telephone Here*. Fairly close by is a tiny shop (*See* **Commercial Shopping Area, A To Z**) who also has an international phone, as does the Travel Information Bureau, on the Bourtzi side of the Commercial Bank (*Tmr* 27D4/5).

PETROL There is a Petrol station (*Tmr* 49D1/2) towards the east end of the ring road and yet another at the outset of the road to Koukounaries (*See* **Route One**).

PLACES OF INTEREST

Airfield More correctly where the Ormos Xanema road squeezes between the water's edge and the upward sloping bottom end of the runway. The great, but very risky sport is to crouch down on the seashore side of the road, where there is a smidgin of sand spotted with bits of building brick and an old trestle table. The 'chaps' gather here, smack on the flight path and wait for an incoming international flight. These turn and line up on Daskalio rock, thundering just over an intrepid watcher's head, to thump down on the adjacent runway. A more exciting activity than watching ferry-boat arrivals but not, as the financial pundits say, one for the nervous (or widows and orphans). The local flight aircraft are an anticlimax after the real thing (Did the earth move? No, just the dressing table).

Oh, and don't carry the 'sport' a stage further, as did yours truly, by remaining *in situ* whilst an aircraft takes off. That is a very dangerous and stupid pursuit. We were lucky to escape serious injury, even if Rosemary was pinned beneath the scooter! You have been warned.

Bourtzi promontory Hardly a peninsula, this pleasantly wooded outcrop was once an islet. The approach is dominated by a memorial to Alexandros Papadiamantis (1851-1911), an island author and essay writer. His house is preserved as a Museum (*Tmr* 3D4, *See* **Museum**). The once famous school that dominates Bourtzi, and now abandoned, was itself built on the remains of a Venetian Castle. A walk circumscribes the promontory. On the southern end is the *Bourtzi Dance Bar*, just beyond which, walking in an anticlockwise direction and down some steps, are a pair of public toilets in an acceptable, clean, sweet-smelling condition. They are 'sit-on jobs', not 'squatties', with loo-rolls but the seats are missing. Where does the outflow emerge?

Churches & Cathedrals Neither of the two churches declared to be of interest, Tris Ieraches (*Tmr* 43C/D4/5) and Panaghia (*Tmr* 38C5), are very old or visibly outstanding.

Excursion Boats *See* **Taxis, A To Z**.

Monastery Evangelistrias When I first traversed the ring road, I naively assumed that the donkeys and mules, marshalled in one of the fields, indicated that pack-animals were still in use. My spirit lifted, but only momentarily for it soon became obvious that they are the sole preserve of the 'Monastery donkey rides' circuit. Oh well, there you go. The organised rides depart at 0900hrs at a cost of 1400drs. For details of the Monastery *See* **Excursions To Skiathos Town Surrounds**.

Alexandros Papadiamantis Museum (*Tmr* 3D4) The writer's simple house, situated off to the right (*Sbo*) of the Main St, is now a 'twee' museum, open daily, morning and afternoon.

POLICE
Port The first floor office is in an alley off the Paralia Esplanade.
Town (*Tmr* 15C3/4) The first floor office is above a store with a prominent fruit and vegetable display, towards the top of the High St and on the left, (*Sbo*), diagonally across the road from the School.

POST OFFICE (*Tmr* 14C/D3/4) On the right (*Sbo*) of the High St and open between 0800-1500hrs, Monday to Friday. On islands where the banks are as busy as here do not forget the Post Office, which in any case charges half the commission 'extracted' by the banks for currency transactions.

TAXIS The wheeled variety park (*Tmr* T) on the Square, across the way from the Ferry-boat Quay (*Tmr* 1E4).
The Water Taxis and Excursion boats operate from the Paralia Quay. Destinations include Esperides Beach. These departures are on a timetable basis, starting at

0850hrs and stopping at 2300hrs, setting out approximately every hour on the hour. The service from the beach starts at 0830hrs to end at 2220hrs.

TELEPHONE NUMBERS & ADDRESSES

Hospital (*Tmr* 47B/C5)	Tel 22040
Olympic office (*Tmr* 26D3/4)	Tel 22200
Police, port	Tel 22017
Police, town (*Tmr* 15C3/4)	Tel 22005
Taxi, rank (*Tmr* T)	Tel 22589, 22355 & 22758

TOILETS *See* **Bourtzi promontory, Places of Interest, A To Z.**

TRAVEL AGENTS & TOUR OFFICES Any number, of which the following are but a representative cross-section. The most prominent, and across the way from the Ferry-boat Quay, are:-

Alkyon Tours (*Tmr* 44D/E4) Papadiamanti/Filokleous Georgiadou Sts Tel 22029

Directions: On the corner of the High St and Nea Paralia Esplanade.

This office does (almost) everything

and:-

Mathinos Travel Agency (*Tmr* 20D/E4)

Directions: On the opposite corner to Alkyon.

This office does everything Alkyon does and possibly more. They are involved in property and, in 1987, could have sold a client The Admiral Benbow Pub.

To the right (*Sbo*) of the Ferry-boat Quay (*Tmr* 1E4), and edging Nea Paralia, is a row of Tourist and Travel offices including Skiathos Holidays (*Tmr* 5E4), Theofanidis Hellas, Rent A Car Skiathos and the Papadiamantis II office. The first two sell a punter anything to anywhere, any time. Rent a Car Skiathos also hires speed boats and larger craft (*See* **Watersports, A To Z**).

Another concentration of travel offices,amongst which are Skiathos Tours and Vanda Travel is centred in the narrow streets of Nifonos and Nikotsara,which are located in the area behind the junction of the two waterfront Esplanade, to the left (*Fbqbo*) of Papadiamanti St.

On the Bourtzi side of the Commercial Bank (*Tmr* 27D4/5) is a Travel Information Bureau that rents villas and apartments, plus anything else to anywhere else, as well as exchanging foreign currency.

WATER To reiterate do not drink tap water but *See* **Excursion To Ormos Xanema...** for details of a tap that appears to deliver the goods.

WATER SPORTS An aficionado's dream. Amongst others, Rent A Car Skiathos, on Nea Paralia, hires speedboats and larger craft, but a cautionary tale may not go amiss. We were told a horror story regarding some Germans who rented a boat from an unknown firm for 12,000drs a day. Having paid they also gave up their passports. The craft broke down through no fault of theirs, but in order to get their passports back they had to pay another 12,000drs!

EXCURSIONS TO SKIATHOS TOWN SURROUNDS

Excursion to Ormos Xanema via the Pounta Peninsula and the Airfield using the ring road (about 9km) The ring road or bypass circles the town from the junction with the Koukounaries road (to the west) all the way round to a junction with the Airport road, to the east of the Town. Frankly the ring road is rather squalid and for those package tourists corralled at the east end of this road, it is a jolly long, dusty walk round to the Town Beach, Megali Ammos. Close to an Anderson shelter, where a path climbs into the hillside, a 'little-bit-of-a' marble works and a building materials yard, there is a water tap (*Tmr* 50C2) on the left-hand wall. The locals fill their containers here so it must be safe. Further on round is a petrol station (*Tmr* 49D1/2), on the right, which stays open throughout the siesta. On the left, alongside a bakery (*Tmr* 33D1), a track branches off to Monastery Evangelistria. Local knowledge advises that this route is only any good for 'descending'. To ascend it is best to proceed to the next metalled road that turns off towards the Monastery. Beyond this the ring road makes a junction with the turning to the Airport, to the left, and back towards the head of Skiathos Bay, to the right. At the far end of the Nea Paralia Esplanade, from whence it would be quite acceptable to start off, turn right (*Sbo*) along the top of Skiathos Town Bay. The surrounds are rather 'hillbilly', shanty-town sprawl. The road passes a motorbike rental business; a taverna or three, the first one of which is very good, if a little out of the way; a number of discos, which include the BBC Disco; a windmill, opposite which is the *Taverna O Miltos* (or mill) as well as some package holiday accommodation. This really is a disgraceful location for the industry to place tourists, for not only is it the sleazy end of town but the incoming jets 'wang' over, close by, as the start of the runway is not far away.

The road manages to snake through between the shoreline and the beginning of the airfield, beyond which is a simple boatyard. If the boatyard is engaged in pulling a craft out, traffic must come to a halt. This is because the power winch is located in a wooden hut on the other side of the road from the foreshore, resulting in the winch wire stretching taut round a few trees and over the byway. Ho, hum! A little further on a messy lake, which drains into the sea, is trapped on the left of the road, after which the Charlio Disco is on the right, as is the track down the length of the:-

POUNTA PENINSULA A signpost indicates the direction for the *Hotel Pounta* and the unsurfaced track starts out alongside a gravel workings, climbing on to the spine of the promontory. Unless the smart *Hotel Pounta* operates a water taxi, residents will have a long, dusty, rutted trek to Skiathos Town. There are marvellous views out over the islets off the Skiathos coastline with Skopelos in the distance. The track, now threading through thickly wooded tracts of pine trees, comes to a dead end against a gate and barbed wire fence.

Back at the unsurfaced lakeside track, the route strikes northwards and, once having left the shores of the lake, makes a 'T' junction with a rough track that continues on between the lake and the runway, in an anticlockwise direction, and a surfaced road to the right. The latter passes through pleasant farmland with groves of olives on the left-hand but rather despoiled by a cement works. At about 4½km, a metalled road spurs off to the right, running out beyond the OTE dish in a hillside quarry, from whence there are quite dramatic sea views.

Another short track to the right (5km), terminates on a crumbling cliff-edge. This overlooks a windblown, wild section of coastline edged by a narrow, fine shingle beach dotted with rocks and down to which a goat track tumbles.

There is a certain amount of sea swept debris and the electric power lines used to slither ashore here. Beyond this turning is a new development underway, on the right, but plonked down in a very scrubbly setting with a certain amount of 'plastic' farming in evidence.

The still surfaced road now curves round past a taverna, on the right, to the back of the large, almost circular:-

ORMOS XANEMA This bay is confined by rocky headland horns of about 120m height. The backcloth to this shadeless, broad, gritty sand and rubbish strewn beach is a large, unattractive quarry.

The sea-bed is initially sandy and quite steeply shelving but any sort of a blow makes for tumultuous seas.

The campsite, drawn on one or two maps in this area, has long gone, which is not surprising considering the possibility of a DC9 landing on the tents. Part of the quarry is used for storage of civil engineering pipework.

The now, unsurfaced track completes a reversal of direction round the top end of the runway, to head south on the west side of the airfield through bamboo groves on the left and olive trees on the right. The countryside is a scrubbly combination of olive groves and 'hillbilly' farmsteads, with the ever menacing presence of the airfield runway occasionally glimpsed to the left.

The old airport transit sheds and shacks are being replaced by gleamingly modern airport buildings and a 'super-duper' control tower. Almost opposite these, on the other side of the dirt track that borders the runway, is the almost ludicrous contrast of a rustic shambles of a peasant's single storey farm homestead and small holding, beset by goats, chickens, cockerels, horses and ducks. How very Greek.

From the Airport towards Skiathos Town, the road is surfaced again, passing a very smart stadium complete with stands and, unbelievably, a hotel sandwiched between the road and the airfield. Must be a fun place during the day, but at least there are no night-flights, yet!

Excursion to Monastery Evangelistrias (circa 5km) Refer to the previous Excursion for the turnings off the ring road. The signposting is excellent but, in places, the very steep ascent alternates between a concrete strip and acceptable track. There are wide ranging views of the airfield to the right and out over the sea as far as Skopelos, on which it is quite easy to pick out Glossa and its port. The road ends at the:-

Monastery Evangelistrias (circa 5km from Skiathos Town) The immediate surrounds, of this now unoccupied monastery, are scrubbly. On the other hand, the overall setting is stunning with lovely views to the north down to the tiny, 'U' shaped Ormos Nikotsara, which is edged by a small, pebbly shore down to which winds a river bed/track. The buildings, partially screened by cypress trees, were erected in the 18th century and they are set to one side of a summer trickling, rocky gorge that cleaves the tree clad mountainsides. The still running fountain, round to the right, was once channelled to feed the now derelict, drinking water cisterns, the various mechanisms of which are also in disrepair.

Tatty bus seats are incongruously scattered about the forecourt of the Monastery, which is reputed to be the first flag-raising, rallying point of the War of Independence – but don't let the natives of Spetses, amongst others, hear you repeat that particular heresy. The building should open between 0800-1200hrs and 1600-1800hrs, but note 'should'. The management wish visitors to be respectably clothed – *We beg you please to be properly dressed.* The walk takes about 1¼ to 1½hrs.

Excursion to The Kastro & Lalaria Beach (circa 8km)

Unless a traveller is an intrepid walker, it is best to take an excursion boat, apart from which the route defies my powers of description (what powers of description?). There is a recently bulldozed track to the north-west coast but it is not yet drawn on the maps.

The boats cost 400drs but won't depart in adverse (northerly) winds. They land at the:-

KASTRO BEACH It is a twenty minute hike to the pile of rubble and couple of churches – all that is left of the once majestic fortifications. The views are magnificent.

LALARIA BEACH This famed, fabled and vaunted beach is pebbly and it is doubtful if the journey is worthwhile. The sea is beautifully clear but then it is all the way round the island. There is a natural, sea-formed rock arch and a couple of small, water filled caves in the locality.

ROUTE ONE

To Koukounaries (13 km) via the Kalamaki Headland & including other excursions to Kounistra (Panaghia) Monastery & Megas Asselinos Beach

The island's main road skirts the south coast from east to west, passing, after 200m, a petrol station on the left. This first stretch of the road is bordered by villas, apartments, flats, small hotels and ***Rooms***, many of which are booked by holiday tour companies. A house on the left has a sign *Dog's bite*. (Bites who?).

From the hill above **Vasilias** are very pretty offshore views to the south-east, due to the number of small islands speckled about in the surrounding seas.

About 3 km out of Skiathos Town, beyond Vasilias and just prior to Achladias Beach, a sharply inclined turning off to the right heads for the beautifully wooded interior. It is signed Kechrias Beach, about a 6km trek. I don't find the Skiathos countryside as attractive as that of Skopelos. Perhaps it is because it does not possess such magnificent, pine tree covered mountains, rather more moth-eaten, softer hillsides. The problem with these inland incursions is that, apart from the quite appalling track conditions, the crude, red daubed direction signs have, in many cases, been dislodged. Added to which various pioneering firebreaks and unexplained civil engineering works have muddled the choice of direction. In plain language, once into the interior, its an absolute jumble. Those who do venture must, I repeat, must have a hand compass and several maps. The best available map is that incorporated in the small, blue coloured, island guide.

The first section of this route is very rough and quite steep in places, passing through lovely, pine tree clad countryside. Keep left at the first and second forks. Kechrias Beach is still signed, after which the now appallingly surfaced track is deeply and dangerously rutted, with a lot of loose surface scree. Scooterists beware. The roadway descends to an agricultural valley on which are dotted about a number of homesteads. At the lone deciduous plane tree, with the remains of tattered signs hanging from its trunk, take the right-hand turning. The left-hand track curves back round to Platanias, alongside a water running river-bed, bordered by lush countryside with cypress, deciduous and olive trees set in grasslands grazed by cows.

After the right-hand turning, take another right as left leads back to Kounistra Monastery.

KECHRIAS BEACH It may be isolated but it is made up of stony pebbles. Another kilometre or so to the right (*Fsw*), and in an inland direction, leads along a river-bed gorge to the 16th century Kechrias Monastery.

Back on the coastal road, the next important location is:-

ACHLADIAS BEACH (4km from Skiathos Town) This once pleasant, and still pretty spot, is now dominated by the monstrous *Hotel Esperides*, beside which a track leads to a lovely, sandy if not very wide beach. This stretches out for some 200m, bordering a shallow bay. Ranks of old-fashioned deck-chairs are set out for hire but if the occupants of the hotel were not enough to fill every available space, water taxis ply between here and Skiathos Town on a timetable basis. The first boat departs at 0830hrs and the last 2220hrs, running approximately every hour.

The small *Pharos Taverna* edges the middle of the beach backshore, where the track down from the main road runs out on some dangerous 'bits of concrete' steps to the sand. A number of apartments, hotels, the occasional taverna and a Rent A Motorbike are also in the area.

TZANERIAS BAY (5½km from Skiathos Town) The bay is divided into two small coves, the first of which is very narrow and pebbly with some sand at the top, west end.

The second cove is overlooked by the large *Nostos Hotel*, the chalets of which spread down the far hillside surrounds. It is an idyllic location with a very lovely, sandy beach off which juts a low, wooden jetty. Despite the 'smarty-pants' appearance of the cove from the main road above, the backshore surrounds are rather scrubbly.

Access to Nostos beach is along a track from the road that circumscribes Kalamaki Headland. To the left (*Fsw*) of the beach is a firm renting boats and pedaloes and to the right, about the middle of the backshore, is a taverna. Immediately beneath the *Hotel Nostos* is a smart taverna. Offshore is the tiny, navigation light topped, rocky outcrop of Prasou. The various islets and distant Skopelos island form an attractive vista.

To proceed round the *Kalamaki Headland* turn left off the main road. The first undulating section of the road passes a number of smart villas prior to:-

KANAPITSA BEACH (6km from Skiathos Town) From the nearside, steps descend to the neat, nice, sandy beach backed by a field and set in a small curved bay. *Welcome to Kanapitsa. Barbeque on Thursday, RegattasurfonSunday*. (Yes one word). There is no need to take to the steps as the road drops down to sea-level. Here a track wanders across the field and runs out alongside a ramshackle, 'chicken shed-like' taverna with a hammock slung and around which are scattered bits and pieces of water sport apparatus for hire. Unfortunately for this quiet location, across the road from where the track branches down to the beach, a brand new hotel is under construction.

The headland road climbs another hillside, still paralleling the coastline, which is now some way down below. There are chic villas on both sides of the road, with the occasional one appearing to be available for letting.

After the route has rounded the south end of Kalamaki Headland, the countryside becomes boulderous, more *au naturel*, with little tree cover. The rocky coastline is punctuated by the occasional sandy cove. There is quite a large beach in the area marked on some tourist maps as Koutsouri but, as with the previous coves, there is no apparent way to gain access, although a goat track appears to 'totter' down to the far end.

The road forks where it turns in a northerly direction to edge the western, tree growing flank of Kalamaki Headland. It is possible to take the steeply descending, left-hand turning, but this peters out amongst some villas facing over a 'crocodile country' swamp, backing the left, southern end of:-

VROMOLIMNOS BEACH (9½km from Skiathos Town) A footpath emerges at the left-hand end (*Fsw*) of a lovely, sandy, sweep of wide beach with a small pebble foreshore and divided into two by a rocky outcrop. At this southern end there is a water ski school, surfboats and old-fashioned deck-chairs. Despite protestations with regard to other Skiathos locations, I consider this the most all-round attractive beach of the island. At the far, right-hand end of this first section of the beach is a rather modern taverna, behind which is an open space on to which the main track from Kolpos (or Kolios) decants. Despite the modernity of the establishment a Nes meh ghala only costs 75drs.

Just to muddle matters the southern section of the beach is often called Argirolimnos

As indicated it may well be easier to get to Vromolimnos/Argirolimnos Beach from the main road and make the ¼hr walk from the turning off at:-

KOLPOS (KOLIOS) BEACH (7km from Skiathos Town) Naturally it is not necessary to proceed round the Kalamaki Headland. It is more direct, but not so attractive, to keep to the main road. Kolpos is less fortunate than its near neighbours. A nasty little 'Amazon' stream festers away during the summer months. The beach is sandy but the foreshore has a certain amount of kelp and the surrounds are seedy. A number of yachts are anchored at the left-hand side (*Fsw*) of the bay.

There is a campsite, probably mosquito ridden. Unfortunately the treeless aspect gives the appearance of a concentration camp, without the huts.

The main road is bordered by villas and apartments for rent as well as a scooter and car hire businesses. A 'reader recommended' restaurant is *The Stathis...* 'excellent meal and colourful service'.

PLATANIAS BEACH (8km from Skiathos Town) The approach to this popular, package tourist beach is via a rough track, over what was once marshland, now effectively drained. There is still a little bit of a swamp, the other side of the beach backshore. The lack of any tree cover detracts from the allure of this lovely sweep of broad, sandy beach. There is a taverna, the *Platanias*, to the left (*Fsw*). An outfit hires out pedaloes and umbrellas (400drs a day), canoes (400drs an hour), bicycles (600drs an hour), wind surfers (800drs per hour) and offers water skiing tuition (1200drs an hour) – *Christos he gives 99% success.*

Bordering the main road is a taverna and a scooter rental business. The interior road system rejoins the main road at Platanias.

Inland Excursion To Megas Asselinos, Kounistra Monastery & Mikro Asselinos At the outset of **Troulos** settlement (9½km from Skiathos Town), a surfaced turning to the right climbs through fire damaged countryside. This has left the reddish coloured soil resembling crumbling molars.

At a fork (11¾km from Skiathos Town), the left-hand, dusty and now unsurfaced track advances between chestnut and hornbeam trees set in pine tree clad hillsides. To the left is a summer-dry stream which, no doubt, accounts for the richness of the tree growth.

Camping Asselinos Beach (13¾km from Skiathos Town) Tel 49312
Directions: The campsite is to the right of the road, immediately prior to the beach.

The site is very pleasantly set in an area of grassland on which are planted olive trees. There are a number of old buildings scattered about the entrance, amongst which is a shower block as well as a camp shop and taverna. They exchange currency. I consider it unfortunate that the 'kiddies' playground has a model of the Red Baron's aeroplane for children to sit on. What's wrong with Biggles? The owner speaks good English and charges 250drs per person per night and 100drs for a tent. His card charmingly refers to *Tree Shadows* and a sign at the gate intones *No Motor Bikes After Midnight*. A private bus service shuttles between the campsite and Skiathos Town. The bus departs at 0915, 1100, 1500 & 1800hrs. (*See* **Buses, A To Z, Skiathos Town**). If all this were not enough, the site has access to:-

MEGAS ASSELINOS BEACH (14km from Skiathos Town) The main track spills out on to the reverse side of the backshore of a clean, wide, steeply sloping, 200m long sweep of fine grit beach. There are bamboo sun shelters and, bordering the backshore, a very large taverna with a bamboo enclosed and covered patio. There isn't any tree cover but the horns of the shallow, wide 'U' shaped bay enclosing hillsides are clad with olive trees and scrub. In front of the taverna are some beach showers. There are, more often than not, two or three camper-vans parked at the far, east side of the sweep of beach.

Unfortunately the beach is the target for daily excursion boats. On disembarking a large number of the passengers immediately head for the:-

Taverna Asselinos
Despite, or perhaps because of the size of the place, the service, especially if a new influx has taken their seats, is pot-luck, and you know how rarely one wins on a one-armed bandit. The general and usual state of confusion is magnified by one waiter taking the order whilst shouting the drinks order to another waiter with yet another waiter rendering the bill. What was ordered and what is served may bear little relationship to each other. Mind you the food appears fresh, but then the time taken to serve it as near as not allows enough of an interlude to grow some of the constituents!

If a price list is not available potential diners are advised not to order unless they do not mind 'confusion' at the magnitude of the bill. On our last visit we ordered a tzatziki, a Greek salad, a bottle of beer, a lemonade and bread which the owner, he of an unpleasant demeanour, first attempted to charge 800drs. After I expressed disgust and disbelief, the bill was reduced to 680drs, but he would not show me a printed price list or even write the amounts down on a bill. However, we did manage to extract the information that the tzatziki cost 190drs, the Greek salad 290drs (yes 290drs), the beer 100drs, the lemonade 60drs and the bread (for two) 40drs. On the price of the Greek salad being queried he announced with finality *Special*, and so it would have to be at 290drs. In the continuing 'argy-bargy' he spat out that he thought we had been served with two tzatziki, an accusation only denied and reluctantly accepted after several plate counts. I was not quick-witted enough to add a further 190drs to the revised bill of 680drs and realise the accountancy was a myth or that my bill, even at those prices, should have been 610drs. An establishment to be avoided as I observed other clients experience a severe 'pain' of disbelief when informed of the cost of their meal.

Back at the fork in the route, the right-hand direction is signed to *The Monastery* and the *Cool Beach*. The road climbs and is metalled for another kilometre after which it degenerates to an unsurfaced, but wide track.

Kounistra (Panaghia) Monastery (13¼km from Skiathos Town) A small, homely monastery to the side of the road and distinguishable by an eye-catching, attractive, semicircular painting on the wall above the main entrance door and the taverna tables set out on the courtyard. Yes, it is possible to purchase a simple meal at this 17th century, ex-nunnery, originally named Panaghia Ikonistra. A sign proclaims *Ikonistra (Monastery) you can find drinks, salad and omelette*. So much better to dine here than at the taverna on Megas Asselinos Beach. The monastery possesses a number of superb frescos.

The wide, exposed track continues on beyond the monastery, with views down over the east side of Megas Asselinos Beach. almost as far as:-

MIKRO ASSELINOS BEACH (15km from Skiathos Town) The road peters out on the hillside, just round the corner from the steep path down to a triangular shaped, gritty beach set in a 'U' shaped cove, bordered by bare, rocky hillsides. The beach backshore is extensively piled with seaborne, but clean rubbish in amongst which are lengths of sun-bleached timber and other flotsam. The sea is clear (as elsewhere around Skiathos) and the location is popular with adventurous nudists.

Back at the southern coast main road and still proceeding westwards, it is only ¾km to:-

TROULOS BEACH (10km from Skiathos Town) The track to the beach emerges at about the centre of the backshore, with the *Taverna Troulos* on the right. A rather 'tired' sign inveighs *No nudism, No camping*. The smallish, very sandy, if somewhat messy and not overly attractive beach is set in a shallow bay of about 150m in length. There are lots of deck-chairs and seats, which is understandable as Troulos is a popular, package holiday centre. There is a block of apartments up against the left-hand beach backshore and a couple more across the main road. In strict Hellenic contrast, a black swathed old lady is just as likely to be labouring in the fields behind these manifestations of 20th century affluence. *Plus ca change, plus c'est la même chose.* Not far offshore is Troulonisia islet and, to the left (*Fsw*), the Marines. No mother, not the commandos, just a few lumps of sea-bound rocks.

Another 2km further along the main road is:-

MARATHA BEACH (12km from Skiathos Town) Only accessible down a track which emerges towards the right-hand side (*Fsw*) of the narrow, sandy beach. The backshore is hemmed in by conifer trees, so much so that the much abused cliché about the boughs kissing the sea's surface is almost true. The sea-bed has a patch of pebble about a couple of metres from the foreshore and there is a just discernable kelp line along the middleshore. To the left is conveniently perched a small *Cantina*.

On the approach to Koukounaries a banner spanning the road (Skopelos fashion) exhorts visitors to appreciate the benefits of the forests. One side announces *The forest I give you everything*. The route passes above a well-patronised marina harbour to the left, situated at the nearside of Koukounaries Beach. Amongst the more usual, fibreglass, run-of-the-mill yachts is a shapely vessel, irresistibly reminding me of the reconstructed *Argo**, without the oars, but with a similar, great pair of eyes painted on either side of the bows.

**As described in The Jason Voyage, a quest for the Golden Fleece, By Tim Severin.*

The right-hand side of the route is dominated by a modern hotel, *The Pallas*. To the left stretches away the renowned sweep of:

KOUKOUNARIES BEACH (13km from Skiathos Town) The road, edged by spaced out gum trees, skirts the inland side of a very clean, sea-fed lagoon, around the surrounds of which a small golf course has been laid out. Nothing like the unwholesome swamp I expected from previous experiences. The inland side of the road is bordered with apartments, flats, and ***Rooms***. Much new construction is underway but there are perhaps not so many hotels as might be expected. The real problem is that the much lauded beach just cannot take any more people.

There are two turnings off to the right of this road, one to Ag Elenis Beach, the other to Krassa Beach, for details of which read on.

The road peters out at the far end of Koukounaries Beach, adjacent to a jetty. The lovely, wide, beautifully sandy 1000m or so sweep of the shore stretches away to the left, set in a large bay. The attractiveness of the spot is enhanced by the band of thick-set pine trees that border the backshore. On the other hand the serried ranks of deck chairs, sun-beds, beach umbrellas and holiday-makers, the latter in every state of dress and undress imaginable, makes it rather difficult to see the sand. In case there aren't enough people *in situ*, water taxis ply their service, bringing ever more fun loving hedonists. To look after the inner person, two or three *Cantinas* are strung out along the backshore. The sea-bed gently shelves and, in the absolutely clear sea-water, every known type and diverse form of water sport known to man takes place. About 30m out, over to the left (*Fsw*), is a crescent of yachts moored at anchor.

Despite the praise heaped on the spot as possibly the greatest Greek island beach (amongst many other possible claimants), I would like to put forward Milopotamos Beach, Ios and some of the lovely and much quieter sweeps of sandy beach on the south-west coast of Naxos.

Round to the right (*Fsw*) from the jetty, beyond a rocky outcrop, are a couple of small coves that 'support' wind surfing activity.

If all this sunbathing and sporting activity is too much, there are alternatives close by. These are:-

KRASSA (or BANANA) BEACH (13km from Skiathos Town) The road climbs steeply from the main road. About half-way to this beach, at the height of the ascent, the authorities have ensured powered vehicles can proceed no further by erecting gates to bar the way. There is a slip path for pedestrians who have to wander down through pleasant groves of olive trees. Despite these precautions some scooters manage to get through. The track edges over on to the backshore of the 120m long, broad, sandy beach on which are 'plonked' lots of beach umbrellas and deck-chairs. The backshore is pleasantly shaded by mature pine trees, amongst which is a small taverna to the left (*Fsw*) as well as another alongside the track. Surfboards and a buoyed speedboat run are at the right-hand end of the beach. Cooling onshore breezes bring welcome relief from the intense midday sun, as they do on other, west facing Skiathos beaches. Water taxis include Krassa (or Banana) Beach on their schedule. Well, they would, wouldn't they. And why Banana? Are they being rude?

AG ELENIS BEACH (13km from Skiathos Town) A surfaced road off the main route terminates close to the right-hand side (*Fsw*) of this crescent shaped, quite broad beach. Apart from a shingle foreshore, the beach is very sandy and pleasantly set in pine clad, low hillsides. To the right of the access road is an ethnic *Bus Cantina*. This is draped over and around with bamboo to shade the tables, chairs and upright logs (that serve as seats), set out to one side. This self-service operation offers sandwiches, Greek salads, freshly made meatballs, kalamares, breakfast, ice-cream, drinks and salat (*sic*). I'd love a salat. A beer and lemonade cost 160drs.

A couple of other *Cantinas* are spaced out to the left (*Fsw*) of the beach backshore.

A 'billy' goat with a devilish look in his eyes on the side of the road, Evia.

INDEX

A
AA, the, 23
A to Z,
Aegina, 202-206
Alonissos, *See Patitiri Port*
Angistri, *See Skala Angistri*
Athens, 98-115
Chalkis(Evia), 253-256
Chora(Kithira), 231-234
Chora(Skyros), 299-303
Eretria(Evia), 258-261
Evia, *See Chalkis, Eretria, Paralia Kymi(Evia)*
Hydra, 172-176
Kithira, *See Chora(Kithira)*
Linaria(Skyros), 293
Loutraki Port(Skopelos),354-355
Paralia Kymi(Evia), 268-270
Patitiri Port(Alonissos), 317-323
Piraeus, 122-125
Poros, 187-192
Skala Angistri(Angistri), 218-220
Skiathos, 366-374
Skopelos, 338-346
Skyros,*See Chora,Linaria(Skyros)*
Spetses, 152-159
Accommodation, 37-42
Aegina,198-201
Alonissos,*See Patitiri Port* (Alonissos)
Athens,81-92,110-111
Chalkis(Evia),251-253
Chora(Kithira),230
Chora(Skyros),296-298
Eretria(Evia),258
Evia,*See* Chalkis,Eretria, Paralia Kymi(Evia)
Hydra,166-170
Kithira,*See Chora(Kithira)*
Linaria(Skyros),291
Loutraki Port(Skopelos),352-354
Paralia Kymi(Evia),265-267
Patitiri Port(Alonissos),312-315
Piraeus,119-122
Poros,181-184
Skala Angistri(Angistri),214-217
Skiathos,360-363
Skopelos,332-336
Skyros,*See Chora,Linaria(Skyros)*
Spetses,146-149
Achladias Beach(Skiathos),378
Acropolis, The,79 (Athens)
Addresses, *See Useful...*
Aegina island,197-211
Aegina town & port,198
After-sun,4
Ag (Agios)
Anargyri(Spetses),159,160
Anna(Evia),273
Apostoli(Evia),280
Dimitrios(Evia),281
Elenis Beach(Skiathos),383
Fokas(Skyros),306
Georgios(Evia),256,277
Georgios(Salaminas),244
Ioannis Church(Skopelos),352
Konstantinos(Skopelos),348
Marina(Aegina),197
Nikolaos(Evia),276
Palagia Port(Kithira),226
Paraskevi(Spetses),160
Ag Konstantinos Port(M),129
Ag Marina Port(M),129,282,283-284
Agiokampos(Evia),274
Agios(Evia),275
Aghistri, *See Angistri*
Agious(Aegina),207-208
Agistri, *See Angistri*
Agnotas Port(Skopelos),349
Agora, The Greek,80 (Athens)
Agora, The Roman,80 (Athens)
Agriovotano(Evia),273
Airline flights
Athens,75,98
Domestic,31-32
international,11-14
fares,11-14
Airports
Athens,15*See Athens*
Kithira,226
Skiathos,360,372
Skyros,291,305
UK,14
Air temperatures, *See Weather*
Alarm clock, *See Clocks*
Alcohol, *See Drink*
Alexandros Papadiamantis Museum (Skiathos),373
Aliverion(Evia),263
Allowances,5,25
Almyropotamos(Evia),282
Alonissos island,309-329
Alonnisos, *See Alonissos*
Alonnissos, *See Alonissos*
Alphabet, Greek, *See Language*
Amarinthos(Evia),262
Ancona,19,24,25,27 (Italy)
Ano Vathia(Evia),262
Angistri island,213-223
Aphrati(Evia),257
Argiro(Evia),281
Argo-Saronic islands, *See Mainland islands*
Arkitsa Port(M),128,275
Aroniadiki(Kithira),238-239
Aronisos(Angistri),223
Arrival by Air, *See Airline flights & Airports*
Arrival by Ferry-boat, *See Ferry-boats*
Arrival by Train, *See Trains*
Artemision(Evia),273
Askeli Beach(Poros),195
Asminion(Evia),274
Aspirin,4
Athens,75-115
airport,15
camping, *See Camping*
Atsitsa(Skyros),305
Australia,14
Avlemonas(Kithira),238
Avlonarion(Evia),263

B
Backpacks,3
Bad buys,61
Bakers,62
Banks,5,64
Bank cards,5
Bari,19,24,27 (Italy)
Bathrooms,38-39
Beach Frigani(Evia),273
Beaches,39,43
Bedroll,3

Bedrooms, *See Accommodation*
Beer, *See Drink*
Bekiris Cave(Spetses),161
Best buys,61
Beverages, non alcoholic,51
Bicycles,46-47
Bin liners,5
Books,5
Bottle-opener,3
Bouros Beach(Evia),286
Bourtzi promontory(Skiathos),368
Brandy, *See Drinks*
Bread shops, *See Bakers*
Brindisi,18,19,23,24,25
(Italy)
Buphalo islet(Evia),281
Buphalon Harbour(Evia),281
Buses
Athens,75,100-102,113,114
domestic,32,45
international,20-21,75,116
Piraeus,117,122
Butchers,63

C
Cafe-bars,53,54
Calamine lotion,4
Cameras,5
See Photography
Camping,39,91-92(Athens)
Canada,13
Car
hire,46-47
travel by,21-25
Cards, playing,5
Chalcis, *See Chalkis*
Chalki, *See Chalkis*
Chalkida, *See Chalkis*
Chalkis Town(Evia),250
Charter flights,11-14
Chemists,4
Chora, The
Kithira,228
Skyros,294
Chrisi Milia Beach(Alonissos),327
Cigarettes,5,25
Cigars,5,25
Climate,5
Clocks,5
Clothes pegs,3
Clothing,3
Coaches, *See Buses*
Coffee, *See Beverages*
Compass,5
Condiments,3
Containers,3
Conversion tables,6
Cooking equipment,3
Creams,4
Credit cards,5
Cruise ships,34
Currency,5,25,64
Cythera, *See Kithira*

D
Daphni(Evia),271
Dapia, *See Spetses*
Denmark,14,20,24,29
Department of Health,
See National Health Cover & Insurance matters & policies
Diakofti(Kithira),239
Dialling Codes, *See OTE*
Diasello(Alonissos),329
Disinfectant,4
Dokana(Kithira),238
Donkeys,45
Drink,5,25,52-53,61
Drinking Places,53
Drivers & driving
requirements,24-25
Duty free,5,25

E
Eandio(Salaminas),245
Eating Out,53-55
Aegina,201-202
Alonissos, *See Patitiri Port*
Angistri, *See Skala Angistri*
Athens,92-98
Chalkis(Evia),253
Chora(Kithira),230
Chora(Skyros),298-299
Eretria(Evia),258
Hydra,170-172
Kithira, *See Chora(Kithira)*
Linaria(Skyros),291-293
Loutraki Port(Skopelos),354
Paralia Kymi(Evia),267
Patitiri Port(Alonissos),315-317
Piraeus,122
Poros,185-187
Skala Angistri(Angistri),217-218
Skiathos,363-366
Skopelos,336-338
Skyros, *See Chora,Linaria(Skyros)*
Spetses,149-151
Eating Places,53-55
Edipsos(Evia),275
Egina, *See Aegina*
Electricity supply,6
Elios(Skopelos),350-351
Ellinika(Evia),273
Episkopi(Hydra),178
Eretria(Evia),258
Euboea, *See Evia*
Eurorail pass, 185
Eurocheque card,5,64
Evia island,249-287
Evoia, *See Evia*
Exchange rates,1
Eyboia, *See Evia*

F
Fatsadika(Kithira),237
Ferry-boats(& Flying Dolphins)
Aegina,204
Agiokampos(Evia),274
Almyropotamos(Evia),
See Panaghia
Ag Pelagia(Kithira),227,232-233
Angistri, *See Skala Angistri*
Athens, *See Piraeus*
Brindisi,25
domestic,32-34
Eretria(Evia),261
Hydra,166,173-174
Kapsali Port(Kithira),234-236
Karistos(Evia),286
Linaria(Skyros),293
Loutra Edipsos(Evia),275-276
Loutraki Port(Skopelos),355
Mamari Port(Evia),284
Nea Styra(Evia),283-284
Paloukia(Salaminas),244
Panaghia(Evia),282
Paralia Kimi(Evia), *See Paralia Kymi*
Paralia Kymi(Evia),269

Patitiri Port(Alonissos),319-321
Piraeus,123
Poros,
Selinia(Salaminas),242
Scopelos,*See Skopelos*
Skala Angistri(Angistri),219-220
Skiathos,371
Skopelos,340-343
Skyros,*See Linaria*
Souvala(Aegina),207
Spetses,155
Finland,20
Fish,*See Food*
Flats & houses,42
Flying Dolphins,*See Ferry-boats*
Fokionos Negri,81
(Athens)
Food (& drink),49-59
Foot,On,44
Footwear,3
France,15-17,21,23,24
Frozen food.51

G
Galaktopoleio,53
Galaktozacharoplasteion,54
Galatos(Poros),192
Gasoline,*See Petrol*
Geraka Bay(Alonissos),329
Germany,20
Gialtra(Evia),276
Gialos Beach(Skyros),300
Girismata Bay(Skyros),304
Glifa(M),129
Glossa(Skopelos),351
GMT,7
Good buys,*See Best buys*
Gouves(Evia),273
Greece
Climate,*See Weather*
Currency,64
driving requirements,25
history,69
holidays,69-72
language,*See Language*
mythology,69
people,70-71
religion,70
Guides & maps,*See Maps*

H
Hair curlers,3
Halkida,*See Chalkis*
Hire
bicycle,moped,scooter,
car rates,46-47
History,*See Greece*
Hitching,44
Holidays,Greek,*See Greece*
Holiday Insurance,*See Insurance*
Hotels,55,*See Accommodation*
Hotline,Greek island,viii,2
Hydra island,163-178
Hydra village & port,166

I
Ilia(Evia),278
Insect cream,4
Insurance matters & policies,4,47
Interail pass, 18
International Driving Licence,
See Driving Requirements
Ireland,14
Island
accommodation,37-42
See Accommodation
place names,34
maps,*See Maps*
Istiaea(Evia),274
Italy,17,18,19,20,21,22,23,24,25,26

J
Jellyfish,43

K
Kafeneions,53
Kalamaki Headland
(Skiathos),377,378,379
Kalamakia(Alonissos),329
Kalamitsa(Skyros),307
Kamini(Hydra),177-178
Kanakia(Salaminas),246-247
Kanapitsa Beach(Skiathos),378-379
Kaningos Sq,77
(Athens)
Kaolin (& morphine),4
Kapsali Port(Kithira),234-236
Karalides,Ormos(Evia),
See Ormos Karalides
Karavas(Kithira),240
Karistos(Evia),285-286
Karvounades(Kithira),237-238
Karystsos,*See Karistos*
Kastro Beach(Skiathos),377
Katheni(Evia),270
Kato Steni(Evia),270
Kechrias Beach(Skiathos),378
Keramikos,80
(Athens)
Khalkis,*See Chalkis*
Kiosks,*See Street Kiosks*
Kirinthos(Evia),272
Kithira island,225-240
Kithira town,*See Chora,the*
Klafthmonos Sq,80
(Athens)
Klima(Skopelos),351
Kokkinokastro(Alonissos),327
Kolimbadas Bay(Skyros),307
Kolonaki Sq,78
(Athens)
Kolpos Beach(Skiathos),379
Kondolianika(Kithira),237
Konistres(Evia),264
Kontos(Aegina),210
Koskina(Evia),280
Kotzia Sq,80
(Athens)
Koukounaries Beach(Skiathos),382
Krassa Beach(Skiathos),382
Kria Vrysi(Evia),272
Krieza(Evia),280
Kronia(Evia),278
Ksilokeriza Bay(Spetses),161
Kymi Port,*See Paralia Kymi*
Kymi Town(Evia),264
Kythera,*See Kithira*
Kythira,*See Kithira*

L
Lalaria Beach(Skiathos),377
Lampara Beach(Spetses),159
Lampsakos,N(Evia),256
Language,
Greek,7-9,35-36,42,47,58-59,66-67
Lefkandi Beach(evia),257
Lefto Gialo Bay(Alonissos),328
Lemonodassos(Poros),192
Leandi(Aegina),207
Lepoura(Evia),263
Ligoneri Beach(Spetses),152

Limenari(Angistri),222
Limnaria(Kithira),237
Limni(Evia),279
Limnonari Beach(Skopelos),349
Linaria Port(Skyros),291
Liquid containers,3
Livadi(Kithira),237
Lotions,*See After-Sun*
Louli Beach(Evia),257-258
Loutra Edipsos(Evia),275-276,277
Loutra Gialtron(Evia),277
Loutraki Port(Skopelos),352
Lutra Aedipsos,*See Loutra Edipsos*
Lycabettus,Mt,78
(Athens)

M

Magazia(Skyros),303-304
Magazines,*See Newspapers*
Magoula(Evia),262
Mainland Ports,*See Piraeus & other Mainland Ports.*
Mainland Islands,
(Argo-Saronic & Sporades)
Introduction,137-138
Islands,141-142
Malakonda(Evia),257
Mandoulion(Evia),272
Mandraki Beach(Hydra),177
Maps,44,62
Map names,34-35
Maratha Beach(Skiathos),381
Markets,63
Marmari Port(Evia),284
Marpounta Cove(& Hotel)
(Alonissos),326
Mealos Bay(Skyros),294,307
Medical matters & medicines,4
Megalochorio(Angistri),221
Megalo Neorion Bay(Poros),193
Megali Ammos Beach(Skiathos),367
Megas Asselinos Beach(Skiathos),380
Mendulis(Evia),264
Menu, sample,55-58
Mesochoria(Evia),282-283
Messagros(Aegina),206,210
Metochi(Angistri),221
Metochi(Evia),286
Metro
Athens,105,114
Piraeus,117,125
Mikro Asselinos Beach(Skiathos),381
Milia Beach(Skopelos),350
Milia Gialos Beach(Alonissos),327
Milopotamos(Kithira),238
Molos Beach(Skyros),303-304
Monastery of:
Ag:
Georgiou Arma(Evia),257
Matrona Convent(Hydra),178
Nikolaos(Hydra),178
Nikolaos(Evia),262
Nikolaos(Salaminas),246
Reginos(Skopelos),348
Trias Convent(Hydra),178
Analipseos(Skopelos),348
Chiliadon(Evia),271
David Geronta,278
Evangelistria(Skiathos),373,376
Evangelistria(Skopelos),347
Kounistra(Skiathos),381
Lefkon(Evia),263
Metamorphosis(Skopelos),347
Prodromos(Skopelos),347
St Nicholas(Galataki)(Evia),279
Varvaras(Skopelos),347
Zoodochos Pighi
(Poros),193,194,195
Zourvas Convent(Hydra),178
Monastiraki Sq,77
(Athens)
Money,5
Monodrio(Evia),264
Mopeds,46-47
Morphine,*See Kaolin..*
Mosquito,38
coils,3
Motorists,requirements,24-25
Mt Lycabettus,*See Lycabettus,Mt*
Museums,65
Mythology,*See Greece*

N

Names & addresses,*See Useful...*
National Gardens,79
(Athens)
National Health Cover,4
Nea Artaki(Evia),270
Nea Chora(Poros),187,188,193,194
Nea Styra(Evia),283
Neos Pirgos(Evia),274
Nerotrivia(Evia),271
Newspapers & Magazines,62
New Zealand,14
Norway,14,20

O

Official guides,*See Maps*
Olympic Airways,*See Airline flights*
Omonia Sq,76-77
(Athens)
Opening hours,61
Orei(Evia),274
Ormos Acherounes(Skyros),294
Ormos Karalides(Evia),282
Ormos Vagionia(Poros),194
Ormos Xanema(Skiathos),376
OTE,65
Otranto,22
Ouzeries,53
Overseas phone calls,*See OTE*
Oxilithos(Evia),263

P

Package tours,11
Packing,3-4
Paleochora(Aegina),210
Paloukia(Salaminas),244
Panaghia(Evia),281
Panaghia Mirtidiotissa(Kithira),237
Panormos Beach(Skopelos),350
Pappades(Evia),273
Paradise Beach(Angistri),221
Paralia(Evia),264
Paralia(Salaminas),246
Paralia Koskinon(Evia),280
Paralia Kymi(Evia),265
Paralia Politika(Evia),271
Passport,5,37,64
Patitiri Port(Alonissos),310-312
Pavement cafes,*See Cafe-bars*
Pefkos Bay(Skyros),306-307
Pensions,*See Accommodation*
Perani(Salaminas),246
Perdika(Aegina),210
Periptero,*See Street Kiosks*
Peristeria(Salaminas),246
Personal possessions,3-5,43
Petries(Evia),280
Petrol,46
Pharmaceuticals,4

Pharmacies,4
Photography,25,62
Phylla(Evia),257
Piraeus(M),117-135
& other Mainland Ports
Pizzerias,54
Place names,34
Plaka,the(Athens),*See Monastiraki*
Plasters,4
Platana(Evia),264
Platanias Beach(Skiathos),379
Platia Ammos(Kithira),240
Plumbing,*See Bathrooms*
Police,31,33,37,39,40,46,65,66
Politika(Evia),271
Poros island,179-195
Poros town & port,181
Portes(Aegina),209
Ports,mainland,*See Piraeus & other Mainland Ports*
Post Office,65
Potamos(Kithira),239-240
Pounta peninsula(Skiathos),375-376
Prokopion(Evia),272
Psachna(Evia),271
Public Services,*See Services*
Pyrgaki(Evia),281

Q

R
Rafina port(M),126
Rainfall,*See Weather*
Railway Stations,*See Trains*
Razors,3
Religion,*See Greece*
Religious holidays & festivals,72
Renes Bay(Skyros),307
Restaurants,53-54
Retsina,*See Wine*
Retsinolakkos(Evia),278
Rizokastelliotissa(Evia),257
Roads
international,21-25
island,44
signs,48
Roll-bags,3
Roman forum,80
(Athens)
Rooms,*See Accommodation*
Rotisserie,*See Restaurants*
Rovies(Evia),278
Rsoum Gialo Bay(Alonissos),323
Rural Centres,*See Restaurants*
Russian Bay(Poros),193

S
Saint,*See Ag*
Salamina,*See Salaminas*
Salaminas island,241-247
Salamina town(Salaminas),243
Salaminos,*See Salaminas*
Salamis,*See Salaminas*
Scandinavia,14,20
Scooters,46-47
Scopelos,*See Skopelos*
Sea temperature,*See Weather*
Sea urchins,43
Selinia(Salaminas),242
Services,61-66
Shoes,*See Footwear*
Shopping,61-64
Shops,*See Shopping*
Siesta,*See Opening hours*
Sink plugs, 5,38
Sipias(Evia),278
Skala Angistri port(Angistri),214
Skala Oropou port(M),129
Skiathos island,357-383
Skiathos town & port,358
Skiros,*See Skyros*
Skopelos island,331-355
Skopelos town & port,332
Skyros island,289-3-7
Skyros town,*See Chora*
Sleeping bags,3
Smokers,5,61-62
Snackbars,54
Soap powder,3,4
Solar energy,38-39
South Africa,14
Souvala(Aegina),207
Speciality shops,63
Spetsae,*See Spetses*
Spetsai,*See Spetses*
Spetses island,143-161
Spetses town & port,146
Spetsopoula islet,161
St,*See Ag.*
Stafilos Beach(Skopelos),339,348
Steni Dirphos(Evia),270
Steni Vala(Alonissos),328
Stomach upsets,4
Street kiosks(& peripteros),63
Strefilia(Evia),273
Students,13,18
Styra(Evia),283
Summertime,7
Sunburn,43
Sunglasses,3
Sun-tan oil,4
Supermarkets,63
Sweden,14,20,24,29
Switzerland,23,24
Symbols,keys & definitions,139-141
Syntagma Sq,76
(Athens)

T
Tavernas,40,54-55
See Restaurants
Taxiarchi(Evia),264
Taxis,45
Athens,109
Tea,*See Beverages*
Telegrams,*See OTE*
Telephone office,*See OTE*
Temple of Aphaia(Aegina),208
Temple of Poseidon(Poros),194
Temperatures,*See Weather*
Time,7
Timetables,*See individual services*
Tin opener,3
Tobacco,*See Smokers*
Toilets,*See Bathrooms*
Toilet rolls,3
Torch,5
Tourist guides & maps,*See Maps*
Tourist police,*See Police*
Trains
Athens,110-115
international,15-20
metro,*See Metro*
Piraeus(M),119,125
Transalpino tickets,18-19
Travel
Around an island,43-48
Athens to the Mainland islands,31
Travellers cheques,5,64
See Banks & Post Office
Tris Boukes Bay(Skyros),307
Trolley-buses,(Athens),*See Buses*
Troulos Beach(Skiathos),381
Tweezers,4
Tzanerias Bay(Skiathos),378
Tzortzi Gialo Bay(Alonissos),327-328

U
USA,13,18
Useful Greek,*See Language*
Useful names & addresses,28-29,42,47

V
Vagia(Aegina),208
Vasilias(Skiathos),377
Vasilikon(Evia),257
Vassilika(Evia),273
Velanio Beach(Skopelos),339,348
Velos(Evia),263
Venice,17,23
Vithisma Beach(Alonissos),325
Vlichos(Hydra),178
Volos port(M),132
Votsi Bay(Alonissos),324
Voudoro(Salaminas),244
Vrellou Beach(Spetses),159
Vromolimnos Beach(Skiathos),379

W
Walking,*See Foot,on*
Washing
 line,3
 powder,3,4
Water,drinking,44,51-53,63
WC (toilet),*See Bathrooms*
Weather,5-6,43
Wind,5
Wine,52
Wire hangers,3
Women,43

X
Xanema Bay(Skiathos),
 See Ormos Xanema(Skiathos)
Xenias,*See Accommodation*

Y
YMCA,YWCA & Youth
 hostels,39,83(Athens)
 90-91 (Athens)
Yugoslavia,17-18,19,20-21,
 23,24,25,26,28

Z
Zacharoplasteion,54
Zogeria Bay(Spetses),160

Artwork by:Jonathan Duval & Geoffrey O'Connell
Plans & maps by: Graham Bishop & Geoffrey O'Connell
Typeset by:Disc preparation by Willowbridge Publishers
Output by Unwin Bros.